"Scott is a great writer, and there's so much good stuff here. For me, it brings back some beautiful memories of guys like Duane Allman and Toy and Tommy Caldwell. If you want to know what Southern rock was all about, read this book."

—*Elvin Bishop, guitarist and recording artist, "Fooled Around and Fell in Love"*

"Scott B. Bomar has dug deeply into a special time in my career and my life, and the lives and careers of some people who are very dear to me—the bands who were involved in what has become known as Southern rock. We so often see only the professional side of entertainers, but Scott has also exposed the personal side—up-close and intimate looks at some of the people I admire the most."

—*Charlie Daniels, Grammy-winning vocalist and multi-instrumentalist*

"I'm overwhelmed by the effort that Scott invested in this book to remind us, not only of our history, but to help point us on to what's next. I've got all the confidence in the world in his ability to tell the story, from its earliest roots to its ongoing and unfolding future."

—*Doug Gray, vocalist and founding member of the Marshall Tucker Band*

"Scott B. Bomar has done his research! The chapters about Lynyrd Skynyrd are as accurate as can be. His matter-of-fact style makes *Southbound* a good resource . . . and a great read."

—*Ed King, guitarist for Lynyrd Skynyrd and member of the Rock and Roll Hall of Fame*

"In *Southbound*, Bomar captures the golden age of Southern rock and takes the reader on a wonderful journey that some of us were privileged to experience."

—*Chuck Leavell, Grammy-winning keyboardist for the Allman Brothers Band and the Rolling Stones*

"It's apparent that Scott took the extra initiative with respect to the truth regarding this genre of music. The players who struggled against impossible odds to reach their dreams and goals are grateful for that truth. He fully fleshes out the passion, the persistence, the underdog spirit, and incredible fortitude it took for these relatively few musicians to make their mark in the highly competitive music world. Scott gets it right."

—*Don Barnes, vocalist, guitarist, and founding member of 38 Special*

"I thought I knew everything I'd ever need to know about Southern rock until I read Scott B. Bomar's *Southbound*. Filled with great photos and insightful information culled from his interviews with many of the genre's most important figures, Scott brings the Southern rock era roaring back to life in this extremely entertaining and well-written book."

—*Randy Poe, author of* Skydog: The Duane Allman Story

"We are very fortunate to have Scott B. Bomar telling our story. His passion for the music—and all the details behind it—makes this book an accurate and worthy resource for generations to come."

—*Jimmy Hall, vocalist for Wet Willie*

"Thanks a million to Scott for his tireless efforts in the pursuit of factual information. He rocks!"

—*Dave Hlubek, guitarist and founding member of Molly Hatchet*

"Thank God for people like Scott, who love and appreciate this beautiful music and the musicians who have created it . . . and continue to create it. It is a fascinating art form and is as deeply and truly American as the culture that influenced it. We in Blackberry Smoke feel honored to be included."

—*Charlie Starr, vocalist and guitarist for Blackberry Smoke*

"Thanks to Scott for shedding new light on a bright spot in our lives. His approach is very respectful and insightful, and I know the fans will love it!"

—*Henry Paul, vocalist and guitarist for the Outlaws*

"Southern rock gets the detailed historical treatment it's long deserved in this fascinating, well-written book. Not only does Scott B. Bomar attempt a solid definition of the elusive genre that came to prominence with the rise of the Allman Brothers Band in the late 1960s, but he follows the music's trajectory straight up to present-day country. Meticulously researched and reported, with proper attention to the culture of the South and the social and political mood of the times, Bomar traces Southern rock from its blues, country, and R&B roots in the 1950s to its FM-radio heyday of the 1970s, with full stories (and loads of stunning photos, many rarely seen) of every important act that came in the Allmans' wake: Wet Willie, the Marshall Tucker Band, Lynyrd Skynyrd, Charlie Daniels, Blackfoot, 38 Special, Molly Hatchet, and more. A welcome addition to the rock canon."

—*Mark Kemp, former senior music editor for* Rolling Stone *and author of* Dixie Lullaby: A Story of Music, Race, and New Beginnings in a New South

"There've been quite a few books written about the Southern rock genre, with varying degrees of accuracy. In *Southbound*, Scott B. Bomar gets down in the trenches with the Southern rock soldiers and chronicles their stories—from being hungry, struggling hopefuls, to staying the course and finally 'making it' against all odds. And Scott gets it right!"

—*Paul Hornsby, musician and producer of the Marshall Tucker Band, Charlie Daniels, and Wet Willie*

"Scott B. Bomar digs deep into the history of one of America's most misunderstood musical genres, writing not only about the well-known bands such as the Allman Brothers and Lynyrd Skynyrd, but also fantastic bands like Grinderswitch, Hydra, and Cowboy. Richly illustrated with rare and never-before-seen photographs, this one is a must read for all of us fans of good ol' Dixie rock!"

—*Michael Buffalo Smith, author of* Rebel Yell: An Oral History of Southern Rock

"Scott's dedication to the truth and to the music is unmatched. His revealing look at Southern rock will certainly become the standard by which future works on the subject are viewed and valued."

—*Tommy Talton, founding member of Cowboy and former guitarist for Gregg Allman*

Southbound

AN ILLUSTRATED HISTORY OF SOUTHERN ROCK

Southbound

AN ILLUSTRATED HISTORY OF SOUTHERN ROCK

Scott B. Bomar

Backbeat
Books

An Imprint of Hal Leonard Corporation

Published in 2014 by Backbeat Books
An Imprint of Hal Leonard Corporation
7777 West Bluemound Road
Milwaukee, WI 53213

Trade Book Division Editorial Offices
33 Plymouth St., Montclair, NJ 07042

Images are from the author's collection, unless
otherwise noted.

Excerpts from *My Cross to Bear* copyright © 2012
by Gregg Allman. Reprinted by permission of
HarperCollins Publishers.

Every reasonable effort has been made to contact
copyright holders and secure permissions.
Omissions can be remedied in future editions.

Printed in the United States of America

Book design by Patrick Crowley

Library of Congress Cataloging-in-Publication
Data is available upon request.

ISBN 978-1-48035-519-4

www.backbeatbooks.com

To Melanie, the love of my life, who is as familiar
as a best friend, yet full of happy surprises. After all these
years together, these are still the salad days.

And to Randy Poe, a mentor and friend
who came along when I needed both.

Contents

CONTENTS

Foreword

 HEN YOU GROW UP in the South, you know there's going to be *something* every Sunday where the whole family gets together. When I was a kid, it was an understood thing. There's going to be food, everybody's going to be there, and you're expected to participate in the conversation, whether you brought a dish or not. It was almost like a ritual that pulled us all together in a shared bond, and it helped define us as people.

Because of that tradition, there was a real sense of family connection that extended outward to the whole community. You'd see people out fishing with each other, or see little kids riding their bicycles. Growing up, we'd go over to somebody's house, knock on the door, go inside, and just have that shared familial spirit. Even today, people will ride down the road in this part of the world and say, "I've never seen so many churches in all my life." My personal opinion is that you don't have to go to church to believe in God; *my* thinking is that all these churches are significant because they're *gathering* places. They're places where people come together and find something that connects them with one another.

Of course, growing up in the South wasn't always perfect. It wasn't quite like *The Andy Griffith Show*. You did have the uncle who was drunk all the time, and you did have the cousin who lived down the street and talked weird and didn't know anything. We had our problems, but we still made it work. If somebody needed help, we rallied around. We all looked out for each other.

That same spirit kept us going when the Marshall Tucker Band were just starting out. Tommy Caldwell was the guy in charge of the money. He'd collect what we were owed and then pay for the hotel and the gas for the van to get back home. We'd go to the grocery store to buy hoop cheese, Saltine crackers, and Jack Daniels, which is what we lived on. Tommy would then divide up among us whatever was left over. I remember when we went and played a show one night at a club called the Yellow Bandana in Macon, Georgia. After the expenses were taken care of, Tommy said, "Well, boys, we really broke the bank today," and handed everybody one penny. Even in the early days, however, we felt like a success, because we were doing what was in our heart. Those were emotional ties that pulled us all together as a family, and those are the ties that really bind.

When Southern rock began to take off in the early 1970s, all of us musicians continued to carry that tradition of camaraderie and mutual support with us. We all looked out for each other, because that's who we were and how we were raised. The Southern rock community became yet another family that was shaped by those formative years in South Carolina or Georgia or Florida, or all the places where these folks came from. It was almost like a celebra-tion, or maybe even a fellowship. We invited Charlie Daniels and Elvin Bishop and all these friends to come play on our records. We'd walk into the Capricorn studios in Macon, Georgia, and there's Dr. John sitting out front, or Gregg Allman in the back room working on a song. There was a real sense that we were becoming a part of something that was special, and we looked forward to seeing these people at the next show where we were sharing the bill. None of us Southern bands competed with one another. We just knew that if we didn't get up there and blow *their* ass off the stage, somebody else would blow *our* ass off the stage!

All of us—the Allmans, Wet Willie, Charlie Daniels, Marshall Tucker—were spreading that love and extending that sense of family to the fans, one by one. It was almost like an awakening. People started to realize that Southerners aren't just a bunch of dummies. They were realizing that we've actually got some talented musicians down here who can really play and can write songs that mean things to people. It was like a stamp of approval for us. We were on the road over 300 days a year for the first five years of the Marshall Tucker Band, so the fans were all we had. There was an understanding that we were all involved in something greater than ourselves.

Obviously, Southern rock wasn't just popular in the South. It made an impact all around the world, and I believe that has a lot do with the fact that people are searching for that *connection*. There's a soulfulness in Southern music that makes the heart feel good, be it R&B, blues, or country. They're all tied together, and everybody wants a little piece of that good feeling. The music is just a way for people to relate to the underlying spirit. The moment this really hit home for me was when the Marshall Tucker Band were in Myrtle Beach, South Carolina, to play at the Convention Center. We were staying at this hotel by the ocean, and we were all out there on the beach, having a good time like a bunch of redneck boys on the road who didn't know wrong from right—much less what we'd smoked that day! We were out in the water, and Joe McConnell, our road manager, waved his hands for us to come up to the hotel room. He said, "I just got word that your first record went gold." We didn't know what to say. It was amazing to think that a half-million people had bought our album, and that every single one of them was woven into our story, and had become a part of that growing Southern rock community. But there was more to accomplish. The next day, we got back in that Dodge van that smelled like hoop cheese and beer and drove to New York City for a concert.

And it just kept growing from there. When we got invited to open for Santana, we stopped somewhere and bought a cowboy hat to give to Car-los. He came out with that hat on and played with us during our set! We'd go all over the country—and all over the world—and people would accept us. They might have looked at us a little funny in those Northern restaurants when they heard our accent, or when they had to explain that they didn't have *sweet* tea, but we didn't really encounter any problems anywhere we went. I think it's because we extended a hand without expecting anything back. I don't just mean Marshall Tucker, but the Allman Brothers, Wet Willie, and all of them. When someone extends a hand without expecting anything back, that's when you know you've got a true brother or sister.

Thinking back on those years, it's like we were riding a wave. But it's a wave that's still rolling on, even today. Skynyrd still goes out and draws a good crowd, we go out and draw a good crowd, Charlie Daniels goes out and draws a good crowd. There are some people now who don't want to admit that Southern rock was part of their history, but we were one of the bands that said, "We're Southern, and we'll stick with it!" That unity is going to be there, and that wave will go on and on, because there are still Southern bands keeping the flame alive. We'll look back thirty years from now, and it will be obvious to historians that people like Zac Brown, Blackberry Smoke, and other great Southern artists were keeping it going because they learned to absorb the spirit of Southern rock without being imitators.

I'm overwhelmed by the effort that Scott invested in this book, not only to remind us of our history but also to help point us to what's next. I've got all the confidence in the world in his ability to tell this story, from its earliest roots to its ongoing and unfolding future. When we look back, it helps us look ahead. People still travel to Macon to see where Berry Oakley and Duane Allman are buried. They come to Spartanburg to see where Toy and Tommy Caldwell are buried. I miss those guys. Some nights I'm up on that stage knowing they're pushing me. But I don't dwell on the point that they're no longer with us. Instead, I celebrate the fact that we all got to know each other, and that they left a legacy where you still see thirteen- or fourteen-year-old kids who want to learn to play music because of the inspiration they got from someone like Duane.

None of us are going to live forever, but I do believe that we're all going to come back and join each other again one day—the musicians, the fans, the visionaries, and everyone who made up the Southern rock community in each generation. I don't know if you call it heaven or what, but I think we'll all be back together as one united family. I just hope I come back as a dog, so I can lie around and listen to the blues all day!

—Doug Gray of the Marshall Tucker Band

Introduction

BROTHERS AND SISTERS: DEFINING SOUTHERN ROCK

★ ★

Dave Hlubek and Duane Roland of Molly Hatchet. (Photo by Larry Hulst/Michael Ochs Archives/Getty Images)

ROCK AND ROLL was born in the American South. Elvis Presley, Little Richard, Fats Domino, Buddy Holly, and the overwhelming majority of rock's pioneering artists of the 1950s emerged from below the Mason-Dixon Line. But by the following decade, it was the British Invasion that assured rock music's place as a permanent cultural fixture. Though Southern music was a major influence on the Beatles, the Rolling Stones, and the myriad of British and American bands that rose up in their wake, the rock-and-roll revolution ultimately transcended any region. Instead, rock and roll belonged to

> *"Everybody that's seen Easy Rider now trembles in their shoes to go down South, man. Everybody should spend some time on our farm . . . see what it's like before they go making those solid opinions about things they don't know anything about."*
>
> —DUANE ALLMAN,
> THE ALLMAN BROTHERS BAND

an emerging national youth culture in need of visceral musical expression.

Ironically, the land that gave birth to rock and roll was perceived as the most resistant to the cultural changes that accompanied the soundtrack of the era. The South came to be viewed not as the spiritual homeland of rock's roots but as a mysterious backwater that didn't cotton to the ways of young rockers with shaggy hair. By the time potent new rock bands from the Southern states were rising to prominence in the early 1970s, their geographic origin was regarded as a peculiarity that necessitated the designation of a distinct subgenre. *Southern* rock became the battle flag under which long-haired kids from states like Florida, Georgia, Alabama, and Tennessee, were able to rally.

As much as it was a new movement, so-called "Southern rock" was a renaissance. "We didn't invent something that was already there," Allman Brothers Band drummer Jai Johanny "Jaimoe" Johanson remarked in Candice Dyer's *Music from Macon*. "If we supposedly invented 'Southern rock,' what the hell was Little Richard, Elvis—who was a disciple of Little Richard—Brenda Lee, and . . . Hank Williams? If 'Jambalaya' wasn't Southern rock then tell me, what is? Don't get me wrong—I'm very proud of our achievements, but, shit, Southern rock was going on fifty years before we came along."

What Jaimoe's comments illustrate is the ongoing reality that Elvis and Little Richard, both Southerners, are simply considered rock-and-rollers, while the Allman Brothers Band, Lynyrd Skynyrd, the Marshall Tucker Band, Wet Willie, the Charlie Daniels Band, and the Outlaws are almost always identified as *Southern* rockers. While stereotypes of Southerners date back even further than *Uncle Tom's Cabin* and the writings of Mark Twain, it was the proliferation of mass media in the 1960s that helped solidify a pervasive Southern caricature. Television programs—including *The Andy Griffith Show*, *The Beverly Hillbillies*, *Gomer Pyle, U.S.M.C.*, *Green Acres*, and *Hee Haw*—portrayed white working-class Southerners as affable simpletons whose out-of-step-with-modern-times eccentricities were played for comedic effect.

By the latter part of the 1960s, and into the 1970s, movies like *In the Heat of the Night*, *Easy Rider*, and *Deliverance* built on this image, adding frightening stereotypes of big-oted and menacing white Southerners that captured the popular imagination and helped cement an image of the South as a culturally deprived wasteland that was populated primarily by idiots and racists. As a result, the region's artistic exports—including its rock music—were increasingly treated as something distinct from the culture at large.

Sadly, some of the Southern stereotypes were not simply media inventions but reflections of real-life bigotry. Highly publicized battles of the civil rights movement, for instance, found high-profile politicians defiantly embracing racist, regressive attitudes that cast a shadow over the entire region.

Over the years, the term "Southern rock" has suggested a number of connotations. For many, it simply suggests the authentic good-time working-class music that's rooted in the Southern traditions of blues and country. It's music that remains free from the pretensions of heavily produced performers who rely on theatrics and studio trickery over honest-to-God-shake-your-butt-'cause-it's-Saturday-night rock and roll. For others, the term "Southern rock" has conjured images reminiscent of decidedly urban rock critic Lester Bangs' characterization of the members of Lynyrd Skynyrd as "crude thunderstomper hillbillies whose market value rested primarily on the fact that they could play their instruments about like they could plant their fists in your teeth."

Despite these negative stereotypes, the world of Southern rock was built on a rich foundation of musical traditions that covers a complex system of roots and branches, including the blues-heavy, jazz-tinged improvisations of the interracial Allman Brothers Band; the choreographed triple-guitar attack of Lynyrd Skynyrd; the country-oriented instrumental subtleties of the Marshall Tucker Band; the lean, Stones-influenced boogie of Wet Willie; the lushly harmonious pop strains of the Atlanta Rhythm Section; or the foot-stompin' stage show of the Charlie Daniels Band.

The majority of the players widely recognized as pillars of the Southern rock genre, however, have long grappled with the label and its associated presuppositions. "There's something about the perception of how folks look at Southern people," Marshall Tucker Band lead singer Doug Gray sighed in 2013. "The Marshall Tucker Band is Southern, but it ain't about Honey Boo Boo, and it ain't about making moonshine!"

Many of the musicians who are squeezed into the category insist the term is little more than a music industry invention. "'Southern rock' is an expression I don't know if I ever fully understood," mused Phil Walden, who helmed Capricorn Records, generally regarded as the quintessential label in the genre's history. "I never really saw the close identity that was drawn between those bands," he elaborated to Robert Gordon in 1995. "But I guess it's just easier to heap everybody into one category."

To a large degree, Walden benefited from the term by establishing a unique identity in the marketplace for his Macon, Georgia–based record label in the 1970s. "Around this time," Allman Brothers Band guitarist Dickey Betts explained to journalist Alan Paul, "everyone started calling us 'Southern rock,' which I always had real mixed feelings about, and which I don't think any of us ever liked." The Outlaws' guitarist, Hughie Thomasson bristled at the categorization. "That's a label that was stuck on us," he insisted to author Marley Brant. "We didn't put it on ourselves."

The very diversity of the Southern rock landscape, however, has proven to be a complicating factor when it comes to defining *what*,

Jai Johanny "Jaimoe" Johanson of the Allman Brothers Band. (Courtesy of Fame Studios)

Hughie Thomasson of the Outlaws. (Courtesy of Carl Lender)

The Allman Brothers Band, 1969. *Left to right:* Jaimoe, Berry Oakley, Duane Allman, Butch Trucks, Gregg Allman, and Dickey Betts. (Photo by Twiggs Lyndon, courtesy of the Big House Museum, Macon, Georgia)

exactly, Southern rock is, and *who* should fall into the category. For the purpose of this book, the term "Southern rock" refers to music that was rooted in a specific time, belonged to a particular place, was created by musicians with similar formative and cultural experiences, and served as a key expression of a uniquely countercultural movement in the South.

SOUTHERN ROCK REPRESENTS AN ERA IN HISTORY AS MUCH AS A MUSICAL GENRE THAT CAN BE DEFINED BY CHARACTERISTICS LIKE MELODIC STRUCTURE OR SPECIFIC INSTRUMENTATION.

With its roots in blues and country music, the electric guitar is a key component of most Southern rock bands—the majority of which feature two and sometimes three guitars. Beyond that common feature, however, Southern rock belongs primarily to a specific age in music history. This period began in 1969, with the Allman Brothers Band's debut album on Capricorn Records, and lasted into the early 1980s, when musical tastes began to shift toward synthesized pop sounds. In contrast, the rock music that emerged from the South during the Southern rock era was heavily rooted in blues, country, and R&B, but often featured a generous side serving of jazz-inspired improvisation.

Plenty of new groups emerged from the South in the 1980s and beyond, and while many of them were certainly Southern bands that played rock music, they weren't playing *Southern rock*. The B-52s, R.E.M., and Creed, for example, are all bands that came from the South, but the sound of their music isn't rooted in the classic Southern rock era. Other groups, like the Georgia Satellites, the Screamin' Cheetah Wheelies, the Black Crowes, Widespread

Panic, and Drive-By Truckers, share a musical commonality that is significantly—though not *exclusively*—influenced by the sound and spirit of Southern rock's golden age.

SOUTHERN ROCK BELONGS TO A PARTICULAR PLACE.

While many performers gravitated to the music-business centers of Los Angeles and New York City, the South remained the home base for most of the groups that fall into the Southern rock genre. Much of their recording was done in places like Atlanta, Nashville, Macon, Miami, Memphis, and Muscle Shoals, rather than on the coasts. Additionally, the majority of the performers chose to continue to live in the South following their rise to national prominence. The members of the Marshall Tucker Band, for instance, remained in their small hometown of Spartanburg, South Carolina, while the members of Lynyrd Skynyrd continued to live in Jacksonville, Florida. Though the Allman Brothers Band members would splinter in later years, they stayed in their adopted hometown of Macon, Georgia, during their most successful period. "When we first formed," recalled ZZ Top bassist Dusty Hill, in *Recycling the Blues*, "they told us at the record company . . . 'You have to move to New York or L.A. You can't live in Texas, it's not done.' We said, 'Sure we can.' I don't see any reason why not."

Declaring that Southern rock belongs to a particular place begs the question, "What states constitute the South?" Not wanting to get too bogged down, I am simply defining the South as the eleven states that formed the Confederacy during the Civil War. These are South Carolina, Mississippi, Florida, Alabama, Georgia, Louisiana, Texas, Virginia, Arkansas, Tennessee, and North Carolina. There are several high-profile artists whose sound and

aesthetic *seems* to fit with the Southern rock genre, but whose geographic location outside this eleven-state radius excludes them from the category. Credence Clearwater Revival, for example, are often mistaken as a Southern rock band, thanks to their embrace of the swampy sounds of the bayou. In reality, they hailed from the San Francisco Bay Area. Likewise, Little Feat came from Los Angeles.

Some fans of Southern rock will be disappointed that I chose not to include the Ozark Mountain Daredevils here. The group, best known for the excellent singles "If You Wanna Get to Heaven" and "Jackie Blue," had a Southern rock sensibility but were based in Missouri. Sticking to my definition of which states constitute the South (which pains me as a fan of the band) excludes them from my parameters.

An even thornier example is Tom Petty & the Heartbreakers, who started out in the 1970s as Mudcrutch in the inarguably Southern locale of Gainesville, Florida. Petty's subsequent relocation to the West Coast and embrace of its jangly folk-rock aesthetic distanced him and his band from a Southern rock identity. "I love the South," Petty told *Rolling Stone* magazine in 2013. "A lot of people associate us with Florida, but I really feel like we're an L.A. band."

SOUTHERN ROCK WAS CREATED BY MUSICIANS WITH SIMILAR FORMATIVE AND CULTURAL EXPERIENCES.

The music that marked the Southern rock era was created by generally like-minded young working-class Southerners with similar backgrounds. "Some of my success and career, I know," noted Allman Brothers keyboardist Chuck Leavell, "has been due to the fact that I'm a Southern musician. It's in my

Charlie Daniels signing autographs for fans in New Haven, Connecticut. (Courtesy of Carl Lender)

Southern rock superstars gathered at Studio One in Doraville, Georgia, 1978. Standing, *left to right:* Lenny LeBlanc, Garry Rossington, Jimmy Hall, Barry Bailey, unknown, Artimus Pyle, Dickey Betts, Charlie Daniels, unknown, Taz DiGregorio, and Allen Collins; Billy Powell (kneeling), Bonnie Bramlett (sitting). (Photo by Tom Hill/WireImage)

Brothers Toy Caldwell and Tommy Caldwell of the Marshall Tucker Band, 1976. (Courtesy of Peter Cross)

Bassist Jerry Jemmott, Aretha Franklin, and Duane Allman recording "The Weight" at Atlantic Studios in January of 1969. (Photo by Michael Ochs Archives/Getty Images)

blood, in my veins." As Leavell's observation suggests, the performers who made up the Southern rock community of the 1970s are what Charlie Daniels called "a genre of people more than a genre of music."

The unique culture of the South has often seemed mysterious to those who weren't raised there. It's a culture of contradictions, where religious reverence and mannerly hospitality are expected but are often accompanied by fierce independence, pride, rowdiness, and a defiant mistrust of outsiders. To grow up in the South is to understand both the power of Sunday morning and the lure of Saturday night. It may be the Bible Belt, but it's also the home of the blues and the honky-tonk. It's a place where both sin and salvation are serious business.

"You know," Charlie Daniels explained, "I could sit down with Ronnie Van Zant or with Dickey Betts of the Allman Brothers, or with Jimmy Hall of Wet Willie, and we all liked the same things. We all ate grits for breakfast. We all went to basically the same kind of schools." As Daniels' observation suggests, Southern rockers were generally blue-collar family people who grew up attending

like-minded churches, listening to the same radio stations, and adopting the same values of hospitality, unpretentious simplicity, and fierce loyalty. Perhaps this emphasis on personal relatability explains, in part, the unusual tendency of Southern rock groups to choose names that sounded misleadingly like the names of individuals. Bands like Lynyrd Skynyrd, the Marshall Tucker Band, Wet Willie, Barefoot Jerry, Molly Hatchet, Doc Holliday, Eric Quincy Tate, Mose Jones, and Cooder Browne included nary a Leonard, Marshall, Willie, Jerry, Molly, Doc, Eric, Mose, or Cooder among them.

Whether or not the choice of band names had anything to do with it, the similar experiences of Southern musicians created a connection that bound them together in a tight-knit community. "Man, you get tight with a Southerner," Duane Allman told *Rolling Stone*'s Alex Dubro, "and he'll jump in front of a fucking car for you."

"Southern rock is just a name somebody came up with to market the music that was coming out of Jacksonville, Macon, and Atlanta," observed Grinderswitch guitarist

Dru Lombar, in an interview with Ella Wirtz. "It's all different, but it comes from the same place. *It comes from deep within the man or the woman.*" As a result, most of the veterans of Southern rock's golden age regard their fellow musicians like family. "What it was all about was a community of people," Wet Willie's Jimmy Hall explained. "The groups that played together always tried to encourage and help each other. There was never a problem with being confrontational or backstabbing."

The family atmosphere was likely created, in part, by the fact that an unusually high number of *actual* family members were involved in the music. Brothers Phil and Alan Walden were the architects of the music business in Southern rock's musical mecca of Macon, Georgia. The first act on the Waldens' Capricorn label was the Allman Brothers Band, who took their name from real-life brothers Duane and Gregg Allman. Brothers Toy and Tommy Caldwell anchored the Marshall Tucker Band, while siblings Dennis and Donnie formed the Winters Brothers Band and became staples of Charlie Daniels' annual Volunteer Jam concerts. Brothers Jack and Jimmy Hall launched

Wet Willie, and were later joined by their sister Donna Hall on backup vocals. Lynyrd Skynyrd backup singer Cassie Gaines convinced the band to recruit her brother Steve Gaines on guitar, while Skynyrd front man Ronnie Van Zant's brother, Donnie, became a founding member of 38 Special.

Though their music was diverse, the shared spirit of many Southern rock bands was concretely reflected in a shared stage persona. In the flashy era of Alice Cooper and David Bowie, most Southern rockers appeared onstage in their jeans and street clothes, prizing pure musicality over dramatics. In this way, they were immensely relatable, first to fellow Southerners and eventually to fans all over the country.

"If you're a woman and you're on that stage in a Southern rock band, it's not because you have boobs," explained Bonnie Bramlett, who recorded for the Capricorn label in the mid-1970s. "It's because you're a significant part of that group." Prizing hard work and genuine community over image bonded the like-minded performers together in a common goal of honest musical expression whose roots were deep. "We were all closer than family," Marshall Tucker Band lead singer Doug Gray reflected years later. "Family will get competitive. We were partners, and we all shared something *real*."

SOUTHERN ROCK SERVED AS A KEY EXPRESSION OF A UNIQUELY COUNTERCULTURAL MOVEMENT IN THE SOUTH.

In some circles, Southern rock is simply dismissed as "redneck music" and not afforded the same critical respect as other popular genres. "While white critics generally praise the music of poor black Southern musicians," journalist Mark Kemp observed, "many of those critics freely mock the music and character of working-class white Southern artists."

While covering Southern rock artists, for example, many journalists condescendingly chose to transliterate their subjects' interview responses phonetically to spotlight their unique accents. In a profile of ZZ Top, for example, Barney Hoskyns offered drummer Frank Beard's response to why he was the only member of the group without facial hair in an embarrassingly literal rendering: "Ah cain't! Ah'm jist so far behind! Ah use to say I was too yerng, but after twelve years that stopped working. Then ah said it was doo to female thigh-burn, but I got married and ah cain't say that no more! So now I say ah'm jist too far outta the race." Mike Hyland, who headed the publicity department for Capricorn Records in the 1970s, still bristled, decades later, at the journalistic practice. "They loved to do that shit," he sighed, "and we *hated* that."

The tendency to dismiss white working-class Southerners as white-trash bumpkins has fueled the fire of Southern rock's devaluation as rock music's embarrassing cousin. "A whole vein of human experience . . . is dismissed as a joke," Jim Goad wrote in *The Redneck Manifesto*, "much as American's popular notions of black culture were relegated to lawn jockeys and Sambo caricatures a generation or two ago. The redneck is the only cardboard figure left standing in our ethnic shooting gallery."

What some outside observers who gleefully typecast Southern rockers as degenerate hayseeds failed to recognize, however, is that many of them actually *challenged* the attitudes and stereotypes that came to be associated with Southern culture. At the time that Southern rock was rising to prominence, those who were most often identified as "rednecks" were strictly conforming traditionalists with crew-cut hairstyles and an aversion to the rebellious attitude of rock and roll. Southern rockers were often regarded with great suspicion by the so-called rednecks of their day. Most Southern rockers, for example, cut their teeth on the blues and R&B, which was the territory of black America in that time. They were *countercultural* figures in a Southern society that was still grappling with desegregation and the evolution of race relations.

"After I got this gig," African American bassist Oteil Burbridge told Alan Paul of his joining the Allman Brothers Band in 1997, "my sister said, 'Southern rock? I don't know if I like that.' Then I opened up an Aretha Franklin album at her house, and there's a picture of Duane Allman, who had played on it. She had an image of the Allman Brothers Band as racist, redneck, Southern boys. Bands and studios were some of the first places to integrate in the South. Honestly, it tripped me out that there are these older white guys with thick Southern accents who are so hip to black music. They shatter a lot of stereotypes."

Additionally, the fashion choices of some Southern rockers invoked the ire of traditional Southern society. "If you were a long-haired boy, you were thought less than a black person," explained Muscle Shoals musician Jimmy Johnson, who worked with Duane Allman and Lynyrd Skynyrd, among others. Though Southern rockers shared similar formative traditions, they deviated from cultural norms by crossing racial boundaries, adopting a new appearance, embracing elements of the hippie lifestyle, and experimenting with drugs.

Southern rockers were not only countercultural within Southern society, but also found ways to proudly assert their regional identity

Lynyrd Skynyrd, as pictured on the back of their *Nuthin' Fancy* album, 1975. *Left to right*: Ed King, Leon Wilkeson, Billy Powell, Johnny Van Zant, Gary Rossington, Allen Collins, and Artimus Pyle. (MCA Records)

Grinderswitch, *left to right*: Dru Lombar, Larry Howard, Joe Dan Petty, and Rick Burnett. (Photo by Terry Milam, courtesy of Larry Howard)

within the larger world of rock and roll. The 1960s and early 1970s was a time when outlandish rock bands were letting their freak flags fly. For Southern rockers, however, it was sometimes a literal flag—a flag that allowed them to assert their regional pride, as well as their identification as "rebels." The "stars and bars" that served as the official flag of the Confederate States during the Civil War eventually morphed into what is now known as the Rebel flag. Today, it is perhaps one of the most contentious symbols in America. The flag's apologists insist it celebrates Southern heritage, regional pride, and an independent spirit of rebelliousness. Its detractors, however, point to its use as a symbol that is associated with the pro-slavery sentiments of the Confederacy, a defiant representation of anti-segregationist attitudes that was employed during the civil rights era, and a hateful emblem of the Ku Klux Klan and neo-Nazi fringe groups. For many, it is a painful reminder of the nation's racially trouble history.

In 2012, members of Lynyrd Skynyrd appeared on CNN to discuss their current album and tour. When host Fredricka Whitfield asked if they were distancing themselves from the Confederate flag, founding member Gary Rossington explained, "It became such an issue, you know, about race and stuff.... Through the years, you know, people like the KKK and skinheads and people have kind of kidnapped the Dixie—or Rebel—flag from the

Southern tradition and the heritage of the soldiers—you know, that's what it was about—and they kind of made it look bad in certain ways. So, we didn't want that to go to our fans, or show the image like we agree with any of the race stuff, or any of the bad things."

While many fans applauded the band's decision to move on from a potentially painful symbol, others erupted in outrage and accused them of selling out to political correctness. Within days, Lynyrd Skynyrd appeared to backpedal when Rossington posted a message on the band's official website to reassure concerned fans. "We still utilize the Confederate (Rebel) flag onstage every night in our shows," Rossington noted. "We are, and always will be, a Southern American rock band, first and foremost.... The Confederate flag means something more to us—heritage, not hate."

As Rossington noted, not everyone who embraces the Confederate flag intends to send a racially charged message, though it's clear why the symbol can lead to misunderstanding and disagreement. "I know none of us viewed the confederate flag with any political significance," Henry Paul of the Outlaws explained. "I think, to us, it was a banner that just represented geographical pride. Time has played a significant role in redefining its meaning, and I understand the sensitivity connected to it."

Even while kicking against established Southern social guidelines, like hair length and racially homogeneous musical pref-

erences, Southern rockers were rebelling against a growing urban elitism in music centers like New York and Los Angeles that put them in a defensive posture against broad assumptions about Southern identity. "And so it is today," author Frey Gaillard noted in her 1978 book *Watermelon Wine*, "as the South emerges from twenty years of turmoil, and the young people who were estranged from their region and heritage during the years of upheaval begin to realize that once a few key sins are purged, theirs is not, in fact, a place to be ashamed of." Perhaps no one embodied the tension of that transitional attitude more than Duane Allman. "We're just plain ol' fuckin' Southern cats, man," he testily told sneering journalist Grover Lewis in an unflattering *Rolling Stone* profile of the band. "Not ashamed of it or proud of it, neither one."

In the spirit of Duane Allman, this book attempts to present the stories of the musicians who contributed to Southern rock's rich history. That isn't necessarily a simple task. "People have tried to tell the Southern rock story in all kinds of ways, but I can tell you the real story will never be told," Grinderswitch's Larry Howard once declared. "All the Southern rockers are taking the true story to the grave with them one at a time."

Tantalizing as that sounds, the research for this book revealed something different. Instead of the real story being withheld, I came across countless "real stories" and versions of events that often collided with and contradicted one another. Oftentimes, the eyewitnesses to the exact same situation reported widely varying details. Accordingly, I make no claim that this is *the* definitive history of Southern rock. Instead, it's *a* history. As a student of the music, I've put the events in the words of the musicians as much as possible. Where memories conflicted, I've sometimes presented varying perspectives. Other times, I went with the consensus view. Some might think I've gotten it wrong. Some might think I've woefully neglected certain performers, while overemphasizing others. In such instances, I hope I at least start some interesting discussions.

My ultimate hope, however, is that you'll simply enjoy this history as a companion piece to the music itself. What really matters is appreciating the music on its own terms without getting hung up on anything that might serve as a distraction from the fact that there is some great Southern rock music that is best enjoyed by being experienced firsthand. As you read the stories of the performers, don't forget to fire up the stereo and, as Lynyrd Skynyrd's Ronnie Van Zant urged, turn it up! ★

Southbound

An Illustrated History of Southern Rock

Part One

SHAKE, RATTLE, AND ROLL: SETTING THE SOUTHERN STAGE

OF THE FIRST twenty performers inducted into the Rock and Roll Hall of Fame, fourteen of them—a full 70 percent—came from the South. "When you trace the roots," Charlie Daniels explained, "you'll find it's all got a Southern accent to it, every dad-blamed bit of it."

Southern music in general—and rock and roll in particular—is the story of Anglo-American traditions and African American influences colliding, intersecting, butting up against one another, and shaping each other into new forms. The uneasy relationship between blacks and whites provided the heat that fueled the furnace in which Southern music first formed—and continued to form—well into the rock-and-roll era. Born at a time of racial unrest when legal segregation was still a way of life in the Southern United States, rock music brought blacks and whites together in a way that some saw as hopeful and others saw as an alarming threat.

By the 1960s, the musical culture clash shifted from white and black to British and American. The British Invasion flowered into a psychedelic music explosion that ultimately buckled under the weight of its own pretensions. When audiences began craving the purity of American roots music once more, they turned their attention southward, where a bourgeoning community of Southern rockers was poised to take over once again.

"'Southern rock' is like saying 'rock rock.' Rock and roll was born in the South."

—GREGG ALLMAN, THE ALLMAN BROTHERS BAND, 2005

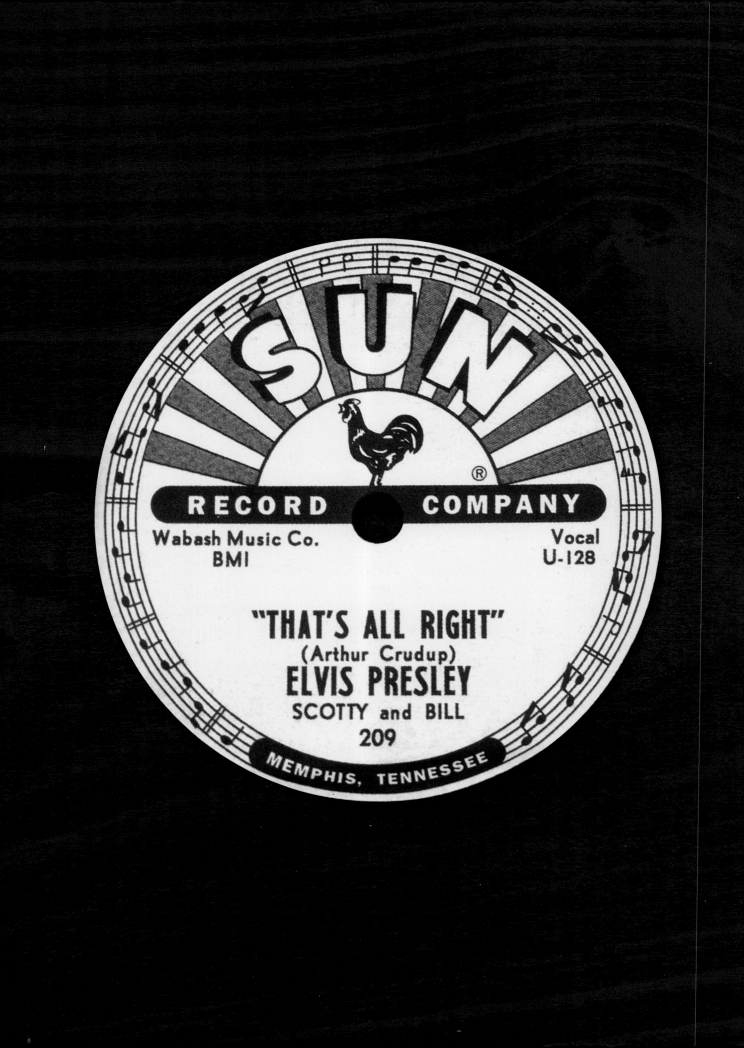

CHAPTER 1
Good Rockin' Tonight: A Sweet Southern Stew of Country, Blues, and R&B

THOUGH HIS MUSIC was fairly polished, it was Alabama-born African American bandleader and composer W. C. Handy who first popularized the concept of twelve-bar blues with his hit "Memphis Blues" in 1909. Though he borrowed heavily from street singers and rural bluesmen, his orchestrated music was considerably more refined. Many popular early blues records—mostly by black Southern women like Ma Rainey and Bessie Smith—incorporated these more sophisticated big-band elements into their style.

During this period of innovation and development in the world of black music, there was a parallel explosion of interest in the music of the working class. Starting around 1910, and stretching into the teens, the public became fascinated with the Appalachian Mountain ballad tradition, as researchers like Mississippi-born John Lomax scoured the country making invaluable early recordings of both white and black folk music for the Library of Congress. Later, important Southern performers such as Leadbelly and Muddy Waters were first captured on disc thanks to Lomax's efforts.

With the 1920s came the advent of radio and an explosion in the popularity of 78-rpm records. In August of 1920, Mamie Smith became the first black artist to record a vocal blues when she cut "Crazy Blues" for Okeh Records. It sold over a million copies and alerted the record companies that there was a market for "race" records.

They soon discovered that working-class whites were eager to purchase records of their own music as well. In August of 1927, the seeds were sewn that launched commercial country music into a major industry when Ralph Peer traveled to Bristol, Tennessee, where he recorded both the Carter Family (from Virginia) and Jimmie Rodgers (from Mississippi) for the Victor Recording Company. Peer was the first to bring commercial recording crews to the South. That same year, he traveled to Memphis, where he captured the music of black blues singers and jug bands.

At the close of 1928, Pinetop Smith recorded "Pinetop's Boogie Woogie," popularizing a propulsive piano style that appealed to both white and black listeners and helped lead the way to the influential "jump blues" style of the 1940s. At the same time, rural-themed barn-dance radio shows like Nashville's *Grand Ole Opry* brought country music into the homes of black and white Americans every Saturday night. In

Though Huddie Ledbetter wrote his stage name as "Lead Belly," his records were usually released under the name "Leadbelly." (Capitol Records)

large part because of the *Opry*, a country-music industry grew up in Nashville in the 1930s and '40s around performers like Roy Acuff, Eddy Arnold, and Hank Williams.

As early as the 1920s, blues and other popular-music forms began employing phrases like "rocking" or "rocking and rolling" in their lyrics. By the close of the 1930s, the term "rock and roll" was used, primarily by black Americans, to refer to both religious and sexual ecstasy. The genre of music that would adopt the term as its label would not emerge for nearly a decade and a half, but these intervening years served as a pressure cooker of influences that intermingled and eventually simmered into a new sound that changed the world.

The middle of the 1940s gave birth to the rise of jump blues, with singers like Louis Jordan finding widespread interracial acceptance. The Arkansas-born Jordan saw his "Ration

Sheet music for W. C. Handy's "Memphis Blues." The song was a hit as "Mr. Crump" in 1909 before Handy, an Alabama-born African American musician and composer, reworked the song and published it under its new title in 1912.

Blues" ascend the race, hillbilly, and pop charts in February of 1944. This era of blues shouters and jump-blues performers was the direct precursor to rock and roll. In 1945, *Billboard* magazine characterized Erskine Hawkins' recording of Caledonia as "rhythmic rock and roll music." The race charts were soon flush with songs that featured a "rocking" theme. Louisiana-born Roy Brown recorded "Good Rockin' Tonight" in 1947. While the lyrics were suggestive, Brown's vocal delivery was somewhat formal. Wynonie Harris, who called himself the "hard-drinkin', hard-lovin', hard-shoutin' Mr. Blues," recorded the same song the following year. His vocal delivery was considerably earthier, with the backing band sounding looser and funkier. It hit #1 on the R&B charts in June of 1948 and would be reinvigorated in the following decade as one of the first classics of the rock era.

As both black and white record buyers embraced the rhythm-and-blues aesthetic, white country artists increasingly incorporated the beat into their folk tunes. At the end of 1946, the Alabama-born Delmore Brothers had a country hit with "Freight Train Boogie," while South Carolinian Arthur Smith hit with "Guitar Boogie" in 1948. Texan Moon Mullican first charted in 1947 with his brand of hillbilly boogie. "We gotta play music that'll make them goddamn beer bottles bounce on the table," Mullican once said of his hopped-up brand of proto-rockabilly.

By the 1940s and early 1950s, more than a thousand independent record companies had begun to spring up to target the market of working-class blacks and whites that were ignored by the major labels' emphasis on sophisticated pop sounds. These independent companies were critical in further exposing the nation to Southern music.

Atlantic Records emerged in late 1947 in New York but didn't have a hit until early 1949, when Tennessean Stick McGhee's "Drinkin' Wine Spo-Dee-O-Dee" became a hit. Its earliest consistent success was with Ruth Brown of Portsmouth, Virginia, who placed more than twenty singles on the R&B chart and helped establish Atlantic as an independent powerhouse.

Perhaps one of the most influential of the independent labels was Chess Records in Chicago. Between 1940 and 1950, the black population of Chicago grew from 278,000 to 492,000—an increase of 77 percent. Many of the new Chicagoans were Southerners who moved north in search of job opportunities and the promise of a better life. Chess stars like Mississippian Muddy Waters brought the

McKinley Morganfield, better known as Muddy Waters, was first recorded at his modest home in Stovall, Mississippi, in 1941 by John Lomax's son Alan.

An advertisement for song folios produced by the Southern Music Publishing Company, a firm launched by Ralph Peer, who first recorded both the Carter Family and Jimmie Rodgers at a 1927 session for the Victor Recording Company.

Louis Jordan's "Ration Blues" climbed the race, hillbilly, and popular music charts in 1944, foreshadowing the cross-genre appeal of rock and roll.

Delta blues to the city and electrified it in a way that would serve as the blueprint for the rock-and-roll instrumental lineup of drums, electric guitar, bass, and piano.

Imperial Records' Fats Domino, who emerged from New Orleans, appeared on the charts for the first time in February of 1950. Hits like "Blueberry Hill," a song originally recorded by Texas-born cowboy singer Gene Autry, landed him in the Top 5 of both the R&B and pop charts.

In July of 1951, white DJ Alan Freed, using the name Moondog, launched a radio show in Cleveland, Ohio, that helped introduce R&B music to white teenagers. He adopted the term "rock and roll" for the R&B platters he was spinning. When he moved to New York in 1954, he renamed his show *Rock 'n' Roll Party*, forever linking the term with a genre of music.

In June of 1954, black blues shouter Big Joe Turner topped the R&B chart with "Shake, Rattle and Roll." White country singer Bill Haley and his band the Comets covered the song, taking it to #7 on the pop chart. His version, however, was heavily edited, omitting an entire verse and sanitizing another. Apparently unaware of the explicit sexual innuendo, Haley preserved the refrain, "I'm like a one-eyed cat, peepin' in a seafood store." Haley enjoyed additional singles on both the pop and R&B rankings but is best remembered for "Rock Around the Clock," which went to #1 on *Billboard*'s Best Sellers chart in July of 1955 and stayed in the top slot for two months. It also made the Top 5 on the R&B chart.

As teenagers embraced R&B and early rock-and-roll records, white parents, teachers, administrators, and religious authorities grew increasing concerned about the effects of "vulgarity" on impressionable young minds. Boycotts and protests only served to make the music more attractive to teenage audiences.

As Haley was topping the charts with his sanitized version of R&B, black Southern artists were continuing to break through to national prominence. On May 7, 1955, Floridian Ray Charles had his first #1 R&B hit with "I Got a Woman." Though he'd had nearly a half-dozen Top 10 hits since first charting in 1951, this was the song that put him on the map with a wider audience. Another product of the melding of black and white musical traditions, Charles spent a portion of his early career playing with a white country band called the Florida Playboys.

The same week that Charles hit the top position with "I Got a Woman," Mississippian Bo Diddley appeared on the charts for the first time with his Chess Records recording of "Bo

Diddley." It eventually climbed to #1 on the R&B chart and established the famous syncopated "Bo Diddley beat" that was highly influential on early rock and roll.

Memphis was the home base of successful country acts like the Louvin Brothers and the Delmore Brothers, but after World War II the city became a mecca for Southern blacks who, reflecting a changing economy, increasingly migrated from rural farms to urban centers where there were more job opportunities. By 1949, WDIA became the first exclusively black-oriented radio station in the country. The success of WDIA—and other stations that soon followed suit—had the unintended byproduct of introducing white teenagers to black music.

One Memphis DJ, Sam Phillips, grew up on a farm near Florence, Alabama, and eventually settled in Memphis in 1945. He took a job with WREC, and by 1950 he had launched a recording studio in a small building at 706 Union Avenue. "I opened the Memphis Recording Service," Phillips later explained to writer Colin Escott, "with the intention of recording singers and musicians from Memphis and the locality who I felt had something that people should be able to hear. I'm talking about blues—both the country style and the rhythm style—and also about gospel or spiritual music and about white country music. I always felt that the people who played this type of music had not been given the opportunity to reach an audience."

In the early years, Phillips was barely scraping by, but he was finally able to get some traction when he set up arrangements to record artists for various independent labels, including Modern and Chess. He cut several sessions in 1950 and 1951 featuring a Mississippi-born blues singer and guitarist named Riley King, who'd moved to Memphis a few years earlier and started performing under the name B. B. King.

While on tour, King mentioned Sam Phillips' recording studio to a radio personality and bandleader from Clarksdale, Mississippi, named Ike Turner. In June of 1951, Ike and his band, which included lead singer Jackie Brenston, traveled to Memphis to record "Rocket 88" under Sam's direction. Many critics regard it as the first true rock-and-roll record. That same summer, Phillips began recording a handful of additional acts for Chess Records, including Mississippian Chester Burnett, known as Howlin' Wolf, and Bobby "Blue" Bland.

By 1952, Phillips chose to start his own label, which he named Sun Records. His first national hit came the following year when Rufus Thomas recorded the Phillips-penned "Bear Cat," an answer song to Big Mama

Wynonie Harris' 1948 recording of "Good Rockin' Tonight" helped set the blueprint for early rock and roll. (King Records)

In the mid-1940s, the Alabama-born Delmore Brothers helped popularize country boogie, which, along with black R&B, would contribute to the birth of rock and roll as a uniquely Southern phenomenon. (King Records)

Fats Domino headlined this 1956 traveling revue, which also included Atlantic Records' Ruth Brown and Macon native Little Richard.

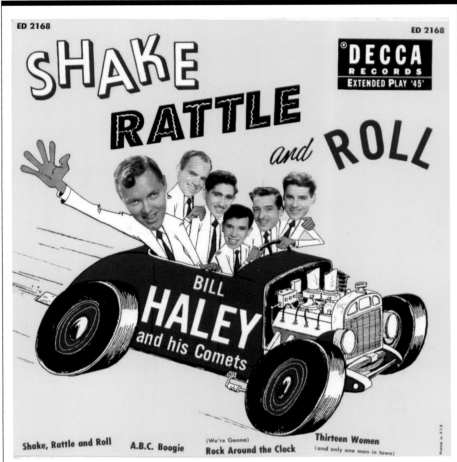

ED 2168

Shake Rattle and ROLL

DECCA RECORDS
EXTENDED PLAY '45'

ED 2168

BILL HALEY and his Comets

Shake, Rattle and Roll   A.B.C. Boogie   (We're Gonna) Rock Around the Clock   Thirteen Women (and only one man in town)

Bill Haley & His Comets covered Big Joe Turner's "Shake, Rattle and Roll" in 1954, as the first rumblings of rock and roll began to transform popular music.

THE GENIUS OF RAY CHARLES

Floridian Ray Charles, who spent time performing with a white country band known as the Florida Playboys, was another R&B star with cross-genre appeal who found success as the rock-and-roll era dawned.

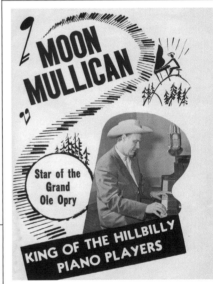

MOON MULLICAN

Star of the Grand Ole Opry

KING OF THE HILLBILLY PIANO PLAYERS

Texan Moon Mullican was another popular country artist who incorporated boogie elements into his brand of pre-rockabilly recordings.

B.B. KING "The blues boy"

R.P.M. RECORDING ARTIST

And His

3-O-Clock in the Morning ORCHESTRA

One of the artists Sam Phillips recorded early on was Mississippi's B. B. King.

Thornton's "Hound Dog." As the 1950s progressed, however, Sam was having less success recording blues music. Though he worked with legends like Little Milton and James Cotton, Phillips had his eye out for something new. He knew that white Southern teens were drawn to the propulsive rhythms of black R&B, but it seemed like forbidden fruit in the racially segregated South. Phillips has often been attributed with the adage that if he could find a white boy who could sing like a black man he'd make a million dollars.

In the summer of 1953, a white Memphis teenager named Elvis Presley stopped by Sam Phillips' Memphis Recording Service and paid a few dollars he'd earned driving a truck for the Crown Electric Company to record a couple of songs. Sam eventually introduced the fledgling performer to a couple of Memphis musicians named Scotty Moore and Bill Black, who helped Presley develop a unique sound. It wasn't exactly country, blues, or R&B, but it had a crackling energy that sounded fresh. "It just sounded sort of raw and ragged," Moore told Elvis' biographer, Peter Guralnick. "We thought it was exciting, but what was it?" Phil-

lips knew in that moment that he'd stumbled on something special, but he wasn't exactly sure what to do with it. "What I was thinking," Sam reflected to Guralnick, "was, where you going to go with this? It's not black, it's not white, it's not pop, it's not country."

What it was, was rockabilly. A white country boy embracing the verve of R&B— but stripping away the horns and ornamentation to get to the raw energy of the music— sounded a little dangerous—and more than a little exciting. In that moment, the simplicity of country, the vibrancy of gospel, and the sexual vitality of R&B collided as Elvis Presley discovered his musical identity.

Elvis readily admitted that those black artists laid the foundation for his breakthrough. "The colored folks been singing and playing it just like I'm doing now, man, for more years than I know," Presley explained in a 1956 interview with the Charlotte *Observer*. "They played it like that in the shanties and in their juke joints and nobody paid it no mind until I goosed it up. I got it from them." It would be a disservice to Presley, however, to simply write him off as a white boy who could imi-

DJ Alan Freed is credited with linking the term "rock and roll" with a specific genre of music.

Publicity photo of the Alabama-born DJ Sam Phillips, who moved to Memphis in 1945 and subsequently founded the Memphis Recording Service and Sun Records.

Jackie Brenston's version of "Rocket 88" is regarded by many as the first true rock-and-roll recording.

Elvis Presley in the film *Jailhouse Rock*. (Metro-Goldwyn-Mayer)

tate black singers. Instead, he was a sensitive performer who wholly absorbed both country music and the blues, channeling them into a unique sound that possessed all the passion and intensity of the best performers in any genre. Sun Records #209, featuring "That's All Right" and "Blue Moon of Kentucky," was released on July 19, 1954, and the future King of Rock and Roll was born.

Elvis' contract was eventually purchased from Sam Phillips in a joint deal between RCA Records, Hill & Range Music Publishing, and Colonel Tom Parker, who became Elvis' lifelong manager. On April 21, 1956, Elvis' "Heartbreak Hotel" became the #1 bestseller in the country as ranked by the *Billboard* chart. He dominated the top slot for twenty-five of the remaining weeks that year with hits like "Hound Dog," "Don't Be Cruel," and "Love Me Tender." Bill Haley might have come first, but Elvis had the magnetism and raw sexual energy that would come to define rock and roll. Presley, a quintessential Southerner with his mix of "yes ma'am" charm and snarling rebelliousness, had become the first real rock-and-roll icon. ★

Arkansas-born Levon Helm of the Band onstage in Hamburg, Germany, May, 1971. (Courtesy of Heinrich Klaffs)

CHAPTER 2
Across the Great Divide: The Growth, Death, and Rebirth of Southern Rock and Roll

★ ★

S ELVIS PRESLEY began his ascent to the throne of rock-and-roll royalty, black artists increasingly crossed over onto the white-dominated singles charts to become identified with the genre. In August of 1955, Chuck Berry entered both the R&B and pop charts with "Maybellene." The song was based on western-swing pioneer Bob Wills' recording of the country fiddle tune "Ida Red." It was the selection that landed Berry his deal with Chess Records when, like Sam Phillips, label head Leonard Chess became intrigued by cross-racial appeal. As Berry recounted in his autobiography, "He couldn't believe that a country tune (he called it a 'hillbilly song') could be written and sung by a black guy." Thanks to his distinctive guitar style and uncanny ability to craft clever lyrics aimed at the teen market, Berry became one of the most important pioneers of early rock and roll, and a kindred spirit with Elvis in the transcendence of his racial appeal.

Like Berry and Presley, the flamboyant Little Richard did much to integrate rock and roll. His "Tutti-Frutti" entered the charts in November 1955, ushering in an era of R&B and mainstream success with songs like "Long Tall Sally," "Keep A Knockin'," and "Good Golly, Miss Molly" that appealed to both black and white audiences. Little Richard, along with Fats Domino and other R&B and early rock-and-roll performers, made important records in Cosimo Matassa's studio in New Orleans. Aside from Sam Phillips, Matassa, an Italian American, was the most important independent Southern-based music-business figure of the 1950s.

Following the success of Presley, Phillips went on to work with Arkansas-born Johnny Cash, who racked up several rockabilly-flavored country hits, including "Folsom Prison Blues" and "Guess Things Happen That Way." Most of his hits were successes on the country chart, though "I Walk the Line" moved into the Top 20 on the mainstream charts at the end of 1956.

Cash toured frequently with another Sun labelmate, Carl Perkins, who grew up in West Tennessee. Perkins learned to sing and play guitar by listening to the *Grand Ole Opry* and sitting at the feet of John Westbrook, a black sharecropper who lived nearby. Carl characterized early rock music as "a country man's song with a black man's rhythm." Despite Elvis' achievements, it was actually Perkins who provided the first million-seller for Sun Records with "Blue Suede Shoes" in 1956.

By 1958, both Cash and Perkins were lured away to Columbia Records, but Sam still had other artists in his stable. Texan Roy Orbison had come aboard in 1956 and scored a hit with "Ooby Dooby." Ultimately, though, rock novelties were not Orbison's preferred material, and he bought out his Sun contract.

One day, when Orbison was in the studio working with Sun producer Jack Clement, a braggadocios fireball of kinetic energy from Ferriday, Louisiana, showed up unexpectedly. Clement recorded him and played the audition for Sam. Phillips liked what he heard and booked an official session with Jerry Lee Lewis. The kinetic sexual energy captured on Lewis' Sun recordings seemed both alluring and dangerous. Teenage record buyers couldn't get enough. When Jerry Lee

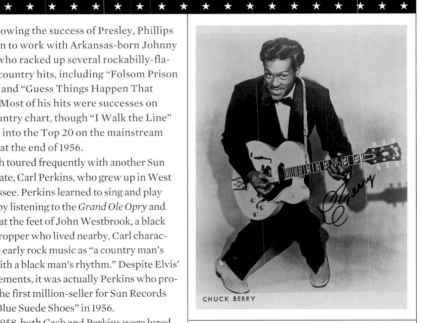

CHUCK BERRY

appeared on Steve Allen's TV show in the summer of 1957 to play "Whole Lotta Shakin' Goin' On," he was a man possessed with the power of rock and roll. The song went to #1 on both the country and R&B charts, and almost reached the top of the pop rankings.

Like Elvis, Carl Perkins, and Jerry Lee Lewis, many of the significant white rock-and-roll artists who emerged in the mid-to-late 1950s were Southerners who were able to draw from both black and white sounds to ignite the interest of young record buyers. Virginian Gene Vincent moved into the Top 10 on the country, R&B, and mainstream charts in the summer of 1956 with "Be-Bop-A-Lula," followed by Texan Buddy Knox, who scored on both the pop and R&B charts in the early

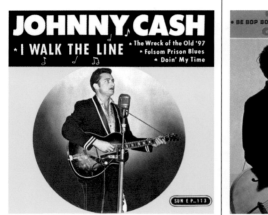

Little Richard's 1957 debut album. (Specialty Records)

took on a political dimension as civil rights activists seized on its potential for influencing integration efforts. Nowhere was this more evident than in the South. The mixing of black and white musical influences played an important part in helping to deconstruct racial barriers, as the hearts and minds of white teenagers were opened to the dawning of a new era of racial reexamination in the 1950s. With rock music, black American culture was mainstreamed into white teen fashion and tastes. "I doubt that many Caucasian persons," Chuck Berry speculated, "would come into a situation that would cause them to know the feeling a black person experiences after being reared under old-time Southern traditions, and then finally being welcomed by an entirely unbiased and friendly audience, applauding without apparent regard for racial difference."

But not everyone was applauding. Rock and roll's opponents believed the music was a tool that was rapidly undermining the traditional moral fabric of America. As the decade drew to a close, those who disliked the influence of rock and roll were delighted by what appeared to be a series of events that led to its apparent unraveling. By the start of 1958, Little Richard unexpectedly announced that, after a born-again experience, he was leaving secular music to study theology and dedicate himself to Christian ministry. In March of that year, Elvis Presley was inducted into the army, leaving many to wonder if his career would survive the two-year hiatus. Two months later, Jerry Lee Lewis was on tour in Europe when the British press discovered that his third wife, Myra, was also his thirteen-year-old cousin. By the time he returned to the States, Jerry Lee was regarded as a public disgrace. In February of 1959, Buddy Holly died in a plane crash along with Ritchie Valens and fellow Texan J. P. Richardson, known as the Big Bopper. In December, Chuck Berry was arrested under the Mann Act for transporting a fourteen-year-old girl across state lines to work in his club. Allegations of a sexual relationship, and Berry's ongoing trials and eventual prison term, discredited him in the eyes of some observers. By the close of the decade, it seemed as if rock and roll was finished.

With Little Richard, Elvis, Jerry Lee, Buddy Holly, and Chuck Berry out of the picture, polite, pop-oriented fare with smoothly rounded edges like "It's All in the Game" by Tommy Edwards and "To Know Him Is to Love Him" by the Teddy Bears ascended to the top of the charts. Though crooner Pat Boone had given birth to the squeaky-clean teen idol movement as early as 1955 with

part of 1957 with his hit "Party Doll." In May of that year, the Everly Brothers debuted with "Bye Bye Love," which went to the Top 5 in the country, R&B, and pop rankings. Their father was a pioneering country guitarist, and the family had settled in Knoxville, Tennessee, where Don Everly and his younger brother Phil attended high school. The Everlys toured extensively with a Texas act called Buddy Holly & the Crickets. There was an instant kinship between Holly and the Everlys, with Phil explaining the connection to Holly's biographer: "We were all from the South."

By the end of 1957, rock and roll almost completely dominated the top of the charts as it developed from a Southern phenomenon into a national craze. Between 1954 and 1959, record sales in America nearly tripled, due in part to the rise of rock and roll and a growing teen market that resulted from the postwar baby boom. For many teens, buying records that their parents found objectionable was an assertion of independence, which only fueled rock and roll's image as a controversial medium.

It wasn't just rebellion for rebellion's sake that parents found unsettling. Rock and roll

JERRY LEE LEWIS   SUN RECORDS

insipid covers of R&B hits like "Ain't That a Shame" and "Tutti Frutti," the sanitized sounds of acts such as Tommy Sands, Frankie Avalon, Fabian, Paul Anka, Neil Sedaka, and Bobby Darin soon dominated the charts.

That same year the payola scandal came to light, in which it was revealed that radio DJs were often accepting money in exchange for airplay. Alan Freed, the man who'd helped popularize the term rock and roll, bore the brunt of the scandal. Amazingly, Dick Clark, whose *American Bandstand* became a nationally broadcast TV show in 1957, emerged relatively unscathed. The clean-cut and well-scrubbed dancers on Clark's tightly controlled program helped neuter rock and roll, making it less threatening to middle-class parents. As the 1950s came to a close, the rough-around-the-edges Southern rockers who defined the genre were pushed to the sidelines in favor of inoffensive alternatives from Philadelphia and New York.

But then everything changed. On January 18, 1964, the Beatles' "I Want to Hold Your Hand" debuted on the US charts. By the beginning of February it was sitting in the #1 position, and by the time they appeared on Ed Sullivan's TV show on Sunday, February 9th, America, too, was caught in the full throes of Beatlemania. By April 4th, the Beatles occupied all five of the top slots on the *Billboard* Hot 100 singles list, opening the floodgates for a British Invasion that dominated popular music in the mid-1960s. Rock and roll would never be the same.

Suddenly, American teenagers were desperate for any music coming from the UK. Dusty Springfield, the Dave Clark Five, Peter & Gordon, the Animals, Manfred Mann, the Kinks,

Dick Clark, as profiled in a DC Comics series in the 1960s.

Herman's Hermits, the Zombies, and Petula Clark all scored significant US hits. The only British band to seriously rival the popularity of the Beatles, however, was the Rolling Stones. The Stones debuted on the US charts in May of 1964 with a cover of Buddy Holly's "Not Fade Away" before breaking out at the end of the year with their first Top 10 hit, "Time Is on My Side," which they learned from a record by New Orleans soul queen Irma Thomas.

The trend continued, with significant British bands like Eric Clapton's Cream and Led Zeppelin emerging by the end of the decade. The common bond among most of the British rock acts was their devotion to the blues, R&B, and early rock and roll that had emerged from the American South. The Beatles, for example, recorded songs by Carl Perkins, Little Richard, Arthur Alexander, Buddy Holly, Elvis Presley, the Everly Brothers, and Ray Charles. Ironically, artists from the American South were virtually absent from popular music during the majority of the 1960s, but their presence lingered under the surface as it crept from the airwaves through a British filter. "The most bizarre part of the whole story," Rolling Stones guitarist Keith Richards noted in his autobiography, "is that having done what we intended to do . . . which was to turn people on to the blues, what actually happened was we turned American people back on to their own music. And that's probably our greatest contribution to music."

"When the British Invasion hit the South, it influenced everybody," recalled Chuck Leavell, who later played keyboards for both the Allman Brothers Band and the Rolling Stones. "I used to go hear Duane and Gregg Allman when they were starting out as the Allman Joys. They had a psychedelic version of 'Satisfaction,' and Duane had two or three Fuzz Face pedals in a row. He would, like, distort his distortion. I remember that they would do their own arrangements of Beatles covers. All of us were being influenced by this influx of the British Invasion."

In August of 1965, the 13th Floor Elevators, a Texas-based band, released an album called *The Psychedelic Sounds of the 13th Floor Elevators*, introducing the term psychedelic as a new offshoot of rock music. British groups like the Yardbirds, Cream, and Pink Floyd quickly associated themselves with psychedelic or "acid" rock, while American bands, including Jefferson Airplane, the Jimi Hendrix Experience, and the Doors, embraced the aesthetic. The Byrds' recording of "Eight Miles High" epitomized the psychedelic sound that would dominate the era. Donovan, the Strawberry Alarm Clock, and other groups adapted psychedelic influences for a pop audience and, by 1967, the psychedelic-fueled hippie counterculture was in full swing.

But the era was relatively short-lived. In February of 1968, the Beatles traveled to India to devote themselves to transcendental meditation under the teachings of the Maharishi Mahesh Yogi. They gave up LSD during this period, but eventually returned home when some band members became disillusioned with the guru. Renewed and refocused, they shed the psychedelic excesses of the *Sgt. Pep-*

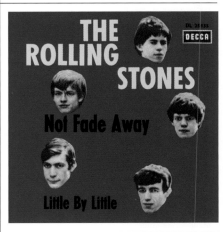

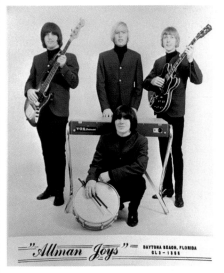

The Allman Joys, *left to right:* Mike Alexander, Gregg Allman, Maynard Portwood (kneeling), and Duane Allman. (Courtesy of the Big House Museum, Macon, Georgia)

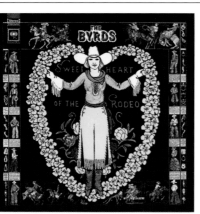

per and *Magical Mystery Tour* albums in favor of the lean, rock aesthetic of the self-titled LP that's come to be known as *The White Album*. A month later, the Rolling Stones returned to an unadorned sound with their *Beggar's Banquet* LP, which explored blues, country, and gospel.

Just before the release of *The White Album* and *Beggar's Banquet*, LSD was made illegal by the federal government of the United States. As the 1970s dawned, the excesses of drug abuse claimed the lives of Jimi Hendrix, Janis Joplin, and Doors lead singer Jim Morrison. The promise of the psychedelic age had proven hollow. As that era wound to a close, music fans were hungry once again for the authentic blues and country roots of early rock and roll.

Bob Dylan had begun to seriously explore American roots music after hiring the group that came to be known as the Band to back up his live performances in the mid-1960s. Dylan and the Band moved to upstate New York together and began recording the Basement Tapes, out of which emerged the latter's debut album, *Music from Big Pink*. With the exception of drummer and vocalist Levon Helm—who hailed from Arkansas—the group was made up of Canadian musicians who were captivated by a romantic vision of the South.

By the time the Band released their self-titled follow-up, with titles like "Cripple Creek" and "The Night They Drove Old Dixie Down," Southern simplicity was the envy of psychedelic superstars who felt like their music had become bloated. "The Band brought things back into perspective," Eric Clapton told *Guitar Player* magazine in 2001. When he inducted them into the Rock and Roll Hall of Fame in 1994, Clapton commented, "For someone like me, who had been born in England . . . and worshiped the music from America . . . this band . . . had it all. They were white, but they seemed to have derived all they could from black music, and they com-

bined it to make a beautiful hybrid. . . . I wanted to be in the Band."

Released the same month as the Band's *Music from Big Pink*, the debut album from Creedence Clearwater Revival channeled the swampy Southern sounds of the Louisiana bayou, setting the stage for subsequent albums like *Bayou Country* and *Green River*, which explored country-leaning material such as "Lodi." Though based in San Francisco, primary songwriter John Fogerty embraced the imagery of the South more extensively than other rock musicians had done. "If the earliest icons of rock and roll are all from the South," Fogerty reflected, during a 2013 interview with Bob Santelli at Los Angeles' Grammy Museum, "that was, at least, the map of where I should go."

A month after the debut albums from the Band and Creedence appeared, the Byrds shocked fans and critics by releasing the explicitly country-themed *Sweetheart of the Rodeo* album. Driven largely by new recruit Gram Parsons, who was raised in Georgia and Florida, and founding member Chris Hillman, who'd started out as a bluegrass musician, the LP was partially recorded in Nashville, and featured covers of songs by Merle Haggard and the Louvin Brothers.

In the wake of Bob Dylan, the Band, CCR, and the Byrds, the rustic sounds of Southern-influenced rock continued to resonate with listeners in the late 1960s and early 1970s. Groups like Buffalo Springfield and the Beau Brummels (who recorded an entire album in Nashville at famed country producer Owen Bradley's studio) sprinkled their albums with rural overtones, while former Monkee Mike Nesmith's First National Band and husband-and-wife duo Delaney & Bonnie promoted an explicit hybrid of rock roots and country sounds. With romanticized notions of Southern life capturing the musical imagination, the stage was set for an authentic rock band from the South to rise to the forefront of the movement. ★

The Muscle Shoals Rhythm Section in the parking lot outside Fame Studios, 1968. *Left to right*: Barry Beckett, Jimmy Johnson, David Hood, Roger Hawkins, and Junior Lowe. (Courtesy of Fame Studios)

CHAPTER 3
Can't Turn You Loose: From Memphis to Muscle Shoals and Back

★ ★

 HILE THE PSYCHEDELIC craze ruled the counterculture in the 1960s, many young white professional recording musicians in the South—those who weren't making a living playing country music in Nashville—were creating soul music alongside African American performers in a musical environment that was considerably more racially integrated than many would have expected. Southern soul—concentrated primarily in Memphis, Tennessee, and Muscle Shoals, Alabama—was emerging as a vibrant genre that was heavily integrated.

In 1960, Stax Records set up shop in a converted movie studio in Memphis. Launched by white siblings Jim Stewart and Estelle Axton, the company got off to a slow start until Jim met a young white guitarist from Georgia named Chips Moman. Chips, who'd moved to Memphis as a teenager, had toured with early rock-and-rollers Johnny Burnette and Gene Vincent before relocating to Los Angeles to pursue work as a studio musician. After returning to Memphis, he eventually wound up doing some recording for Jim Stewart's fledgling operation.

In the fall of 1960, Carla Thomas, daughter of Memphis DJ and singer Rufus Thomas, recorded "Gee Whiz" at Stax. Produced by Chips Moman, it became a nationwide hit and earned the label a distribution deal with Atlantic Records. The nucleus of the Stax rhythm section became guitarist Steve Cropper, keyboardist Booker T. Jones, bassist Lewis Steinberg, and drummer Al Jackson. The racially integrated group made records of their own as Booker T. & the M.G.'s, including the instru-

mental hit "Green Onions," which climbed to #1 on the R&B chart and went Top 5 pop.

In 1962, Otis Redding recorded a couple of songs at Stax, including "These Arms of Mine." Jim Stewart pressed it on Volt Records, a Stax subsidiary, and watched as Redding emerged as the quintessential Southern soul artist. With Otis Redding leading the charge, Stax became an important headquarters of Southern soul in the mid-1960s, producing hit records by Sam & Dave, Eddie Floyd, the Bar-Kays, Albert King, and others. Stax emerged as a unique interracial talent pool of soulful Southern cats who composed timeless hits including "Soul Man,"

Chips Moman (standing, *second from left*) in the studio with Junior Lowe (kneeling), Tommy Cogbill, Spooner Oldham, Wilson Pickett (sitting), Roger Hawkins, and Jimmy Johnson. (Courtesy of Fame Studios)

CARLA THOMAS

The Atlantic/Stax Appreciation Society.

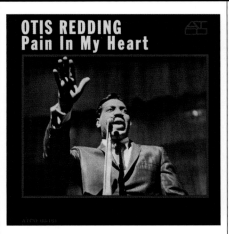

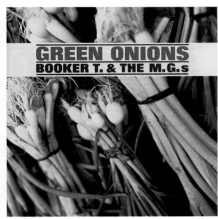

"When Something Is Wrong with My Baby," "Hold On, I'm Comin'," and "Knock on Wood." While many of the songs recorded at Stax were released on either the Stax or Volt imprints, outside artists also found success with the studio's sound. Atlantic Records' Jerry Wexler brought Wilson Pickett to Memphis in 1965 to record with the Stax team, and scored with the #1 R&B singles "In the Midnight Hour" and "634-5789."

Eventually, Stax's Jim Stewart grew more protective of his stable of songwriters and musicians. Wexler and Atlantic, however, were sold on the Southern sound and sought out a fresh well of talent from which to draw. He found it in northwest Alabama, in a region made up of four cities: Muscle Shoals, Florence, Sheffield, and Tuscumbia. The entire region, commonly referred to as Muscle Shoals, had a rich musical history prior to the emergence of soul music. Both black bandleader and composer W. C. Handy and white Sun Records founder Sam Phillips hailed from the city of Florence. But it was a loose coalition of young white musicians who transformed Muscle Shoals into the successor to Memphis' soul music throne.

Tom Stafford, a local music enthusiast, invested in a company launched by local musicians Rick Hall and Billy Sherrill, who played together in a group called the Fairlanes. They named it Florence Alabama Musical Enterprises (FAME) and set up shop above Florence's City Drugstore in the summer of 1959. Their makeshift studio quickly became the focus of a budding regional music scene that attracted a community of young musicians including Donnie Fritts, Spooner Oldham, and Dan Penn. "We all met right there at that drugstore," Penn recalled, years later, in the pages of *Sweet Soul Music*. "Everyone I knew met there."

Dan Penn, from the town of Vernon (an hour and a half south of Muscle Shoals)

became the Fairlanes' lead singer. "He knew more about black music than the rest of us put together," Rick Hall told writer Peter Guralnick. Dan cut his teeth on R&B by soaking up DJ John Richbourg's nightly radio show. Broadcast on Nashville's powerful WLAC, Richbourg—who appeared on the air as "John R."—was a South Carolinian who'd spent time in New York City as a radio soap-opera actor. Though he and fellow WLAC personality Hoss Allen affected black slang and speech patterns that led many listeners to believe they were African American, both men were white.

WLAC's role in introducing white Southerners to the music of Muddy Waters, Sonny Boy Williamson, Fats Domino, and other important black R&B and blues performers

cannot be overstated. Penn exuded a natural soulfulness that seemed to seep from his pores. "The South is an old romantic place, no doubt about it," he reflected, in the liner notes to 2003's *Country Got Soul* compilation. "I think it had a lot to do with the arts, and especially the music. People are slower and more laid-back down here. It's just a romantic place, and that got into the music somewhere."

By the end of 1960, Rick Hall parted ways with Sherrill and Stafford, setting out on his own with a burning ambition to create a music empire. Keeping the FAME name, he put together a studio in an old warehouse outside of town and began hustling for recording projects. The Fairlanes fell apart, and Dan Penn formed a band of his own called the Mark V, which included David Briggs, Norbert Putnam, and Jerry Carrigan. The group formed the backing band on Arthur Alexander's "You Better Move On," which Rick placed with Dot Records. The single went to #24 on the *Billboard* chart and provided the money Rick needed to break ground on a proper studio.

Rick Hall hired Penn, and in the fall of 1962, FAME studio officially opened. In 1964, Rick launched his own label, releasing black soul singer Jimmy Hughes' "Steal Away," which became a Top 20 hit on the *Billboard* Hot 100. Outside soul artists like Joe Tex, Etta James, and others continued to flock to the Muscle Shoals area to record at Rick Hall's facility. When the initial FAME rhythm section of

The Fairlanes, *left to right*: Randy Allen, Charlie Senn, Bill Sherrill, Rick Hall, and Terry Thompson. (Courtesy of Fame Studios)

WLAC's John Richbourg, better known as John R., was one of the most influential R&B disc jockeys in the South. Many listeners were shocked when they learned that Richbourg was white.

The second Fame Studios facility, built following the success of Arthur Alexander's "You Better Move On." (Courtesy of Fame Studios)

After the Mark V, Dan Penn assembled a group in the Muscle Shoals area known as the Pallbearers. *Left to right:* Junior Lowe, Spooner Oldham, Dan Penn, Roger Hawkins, and Donnie Fritts. (Courtesy of Fame Studios)

A publicity photo of Arthur Alexander. (GAC)

Briggs, Putnam, and Carrigan moved to Nashville, it didn't slow Hall's ambitions. He continued on with Jimmy Johnson, Roger Hawkins, Junior Lowe, David Hood, Spooner Oldham, and a handful of others. "The sounds that were coming out of Rick Hall's FAME studios there in Muscle Shoals were unique," ZZ Top's Billy Gibbons observed, "because the musicians were white guys. It was only the singers that were the black guys. Steve Cropper always said, 'Find me the white guys to play it and the black guys to sing it and express it, and that's the winning combo.'" The combination worked so well that work was flowing in during the mid-1960s, and Hall couldn't manage it all by himself.

Local DJ Quin Ivy had written songs for Rick's company, and now sought Hall's blessing to open up a studio of his own with the objective of picking up the scraps of work that FAME couldn't take on. Rick agreed. When Jimmy Hughes' cousin, a local hospital orderly, was referred to Ivy's studio, the musicians cut a track engineered by Jimmy Johnson and featuring Spooner Oldham playing a distinctive organ part. The result, "When a Man Loves a Woman," was Percy Sledge's recording debut. Rick Hall sent the tape to Atlantic Records on Quin's behalf, and it became the first Southern soul song to cross over to #1 on the pop chart.

Impressed by the success of "When a Man Loves a Woman," Jerry Wexler brought Wilson Pickett to FAME in early 1966, where they cut "Land of 1000 Dances." He asked Chips Moman to come in from Memphis to play on the Pickett session. Dan Penn and Chips Moman were kindred spirits, and though they had met in Nashville previ-

ously, their time together in Muscle Shoals strengthened their mutual admiration.

Chips eventually launched American Studios in Memphis. In 1966 he was assembling a permanent house band and hoped to recruit Dan to join him there. Chips began hanging out and playing sessions in Muscle Shoals in an attempt to woo his friend to Memphis. Penn wanted to produce records, but Rick Hall maintained tight control of the FAME studio. Convinced he'd never get the opportunity in Muscle Shoals, Penn defected to Memphis with Chips in the summer of 1966. Spooner Oldham, who'd co-written James and Bobby Purify's Top 10 pop hit "I'm Your Puppet" with Dan, joined them in Memphis the following year.

The Memphis Boys, as Chips and his musicians came to be called, recorded well over one hundred charting hits. He perfected a sound that blended the best of black and white musical influences. "It's the dead center between Delta blues and Nashville country," Memphis Boy Reggie Young said of his city, with a nod to both the geographical and stylistic significance of his observation.

During 1967, Chips and Dan bounced back and forth between Memphis and Muscle Shoals for recording sessions. That same year, Little Esther Phillips recorded at American, which marked the studio's first work for Atlantic Records. Before long, Wilson Pickett, King Curtis, and others were making the trek to Memphis to work with Chips Moman and his team. While the American Studio was still significantly involved in soul music, the Memphis Boys were a versatile assemblage of musicians who could find success in multiple genres.

Their greatest success that year came from a local band of white rock musicians.

Dan Penn had moved to Memphis in hopes that he would have the opportunity to produce records. He asked Chips to assign him any act that Moman wasn't interested in working with. Moman thought of a local rock group called the Devilles, fronted by a teenager named Alex Chilton. By the time the Devilles showed up at American for their recording date, they'd changed their name to the Box Tops. They recorded a Wayne Carson song called "The Letter" that soon climbed to the #1 position on the *Billboard* chart. It stayed there for four weeks.

"Alex and I wanted to cut 'Wang Dang Doodle,' that old Willie Dixon song," band member Gary Talley recalled, in an interview with author Roben Jones. "Dan said, 'Oh, no, we can't cut that, that's about razor totin' and carryin' guns.'" In 1968, the Box Tops had another major hit with Dan Penn and Spooner Oldham's "Cry Like a Baby," but they may well have become the first real Southern rock band, were it not for Dan Penn's desire to keep them oriented toward the sound that was bringing them success on pop radio.

A month after "Cry Like a Baby" debuted on the *Billboard* chart, a national tragedy struck Memphis that changed the musical landscape of the South and ultimately gave birth to the circumstances that ushered in the Southern rock era.

On April 4, 1968, civil rights leader Martin Luther King, Jr., was in Memphis in support of black sanitation workers who were on strike to protest unequal wages and inequitable working conditions. When he stepped out onto the second floor balcony of his motel room in the early evening, he was struck by an assassin's bullet. Following the pronouncement of King's death, riots broke out in major US cities, including Washington D.C., Baltimore, and Chicago. "The whole complexion of everything changed," Rufus Thomas explained, in a 2007 Stax Records documentary. And *everything* included the music business.

The continued fallout from King's assassination rippled through every segment of American society. Southern recording studios, which had previously been oases of harmony within otherwise racially troubled communities, were no longer immune to societal tensions. "We never did have any problem with the KKK," explained Muscle Shoals mainstay Jimmy Johnson. "We figured out the reason was that they loved 'Mustang Sally.' They didn't want to change that. We never had one moment where any-body got out of line, except for looks. No cat-calls or 'n' word. Nothin'."

Following King's death, however, mis-trust and racial unrest began to infect even the sanctuaries of musical integration that existed in Memphis and Muscle Shoals. "I can tell you that prior to that," Stax producer and musician Steve Cropper tearfully explained, in the 2007 film *Respect Yourself,* "there was never, ever any color that came through the doors. Didn't happen. After that, it was never the same." American Studio mainstay Bobby Emmons agreed. "I thought, musician-wise, there was no segregation in music circles that I experienced, until after the assassination," he revealed, in *Memphis Boys.* "After that, it seemed like everybody felt an obligation to divide down racial lines for one reason or another."

Four months after the civil rights leader's death, tensions reached a boiling point at the National Association of Television and Radio Announcers' annual convention in Miami. King himself had addressed the trade organization for black DJs at the previous year's gathering. Discussions at the event included reflections on the state of an industry with many powerful white-owned radio stations and record labels succeeding on the backs of black DJs and per-formers. In the wake of civil rights advances, African Americans understandably wanted a larger piece of the pie that they had helped create. As NATRA called for change, some of its leaders were subjected to harassment and anonymous threats from whites. At the 1968 convention, with the sting of King's death still fresh, some attendees grew more militant. An unsanctioned group calling themselves the Fair Play Committee appeared at the conference, loudly declaring their intent to wrest power from the "white colonialists" who controlled black music, and threatening violence against those who refused to cooperate. Rumors of kid-nappings, physical confrontations, pistol-whip-pings, and death threats spread throughout the hallways of the Sheraton Four Ambassadors Hotel where the event was being hosted. "I was threatened," Jerry Wexler—who was report-edly hung in effigy—confirmed to author Peter Guralnick. "They hustled me out of there when somebody with a gun appeared at the registra-tion and said, 'I'm looking for Wexler.'"

Otis Redding's white manager, Phil Walden, was also threatened. "I went to the conven-tion," Walden added. "Marshall Sehorn [a white New Orleans music promoter] got beaten up in the shower. I got threatened.... I saw all the things I worked for being destroyed, Dr. King killed, and someone like me being

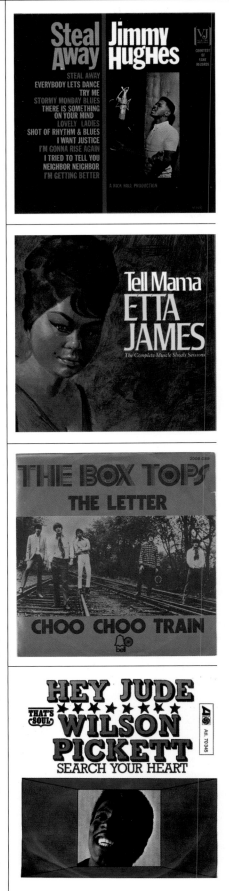

Steve Cropper. (Stax Records)

hit with more racist stuff than George Wallace ever was. It made me *sick*. You know, if I was a young black, I'd probably have been the most militant son of a bitch in the black race. But I just got tired of being called 'whitey' and 'honky.'" Homer Banks, a black songwriter at Stax, believed the shift in the R&B business was inevitable. "A lot of people had to get out of Miami for safety reasons," he confirmed to Guralnick. "It was heavy, but it was destined to come. If not at Miami, then somewhere else.... Blacks made the music, blacks made the audience, but the ownership was white."

"All of a sudden," Jimmy Johnson recalled, "blacks took over their own music at all the record labels. All the A&R people were black, when before that it had been white. We thought, 'Man, our lives have ended. Ninety-eight percent of what we did was black, and it was like, 'Oh shit, what are we gonna do now?'"

What most white Southern music-industry professionals did was search for new avenues to stay viable in a musical climate that had suddenly shifted. "I just decided I'd get into white rock and roll," Phil Walden explained, following his experience at the Miami convention, "and that's what I did." Walden's first signing was a young white musician from Florida named Duane Allman, who'd been working as a guitarist at Rick Hall's FAME studio. Allman had generated considerable attention with his wild guitar solo during the long vamp at the conclusion of Wilson Pickett's recording of "Hey Jude." "Do you know what happened at that moment?" remarked Jimmy Johnson, who was in the studio for the Pickett session. "Duane Allman went fuckin' bananas, and Southern rock was born." ★

AIN'T WASTIN' TIME NO MORE: THE ALLMAN BROTHERS BAND AND THE RISE OF THE SOUTHERN ROCK ERA

"The Allmans were the great Southern rock band, but they were more than that. They defined the best of every music from the American South in that time. They were the best of all of us."

—BILLY GIBBONS, ZZ TOP, 2005

THE ALLMAN BROTHERS BAND

- **DUANE ALLMAN** guitar
- **GREGG ALLMAN** vocals, organ, guitar
- **JAI JOHANNY "JAIMOE" JOHANSON** drums, percussion
- **BERRY OAKLEY** bass, vocals
- **BUTCH TRUCKS** drums
- **DICKEY BETTS** guitar, vocals
- **CHUCK LEAVELL** keyboards
- **LAMAR WILLIAMS** bass

The Allman Brothers Band in 1969. *Left to right*: Dickey Betts, Berry Oakley, Jaimoe, Duane Allman, Butch Trucks, and Gregg Allman. (Photo by Twiggs Lyndon, courtesy of the Big House Museum, Macon, Georgia)

"ANYBODY IN THIS room who's not going to play in my band, you've got to fight your way out," Duane Allman declared breathlessly as he moved to block the exit door. Covered in sweat, and with his instrument still draped around his neck, the twenty-two-year-old guitarist was practically giddy. Three hours earlier, a half-dozen musicians had gathered at a house in Jacksonville, Florida, for a Sunday jam session. Once they'd started, the music flowed with an effortlessly euphoric synergy that, when they finally wound to a close, left everyone in the room speechless.

It was March of 1969, and those gathered were already key figures in Jacksonville's budding hippie culture. Drummer Butch Trucks was in a regionally popular folk-rock group called the 31st of February that had recorded for Vanguard Records. Guitarist Dickey Betts, bassist Berry Oakley, and keyboardist Reese Wynans played in a well-known local band called the Second Coming. Additional drummer Jai Johanny "Jaimoe" Johanson had been in Otis Redding's touring band before joining up with Duane Allman and Berry Oakley to experiment with new sounds that blended blues, rock, R&B, and jazz.

"Nobody'd ever done anything like that before," Duane later said of the afternoon jam. "It really frightened the shit out of everybody. Right then, I knew. I said, 'Man, here it is, here it *is*.'" It was exactly the sound Duane had been searching for but hadn't yet been able to articulate until stumbling upon it in Jacksonville. It may have been the "big bang" of Southern rock, but the newly formed group still needed a singer. Duane contacted his younger brother Gregg, who was still in California following the brothers' failed attempt to find success with an earlier band called the Hour Glass. "One Sunday morning," Gregg told *Guitar Player* magazine, "Duane called me on the phone, and he said he had this band together with two lead guitar players, and I thought, 'Well, that's weird.' Then he says, 'And two drummers.' And I said, 'That's *real* weird!'" But Duane was persuasive. Within days, Gregg had arrived in Florida. Since he also played organ, Duane broke the news to Reese Wynans that the group wouldn't need two keyboardists.

With that, the Allman Brothers Band was born. "Our thing was so perfect," Gregg explained, in his autobiography, "and on paper, it shouldn't have been—we had two drummers, not to mention that one of them was a black man and we were in the Deep South, 1969. The way I saw it, fate brought a certain group of musicians together who just blended perfectly." So perfectly, in fact, that they would become one of the most popular American bands of the 1970s, surviving an avalanche of addictions, rehab stints, marriages, divorces, deaths, legal troubles, tragic accidents, arrests, breakups, and reunions that would be too unbelievably melodramatic for the storyline of a credible Southern Gothic novel.

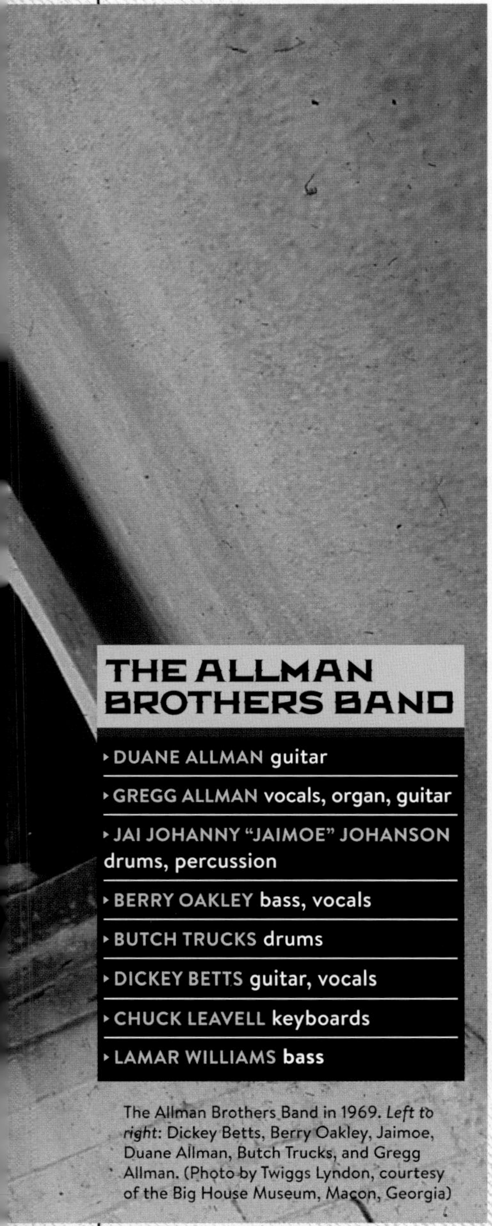

Dial Records publicity photo of the Allman Joys. *Left to right:* Gregg Allman, Duane Allman, Bob Keller, and Bill Connell. (Courtesy of the Big House Museum, Macon, Georgia)

CHAPTER 4
Changing of the Guard: The Allman Joys

★ ★

 OWARD DUANE ALLMAN and Gregory LeNoir Allman were born in Nashville, Tennessee, in 1946 and 1947 respectively. They were the only children of Geraldine and Willis "Bill" Allman, who'd served in World War II before coming home and relocating the family from Nashville to an assignment at Fort Story near Norfolk, Virginia. On the day after Christmas 1949, Bill and a friend agreed to give a ride to a fellow army veteran they'd met in a bar. The stranger pulled a pistol on the two men in an attempted robbery. Duane and Gregg's father was shot and killed.

As their mother struggled to support them, Duane and Gregg wound up spending a lot of time with their grandmother in Nashville. She was one of the first to expose the Allman brothers to music. "The first stuff I heard," Duane recalled years later, "was Hank Williams and Flatt & Scruggs on my grandma's old 78 player." Duane and Gregg's first taste of live performance was also rooted in country music. "When we lived in Tennessee," Gregg told *Rolling Stone* magazine, "my grandmother drug us off to that damn *Grand Ole Opry* every Saturday night."

Eventually, Geraldine sent her sons to Castle Heights Military Academy in Lebanon, Tennessee, so she could focus on getting an education to become a CPA. Duane and Gregg, who were in the third and fourth grade, respectively, were roommates with a typical brotherly relationship. "He pretty much whipped my ass every day of my life when we were little," Gregg explained. He was relieved, in 1959, when Geraldine found a good job in Daytona

THE ALLMAN JOYS

- DUANE ALLMAN vocals, guitar
- GREGG ALLMAN vocals, guitar, organ
- VAN HARRISON bass
- MAYNARD PORTWOOD drums
- BOB KELLER bass
- MIKE ALEXANDER bass
- BILL CONNELL drums
- RALPH BALLINGER bass

Beach, Florida, and moved there with her boys.

Though they were now Floridians, Duane and Gregg would spend a few weeks each summer visiting family back in Tennessee. It was there, in the summer of 1960, that they attended a package concert at Nashville's Municipal Auditorium, featuring Jackie Wilson, B. B. King, and others. "My brother was just mesmerized," Gregg recalled, in his memoirs.

Later that summer, Gregg spotted a cheap guitar on the front porch of his grandmother's neighbor's house. Jimmy Banes was no virtuoso, but he taught twelve-year-old Gregg an E chord, and the younger Allman brother was hooked. When he returned to Daytona at the end of the summer, Gregg found a paper route and, within weeks, was at Sears, purchasing a $21 Silvertone guitar. It wasn't long before Gregg's big brother became intrigued, too. "I was about fourteen," Duane remembered, in an interview with *Crawdaddy!*, "and I had a motorcycle and I wrecked it, and

Gregg got a guitar so I traded the parts for a guitar and got him to teach me to play."

From their earliest years as musicians, the boys were trying to master the blues. "We listened," Gregg recalled, in a 1979 *Rolling Stone* profile, "to Elmore James, Sonny Boy Williamson, Howlin' Wolf, Ray Charles, B. B. King. I guess Little Milton was about my favorite." In addition to the influence of records, Duane had a friend named Jim Shepley, who mentored the brothers in their guitar education. "From the first day I showed him Jimmy Reed licks," Shepley recounted in an interview with *Guitar Player* magazine, "Duane knew that he only wanted to be one thing: a rock-and-roll star."

While Gregg was generally shy and reserved, Duane was charismatic and crackling with hyper energy. "Him and I did a lot of outrageous things together," Shepley told writer Jas Obrecht. "We partied pretty hard. He was always taking a lot of chances, whether it was motorcycles or climbing up to the top of a newly finished building.... He was a pretty outrageous type, man."

As they worked up their instrumental chops, Duane and Gregg played with each other, and with other friends, in groups with names like the Y Teens. "The first band that we put together ourselves was called the Shufflers," Gregg remembered, in 1981, "and I played lead guitar and Duane sang." Once the music had captured Duane's attention, he took much more interest in playing guitar, sniffing glue, and getting rowdy than he did in getting an education. Thanks to his shenanigans, he was back at Castle Heights Military Academy by his junior year of high school. Gregg soon followed. While there, they formed a

The Escorts, *left to right*: Van Harrison, Duane Allman, Maynard Portwood, and Gregg Allman. (Courtesy of the Big House Museum, Macon, Georgia)

band called the Misfits with their friend Mike Johnstone on bass. "We did what I call black rock and roll," Johnstone recalled in Randy Poe's autobiography of Duane Allman, "the early R&B things: Bobby 'Blue' Bland and Ray Charles and James Brown." Duane practiced religiously and taught himself every guitar lick on every record he owned.

Sometime in late 1963 or early 1964, Duane returned to Daytona. Before long, Gregg was back in Florida, too, and he and Duane spent their free time working themselves into the local scene. "Musicians find musicians," Gregg explained, in his book, "and I met every one of them in Daytona—black, white, and everything in between. . . . If a musician could play, we didn't look at his skin color, but unfortunately we were in the minority back then, since when it came to racism, that shit was boiling up in the South."

Jim Shepley played in a band led by Bob Greenlee called the Houserockers that regularly backed a vocal group known as the Untils. "The Untils were the singers, four black guys," explained Floyd Miles, who was one of those black singers, "and the Houserockers were all white. Eventually, Gregg and Duane started sitting in with the band." It would prove to be a great experience for the budding guitarists. "We were a smokin' band," Duane remembered. "Boy, I mean we would set fire to a building in a second. . . . Sixteen years old, $41 a week. Big time."

"Gregg and the drummer and the bass player, Van Harrison, left and formed the Escorts," Houserockers leader Bob Greenlee recalled to Obrecht. The drums were covered by Tommy Anderson or Maynard Portwood, who switched in and out of the band. In their earliest days of playing together, Duane handled most of the vocal duties, but it was during this era that Gregg started singing, too. It would take some time, however, before he perfected his gravelly vocal style by imitating Lit-

tle Milton. "I still have some tapes of that first time I sang onstage at some club in Daytona," Gregg told *Rolling Stone* magazine in 1975. "It is just purely awful noise. I sound like a cross between Hank Williams with the croup and James Brown with no lips."

When they weren't playing at teen dances, the Escorts could be found hanging around the Surf Bar in Daytona Beach, where Gregg studied local black singers like Charles Atkins and Floyd Miles. "He idolized them," Jim Shepley confirmed. "He tried to sound like them. As a matter of fact, he tried to sing like them, he tried to act like them, he spent time with them." Floyd Miles, in particular, turned Gregg on to a whole new musical world. "Way back in 1960, when I was thirteen or fourteen," Gregg recounted, in a 2000 interview with *Hittin' the Note* magazine, "Floyd started taking me over across the tracks—literally. Blacks lived on the other side of the railroad tracks in Daytona. . . . He took me over there to this place, which was a combination convenience store/drug store/record store. . . . They had this big bin in the middle of the store just full of records, and he said, 'This is James Brown and this is B. B. King and this is Sonny Boy Williamson and this is Howlin' Wolf.'"

By 1965, the Escorts had changed their name to the Allman Joys. "They were unbelievable," Lynyrd Skynyrd lead guitarist and Jack-

sonville native Gary Rossington recalled, while reflecting on the times that he and his bandmates would drive to Daytona to catch the Allman Joys live. "They'd have a new single figured out the day after it came out. . . . We'd just stand there with our mouths open and go, 'Look at those guys.' They were that much better than everyone else."

When the Nightcrawlers—another local group fronted by Sylvan Wells—recorded a single called "Little Black Egg" that dented the *Billboard* charts in the mid-1960s, the Allman Joys were inspired to visit a local studio to record some demos. With Duane handling most of the vocals, they recorded cover versions of popular songs. It helped them book the best venues in town, including the Martinique, where a lot of young musicians hung out. One night at the Martinique, the Allmans heard a band called the Bitter Ind (short for "Individual") who'd come up from Jacksonville to try to gain some notoriety in Daytona. The group's drummer was future Allman Brothers Band member Butch Trucks. "We started playing our set and in comes . . . some *presence*," Trucks recalled, to Gavin Edwards, in a 1999 *Rolling Stone* article. That presence was Duane Allman. "Duane was a ball of fire," Butch continued. "He's the type, you'd be sitting in a room with about two or three hundred people talking, and he walks in and everybody looks. Something just came

The Allman Joys, *left to right*: Duane Allman, Mike Alexander, Maynard Portwood, and Gregg Allman. (Courtesy of the Big House Museum, Macon, Georgia)

The Allman Joys, *left to right:* Gregg Allman, Bob Keller, Maynard Portwood (sitting), and Duane Allman. (Courtesy of the Big House Museum, Macon, Georgia)

through: charisma, whatever you want to call it."

"About three or four weeks later," Trucks remembered, "I get a call from Duane. They're playing downtown at this place called the Beachcomber, a little late-night club in downtown Jacksonville . . . and they needed a drummer." Butch only played a couple of nights with the Allman Joys, but it led to the Bitter Ind becoming the house band at the Beachcomber for over a year. It would be a few years before the Allman brothers crossed musical paths with Butch Trucks once again.

In April 1965, the Allman Joys and the Nightcrawlers were hired as dual opening acts for the Beach Boys at a local ballpark. By that point, Duane had already dropped out of school for a life of music. Within two months, Gregg graduated with a career path of his own in mind. "I had my goal set to be a dental surgeon," he told Alan Paul. "I was already accepted to college in Louisiana." First, however, he decided to take some time off to have some fun with his music. "Hell, I had some adventures in my soul," Gregg told *Rolling Stone* in 1999, "I figured I'd go out and play the chitlin' circuit for a year—the places that had the chicken wire up so the beer bottles wouldn't hit you. I knew we weren't going to make any money. But perhaps we'd meet some fine-looking women."

Van Harrison quit the band to pursue his college studies, so Duane, Gregg, and Maynard Portwood got a booking agent and hit the road with a new bassist, Bob Keller, for $100 per week each. "We had our own sound system, amps, and a fucking station wagon," Gregg told

Cameron Crowe in 1973. "Big time. Our first gig was in Mobile, at a place called the Stork Club. Boy, it was a nasty fucking place. I was homesick and the band had broken up about fourteen times before we got there."

The Allman Joys played a stint at a club called the Briar Patch in Nashville, where they met John D. Loudermilk, an RCA recording artist best known as the songwriter of country hits like Stonewall Jackson's "Waterloo" and George Hamilton IV's "Abilene." Seeing potential in the young group, Loudermilk invited them to stay at his home, where he mentored them and helped develop their talent. "We had the best time," Loudermilk recalled in an interview with author Randy Poe, "sittin' around talking and philosophizing. See, I was a little bit older than them, so they listened very carefully and they learned real quickly."

When they returned to Florida, Gregg got a Vox organ and taught himself to play. Though he still played guitar on many of the songs, it was the first time that he would begin to incorporate keyboards into the band's sound. After playing with the group for around six months, Bob Keller departed, with Mike Alexander replacing him on bass.

As 1966 dawned, the Allman Joys continued to book extended gigs outside the region. "We went to New York for the first time in '66," Gregg recalled, "and we played a place called Trude Heller's, which was on 9th Street and Avenue of the Americas." It turned into an extended gig, and Duane and Gregg started getting serious about being a truly professional unit. They gave drummer Maynard Portwood several hundred dollars to get his rotten teeth fixed, but when the money disappeared and the teeth remained unchanged, they replaced him with Bill Connell, whom they recruited from another Southern group called the 5 Men-Its. "One night," Gregg remembered in *My Cross to Bear*, "the whole damn Rolling Stones filed in, and my brother, being the ballsy son of a bitch that he was, launched into '19th Nervous Breakdown,' and we just smoked it."

Later that summer, the Allman Joys returned to the Briar Patch in Nashville and resumed their relationship with Loudermilk. Around that time, Mike Alexander departed and Bob Keller came back into the band on bass. Loudermilk produced some demos of the group at the famed Bradley's Barn recording studio. When songwriter John Hurley got to know the band through their gig at the Briar Patch, he convinced influential music publisher and record executive Buddy Killen to give them a shot. In addition to the Bradley's Barn recordings, they did some tracks at RCA,

and at Killen's studio, with Hurley producing. The results were what Duane's biographer Randy Poe described as "a mix of the Beatles, Animals, Booker T. & the M.G.'s. and Mitch Ryder & the Detroit Wheels—with a Southern-accented singer and a lead guitarist clearly obsessed with his fuzz box."

Killen's Dial Records released the Loudermilk-produced "Spoonful" and "You Deserve Each Other" as two sides of a single in 1966. The Dial period wouldn't provide the Allman Joys with their big break, and their antics were more memorable than their recorded music. "They shot off a pistol in the studio," Loudermilk recalled. "They shot a hole in the roof, and Owen Bradley called me about two weeks later and said, 'Man, it's raining, and the water's coming right through this hole. I don't remember if I fixed the hole or if I paid to have it fixed or what. It just became part of the myth."

In the summer of 1966, the Allman Joys played a gig at a club called the Spanish Village in Pensacola, Florida. The house band was the Minutes, a group from Tuscaloosa, Alabama, that was originally a five-piece ensemble called the 5 Men-Its before becoming a quartet and changing the spelling to the 5 Minutes. They eventually dropped the "5" altogether. The band consisted of singer and guitarist Eddie Hinton, drummer Johnny Sandlin, guitarist and keyboardist Paul Hornsby, and bassist Fred Styles. "It was just eye opening," Sandlin said of seeing the Allman Joys for the first time. "I couldn't even imagine a band that good. And what a look! This was before long hair was safe to have in the South, and Gregg and Duane both had this shoulder-length blond hair." Bill Connell, who'd played with the Minutes before joining the Allman Joys, made the introductions between the two bands, and the groups stayed in touch. "There was something about Duane," Sandlin noted. "You almost had to know him to understand what it was, because I don't think I can describe it. You could tell Duane had an undeniable passion for music, and something was going to happen with him." ★

The Minutes in 1966. *Left to right:* Fred Styles, Paul Hornsby, Eddie Hinton, and Johnny Sandlin. (Courtesy of Johnny Sandlin)

The Hour Glass, *left to right*: Gregg Allman, Johnny Sandlin, Paul Hornsby, Duane Allman, and Mabron McKinney. (Courtesy of the Big House Museum, Macon, Georgia)

CHAPTER 5
Got to Get Away: The Hour Glass

★ ★

BY **EARLY 1967,** the Allman Joys were the standard by which other Southern cover bands were measuring themselves. Great admiration, however, didn't necessarily translate into great financial reward. The Allman Joys were barely limping along with an extended gig in St. Louis. When Bob Keller left the band, he was replaced with bassist Ralph Ballinger. Then drummer Bill Connell joined the navy, and the group fell apart.

Meanwhile, the members of the Minutes were experiencing declining bookings and lineup changes of their own. "We were starvin' for a few weeks, livin' out of Johnny Sandlin's parents' garage," Paul Hornsby recalled. "Duane called me and said, 'Paul, how'd you like to have me and Gregg in your band?' He said, 'Our bass player quit and Bill Connell's getting drafted, so it's just me and Gregg.' Within a day or two they were in Decatur, Alabama, in the garage with the rest of us."

Dropping guitarist Pete Carr from the lineup, Johnny Sandlin, Paul Hornsby, and Minutes bassist Mabron McKinney joined forces with the Allmans to build a new band. "We rehearsed a lot," Sandlin recounted. "It was a week or two that we were there. It didn't take us too long, because our bands had a lot of the same songs in common. We just focused on getting ourselves ready to go out and play."

The newly formed group returned to St. Louis in the late spring to hone their sound and play local gigs. "There was an area there called Gaslight Square," Hornsby explained, "that was kind of like Bourbon Street in New Orleans. It was a very touristy place. They said they could get us a two-week booking there. We stretched that into a monthlong gig."

One day in St. Louis, Mabron McKinney ran into the members of the Nitty Gritty Dirt Band, who were in town for a gig at the Kiel Auditorium. Though it would be a few years before the Dirt Band would break through with their hit single "Mr. Bojangles," they had already released an album on Liberty Records and were promoting the single "Buy for Me the Rain," which was a moderate hit. McKinney invited them to come see the Allman-Act, as Johnny Sandlin remembered they were calling themselves at the time, at Pepe's a Go Go in Gaslight Square.

The Nitty Gritty Dirt Band did, in fact, show up to the club, and Bill McEuen, who managed the Dirt Band, was impressed when he heard the Allmans. "He got real excited and said we were the best band he'd ever heard," Hornsby recalled. "He called them in L.A. and said he'd just discovered the next Rolling Stones. He told us, 'I can get you a record deal if you'll come out to California.' He was ready to manage us."

GIGANTIC
SHOW and DANCE
The Allman Joys

Playing their smash hit "SPOONFUL"
on Dial Records

Fort Brandon Armory
TUSCALOOSA
Friday, November 25
Admission $1.50   8:00 — 12:00 —
Don't Miss the NEW Psychedelic Sound

An Allman Joys concert poster for a show at the Fort Brandon Armory in Tuscaloosa, Alabama, 1966.

Deciding to try their luck in the Golden state, the Allmans and their bandmates packed up and headed west. It might have been the Summer of Love at their California destination, but the rest of the country wasn't always as friendly to long-haired hippies. "When we were first driving to Los Angeles," Sandlin remembered, "we pulled up to get gas at this little place, and the people in the service station came out running with an axe handle toward us. We drove right on!"

When the Allmans arrived in Los Angeles, Bill McEuen got them a contract with Liberty Records and set about trying to attract local attention. "The first gig we did when we got out to L.A. was opening for the Doors at the Hullabaloo Club," Gregg recounted in his autobiography, "and that scared me to death—I could barely sing!" Liberty enlisted a pro-

THE HOUR GLASS

▸ DUANE ALLMAN guitar

▸ GREGG ALLMAN guitar, vocals, organ

▸ PAUL HORNSBY keyboards, guitar

▸ JOHNNY SANDLIN drums

▸ MABRON MCKINNEY bass

▸ BOB KELLER bass

▸ PETE CARR bass

The Minutes in the fall of 1966. *Left to right:* Paul Hornsby, Eddie Hinton, Mabron McKinney, and Johnny Sandlin. Eddie Hinton would soon be replaced by guitarist Pete Carr. (Courtesy of Johnny Sandlin).

Duane Allman, Gregg Allman, Johnny Sandlin, Paul Hornsby, and Mabron McKinney, 1967. (Courtesy of the Big House Museum, Macon, Georgia)

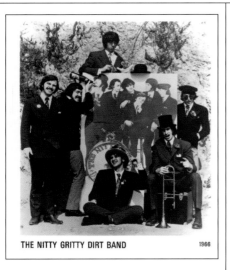

THE NITTY GRITTY DIRT BAND   1966

the record company had different ideas than they did about what the band should be. Hoping to cast them in the mold of a psychedelic pop group, the label presented them with a limited number of songs from which to choose, as Paul Hornsby recalled:

> Here we were in L.A., ready to do an album, and all we knew was our club set. We hadn't had time to put anything together yet. They had to throw something at us, 'cause we didn't have anything else. But the shit they were throwin' at us . . . the producer had no earthly idea what we were like. For whatever reason, this guy never noticed Duane. I don't know why. I mean, Duane was the shit. He thought Gregg was a soul singer and we were the backup band. He kept referring to us as a Motown band.

The band members were dismayed by the label's choice of songs. "Recording that album was a horrific experience," Gregg remembered in his autobiography. "We hated the whole process, because every time we tried to loosen it up a little bit, they would stiffen it right back up. They'd force us back into the pop bullshit that they wanted us to do." From the get-go, the band members were at odds with their producer and had little faith in his understanding of what they were about. "Our producer had done Jan & Dean's surf-type stuff," Paul Hornsby continued. "Now he's hearing the very first Southern rock band and doesn't know what in the hell it is. It's like we'd come from Mars or something, and he absolutely didn't know what to do with it." Gregg summed up his opinion of their producer when he noted, "Dallas Smith had a background as a shoe salesman. And as a producer, he was a hell of a shoe salesman."

Despite the subpar quality of the recorded material, the Hour Glass became a live force to be reckoned with. "Back then, nobody in L.A. knew what the word 'jam' meant," Paul Hornsby explained, "and we kind of started that." They earned a fierce local following, and would regularly have friends like Janis Joplin, Neil Young, Stephen Stills, Jackson Browne, and others join them onstage for extended jam sessions at venues like the Whisky a Go Go. "It was obvious," Dirt Band member John McEuen related, "that this Duane Allman guy was either transported from a different age or he was going to be a leading commentator on the guitar for our age."

The self-titled Hour Glass album came out in October 1967. It featured only one original song, Gregg's "Got to Get Away," which was recycled from the Nashville sessions. Duane's

ducer named Dallas Smith, who had produced the Dirt Band's album, to work with them on their debut LP. The first thing the label did was change the band's name. "There were was a bunch of silly names thrown around," Paul Hornsby remembered. "Everything was psychedelic stuff, like Strawberry Alarm Clock. Whether you were eating mushrooms or not, they wanted to give you that persona. Hour Glass was a name that we didn't dislike as much as some of the others they suggested."

In August 1967, the Hour Glass went into the studio to begin work on their first album. "We were probably the very first Southern rock band," Paul Hornsby reflected. "I can't think of another one." The members of the Hour Glass quickly discovered, however, that

NOTHING BUT TEARS
HEARTBEAT
#56002
LIBERTY RECORDS
HOUR GLASS

Duane Allman and Bob Keller onstage during Keller's brief stint in the Hour Glass. (Courtesy of Johnny Sandlin)

THE HOURGLASS IS TICKING

A promotional poster for the Hour Glass' Liberty Records debut. (Courtesy of the Big House Museum, Macon, Georiga)

considerable guitar prowess was consistently deemphasized, and the band virtually ignored the album when they performed in the clubs. After the LP's release, the label cracked down on the band's extensive local appearances, citing fear of overexposure. "They didn't want us to go out and play too much," Sandlin confirmed. "It was like, 'We're not gonna let you play, and that way you'll become popular.' It made no sense." The restriction only caused further tension between the Hour Glass and Liberty Records. Despite an appearance by the band on *The Merv Griffin Show* and their inclusion on the lineup of some major music festivals, the *Hour Glass* album and accompanying single "Nothing but Tears" completely bombed. "The story is," Sandlin quipped, "if Patty Hearst had been on Liberty, they'd have never found her."

By the end of the year, bassist Mabron McKinney had departed following a bad acid trip that took a toll on his mental health. Former Allman Joy Bob Keller came back to play with the brothers for the third time, but he didn't last more than a few weeks before returning home to Florida without warning. Guitarist Pete Carr, who lost his gig in the Minutes when they merged with the Allman Joys, happened to be

visiting his former bandmates in Los Angeles, and though he'd never played a bass, they recruited him to step in for the night to cover for the missing Keller. Carr wound up staying on as the Hour Glass' permanent bassist.

In January 1968, the band recorded their second album, *Power of Love*, which was a marked improvement over the first effort. Seven of the twelve songs were written by Gregg. But while the material was better, Dallas Smith was still in the producer's chair, and the process was an uphill climb. "I remember we were driving up into the parking lot of the studio out there one day," Paul Hornsby recalled, "and I remember Duane telling our manager . . . 'Look, I feel like I'm close to the top of my field as a guitar player, and I don't feel like he's at the top of his field as a producer, and he's in there trying to tell me what to do.' That pretty well summarized his feeling of the whole L.A. scene." At one point during the recording process, Duane gave up and returned to Daytona. "Duane was just not into it," Johnny Sandlin recalled. "He couldn't take it anymore. He said, 'Get somebody else. I'm not playing anymore,' and he left. We didn't know what to do. We were halfway through a record, and it was gonna be a better record." Within a few weeks, however, Duane returned to California.

While the song selection was improving, the band members were uncomfortable with the visual image the label was trying to create. "They'd dress us up in these funny fucking duds and we just felt silly," Gregg told *Rolling Stone*'s Cameron Crowe in 1973. Duane was already disillusioned with the Hollywood scene. "We tried it," he later said, "fig-

Hour Glass publicity photo, 1968. Standing, *left to right*: Johnny Sandlin, Gregg Allman, and Paul Hornsby, with Duane Allman (kneeling) and Pete Carr. Gregg is holding a cane, the result of the "foot shootin' party." (Liberty Records)

The third lineup of the Hour Glass performing on television. *Left to right*: Duane Allman, Gregg Allman, Johnny Sandlin, Pete Carr, and Paul Hornsby. (Courtesy of Johnny Sandlin)

ured maybe we could squeeze an ounce or two of good out of this crap. We squeezed and squeezed, but we were squeezing rock. Those albums are very depressing for me to listen to."

After the second album was recorded, Duane began experimenting with slide guitar. "I know exactly how Duane got into bottleneck," Pete Carr remembered, in a *Guitar Player* interview. "We were in L.A. and saw Taj Mahal playing in a club. Jesse Ed Davis was with him, and they did 'Statesboro Blues,' which was on one of their albums. Jesse played slide guitar and really turned Duane on." While recuperating from a cold at home, Duane started working on his chops. "I went and bought him a bottle of Coricidin," Gregg remembered, "a bottle of pills that said it was for colds. Then I went by the record store and got that first Taj Mahal album." Duane dumped the pills from the bottle, washed off the label, and got to work teaching himself slide guitar. "The first song I learned was 'Statesboro Blues,'" Duane recalled, in a 1971 *Rolling Stone* interview. "I just sat around for three weeks and practiced. It still sounded terrible."

Drummer Johnny Sandlin recalled that Gregg received his draft notice in early 1968. "Gregg had been dodging the draft board for a while," Paul Hornsby confirmed. "That was going to be the death of the band if he got drafted. Boy, we had our fingers crossed to the elbows. I don't know how many trips back to the draft board he had made, but this seemed like the big one. Duane flew back to Daytona with him." Duane had earlier dealt with his

own draft notice by showing up to the induction center wearing a pair of panties. "Duane would never tell us exactly what happened," Hornsby continued, "but it had something to do with lace underwear. Duane never elaborated when we asked him. He'd change the subject real quick."

Knowing the same trick wouldn't work twice, Duane hatched a desperate plan to keep the band together and save his baby brother from getting shipped off to Vietnam. Once they were back in Daytona, Gregg and Duane and some friends gathered for a "foot-shootin' party." With the help of a lot of liquid courage, Gregg put a bullet through his own moccasin in an effort to fail the army's health exam. Gregg appeared at the army induction center the following day with his bandaged foot. He told them he'd accidentally shot himself while cleaning his gun, and they dismissed him. "When he returned . . . he used a crutch for a while and played some with his foot propped up," Sandlin recalled. "Then he hopped around with a cane as his foot started to heal."

The *Power of Love* album came out in March 1968, and the band hit the road to promote it. While traveling that April, Hornsby and Sandlin suggested they try recording some material at FAME Studios in Muscle Shoals. They recorded "Ain't No Good to Cry" and a B. B. King medley, with Jimmy Johnson engineering and former Minutes lead singer Eddie Hinton, who was now a respected Muscle Shoals guitarist and songwriter, serving as a production advisor and cheerleader. For the first time,

the band members were happy with what they'd committed to tape. "They knew our style of music, and they knew how to record us," Hornsby said of the Muscle Shoals team. "They got a much better sound for what we were trying to do." The result was much closer to their vision than what Dallas Smith was doing on the West Coast. "It was a hell of a session," Gregg recalled, in his book. "It felt so good, because we were back down South, on our own turf."

"We carried the tapes back out there to L.A. and presented them to the label," Paul Hornsby recalled. "We said, 'This is the way we sound, and this is what we want.' They were just appalled. They thought it was the worst thing they'd ever heard." While the band members were playing the tapes, their producer, Dallas Smith, started talking to other people in the room. "He didn't like them," Pete Carr said

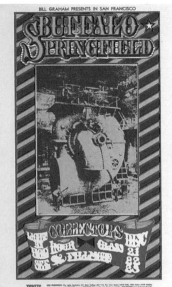

A ticket for a Buffalo Springfield performance, featuring the Hour Glass as the opening band. (Courtesy of the Big House Museum, Macon, Georgia)

The Hour Glass onstage in Tuscaloosa, Alabama, 1968. *Left to right:* Johnny Sandlin, Gregg Allman, Pete Carr, Paul Hornsby, and Duane Allman. (Courtesy of Paul Hornsby)

An advertisement for an Eric Burden performance at the Fillmore West that included the Hour Glass as a support act. (Courtesy of the Big House Museum in Macon, Georgia)

of the recordings, "and we were all upset about him being so closed-minded." Nobody was more upset than the elder Allman brother and band visionary. "Duane stood up and pointed at the Liberty guys in the room," Gregg remembered. "'I'll tell you what,' he said, 'you, you, you, and you and Liberty Records can kiss my fucking ass. Me and the guys are picking up and going . . . back down South, or anywhere but here. Fuck this place, and all the tinsel, and all the other bullshit. Stick your papers and contracts up your ass, we're outta here.'"

With that, Duane, Gregg, Paul Hornsby, Johnny Sandlin, and Pete Carr left California behind in May of 1968, as Hornsby recalled:

> We all came back together. We played a gig in St. Louis, then we headed on down and played a gig in Nashville at one of our favorite clubs that the Allman Joys and the Minutes always played. Then we went on to Mobile. Those were the strongholds of the Allman Joys. Mobile was our last gig. All they wanted to hear was "Mustang Sally" and "Gloria." We had just spent a year and a half in L.A. playin' for ten- and fifteen-thousand-seat pop festivals, playin' with Jefferson Airplane, playin' with the biggest people in the world. Duane wanted to come back to the South, where he'd been looked upon as a god, but it wasn't quite as rosy as he remembered. That week in Mobile probably goes down as the most depressing gig I ever played. It was such a bummer. After that, we broke up. The Allmans went back to Daytona, and I returned to Tuscaloosa.

That was it for the Hour Glass, though Gregg's L.A. sojourn wasn't over for good. The label was much more interested in him as a singer than it was in which musicians backed him up. Though his big brother was furious, Gregg maintained his ties with Liberty Records, in part because the group were still under contract, and he wanted to avoid legal troubles. That June, Dallas Smith took Gregg in the studio to record an ill-advised cover version of country queen Tammy Wynette's "D-I-V-O-R-C-E." It was released as a single, credited to Greg (with one "g") Allman and the Hour Glass. Not surprisingly, it was a flop.

Gregg headed back to Daytona, and it was during this time that Butch Trucks, the drummer from the Bitter Ind who'd played with Duane and Gregg for a couple of nights in Jacksonville two years prior, came back into the Allmans' lives. Trucks was still playing with Bitter Ind bandmates Scott Boyer and David Brown,

Liberty Records attempted to turn Gregg Allman into a solo star with a cover of "D-I-V-O-R-C-E." The label spelled his first name incorrectly.

but they'd changed their name to the 31st of February, and had released an album on Vanguard Records that tanked. Duane and Gregg ran into the 31st of February in Daytona and briefly joined forces with the trio.

"Our band was kind of stuck in a rut," Butch Trucks noted years later on his personal blog, "and Duane said we should join forces. Well, hell, this was incredible. We did and worked up a bunch of material that they played and a lot that we played and started touring as the Bitter Ind, the Allman Joys, or the Hour Glass, depending on where we were playing." In September, they all went to TK Studios, just north of Miami, to experiment with some demo recordings, to see if anything might come of it. One of the tracks they recorded was the original version of Gregg's song "Melissa." It was Duane Allman's recording debut as a slide guitarist.

Before long, Liberty Records came calling once again, and Gregg returned to Los Angeles. "[They were] telling me to get my ass back to California, or they'd sue us for $48,000 that Hour Glass still owed them," Gregg explained to Cameron Crowe in 1973. Gregg claimed he didn't have many options, though most friends believed there was a part of him that enjoyed the Southern California lifestyle. Either way, the label threatened to freeze the band for the next seven years, effectively preventing any other label from signing them unless he recorded with their studio band. "I remember us sitting in the living room," Butch Trucks told *Hittin' the Note* in 1996, "and the phone rings, and it's Gregg. And he's telling Duane that he's gonna be doing a solo thing out in California, that this [Bill] McEuen guy will let Duane and the rest of them out of their Hour Glass contract if Gregg will stay and do this solo thing. And I remember if Duane could have got through that telephone . . . I mean he was *so mad* at Gregg that night, good God!" ★

The Allman Brothers Band in Piedmont Park, Atlanta, Georgia, 1969. (Photo by Twiggs Lyndon, courtesy of the Big House Museum in Macon, Georgia)

CHAPTER 6
Dreams:
The Birth of the Brothers

★ ★

HEN GREGG ALLMAN returned to California to fulfill the Liberty Records contract, Duane kicked around Jacksonville jamming with local players who gathered in Willow Brook Park each Sunday. Butch Trucks was usually there, as was a Chicago-born bassist named Berry Oakley, who was a member of the Second Coming. He'd played lead guitar for a band called the Shaynes in high school, but got a break in 1965 when he joined Tommy Roe's backing group, the Roemans, and relocated to New Port Richey, Florida. Roe, who is best known for his #1 pop hits "Sheila" and "Dizzy," eventually fired Oakley. It was then that Berry went to live in Sarasota, where he met a guitarist named Forest Richard "Dickey" Betts.

Dickey Betts was born in West Palm Beach but moved to Sarasota with his family while still in elementary school. He was raised on the country music of Hank Williams and Lefty Frizzell, and from an early age he was jamming with his father and uncles, all of whom were amateur musicians. "I always said when I was a kid," Dickey recalled in an interview with Kristen West, "that I was going to play on the *Grand Ole Opry*." As a teenager, however, Betts discovered the blues, and his interests turned toward black music. "I used to listen to Chuck Berry almost religiously," he explained. When Dickey was sixteen he was offered a job playing with a group called Teen Beat in a sideshow with a traveling fair called the World of Mirth. "This guy would bring our band out," Betts recounted, "and tell all these lies to the people about us. We were pretty good, though."

At eighteen, Dickey joined an Indiana group

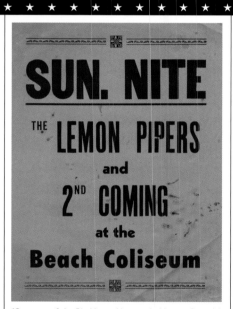

SUN. NITE

THE **LEMON PIPERS**

and

2ND COMING

at the

Beach Coliseum

(Courtesy of the Big House Museum in Macon, Georgia)

called the Jokers that was later immortalized in the first verse of Rick Derringer's hit "Rock and Roll Hoochie Koo." Dickey eventually began putting together his own groups and hitting the club circuit back in Florida. "I met Oakley at a club in Sarasota," Betts remembered. "Pretty soon, Oakley was sitting in a lot, and he and I began to talk about putting something together." They would go through several incarnations before establishing themselves in Jacksonville as the Second Coming. "Berry and I started with a band called the Soul Children, which later became the Blues Messengers," Betts recalled, in a 2007 interview with *Guitar World* magazine. "Eventually Oakley and I ... went to Tampa ... and we really started coming up with some very inter-

esting stuff. We were doing a lot of off-the-wall Jefferson Airplane stuff, stuff that was way out there." They spent about a year in Tampa before moving on. "By 1967, '68, we moved to Jacksonville, and our band had become the Second Coming, so named by a club owner because he thought Berry looked like Jesus Christ.... The club was called the Scene, and it was the *only* place in Jacksonville like that, and we were the *only* people in town with long hair. We'd drive somewhere, and people would throw shit at us!"

In the summer of 1968, the Hour Glass played at the Comic Book Club in Jacksonville, and Second Coming bassist Berry Oakley had the chance to hear Duane Allman for the first time. "I talked Berry into going," his wife Linda remembered, in an interview with John Ogden. "I had seen Duane a couple of years ago when they were the Allman Joys.... Berry was knocked out by his playing!" The two musicians got together after the show to compare notes, and within a few days Duane was over at Berry's house, where they jammed until dawn.

A hip local scene was beginning to form in Jacksonville, and Berry was doing everything he could to nurture it. In a 2010 interview with *Hittin' the Note*, Dickey Betts recalled:

> Berry Oakley was a visionary. He was the one who put together all the free concerts in Jacksonville. When we got to Jacksonville, we were literally the first people to look like we looked. Jacksonville was really backward at that time, and people didn't know what to think of us.... He wanted to bring everybody together and show the people of Jacksonville that there

were people in the city who thought a certain way, and that there was a lot of us. We were there for about a year, and it went from people thinking that we were going to get run out of town on a rail because of our long hair to the point where there were thousands of people coming to the parks to listen to our music.

One of the musicians who appeared regularly at the park on Sundays was Oakley's new jamming buddy. "Duane started showing up, and he'd sit in with us," Betts continued. "That was when I really started to get to know Duane."

While Duane enjoyed the flowering Jacksonville scene and was particularly impressed with Oakley's melodic bass style, he wasn't making any money or moving forward with his music. Without a band of his own, Duane needed a new challenge and a way to make a living. He packed up his Fender Stratocaster electric guitar and headed for Alabama.

In the late summer of 1968, Duane arrived at Rick Hall's FAME Recording Studio in Muscle Shoals, where he and the Hour Glass had cut their last session. "He came here," Hall recounted to Randy Poe, "wanting to break into the business as a studio musician. He was a huge fan of the things I was doing—Jimmy Hughes, Arthur Alexander, Clarence Carter, Joe Tex. He knew about all the records I was cutting, and was heavy into black music."

Rick Hall wasn't necessarily looking for a new guitarist, however, as he already had a stable of highly capable staff musicians. "I said, 'I don't have need of a session player,'" Hall remembered, in an interview for documentary producer Anne Fentress. "He said, 'Well, do you mind if I stick around anyhow? I'll just pitch my pup tent out in the parking lot and I'll just hang out.'"

Always persuasive, Duane convinced Rick to let him hang out in case he ever needed someone in a pinch. "I rented a cabin and lived alone on this lake," Duane remembered. "I just sat and played and got used to living without a bunch of jive Hollywood crap in my head."

Within weeks, Allman was playing on Clarence Carter sessions, thanks to his impressive slide abilities. "When Duane played bottleneck guitar on a session," Hall told Poe, "you had to have plugs in your ears, because he would rattle the shingles. It was all full volume."

Musically and stylistically, Duane was like nothing the Muscle Shoals studio musicians had seen before. "The rest of us had short hair and button-down collars," FAME bassist David Hood explained. "Even though we were in the music business, we looked pretty straight. All

Wilson Pickett and Duane Allman in the studio. (Photo by Michael Ochs Archives/Getty Images)

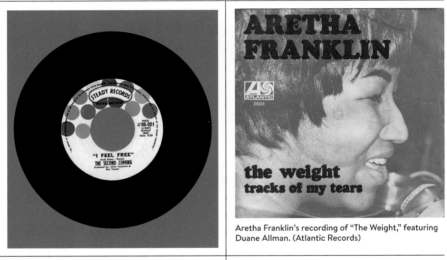

Aretha Franklin's recording of "The Weight," featuring Duane Allman. (Atlantic Records)

of a sudden, this guy comes in with bellbottom pants and long hair and mutton-chop sideburns and flowered shirts and everything. Duane was like a guy from another planet, almost."

"Back then there was so much problem with blacks going out to eat with the white boys," explained Jimmy Johnson, who engineered the Hour Glass' FAME recordings. "And you know what was one step worse? Long-haired boys. What they got was looks.... I know it happened to every artist that came through back then."

One of those artists who came through was Wilson Pickett. Atlantic Records' Jerry Wexler sent him to FAME Studios to record an album, and Duane was there for the session. "A lot of times," Johnson continued, "the blacks would stay back at the studio and say, 'Y'all bring me some food,' just because of the looks they'd get. Duane and Pickett stayed back. We had played on a few tracks one after-

noon and then we left to have supper. When we came back we brought 'em food. But while we were gone, Duane had talked him into doin' 'Hey Jude.' It was unbelievable."

When Rick Hall finally rolled the tape, Duane Allman officially served notice that he was a musical force to be reckoned with. "All through the record he was just playin' blues," Jimmy Johnson recounted, "but when he hit that vamp he just stretched out. When we got through with that cut we all just couldn't believe it. The first Southern rock inspiration was from 'Hey Jude.' Turn that sucker up till your roof shatters."

Pickett was thrilled with the result and started calling Duane "Skyman" for his stratospheric guitar chops. The other guys around Muscle Shoals already called him "Dog," a nickname he earned in the Hour Glass days for his shaggy appearance. Before long, the two nicknames merged, and everyone was calling him "Skydog." Duane Allman had officially become part of the Muscle Shoals inner circle.

As soon as it was recorded, Rick Hall called Jerry Wexler and played Wilson's version of "Hey Jude" for him over the phone. Wexler loved it. In December 1968, Hall signed Duane to recording, production, and publishing contracts, though it would take of bit of wrangling for Duane to disentangle himself from the management and recording agreements he'd signed in California as part of the Hour Glass. While he sorted everything out, Hall continued to use Duane on sessions backing King Curtis, Arthur Conley, and others.

In January, Jerry Wexler brought Duane and the rest of the house band from FAME to New York to back Aretha Franklin on a handful of songs, including her hit version of "The Weight." "Duane is one of the greatest guitar players I ever knew," Wexler reflected, in an interview with Jas Obrecht. "He was one of the very few who could hold his own with the best of the black blues players, and there are very few—you can count them on the fingers of one hand if you've got three fingers missing."

Meanwhile, down in Georgia, artist manager Phil Walden was watching Duane Allman. He knew Rick Hall was working with Duane on his first solo album and suggested a black

drummer from Ocean Springs, Mississippi, go up to Muscle Shoals to jam with the remarkable guitarist. Jai Johanny "Jaimoe" Johanson, who was born Johnnie Lee Johnson, had played for Otis Redding, Percy Sledge, Joe Tex, Clarence Carter, and a slew of other important soul artists. Jackie Avery, a friend of Jaimoe's who was working with Wilson Pickett, called him and told him that Walden thought Jaimoe should go meet Duane to see if there was any chemistry. Frustrated by the small paychecks he was earning backing soul artists on the road, Jaimoe thought back to something his mentor Charles "Honeyboy" Otis had instilled in him early on. "He said, 'If you want to make some money, you go play with them white boys,'" Jaimoe recalled in a 1998 interview with John Lynskey. "So when Avery was talking to me over the phone, I saw dollar signs in my head. Plain and simple. I just said, 'Fuck this—I'm going to go make some money.'"

When Jaimoe arrived in Muscle Shoals, he and Duane discovered they had a strong musical chemistry. They began experimenting with lengthy jam sessions, and the drummer, whose first love was jazz, turned Duane on to Miles Davis and John Coltrane. "Complexity is the only difference between blues and jazz," Duane would later explain in an interview published in *Guitar Player* magazine. "It's all the portrayal

Jai Johanny "Jaimoe" Johanson. (Courtesy of Johnny Sandlin)

of the feelings and the soul in a medium other than words." Soon, Duane invited the Second Coming's Berry Oakley over from Jacksonville to join them in their jam sessions. "When Berry Oakley came down to Muscle Shoals," Jaimoe told *Hittin' the Note*, "it was like, 'Holy shit! Where did this motherfucker come from?' It became a whole different ballgame."

Rick Hall liked Oakley's playing, but Jaimoe's drumming was too jazz-oriented for his tastes. Instead, the lineup of backing musicians for Duane's solo album became Berry Oakley, Johnny Sandlin, Pete Carr, and Paul Hornsby, who recalled:

> Phil Walden was there. He had just come on board as Duane's manager. He saw something in Duane that nobody in California seemed to notice. He was wantin' to put a band around Duane, and wanted to put me and Johnny Sandlin back in the band—essentially it was re-forming the Hour Glass. I couldn't get enough emotional energy to get behind that again, and Sandlin couldn't either. I had just gotten established back in Tuscaloosa. I was playing and making a living. My wife was going back to college, and here they wanted us to go starve again. It was too soon for me.

While the former Hour Glass members weren't interested in going back on the road, they were happy to work with their friend in the studio. Duane Allman's approach to recording—slowly, and aided by copious amounts of drugs—wasn't Rick's style. "I was more mainstream," Hall admitted. "I want a hit record tomorrow. I don't have time to fart around. I was on a roll, and I didn't want to be bothered." Though they got several songs in the can, the process soon stalled out. But Jaimoe, Duane, and Berry Oakley were

Berry Oakley, Jaimoe, Johnny Sandlin, and Duane Allman listening to records and jamming at Fame Studios. (Courtesy of Fame Studios)

Rick Hall and Duane Allman in the studio. (Courtesy of Fame Studios)

Johnny Sandlin and Duane Allman working on Duane's aborted solo album. (Courtesy of Fame Studios)

still energized by their regular jam sessions, and were in search of another outlet. "Duane was always looking for a challenge, for something new," Jaimoe remembered in a 1999 interview with John Lynskey. "He never grew tired of learning, of developing new ideas, exploring, and I always admired him for that."

Atlantic's Jerry Wexler partnered with Phil Walden to buy Duane out of his various contracts with Rick Hall. It cost $15,000. "Without Phil, Duane, and Jerry Wexler," Johnny Sandlin observed, "I don't think the whole Southern music scene would have happened."

At first, Walden set his sights on something akin to the lineup of Cream. "Phil wanted him to put a trio together," Berry's Second Coming bandmate Dickey Betts remembered, in a 2011 profile by Kirk West, "and Berry Oakley was thinking about going with Duane, and so was Jaimoe. It was going to be those three: Duane on guitar, Oakley on bass, and Jaimoe on drums. So, with that in mind, Duane started showing up in Jacksonville a lot, because he and Oakley were really working on some stuff."

Back in Jacksonville, Duane was drawn, once again, to the weekly gathering of hippies and local musicians that had begun the previous year. "We'd just go down and set up at Willow Branch Park and do a free jam session," recalled Reese Wynans, who played with Dickey and Berry in the Second Coming, and would go on to work with Stevie Ray Vaughan as a member of Double Trouble. "When Duane and Jaimoe came down, they'd play at the jam session every Sunday. That's when a lot of the local bands would come out—particularly people like the 31st of February. That's what Butch was doing at that time."

Duane was soon on a quest to expand his band beyond a trio. "Duane came to me," Phil Walden remembered, in a 2005 documentary. "He said, 'I need to ride around and jam with some people and play, and see who's out there, and see who thinks like I think, and come up with something.'"

"One day there's a knock at my door," Butch Trucks recounted, in an interview with Kevin Spangler and Ron Currens, "and it's Duane. And he's got this big black guy with him with this tank top on him, you know, and he looked like Schwarzenegger or something. Really muscle-bound, and he's got these bear claws around his neck and everything. And Duane introduced me as his *old* drummer. He says, 'Hey Jaimoe, this is my old drummer, Butch. Butch, this is my new drummer, Jaimoe.'" Trucks didn't know what to think. "I think I scared the hell out of Butch," Jaimoe later laughed, in a 1996 interview with *Hittin' the Note*.

"Berry and Duane were getting ready to go into this new venture," Dickey Betts explained to *Guitar Player*. "As we started jamming, we realized that Duane and I playing harmony guitars together was something that we weren't expecting to hear. Western swing bands from the '30s always used that twin-harmony guitar, and a lot of the songs that we did were strongly influenced by that."

Everything finally came together on March 23, 1969. Sometimes, if the Jacksonville musicians couldn't gather in the park, they'd congregate at various homes. That particular Sunday, Duane, Jaimoe, Butch Trucks, and Second Coming members Berry Oakley, Dickey Betts, and Reese Wynans assembled for a private jam session at either Butch or Berry's house, depending on whose version of the story is told. "We set up the equipment," Duane remembered, "and whipped into a little jam, and it lasted two and a half hours. Nobody said a word, man. Everybody was speechless."

It was a powerful experience for everyone in the room. "One minute I got chill bumps up and down my neck," Trucks recalled. "The next minute I was crying, and the next minute laughing. I just went through all of the emotions. I finished and just sat there stunned. I'd never felt anything like that."

"Duane called Gregg," Betts recalled, in an interview with *Hittin' the Note*, "and by the time he showed up . . . we blew his socks off, man! We had worked up 'Statesboro Blues,' 'Trouble No More,' and 'Don't Want You No More,' and Gregg brought some things with him, including 'Not My Cross to Bear' and 'Dreams,' so we went from there."

Gregg, who managed to hightail it back to Florida from California in just a few days, was immediately inspired. Suddenly, he was flush with ideas. "Within the next five days I wrote 'Whipping Post,' 'Black-Hearted Woman,' and a couple of others," he told Alan Paul. "I got on a real roll there."

"People say things like, 'Gregg Allman, one of the greatest white blues singers ever to come along,'" Jaimoe explained, to *Hittin' the Note*. "I disagree. Gregg Allman is one of the greatest blues singers ever to come along—period. Blue, red, ever what the hell color—the man is a great singer . . . a genius." Gregg was the final puzzle piece in Duane's outrageous new venture, with its unorthodox instrumental lineup of two lead guitarists and two drummers. "Duane had that real clear sound," Dickey Betts explained to Kirk West, "although it had more of a blues edge to it, and my style had that country kind of thing, but they worked together." The drummers, too, worked in complimentary ways. Butch kept solid time while Jaimoe threw in

the wild flourishes that added a decidedly jazz vibe to the band's rhythm section. "We all dug this different stuff," Gregg revealed to *Hittin' the Note*, "but then we all started listening to the other guys' music. What came out was a mixture of all of it."

Behind the whole enterprise was the driving force of Skydog Allman. "It would be real accurate to say that Duane was the father of the band," Gregg explained to *Guitar Player*. "He had a lot to do with the spontaneity of the whole thing. He was like the mother ship. Somehow he had this real magic about him that would lock us all in, and we'd all take off." His former Hour Glass bandmate, Johnny Sandlin, concurred. "More than anyone else," Sandlin told *Rolling Stone* in 1971, "Duane was responsible for the musical revolution in the South."

With Gregg there to play keys, Reese Wynans returned to the Second Coming, which, without Dickey and Berry, reinvented itself as the New Second Coming. "We knew we had something right off the bat," Dickey explained, to Kirk West, of his new venture with Gregg and Duane. "We knew it was great, and if nobody liked it, that was their loss. That was the attitude we had." They dove right in, rehearsing at the empty Comic Book club during the day before it opened to the public each night. Within a week after Gregg arrived in Jacksonville, the band gave their first public performance and began building a strong local following. That first gig, at the Beach Coliseum, was billed as "Duane and Gregg Allman, Berry Oakley, Dickey, and all the rest formally [sic] of the Second Coming." Soon, they were calling themselves Beelzebub, before becoming the Allman Band and, eventually, the Allman Brothers Band. The name was not a reference to the fact that Duane and Gregg were brothers by birth. Instead, it was a reference to the idea that they'd created a true brotherhood based on a shared musical vision. "I'd rather be known as ABB," Gregg complained to *Creem* in the mid-1970s, "because people always call us the Allman Brothers, and we're not. We're the Allman Brothers Band."

With the Allman Brothers Band lineup now in place, Phil Walden sent Twiggs Lyndon, who worked for Walden's management and booking firm, down to Jacksonville in the spring of 1969 to assist Duane, Jaimoe, Berry, Dickey, Butch, and Gregg with their relocation to Macon, Georgia, where Phil ran his businesses and was in the process of launching a new label called Capricorn Records. Walden found them a two-room apartment at 309 College Street, where they set up a temporary

Dickey Betts and Duane Allman onstage during the earliest days of the Allman Brothers Band. (Courtesy of the Big House Museum, Macon, Georgia)

crash pad. He signed them to a management contract for 25 percent of the proceeds and waited for Atlantic Records, which was bankrolling the Capricorn venture, to give the signal that it was time to record an album. The scraggly hippies and their crew were a conspicuous addition to the relatively quiet town.

At first, there wasn't much going on in Macon. The band would congregate at the H&H Restaurant or walk to their favorite outdoor hangout. "At the foot of College Street," Twiggs Lyndon explained to *Rolling Stone* in 1973, "is this old cemetery, Rose Hill. We all used to go down there and have a good time. Dickey would sometimes go down there at night with his acoustic guitar and write songs."

It was in Macon that they started using psilocybin mushroom extract pills. "The mushroom logo for our band," Gregg later wrote, "came out of this early experience.... There's no question that taking psilocybin helped create so many spontaneous pieces of music. The music would come oozing out of our band.... Our musical puzzle was coming together, and mushrooms certainly enhanced that whole creative atmosphere." Each of the Brothers eventually got a tattoo of a mushroom on his calf as a sort of identifying mark of their affiliation.

In a 1999 *Rolling Stone* interview, Butch Trucks recalled the band's initial arrival in Macon:

> After about four weeks, we said, "We gotta go play for somebody." So we piled into this Ford Econoline van, drove up to Atlanta, and drove around Piedmont Park until we found a nice spot, with some flat concrete and some power not far from it. We didn't say shit to anybody. We just set up the gear, plugged in, and started playing. Within the hour, there's a couple of thousand people.... The next week in this underground newspaper, the *Great Speckled Bird*, there's this article about the Allman Brothers, and all of a sudden, we became the band of the revolution, you know?

It was May of 1969, and a scene was forming in Atlanta, with bands like Eric Quincy Tate, the Hampton Grease Band, Radar, and others knitting together a community of Southern hippies. "Playing concerts in the park was one of the smartest things the Allmans ever did," future Capricorn publicist Mike Hyland reflected. "That's what won the locals over. They became like gods to these kids, and everybody started growing their hair long."

In 1970, Duane told an interviewer for

Gregg Allman with roadies Kim Payne, *left*, and Joseph "Red Dog" Campbell, *right*, during the band's early days in Macon. (Courtesy of W. Robert Johnson)

Crawdaddy! magazine that it was the best place he'd played. "You got up onstage," he explained, "and it'd be covered with dope. Piles of reefer on the stage. Acid tabs, every color you could see. The people down there ... they just go fucking crazy whenever they want to." A hippie transformation was in the air down South, and the Allman Brothers were leading the way. "Eventually, we became like the Dukes of Macon," Gregg recalled. "People followed us home, and the women would chase us down."

Between rehearsals and shows, Duane continued to play on sessions for other artists. As a live act, the Allman Brothers Band were gaining steam. They hit the road with Twiggs Lyndon serving as their first tour manager.

Lyndon had once been Little Richard's road manager, and was the most touring-savvy member of the bunch. Kim Payne and Mike Callahan became the Brothers' first roadies, and they soon added Joseph Campbell, better known as Red Dog, to the mix. "It was kind of a collective deal between the roadies and the band," Gregg noted. "We'd throw our backs into it, right along with them."

With Atlantic not yet ready to spend the money to record the first album, Duane pushed to keep the Brothers on the road. "For a long time," Butch Trucks told Cameron Crowe in 1973, "our only mode of travel was an Econoline van. Eleven of us, with nine sleeping in the back on two mattresses. The only way we made it was with a great big old

Duane Allman onstage in Piedmont Park, Atlanta, Georgia, 1969. (Photo by Twiggs Lyndon, courtesy of the Big House Museum, Macon, Georgia)

bag of Mexican reds and two gallons of Robitussin HC. Five reds and a slug of HC, and you can sleep through anything."

At every new gig, and with every new audience, the Allman Brothers were like door-to-door salesmen for their new brand of rock and roll. "We were the first band to sound like we were from the South," Dickey explained to journalist Alan Paul in 1999. "We fought tooth and nail to prevent Atlantic Records from moving us out of the South, when they said

we'd never make it living in Macon, Georgia, and playing that type of music. They insisted we had to go to New York or L.A., and that they'd break us out of there."

At first, Atlantic Records didn't seem to grasp what was special about the Allman Brothers Band. "They wanted us to get Gregg out from behind the organ," Butch Trucks explained, "put velvet pants on him, stick a salami down his pants, and get him to jump around like an English sissy boy. But we

wouldn't do it—said, 'To hell with it.'"

The Brothers' fierce commitment to their unique vision paid off. "Thank God we, along with Phil Walden, our manager, were smart enough to know that that would ruin the band," Betts told *Hittin' the Note*. "We stuck with it and stuck with it, and finally got to make a record. Atlantic kept holding off, so we kept touring. Even without a record contract, we developed a strong grassroots support system that eventually impressed the label." ★

Berry Oakley, Jaimoe, Dickey Betts, Gregg Allman, Butch Trucks, and Duane Allman. (Photo by Twiggs Lyndon, courtesy of the Big House Museum, Macon, Georgia)

CHAPTER 7
Trouble No More:
The Allman Brothers Band
Keep Hittin' the Note

AFTER WHAT FELT like an eternity to the members of the group, the Allman Brothers Band traveled to New York in August 1969 to cut their first album at Atlantic Studios. Following the recording dates, photographer Stephen Paley was dispatched to Macon to take some shots for the LP. Several iconic nude photos of the band were taken in the local Ocmulgee Creek. "That's on Otis Redding's farm," Duane explained in a 1970 interview. "We took off our clothes to take the picture and he took off his clothes to snap us." Band roadie Red Dog Campbell told journalist Barney Hoskyns that the first orgy ever to take place at their College Street apartment occurred later that night. With an album set for national release, the world was about to be introduced to a new breed of rock-and-roll hedonists with a Southern drawl.

The band's eponymous debut LP was released in early November. Capricorn Records was still so new that it didn't have a logo, so the album was released on Atlantic's Atco imprint instead. "The first album sold less than 35,000 copies when it was released," Phil Walden recalled years later. "Black Hearted Woman" was issued as a single, but failed to chart. Other than two cover songs—an instrumental take on the Spencer Davis Group's "Don't Want You No More," and Muddy Waters' "Trouble No More"—all the titles on the first album were credited to Gregg. The second side closed with "Dreams" and "Whipping Post," which were becoming staples of the band's ambitious live jams. Lester Bangs, in his glowing *Rolling Stone* review, wrote, "Sometimes it sounds like what

Butch and Duane onstage. (Photo by Twiggs Lyndon, courtesy of the Big House Museum, Macon, Georgia)

Led Zeppelin *might* have been if they weren't hung up on gymnastics."

With the debut album under their belt, the Brothers ditched the Econoline van for a Winnebago, which they nicknamed the Windbag, and hit the road with a vengeance.

As 1969 wound to a close, the Allman Brothers Band played at the Fillmore East, Bill Graham's legendary concert venue, for the first time. They performed for three nights, opening for Blood, Sweat & Tears. "It was the temple of rock and roll," Dickey Betts said of the

venue in a 1994 interview. "It was the lowest paying gig out there . . . but everybody wanted to play the Fillmore, because it was the artistic presentation of rock and roll music." The Fillmore would become one of the band's favorite haunts as they built a reputation as a formidable live act. "For ten years," Duane told a reporter for the New Orleans *Free Press* that same week, "I've been playing bars, night clubs, lounges, and—before that—high school dances, little Y teen dances, and—before that—for anybody who would listen. Just learning things. . . .

Butch Trucks, Jaimoe, Gregg Allman, Dickey Betts, Berry Oakley, and Duane Allman. (Photo by Twiggs Lyndon, courtesy of the Big House Museum, Macon, Georgia)

often hard won. At the end of April, the band played a club in Buffalo, New York. The owner, Angelo Aliotta, informed road manager Twiggs Lyndon that the group had been late for the gig and refused to pay them unless they agreed to play a second night. Their schedule made that an impossibility. A scuffle broke out, and Twiggs stabbed Aliotta to death. He spent eighteen months in jail before being found not guilty for reasons of insanity. His defense attorney successfully argued that touring with the Allman Brothers Band was enough to lead any reasonable person to snap. Twiggs did six more months in a mental hospital and eventually rejoined the band on the road in 1972.

The Allmans played the Fillmore in February 1970 for a series of shows supporting the Grateful Dead before returning home to begin work on their second album. "Tom Dowd wanted us to go to Miami and work at Criteria," Gregg remembered, in an interview with John Lynskey. "Duane told me, 'It's his idea, so let's go to his town and see what he's got.'" Though they recorded the second album primarily in Miami, the band also managed to fit in studio time in Macon and New York when they could find short bursts of time in their relentless schedule. They were thrilled to get to work directly with Tom Dowd. "We've got the best producer in the world," Duane told the *Free Press*.

The resulting album, *Idlewild South*, was named after the Georgia farm where Dickey

We're just working our way up, trying to perfect what we think is right."

In January 1970, Berry Oakley's wife Linda rented a stately grand Tudor home at 2321 Vineville Avenue in Macon that soon became the band's headquarters. It was officially home to three couples: Berry and Linda Oakley and their daughter, Duane and his girlfriend Donna and their daughter, plus Berry's sister Candace and Gregg, who was her boyfriend at the time. Known as the Big House, it became a central meeting place, where Berry presided over family style gatherings. "He took great pleasure in supervising all the meals, including the planning and preparation," Candace told journalist Scott Freeman. "Berry was like the self-appointed master of ceremonies." The role was crucial to the harmony of the band during this era. "Berry was a family kind of person," Jaimoe confirmed to *Hittin' the Note*, "the head of the family, the godfather, and that made him so special. Berry cared about everybody, didn't dislike anybody."

"Our family thing only grew stronger, Gregg explained, "and that included dealing with the perennial redneck questions.... Keep in mind, this was the 1960s, and we were in the Deep South, so having a black guy in the group came up a lot. But Jaimoe was one of us, and we weren't going to change that for nobody.... Any kind of problem that came from the outside, we met head-on. It was like we had a force field around us. It was us against the world, man."

Everyone associated with the band looked back on that period as the golden era. They were still hungry, but things were beginning to break loose, and everyone could feel the energy building. "In 1970 we worked 256 dates," Gregg recounted in a 1974 interview with *Melody Maker*, "and neither one of us made $1,600."

What money they were able to earn was

The Brothers in Macon. (Photo by Twiggs Lyndon, courtesy of the Big House Museum, Macon, Georgia)

Duane Allman and Dickey Betts onstage. (Courtesy of Johnny Sandlin)

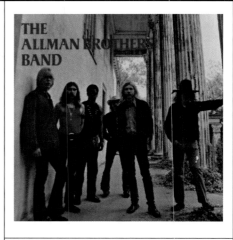

Gregg and Duane Allman onstage. (Courtesy of Johnny Sandlin)

In July, the Allman Brothers Band appeared at the Atlanta International Pop Festival, alongside Jimi Hendrix, B. B. King, Johnny Winter, Bob Seger, and others. The crowd, which numbered more than 350,000 people, was the largest for which the Brothers had played up to that point. It gave a nice boost to the regional success of *Idlewild South*, and helped establish the group as the first important Southern rock band of the era.

On August 26, 1970, the Allman Brothers Band played a free concert on an outdoor stage in Miami Beach. Duane was in the middle of a guitar solo when he looked down and spotted Eric Clapton sitting up front with the rest of the band that would come to be known as Derek & the Dominos. They were in town to record an album at Criteria Studios with Tom Dowd, who attended the show with them. "Duane's in the middle of a solo," Dowd told Alan Paul, "when he opens his eyes, looks down, sees Eric, and stops playing cold, in shock." Dickey instinctively took over the guitar solo—but then he, too, saw Clapton, and had to turn his back to keep it together.

After his monstrous success with Cream, Eric Clapton had toured with Delaney and Bonnie Bramlett, and it was with their band that he got to know keyboardist Bobby Whitlock. After Whitlock left the Bramletts, he headed to England to hang out with Clapton. George Harrison wound up recruiting the two of them, along with fellow Delaney & Bonnie veterans Jim Gordon and Carl Radle, to play on *All Things Must Pass*. When they were finished working with Harrison, the guys headed for Miami to begin working on an album of their own.

"I've been an admirer of Eric Clapton for a long, long time," Duane told interviewer Jon Tiven. "I've always dug his playing. He inspired me a lot." When Eric heard from Tom Dowd that Duane wanted to meet him, he called a

was living with his family, and which the band sometimes used for rehearsals, or just to party. Released in September, the album included a cover of Willie Dixon's "Hoochie Coochie Man," featuring a rare vocal performance by Berry Oakley. The remaining songs were originals, with Gregg contributing four titles, including "Midnight Rider," which he called "the song I'm most proud of in my career." Dickey Betts emerged as a songwriter on the second album with "Revival" and the complex instrumental "In Memory of Elizabeth Reed."

"I wrote 'In Memory of Elizabeth Reed' in

Rose Hill [Cemetery]," Betts told Kirk West. "The name came from her grave marker. At the time I wrote that song I was having a little affair with Boz Scaggs' girlfriend, and I wrote it for her.... I couldn't name it for her, so I called it 'Elizabeth Reed.'"

Overall, *Idlewild South* was a more nuanced record than its predecessor. It showed off some of the complex elements that would come to define the Allman Brothers Band as more than just a heavy blues-rock outfit. Though it wasn't a runaway hit, it was a very good album, and it managed to crack the Top 40.

Publicity photo for the Allman Brothers Band's *Fillmore* album. *Left to right:* Jaimoe, Duane Allman, Gregg Allman, Berry Oakley, Dickey Betts, and Butch Trucks. (Capricorn Records)

Duane backstage with Derek & the Dominos at the Onondaga County War Memorial Auditorium in Syracuse, New York, December 2, 1970. *Left to right:* Carl Radle, Jim Gordon, Eric Clapton, Bobby Whitlock, WOLF radio's Ron Wray, and Duane Allman. (Courtesy of the Ron Wray collection)

The *Rolling Stone* piece came out in November and, while not an absolute train wreck, it certainly wasn't a flattering profile. Lewis wrote about the musicians' cocaine use in explicit detail, and made little effort to conceal his assumption that the band was made up of a bunch of ignorant rednecks. He chose to print their quotes in a literal rendering of what he called their "buttery drawl," making Georgia "Gawgia," guitars "git-tars," pretty "purty," and so on.

The *Rolling Stone* article was a snapshot of a band burning the candle at both ends. They came across as surly and drugged out. By this point, hard drugs were a regular part of life in the band. Duane and some of the others were doing heroin. "We had a band policy about it—it was OK to snort it, but no needles," Dickey recalled in a 2011 *Hittin' the Note* article. "Duane was really emphatic about that; it was one thing that he tried to make a rule about."

But it was getting out of control. In October of 1971, at the conclusion of the tour, Phil Walden checked Duane, Gregg, Berry, Red Dog, Kim Payne, and several of the others into a rehab facility in Buffalo, New York. None of them were serious about kicking drugs, but if nothing else, Duane needed the rest. When he checked out, he headed to New York City for a few days to hang out with John Hammond and some other friends before flying home to Macon on October 28th.

The next day, Duane rode his Harley Davidson motorcycle over to the Big House to hang out for a bit before Linda Oakley's surprise birthday party that evening. In the late afternoon, Duane, Berry, Candace Oakley, and Duane's girlfriend Dixie Meadows set out for Duane's house to pick up the presents and cake for the surprise celebration. Duane was on his Harley, Berry took a car along a different route, and the girls followed in a separate car behind Duane.

While en route, an oncoming truck started to make a left turn in front of Duane. He

At that moment, Marshall snapped the iconic shot that became the album's classic cover.

More important to the band than the front cover of the album was the reverse side. Duane suggested that the roadies be photographed for the back of the LP, pointing out that they worked just as hard as the band. Red Dog Campbell, Kim Payne, Mike Callahan, Joe Dan Petty, and Willie Perkins were pictured on the back. A photo of the then-incarcerated Twiggs Lyndon was superimposed on the brick wall for the album's release.

In October, *Rolling Stone* dispatched Grover Lewis, with photographer Annie Leibovitz in tow, to spend time traveling with the band and write the magazine's first feature piece on the group. Road manager Willie Perkins noted in his own book about the Allmans that "the rapport with the writer was terrible, and the article proved to be a major disappointment."

Capricorn Records publicity photo of Duane Allman. (Courtesy of Bill Stewart)

swerved left to go around it, but the truck suddenly stopped, blocking most of the lane Duane was aiming for. He lost control. The motorcycle bounced off the pavement and slammed down on top of him before skidding off and coming to a rest on the curb. Dixie and Candace arrived on the scene to find him with only a few scrapes and scratches.

By the time medical help arrived, however, Duane was unconscious. He was resuscitated twice in the ambulance, and when they arrived at the hospital, the doctors took him right into surgery. But there was little that could be done for the multiple internal injuries he'd suffered. Within three hours, Duane Allman was dead. He was twenty-four years old. It had been one year since Berry Oakley had cried out to God in a Nashville hospital to give Duane another year of life. "That's when Duane died," Butch Trucks confirmed in *Midnight Riders*. "It was a year to the day when he got in the wreck. I mean, it was *to the day* a year." The Macon music community experienced a collective stunned silence.

"Duane always used to say, 'I'll be the first one to go in this band,'" Jaimoe told Gavin Edwards. "I remember this shit coming up three or four times." Perhaps Duane sensed his fate. "I think that's one reason he lived so intensely," Jaimoe continued. "Duane loved life, and he lived his life to the fullest." Duane accepted the fact that he was a risk-taker, and recognized it was just the way that he was wired. "I dropped three tabs of good red acid on a motorcycle going a hundred miles an hour down the road," he told *Crawdaddy!* magazine in 1970, "no shoes and no helmet on. And, of course, you've got to pay dues for stuff like that." It was an eerie foreshadowing of the ultimate dues he finally paid.

The rest of the band performed at the funeral at Snow's Memorial Chapel in Macon on November 1st, as did Dr. John, Delaney Bramlett, and harmonica player Thom Doucette, who'd appeared with the band on the *Fillmore* album. Jerry Wexler delivered an emotional eulogy. "After we played at the chapel, we all went out back to smoke a joint," Gregg wrote. "We were standing together, and I think we were all wondering what we were going to do. 'Look, boys,' I said. 'If you're thinking about stopping, don't. . . . If we don't keep playing, like my brother would've wanted us to, we're all gonna become dope dealers and just fall by the wayside. I think this is our only option." The others agreed. "There was never any thought of not continuing," Butch Trucks explained, "because Duane had given us the religion, and we were going to keep playing it." ★

The Brothers after Duane. *Left to right*: Butch Trucks, Gregg Allman, Berry Oakley, Jaimoe, and Dickey Betts. (Courtesy of the Big House Museum, Macon, Georgia)

CHAPTER 8
One Way Out: The Allmans Soldier On…to the Top

LTHOUGH THE FILLMORE album had already been certified Gold before Duane's death, its popularity continued to soar in the wake of his passing. "It's really hard for me to believe that what we accomplished with Duane happened in two years—beginning to end," Butch Trucks marveled in an interview with *Mojo* magazine. He had built the foundation and created the archetype of what music journalist Barney Hoskyns called "the walkin', talkin' embodiment of New Southern Manhood— the original Longhaired Redneck, the Righteous Brother of blue-eyed blues and moonshine soul." Duane's vision would cast a long shadow over the Allman Brothers Band for years to come. "Duane played music the same way that he rode his motorcycle and drove his car," Dickey explained in a 2007 interview. "He was a daredevil, just triple-Scorpio, God's-on-my-side wide open. That was part of the romance. And I loved Duane."

On November 25, 1971, the Brothers appeared for a scheduled show at Carnegie Hall in New York. In December, the band returned to Criteria Studios in Miami to resume recording their fourth album. They'd already committed "Stand Back," "Little Martha," and "Blue Sky" to tape prior to Duane's accident. "Blue Sky" marked Dickey Betts' debut as a vocalist with the band, a leadership role that would take on more meaning in the months and years ahead. At first, it fell to Dickey to take over the signature slide-guitar work that marked many of the Brothers' recordings.

"I remember Dickey diligently practicing and rehearsing his slide in the studio and at

The Allman Brother Band in early 1972. *Left to right:* Butch Trucks, Gregg Allman, Dickey Betts, Berry Oakley, and Jaimoe. (Courtesy of Mike Hyland)

the Thunderbird Hotel, which was our base in Miami for the Criteria Studio sessions," Willie Perkins recalled in his book. Everyone was amazed at how quickly Betts mastered Duane's sound. "I played with the opening band on the first gig in Miami that they did without Duane," Macon drummer Bill Stewart recalled. "I remember thinkin', 'Damn! I didn't know Dickey played slide!'"

In addition to what they'd done with Duane, the Brothers cut three more songs, including Dickey's "Les Brers in A Minor,"

and Gregg's songs "Ain't Wastin' Time No More" and "Melissa." The latter was one of Duane's favorite songs, and Gregg had sung it at his big brother's funeral.

The original title for the Allman Brothers Band's fourth album was *The Kind We Grow in Dixie*, but it was changed to *Eat a Peach* as a tribute to Duane, who once told an interviewer, when asked what he was doing for the revolution, that he liked to "eat a peach for peace" whenever he was in Georgia. For years, an urban legend persisted that the truck involved

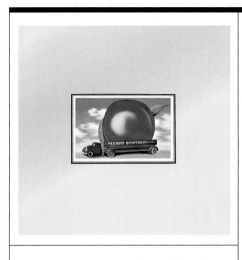

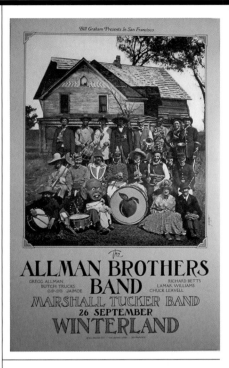

in Duane's death was a peach truck like the one pictured on the LP's cover, but the vehicle involved in the accident was actually a flatbed lumber truck. The album cover image was unrelated to the collision.

The LP opened with the three songs recorded after Duane's death. It was a powerful statement that the band would continue on the path that their leader had set out for them. Next came three live songs taken from previously unissued recordings of shows at the Fillmore East, including the nearly thirty-four-minute "Mountain Jam," which was based on Donovan's "There Is a Mountain." The double LP concluded with the final three studio tracks featuring Duane, ending with "Little Martha," a beautiful acoustic instrumental that Duane had written for his partner, Dixie. It was the only song he ever wrote for the Allman Brothers Band.

Released in February of 1972, *Eat a Peach* was the group's biggest album to date. It hit #4 on the *Billboard* chart and was eventually certified Platinum. But with the band enjoying their greatest commercial success yet, small cracks began to appear in the foundation. Gregg sank deeper into heroin use and didn't seem to have a problem taking a backseat following the death of his brother. "You might say he was born to lead," Geraldine Allman said of her eldest son, Duane, in a *Rolling Stone* interview. "Gregg is a lover, and laid-back—he'd rather have a leader." As Gregg grew increasingly distant and disengaged, Dickey Betts stepped further into the leadership gap left by Duane. "When my brother died, Dickey really stepped up," Gregg admitted. "He woodshedded like crazy.... Dickey was capable of handling things, but he would overdo it every time. He'd just want to get into a fistfight."

Though they needed his assertive leadership, Dickey was quickly gaining a reputation among his bandmates for his volatile personality and drunken behavior. "He was kind of an independent loner biker," roadie Kim Payne elaborated to Scott Freeman. "He was rough and rowdy. You could say he had a bad attitude." Musically, the Brothers weren't all on the same page in the way they'd once been.

"Duane was a very strong leader," Phil Walden explained in 1985. "After he died there was a real struggle between Dickey Betts, who leaned very strongly toward country, and Gregg, who probably found country music offensive." Despite his unpredictability,

most everyone involved with the group during this era acknowledged that Dickey became the driving force of the Brothers. "Dickey became the de facto leader of the band," Willie Perkins explained. "I think even he would agree it was a position for which he was not psychologically equipped.... He was a real chameleon ... he would turn from a smiling, friendly, convivial individual into an angry, brooding, violent hellion at the blink of an eye."

By 1972, the Allman Brothers Band were making serious money, but touring less often, jamming less often, and no longer living together. Meanwhile, Berry Oakley, who'd always played the role of nurturing big brother, seemed unable to recover from the loss of Duane. "When Duane was alive," Kim Payne explained, "he carried the load for the band, but it never affected him that much. When he died, Berry felt that the whole weight had dropped on his shoulders, and he just couldn't carry it. For him it turned out to be a big, long, bad bummer." Oakley's bandmates became concerned about his state after they lost Duane. "It absolutely destroyed him," Butch Trucks told Barney Hoskyns. "The next year, for the whole year, he was just a zombie—always just completely fucked up and unable to deal with life." Berry's playing suffered as a result. On more than one occasion, he fell off the stage while performing.

In the post-Duane era, Gregg started bringing new songs to the band that met with a lukewarm reaction. Frustrated that the others weren't interested in some of his

The Allman Brothers Band with new member Chuck Leavell (*far left*) taping a performance for Don Kirshner's *In Concert*. This was the only live show Leavell and Berry Oakley played together. (Courtesy of the Big House Museum, Macon, Georgia)

The fourth lineup of the Allman Brothers Band. *Left to right*: Jaimoe, Gregg Allman, Butch Trucks, Chuck Leavell, Lamar Williams, and Dickey Betts. (Courtesy of the Big House Museum, Macon, Georgia)

new material, he decided to start working on a solo album. Johnny Sandlin produced the tracks at the Capricorn studio in Macon that would eventually be released as *Laid Back* in October of 1973. "I worked with a band called Cowboy on the album, and a guy called Paul Hornsby who was in Hour Glass," Gregg told *Melody Maker* magazine. "I skipped around a lot and used some very good bass players. It took so long because I was working my ass off with the Brothers Band."

While recording *Laid Back*, Gregg worked with a young keyboard player named Chuck Leavell from Tuscaloosa, Alabama. Leavell had played on Freddie North's' R&B classic "She's All I Got" in Muscle Shoals, but he wasn't able to secure enough studio work to make a living. "They already had great play-

ers who were older than me and more experienced than me," Chuck explained. "I played on a minor session or two but couldn't get anything going. When I heard the Allman Brothers' first record, I went, 'Holy shit! What is this? This is awesome! This is great!' I decided to go over to Macon, Georgia, to check it out."

Leavell was in the right place at the right time. "He was hanging around the studio, and he certainly looked the part," Gregg recalled, in his memoirs, "but when I heard him play, I knew he was there for a reason. . . . I introduced Chuck to the other guys in the band. After *Eat a Peach* we needed something, and adding keyboards was the right thing to do. He started jamming with us, and everybody liked him right away."

Leavell recalled his invitation to join the

band with amazement. "I got a call to go into the offices of Phil Walden," he recounted. "I walked in for this meeting, and there's all the Allman Brothers Band, there's Phil Walden. I'm this kid who was, at the time, barely twenty years old—and next thing I know, I'm asked to be in the Allman Brothers Band. After picking myself up off the floor, I said, 'Yeah! I'd like to do that.'"

As soon as he came into the band, Chuck was a full-fledged part of the family. "It was a very definite brotherhood," he recalled. "It was a harmonious all-for-one and one-for-all." Despite the growing struggle for control of the group, the members were still very much rooted in the spirit of Duane Allman. "Duane was this huge leadership figure," Chuck explained. "Not only to that band, but to us as musicians that had come to engage in Macon, Georgia. Duane was king. I never really knew Duane. I met him once in a hallway in Muscle Shoals, Alabama, but this guy was *the king*. He was like Count Basie. He was so respected because of his musicianship. We all loved and respected him."

Chuck's first public performance with the group was at Hofstra University in New York, where the Allman Brothers Band filmed what would be their first television appearance. It would become the debut broadcast of Don Kirshner's *In Concert* on ABC, and everyone was excited about the new lineup. Berry Oakley, especially, seemed energized by Chuck's arrival and immediately took him under his wing. "When we got Chuck in the band it was like seeing the light," Jaimoe revealed to *Rolling Stone* in 1973. "He was back being the old Berry again, playing his ass off." Unfortunately, Berry's emergence from the funk he had been in since Duane's death would be short-lived, and the concert would be the one and only Allman Brothers Band show he and Chuck would play together.

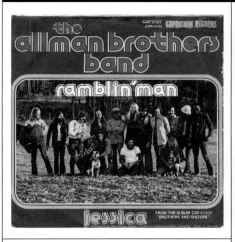

Chuck Leavell, Jaimoe, Butch Trucks, Gregg Allman, Lamar Williams, and Dickey Betts. (Courtesy of Mark Pucci)

On November 11, 1972, Berry overshot a turn on his motorcycle and collided with a Macon city bus, just blocks from where Duane was killed. Berry was drunk, and most everyone associated with the band admitted that he wasn't as skilled a rider as most of the others. The bike came down on top of him, just as had happened with Duane. Remarkably, he was able to get up. He chose to return home to the Big House instead of seeking medical attention. Within a short time, however, Berry was in serious pain and speaking incoherently. He was taken to the hospital and pronounced dead within an hour. His skull had been fractured in the accident, and he died of a brain hemorrhage. Like Duane, he was twenty-four years old.

Suddenly, the band members were reliving the events of just one year prior. Duane had been the spiritual leader of the band's musical direction, but where Duane could be confrontational and uncompromising, Berry was gentle and accommodating. Duane set the tone for the band's vision, but Berry was at the heart of the communal spirit that defined their brotherhood. Everyone in the band was reeling.

The surviving Brothers couldn't help but wonder if the band was cursed. "Many of us felt like we were actually living and breathing some sort of strange, tragic Southern Gothic novel," Willie Perkins confessed. He wasn't the only one who was freaked out. "I caught myself thinking that it's narrowing down," Gregg admitted, "that maybe I'm next."

Just as was the case following Duane's fatal accident, the band chose to push ahead. Before Berry's death, the Brothers had recorded "Wasted Words" and "Ramblin' Man." Once again, they found themselves trying to figure out how to fill some very big shoes. Chuck Leavell recalled:

We were auditioning bass players. We had Mark Andes, who has played with Heart,

Capricorn publicity photo of Dickey Betts. (Mark Pucci)

and we had Kenny Gradney, who had played with Little Feat. Dickey brought this guy in named Stray that was somebody he'd played with. Then Jaimoe says, "I've got this guy in Mississippi I'd like to bring in." Lamar Williams came in with confidence and with gratitude. Lamar was a really sweet guy. He came from a gospel background. His family was rooted in the church, and he played bass in a gospel band. Immediately, we all knew he was the guy. What sort of interested me was that he got Berry's melodic bass style, whereas others came in playing *their* styles. Somehow Lamar adapted an understanding of the style that Berry had, and it was not that difficult for him. He didn't have to work at it. It came naturally.

Lamar had known Jaimoe from their years growing up together in Gulfport, Mississippi. Accordingly, there was already a foundation of trust in the rhythm section on which the rest of the brotherhood quickly built. "He came in and everybody took to him," Johnny Sandlin, who was working as the Allmans' producer, explained. "He was an excellent bass player." The resulting album, *Brothers and Sisters,* became even more successful than *Eat a Peach.* Released in August of 1973, the LP went to #1 on the *Billboard* album chart and stayed there for more than a month.

With Gregg having written just two of the seven songs, Dickey's influence took center stage. "After Duane died, we started heading in a country direction," Butch explained to band historian Alan Paul, "because that was Dickey's background." Billed as "Richard Betts" in the liner notes, Dickey contributed the classics "Jessica," "Southbound," and "Ramblin' Man." The latter, which was sung by Dickey, became the Allman Brothers' only major hit single.

Guitarist Les Dudek, who'd emerged from the Jacksonville club scene, played the distinctive twin-lead guitar with Dickey on "Ramblin' Man." "Les was hangin' around with Dickey," drummer Bill Stewart recalled. "I think he was tryin' to get with Capricorn." Nobody seems to remember for sure if permanently adding Les was part of the plan. "I think the window was open, and the band was kind of considering options," Chuck Leavell recalled. "Dickey brought him in, and he respected his playing. I think the feeling was, 'Gosh, if we need some twin-guitar stuff, what do we do?' Dickey said, 'I know this guy, Les, and let me bring him in. If we need to do that kind of thing, he can help us cover it.' It was just sort of whatever happens, hap-

Gregg Allman the solo artist. (Capricorn Records publicity photo by Elissa Mallin, courtesy of Mike Hyland)

pens." Producer Johnny Sandlin was not in favor of Les becoming a permanent fixture. "I know he *thought* he was being considered to join the Allman Brothers," Sandlin explained. "He played well, but he was not easy to work with."

"Ramblin' Man" climbed to the #2 position on the *Billboard* singles chart but was kept from the top spot by Cher's "Half-Breed." "AM radio didn't have much to do with the Allman Brothers," Dickey remembered. "When 'Ramblin' Man' became a hit, everything changed; the band reached a whole other level. The places we played got bigger, the crowds were huge, and the money was just pouring in."

A month before *Brothers and Sisters* was released, the Brothers hit the road for an extended tour. The new lineup breathed some life into the group after two years marked by tragedy. They played a legendary show in Watkins Glen, New York, to 600,000 fans—as co-headliners with the Band and the Grateful Dead—that set a Guinness World Record for attendance at a rock concert.

With Lamar on board, the band now featured two African American musicians. "People asked me whether I had any problems with an integrated band," Phil Walden revealed to journalist Chris Charlesworth in a 1974 interview, "but I'd never even thought about it until I was asked. I don't think the band realized they were integrated until it was pointed out to them. They were picked because of their musical ability and the bulk of American musicians, whether black or white, have always come from the South." It was a new era for a new South, and the Allmans were leading the way. *Rolling Stone*

named them "Band of the Year" in 1973, and it seemed their popularity had no end.

By the time the 1973 tour had ended, however, the brief respite of peace, harmony, and "hittin' the note" was fading. Longtime roadies Kim Payne and Mike Callahan were fired at the insistence of Capricorn, following a confrontational incident with one of its executives. It was another crack in the foundation of the brotherhood. In addition, some of the band members began to grow restless with the group's evolving sound. "After *Brothers and Sisters*, it did become less of the Allman Brothers Band and more of the Dickey Betts Band," Butch Trucks confessed to Barney Hoskyns. "It came to where he wasn't just leading us, but to where he was dominating us. And most of that was our fault: we were so fucked up, he was the only one *doing* anything." Kim Payne concurred. "Dickey was kind of a loose cannon, just bristling with talent and piss and vinegar," he revealed to Scott Freeman. "He was pretty agitated by the unrest and the lack of direction. There was a lot of dissension going on."

After the tour, Gregg finally released his solo album. The following year, Dickey began work on his first solo project, *Highway Call*, which he co-produced with Johnny Sandlin. The Allman Brothers Band hit the road again from May through August of 1974, but everyone was continuing to move in different directions, and many of the shows were lackluster. When they came off the road in August, they didn't tour together again for a full year. "Everybody in the Brothers wants to expand their activities and go off in other directions," Chuck Leavell told *Melody Maker* earlier that year. "It seems that every month or so we have to get away from each other to try something different." Gregg and Dickey both went on separate tours in the fall of 1974—Dickey to support *Highway Call* and Gregg to support *The Gregg Allman Tour*, a live album taken from shows he did following the release of *Laid Back*. "It seemed like things between us became a sibling rivalry of sorts," Gregg admitted, "which was ironic because when I'd had a sibling, we'd never been rivals over anything."

The Allman Brothers Band had become one of the most successful groups in America, and were regarded as the spiritual leaders of the Southern rock movement. But having survived the mounting pressures of fame and the death of two key members, the Brothers were now left wondering if they could survive one another. By the time they paused to figure it out, a significant Southern rock community had bloomed around them. ★

Part Three

REACH FOR THE SKY: THE ODYSSEY OF PHIL WALDEN AND CAPRICORN RECORDS, PART ONE

LOCATED EIGHTY MILES south of Atlanta, along the banks of the Ocmulgee River, the central Georgia town of Macon rose to prominence as an important—though unlikely—musical center in the late 1950s. The first black DJ in town was Hamp Swain who, using the name King Bee, took to the airwaves over WBML in 1954. When he wasn't behind the microphone at the station's studio, Swain was hosting local talent competitions and playing the saxophone at regional gigs with his own band, the Hamptones. Swain was managed by Clint Brantley, a bass player, booking agent, and local black music entrepreneur who owned two nightclubs, the Two Spot and the Key Club. "He was a character who knew everybody that needed to be known," Macon trumpet player Newton Collier recalled of Brantley in *Music from Macon*. A thriving local R&B scene began to form around Hamp Swain and Clint Brantley. It soon came to include Little Richard, James Brown, Johnny Jenkins, Otis Redding, and an ambitious white kid named Phil Walden.

"The musical heritage of Macon is as rich as the soil it sits on, and what's happening there now may well serve as the basis for a future historical view."

—BEN EDMONDS, *CREEM* MAGAZINE, 1972

Otis Redding with manager Phil Walden. (Courtesy of the estate of Otis Redding, www.otisredding.com)

CHAPTER 9
Rip It Up: Phil Walden and the Seeds of a Macon Music Empire

ORN IN DECEMBER 1932, Macon's Richard Penniman made his first public appearances with an a cappella gospel group known as Ma Sweetie & the Tater Tots. As a teenager, he went to work selling soft drinks at concerts booked by Clint Brantley in the Macon City Auditorium. Before one such show, Richard sang for Sister Rosetta Tharpe while her band were setting up for the evening performance. Impressed by his abilities, Tharpe invited him onstage to sing that night. The crowd loved him, and "Little Richard" was hooked.

Richard left home at fourteen and toured with a variety of minstrel shows, where he honed his eye-catching stage persona, complete with flashy outfits and heavy makeup. Sometimes performing in drag under the name Princess Lavonne, Little Richard defined "outrageous" in an era when men simply didn't behave flamboyantly. Blues singer Billy Wright, who served as a mentor to Richard, helped him land a recording session with RCA Records. Failing to make a splash with RCA, Richard returned home to Macon, where he took a job washing dishes at the Greyhound Bus Station. Forced to help support his family following the shooting death of his father in 1952, Penniman worked hard at his day job. Unable to stay away from the spotlight, however, he began singing with several local groups, including Hamp Swain & the Hamptones.

Richard recorded a few sides for the Peacock label, but—like his work for RCA—none of the songs caught on. Though he continued to perform with Swain, he formed his own band,

Little Richard. (London Records)

the Upsetters, managed by Clint Brantley. In 1955, Richard and Clint sent a demo tape of the Upsetters to Specialty Records, where it found its way to producer Bumps Blackwell. Penniman had finally caught his break. Blackwell was searching for a gospel-fueled blues shouter to compete with Ray Charles, and he brought Richard down to Cosimo Matassa's studio in New Orleans. Seeing his big chance, Little Richard didn't hesitate to walk away from a previous engagement. "We were supposed to pick him up in Dothan for a show," Hamp Swain remembered, "but he'd flown off to New Orleans and recorded 'Tutti Frutti.' After that, his career just took off, and the rest is history."

When Little Richard became a star, Clint Brantley needed to find a new singer to front the Upsetters. He found a gifted recent parolee

named James Brown. Convicted of petty theft at age sixteen, Brown spent three years in the Georgia Juvenile Training Institute before being released on parole and finding work as a janitor in Toccoa, Georgia. He soon gained a reputation as a skilled gospel and R&B singer, leading Brantley to bring him to Macon to work as a singer at his club, the Two Spot. In 1956, Brown recorded a demo of the song "Please, Please, Please" in Macon. The recording was heavily promoted on Hamp Swain's radio show, and caught the attention of the King label in Cincinnati. The future Godfather of Soul—like Little Richard before him—departed Macon for superstardom.

Once again, Clint Brantley needed a singer for the Upsetters. One of several front men who spent a brief time in the band was an ear-

Phil Walden. (Courtesy of
Rose Lane White Leavell/
Center for Public History,
University of West Georgia)

CHAPTER 10
I'm a Changed Man: Capricorn Rising

★ ★

EFORE OTIS REDDING'S tragic death in 1967, he and Phil Walden had been planning to open a first-rate studio in Macon, in the hope of establishing the town as a Southern recording destination. Walden contacted Jim Hawkins, a musician and electronics whiz from Athens, Georgia, who had the technical know-how to help Otis and Phil realize their vision.

By 1968, the musical landscape that Phil and Alan Walden loved so deeply was rapidly changing. The loss of their friend Otis Redding, combined with the mounting tension and mistrust following Martin Luther King, Jr.'s, assassination, signaled the close of a golden age for the Waldens. "By the end of the decade, a lot of the results of the civil rights era had served to urbanize black music," Phil told journalist Barney Hoskyns in 1985. "A lot of the people we had considered friends were suddenly calling us blue-eyed devils." Finding themselves increasingly demonized by some of their black colleagues was just too much for the Walden Brothers. "Some of us got tired of it and started looking in other directions," Alan Walden confessed. "And that's when Southern rock started to emerge."

"Phil and I had already purchased the building for the recording studio," Alan explained to Michael Buffalo Smith in 2002, "and we decided to go forward with it. With our new direction he signed Duane Allman and I signed Boz Scaggs. Into rock and roll we went." Though he recorded one album in Muscle Shoals for Atlantic in 1968 that featured Duane Allman, Boz Scaggs' sojourn in Macon was just a stopover between his late 1960s success with

Boz Scaggs publicity photo. (Courtesy of Chuck Perkins)

the Steve Miller Band in San Francisco, and his subsequent solo career as a recording artist for Columbia Records. By early 1970, after living in Macon for only a few months, he was gone.

By the beginning of 1969, the studio at 536 Broadway was nearing completion, and Phil began scouting for engineers and musicians to staff it. Jim Hawkins was hired as the first studio engineer. "Initially, we saw ourselves as Muscle Shoals and Stax, with a house rhythm section," he explained. "Phil had a ton of artists that he was managing. I hit the ground running." Phil was now both a manager *and* studio owner, but he would soon

further widen the platform from which he would launch Duane Allman's career.

"I had been fishing in Florida with Jerry Wexler right after I finished the studio here in Macon," Walden told *Creem* in 1972. "He told me I should have a label. I told him I didn't want a label, but he said, 'Aw, c'mon, have a label.' I finally said OK, but I didn't know what to call it. Jerry asked me what my sign was, and when I told him Capricorn, he said, 'I'm a Capricorn too. Call it Capricorn.' And that's the way it happened." With the backing of Jerry Wexler and Atlantic Records, Capricorn Records was born. Walden signed a three-year deal for Atlantic to function as the exclusive distributor of the Capricorn label in exchange for a $75,000 advance. "I had an absolutely solid belief in Duane Allman," Wexler explained as one of the motivations for encouraging Walden to launch Capricorn.

When Johnny Sandlin and Paul Hornsby turned down Duane's invitation to join his band during their Muscle Shoals sessions, Johnny Sandlin took a job in Miami at Tone studio, and convinced fellow former Hour Glass member Pete Carr to join him. Paul Hornsby returned to Tuscaloosa, where he played with a rotating collective of musicians known as South Camp. Phil still had his eye on the talented musicians, as Hornsby recalled:

> Walden kept courtin' me for a few weeks, and he said, "Well, if you won't be in this band with Duane, I'm building a studio in Macon. Would you consider coming and working at my studio?" I said, "Macon? What's that?" I'd never even heard of Macon. I didn't know what state it was in!

The interior of the Capricorn Studio in Macon, Georgia. (Courtesy of Jim Hawkins)

bunch of lumber and other stuff lying around. Down the hallway was the door to the studio. It seemed the studio would be a wreck, too, but then you opened the door, and there was this beautiful studio. The contrast was shocking." Once they began recording operations, the musicians took a hands-on role in fine-tuning the facility. "We'd play sessions and then we'd glue tile," Paul Hornsby laughed, "and we'd play another session and we'd say, 'Well, that doesn't sound quite right, let's put a little more padding over here.'"

When Hornsby first appeared in Muscle Shoals, he brought a Tuscaloosa bassist named Charlie Hayward with him. Hayward played with Hornsby in South Camp and had deep roots in R&B music. "We used to pick up WLAC from Nashville down there in Tuscaloosa," Hayward recalled. "DJs like John R. and Hoss Allen played a lot of the great old R&B and blues stuff. Growing up in the South, there were some issues with race and all, and it was probably not cool to listen to that, but me and my brothers always did anyway. We were just not fearful of the guys with the pointy hats."

"I tried out for the gig of being the session bass player," Hayward recalled of his sojourn to Macon, "but I was not ready for it yet. I had been playing clubs, but I had no idea what it was like to be tight with a rhythm section, and stuff like that. I was still pretty green and it just didn't work out."

When Charlie Hayward moved on, Floridian Robert "Pops" Popwell, who had been a member of the Young Rascals, joined Hornsby, Sandlin, and Carr to serve as the bassist for the studio's house band. "Duane recommended him," Hornsby recalled. "He was a hell of a bass player. He was almost too good. He was real flashy and he was just all over the place. We called it 'bumblebass.'" When the musicians heard Popwell's style, they were floored. "He showed up and started playing, and he was just amazing," Johnny Sandlin recalled. "We said, 'Oh man, we're gonna have to get this guy tired before we can cut any tracks.'"

When Cosimo Matassa's New Orleans studio closed down as a result of tax problems in 1969, the Meters traveled to Macon to record at the Capricorn facility. Their New Orleans funk influence stuck with Sandlin and Hornsby, in particular, and the percussive flavor of the Crescent City would linger on with the strains of blues, soul, and country that gave the Capricorn house band its early identity.

With the studio team solidified, one of the first people Phil brought into the fold to help run the new label was Frank Fenter. Fenter grew up in Johannesburg, South Africa, where

It didn't sound very exciting to me to go someplace I'd never heard of, in the middle of Georgia. But Phil could sell anything in the world, and over the next few weeks he'd call me. Eventually, Johnny and Pete Carr and I said we'd go.

It was the early summer of 1969 when they arrived. "When I first started working at Capricorn," Johnny Sandlin recalled, "the name of the studio was the Otis Redding Memorial Studio. When you walked in the front door, it looked like a vacant building with a whole he, like Walden, became obsessed with black R&B music from an early age. He landed in London in 1958 and got involved in booking bands like the Animals and the Rolling Stones, who were in the early stages of their rise to fame. By 1966, Frank was overseeing Atlantic Records' operations in the UK, and was soon named managing director of the label's entire European division. He discovered the band Yes and was instrumental in Led Zeppelin's early career. It was when Fenter assembled the legendary Stax Records tour of Europe in 1967 that he first came into contact with Phil Walden, who was managing tour participants Otis Redding and Sam & Dave.

Walden approached Fenter with a unique vision for what he wanted to accomplish. "Capricorn, right from the outset, had a different approach and different attitudes to other

record companies," Walden explained to Chris Charlesworth in 1974. "We wanted it to be a company rather than a label. Anyone can have a label; you can start one tomorrow. . . . We have in-house producers, in-house press office, and an in-house promotion department, which makes us a *company* instead of a label."

What Walden wanted was a self-contained enterprise that encompassed management, booking, publishing, and all other aspects of an artist's career. "Phil was always inspiring," Johnny Sandlin noted. "He'd say, 'Oh man, we're gonna do this . . . we're gonna do that,' and he would. He'd get you all fired up to do whatever it was, and you really believed you could do it. . . . He'd plan the whole thing and he'd make it work. I came to love and respect him." To pull it off, however, Phil needed someone with Fenter's label expertise.

"Frank was a brilliant record man," remembered Dick Wooley, who worked with Fenter at Atlantic and, later, at Capricorn. While Phil Walden was the public face of Capricorn Records, Fenter's ability to run day-to-day operations was crucial. "Frank was the strength behind the scenes, and Phil took the spotlight," explained Capricorn's former head of production Keith Crossley. "He signed the acts and Phil managed them. Phil was the wonder boy who dined at the White House and told raunchy stories, and Frank was the power that ran the company. He was the man who knew how to deal with the movers and shakers in the record industry." At first, they seemed an unlikely pairing. "In the beginning," Fenter told journalist Louis Kraar in 1975, "no one believed in us at all. Who ever heard of two guys in

Robert "Pops" Popwell. (Courtesy of Jim Hawkins)

Pete Carr. (Courtesy of Jim Hawkins)

Johnny Sandlin. (Courtesy of Johnny Sandlin)

Left to right: Johnny Sandlin, Tyrone "Little Tommy" Thomas, Pops Popwell, Jerry "Swamp Dogg" Williams, and Pete Carr, with Paul Hornsby (seated). (Courtesy of Jim Hawkins)

Frank Fenter. (Courtesy of Robin Fenter)

Macon, a cracker and a South African, with a record company?"

By the middle of 1970, Walden was overseeing Capricorn Records, No Exit Music Publishing, Redwal Music, Phil Walden & Associates Management, Aura Publicity & Public Relations, and a partnership with "Polk Salad Annie" singer Tony Joe White called Swamp Fox Productions. He was still managing Clarence Carter, Johnnie Taylor, Eddie Floyd, Al Green, Candi Staton, Arthur Conley, Percy Sledge, Doris Duke, Jimmy Hughes, and others. He had recently signed the Allman Brothers Band to a management deal and was closing new management agreements with white artists like Danny O'Keefe, whose "Good Time Charlie's Got the Blues" became a major hit at the end of 1972. It was time for Capricorn Records to start branching out beyond the Allman Brothers Band.

At first, Phil looked to a key figure from his early career as a possible bridge to his future. The second Capricorn album was Johnny Jenkins' 1970 release *Ton-Ton Macoute!* Following his failed 1962 session at the Stax studio in Memphis—and the subsequent rise of Otis Redding—Jenkins had grown bitter and insular. "I have no doubt that if I were Jenkins, and I witnessed the phenomenal rise of my singer to world status, I'd have resented it, too," Walden conceded in an interview with Fred Shuster. Perhaps partially to make up for the mistrust that had grown between them, Walden found an opportunity to record Johnny Jenkins for Capricorn in 1970. Several of the tracks that eventually formed Jenkins' *Ton-Ton Macoute!* LP were originally recorded as the foundation for the abandoned Duane Allman solo album back at FAME Studios in Muscle Shoals.

With Duane listed as a co-producer along-

Berry Oakley, Duane Allman, Arthur Conley, Johnny Sandlin, and Paul Hornsby during a recording session at Capricorn Studios. (Courtesy of Johnny Sandlin)

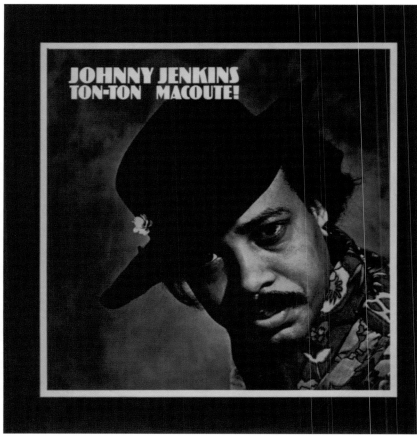

The Capricorn Rhythm Section that backed Johnny Jenkins live and in the studio. *Left to right*: Sandlin, Popwell, Hornsby, and Carr. (Courtesy of Johnny Sandlin)

side Johnny Sandlin, the album featured fellow Allman Brothers Berry Oakley, Jaimoe, and Butch Trucks, as well as the core group that formed the first house band at Capricorn Studios: Sandlin, Paul Hornsby, Pete Carr, and Pops Popwell. The LP captured the Southern rock aesthetic for which Capricorn and the Allmans would become known. Dr. John's "I Walk on Gilded Splinters" opened the album, which also included excellent cover songs by Bob Dylan, John D. Loudermilk, Muddy Waters, and others.

The Capricorn crew had high hopes for Johnny's appearance at the July 1970 Atlanta International Pop Festival, which was actually held in the town of Byron, just a few miles outside Macon. With Jimi Hendrix, Johnny Winter, B. B. King, and other high-profile performers on the bill, the concert was an important breakout moment for the Allman Brothers Band, but was pivotal in a different way for Jenkins. The Capricorn studio players formed Johnny's backing group for the appearance. "We rehearsed for weeks," Walden recalled, "and then Johnny got up there and abandoned everything we had worked on and began to play songs. I was a little startled and confused to say the least. Then, someone who had ingested too many chemicals jumped onstage nude and began dancing around him. It wasn't the success we thought it would be."

As it became clear that promoting Jenkins would be an uphill battle, Capricorn cut its losses. "We just didn't sense that the commitment was there from Johnny in the long run," Walden acknowledged, "so we agreed to tear up the contract." Following the failed effort with Johnny Jenkins, Walden turned to Duane Allman, keen to find out what else was going on down in Jacksonville when the Allman Brothers Band was being formed. ★

Cowboy onstage at the Fillmore, 1971: Bill Pillmore, Pete Kowalkie, Scott Boyer, George Clark, and Tommy Talton. (Courtesy of Joe Bender)

CHAPTER 11
Livin' in the Country: Cowboy

I **N 1970,** on the recommendation of Duane Allman, Phil Walden signed the band Cowboy to a record deal. The core of the group was built around musicians and songwriters Scott Boyer and Tommy Talton, both of whom emerged from the same Florida music scene that nurtured Duane and Gregg in their formative years. Musically, however, Cowboy were no Allman Brothers clone. The band represented an important country-rock strain of the Southern music that was beginning to emanate from the South in the early 1970s.

Scott Boyer was born in upstate New York, but his family moved to Louisville, Kentucky, when he was five. By the time he reached the sixth grade, his folks had relocated to Jacksonville, Florida. Scott finished high school there before moving on to Florida State University, in Tallahassee, to study viola. While in college, he joined forces with David Brown and future Allman Brother Butch Trucks to form the folkrock flavored Bitter Ind. "We made a ton of money," Boyer explained to Michael Buffalo Smith. "We were making $300 per night in a three piece band back then. This was in 1965. I bought a Jaguar and we were playing three to four nights a week. I dropped out of college at the end because I was making good money."

The members of the Bitter Ind eventually changed their name to the 31st of February. After recording one album for Vanguard Records, they began working on demos for a follow-up. Gregg and Duane Allman, who had recently returned from their Hour Glass period in California, joined forces with the 31st of February to record some new mate-

COWBOY	
▸ SCOTT BOYER guitar, vocals	
▸ TOMMY TALTON guitar, vocals	
▸ TOM WYNN drums	
▸ GEORGE CLARK bass	
▸ BILL PILLMORE guitar, keyboards	
▸ PETE KOWALKE guitar	
▸ DAVID BROWN bass	
▸ BILL STEWART drums	
▸ RANDALL BRAMBLETT horns, vocals	
▸ CHIP CONDON keyboards	
▸ CHARLES MILLER drums	
▸ ARCH PEARSON bass	

rial. When the label failed to get excited, the group splintered. Butch Trucks went on to form the Allman Brothers Band with Duane and Gregg, while David Brown would eventually go on to play with Boz Skaggs. Scott Boyer would find his success after joining forces with Tommy Talton.

Talton grew up near Orlando, Florida, where like many of his peers he soaked up the black music of the era. "Growing up on R&B was just an automatic," he explained. "It was the stuff to hear. We were enthralled with it. We would go down to the black area and go to the record stores there. I snuck in to hear James Brown at a place called Club 436 in Orlando. I was one of four little white kids there."

As a teenager, Tommy formed his first garage band. "I had a band called the Keyes," he remembered, "soon to be changed to the

Tommy Talton publicity photo. (Capricorn Records)

Scott Boyer publicity photo. (Capricorn Records)

Chessmen. We all wore white shirts and black pants, and I played my first gig with them at a school dance." Performing cover songs by groups like the Kinks, the Chessmen also worked on original material for their gigs at venues in Cocoa Beach. "I ran across Duane and Gregg when they were the Allman Joys at a place called the Tiger's Den," Talton explained. "We just generally kind of knew each other because we musicians were a pretty small genre of humans back then. It was like you had to stick together, 'cause you were targeted by all the rednecks down there."

Eventually, Talton joined another band that had a larger following. We the People were a legendary central Florida garage band. With Talton functioning as one of the principal songwriters, the group landed a recording contract at Challenge Records. In the late 1960s, they moved on to RCA, where they recorded with Elvis Presley's producer, Felton Jarvis, in Nashville. Though they never had a national hit, We the People were considered one of the top Florida bands of the era, alongside the Nightcrawlers and the Allman Joys. "We played regularly," Talton remembered, "in Cocoa Beach, Daytona, Orlando, Winterhaven, Kissimmee, Gainesville—all the central Florida area. In 1967 I remember driving up and down Highway 441 very often. So did Tom Petty, by the way. Petty and his Mudcrutch band would be playing right across the campus while We the People would be playing at another fraternity house. Around the corner would be the Maundy Quintet, which was Bernie Leadon

Tommy Talton (*second from right*) and We the People, as featured in a 1966 newspaper profile.

and Glenn Fry, who later started the Eagles. A lot of talent was going on."

By the late 1960s, Talton was ready to get out. "I was going through more inward changes, and I started liking a different type of music. I said, 'I don't want to do this anymore,' and sold my cherry red 1968 Gibson 335 guitar. I walked into a music store in Orlando and traded it in for a new guitar that had just come out, an acoustic guitar called an Ovation." Tommy was ready to try his hand at songwriting. "When I traded my guitar in for the Ovation," he recalled, "me and my friend Ovie Sparks—who's an electronics genius, so it's funny that his last name is Sparks—left Orlando in his little '65 green turtle Porsche and went up to Nashville. We banged around there for two or three months. . . . Nothing was happening. I wasn't country, so I left."

In 1968, Talton and Sparks headed to

Southern California, where Tommy devoted himself to his music. "I was staying at home and writing a lot," he recalled, of the year he spent in Los Angeles. "That was a spiritual time for me . . . I was searching my inward self and doing some real reflection. A lot of songs came out of that time." After experiencing some setbacks, including a two-week jail stint for possession of half a joint, Tommy decided it was time to return home.

"I came back to Florida from California to regroup and make decisions about my next musical direction," he remembered. Playing the coffeehouse and folk-club circuit, Talton began performing the songs he'd been writing in California. While most would-be troubadours of the time were heavily reliant on Bob Dylan covers and standard folk songs, he distinguished himself as one of the few who was concentrating on original material. "That's when I met Scott Boyer," Tommy continued. "I was introduced to him by a mutual friend. This girl said, 'I know another guy who writes his own stuff, and he's pretty good, too. You guys ought to meet.' We met and we sat down at this table at her house in Winterpark, Florida. Scott had come down from Jacksonville. We got our guitars and each played a song for each other. Then it was like, 'OK. Who else is gonna be in the band?'"

Talton brought in Tom Wynn, who'd played drums with him in We the People. He also recruited an Orlando bassist named George Clark. Boyer brought in Bill Pillmore and Pete Kowalke, who were friends from his days at Florida State. Pillmore and Kowalke both played guitar, but Pillmore switched to keys when the band came together. The members of the group that would eventually become Cowboy moved into a house in Jacksonville that they called the Crab House and committed themselves to nonstop writing and rehearsing.

"We threw papers at two in the morning to pay the rent while we were working up songs," Tommy explained. "That's all we did. We all lived together, woke up in the morning, and played all day. Two or three kids from the neighborhood would drop by and ask if they could sit there and listen. We said, 'Yeah, as long as you shut up.' One of 'em was Ronnie Van Zant from Lynyrd Skynyrd. He must have been fifteen, maybe sixteen. The rest of us were all nineteen and twenty."

Boyer, Talton, and the others originally called their band Easy and were part of the second wave of the Jacksonville music community that formed around the Second Coming, Duane Allman, and other like-minded musicians who were beginning to populate the

The Allman Brothers Band jamming on the front lawn of the Cowboy farm in Cochran, Georgia. (Courtesy of Tommy Talton)

An early Cowboy publicity photo. *Left to right:* Scott Boyer, Bill Pillmore, Pete Kowalkie, George Clark, Tom Wynn (in front), and Tommy Talton. (Courtesy of the Big House Museum, Macon, Georgia)

Cowboy onstage at the Fillmore, 1971. *Left to right:* Scott Boyer, Bill Pillmore, Pete Kowalkie, and Tommy Talton. (Courtesy of Joe Bender)

"On nothing more than Duane Allman's recommendation," Tommy Talton explained, "Phil Walden signed Cowboy to a contract, sight unseen. I don't know what Duane said to Phil, but a week later we had management, publishing, and booking contracts in the mail." Though Walden apparently sent producer Johnny Sandlin down to verify Duane's report, the band never met Capricorn's president prior to signing with the label. "Phil asked Johnny Sandlin to come to Jacksonville to hear the band," drummer Tom Wynn told *Gritz* magazine. "He did. And when he went back to Macon, he apparently told Phil Walden he thought we had something worth hearing. So that was it—Duane told Phil; Phil sent Johnny. Phil signed the band, Johnny was our producer, and Duane got famous. The lesson must be—always help your friends."

Soon after signing with Capricorn in 1970, the band relocated. "We moved up into Cochran, Georgia, thirty miles south of Macon," Talton recalled, "where we had a huge house on 400 acres. We paid something like $75 a month for it. All the band lived there, and all the people we met on the road that followed us home."

Soon after arriving in Georgia, Walden discovered that there was another band called Easy in California, so the group was quickly re-christened Cowboy. "It was always a toss-up between Easy and Cowboy, anyway," Tommy revealed. "Easy was decided upon originally by playing a game of horse, the old basketball game, with the band. George Clark, the bass player, won that game and chose Easy. Cowboy automatically became the second choice, so we just went with that."

Cowboy entered the Capricorn studio to begin work on their first album in mid-1970. "The songs were fun, light, hippie, good-feeling music," producer Johnny Sandlin recalled. "Innocent folk with a little country-rock flavor, and great harmonies along the lines of the Eagles." The partnership between Cowboy

fledgling hippie scene in Florida. It was Duane who would give the new group their big break when he stopped by unexpectedly one day.

"He pulled up in our driveway about 7 a.m.," Scott Boyer remembered. "He was on his way from Daytona back to Macon. He woke me up and said, 'I hear you got a band.' I said, 'Yeah,' and he said, 'Well, play something for me.' So I woke everybody up, and we went down into the music room and played a few songs for Duane. He said, 'OK, I like your stuff, man. I'm gonna go back and talk to Phil Walden about it.'"

71

and Sandlin was a great fit. "It was wonderful working with Johnny," Talton recalled. "He was just like another member of the band."

The label gave the band members the freedom to express themselves without trying to micromanage the sound. "The Capricorn offices were two or three blocks away, up the hill from the studio," Talton recalled. "The booking agency and the record company and the publishing company were all in one little building up there. They stayed up there, and the musicians had our clubhouse down on Broadway." It was like a musical Utopia for the young band.

"The studio was just plain funky," drummer Wynn recalled:

> It was housed in an old storefront building right in the middle of downtown. There was no sign, and walking up to it, it looked like just another dust-crusted vacant building. The front was vacant; the studio area was a big room with a control booth in the back of the building. . . . Most of the other buildings in the neighborhood were vacant. Seemed like they probably had been vacant for a long time. I remember the "Heart of Georgia Diner" was across the street, and I never worked up the nerve to actually eat there. I remember the red neon lights on the mission building's cross that said "Jesus Saves" would glow huge in the fog. We

could see it from several blocks away coming out of the studio late at night. It was the heart of old Georgia.

The first Cowboy album was recorded in a series of marathon sessions, as Sandlin recalled in *A Never Ending Groove*:

> I think we were there for a couple of days straight between good things to smoke and a few amphetamines. Toward the end of our two days in the studio, about the time the effect of the Black Beauties was starting to wear off, some of the guys got to thinking of some ways to keep the session moving along. One of them said, "Hey, let's do a track naked." I thought to myself that certainly wasn't necessary, and wasn't something I even wanted to envision. I told them, "I'll turn the lights out and you can do what you want, but y'all can't come into the control room naked." All the guys took off their clothes and we cut a track or two. I could see them from the waist up, but I didn't look down.

Tommy Talton laughed at the memory. "It's all true," he confirmed. "How could he forget that?"

The album, *Reach for the Sky,* was released soon after, and featured the same brand of country-infused earthy harmonies that would dominate early-'70s folk-rock. "Many people

A later incarnation of Cowboy, *left to right:* David Brown, Scott Boyer, Bill Stewart, Randall Bramblett, and Tommy Talton. (Courtesy of the Big House Museum, Macon, Georgia)

have said that we were ahead of the Eagles in what we were doing," Talton remarked.

Thanks to the Capricorn connection, Cowboy were able to reach a wider audience by opening shows for the Allman Brothers Band. Duane, in particular, enjoyed his relationship with the group. "We'd sit down, just the two of us, at the old Capricorn Studio in Macon," Talton remembered, "and enjoy playing for each other for hours and hours. There was never any jealousy or envy. We just liked to show each other things that we were working on."

When it came time for Cowboy to record their second album, *5'll Getcha Ten,* the Capricorn studio was in the middle of a renovation and expansion. Producer Johnny Sandlin took them to Muscle Shoals Sound in Alabama to work on the project. Duane showed up at the studio and played dobro. "One of the last things he recorded just before the *Eat a Peach* sessions," Butch Trucks told Alan Paul, "was Cowboy's 'Please Be with Me,' with Scott Boyer and Tommy Talton." In fact, it would be Duane's very last non–Allman Brothers Band recording. The Scott Boyer–penned tune is likely Cowboy's best-known song, thanks to the cover version that Eric Clapton recorded for his *461 Ocean Boulevard* album in 1974.

"One day I got a phone call from Johnny [Sandlin]," Boyer told Michael Buffalo Smith, "and he said, 'Man, you aren't going to believe it. Eric Clapton is going to record your song, "Please Be with Me"'! I told him that wasn't funny, because I was having a hard time. Johnny was having to convince me that he was not kidding and it was for real."

When Gregg Allman launched his solo career in 1973, Cowboy's Scott Boyer and Tommy Talton were heavily involved. "We played their album *5'll Getcha Ten* quite a bit at the Big House," Allman explained. It was

Scott Boyer, Bill Stewart, Tommy Talton, David Brown, and Randall Bramblett. (Courtesy of Bill Stewart)

Johnny Sandlin, Bill Stewart, and Tommy Talton. (Capricorn Records)

Cowboy onstage, *left to right*: Tommy Talton, Pete Kowalkie, Tom Wynn, Scott Boyer, and George Clark. (Courtesy of Tommy Talton)

the same setup in the studio for both albums, in terms of drum mics and everything."

Despite working as artists, the two principle members of Cowboy became increasingly focused on side projects and studio work for others. The duo eventually became de facto members of the Capricorn house band, backing everyone from soul legend Arthur Conley to country queen Kitty Wells. It was Talton who obtained an advance copy of Bob Dylan's *Planet Waves* album and convinced Wells to record Dylan's "Forever Young" as the title track for her Capricorn LP.

Around the same time, Tommy Talton, Bill Stewart, and Johnny Sandlin released an LP called *Happy to Be Alive* that was practically a Cowboy album without any Scott Boyer songs. "One night," Talton explained, "Johnny, me, and Bill Stewart were sitting around the studio waiting for Dickey to come overdub some part on an Allman Brothers project. He was late and never showed up, so Johnny said, 'Tommy, you got a new tune? Let's record something.'" As it turned out, Talton had a song he'd recently written. "Bill and Johnny and I recorded this song called 'Help Me Get It Out,'" he continued. "We recorded it, and just off the cuff, Johnny showed it to Phil a few days later after he had mixed it. So Phil said it sounded pretty good and that we should just go ahead and do an album."

In 1977, Boyer and Talton released the fourth and final Cowboy album for Capricorn with a new lineup that included Chip Condon on keyboards, Charles Miller on drums, and Arch Pearson on bass. Simply titled *Cowboy*, it was a fairly lightweight pop affair that was not as well received by critics as the band's earlier work.

By the late 1970s, Cowboy had broken up, having failed to ever achieve mainstream notoriety. Their place in the Macon community was historic, but their failure to find major success left the band members with mixed feelings about the experience. "Phil Walden loved us," Tommy Talton enthused:

> He liked our music, but when it came to publicity and marketing and stuff, Capricorn didn't know what to do with us. Phil was of the school of, "You get out there and you play 250 nights a year, and we'll give you a station wagon to travel in, and you just work and make sure I have some money in my pocket from my percentage of your gig. And then *maybe* I'll let you go in my studio, and I'll charge you $30,000 that you'll all of a sudden owe me, 'cause I let you go in there." He had a kingdom going there in Macon. But in the end, I really loved him. ★

a sound that Gregg would embrace when he invited Boyer and Talton to play on his *Laid Back* album, alongside Capricorn studio staffers Johnny Sandlin, Paul Hornsby, and a handful of others. Gregg also recorded Boyer's "All My Friends," which had appeared on *5'll Getcha Ten*, and when he toured in support of his solo album, the members of Cowboy formed the core of his band.

"That tour was just wonderful," Talton recalled. "We played all the best venues in every large city in the United States. We did thirty-five gigs in fifty days.... Cowboy would start out the show, and we would play for about an hour or so. Then we would take a short intermission and come back to support Gregg." The *On Tour* album, released in 1974, was credited to "Gregg Allman with Special Guests Cowboy/Boyer & Talton," and featured two Cowboy songs in the middle of the LP.

By the mid-1970s, only Boyer and Talton remained from the original Cowboy lineup. David Brown, from Boyer's 31st of February days, joined them on bass, while Capricorn studio drummer Bill Stewart, who took over for Johnny Sandlin when Sandlin began focusing on his production work, rounded out the rhythm section. Soon after, multi-instrumentalist Randall Bramblett, who'd been part of the Gregg Allman tour, came into the group to add horns and vocals. In 1975, Cowboy released their third album, appropriately titled *Boyer & Talton*. "We cut that album about the same time we cut *Laid Back* with Gregg," Bill Stewart recalled, "and, in my head, it's almost like a double album. It was

The second wave of
Capricorn studio and
road musicians, known as
Friends and Neighbors.
Left to right: Charlie
Hayward, Bill Stewart,
Jimmy Nalls, Earl "Speedo"
Sims, and Chuck Leavell.
(Courtesy of Bill Stewart)

CHAPTER 12
Sunshine to Sundown: Searching for a Sound

 Y THE END of 1970, Capricorn had released five albums: the first two Allman Brothers LPs, plus the debut offerings from Johnny Jenkins, Cowboy, and folk singer Livingston Taylor. Up to that point, the Capricorn releases were still technically on Atlantic's Atco label imprint, with "Capricorn Records Series" appearing beneath the Atco logo on the album jacket. In 1971, Capricorn, while still distributed by Atlantic, became a proper label with its own logo and design.

Capricorn was still defining itself. Alan Walden had departed the label due to an increasingly tense relationship with his brother Phil. The Allman Brothers were not yet major stars, and the concept of "Southern rock" was only beginning to take hold. Despite being home to the Allmans and Cowboy, Capricorn was not nurturing a singular identity. In the early 1970s, for example, they invested in a small cadre of singer-songwriters, two of whom happened to be James Taylor's brothers.

Emerging from the Boston coffeehouse scene, Livingston Taylor signed with Capricorn in November of 1969, before James had experienced major success. "Atlantic suggested to Phil that he sign Livingston," Capricorn publicist Mike Hyland recalled. He recorded his album in Macon over a two-week period around the same time that his brother's *Sweet Baby James* was just hitting stores. Livingston's self-titled album wasn't released until July, by which time James had exploded on the scene. Produced by music critic–turned–record producer Jon Landau, *Livingston Taylor* featured the regular lineup of Capricorn

musicians, including Pete Carr, Paul Hornsby, Johnny Sandlin, and Pops Popwell.

Capricorn then snatched up Alex, the oldest Taylor sibling, who recorded his debut album in Macon in the fall of 1970. Alex's first album, *With Friends and Neighbors*, was produced by Johnny Sandlin. Paul Hornsby played keys, while Scott Boyer and Tommy Talton from Cowboy appeared as backing musicians. The end result of Alex's recording sessions was reminiscent of a bluesier version of brother James, but with a distinct early Southern rock flavor.

"In a way, the Taylors are becoming the Kennedy family of folk music," *Rolling Stone* mused in December of 1970. It would have been impossible for them to live up to the hype. "It was scary in the beginning," Alex told journalist David Browne in 1987. "*Time* magazine and the cover of *Rolling Stone*—the first family of rock? That's quite a moniker when you're not sure of your identity at all." Livingston recorded two more albums for Capricorn, *Liv*

and *Over the Rainbow*, in 1971 and 1973, respectively, but found greater success later in the decade, after he'd moved on to another label.

Capricorn signed another artist in 1971 who was firmly in the Taylor vein, if not part of the actual Taylor family. Jonathan Edwards was born in Minnesota but raised in Virginia. Though Edwards had provided Capricorn's first successful single with the #4 hit "Sunshine," he faded away from the fold, signing with Atlantic Records for his follow-up.

The Allman Brothers Band's *At Fillmore East* album was released in July of 1971. It was certified Gold in October, four days prior to Duane Allman's death. Following Duane's accident, interest in the band continued to grow, pushing the LP to #13 on the *Billboard* album chart. It was Capricorn's first hit album, and the money began flowing freely.

At the close of 1971 Capricorn ended its distribution agreement with Atlantic Records and entered into a new contract with Warner Bros. at the start of the New Year. Capricorn's deal with Atlantic earned Walden's label a royalty rate of about 13 percent. He wanted a bigger percentage, but Jerry Wexler wouldn't budge.

"Jerry had this paternalistic view of Southerners," Walden told *Fortune* magazine in 1975, "as people that he brings to the forefront, and after that they desert him. But anyone will leave when he's not getting an ample share of the profits." With the Warner deal, both companies shared the profits equally. With $75,000 in advance money from Warner Bros. they expanded the roster. With a new label handling manufacturing, distribution, and merchandising of Capricorn releases, Walden and company found new energy.

(Courtesy of Bill Stewart)

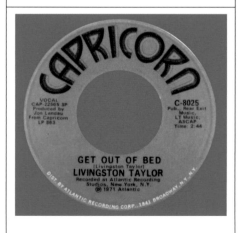

The first LP released under the new Warner deal was Alex Taylor's sophomore Capricorn album, *Dinnertime*. It was recorded in Muscle Shoals, with Johnny Sandlin returning to the producer's chair. A little more raw and rooted in the Allman Brothers' style than his debut LP, it was well received by critics. The second was the Allman Brothers Band's phenomenally successful *Eat a Peach*. When the latter climbed to #4 and was certified Gold, it signaled a new era of success for Capricorn.

Walden and executive vice president Frank Fenter continued to expand the company. Johnny Sandlin was promoted to vice president and head of A&R. He was joined in the studio by Terry Kane, who had left Criteria Studios in Miami to come aboard as Capricorn's chief engineer. With Mike Hyland directing publicity, Capricorn had assembled a crack team to lead it into 1972. "Phil was in charge of everything," Hyland explained. "He owned the booking agency, the record company, the publishing company, the studio. He owned a travel agency to move these people around, and he owned liquor stores to sell 'em booze when they were home. It was brilliant!"

By that time, the approach to staffing the studio had changed. "It became apparent," Sandlin explained, "there wasn't a need for a dedicated studio band since most of the artists on Capricorn were self-contained groups." Guitarist Pete Carr departed for Muscle Shoals, where he eventually joined forces with Lenny LeBlanc as LeBlanc & Carr, before moving on to play guitar with Paul Simon. Robert "Pops" Popwell headed to California, where he ultimately joined forces with the Crusaders.

"The more and more white rock-and-roll bands that were comin' in there," Paul Hornsby explained, "meant there was less and less playing to be done, because they already had their own players. I figured if I was gonna keep a job in the studio, I was gonna have to learn some other duties. I never had any inclination to be a record producer. I just wanted to play. I wasn't even quite sure what a real record producer did, but I figured it out and Johnny and I were the only two staff producers at Capricorn."

One of Hornsby's first production projects was for a band called Sundown. When

Chuck Leavell, Jimmy Nalls, Alex Taylor, Charlie Hayward, Bill Stewart, and Earl "Speedo" Sims. (Courtesy of Bill Stewart)

the group began to disintegrate during the recording process, he called on a handful of his musical buddies from his old band South Camp in Tuscaloosa, which included a pre–Allman Brothers Band Chuck Leavell. "Sundown," Leavell explained, "was a combination of a group called the Boogie Chillen'—a local Macon, Georgia, outfit led by a guy named Asa Howard—and the Tuscaloosa constituency, which was Lou Mullenix, Court Pickett, and myself."

By the time Sundown's album was completed, bassist Ronnie Chambley had departed the band. "I actually came in to replace the bass player," explained Charlie Hayward, who returned to Macon despite his earlier failed audition for the job as house bassist in the Capricorn rhythm section. With the official Capricorn rhythm section now disbanded, the influx of Tuscaloosa musicians created a flexible stable of players who were available to step in for studio work or touring duties. After

Sundown, the Tuscaloosa contingent took over from Hornsby, Sandlin, and Bill Stewart as Alex Taylor's road band.

Ultimately, Alex Taylor and Walden clashed over the grueling tour schedule that Walden's team had booked. "I don't really know how this is going to be resolved," Taylor told *Creem* magazine in 1972, "but I'll tell you one thing. Regardless of what might happen in the future, I have the utmost respect for Phil Walden as a manager and a man. Our philosophies might not exactly match up, but what he's done down there is tremendous." Taylor broke ties with Walden and didn't record for Capricorn again.

"Shortly after Alex Taylor had a falling out and went off the booking agency in Macon," Hayward recalled, "Dr. John's guys had quit. So we went out and did that gig." New Orleans–born Mac Rebennack had made a name for himself as a Los Angeles session musician in the 1960s before reinventing himself as Dr. John, the Night Tripper. Cultivating an elabo-

rate stage show that was one part voodoo ceremony, one part psychedelic rock concert, and one part over-the-top theatrical performance, he is best known for his 1973 album *In the Right Place*, which spawned the singles "Right, Place Wrong Time" and "Such a Night."

"Just before I recorded *In the Right Place*,"

77

Dr. John. (Photo by David Warner Ellis/Redferns)

Rebennack noted in his autobiography, "I hooked up with yet another high-flying low-balling manager I thought would kick me into the super-stratosphere of rock and roll. This time, the character was Phil Walden, who managed the Allman Brothers, the Meters, and a bunch of other people." Several members of the Capricorn community were big fans, and they were excited when Mac moved to Macon. "My whole inspiration for that Johnny Jenkins album," Johnny Sandlin revealed, "was from Dr. John's records."

"When Dr. John moved to town," Paul Hornsby recalled, "I went out and played organ on weekends behind him. When I came off the road with Dr. John, I handed the keys to Chuck once again. Chuck and all those guys just moved from Alex Taylor's band to Dr. John. That's how close-knit we all were here."

"The band with Dr. John was me, Chuck Leavell, Charlie Hayward, and Jimmy Nalls on

guitar," Bill Stewart remembered. Lou Mullinex and I switched back and forth on drums. I played mostly drum set, and he played percussion, but sometimes we'd switch. With Dr. John, we had wardrobe, so we dressed up in all these crazy clothes. I wore a red graduation gown with a hat and a tassel." Chuck Leavell concurred. "Playing with Mac was like going to the University of Funkology," he enthused.

"I always thought it was really funny," Cowboy's Tommy Talton laughed, "that Dr. John, the Night Tripper, is living on the second floor of the Crestwood Apartments in a two-bedroom little place, just like the rest of us." Regardless of the theatrical aspect, Mac infused the Macon crowd with a hearty dose of musical sophistication. "It was such a different kind of approach, rhythmically," Charlie Hayward said of his work with Dr. John. "We were on the road with him for about four months, and then he got the Meters after us." It wasn't long after that that Rebennack's relationship with Phil Walden deteriorated, and he left Macon. "Phil's hustle was he wanted total control of his acts," Rebennack reflected. "He owned not only your management, but the booking agency that set up your gigs and the travel agency that sent you on your way—he had an angle on every piece of your business."

By that time, the Tuscaloosa crowd had become a key part of Macon's musical landscape. "We were hanging out together, playing on each other's records, and going to the H&H Restaurant, and Grant's Lounge, and Le Carousel, with the famous hot chicken," Chuck Leavell reminisced. "It became this huge social scene. . . . Everybody was just so happy to be playing music. It was a true community." ★

DRINKING MAN'S FRIEND: ERIC QUINCY TATE

—

WHILE CAPRICORN BOASTED a diverse roster, Eric Quincy Tate were one of the groups that truly embodied the early Southern rock aesthetic. An effortless blending of R&B, country, and funky swamp-pop, their music was some of the most organically appealing of the Southern rock era.

Guitarist Tommy Carlisle and singing drummer Donnie McCormick met in 1963 when Carlisle joined McCormick's band, the Kings, near Corpus Christi, Texas. The following year, they joined the US Navy Reserve. Stationed on the USS Essex in Rhode Island, the two formed Eric Quincy Tate on the ship. "Donnie made that name up," future bassist David Cantonwine explained. "They wanted something British sounding, like the Spencer Davis Group." According to Donnie, "Eric" referred to Eric Burden of the Animals, while "Quincy" was a nearby town, and "Tate" was the name of a fellow sailor. They performed for troops in Europe, and were named official Goodwill Ambassadors for the US Navy.

Eric Quincy Tate returned to Texas in 1968, where McCormick bought a nightclub called the Muddy Turtle. It was there that Cantonwine and keyboardist Joe Rogers came into the group. Tony Joe White—known for his hit "Polk Salad Annie"—became a fan of the band's brand of soul-infused boogie and convinced Phil Walden to manage them. "We drove up to Macon from Corpus," McCormick told Bill DeYoung, "and that's when we cut the first version of 'Comin' Down.'" Duane Allman showed up at the studio and spontaneously joined the demo session. "He just strolled in the studio and asked if we minded if he played," McCormick recounted. "He broke the neck off a whiskey bottle and sat down."

Jerry Wexler signed Eric Quincy Tate to Atlantic's Cotillion label. Their first album was co-produced by Wexler, White, and Tom Dowd in Memphis, where the band had relocated. "The first album we always called the monkey album," Cantonwine laughed. "They wanted to get this thing done real quick as a favor to Tony Joe. They just hired studio musicians and recorded all our songs, which hurt. They let Donnie sing and Tommy play a few guitars, but that was it."

The self-titled debut was released in January of 1970, and showcased a uniquely Southern blend of blues, rock, soul, and funky pop. They relocated from Memphis to Atlanta soon after. "We finally got a gig on the strip at the Bowery," Cantonwine recalled, "and played for nothing. . . . I grew up a lot in that place. I saw a guy get shot—just blown right out the door there."

Eric Quincy Tate soon became a staple on the Atlanta scene, and they were local celebrities by the time their second alum, *Drinking Man's Friend*, was released on Capricorn Records in April of 1972. Paul Hornsby was tapped to produce. In reviewing the album, *Billboard* called Tommy Carlisle's guitar playing "exceptionally memorable and liquid."

Eric Quincy Tate toured with a vengeance. "Capricorn actually went out and spent $10,000 on equipment, on a van, on a truck, and put us on the road," Cantonwine recalled. "We went and played the major venues throughout the country. We opened up for everybody from A to Z. Literally, the Allman Brothers to Frank Zappa!"

Despite the critical acclaim, they struggled to find sustained success. "It got to where the more or less crappy gigs were comin' our way," David acknowledged. "We were supposed to do another record, but Capricorn was holding back and hemming and hawing about that. We were complaining, 'Either do something with us, or let us out of our contract.' Phil Walden jumped up and said, 'What do you guys think you are? A fuckin' million-dollar act?' Joe, our keyboard player, who had a little temper, went over Phil Walden's desk and started chokin' him right there. . . . We never really talked with Phil anymore after that."

Frustrated, guitarist Tommy Carlisle

Eric Quincy Tate, *left to right:* Donnie McCormick, Tommy Carlisle, Joe Rodgers, David Cantonwine, and Wayne "Bear" Sauls (Courtesy of David Cantonwine)

departed in 1973, and was replaced by Wayne "Bear" Sauls. Eventually, the band caught the attention of Atlanta's most preeminent music impresario. "Bill Lowery hooked us up with GRC Records," Cantonwine recalled. "We started working on our next album in 1974." *EQT* was released the following year.

They hit the road again, with a little boost from an old friend. "Gregg Allman got in his Volkswagen van and went and played two weeks with us," Cantonwine recalled:

The last gig on that tour was opening up for Ted Nugent in Hollywood, Florida. We had played with Ted before, and during our show he came out and went around hollerin' and screamin' and took all the attention away from us. He was pretty much an asshole. For this show in Florida, Gregg got everybody seats in a 747. We flew down there, snortin' coke and smokin' pot in the lounge of the plane. That night we got to the gig and they took us in the dressing room and told us, "You've got forty-five minutes for your set. If you don't stop in forty-five minutes on the button, we're pullin' the plug on you."

When the guy signaled that it was our last song, we did that song, and then I got up to the microphone and said, "Now we'd like to welcome Gregg Allman to the stage." The place went berserk. Ted Nugent comes out of his dressing room yelling, "What the fuck?" He was beatin' on the walls. We kicked into "Statesboro Blues," and the people went nuts. Ted was so pissed off. Gregg stole

the damn show from him. There was no way they were gonna pull the plug on us. There would have been a riot! We finished up and headed straight for the limos and took off, with Ted still screaming like a five-year-old.

It was a small but satisfying triumph for the band, but their luck didn't hold out. "Michael Thevis, who owned GRC Records, got popped," Cantonwine explained. "He had all these porno clubs in Atlanta, and got hit for income tax evasion or something like that. His ass was in jail, and the record company was stripped. Anything of value was taken by the IRS. We had a tune called 'No Rollin' Boogie' that was in the Top 100 of *Billboard* magazine that week. We'd been working for about seven years, and I think it crushed everybody in the band that we were that close, and then it fell apart."

While Eric Quincy Tate failed to find a significant audience in their heyday, their music endures as a snapshot of a quality band that helped define the sound of the emerging Southern rock genre in the early 1970s.

ERIC QUINCY TATE

- DONNIE MCCORMICK drums, vocals
- TOMMY CARLISLE guitar
- JOE ROGERS keyboard
- DAVID CANTONWINE bass
- WAYNE "BEAR" SAULS guitar

Ricky Hirsch and Jimmy Hall onstage. (Photo by A. K. Burton, courtesy of Mike Hyland)

CHAPTER 13
Keep On Smilin': Wet Willie

 ET WILLIE MAINSTAYS Jimmy and Jack Hall were born in Birmingham, Alabama, but moved to the city of Mobile with their family at a young age. Jack, the eldest of the family's six children, recalled that their initial music experiences were firmly rooted in the gospel tradition. "We give our mom credit for the musicality in our family," he explained. "It's a typical story—mom at the piano, the church choir, singing hymns and gospel songs around the piano at home."

Their father, too, encouraged his children in their melodic pursuits, as younger brother Jimmy explained:

> My dad was quite the record collector. I remember one of them was Ray Charles' album *Modern Sounds in Country and Western Music*. Just hearing a black guy sing Hank Sr. was mind blowing to me. And, of course, I grew up in a time when rock and roll was coming out with Elvis and Jerry Lee Lewis, and a lot of rockabilly. That was pretty exciting music to me. My dad knew what was going on. Elvis would come on TV and my dad would say, "You kids need to come check this guy out. This is an important artist and you need to pay attention." We'd all gather around the TV.

By junior high, Jack was playing the clarinet, while Jimmy had embraced the saxophone. "We'd take our horns home from the school band and practice Dixieland," Jimmy recalled. "At some point, my dad bought Jack

WET WILLIE
▸ JIMMY HALL vocals, harmonica, sax
▸ JACK HALL bass
▸ LEWIS ROSS drums
▸ RICKY HIRSCH guitar
▸ JOHN ANTHONY keyboards
▸ FRANK FRIEDMAN guitar
▸ WICK LARSEN guitar
▸ MIKE DUKE keyboards
▸ ELLA AVERY background vocals
▸ DONNA HALL background vocals
▸ ELKIE BROOKS background vocals
▸ LESLIE HAWKINS background vocals
▸ MARSHALL SMITH guitar
▸ T. K. LIVELY drums
▸ LARRY BERWALD guitar

an acoustic guitar and he learned how to play it. We were getting songbooks and learning songs and singing together. These were folk songs and that sort of thing. Pretty soon, he got asked by some fellow musicians to join a band called the Vibrations. They rehearsed at our house, and I thought that was cool. I was hanging around at their rehearsals and they'd let me sing a little every now and then."

In those early years, however, Jack didn't yet have a vision for what he and his brother might accomplish together. "I'm a little bit older than Jimmy," he explained, "so I

started playing in bands in Mobile a little before he did. I knew he was talented, but it wasn't apparent how extremely talented he was. At first, he was just my kid brother that was gettin' in the way sometimes."

While Jack was off playing music, Jimmy was getting his own education in entertainment. "I got the opportunity to see James Brown when I was in high school, probably around 1965," Jimmy remembered. "It was quite an eye-opening experience, an epiphany to see that kind of showmanship and excitement all in one package." Before long, Jimmy was playing with different groups around Mobile. "When I was fifteen or so I found some guys about my age, and they wanted me to sing with them," he recalled. "The first name we had was the Squires, 'cause we thought it sounded English, you know. We dressed alike and had these matching caps and everything. We played copy stuff, mostly what was on the radio, leaning toward R&B, plus some Stones and Yardbirds."

When Jack completed high school he continued to pursue his love for music while continuing into higher education. "I was in college bands with guys at the University of South Alabama," he explained. "We had a band called the Pagans. We were so naïve at the time we weren't aware of the impact our name might have in the Bible Belt. We even had a band called the Devil's Disciples at one point that we thought just sounded so cool. When we weren't getting any more of those church gigs after a while, we finally figured it out."

Eventually, Jack and Jimmy were playing together in a band with drummer Lewis Ross that also included guitarists Wick Larsen

Left to right: Donna Hall, Ella Avery, Jack Hall, Jimmy Hall, Ricky Hirsch, and John Anthony. (Photo by Michael Ochs Archive/Getty Images)

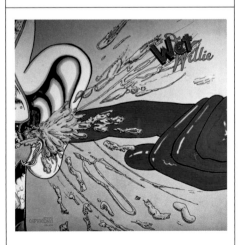

and Marshall Smith. When Smith was drafted, the group splintered. Unwilling to give up his rock-and-roll dream, Ross began assembling a new band in 1969 with guitarist Ricky Hirsch. Hirsch had graduated from the University of Alabama and returned home to Mobile in 1968. "When he came back," Jack remembered, "he and Lewis kind of got together and started kickin' around. Then I got involved." John Anthony, a classically trained multi-instrumentalist who'd been in a group called the Sons of Creation, soon joined on keyboards. "We started to work on a set list and a repertoire," Jack added, "but nobody in the band had a very strong voice. None of us were 'lead singer' material, so that's when the other guys and I started to think about needing somebody who really could sing well."

Initially, Jimmy Hall was unavailable, as he was performing with his own group after floating in and out of various bands with exotic names like Tequila Mockingbird. "One band would morph into another," Jimmy explained, "but the first real serious band I was in was about 1967 or '68. It was a band of guys and one girl singer called Mrs. O'Leary's Cow. We played a mixed bag of stuff, and it was really well rehearsed. We dressed in the latest mod fashions, and we ended up in a Battle of the Bands contest in New York City, and damn if we didn't win. We came back to Mobile as conquering heroes."

"I didn't want to do copy music," Jimmy said of his stint with Mrs. O'Leary's Cow. "I wanted to work on original material." He eventually joined up with his brother's band, handling lead vocals, saxophone, and harmonica. "We were listening to everything from Led Zeppelin to Wilson Pickett and James Brown," Jack Hall explained. But while absorbing various influences, they weren't looking to imitate their heroes. "We didn't form with the intention of playing any specific kind of music, just good music which we hope everybody likes,"

Lewis Ross reflected, in a 1974 interview with *Melody Maker*. "You can't say that we're definitely a hard rock band or a rhythm and blues band, but I suppose we're heading in that direction. We're into black music as well."

Booking gigs around Alabama, they had to come up with a name for the group, and they landed on Fox. "Not that we thought we were great looking," Jack Hall laughed. "It just sounded smooth."

"Ricky Hirsch had a college buddy," Jack continued, "a fraternity brother in the Jewish fraternity named Frank Friedman. Frank was the person who was responsible for us coming up from Mobile to check out the scene in Macon. He had gone over to Macon himself, to see what was going on once the Allman Brothers were just starting to get off the ground, and musicians were starting to get wind that something was happening there."

Friedman had a group known as the Willie Band, and later the Wet Willie Band, that included, at various times, Court Pickett, Joe Rudd, Bill Stewart, Chuck Leavell, Lou Mullenx, and Ronnie Brown. When the band dwindled to just Frank and Lou, he recruited Fox and arranged an audition with Capricorn's Frank Fenter. "We all came to Macon and set up in an old warehouse next door to the Capricorn Studios," Ricky Hirsch recounted. "I remember there were two bare lightbulbs suspended on wiring hanging from the ceiling, and Frank sat quietly on a cardboard box off to the side. After we played two songs, Frank said, 'Delightful. Come in Monday morning and we will sign the papers.' . . . He was the elegant captain of the ship."

The group signed an artist deal with the label and a management contract with Phil Walden in July of 1970. Before finalizing the agreement, however, there was one obstacle they needed to overcome.

"They told us there was another band called Fox," Jimmy recounted. The group quickly reverted back to using the name of Frank Friedman's previous band, Wet Willie. Over the years, the choice raised a few eyebrows, especially among British audiences, as Jack Hall recalled with a laugh:

> To us Southern guys, there was no other connotation with that term, except to wet your finger in your mouth and stick it in someone's ear. That's giving somebody a wet willie. We were very naïve. Later on, we became aware that there might be other meanings. What really brought it home was when we went to England. We had a number of our guitar cases and

THE WET WILLIE BAND   CAPRICORN

An early incarnation of Wet Willie. *Left to right:* Joe Rudd, Frank Friedman, Court Picket, and Bill Stewart. (Courtesy of Bill Stewart)

equipment cases that had "Wet Willie" stenciled all over them. The baggage handler guys in England were snickering, and we said, "What's so funny?" They said, "Don't you know what it means to get your willie wet?"

With Friedman as the primary songwriter, Wet Willie began conceptualizing their first album, while the boys from Alabama threw themselves into the burgeoning Macon scene. "We'd been in Mobile all our lives," Jimmy pointed out, "and were ready to see some new scenery and meet some new people. We let Phil Walden sort of guide us through the things you do to set up a band. We rented this big house, like the Allman Brothers did. We had a pay phone in our hallway. Various girlfriends were in there with us. It was communal living—which most of us had had enough of after about a year!"

"We did a few demos, but we weren't real happy with them," Jack Hall explained. Frank Friedman liked the sound, but it wasn't what the rest of the guys were looking for. "Frank wrote those songs that we recorded," Jimmy Hall elaborated, "but the question of who would be the producer came up. Frank was really close to Paul Hornsby, and he wanted Paul to produce. The label was going, 'How about this really cool English producer, Eddy Offord? We could make you the American Rolling Stones if we had an English producer like this.' That was the direction the label was

going. Ultimately, Frank just opted out of being in the band at that point."

The first album was 1971's *Wet Willie*, which included four of Frank Friedman's songs. The decision to bring in Eddy Offord worked out well for the band. "He actually did a real decent job, working with what he had to work with," Jack reflected. "We were very new to the studio scene and techniques and all that. He was quite a character. He was a little guy with big stack heels and a beard and a pipe. The Southern females in Macon were really impressed." Jimmy Hall laughed at the memory. "It was like a freak show to Eddy being down South with these crazy talking Southern boys."

Recorded at Capricorn's studio in Macon, *Wet Willie* presented the band as a collective of blue-eyed soul-influenced Southern rockers with a pronounced Rolling Stones edge. "What the band was all about was energetic, funky, greasy, bluesy, R&B-based rock," Jack said of their sound. Anchored by rollicking songs like "Have a Good Time" and "Shame, Shame, Shame," the debut LP was a solid offering of Dixie-fried rock and roll. *Rolling Stone* magazine declared that Jimmy Hall had "a voice strut and an air of raucous elegance not unlike Jagger."

The second LP, *Wet Willie II*, was recorded with guitarist Wick Larsen, who was brought in after the first album was completed to replace Friedman. Capricorn producer Johnny Sandlin took over initial production duties

from Eddy Offord, and moved the sessions to Muscle Shoals while the Macon facility was being renovated. Several additional musicians were added for the sophomore outing, including Cowboy's Scott Boyer on steel guitar, the Allman Brothers Band's Jaimoe Johanson on percussion, and African American background vocalist Ella Avery. Avery's husband Jackie was the staff songwriter at Walden's No Exit Music who'd originally encouraged Jaimoe to play with Duane Allman.

Opening with a raucous cover of Otis Redding's "Shout Bamalama," *Wet Willie II* was a more cohesive set of good-time soulful rock than its predecessor. "We really didn't fit in," keyboardist John Anthony told journalist Lawrence Specker of the band's Southern rock categorization. "We were Southern but we were more R&B." Though the quality was strong, the second LP, like the first, failed to make a big splash outside the immediate region.

By 1973, Wet Willie needed to try something different. Capricorn decided to release a live album, *Drippin' Wet*, which captured the spark of the group's raw dynamism onstage at the Warehouse in New Orleans. "That was on New Year's Eve of 1972, bringing in 1973," Jimmy recalled. "It was the Allmans, us, and Elvin Bishop on the bill. We recorded two nights, and took the best from each night. The venue was really cool—in the bowels of New Orleans, literally, in a warehouse."

It was a magic moment for the band. "There was a lot of energy," Jack remembered, "and some of it might have been fueled by other substances, but the crowd was really enthusiastic, and we were feeding off that."

Having truly captured Jimmy Hall's rock-and-roll swagger, *Drippin' Wet* was the first album to crack the *Billboard* chart, though it only reached #189. By the time it was recorded, Wick Larsen was out of the band. "He had diabetes, and the problem was that he wasn't keeping his meds right," Jimmy recalled. "He

would drink, and in combination with that disease he would just go nuts. He'd have temper tantrums and mood swings. We had to fire him after a certain incident in a hotel when he got real destructive. I'd rather focus on his legacy, because he was a very talented and creative guy, and a great blues player." With Wick out of the picture, Wet Willie was stripped down to the core members who'd originally come together as Fox: Lewis Ross, Ricky Hirsch, Jack Hall, John Anthony, and Jimmy Hall.

The following year, Wet Willie's *Keep On Smilin'* LP climbed to #41 on the strength of the single of the same name. Working with legendary producer Tom Dowd, Wet Willie were able to flesh out a more laid back and nuanced sound that was crisper and more arranged than their first two studio efforts. "With Tom Dowd," Jack Hall remembered, "it was like, 'School's in session, and the professor is here.'"

The cover of the *Keep On Smilin'* LP depicted a blind Macon street musician named Rev. Pearly Brown, whose gospel-blues style was a huge influence on the local music scene. It was a nod to the importance of Macon and the group's regional identity—they'd stayed loyal to their Southern roots and finally found national acceptance. In August of 1974, "Keep On Smilin'" became a Top 10 single, and the band's greatest success. Written by Jimmy Hall, the upbeat anthem came from a personal place. He recalled:

> I was going through relationship difficulties with this girlfriend. We had been goin' together for a few years and just kind of hit a hard spot in the road and trying to decide what to do, and times being like they were—everything was like "Love the One You're With" and, you know, groupies and stuff. To be a good boyfriend and try to be faithful—there were some problems. I was writing this letter to myself, a song to myself, saying, "Buck up, keep on smilin', it's all gonna work out, and you can do it and stay strong," and it really resonated with a lot of the country and a lot of the world.

With the release of *Keep On Smilin'*, Wet Willie introduced the Williettes, the two-woman backup vocal team that included Ella Avery, who'd earlier appeared on *Wet Willie II*, and Donna Hall. Donna was Jack and Jimmy's sister, and she quickly became a fan favorite—and one who, as Ricky Hirsch recounted, "stole the hearts of many male-species Wet Willie fans." Her older brothers weren't always enthused. "Lester Bangs wrote in an article that 'Donna

Hall has lips that could suck the chrome off a trailer hitch,' and blah blah blah," Jack Hall recalled. "Our parents were not amused."

Though Ella Avery eventually moved on, Donna remained a Williette alongside new recruit Elkie Brooks, who became a dynamic presence in the group. "She had a band of her own back then called Vinegar Joe, with Robert Palmer," Jimmy remembered. "Then, after Wet Willie, she went on to record some pretty cool solo albums. She was a rocker, and she liked Jack Daniels. I introduced her to my dad once, when we played down in Mobile, and he said, 'I just can't believe this girl can drink me under the table!'"

Following Elkie Brooks' stint, Leslie Hawkins spent a brief time with the group before going on to join Lynyrd Skynyrd's backup singers, the Honkettes. Such a strong female presence wasn't typical for most bands that were emerging from south of the Mason-Dixon Line. "I believe we were the first Southern rock band to have female background vocalists," Jack asserted.

Touring on the strength of "Keep On Smilin'," Wet Willie impressed audiences wherever they went. Playing their lean and mean brand of high-energy Southern boogie, they won over crowds with working-class appeal rather than bombastic rock-and-roll theatrics. "All I can say is that these people are down home folks, who are sincere, kind, worried about success and life in general, just like the rest of us," wrote one concert reviewer in 1974. "This may sound trite, but it sure as hell is refreshing to know that there are rock stars who are like people I know and hang around with. Wet Willie are the kind of folks you wouldn't mind talking to."

Authenticity was a hallmark of Wet Willie, and it helped them fare a bit better than other groups when the inevitable backlash against

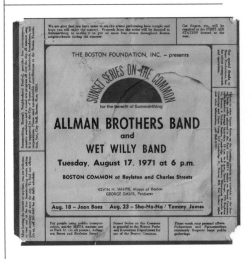

Wet Willie in 1973. *Left to right*: Jack Hall, John Anthony, Jimmy Hall, Ricky Hirsch, and Lewis Ross. (Courtesy of Mike Hyland)

An ad for the 1973 album *Drippin' Wet*. (Courtesy of Walter Vanderbeken)

Southern rock began to flare up in the mid-1970s. "There's no sense hiding the fact that we're Southern," Jack Hall told *Rolling Stone* in 1974. "The point is that we don't want to beat it in their heads with every song." Though stereotypes equate Southern rock with drunken antics, the members of Wet Willie weren't known for their wild ways. "We were known kind of as the nice guys," Jimmy explained, "not too rowdy, but rowdy enough. We didn't tear anything up."

Released in 1975, *Dixie Rock* was another solid collection of gritty blues-tinged good-time music. Though it, too, was produced by Tom Dowd, the album failed to build on the success of *Keep On Smilin'*, signaling the beginning of the decline of the band's Capricorn era. The follow-up, *The Wetter the Better*, found Paul Hornsby in the producer's chair. In addition to the switch in producers, Wet Willie added keyboardist Mike Duke to the lineup. "He was a great songwriter and a strong singer

whose voice complimented mine," Jimmy explained. Like the other band members, Duke's roots were deeply planted in the musical South. "We had known Mike for several years," Jack Hall elaborated. "He was from the northern part of Alabama, and he had his own local reputation. He was a really jolly guy, a big guy with long black hair and a beard. He had quite an image and would run around town in overalls and barefoot. He was a good guy, and we invited him into the band. For a time, John played piano and he played organ." Despite the changes, the resulting LP was a somewhat uneven set of songs that ranged from the appealing guitar-driven sound of "No, No, No" to the disco-oriented "Baby Fat."

By 1977, Wet Willie had grown dissatisfied with their record label. "We became disenchanted with Capricorn," Jack Hall confessed. "They were having financial problems, and probably drug problems, and everything else. The Allman guys had started

lawsuits, and we started to look around for somebody who could help us find another label. We had a good attorney on the West Coast who began to look around discreetly." During that transition time, the personnel shifted, and Wet Willie entered a new era. On leaving Macon, they resettled in Atlanta.

"A couple of guys in the band decided to seek other opportunities," Jack explained. "Ricky Hirsch had been approached by Gregg Allman to come play on one of his albums, so Ricky took that opportunity and moved to California and got involved out there." By the time Epic Records made an official proposal, Jack and Jimmy Hall were the only original members left. "John Anthony gave his notice," Jack explained, "and I still don't know why he decided to leave the band. Lewis, the drummer, had left and wasn't in touch, and we felt like he was just not interested."

The Hall brothers and Mike Duke recruited a new batch of talented musicians. "Marshall Smith, who we played with way back in the early Macon days, had returned from the Army and was playing in Mobile," Jack recalled. "We knew he'd wanted to play with us for years, so we got in touch with him. He said he really thought we ought to consider T. K. Lively as the drummer, and he was right. He's a really talented drummer, and one of the nicest people in the world. So they came up to Atlanta. We started to audition guitarists, different people from Atlanta and around the area, and that's when we found Larry Berwald." With Berwald in place, the second era of Wet Willie was born.

Unlike on the earlier albums, the band's initial work for the new label was not a product of the South. "The first Epic album was recorded in England with Gary Lyons, who'd worked with Queen and Aerosmith," Jimmy recounted. "It was the label's suggestion to try to go for a more commercial pop appeal." The recording process marked a shift in the band's sound. "That first Epic album was very *produced*," Jack Hall explained. "There were backing vocals stacked up way to the sky. It was a departure from our basic rootsy production of the earlier records. We recorded it at Manor Studios, so I came up with *Manorisms*, and that became the title."

"Street Corner Serenade" gave Wet Willie their first Top 40 single since "Keep On Smilin'" when it climbed to #30 on the *Billboard* singles chart. Decidedly slicker and less rooted in the Southern rock tradition than their previous efforts, the LP was still a solid blue-eyed soul-pop album in the Huey Lewis vein. "It was definitely over-produced," Jimmy conceded, "but I think we got some cool stuff out of it." The airplay Wet Willie received seemed to signal a possible new era for the band that would help them survive the decline of Southern rock's popularity. Unfortunately, no further major hits materialized.

"When it came time to do one more," Jack Hall said of the group's second Epic effort, "the producer threw in everything but the kitchen sink to try to get a hit record. One of the songs was called 'Weekend,' and it really had that disco feel to it. That was our Southern rock disco song, but we got some pretty good airplay on it." After reaching #29 on the *Billboard* chart, "Weekend" went on to become a favorite of radio station DJs who would regularly play it on Fridays at 5:00 p.m. to signal the end of the workweek. "Music was pulling away from the more organic bands to dance music, and into disco, really," Jimmy explained. "We were looking at each other going, 'God, I can't believe we're doing this.'"

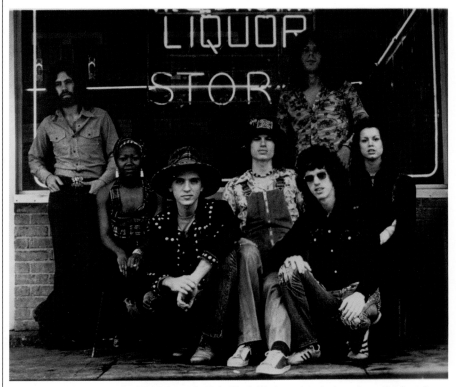
Wet Willie (with the Williettes) in 1974. *Left to right:* Ricky Hirsch, Ella Avery, John Anthony, Jimmy Hall, Lewis Ross, Jack Hall, and Donna Hall. (Courtesy of Mike Hyland)

Wet Willie's music-industry handlers began turning their attention to lead singer Jimmy Hall, who possessed a voice that transcended genre. Jack explained:

> We had left Phil Walden and signed with Joe Sullivan, who was Charlie Daniels' manager. Joe and the folks at the record label were kind of tugging at Jimmy to do a solo thing. It came as a big surprise to me and the rest of the band. I remember Joe called a meeting and we all went in and he basically said, "Look, Epic feels like it's time for Jimmy to do a solo record, so see ya!" At that point, our manager had everybody but Jimmy and me sign releases so that only Jimmy and I retained the rights to the Wet Willie name.

For his part, Jimmy insisted he never intended to break up the band. "Music changed a lot right then. New wave and punk and dance music had come in. Epic was ready for the next project. We played some stuff for them, and I could tell they weren't so thrilled. They wanted to have a meeting, and they came to me and suggested I do a solo project while the band pulled together material for the next Wet Willie album. Some of them blew me off, like, 'How could you do this to us? You're only thinking of yourself.' There was a big rift with some of the guys."

Released in 1980, Jimmy's solo debut album, *Touch You*, was produced by former Muscle Shoals musician Norbert Putnam. Though several Nashville studio players were used to augment the backing band, former Wet Willie members Jack Hall, Mike Duke, Donna Hall, and Larry Berwald also appeared. "We toured behind that album," Jack remembered, "with Jimmy, me, Mike Duke, Larry Berwald and some other guys. It was like 'Almost Willie.'"

A single, "I'm Happy That Love Has Found You," reached #27 on the *Billboard* chart. "I

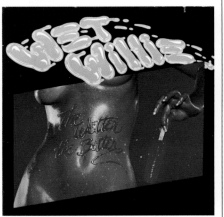

Wet Willie in 1974. Standing, *left to right*: Lewis Ross, Donna Hall, Jack Hall, Ella Avery, and Jimmy Hall. Seated: Ricky Hirsch and John Anthony. (Courtesy of Mark Pucci)

The latter lineup of Wet Willie. *Left to right*: Larry Berwald, T. K. Lively, Jack Hall, Marshall Smith, Jimmy Hall, and Mike Duke. (Photo by Michael Ochs Archive/Getty Images)

thought we would continue to work together for the duration," Jack explained. "When it came time to do Jimmy's second album, we started preproduction and working on material. The producer wanted to use all studio guys, so they said, 'See ya'—and this time for good. So we all sort of went back home. That album didn't do as well, so Epic didn't pursue any more records with Jimmy."

With Southern rock largely out of fashion in the early 1980s, the members of Wet Willie scattered for various projects. Jack Hall went on to work with female country vocalist Terri Gibbs, best known for her 1981 Top 10 single "Somebody's Knockin'." Mike Duke joined the Outlaws, and later found songwriting success, most notably with several Huey Lewis songs, including the Top 10 hit "Doing It All for My Baby." Jimmy had moved to Nashville in the early 1980s when he launched his solo career, and he established a home base there from which he went on to work with a variety of performers. He spent a couple of years in the Southern rock super group BHLT with Dickey Betts, Chuck Leavell, and Butch Trucks. He collaborated with Jeff Beck on the 1985 album *Flash*, contributing vocals to four of the tracks and earning a Grammy nomination. Eventually, Jimmy became the longtime leader of Hank Williams, Jr.'s, band, playing saxophone and harmonica.

In the early 1990s, Wet Willie re-formed with the Hall brothers, sister Donna, T. K. Lively, and a handful of new members, working primarily as a live act between Jimmy's various musical commitments as an in-demand vocalist. Jimmy released an excellent solo album, *Rendezvous with the Blues*, in 1996, followed by several independent label releases beginning in the late 2000s. On May 29, 2010, original members Lewis Ross, John Anthony, and Rick Hirsch reunited with the three Hall siblings to play a show in Mobile, Alabama, in celebration of Wet Willie's fortieth anniversary. ★

George McCorkle and
Tommy Caldwell of the
Marshall Tucker Band.
(Courtesy of John Gellman)

CHAPTER 14
Searchin' for a Rainbow: The Marshall Tucker Band

 N SEPTEMBER OF 1973, Don Kirshner filmed a television special at the Macon Opera House called *Saturday Night in Macon*, featuring the Allman Brothers Band. The other two groups selected for inclusion on the televised broadcast were Wet Willie, whose performance was filmed in a Macon park a couple of days prior—an environment that Johnny Sandlin described as "hippies gone wild"—and the Marshall Tucker Band, who opened for the Allmans at the Opera House. After the Allman Brothers Band, The Marshall Tucker Band went on to become the most successful group on Capricorn Records.

It was Wet Willie who first discovered the Marshall Tucker Band while playing a show in Spartanburg, South Carolina. "We didn't really pay attention to who was opening until we got there," Wet Willie front man Jimmy Hall remembered, "but we sat out front and listened to them. They just knocked us out from

the beginning. It was a sound that was totally unique to my ears, and to the other guys in the band as well." Jimmy Hall suspected that Phil Walden and Frank Fenter would be interested. "We came back home after that trip," Jimmy recounted, "and said, 'Man, we want you guys to come to Macon and try to get on our label.'"

With encouragement from Wet Willie, Marshall Tucker Band members Toy and Tommy Caldwell traveled to the Capricorn office. "They came down," Capricorn publicist Mike Hyland remembered, "I brought 'em into my office, and I said, 'Do you have a tape?' They said, 'No.' I said, 'Well you really need to have a tape that we have to listen to first, then if we like what we hear we'll put you in the club downtown and everybody will come and see you.'" The Caldwell brothers returned home and soon sent Capricorn a demo tape they had recorded for $500 at a gospel music studio in Greenville, South Carolina. "I played it for Phil," Hyland continued, "and Phil liked it. Frank liked it, too, so we set up the date for them to do a showcase in Macon at Grant's Lounge. They came and just blew our shit away. They were unbelievable."

"We were telling the Capricorn people, 'Told you so,'" Jimmy Hall laughed. "It was exciting." Walden was impressed after hearing only one song at the showcase. "I said, 'Wow, man, this is the country version of the Allman Brothers!'" Phil recalled. He signed them, and within five years the Marshall Tucker Band had earned six Gold albums.

All six members of the original Marshall Tucker Band were raised in Spartanburg, South Carolina, a blue-collar town whose economy was rooted in the local textile mills. Broth-

Before they became known as the Marshall Tucker Band, the Toy Factory opened for the Allman Brothers Band in 1971. (Courtesy of Pete Howard/PosterCentral.com)

ers Toy and Tommy Caldwell grew up with a father who worked as a plumber by day and pursued music in his free time. "My daddy had his own radio show way before we were born," Tommy Caldwell explained to *Guitar Player* magazine. "We learned all the flatpicking songs, like 'Wildwood Flower,' and the vocals were very country style—them kind of roots. We always played a lot of Hank Williams stuff."

By the early 1960s, however, the country sounds on which the Caldwell brothers were raised were becoming passé among their peers. "One day I looked up and discovered that nobody seemed to be listening to our Hank Williams music," Toy Caldwell told *Country Rambler* in 1977. "That was when the Beatles were beginning to get big, so we

The Marshall Tucker Band in 1973. *Left to right*: Jerry Eubanks, Doug Gray, Paul Riddle, George McCorkle, Toy Caldwell, and Tommy Caldwell. Note the Allman Brothers Band logo sewed on the cuff of Eubanks' jeans. (Courtesy of Mark Pucci)

started changing our music to fit the times. The Beatles did influence us. Our music now is kinda country and kinda rock, and I guess the roots go back to that time."

Rhythm guitarist George McCorkle, like so many white Southerners of his generation, first encountered black music by listening to the powerful WLAC radio station from Nashville. "The blues was like a magnet," he explained, in an interview with Marley Brant. "I liked to listen to B. B. King, Albert King, and guys like that." He soon began jamming with the elder Caldwell brother. "Me and Toy started playing together in the late 1950s," McCorkle recalled. "Nothing that amounted to anything: Ventures songs, some Chuck Berry."

Like McCorkle, lead singer Doug Gray was drawn to R&B in his youth. "Being Southern," he explained, "we had the opportunity to go see black bands. Country music was very influential, especially through South Carolina, but I grew up, besides Spartanburg, down at Myrtle Beach and on the coast of South Carolina, so we had the dance, shag music, and stuff like that. I was listenin' to R&B while Toy and Tommy were soakin' up all that country music from their daddy."

As the 1960s progressed, the Caldwell brothers let their hair get shaggy and embraced the rock culture. "Tommy used to get hell in high school for his long hair," McCorkle told *US* magazine in 1980. "In fact, he was kicked off the football team for that reason. It is because of the country atmosphere where we live, smack in the middle of the Bible Belt." Regardless of their conservative surroundings, the boys were drawn to the emerging counterculture. McCorkle had saved up enough money from his part-time work at a Spartanburg drug store to buy his first quality electric guitar, and by the mid-1960s he was playing in a local garage band called the Rants with Toy Caldwell and a bassist named Franklin Wilkie.

Once the Rants began writing original material, they recorded a demo that made its way to Nashville. John Hurley, the songwriter who convinced Tree Music's Buddy Killen to let him produce some songs for the Allman Joys, was interested in the band. They traveled to the Tennessee capital and recorded a few tracks before the deal fell apart and the Rants returned to the Spartanburg scene.

All the future members of the Marshall

Tucker Band were performing around town in various configurations by the mid-1960s. "We were in different bands," Doug Gray explained, "and we were in competition to get all the frat gigs. You get the frat gigs, and you don't have to worry about nothing. You got the weekend, you got the women, you got the booze, and you actually got *paid* to be there! We'd get up and do '96 Tears' and 'For Your Love' and songs like that." One of the bands, the New Generation, included both Doug

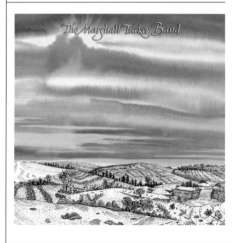

Promotional poster for a Marshall Tucker Band concert in 1974.

Gray and Tommy Caldwell. They released one single for the tiny Sonic label in 1965.

Upon graduating from Spartanburg High School, McCorkle was drafted into the navy. He served on the USS Little Rock in Italy. Around the same time, Toy Caldwell answered Uncle Sam's call and became a marine in 1966. Stationed in Vietnam, Toy experienced a terrifying brush with death. "They sent us out and we were supposed to set up this ambush, but we were the ones who got it," he told Tom Ayres in 1977.

> They really cut us apart. I got shot up pretty good. And when I looked around, it seemed like everybody around me was shot up, too. They had us pinned down there . . . no way to communicate. All we could do was lie out there bleeding and wait for something to happen. . . . By the second day, some of the guys around me had died, and I began to have doubts that I'd get out alive. Then I started telling myself over and over, "You're gonna make it, you're gonna make it." After two days, the choppers finally came to get us. I've never been so glad to see anything in my life.

Caldwell's wounds earned him the Purple Heart. Not long after Toy returned home in April of 1969, Tommy got *his* notice and departed for military duty. "We had a band before Toy went into the service; so when he went in, I kept the group together," Tommy recalled in an interview with Dan Forte. "Then, when I went in, he kept it together. When I got out, in '70, we had another guy on bass, so Toy and I were playing dual guitar parts. Then I left that group and started a band with George McCorkle and Paul Riddle." That band, known as Pax Parachute, was short-lived. "After a few weeks we called up Toy," Tommy continued, "and then Doug and Jerry joined."

With the Caldwell brothers on lead gui-

tar and bass, George McCorkle on rhythm guitar, Paul Riddle on drums, Doug Gray on vocals, and Jerry Eubanks on flute, horns, and keyboards, the band began securing bookings under the name Toy Factory. Though Toy Caldwell wrote most of the songs, his brother Tommy was the driving force of the group. "Tommy's great feature in life was that he was a leader," George McCorkle explained in the book *Carolina Dreams*. "A born leader."

One thing Tommy felt strongly about was that the band should not play cover songs. The members soon discovered that adhering to original material might keep their integrity intact, but it also kept them from the high paying club gigs. "There was resistance all over the South when we started," George McCorkle

recalled in *Circus* magazine. "We got thrown out of clubs left and right for playin' our own music. We'd play one set and the club owner would raise hell because we weren't playin' somethin' by somebody else." They gravitated toward the rougher bars on the outskirts of Southern towns where the patrons were often less discriminating. "You had to play covers to get a gig back then," drummer Paul Riddle confirmed to writer Jac Chebatoris, "but in those biker bars we could play our own music and get away with it." The experience gave them an edge that has come to be associated with the Southern rock genre. "In our part of the country, there's a real hell-raising atmosphere," George McCorkle bragged to the *Chicago Tribune* in 1977. "We used to raise hell all the time. . . . You know, you go to a bar, get drunk, kick hell out of everybody . . . sometimes get your teeth knocked out."

The desire to make a full-time living playing only original music proved to be a difficult proposition, but one that drew the band members into a close fraternity. "We all loved each other," Riddle explained to *Town* magazine. "There was so much trust, with Tommy being the foundation." Each man knew that each of the others was willing to do whatever it took to avoid a life of backbreaking work in the local cotton mills. "My daddy took me through the mill when I was in eleventh grade," Doug Gray remembered. "He wanted to scare the hell out of me, and he did. I went, 'Holy shit, not me!' It was just terrible, all closed in and all, you know?" Nevertheless, economic survival required the band members to hold down traditional jobs. "We all worked days—as plumbers or ditch diggers—then performed on weekends," Tommy confirmed.

In the early part of 1972, Toy Factory got a new name. "We rented this place to rehearse in," Gray recalled, "and the tag on the key said 'Marshall Tucker.'" Tucker was a blind African American musician and piano tuner who had been the previous occupant of the space. "About eight months into us rehearsing three or four nights a week after doing our day jobs," Gray continued, "this promoter came down and said, 'Hey, let's name y'all guys something. We gotta put a name on you.' Well, the name wasn't that important to us as long as we got up there and smoked, you know? Somebody looked at the key and on the chain there was that little tag that said Marshall Tucker. We said, 'OK, this is the name we're gonna be for this weekend only.' And that was forty-one years ago!" Over time, some of the band members wondered if it was the best choice. "The name was a lot of fun for the first three years," Toy laughed, in a 1989 radio interview. "But you can only take so many people coming up to you and saying, 'Great show, Marshall!'"

Taking on any gigs they could in South Carolina, the Tuckers began to build a buzz. Fellow musicians were amazed at Toy's ability to play fiery lead guitar without the use of a pick. "There's no question that my biggest influence was Chet Atkins, but I also listened to Merle Travis," he later remarked, in *Vintage Guitar* magazine. "Both of them were noted for their thumb picking, of course, so that's where I began to develop my playing style. . . . Now, I do use my fingers for some chords, but the lead work is exclusively done with my thumb." Caldwell's approach to his instrument helped define his unique style, best articulated by Charlie Daniels, who observed, "Toy was about half hillbilly, and about a quarter jazz, and about a quarter rock and blues stuff. But no matter how far out he'd get jamming, you could always hear those country licks in there."

A lead guitar player who doesn't use a pick might be somewhat unusual, but it was Jerry Eubanks' presence in the band that was truly unique. Most rock bands didn't feature the flute, but somehow it worked. By the time Wet Willie heard the Marshall Tucker Band at their club gig, Toy and Tommy and the boys were ready to take on the Southern rock world.

"We were like your mama's soup," Doug Gray laughed. "When you didn't have a lot of money, your mama would throw everything from the refrigerator that was about to go bad into the soup. The Marshall Tucker Band was like that, where each individual personality in

Toy Caldwell, George McCorkle, Jerry Eubanks, Doug Gray, Paul Riddle, and Tommy Caldwell. (Courtesy of Chuck Perkins)

The Marshall Tucker Band in Atlanta: Toy Caldwell, Doug Gray, Jerry Eubanks, Tommy Caldwell, George McCorkle, and Paul Riddle. (Courtesy of Mike Hyland)

the band was completely different, and we all brought a different ingredient that made for something special."

Phil Walden contacted the band immediately after their showcase at Grant's Lounge in Macon. "He'd called us before we even got back to Spartanburg, wanting to sign us," Toy remembered. After balancing day jobs with band commitments, the boys finally had the opportunity to dedicate themselves to the music. "The day that Phil Walden offered the Marshall Tucker Band a deal," Doug Gray recalled, "I got offered my own office in Atlanta, working for the bank." Opting for the rock-and-roll life over banking, Gray bet all his chips on Walden.

The Marshall Tucker Band's first Capricorn album was released in the spring of 1973. "Johnny Sandlin took 'em in the studio and cut demos, but nobody got excited about it," producer Paul Hornsby recalled. "But Phil Walden still believed in the band. He said, 'Paul, you take 'em in there.' So we went and spent two months in the studio, and came out with an album."

Hornsby proved a better fit. "I think Paul came more from a country and rock-and-roll background, and then to R&B," Sandlin reflected, "whereas my background was mostly R&B, without much country experience." The pairing with Hornsby proved a winning combination. "Paul Hornsby took us a long way," Gray reflected. "Everybody learned a lot about production in Capricorn Studios. Paul would say, 'Go out there and kick butt.' 'Can't you do any better than that?' He would *motivate* us."

For Hornsby, the experience was a pleasure. "That band had more enthusiasm than any other band I've ever worked with," he recalled.

The *Marshall Tucker Band* LP was a free-spirited romp through breezy country-rock and jazzy improvisation that Lester Bangs, in his *Rolling Stone* review, called "a moving piece of work that bids to put them in the same league as the Allmans damn fast." The comparison made them an obvious choice for an opening slot touring with the Brothers themselves. "Capricorn worked us to death opening shows for the Allman Brothers for four years," Gray remembered, "and that didn't hurt anything. Man, that was a real boost for us. . . . Some of the guys in the band, Butch Trucks and Jaimoe and everybody—we really got to be *good* friends with those guys."

The experience of traveling with Gregg Allman and company provided a break that the band never forgot. "We're six people that nobody had heard of, man," Toy Caldwell observed in 1975, reflecting on the exposure the Allman shows provided. "If you were a group of Southern musicians, up until recently, the most you could ever hope to be was a club band." With the exposure the tour gave them, the Marshall Tucker Band wouldn't be relegated to the clubs for long. "We sold this band through our own constant touring," Toy told Cameron Crowe in a *Rolling Stone* feature story in 1974. "We went out there night-after-night and played our asses off."

Southern rock fans found the Marshall Tucker Band instantly appealing. Their sound was less exploratory blues than the Allman Brothers Band, and less live-wire boogie than the music of Wet Willie. "I don't know what you call it," Toy told journalist Jon East of the attempt to categorize their laid-back approach. "Country-rock pretty well hits it. Or maybe, 'rock with just a little country in it.' Our roots go back to that." The band's debut LP went to #29 on the *Billboard* album chart on the strength of their live performances and appealing songs such as "Take the Highway" and "Can't You See." The latter was one of the few songs where Toy Caldwell handled the lead vocal duties instead of Doug Gray.

From the outset, the band cultivated the image of working-class guys who applied themselves to their music with all the focus they would any traditional occupation. "They were fuckin' *men*," Henry Paul of the Outlaws observed. "They wore United States Marine Corps tattoos. It wasn't like, 'We're in a rock band, fuck you.' It was, 'We're grown men who play the shit out of music.'" Establishing their seriousness was important to the group members. "You know what I'd like people to understand," Toy Caldwell told *Macon News* in 1972. "We are not hippies. Not at all. Sure, we have longer hair

Toy Caldwell and Dickey Betts. (Courtesy of John Gellman)

Tommy Caldwell, George McCorkle, Toy Caldwell, Jerry Eubanks, Paul Riddle, and Doug Gray. (Courtesy of Mark Pucci)

ricorn labelmate Elvin Bishop laughed. "He wouldn't just say, 'I'm hot.' He'd say, 'I'm hotter than a fresh fucked fox in a forest fire!'"

Though they may not have considered themselves hippies, the band members—who maintained their homes in Spartanburg—still had to deal with hassles over their appearance, as Doug Gray recalled.

> They thought we were a bunch of dope-smokin' drinkin' boys. I walked into this pizza joint in Spartanburg in about '73 or '74 with my hair down to my ass—I always kept mine brushed out pretty good so I didn't look like no scrag—but I kinda looked like a Woodstock hippie. I was walkin' in and this woman was checkin' out, and she said, "Well, I *never*!" And I said, "Well, you'll never get a chance to either, baby!" She was gonna make a stand about the longhairs, you know, but the whole place just broke up laughing.... That was sort of our contribution. Black or white or Mexican, gay or lesbian. I couldn't care less. You should be who you are and be able to do what you want to. We sort of fought for that.

When not opening shows for the Allmans, the Marshall Tucker Band played wherever they could. "We told our agent to book anything within twenty-four hours' drive," George McCorkle recalled of their early days. "We hustled, called newspapers, radio stations." Not content to leave everything to their management firm alone, each band member took an active role in promoting the group. "We used to have A, B, and C teams," Gray explained. "We'd roll out of bed and start dialing. We'd talk to anybody. We just wanted to get the message out. We were playing 290–300 dates a year, going places nobody else went.... It made us tight."

than other people around, but we are people with family responsibilities, and we're going to make music our career. We're not into the drug scene either—we're into music and would like people to enjoy what we play."

The Marshall Tucker Band may not have been into the drug *scene*, but they were certainly into the drugs. "Drugs were not a problem for us," Doug Gray confirmed. "It's some-

thing that we just did. We all quit at some point. I quit on August 16, 1989, but we all did drugs. There's no hiding that part." Rather than flaunting their recreational activities or making it part of their identity, however, the band members maintained a down-home persona. What Toy's peers loved about him most was his undeniable good-ole-boy charm. "He had those one liners for all occasions," Cap-

Toy Caldwell, Tommy Caldwell, Paul Riddle, and George McCorkle onstage at the Palace Theatre in Manchester, England, on December 2, 1976. (Courtesy of Peter Cross)

The Marshall Tucker Band backstage in Los Angeles, 1977. Standing, *left to right*: Capricorn's Don Schmitzerle, Paul Riddle, Jerry Eubanks, Phil Rush, Tommy Caldwell, Phil Walden, and Toy Caldwell. Seated, *left to right*: Capricorn's Mark Pucci, Alex Hodges of the Paragon booking agency, Doug Gray, band manager Joe McConnell, Capricorn's Diana Kaylan, George McCorkle, and unknown. (Courtesy of Mark Pucci)

Within weeks of the release of their debut album, they were back in the studio with Paul Hornsby to begin work on their second LP. That album, *A New Life*, came out in February of 1974 and included a guest appearance by Charlie Daniels on "24 Hours at a Time." Charlie would become a special friend to the band. "The first time that we played with Charlie was in Nashville at the Memorial Auditorium," Gray recalled. "Charlie came out and said hello, and him and Tommy got to talking. We didn't actually play together that night, but we created a relationship."

Toy took the lead vocal again on "Blue Ridge Mountain Sky," as he had on "Can't You See." More focused, and featuring less improvisation than the first outing, *A New Life* had strong echoes of basic blues and country that gave the songs a somewhat timeless quality.

By November of 1974, the band had released yet another album, the two-disc *Where We All Belong*. The first disc was a new round of studio recordings from the Capricorn facility in Macon. The second was taken from a live performance from the previous July, and included a fourteen-minute version of "24 Hours at a Time" featuring Charlie Daniels on the fiddle, and showcasing the Tucker boys' chops as an early jam band.

With their first three albums having sold well, the Marshall Tucker Band continued to treat their career as a job, albeit a job they loved doing. "We're a people's band," Tommy Caldwell explained in 1978. "We've got respect for an audience. You can't fool 'em; they're too hip, too smart; they're hitting every lick with you. If you forget the people, you're out on the street pitching pennies."

Having emerged from a working-class upbringing themselves, the Tuckers appreciated the hard-earned money their fans spent to see them perform live. They wanted to reward the investment with a great experience.

"A guy's not paying ten to twelve bucks for a goodnight kiss," Eubanks remarked to *Crawdaddy!* in 1978. "He wants to get laid! So we come out smokin'. We rock because we want to be remembered." The enjoyment was always mutual. "We like to play for people," Gray remarked. "It satisfies us."

Released in August of 1975, the band's fourth LP, *Searchin' for a Rainbow*, kicked off with George McCorkle's "Fire on the Mountain." It was the first time the band had ever recorded one of his songs, and it became a fan favorite—as well as a Top 40 single. As with the previous albums, the members of the band were augmented by guest players, including Chuck Leavell, Charlie Daniels, and Dickey Betts, who played a distinctive guitar solo on the title track. Overall, the sound was a bit more polished than before, with the Marshall Tucker Band becoming something more akin to a straight country group. Reaching #15 on the *Billboard* album chart, *Searchin' for a Rainbow* was the band's highest charting LP. "*Searchin' for a Rainbow* was my favorite MTB album," Jerry Eubanks revealed to Michael Buffalo Smith. "To my ears, the best collection of songs that we ever put together."

In June of 1976, Capricorn released *Long Hard Ride*. With appearances by the Nitty Gritty Dirt Band's John McEuen, on banjo and mandolin, and Charlie Daniels—who by this time was practically a seventh Tucker—it continued to move the group in a country direction. In connection with the album, the band members shot a largely nonsensical cowboy-

themed short film that saw them riding horses, getting in fistfights, shooting guns, and confronting a pack of bandits who looked more like a rock band than the Tuckers did. Their profile continued to rise that year as Toy Caldwell appeared on the cover of *Guitar Player* magazine, while country star Waylon Jennings recorded a cover version of "Can't You See."

The Marshall Tucker Band reached their commercial peak in 1977 with the *Carolina Dreams* album. Featuring the hit "Heard It in a Love Song," the album reached the Top 30 on both the pop and country charts, while the single climbed to #14. Maintaining country roots but featuring pronounced pop flourishes, the LP achieved Platinum status and cemented the band as major players on the mid-1970s music scene. "*Carolina Dreams*," critic Russell Shaw raved in *Circus* magazine, "is quite possibly the

best record to come out of the South since the Allmans' *Eat a Peach*." The boys in the Marshall Tucker Band suddenly found themselves representing the cream of the Southern rock crop, even if the label was getting stale. "This 'Southern music' thing is kind of gettin' just a little bit out of hand," Toy Caldwell told *Rolling Stone* in 1977. "We're all from the South and we all play music, but I don't know what 'Southern music' is."

With six highly successful releases to their name in approximately five years, the band members had enjoyed a rapid rise to fame. They'd started out in an old Dodge van, but it wasn't long before they were traveling in airplanes rather than beating the asphalt. "The last time we rode in that thing to California," Gray told interviewer Jimmy Thomas in 1978, "we said, 'Hell, we got a record selling,' so we left that sucker out there and flew home." While success afforded them some luxuries,

however, the group members never lost their down-home charm. "I think people enjoy that hell-raising image that a lot of Southern bands have," George McCorkle remarked to Lynn Van Matre in 1977. "It's a real unsophisticated kind of thing, and people can relate to it."

Unlike the Allmans and Wet Willie, the Marshall Tucker Band never relocated to Macon. And they certainly never considered moving to the music centers of New York or Los Angeles. "We're real small-town people, and we live like that in our off time," George McCorkle explained to Kurt Loder in 1978. "It's so much more fun at home—we all live within five miles of each other. And I don't think nobody really wants to get caught up in the star thing."

By the time they were ready to enter the studio to begin work on 1978's *Together Forever*, the Marshall Tucker Band had grown tired of the old formula. "All our past records have been similar," McCorkle told *Crawdaddy!* magazine. "They just didn't capture the energy level we had onstage, and we were scared we were getting into a rut." Instead of working with Paul Hornsby in Macon, they enlisted jazz producer Stewart Levine. Setting up camp at Criteria studios in Miami, the group made the decision to forego additional musicians and strip the band down to its essence. The liner notes indicated that all of the music was performed *solely* by the Marshall Tucker Band. It was also captured more spontaneously. "We're a live band," Jerry Eubanks explained to journalist Lee Abbott, "so we tried to record it live, tried to get that live feeling." The idea was not to obsess on

the details. "First takes have always been best for us." George McCorkle elaborated. "We're a first-take band. We lose it otherwise, and that showed up in our early records when we would spend hours on one song."

Together Forever featured "Last of the Singing Cowboys," which became one of the band's signature songs, as well as "Melody Ann," which was Tommy Caldwell's one and only lead vocal performance with the group. It was the Marshall Tucker Band's last Gold record, and their last album for Capricorn.

The 1979 LP *Running Like the Wind* marked the band's debut for Warner Bros. Gray recalled:

> When we signed with Warner Bros., they asked us if we wanted to move to L.A. That would have been like an inside cat without any cat litter! We didn't do it. Different companies were trying to get us at that point, and one of 'em said, "We'll buy you all Ferrari's. What color do you want? They'll be sittin' there waitin' on you." Well, we all lived in the country. We thought, "Let's see how that works before we go and accept the Ferrari. That might be the only thing we get, and we might not be able to sell the Ferrari for as much as we *think* we're worth."

As 1980 dawned, Southern rock's popularity was on the wane. The band's tenth studio album—simply titled *Tenth*—had a considerably slicker sound as they sought a wider pop audience in a rapidly changing marketplace. "We wanted to modernize the Marshall Tucker Band," Doug Gray admitted. "Make it nationwide. We wanted to let people know that we don't walk around with corn on our boots." The in-your-face Southern pride of the 1970s gave way to a general downplaying of regional identity in the new decade. For Gray, however, musical taste was not something to be limited. "I'd listen to the Pointer Sisters," Gray confessed, "and everybody'd look at me like, what the hell?"

To their credit, the Marshall Tucker Band had always drawn from a wide range of influences. "You can listen to our music," drummer Paul Riddle told the Los Angeles *Daily News*

The Marshall Tucker Band toward the end of the Capricorn era. *Left to right*: Tommy Caldwell, Paul Riddle, Toy Caldwell, George McCorkle, Jerry Eubanks, and Doug Gray. (Courtesy of Chuck Perkins)

A Marshall Tucker Band publicity photo from 1980: Jerry Eubanks, Toy Caldwell, Paul Riddle, Frank Wilkie, Doug Gray, and George McCorkle. (Warner Bros. Records)

in 1977, "and you'll find some of every kind of music." It was the dedication to their craft— substance over form—that ultimately made it difficult for the band to thrive in the attention-grabbing MTV era. "They don't get the headlines other bands get," Capricorn's public relations head Mark Pucci had observed as early as 1978. "They don't tear up hotel rooms, they don't dress weird. They just get out and play."

In April of 1980, a month after *Tenth* was released, a tragedy struck from which the band would never fully recover. Tommy Caldwell was involved in a traffic collision in Spartanburg. He slipped into a coma and died six days later. He was thirty years old. Just one month prior, Tommy and Toy's brother Tim was killed in a similar accident. The band members—especially Toy—were devastated.

Former Toy Factory bassist Frank Wilkie, who went all the way back to the Rants with McCorkle and Toy Caldwell, joined the group following Tommy's death. "He was already a friend," Paul Riddle explained. "We had known him for years. He was hurting just like we were, and he worked extra hard to overcome the pain, just like we did." The first album they made without Tommy was 1981's

Dedicated. Though Charlie Daniels was back in the studio with the band, Tom Dowd's production steered the sound toward the slicker pop aesthetic that was selling at the time. Dowd came up with the title in homage to Tommy, and as a statement that the band would soldier on out of loyalty to one another, the music, and their fans. The closing track, "Ride in Peace," was an especially touching parting blessing for their fallen brother.

After nearly a decade of recording, and following the loss of their spiritual leader, the members of the band were beginning to drift. They developed outside interests that pulled them away from a singular focus on music. George McCorkle became heavily involved in building and racing cars, while Toy raised and showed Arabian horses. These distractions showed on the next album, 1982's *Tuckerized*, which was made up primarily of songs by outside writers. It simply lacked the vitality of much of their other work. The next release, 1983's *Just Us*, was the first to be produced entirely by the band members themselves. It was a solid release, but the follow-up, *Greetings from South Carolina*, was largely forgettable. Everyone knew the magic was fading. "I cut my

own record right when Tommy died in 1980," Gray explained. "It was kind of pop rhythm and blues. Even though we went back out for a couple of years, it just never was the same."

By 1984, Toy Caldwell, George McCorkle, and Paul Riddle had had enough. They retired from the band. Doug Gray and Jerry Eubanks eventually continued on with new members, though the reconstituted Marshall Tucker Band didn't record again until 1988, and never returned to the album charts. Toy Caldwell died in his sleep in 1993 after suffering a cardiorespiratory arrest, and Jerry finally departed in 1996. Doug Gray continued to keep the band going with various musicians.

"I think the term Southern rock is great," Gray reflected in 2013. "I think it should still be here. I think it should be busted out all over. *Southern* rock is exactly what it was. Gladys Knight and all these people had to go off to Philadelphia to get heard, but Phil Walden had us be in Macon, Georgia. We were all from Alabama, South Carolina, Florida, Georgia—all those places. All of these other people would have to go—especially the R&B acts—to different places. Phil made it to where it was *accessible* for us." ★

Part Four

SIMPLE MAN: LYNYRD SKYNYRD AND THE RISE OF REDNECK ROCK

Allen Collins and Ronnie Van Zant of Lynyrd Skynyrd onstage in 1976. (Photo by Richard E. Aaron/Redferns)

"Ronnie Van Zant was stronger than ten men. He just had this fortitude, and he was gonna be something. He came from the wrong side of the tracks, from Shantytown in Jacksonville, Florida, and made the whole world listen to him."

—DON BARNES, 38 SPECIAL, 2013

IN THE DIM light of dusk, on a cool autumn evening in 1977, Mississippi farmer Johnny Mote spotted three shadowy figures emerge from the woods at the edge of his barnyard. He could see the members of the bedraggled trio were limping, and it appeared that their long hair and beards were damp with blood. Thinking they were escaped convicts from a nearby penitentiary, and spotting a helicopter that had just begun circling overhead, Mote reached for his shotgun and fired a warning shot above the approaching men's heads.

"Plane crash!" Lynyrd Skynyrd drummer Artimus Pyle managed to call out, despite the three broken ribs protruding from under his dirt- and sweat-soaked shirt, as he stumbled toward Mote. "Is that what that was?" Mote shouted as he set the gun down and hurried to offer his assistance to Pyle and roadies Marc Frank and Ken Peden. Everyone in the remote area just outside Gillsburg, Mississippi, had heard an earth-shaking commotion a short while earlier. It was the sound of the world crashing down around Lynyrd Skynyrd.

When Lynyrd Skynyrd first took to the road in 1973 to promote their debut album for MCA's Sounds of the South imprint, they quickly established themselves as one of the rowdiest and most cantankerous rock bands in America. "The seven individual members of Lynyrd Skynyrd all drank like fishes, took all known illegal drugs, fucked anything female on two legs, and liked nothing better than to fight with their fists, either against others or amongst themselves," remembered Chris Charlesworth, who worked with the band's management company in the late '70s. Skynyrd's tours were a disorderly three-ring circus of food fights, physical fights, rivers of booze, mountains of coke, and legions of loyal fans who couldn't get enough of lead singer Ronnie Van Zant as he methodically prowled the stage, commanding his three-guitar army and tightly honed rhythm section.

Skynyrd created a new archetype of hell-raising Southern rockers and virtually redefined the word "redneck" to refer to an aggressive, long-haired misfit who turned up the volume, turned up a bottle, and turned up the intensity level, with blazing guitars and ready fists, all while fiercely defending the honor of loyalty and regional identity. But despite their highly publicized (and well deserved) reputation for raucous self-destruction, they were extraordinarily hard workers with a meticulous dedication to their craft. It wasn't uncommon for the group to work out new songs and arrangements in marathon sessions that might stretch for days.

Lynyrd Skynyrd was all about mixed messages. Part roughneck cowboy and part rock-and-roll hippie, Van Zant was no one-dimensional Southern stereotype. In his custom-made Stetson hat, he was reminiscent of what one journalist called "a poolroom rumbler with an irrepressible tongue and a highly volatile temper." On the other hand, he always performed barefoot ("I love to feel the stage *burn*," he used to say), and wrote progressively minded lyrics that could be interpreted as pro-environment ("All I Can Do Is Write About It") and anti-gun ("Saturday Night Special").

"The stories of drinking and fighting, the one-night stands and jail stints, were the stuff of rock and roll myth," wrote John Swenson soon after Ronnie's death. "All of it was true, but it wasn't all there was to Van Zant."

"If Ronnie wanted to kick your ass, he would," recalled Skynyrd roadie Craig Reed, whose own escapades as a crew member were immortalized in the lyrics of "What's Your Name." "He was mean. He used to say to us, 'When I've been drinking, I'm nobody's friend.' But when he was sober, he was the nicest, kindest man you'd ever meet. Quiet, and thoughtful.... That's why he was so complicated."

With their Confederate flag stage backdrop, blaring guitars, and straightforward, everyman lyrics, Skynyrd hit the scene as heroes to boisterous Southern rock kids, steadily expanding their influence to connect with disenfranchised working-class fans around the world. For their legions of loyalists, Skynyrd may have been America's answer to the Rolling Stones, but many critics—the majority of whom likely regarded themselves as urban sophisticates—failed to resonate with the band in the same way their dedicated fans did. "The very plain-spokenness that was Skynyrd's glory," Dave Marsh commented in 1978, "was also what kept them from critical acclaim. They always seemed too vulgar." Nevertheless, Lynyrd Skynyrd sold millions of albums and become a staple of the classic-rock radio format. In many ways, they remain the standard by which all post–Allman Brothers Southern rock bands are measured.

LYNYRD SKYNYRD

- ▸ **RONNIE VAN ZANT** vocals
- ▸ **GARY ROSSINGTON** guitar
- ▸ **BOB BURNS** drums
- ▸ **LARRY JUNSTROM** bass
- ▸ **ALLEN COLLINS** guitar
- ▸ **GREG T. WALKER** bass
- ▸ **RICKEY MEDLOCKE** drums
- ▸ **LEON WILKESON** bass
- ▸ **BILLY POWELL** piano
- ▸ **ED KING** bass, guitar
- ▸ **ARTIMUS PYLE** drums
- ▸ **STEVE GAINES** guitar

CHAPTER 15
Down South Jukin':
The Roots of Lynyrd Skynyrd

THE WESTSIDE neighborhood of Jacksonville, Florida, was an unforgiving place to grow up in the 1960s. The autoworkers and Navy enlistees who populated the working-class area known as "Shantytown" were no strangers to a good fight. Ronnie Van Zant was born there on January 15, 1948. His father, Lacy, was a truck driver and former Golden Gloves boxer who taught his son how to use his fists from an early age. "They were all mean around here," Ronnie's mother, Marion, told journalist Jaan Uhelszki, "but Ronnie was one of the meanest."

As a kid, Van Zant soaked up the music of Hank Williams and other country artists of the day while riding along in his dad's big rig. Ronnie's mother recalled that he got in trouble for singing "Ricochet Romance" and "Beer Drinkin' Daddy" in the classroom on his first day of school. As he grew into his teens, however, his interests turned to baseball, and he earned a reputation as an accomplished local player.

Like Ronnie, guitarist Gary Rossington was an avid baseball enthusiast, but he began to get sidetracked by rock and roll after seeing the Rolling Stones on Ed Sullivan's TV show. Gary's buddy Bob Burns got a drum set, and the boys began messing around with music at Bob's parents' home. "I'd learned some chords," Rossington remembered, "and me and Bob started playing. We started a band called Me, You, and Him."

One day in the summer of 1964, Gary and Bob were hanging out around the third base line at the local ballpark when Ronnie Van Zant—two years their senior, and a casual acquaintance—stepped up to bat for his team, the Green Pigs. Ronnie nailed a foul ball that hit Bob in the head and knocked him out. Feeling bad about the incident, Ronnie struck up a conversation with the two younger boys after the game. The discussion eventually developed into a jam session back at Bob's house. "If Ronnie wouldn't have hit that foul ball," Rossington mused in 1992, "there wouldn't be no Skynyrd."

Ronnie had been singing in a local teen band called Us that had recently broken up, so the boys decided to get a new group together. Allen Collins, a guitarist Gary had met in the eighth grade the previous year, had decent skills and—perhaps even more importantly—some decent equipment. Ronnie and the boys went looking for Allen to recruit him for their new group. Collins was riding his bicycle down the road when he noticed Ronnie's car pull up beside him. "Everyone knew Ronnie in Jacksonville because he was Mr. Badass," Rossington explained in 1976. "He would just stand on street corners, flipping people off." Allen didn't know what Ronnie wanted, but he wasn't taking any chances. He took off, eventually ditching the bike and escaping into some nearby woods. "We had to chase him on foot," Rossington remembered, "and we finally caught him. We went, 'Allen, we ain't gonna hurt you, we just wanna play.'"

Ronnie Van Zant, Gary Rossington, Allen Collins, Bob Burns, and Jimmy Parker became My Backyard. Jimmy was soon replaced by Larry Junstrom, who'd played with Bob and Gary in Me, You, and Him, and the band changed their name to the Noble Five. It didn't take long before they began to land some gigs

The original lineup of Lynyrd Skynyrd. *Left to right:* Allen Collins, Gary Rossington, Ronnie Van Zant, Bob Burns, and Larry Junstrom. (Courtesy of W. Robert Johnson)

playing church socials and area high schools.

They may have been Southern boys, but the band's earliest influences were from overseas. "You know, we came from English music," Gary explained, "We'd listen to . . . Clapton, you know, and Jeff Beck, the Beatles and the Stones, the Animals, all those groups. They were our idols and gods at the time." It was also the music that Jacksonville kids from Shantytown wanted to hear at their dances, which went a long way to reinforce the Noble Five's local reputation.

As the band improved and progressed, they graduated from teen gatherings to club gigs. "The scene had so many musicians at that time," recalled Rickey Medlocke, another Florida native who briefly played with Lynyrd Skynyrd before going on to form the band Blackfoot. "Jacksonville was a transient town," he told *Mojo* magazine. "It had three Naval bases, a steelworks, the Anheuser-Busch brewery, the shipyards—an industrial town that liked to blow off steam, so it became a hotbed for musicians." In fact, Jacksonville attracted players from all over the state, including the Maundy Quintet (featuring future Eagles Don Felder and Bernie Leadon), the Second Coming (which included future Allman Brothers Dickey Betts and Berry Oakley), and Mudcrutch (featuring future Heartbreakers Tom Petty and Mike Campbell).

"After about four years playing at parties, we played Jacksonville clubs for $20 a week for the next five years," Gary Rossington explained to John Swenson in 1975. "We used to play all night and go to school during the day. Never slept . . . we were playing anything on the radio."

Though they were still teenagers, Ronnie and the boys were beginning to think they could find a way to make an actual living at it. "I can tell you the exact time we committed our lives to music," Rossington revealed to *Mojo* in 1997. "It was in 1967 when we saw the Allman Joys at the Beachcomber Lounge in Jacksonville. They did all these cool songs, but then Gregg got too drunk or stoned and couldn't play. So Duane began to improvise. . . . We fell in love with him, and with the music."

Leonard Skinner—a coach at Lee High School in Jacksonville who seemed to particularly relish enforcing the school's strict dress code, which required boys to keep their hair cut short—had little use for long-haired rockers. "He used to hate our guts, and we hated his guts," future Skynyrd keyboardist Billy Powell explained to VH1's *Behind the Music*. The dynamic between Skinner and the boys was indicative of the culture. "At the time, for them to have long hair, they were constantly getting beat up by the rednecks," John Swenson recalled. "They were not rednecks, they were the target of the rednecks." Tired of the hassling they received from other students

and Coach Skinner, Gary and Bob had both dropped out of high school by age sixteen.

As they played around town, the boys were always toying with the name of the band. They'd been the Wildcats, the Sons of Satan, Conqueror Worm, the Pretty Ones, the Wild Things, and they'd finally settled on the One Percent when Ronnie joked onstage one night that they were changing their name to Leonard Skinner. Since most of the high school kids who followed the band were well aware of Coach Skinner, the name stuck. With a bit of a spelling tweak—"to protect the guilty," as the band would laugh—the group became Lynyrd Skynyrd.

Most of the band members became high school dropouts, which only made them more popular among their growing young fan base in Jacksonville. "We were bad boys, 'cause we'd quit school and we drank, and we would fight," Gary Rossington later recounted. They became favorites at local joints like the Comic Book Club. After winning recording time in a battle of the bands competition, Skynyrd laid down

Lynyrd Skynyrd's first publicity photo, taken at Rose Hill Cemetery in Macon, Georgia. *Left to right*: Ronnie Van Zant, Allen Collins, Gary Rossington, Bob Burns, and Larry Junstrom. (Courtesy of W. Robert Johnson)

Lynyrd Skynyrd signing their management contract with Hustler's, Inc., in Macon, Georgia. Back row, *left to right*: Pat Armstrong, Gary Donehoo, Allen Collins, Alan Walden, Bob Burns, and Larry Junstrom. Front row, *left to right*: Gary Rossington, Eddie Floyd, and Ronnie Van Zant. (Courtesy of W. Robert Johnson)

two original songs, "Michelle" and "Need All My Friends," in a Jacksonville studio.

Another break came when they landed the opening slot on a tour with the psychedelic band Strawberry Alarm Clock, best known for the 1967 hit "Incense and Peppermints." "It was toward the end," Alarm Clock guitarist Ed King remembered, "when the group had really fallen, and we were playing the lowest kind of gig. Skynyrd had just changed from calling themselves the One Percent—February, 1970, I think it was—we did gigs together for these crooked promoters, worked for a couple of months." King saw great promise in the hungry young band. "At that time they only had two originals," he elaborated. "The rest was all cover tunes—Cream, Zeppelin, Hendrix. And, of course, Ronnie always came out with no shoes on, and they would play, and I was really, really impressed—especially with Ronnie."

As the 1970s dawned, Ronnie began a relationship with Judy Seymour, who would become his second wife. She went to work as a barmaid to support them while Ronnie focused exclusively on his music. "Allen Collins, Ronnie, and myself had this dream to be a big rock-and-roll band," Rossington elaborated to journalist Rob Hughes. "We had fire in our eyes, and we vowed never to quit until we made it." Ronnie dedicated himself to building up original material as he began formulating lyrical ideas to put to the original guitar riffs that Gary and Allen were creating. "Just listen to any six tunes that he wrote," Ed King commented. "It doesn't matter which six. Just listen, and you get to know

the guy just from that. The songs *were* him."

In 1970, Alan Walden resigned from Capricorn Records in Macon to launch his own music publishing and management firm. By this time, Lynyrd Skynyrd had a few original songs, and Walden signed them as his first act, hoping to land them a record deal. "Alan brought them up to present them to our production company," Muscle Shoals musician and producer Jimmy Johnson remembered, "and we were so busy at that time that we couldn't even get them in the door for a demo. Well, Quin Ivy had opened up a studio down the street from us, so we made a deal where he would just cut fifteen or twenty songs live. He was hired to make a demo for us to hear."

Jimmy Johnson loved what he heard and was anxious to get Lynyrd Skynyrd into the studio to cut some material to shop for a record contract. Between October 1970 and early 1971, when Johnson began producing them in partnership with Tim Smith, the band entered a period of shifting personnel that would continue through the next few years. The first to depart was Larry Junstrom, who moved to Miami with his family. Greg Walker replaced him. Shortly before their Muscle Shoals Sound sessions began, drummer Bob Burns departed and was replaced by Rickey Medlocke. By the fall of 1971, Medlocke and Walker were out, with both men eventually resurfacing as founding members of the Jacksonville band Blackfoot. Bob Burns returned to the drums, and Leon Wilkeson joined on bass. At some point that year, crewmember Billy Powell was added to

the group when the others discovered that he was a fantastic piano player.

The recording sessions in Muscle Shoals were a learning experience for Ronnie and the band. "We went in there," Ronnie told *Crawdaddy!*, "and they said, 'Don't you know the bass and drums are supposed to play together?' We didn't even know how to count time to songs—we had just two speeds: slow and fast." They may have been a little rough around the edges, but Skynyrd already had a special magic. "It was a joy for me to teach 'em," Jimmy Johnson added. "I started helpin' 'em with just some of the basics. They were learnin' as they went, but on most of the arrangements, these guys put that together—all their riffs and everything—they put together themselves. I was astonished at how well they played. Even back then, I was impressed."

As they continued their sporadic recording efforts, Lynyrd Skynyrd dedicated themselves to rehearsal with the focused discipline and determination of a well-trained militia. They pooled their money and rented an isolated cabin outside Jacksonville, in an area known as Green Cove Springs, for $65 a month. Ronnie picked up the band members early every morning for the daily writing, arranging, and rehearsing sessions that would sometimes stretch into the night. "We'd practice sixteen-hour days with the band," Leon Wilkeson explained, to *Mojo*, "and then an additional six hours just bass and drums."

The tin-roofed cabin had no air conditioning, and temperatures would routinely reach well over one hundred degrees inside. "That was a special place to us," Wilkeson continued. "Most of the Skynyrd hits were written there... . We worked our asses off there, and it paid off." It was, as journalist Jaan Uhelszki described it, "the boot camp where Van Zant molded his raw recruits into musical men."

There was no question as to who was in charge. "If Ronnie quit, it would fall apart," Gary Rossington told *Crawdaddy!* in 1975. "He holds everything together.... Decisions are made jointly ... but he has always made the final decision, 'cause he was a little older and smarter than the rest of us." Jimmy Johnson observed Ronnie's strong leadership in Muscle Shoals as their studio sessions progressed. "He was quite a taskmaster," Johnson mused. "He controlled everything all the time. Everything. If they didn't perform like he wanted 'em to, he'd whip their ass. I mean, he was pretty vicious."

"We figured the Muscle Shoals album would come out and do something and get us started," Gary Rossington confessed, "but it didn't, it never came out, nobody liked it. We sent it to everybody, you name it, but we never got any reaction."

There are multiple theories about why Skynyrd's Muscle Shoals recordings failed to catch on. Some said the songs were too long. Others suggested that the major labels didn't want to compete with Capricorn for the Southern rock market. Band members claimed they couldn't find a deal that was just right. Ronnie would suggest in later years that they'd been offered a Capricorn contract but turned it down because they didn't think they'd be able to get any attention, with the Allman Brothers on the label.

In reality, Alan and Phil Walden's sibling rivalry thwarted any such alliance, as Capricorn staffer Mike Hyland recalled:

> Alan came to me and said, "I really want to see if we can get Lynyrd Skynyrd signed to Capricorn." I said, "Well, why don't we do a showcase?" We had done one for the Marshall Tucker Band, and we ended up signing them. So we did a show-case. The band played incredibly well. They were fantastic. As soon as the show was over, Alan and Phil are talking, and Phil is, like, glib and doesn't really give a shit and whatnot. And Phil said, "I'll take the band if I can have their publishing." Alan said, "No I've got the publishing." And Phil said, "Then I'm not signing the band." And that was that.

During the era when they were working on their initial recordings in Muscle Shoals, Lynyrd Skynyrd were building an ever-expanding fan base throughout the South. They would find a particularly strong reception in Atlanta, which had built up a thriving music scene in the wake of the regular Piedmont Park concerts that the Allman Brothers Band helped pioneer at the close of the 1960s. "There was what they called the Strip at 10th and Peachtree," recalled Eric Quincy Tate bassist David Cantonwine, who was part of Atlanta's alternative music community. "It was just a whole new experience. This was the birth of the hippie generation, and during that period was amazing. It was free love, free everything. There was this big concrete slab in the park that a building used to be on, and people would just set up and play. It was two or three blocks from 10th and Peachtree."

"Atlanta is a hotbed of rock music," future Lynyrd Skynyrd producer Al Kooper told *Rolling Stone* magazine around that time. "Talent is literally breeding here, and it's about time people found out about it. . . . When some of the big record companies hear some

Allen Collins, Ronnie Van Zant, Leon Wilkeson, and Gary Rossington onstage at Funnochios in Atlanta, Georgia, 1972. (Courtesy of Carter Tomassi/messyoptics.com)

Leon Wilkeson, Ronnie Van Zant, Gary Rossington, and Bob Burns onstage at Funnochios in Atlanta, Georgia, 1972. (Courtesy of Carter Tomassi/messyoptics.com)

of the local talent . . . they'll be coming down here signing up everything in sight."

It was while playing a stint at a club called Funnochios in 1972—Lynyrd Skynyrd's first performance in Atlanta—that Ronnie and the boys met Kooper and eventually found themselves with a record deal. Born and raised in New York, Al Kooper was already a seasoned songwriter, musician, and producer by the time he first met Ronnie and the boys. He'd played the signature organ part on Bob Dylan's "Like a Rolling Stone" and was in the backing band for Dylan's famed 1965 Newport Folk Festival per-

formance, when Bob introduced the live audience to his new electric sound. Kooper became a member of the Blues Project before going on to found Blood, Sweat & Tears in 1967. He left the following year to work at Columbia Records. After recording the acclaimed Super Session album with Mike Bloomfield and Stephen Stills, Kooper continued to work as a session musician, backing a staggering list of rock royalty, including Jimi Hendrix, the Who, Cream, and the Rolling Stones.

Al Kooper happened to catch Lynyrd Skynyrd's debut performance at Funnochios when he was producing an album for his backup band at Studio One in the Atlanta suburb of Doraville:

> We recorded about half an album at that studio with various members that were in the Atlanta Rhythm Section. We were there for about three weeks, living in a hotel, and would work from noon to eight and then we would go out to party and listen to music and chase women every night. We would go to the same club, Funnochios, each night, because I knew the guy that owned the place.
>
> It was one of those really dangerous bars where everybody carries guns and there's about three shootings a night. Skynyrd were playing, and they just blew me out of my seat... and then to find that they weren't signed to anybody was marvelous.

There was something about Ronnie, in particular, that held a certain magnetism. "I just couldn't take my eyes off him—he was so unusual," Kooper explained. "I never saw anybody like him—he was a very weird front man." In an age of outrageously complex theatrics, Lynyrd Skynyrd were a refreshingly basic rock band. "They didn't need production," road manager Ron Eckerman noted, "they just needed a stage—the music did all the rest... and Ronnie's magic."

"He came in one night," Ronnie remembered, "and said, 'Hi, I'm Al Kooper,' and we all flipped out. We'd never seen anybody who was a real rock star or anything." Al sat in with

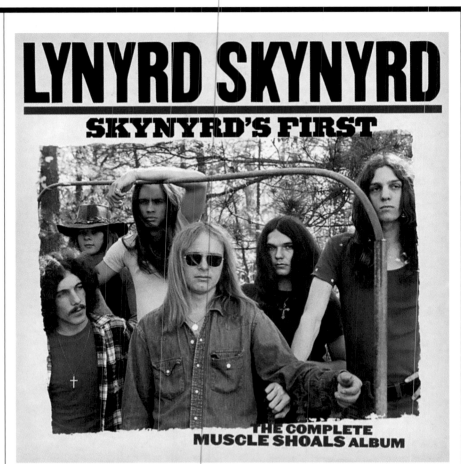

A 1970s publicity photo of Al Ka Al Kooper in the mid-1970s. (United Artists)

the band and started formulating his plan for the future. "I didn't have a label," Kooper explained. "I just wanted to produce them, and I was looking to make a production deal." The negotiations moved slowly at first. "It took me a long time to get them," Kooper confessed, "a long, long time, because their management needed a lot of convincing. They were very careful—the management always knew what they had, even though the group had been turned down by several major companies."

As the negotiation process between Skynyrd and Kooper dragged on, the vision expanded. "In the time it took me to close that deal, I decided to start a label," Al recalled. Kooper declared himself an Atlanta resident and sent his roadies to New York to pack up his belongings. With that, Sounds of the South Records was born, and Kooper focused on a very specific niche. "I said, 'I'd like to be the person they come to after Capricorn turns them down.'"

The first band signed to the Sounds of the South label was Mose Jones. "They had a one-armed bass player named Randy Lewis," Kooper recalled. "His arm ended at the elbow, and he put, like, a leather cover over the elbow and used that to pluck the strings. He was pretty amazing. He also was a great singer. I

really liked them. They were a good band."

Around the same time he signed Mose Jones, Al Kooper finally secured an agreement with Lynyrd Skynyrd. The band's trailer had been broken into, and most of their gear was stolen. Ronnie contacted Al for help. "He called me up," Kooper recalled, "and he said, 'I really need this money to put food on the table.' I said, 'Just tell me where you want the check. It's yours.' I certainly could understand that, and I didn't think he was lying to me. I trusted Ronnie all down the line. When we finished the conversation, he said, 'Al, you just bought yourself a band for 5,000 dollars.'" By that time, Kooper had secured funding for the label. "I went to MCA and, after a while, convinced them to finance me."

Lynyrd Skynyrd finally had a record deal, but in November of 1972, bassist Leon Wilkeson departed, choosing to return to Jacksonville to work for a dairy. They needed to find a bass player quickly. Ronnie tracked down Ed King, from the Strawberry Alarm Clock, whom they'd gotten to know when the two bands toured together. "I told him at that time," King recalled, "'If you ever need a bass player or another guitar player, please look me up.'" Ed eagerly stepped into the role. ★

Ed King and Gary Rossington onstage. (Courtesy of John Gellman)

CHAPTER 16
Freebird: Ronnie and the Boys Conquer America

WITH ED KING on board, Lynyrd Skynyrd rehearsed and played live constantly to prepare to record their first album. Al Kooper spent a lot of time listening to the live show as he formulated a plan for the group's recorded sound. In the process, the band began cautiously letting him into their inner circle. He recalled:

> One time, after we signed the deal, Skynyrd was playing at Funnochios. I was upstairs and they were on a break. Allen and Gary came over to me and they said, "Come with us right now." They were very serious. I said, "OK." They picked me up and lifted me up over the bar and put me behind the bar. They said, "Just crouch down and stay there for about ten minutes unless you want to get the shit kicked out of you." And, sure enough, within five minutes there was a huge fight, which they knew I shouldn't be involved in.

On July 29, 1973, Skynyrd closed the show at a Sounds of the South launch party at Richard's nightclub in Atlanta. It was packed with music-industry representatives and all the bigwigs from MCA Records. Ronnie and Ed King wrote a song just for the occasion, opening the set by tearing straight into "Workin' for MCA." The crowd was captivated. "The Rolling Stones can carry on and dance around and have Southern accents, but these are the real thing," Al Kooper bragged to the press about Skynyrd's personnel. "These boys have a shack in the middle of the Florida swamps, and in their spare time they chase alligators

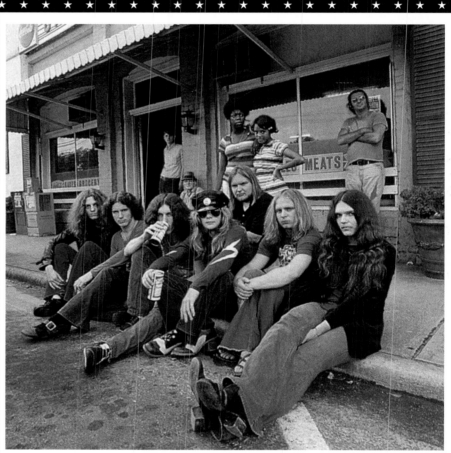

Allen Collins, Billy Powell, Bob Burns, Leon Wilkeson, Ed King, Ronnie Van Zant, and Gary Rossington in Jacksonville, Florida, 1973, as featured in the artwork of the band's first LP. (MCA Records)

and go fishing for catfish." The image of a new brand of Southern good ol' boy was heavily promoted along with the Sounds of the South / MCA release of the band's debut album, *Pronounced 'Leh-'nerd 'Skin-'nerd*.

While it might not have taken long to make

the album, the recording process was intense and not always completely smooth. Lynyrd Skynyrd had been honing their live sound for years, and they were instinctively clannish. It wasn't always easy for them to open themselves to an outside perspective. At one point, Allen Collins bristled at an idea posited by Kooper. "I was making a musical suggestion," Al recalled, "and Allen Collins said to me, 'You know, we know what this song is. You really shouldn't interfere.' Ronnie said, 'You know, Allen, you're right. But I will listen to whatever he wants to say, because if he makes one suggestion in twenty, and we use that and it helps us, then it's worth putting up with the other nineteen.'"

The album was officially released on August 13, 1973, and was packed with what journalist Rob Hughes called "all spring-tight riffage, jukin' country, and delinquent boogie." With instant classics like "Gimme Three Steps," "Simple Man," and "Freebird," listeners were introduced to the band that *Rolling Stone*, in a cautiously positive review, declared a "no-nonsense powerhouse rock unit of modest proportions but considerable promise." That introduction was notably less confusing thanks to the decision to use the album title to inform the public of the correct pronunciation of the groups' name. "It looked like Lie-Nard Sky-Nard when you saw it in print," Al Kooper laughed. In the final analysis, Ronnie was very pleased with the results. "I definitely think the first album was the best," he proclaimed in 1976. The LP climbed to #27 on the *Billboard* album chart, and Lynyrd Skynyrd soon found themselves in front of exponentially larger audiences who were immediately hooked by their electrifying stage show.

Before the first album was even released, Leon Wilkeson had returned to the group. His replacement, Ed King, recalled the lineup change. "After the first album was done. . . . Ronnie and I shared a house together and I was sittin' on the edge of the bed . . . and Ronnie comes in the room and he sits down on the bed, puts his arm around me and goes, 'Man, you're really the worst bass player I ever played with.'" Ed assumed that meant he was out of a job. Instead, Ronnie asked him to stick around. "We got Leon back and Ed switched to guitar," Gary explained to John Swenson. "At first it was really weird, 'cause we didn't know how to do it—all three guitars would play the same thing. We didn't know if it was gonna work, we just tried it out."

On the first day of rehearsals after Skynyrd's famous three-guitar army was assembled, they wrote "Sweet Home Alabama." "When we were done writing it," Ed King recalled, "Ronnie said to me, 'Well, Ed, there's our 'Ramblin' Man.'" The band continued to focus on becoming a tighter unit during marathon sessions at Hell House. "We showed up every day at 8:30 a.m.," remembered King. "Every day. Without fail. . . . And we stayed until past dark, because we didn't have tape recorders. . . . We would literally learn a song until it was burned so far into our brain, literally, you'd be dreaming about it at night."

The hard work continued to pay off. Lynyrd Skynyrd opened for the Who on their *Quadrophenia* tour in November 1973. "We had a whole other tour lined up," King recalled, "but when this tour with the Who came along, we dropped everything else. We turned down a tour with Alice Cooper, but we wanted the Who tour no matter what."

"Before the Who tour," Ronnie explained, "the biggest crowd we ever played to was maybe twelve hundred. The first night at the Cow Palace we faced 18,000 people, and we were shitting." The band got off to a rocky start at first as they learned that Who fans were very loyal to the headliners. "Those kids are there to see one group," Ronnie remarked. "Our first big concert was our first night with them. We got onstage and just lost it. The second and third nights weren't much better." Feeling out of their element, the band were perhaps too hard on themselves. Al Kooper, who went on the road to introduce the group and mix the sound, recalled the Skynyrd boys getting their first encore early on in the tour. The Who's manager, Peter Rudge, was standing at the side of the stage next to Kooper when it happened. "I remember he turned to me," Al enthused, "and said, 'That's the first time I've ever seen an opening act for the Who get an encore.' I said, 'That's because they're the first one that played 'Freebird.' And as long as they keep playing that song, it's going to happen every night.'"

"That's when we started drinkin'," Leon Wilkeson remembered of the tour in an interview with VH1, "'cause we were terrified to go up and perform before the Who. Problem was, we never stopped." Gary Rossington concurred. "We just walked in and said, 'Oh my God. Give us a drink, and make it a *triple*,'" he told *Mojo*. "We had to get drunk beforehand because it was such a scary experience. We always had confidence in the music, but we'd never been in that [arena] situation. The drinking became part of the ritual." Al Kooper wasn't so sure the drinking was really about calming nerves. "Oh, that's baloney," he laughed. "They just had more of a chance to get crazy, and they jumped in. I think that was part of the Southern thing."

It didn't take long for Skynyrd to challenge the Who's reputation for on-the-road destruction, not to mention dominance of the stage. "I really dug it," Ronnie told journalist Barbara Charone. "It was like a challenge, a competition between us and the Who."

Before long, the crowds began to spread the word about the power of Lynyrd Skynyrd. "I hadn't seen many groups explode with such energy," future Skynyrd road manager Ron Eckerman confessed. "Usually you'd have the normal ebb and flow in a concert [but] these guys just powered through until they incited this explosive mass orgasm in the audience when they hit 'Freebird.'"

As the onstage intensity spilled over into the band members' lives, they quickly established a reputation as brawling, drunken delinquents who blazed a path of hotel room damages and left chaos in their wake. "They drank a lot of Jack Daniels," noted writer John Swenson, who spent time on the road with the band, "and, for recreation, almost, they would beat each other up. . . . They were real rough-and-tumble country boys."

Al Kooper was anxious to get Skynyrd back in the studio. By the time they were free to record in early 1974, Kooper had relocated to Los Angeles. "When the Skynyrd album took off," he told *Melody Maker* magazine in 1974, "it changed everything, and got bigger than I thought it would, so I've had to move to Los Angeles to be closer to MCA for the co-ordination, in fairness to the acts on our label."

When Lynyrd Skynyrd headed to the Record Plant recording studio in Los Angeles in January of 1974 to begin work on their second album, the debut LP had already sold 200,000 copies in the US. Highlights of the new sessions included "Don't Ask Me No Questions," "The Ballad of Curtis Lowe," J. J. Cale's "Call Me the Breeze," and "Workin' for MCA," which the band had been using as an opener on their live shows since debuting it at the Sounds of the South showcase the previous year. These titles would form the core of the follow-up album, *Second Helping*, which was released in April 1974.

"Sweet Home Alabama," cut in the sum-

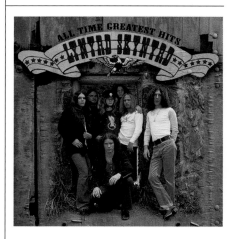

Neil Young onstage in Austin, Texas. (Courtesy of Mark Estabrook)

mer of 1973 before the tour with the Who began, became the band's first charting single, and the first of only two Top 10 hits. Its popularity propelled the album to #12, and it eventually sold enough to earn double-Platinum status. "Sweet Home Alabama" courted controversy, too, as it became the focal point of some of the more complicated aspects of Southern pride in the post–civil rights era.

In 1970, Neil Young released "Southern Man," a scathing indictment of white Southern prosperity built on a historical foundation that was propped up by institutional slavery. In 1972, Young revisited a similar theme on "Alabama," from his *Harvest* album. In response, Ronnie wrote the infamous lines in "Sweet Home Alabama" that dismissed Neil Young for his criticism of the state. Combining this barb with a lyrical reference to Alabama's segregationist governor George Wallace, the ever-present Confederate flag that adorned the back of their stage set, and the band's habit of blasting "Dixie" over the loudspeakers before taking the stage, a growing contingent began to characterize the group as backwoods racists. Others insisted the whole thing was actually a liberal commentary, delivered with tongue planted firmly in cheek.

"They don't like Neil Young," Al Kooper told John Tobler, during the making of the second album in 1974, "and they were very insulted by the lyric to 'Southern Man.'" The members of the band, however, were less dogmatic in interviews. "We thought Neil was shooting all the ducks in order to kill one or two," Ronnie told *Rolling Stone* in 1974. But, he continued, "Neil is amazing, wonderful . . . a superstar."

With the passage of time, the band members would further downplay the idea that they were reacting to Neil Young, and they

brushed the controversy off as a misinterpretation of their humor. "That whole thing was totally fabricated," Gary asserted, in a 2006 *Uncut* magazine profile. "We all loved Neil. . . . [Ronnie] just wrote those lines about 'Southern Man,' which seemed cute at the time, almost like a play on words. But we didn't know that song would turn into such a huge deal." Ronnie insisted that Young took no offense. "Neil thought it was very clever and cute and just laughed," he claimed. "It was a joke. . . . Neil Young's one of our favorite people."

For his part, however, Young expressed regret for the way he articulated his feelings in "Southern Man." "I don't like my words when I listen to it today," he wrote, in his 2012 autobiography. "They are accusatory and condescending, not fully thought out, and too easy to misconstrue."

More unsettling to many critics than the dig at Neil Young was the apparent nod to George Wallace. The Alabama governor started the first of four nonconsecutive terms in 1962, making his famous "segregation now, segregation tomorrow, segregation forever" speech at the inauguration ceremony. He ran for president in 1972 and won every county in Skynyrd's home state of Florida during the primary. Though by the time he sought the nomination for presidency he had renounced his segregationist views, Wallace remained a controversial and polarizing figure. In response to "Sweet Home Alabama," he bestowed the band with plaques that declared them honorary lieutenants in the state militia. It was an association that created some uncomfortable moments, and Ronnie would distance himself from Wallace in the coming years. "The lyrics about the governor of Alabama were misunderstood," Ronnie protested in 1975. "The general public didn't notice the words 'Boo! Boo! Boo!' after that particular line, and the media picked up only on the reference to the people loving the governor."

"I support Wallace about as much as your average American supported Hitler," Leon Wilkeson declared emphatically, in a 1977 *Rolling Stone* article. Then, in typical Lynyrd Skynyrd fashion, he proceeded to muddy the waters, adding, "I respect him, not as a politician—but as a man who hasn't given up what he was after. That's how we all feel." African American journalist Kandia Crazy Horse made the same distinction. "I tend not to think that Ronnie Van Zant was supporting segregation with this song," she observed in a BBC documentary about Southern rock, "but liked this aspect of Wallace's demeanor in telling off northerners and other elites that, yes, you have no right to come down here and tell us how to be."

While Ronnie's lyrics were insightful and often disarmingly socially conscious for a man who could become so unruly, Lynyrd Skynyrd was not an ideological band. Ronnie was often evasive with interviewers, suggesting his own reluctance to be cast as a spokesperson for anything or anyone. Instead, he simply wanted to carve out a space for Skynyrd as a great American rock band whose members did things on their own terms and took great pride in their fierce independence. "We're not into politics, we don't have no education, and Wallace don't know anything about rock and roll," he said, in response to the controversy over "Sweet Home Alabama."

"As far as the Confederate flag is concerned," he explained in 1976, "we've carried that with us for a long time, before we did anything; it's just part of us. We're from the South, but we're not bigots." Ed King, the only non-Southerner in the band, concurred. "Believe me," he explained, "all it was was a *rebel* flag. That's it. That's why we used it. We were rebels." Drummer Artimus Pyle agreed. "I'm a left-wing liberal," he declared in 2013. "I'm a peacenik. I'm a hippie. And I will tell you this: Ronnie Van Zant was not a racist."

All the controversy generated press, and Skynyrd's star only rose further. Their second album was generally well received by both critics and fans. Despite having doubled down on their Southern identity, Bud Scoppa, in his review of *Second Helping* in *Crawdaddy!* magazine, observed that "Lynyrd is closer to London than Macon in its approach, leaving form-expanding progressivism to the Allmans and their kin, and working instead within the well-defined traditions of rock and roll."

As Skynyrd's popularity grew, Al Kooper's relationship with MCA Records deteriorated. After the release of *Second Helping*, the Sounds of the South imprint was dissolved. "I learned I had no business being a record company," Al commented. "The company and I just didn't get along." But while Sounds of the South was no more, the band had grown far too successful for the parent label to let them slip away. Lynyrd Skynyrd signed directly with MCA.

As Kooper's relationship with MCA soured, Skynyrd's association with manager Alan Walden unraveled, too. They felt he was taking too large a percentage of their earnings, and they complained that he was booking them into the same places, rather than pushing into new areas. In 1974, the band bought out their management contract for $250,000 and signed with Peter Rudge, who managed the Who and the Rolling Stones. ★

Drummer Artimus Pyle and bassist Leon Wilkeson onstage in Rotterdam, Holland, 1975. (Photo by Laurens Van Houten/Frank White Photo Agency)

CHAPTER 17
On the Hunt: Ronnie and the Boys Conquer the World

N NOVEMBER OF 1974, with manager Peter Rudge anxious to expand Lynyrd Skynyrd's influence, the band toured Europe for the first time. They were originally slated to open shows for Golden Earring, but it soon became obvious that Skynyrd were no opening act, and adjustments were quickly made.

Despite the positive momentum, Lynyrd Skynyrd were under a lot of strain, and drummer Bob Burns finally snapped during the band's two-week stint in England. "The last time I saw Bob was after a gig," Ronnie later related to Ron Eckerman. "We got back to the hotel—this was a fancy hotel. We were on the third floor. Anyway, Bob went kinda crazy. The last time I saw him, he had jumped out the window and climbed down the vines. . . . then hit the ground runnin'. Just runnin' off . . . never came back."

Nobody was sure what made Bob lose control. Skynyrd lore says he became mesmerized by the film *The Exorcist*, freaked out, threw the hotel cat out the window, and chased the tour manager with an axe. "There's always been talk that Bob Burns was a Satanist," Ed King explained, "though I think it was a case of somebody who was *obs*essed rather than *pos*sessed. . . . He was definitely caught up in the madness of some power I didn't want to know about." For his part, Burns later explained, to the Freebird Foundation, "I left the band in 1974 because of my health. I wasn't feeling good or thinking good at that time. Ronnie never fired me and I never quit, but I just had to leave for my own sake. The touring, the recording, the constant motion was too much."

Lynyrd Skynyrd replaced Burns with Artimus Pyle. After getting out of the marines in 1971, Artimus was living in Spartanburg, South Carolina, hometown of both his wife and the Marshall Tucker Band. "My wife went to high school with Doug Gray and Toy Caldwell," Artimus explained. "The Tucker guys introduced me to Charlie Daniels." Recognizing Artimus' talent, Charlie contacted Ronnie Van Zant and recommended the inventive drummer for Lynyrd Skynyrd.

Artimus recalled his audition with the band:

> Ronnie called me up. He sent me to Atlanta to Alex Cooley's Electric Ballroom, which was the ballroom of the Georgia Terrace that they'd turned into a big rock club. I drove my Volkswagen bus to Atlanta. I was comin' down Peachtree Street and was two blocks from Alex Cooley's Electric Ballroom. My Volkswagen bus, as they often do, got vapor locked. It was hot, and my whole bus just shut down. I left it right in the middle of Peachtree, I opened it up, took out my drums—it took me two trips— walked two blocks up to the Alex Cooley Ballroom, left my van right where it was, and spent three hours setting up and doing the audition process with Ed King and Leon Wilkeson. Ed called up Ronnie right in front of me and said, "This guy's a great drummer. He plays some of our songs better than we recorded 'em. He's got my vote." Leon said, "He's got my vote, too." Ronnie said, "Artimus, you're in."

Pyle was the perfect addition to the wild band of misfits. He was a health-conscious

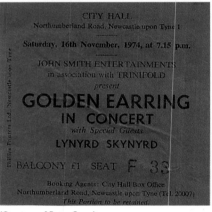

vegetarian who didn't drink but consumed copious amounts of drugs. His approach to his instrument brought an additional layer of sophistication to the band. "Bob Burns was just in the band because he grew up with everybody," Al Kooper speculated. "They told him what to play. Artimus was a much more inventive drummer."

In January 1975, Artimus, Ronnie, Allen, Gary, Ed, Leon, and Billy went to Webb IV Studios in Atlanta to cut the bulk of what would become their third album, *Nuthin' Fancy*. Despite the fact that his Sounds of the South label had been shuttered, Al Kooper was back in the producer's chair. "When the dissolution of Sounds of the South Records happened," Al reflected, "Skynyrd told MCA that they wanted me to produce their third album. So, the label really couldn't get rid of me."

In addition to "Made in the Shade," "Whiskey Rock-a-Roller," and "On the Hunt," the album included "Saturday Night Special," a

Lynyrd Skynyrd publicity photo. *Left to right*: Allen Collins, Leon Wilkeson, Gary Rossington, Artimus Pyle, Ronnie Van Zant, and Billy Powell. (Michael Ochs Archives/Getty Images)

song that had been recorded at Studio One in Doraville in October of 1973, just prior to the start of the European tour. The anti-gun sentiment was an unlikely statement for a self-proclaimed country boy. "Guns? Throw 'em all away," Ronnie declared in 1976. Personal experience kept Ronnie from having much interest in firearms. "I've been shot myself," he declared cryptically in 1975, "and I don't want to get into that, but it happens, you know, every day. . . . I really don't like 'em." He described the incident further in an interview with Harry Doherty the following year. "When I was a kid, I shot myself right there," Ronnie explained as he pointed to his leg, "fucking around with a gun. I'm tellin' you, they hurt. Blew a hole right there in my leg."

Released in March, *Nuthin' Fancy* hit #9 on the album charts but ultimately didn't sell as well as the band's previous two efforts. "*Nuthin' Fancy* maintains the feel, sonically and stylistically, of the first two albums," noted the review in *Rolling Stone*, "but much of it seems stiff next to its direct predecessor, the tough but neighborly *Second Helping*."

The recording process had not been a pleasant experience for either the band or their producer. "The third album was so difficult—we were at each other's throats," Al Kooper revealed. "It really escalated to hell." Part of the tension was attributed to the lack of preparation. While the first two albums were heavy on songs that had been meticulously arranged

and rehearsed at Hell House, the demands of the road prevented the band from doing much advance planning before entering the studio. "No rehearsals, no planned-out guitar solos, and, in fact, *no songs*," Kooper recalled. "I don't mean they had bad songs, they had *no* songs!" Kooper wasn't the only one who was disillusioned. "*Nuthin' Fancy* was probably our poorest showing," Ronnie confessed in 1977. "It was a real rush job, and it wasn't the best thing that we've ever put out. At all."

"They're nice guys except when it comes to recording," Al Kooper told *Crawdaddy!* magazine. "It's a nightmare to work with them in the studio, and I suppose it's the same for them with me. They take their recordings very seriously, and they definitely should produce

themselves." Though their professional relationship came to an end after *Nuthin' Fancy*, Kooper remained friends with the band. "I really liked those guys," he reflected in 2013, "but it was getting hard to work together. Ultimately, it was more important to me to maintain our friendship than our professional association, so we didn't work together again."

In the spring of 1975, Lynyrd Skynyrd embarked on what became known to band insiders as the Torture Tour. The musicians were exhausted, and tensions were running high. But it was the band's live show that won over their fans, and being on the road was important. They kept their loyal crew on the payroll all year—a business model that necessitated constant touring to support it. The steady diet of alcohol, drugs, and fistfights reached legendary proportions during this outing.

Ed King had been dispatched to Los Angeles to represent the band for Al Kooper's remix of the *Nuthin' Fancy* album and was now taking a more proactive role in the business side of the band's activities. During the tour, he became increasingly concerned that there would be no time to come up with new material for their follow-up album. "I went to Ronnie and told him I wanted to cancel the next leg of the tour because it was too much for everybody, and we had that album hanging over our heads," King explained. "He told me, 'If we have to cancel shows, just do it. I can't handle it anymore.' I called Rudge and told him we were canceling some of the upcoming dates, and within two weeks I was gone. He called Ronnie and told him I was trying to ruin the band, and he had to kick me out."

King departed abruptly, following a confrontation with Ronnie in a hotel room in Lake Charles, Louisiana, where Ronnie held a piece of broken glass to Ed's neck and threatened to cut his throat. In his gut, King believed the path of destruction was only going to get worse. "Ronnie treated me real bad," Ed recalled. "As a matter of fact, he was a real asshole. On the road, he just kept drinkin' and

drinkin,' and if you keep doin' that you're going to turn into an asshole. But he was still meaner to the other guys than he was to me. On May 26, I just packed my bags and left."

Ed's departure resulted in another violent altercation between Ronnie and Artimus, but everyone quickly regrouped to keep the Skynyrd train moving forward. The following day they rehearsed for four hours to figure out how to play the songs now that the guitar army had been diminished by one third. Although Ronnie was concerned about how the fans would react, he brushed off questions about Ed's

departure and put on his best who-gives-a-damn face for the press. He told *Creem* magazine that Ed wanted to cancel the tour but that Lynyrd Skynyrd wouldn't be caught "running back home with their tail between their legs." He told others that Ed had inherited a lot of money and didn't need the band anymore.

Ed's resignation apparently wasn't viewed as a wake-up call for the band. "It really was torture," Rossington asserted. "We were gigging every night with no rest, and with constant weather changes. Everybody was sick." Band members were at each other's throats

The inner sleeve from *Nuthin' Fancy*. (MCA Records)

Allen Collins onstage in Sheffield, England. (Courtesy of Peter Cross)

Ronnie Van Zant and Allen Collins. (Courtesy of Peter Cross)

and would show up at concerts refusing to speak to one another. Tour manager Ron Eckerman explained:

> It was rarely with an outside party when the papers read, "those bad boys of Southern rock." No, the fights were usually internal, resulting in one band member punching out another.... These guys all packed a pretty good wallop and were good at throwing sucker punches, resulting in one winner and one loser determined by a single blow.... The next day the whole thing would blow over and everyone would be all lovey-dovey until the next episode. The real problem with the whole mess is the black eyes and swollen faces that resulted, and the fear one of them would do enough physical damage to keep them from performing.

For his part, Ronnie was abusing his voice, sometimes spitting up blood and collapsing backstage. The substance abuse was taking its toll. "They were just partying too much," explained Jon Hornyak, who co-owned the tour's sound company, "doing too much coke and drinking too much."

Ronnie chalked up most of their antics to the adrenaline that came with playing an explosive live show. "We get really hyped up before we go on, and when we do a show, sometimes we don't let the steam off," Ronnie told one journalist during the Torture Tour, "and when we come back, we raise hell. The next day it begins all over again, from hotel to hotel. We're a bunch of hyperactive people gettin' with it. If we don't let it all off at the gig, we're gonna make the hotel a wreck. We usually wind up gettin' thrown out owin' money."

Hotel rooms weren't the only things that suffered the band's abuse. At one point, Ronnie attempted to throw a crewmember out of an airplane at 13,000 feet. The incident resulted in an emergency landing and a quarter-million-dollar lawsuit. On another occasion, he knocked out Billy Powell's front teeth.

"We was at a hotel in Louisville and I heard this terrible goin'-on in the hall," Ronnie told *Rolling Stone*. "It was Billy and our road manager, and they was really gettin' down on each other . . . I just had a towel on and I stuck my head outside and said, 'Cool it.' Then Billy said, 'Fuck you.' So I just walked out and knocked Billy's teeth out, hit the road manager and knocked him down. Then my towel fell off in front of the fuckin' spectators."

Despite the violent behavior, the band members had much more respect than resentment

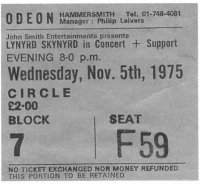

(Courtesy of Peter Cross)

for their leader. "Ronnie would give the shirt off his back for anyone he could," Billy Powell told journalist Rob Hughes. "But he could also get pretty damn mean when he was drinking. He had the 'Jekyll and Hyde' syndrome.... That's how he led the band. But at the same time, if there was trouble from outside, he'd fight for us. He went to jail for us a few times. And when it came down to business, he was always right. We could always trust him."

"Not one of 'em had a true father," Artimus later explained, "and when Ronnie came along, they literally looked at him as a father. And then to see him abuse them . . . I could have argued with Ronnie daily about certain policies and things, but it was his band. It was *his* show." Artimus didn't allow himself to get pulled into that group dynamic. "[Ronnie] had a different relationship with Gary and Allen and Leon and Billy," he continued. "He'd beat them up regularly. I pulled him off of them many, many times."

Powell understood that Ronnie's behavior was not motivated by malice. "That's the way he was raised," Billy to *Mojo*. "When we stepped out of line, he straightened us out."

Ronnie's twisted paternal impulses were likely rooted in feelings about his relationship with his own father. "He is the fairest most beautiful person I have ever known," Ronnie said of his dad in a *Creem* magazine interview. "I learned everything I know from him. He used to say to me, 'Ronnie, if a man says he's never been beaten, it's just because he hasn't fought enough times.' He always wanted me to be something I could never be—and I'm sorry to disappoint him—he wanted me to be just like him."

The root of Ronnie's insecurity remained a mystery to his bandmates. "Ronnie's biggest disappointment in life was that he couldn't please his father," confirmed guitarist Ed King. "I found that so bizarre, because all his father ever did was sing his praises. Yet he felt that way. I could never figure out why, because Lacy

adored Ronnie. Maybe he never told Ronnie."

In the early fall of 1975, the band departed for Europe for yet another extension of the Torture Tour. The craziness continued. "Backstage at our concerts," Artimus revealed, "it looked like an ABC store, with cartons of cigarettes and cases of alcohol of every description, and beer. The guys felt like they had to drink every bit of it and smoke every cigarette. It was *insane*."

By the time they reached Germany, the chaos erupted in full force. "Just getting to the stage is some achievement, considering two of the band look as though they're on an invalids' outing," journalist Tony Stewart wrote of the opening night in Hamburg. What Stewart didn't see was the outrageous scene in the hotel bar the night before. Exhausted, jet-lagged, and drunk on Schnapps, Ronnie smashed a bottle over road manager John Butler's head before turning his attention to Rossington. "Next," crew member Craig Reed told *NME*, "he just turned on Gary, said, 'You think you're a guitar player? I'll do it without you,' and just cut Gary's hands up before he had a chance to answer.... They had to buy the whole carpet in the hotel because there was blood everywhere." Somehow Ronnie also managed to break a few of his own fingers in the melee.

When Artimus found out what happened, he was furious. "I literally broke Ronnie's door down," he recalled. "Ronnie jumped up on his bed and backed into a corner. I jumped up on the bed with him and I grabbed him, and I said, 'How in the *fuck* can you do something like that to somebody that you love? To somebody's that's your brother? What the *fuck*?' Ronnie was like, 'I'm hurt, too. I'm hurt, too. I was

drunk.' I was like, 'That is no excuse!' Being drunk and doing something stupid is no excuse 'cause you could have chosen not to get that drunk." Within several hours, all parties had sobered up, and the band continued on down the road. "The next day, we were the best of friends again," Rossington claimed.

"When he was sober," Artimus insisted, "he was the nicest person. He had beautiful handwriting. He had perfect cursive, like a woman's handwriting. He was a graceful fisherman, and he was a really cool guy when he was sober. When he drank too much, he lost control and he could be very abusive."

What is most striking about Lynyrd Skynyrd is how little self-awareness they seemed to possess about how wild their behavior really was. They would complain that journalists seemed preoccupied with their violent antics—as if all bands behaved the exact same way, and they were somehow being singled out. "Sure, we get in fights," Gary Rossington admitted to Jaan Uhelszki during Skynyrd's heyday. "I think it has to do with being on the road, you're always uptight, so you drink to unwind. If you're drunk and there's any trouble, you're quick to react violently because of the mood. When you're tense and uptight it's just natural to fight."

It didn't seem to occur to the band that their definition of "routine" was completely foreign to the experience of most journalists. "A lot of bands," Ronnie asserted, "won't let that steam off, and then they break up—say, 'Fuck you, I can't get along with you,' and leave. Not us. We'll just throw something through a window, raise hell, and knock hell out of each other, and in the morning get up and start all over." ★

Lynyrd Skynyrd onstage in Rotterdam, Holland, 1975. (Photo by Laurens Van Houten/Frank White Photo Agency)

Allen Collins, Gary Rossington, and Steve Gaines at the Rainbow Theatre in London, England, 1977. (Photo by Ian Dickson/Redferns)

CHAPTER 18

Gimme Back My Bullets: The Rebirth of Lynyrd Skynyrd

ITH LONGTIME producer Al Kooper out of the picture, Lynyrd Skynyrd went in the studio in the fall of 1975 to begin work on their fourth album. "When Kooper left, we were in need of a good producer," bassist Leon Wilkeson explained. "Our manager knew Tom Dowd, and we approached him, not really expecting him to go with us." Dowd was a hero to the entire Southern rock community, thanks to his work with the Allman Brothers Band and Derek & the Dominos. Though he was under contract with Atlantic Records, label head Ahmet Ertegun was hoping to lure Lynyrd Skynyrd to Atlantic when their contract was up with MCA, so he was happy to let Dowd work with the band.

The moment they got down to business in the studio with Tom, the band felt rejuvenated. "Wow, man," Allen Collins exclaimed at the time. "It's so good not to have Kooper breathing down your neck all the time. Tom gives you room to breathe. It's so much easier to come up with ideas, and he'll listen to them, too. Kooper wouldn't even piss on nine out of ten suggestions you'd give him."

The band members knew that their previous album had not been up to the quality of their earlier efforts. In response, Ronnie wrote "Gimme Back My Bullets." The bullets referred to were not ammunition but the symbol that *Billboard* magazine used to designate that a song or album was moving quickly up the charts. The lyrics reflected the start of Ronnie's new resolve to refocus and concentrate more on the music than the offstage drama.

The *Gimme Back My Bullets* album was

Producer Tom Dowd. (Courtesy of Fame Studios)

released in February 1976 and featured fan favorites like "Double Trouble" and "All I Can Do Is Write About It." Unfortunately, not every song was a winner, and the album was released to mixed reviews. Critic Ken Barnes, who noted that he was increasingly drawn to Lynyrd Skynyrd because they continued to sound more and more British, wrote, "There's monotony here, but it's the best kind of monotony—a rock band with a powerful, simple style and no frills (subtleties, yes; frills, no) playing on their strengths.

All in all, they've never sounded better."

Some fans, however, complained that the album was more sterile and lacked the greasy charm of their earlier work. Many were disappointed with Ed King's absence, and it turned out that King had been right to be concerned about the band's lack of preparedness with new material. "We were kind of lost," Gary Rossington confessed. "You know, we just did it, because it was time, and they said do it." Though the LP climbed to #20 on the *Billboard* album chart, it was the first Skynyrd release

the drugs, the hard life." But the focus was changing. "Ronnie had been actively pursuing a new road, a tamer one, as he was getting tired of the fighting and destruction, and especially tired of the damages, which was severely curtailing their income."

September of 1976 was a pivotal month for Lynyrd Skynyrd. Gary and Allen were both involved in separate car accidents over Labor Day weekend. Both were taking Quaaludes at the time, and it was not Gary's first brush with death. In response, Ronnie wrote the lyrics to "That Smell," an ominous warning that drug and alcohol abuse will create an aura of death around a person. "We done things only fools'd do," Ronnie admitted. "If you're into drinkin' and tearin' up hotels and blowin' gigs, that's fine. But it'll take years off your life, too. I ain't as old as I look, and there are plenty of false teeth in our group. There's been treatment by doctors and hospitalizations for our drinkin'."

Rock journalists soon realized they were encountering a more reflective Ronnie Van Zant. "When I was drinkin', I didn't give a shit about nothin'," he told *Rolling Stone* in 1976. "But I've quit the hard stuff. I'll have a couple drinks at the bar socially and that's it. I'm just into wine—it's a lot easier on me. I'm really savin' as much as I can for the tour. I know what happened last year."

Journalist Cameron Crowe mused:

> I think there was an ache inside of him about not wanting to be just a bunch of guys who were partying their way through an incredible opportunity, and who threw away everything they made in hotel damages. Instead he wanted to be like the bands he loved, and become a timeless band like the Stones, or Free or the Allman Brothers. He knew there were sacrifices involved in getting to the top, he knew that he had to give up some of the fun in exchange for true longevity as a band, and he was prepared to do it, but he wanted the band to do it too.

Part of broadening their appeal and ensuring their ongoing success was reinforcing the idea that Lynyrd Skynyrd were a great American rock band that just happened to be from the South. Ronnie wanted to remind everyone that their appeal was not regional. By 1975, he'd grown more agitated with the "Southern rock" label. "Really, I can't see no difference between north and south," he insisted, "and I'd like to see this shit about 'southern man' and 'southern this' just thrown away." The band stopped blasting "Dixie" from the loudspeakers before

---

that failed to eventually reach Platinum status.

With four albums and endless months of nonstop touring behind them, Lynyrd Skynyrd had become big stars by 1976, achieving everything they'd set out to do. Even their namesake, Coach Leonard Skinner, was reaping the benefits of their acclaim. "Leonard no longer teaches school," Gary told *Creem* magazine in 1976. "He divorced his wife and got long hair and sideburns and goes out with chicks. You know, we make him real popular."

Although 1975 may have been the year when the trappings of rock-and-roll excess ensnared the band, Ronnie was beginning to grow up. The Torture Tour had taken its toll, and Ronnie knew that if he and the band didn't get their act together they could easily flame out. After getting in fights, Ronnie had been arrested anywhere between five and nine times in 1975 alone (depending on which report is to be believed), and it was getting old fast.

Van Zant began thinking more seriously about his musical future. "I don't even expect to live very long," he admitted in a 1976 *Creem* magazine interview, "because I'm living too fast. . . . I can see an end to Lynyrd Skynyrd. I know I won't be doing this forever. I can't keep on screaming like this

much longer. I've been doing it for almost ten years, and my body can't take the abuse much longer." He knew exactly what musical direction would be best to preserve his voice. "I get into a lot of country music, but the band won't do that sort of stuff," Ronnie admitted. "I'd like to get into the country thing when I'm thirty-three or thirty-four, after I've had as much fun as I can with Lynyrd Skynyrd."

Those closest to him confirmed that Ronnie was more of a country fan than a rocker at heart. "We had every Merle Haggard album there was," Judy Van Zant recalled. "He didn't come home and listen to rock and roll. It was Merle Haggard. Waylon Jennings. Stuff like that." Haggard, whose "Okie from Muskogee" stirred as much controversy in the country world as "Sweet Home Alabama" did in the rock world, was a model for Ronnie. "He might not like me if I met him," Van Zandt speculated, "but Merle Haggard is my favorite songwriter and performer in the whole fucking world."

As Ronnie looked toward the future, a shift began to take place in the band. "They propagated all of the tales," Ron Eckerman related, "the street-fighting, the drinking, they took the stage, and didn't always use the Confederate flag in their live performances.

Seeking to broaden the appeal of the band's sound, they added three female backup singers in 1976. Ronnie dubbed Cassie Gaines, JoJo Billingsley, and Leslie Hawkins "the Honkettes." He was thrilled with what they brought to the band's sound. "Ronnie's so tickled with the idea," writer John Ingham observed, "he can't look at them onstage for fear of laughing."

Even as Ronnie began to get serious and further professionalize the band, there were still plenty of setbacks. He continued to routinely drink too much and let himself get out of hand. Sometimes he would grow impatient that the others weren't immediately on board with his reform plan and let his temper get the best of him. He could be moody, and there was an increase in concert cancellations as he complained about the damage he was doing to his throat.

At a July 1976 stadium show at the Gator Bowl in Jacksonville, Skynyrd was booked to headline a fundraiser for presidential candidate Jimmy Carter. When Ronnie bowed out of the hometown event on the day of the show with complaints of a sore throat, the concert ended in a riot. A crowd of 15,000 people trashed the stadium. "Cancellations had become a real problem," Ron Eckerman admitted. "I never knew when Ronnie was going to cancel, or when we'd get into some other trouble . . . and I never knew if it was really his throat or not, since he had expressed some animosity to some of the cities in which we were scheduled."

Despite the fits and starts, however, the general trajectory of Ronnie's behavior had significantly improved. He had a renewed energy, but it would take the addition of a new band member to add a fresh dose of excitement and focus back into the band. After sitting with the *Gimme Back My Bullets* album, Ronnie knew they needed to recapture the power of the three-guitar army. "The material was good,"

he maintained, "it was just too . . . refined. We decided immediately to do an honest live album with three guitarists, and get back into the thing that had always worked so well."

The only problem was finding a third guitarist who would ease into the mix the way Ed King had. It had been a year since King had departed when they auditioned a long list of potential new players, including Leslie West (from the band Mountain) and ubiquitous session guitarist Wayne Perkins, who'd been a mainstay in Muscle Shoals before going on to work with Bob Marley, Leon Russell, Eric Clapton, and others. Nobody they auditioned seemed to be the right fit.

Honkette Cassie Gaines had a brother, Steve, who played guitar and worked with his own band. "She kept saying, 'Hey, my brother plays guitar,'" Artimus Pyle remembered. "And we'd go, 'Oh really? That's nice.'" Nobody took her very seriously until a show in Kansas City, when the band begrudgingly agreed to let Steve sit in for a couple of songs. "She convinced us to give him a shot," Gary Rossington related. "So he joined us onstage one night, with no rehearsal or anything, and as soon as he started playing, Allen and I looked at each other, and our jaws dropped."

Steve Gaines was working with a band in Oklahoma at the time he got the call to join Skynyrd as the third guitarist. Though he'd played in some moderately successful bands like Detroit (founded by Mitch Ryder following the breakup of Mitch Ryder & the Detroit Wheels), joining Skynyrd was like joining the major leagues. He had to get up to speed quickly. Steve came aboard on May 31, 1976, in Myrtle Beach, just a few weeks before the recording of the live album. Almost immediately, his presence completely altered the group dynamic for the better.

Steve's abilities forced everyone else to step up their game. "He was a freak of nature, he was so good," Gary Rossington said. "He learned from Motown and blues people that we didn't hear. We were British-influenced, so he played different, and we liked that. He was a great singer, and it sort of kicked Ronnie in the ass a little bit. He had to try harder, because Steve was there." Ronnie didn't disagree. "I expect we'll all be in Steve's shadow one day," he told the *Los Angeles Times*. "This kid is a writing and playing fool. He's already scared everybody into playing their best in years."

In July 1976, the band recorded a series of gigs at the Fox Theater in Atlanta for the album that would become *One More from the Road*. Though Steve Gaines was still new and

Steve Gaines (*far right*) completed the second incarnation of the band's three-guitar army. (MCA Records)

didn't stretch out as much as he would in the coming year, the LP captured the electricity of Lynyrd Skynyrd's live sound and became their best-selling album. It reached triple-Platinum status and climbed to #9 on the album chart. The track listing found them ripping through their best songs, culminating with an explosive eleven-and-a-half-minute version of "Freebird."

The following month, Lynyrd Skynyrd played just before the Rolling Stones at the Knebworth Fair in England to an audience of 120,000. It was the biggest concert they had played, and despite their sharing the bill with 10cc, Hot Tuna, Don Harrison Band, Todd Rundgren, and Mick and the boys, *Melody Maker* declared Skynyrd "THE success of the day."

The band did a three-month tour to coincide with the release of the live album in October. While there were certainly shenanigans on the road that would horrify the average group of musicians, for the most part things had calmed down considerably from the Torture Tour days.

In 1977, the band took time off for the month of March and the better part of April to write, record, and relax. When they geared back up to hit the road again, however, they experienced their fair share of incidents. At one gig in Salt Lake City, a knife-wielding audience member climbed onstage during the set and headed for Ronnie. Roadie Gene Odom tackled him. The attacker was arrested, but not before slashing Gene's arm. As for the band's behavior, Leon was sued at least twice when he broke his bass onstage, threw it into the crowd, and struck an audience member.

By 1977, the other members of the band were getting on board with Ronnie's crusade to mold them into a more mature and respectable rock-and-roll force with wide appeal. "I really get tired with this violence thing associated with us," Gary Rossington confessed to journalist Pete Makowski in February of that year. "I mean, we don't go round smashing up things and beating up people for publicity. Sure, we get into trouble, but we ain't as bad as people make us out to be."

In April, the band traveled to Criteria Studios in Miami to begin work on their first studio album since Steve joined the group. They recorded a handful of songs, including "What's Your Name" and one of Steve's originals, "Ain't No Good Life." That summer they returned to Studio One in Doraville, where they completed the bulk of the album by adding overdubs to—or even re-recording—most of the songs from the April ses-

The band poses by their trailer backstage at a California concert in October of 1976. *Left to right:* Artimus Pyle, Gary Rossington, Leon Wilkeson, Ronnie Van Zant, Billy Powell, Allen Collins, and Steve Gaines. (Photo by Michael Ochs Archives/Getty Images)

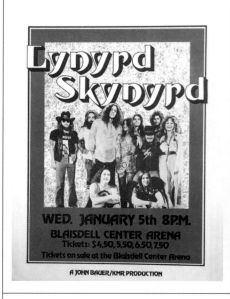

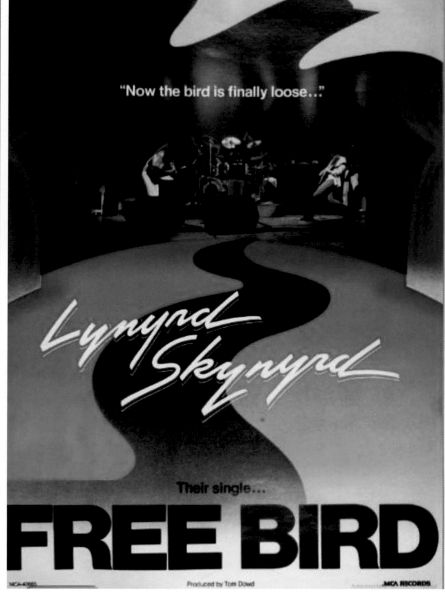

A promotional ad for the single version of "Freebird," as taken from the 1976 LP *One More from the Road*. (Courtesy of Walter Vanderbeken)

sions. In addition, they tackled new tracks like "I Know a Little."

Though Tom Dowd oversaw their work at Criteria, he was unable to make it to the sessions in Doraville. Rodney Mills started producing instead, with Kevin Elson's assistance, while Barry Rudolph, who worked closely with Dowd, served as the engineer. Without an official producer in the room, the band proved that they'd grown to the point where they could try new things on their own, without adult supervision. It was a chance for Ronnie to explore his country side with the recording of Merle Haggard's "Honky Tonk Night Time Man." "I don't think Allen Collins was much into it," recalled engineer Barry Rudolph. "He was pretty much a straight-ahead rock guy." Steve, however, proved adept as a country guitarist. "Sounds like Roy," Ronnie called out on the recording, as Steve launched into his solo. It was a reference to longtime Haggard guitarist Roy Nichols, who was much revered by in-the-know country enthusiasts. "I hope I've created some kind of momentum in the right direction," Steve commented in interview footage that appeared in *Freebird: The Movie*, "on the music side of it I think we're really progressing. That's all I'm lookin' for."

With their sound more in their own control than ever before, Lynyrd Skynyrd had achieved what Ronnie had been hoping for. They were now a versatile group of musicians playing at the top of their game, with an appeal that shattered the barriers of any box in which critics might wish to place them. "Southern rock's a dead label," Van Zant insisted, "a hype thing for the magazines to blow out of proportion. We don't play like the Allmans did, or like Wet Willie. Southern groups are different."

Toward the end of August, the band flew to Los Angeles for photography sessions for the new album cover and promo shots. They gathered at the Universal Studios back lot on a city-scene set to be photographed with flames blazing away all around them. It would prove an appropriate cover for the *Street Survivors* album. "We try to write common songs for what we call the common people, for the street people," Ronnie liked to say. The album cover pictured a ragtag bunch of misfits who'd endured, beaten the odds, and fought their way to the top. The boys from the wrong side of Jacksonville had triumphed.

In September, the band played their biggest headlining show to date when they topped the bill at Anaheim Stadium in Orange County, California, with around 60,000 people showing up to hear Skynyrd, Ted Nugent, and Foreigner. It was the perfect jumpstart for the following month, when they would launch their biggest tour yet—including a headlining slot at Madison Square Garden, scheduled for November.

When *Street Survivors* was released, it climbed to #5 on *Billboard*'s album chart and went on to reach double Platinum status. But not before the band came face-to-face with unspeakable tragedy.

After Peter Rudge took over the band's management, Lynyrd Skynyrd started traveling in their own plane. It was a more effi-

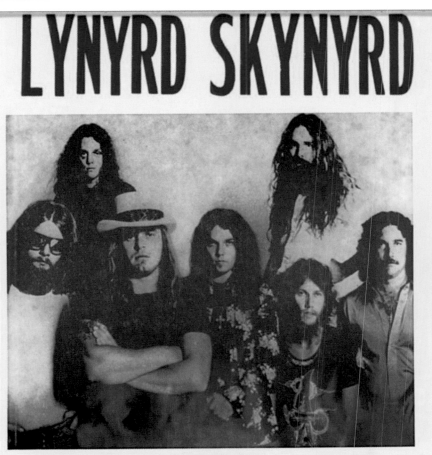

loaded gun mid-flight. When Long retired in 1977, his co-pilot, Walt McCreary, took over. William J. Gray, known as John to the band, came aboard as the new co-pilot.

The *Street Survivors* tour officially launched on October 13, 1977, in Statesboro, Georgia, just two days before the release of the album, and was scheduled to run through February 1 of the following year. After three successful shows in Florida, the band headed to South Carolina for a performance at the Greenville Memorial Auditorium. En route to Greenville, however, a sizeable flame shot from the plane's right engine, giving the band and crew a good scare.

The pilots identified the problem as a faulty magneto in the engine, which was causing it to burn fuel at a rapid rate. The flame had been the result of excess fuel that had ignited, but the issue was not considered serious enough to ground the aircraft. The leasing company agreed to fly a mechanic and a new magneto to Baton Rouge, where the band were scheduled to appear following the show in Greenville. Regardless, Cassie Gaines was so shaken by the experience that she, and perhaps others in the entourage, resolved to either ride in the equipment truck or book a commercial flight to Baton Rouge. But with Ronnie's reassurance that "if it's your time to go, it's your time to go," the band and the crew—twenty-six people in all, including the pilot and co-pilot—boarded the flight for Baton Rouge on October 20th. "She was persuaded," Artimus remembered, "as we all were, to get on board, knowing things were not exactly right. But we were rock and roll." The only person not traveling with them

cient means of transportation, and it helped circumvent some of the delays and hassles that resulted from the band's shenanigans on commercial flights. They leased a converted Convair CV-240 from L&J Leasing in Addison, Texas, that had originally been built as a commercial airliner in 1947. It had been modified to accommodate its use as a means of transportation for rock royalty, and journalist Pete Makowski, who traveled

with them, called it a "nice size machine, equipped with couches and bar, the closest thing to an airborn living room I've seen."

The plane had previously been used by Jerry Lee Lewis, who let it go when he upgraded to a jet. Skynyrd not only got Jerry Lee's plane but also his pilot. Les Long was an experienced professional who was happy to make an exit from his former boss, who had a nasty habit of drunkenly waving around a was JoJo Billingsley, who was home sick and planned to meet up with the group on October 23rd at their Little Rock show.

Roughly two and a half hours after take-off, the pilot contacted Air Traffic Control in Houston, reporting that they were low on fuel and requesting an emergency landing. According to some, the right engine had sputtered to a stop. The pilots knew they could fly safely with just one engine, but they didn't want to take any chances. They were directed to an airfield in McComb, Mississippi, but within moments the left engine, too, ground to a halt. The right engine had been burning fuel more rapidly than anticipated, and the plane had simply run out of gas. The cabin fell silent as it dawned on everyone exactly what was happening.

"Artimus and I raced into the cockpit and saw the pilot was clearly in shock," Billy Powell remembered, years later, in *Mojo* magazine. "His eyes were bugged out with fear, but he managed to tell us all to get back to our seats and make sure everyone was strapped in." Having taken sleeping pills to try to get some rest during the flight, Ronnie was sound asleep on the floor outside the cockpit. The others managed to get him into a seat just as the plane began clipping some trees in a swampy area five miles northeast of Gillsburg, Mississippi. They were only eight miles shy of the McComb airport, but there was no way to make it.

"We hit the trees at approximately 90 mph," Billy Powell continued. "It felt like being hit with baseball bats in a steel garbage can with the lid on. I can't even begin to describe how terrifying it was." The plane blazed a 500-foot-long trail of wreckage through the thick woods. The wings were ripped off, the tail section detached, and the cockpit buckled under, crumpling and causing the fuselage to rip in half. Because there was no fuel left in the wings, there was no fire. Bodies and debris were piled and scattered, with only the sounds of moans and screams breaking the silence of the woods. The sun was setting rapidly, and the woods were already growing dark in the twilight.

"The top of the plane was ripped open," Powell told *Rolling Stone* soon after the accident. "Artimus crawled out the top and said there was a swamp, maybe alligators. I kicked my way out and felt for my hands—they were still there. I felt for my nose, and it wasn't there, it was on the side of my face."

Artimus and two roadies set off through the thick underbrush in search of help. Most everyone else was unable to move. Beloved assistant road manager Dean Kilpatrick's body lay face down with a piece of fuselage twisted through

The revised cover for *Street Survivors* that MCA Records began using following the 1977 crash.

A 1977 publicity photo taken shortly before the plane crash. *Left to right:* Leon Wilkeson, Allen Collins, Ronnie Van Zant, Gary Rossington, Artimus Pyle, Steve Gaines, and Billy Powell. (MCA Records)

his back. The co-pilot's decapitated body hung in a nearby tree. After flagging down local farmer Johnny Mote, Artimus and his companions were able to direct rescuers to the crash site. A helicopter hovered above, illuminating the terrifying and tragic scene. "I remember waking up and hearing people screaming," Gary Rossington recalled in an interview with Rob Hughes. "There were helicopters up there with searchlights and I was hurting real bad, screaming. I had a lot of broken bones and was all screwed up physically."

As rescue workers bulldozed an improvised road through the woods, survivors and bodies were transferred to nearby medical facilities. Of the twenty-six people onboard, nineteen were hospitalized and six were killed, including both pilots, Dean Kilpatrick, siblings Steve and Cassie Gaines, and the heart and soul of Lynyrd Skynyrd, lead singer Ronnie Van Zant.

Though nobody was prepared for it, dying young seemed to be a fate Van Zant himself had accepted. "Ronnie and I were in Tokyo, Japan," Artimus remembered, "and Ronnie told me that he would never live to see thirty . . . the man knew his destiny." Ronnie's father agreed. "Ronnie could see the future," Lacy Van Zant recalled to Jaan Uhelszki. "He told everybody he would not live to be thirty years old. Died at twenty-nine."

Ronnie knew, however, that his hard work had made an impact and he was responsible

for contributing significantly to the legacy of Southern rock. "The last time I saw Ronnie Van Zant alive," Outlaws lead singer Henry Paul remembered, "I was playing a show with him in Winston Salem, North Carolina, and he and I were on the bus drinking whiskey together. He was intoxicated and telling me that he was the Prince of Dixie. I was sitting over there drinking and going, 'Fuck you. What the fuck is the Prince of Dixie?' He said that Duane Allman was the King, and he was the Prince. He had the whole thing figured out."

Following the accident, MCA Records rushed to pull the album from stores. The original cover, which pictured the band surrounded by flames, now seemed inappropriate. Though there was not a fire at the crash site, the image—particularly of Steve Gaines, whose eyes were closed and who appeared to be engulfed in the blaze—was unsettling. The cover was replaced by an alternate shot from the same photo session of the band standing in front of a plain black background.

There was a private funeral service for Ronnie in Jacksonville. Charlie Daniels, Dickey Betts, Al Kooper, and Tom Dowd, plus members of Grinderswitch, the Atlanta Rhythm Section, and 38 Special were there, as were former bandmates Ed King and Bob Burns. Recordings by Merle Haggard and David Allan Coe were played, and Ronnie was laid to rest in a local cemetery where Steve and Cassie were

also buried. Because of their extensive injuries, Billy Powell was the only then-current band member who was able to attend. Allen Collins injured his neck and spine in the crash, while Gary Rossington broke one arm, one leg, and his pelvis, and received puncture wounds to his organs. Leslie Hawkins broke her neck and suffered severe facial damage, which required reconstructive surgery. Leon Wilkeson suffered a punctured lung and came close to having to have both arms amputated.

The aftermath of the wreck plunged many of the remaining members of Lynyrd Skynyrd into profound depression and chaos. Most descended deeper into addiction to cope with the experience. There was survivor's guilt. There was infighting about the legacy of the band. Murky memories and band mythology gave rise to wildly conflicting accounts of what actually happened in the crash. Some maintained that the pilot was drinking, but the autopsies on the pilots found no trace of drugs or alcohol. Some said that Ronnie couldn't be moved to a seat, while others insisted he got to a seat but had no time to strap in. There were reports that Ronnie was thrown from the wreckage and died from a massive head trauma when he hit a tree. Others insisted that he died due to suffocation from bodies and debris piled on top of him in the plane. At least one unlikely version of events put Ronnie in the cockpit beating the pilot mercilessly as the plane descended toward the ground. One band member claimed that Cassie bled to death in his arms, while others insisted that her neck was snapped and she didn't bleed at all.

One of the more persistent claims is that the pilots panicked and accidentally jettisoned the fuel while attempting to transfer it from one engine to the other, but the official National Transportation Safety Board accident investigation report concluded that the fuel cross-feed and dump valves were closed. The NTSB ruled that the likely cause of the crash was "fuel exhaustion and total loss of power on both engines due to crew inattention to the fuel supply." The Safety Board further found that the fuel exhaustion was caused by "deficient flight planning, and an engine malfunction of undetermined nature in the right engine, which resulted in higher than normal fuel consumption."

In the end, the reason why it happened became far less relevant than the implications for the band. "When the crash happened, that was the end of Skynyrd," Allen Collins insisted to the *Los Angeles Times* in 1978. "The band is finished, and that name is finished. . . . That's the way it has to be." ★

Part Five

LONG HAIRED COUNTRY BOYS: WHEN THE DEVIL WENT DOWN TO NASHVILLE

Bob Dylan, Fred Carter, Jr., and Charlie Daniels recording in Nashville's Columbia studio, 1969. (Photo by Michael Ochs Archives/Getty Images)

THOUGH OFTEN ASSOCIATED with country music, Nashville, Tennessee, boasted a vibrant R&B scene as early as the 1940s. A number of independent labels emerged from the city—including Bullet, Dot, and Excello—that helped meet the demands of black record buyers and, eventually, young white kids who were hungry for the blues. Many of the same white session musicians who performed on Nashville's country hits also backed black artists on the city's various independent labels, contributing to a surprisingly integrated recording scene.

Black and white music fans all over the country absorbed the blues and R&B that was broadcast each night over Nashville's powerful 50,000-watt WLAC. Disc jockeys like Gene Nobles, Hoss Allen, and John R. were popular personalities whose hip patter captivated listeners. "It was a most profound culture shock for me many years later," African American journalist and Tennessee native Ron Wynn recalled, "to discover that jocks such as 'Hoss' Allen and 'John R.' weren't gray-haired, big-bellied, African American jocks, but merely good ol' Southern white boys. Back in the late fifties and early sixties, it didn't seem logical or possible—or, for that matter, conceivable—that white guys could have all that soul."

"Ever since those early days,
rock 'n' roll has remained a vital part of Nashville's
youth culture, just the way it has been
a part of so many kids' lives across the country."

—JONATHAN MARX, *THE NASHVILLE SCENE*, 1995

CHAPTER 19
Pledging My Time: Mr. Dylan Goes to Music City

★ ★

 S THE ROCK-AND-ROLL era dawned, Nashville continued to flourish. Artists like Elvis Presley, Roy Orbison, Brenda Lee, and the Everly Brothers made classic recordings in the Tennessee capital. By the late 1950s, what would become known as soul music began to flourish in Music City. Gene Allison's 1957 hit "You Can Make It If You Try" was recorded there, as was Arthur Alexander's "Anna (Go to Him)." Other soul artists who were personally or professionally based in Nashville included Bobby Hebb, best known for his hit "Sunny," Joe Tex, whose "Hold What You've Got" became a pop and R&B hit in 1965, and Joe Simon, who scored big with "The Chokin' Kind" in 1969.

As hit country, soul, and rock-and-roll records emerged from Nashville's studios, young white musicians began forming bands that appealed to the teen club and fraternity crowd. The first serious local rock-and-roll band was the Casuals, a group fronted by Buzz Cason in the mid-1950s that went on to serve as Brenda Lee's backup band at the end of the decade. "Nashville was not a country town in the beginning," Cason told the *Nashville Scene*. "The kids that grew up here, we grew up on Bo Diddley, Joe Turner, LaVern Baker, the Clovers, the Moonglows." In the following years other groups appeared on the scene, including Charlie McCoy & the Escorts. "The Casuals was Nashville's first rock-and-roll band, and the Escorts was Nashville's best rock-and-roll band," laughed guitarist Wayne Moss, who played with both groups. By the mid-1960s, Charlie McCoy & the Escorts were also the most *popular* rock band in Nashville. McCoy

The staff of Nashville's highly influential WLAC radio station, 1968, *left to right*: John "John R" Richbourg, Gene Nobles, Don Whitehead, Bill "Hoss" Allen, and Herman Grizzard. (Courtesy of the Country Music Hall of Fame and Museum, Nashville, Tennessee)

had moved to Tennessee from Florida in 1960 and, by 1962, he and his band operated their own teen club called the Sack in East Nashville.

Thanks to their exceptional instrumental skills, members of the Escorts—including McCoy, Moss, and drummer Kenny Buttrey—soon found work as Nashville studio musicians. They appeared, in various configurations, on classic recordings like "Candy Man" and "Pretty Woman" by Roy Orbison, Charlie Rich's "Mohair Sam," innumerable Elvis Presley movie soundtracks, and, of course, country sessions for artists like Patsy

Cline, George Jones, Dolly Parton, Loretta Lynn, Waylon Jennings, and others.

Wayne Moss opened his own studio, Cinderella Sound, in 1961 and eventually left the Escorts due to his busy schedule as a recording musician. He was replaced by guitarist Mac Gayden, a Nashville native. Whether it was country, rock, or soul, Charlie McCoy and his circle of musical friends were a highly versatile group of behind-the-scenes players in a Nashville music community that was much less homogenized than the public might have thought.

Joe Simon. (Polydor Records)

One of McCoy's more musically eclectic friends was Bob Johnston, a record producer who began his music career in Ft. Worth, Texas, before relocating to New York in the mid-1960s. After a brief stint working for the Kapp label, Johnston moved to Columbia Records, where he produced several artists, including Patti Page, Paul Revere & the Raiders, Simon & Garfunkel, and Bob Dylan. While recording Dylan's *Highway 61 Revisited* album, Johnston invited Charlie McCoy to overdub a guitar on "Desolation Row." Dylan was impressed, and it got Johnston thinking. "I was in the studio in New York with Dylan," he told Edd Hurt in 2012, "and I said, 'Dylan, sometime you gotta come to Nashville. They got great musicians down there. [Columbia executive] Bill Gallagher and a couple more guys were there, and they walked over and they said, 'If you ever mention Dylan and Nashville again, we'll fire you.' And I said, 'Why would you do that?' And they said, 'Because they're a bunch of stupid goddamn people down there, and we don't want that.'"

Johnston returned to Columbia's New York studio with Dylan in the fall of 1965 to begin work on the *Blonde on Blonde* sessions, but the process eventually got bogged down and ground to a frustrating halt. The producer revisited the idea of traveling to Nashville, and against the label's wishes, Dylan agreed. In early 1966, Johnston and Charlie McCoy assembled a crew of Nashville musicians that included, among others, current and former Escorts Wayne Moss, Kenny Buttrey, and Bill Aikins. Robbie Robertson of the Band and Al Kooper, who would later produce Lynyrd Skynyrd, came in from New

York. While Kooper insisted he didn't recall Mac Gayden being there, some of the other musicians confirmed he was present for a few songs. The fact that he was uncredited in the liner notes became a huge frustration for the former Escort throughout his career.

In general, McCoy served as a bridge between the Southern players and Dylan, Robertson, and Kooper. "Charlie was like the quarterback," Gayden explained. "He was the guy who was the mover and shaker. He saw the opportunities and had a good sense of business." As the sessions progressed, it became clear that Bob Johnston's instinct to use Nashville musicians was right on. Their handling of now-classic Dylan material like "Rainy Day Women #12 &35," "I Want You," "Just Like a Woman," "Visions of Johanna," and "Stuck Inside of Mobile with the Memphis Blues Again" was masterful.

"Charlie McCoy blew my mind several times that trip," Kooper recalled in his autobiography, "but my fondest memory was when we were recording 'You Go Your Way and I'll Go Mine.' There was a little figure after each chorus that he wanted to put in on trumpet, but Dylan was not fond of overdubbing. . . . Charlie was already playing bass on the tune. So we started recording, and when that section came up, he picked up a trumpet in his right hand and played the part while he kept the bass going with his left hand without missing a lick in either hand." In a 2013 interview, Kooper added that Dylan was so awed by McCoy's dual-instrument performance that they had to put up a sheet so Bob couldn't see Charlie during the actual take. "Otherwise," Kooper explained, "Dylan would just lose it."

The Nashville contingent that made up the backing band for the *Blonde on Blonde* sessions was comprised of experienced studio musicians who'd played on countless structured sessions that adhered to three-hour time blocks. Unaccustomed to marathon sessions in pursuit of a single song, they found themselves with a good bit of downtime to hang out, play ping-pong, and swap stories in the break area while Dylan tinkered with, and refined, his musical ideas in the main studio. "We could normally go into a three-hour session and turn out a bunch of tunes real fast," Moss recalled. "We got pretty proficient at that. When we were all coffee'd up and ready to go, we ended up spending nine hours at the 'Sad Eyed Lady of the Lowlands' session. It was kind of a 'hurry up and wait' thing on the Dylan recordings." Though the process was different for the Nashville pickers, it was a refreshing change of pace. "I noticed that

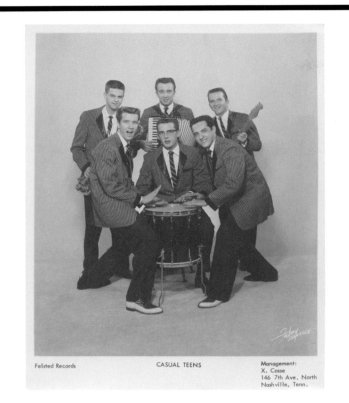

Felsted Records   CASUAL TEENS   Management: X. Cosse 146 7th Ave. North Nashville, Tenn.

Buzz Cason & the Casuals, when they were briefly known as the Casual Teens, 1958. *Left to right:* Joe Watkins, Buzz Cason, Chester Powers, Bill Smith, Johnny McCreery, and Richard Williams. (Felsted Records)

CADENCE RECORDING ARTISTS   Charlie McCoy & The ESCORTS   1511 Stratford Avenue Nashville, Tennessee

Charlie McCoy & the Escorts, featuring Wayne Moss (*upper right*). (Cadence Records)

recording with Dylan was more relaxing and more enjoyable than the usual country things we did," Moss added.

Dylan's approach to the recording process wasn't the only cultural difference the musicians experienced. "The town was like being in a soap bubble," Dylan noted, in his *Chronicles: Volume One*. "They nearly ran Al Kooper, Robbie Robertson, and me out of town for having long hair."

In the studio, the appearance and demeanor of Dylan and his friends was an eye-opening experience for the musicians. "When he came to town we were green as far as the dope culture went," Moss explained. "For one, Dylan looked very strange to us. We were still what you'd call rednecks, and he changed a lot of heads. . . . The new projects that began to spring up in Nashville didn't and couldn't have happened before. . . . All of a sudden it seemed like Nashville was fashionable."

Bob Dylan returned to Nashville to record his next album, 1967's *John Wesley Harding*. Employing a more rustic, stripped-down approach, the LP featured only Charlie McCoy's bass and Kenny Buttrey's drums supporting Dylan's guitar and harmonica. Pedal-steel guitarist Pete Drake was brought in to enhance a few tracks.

In February of 1969, Dylan returned to

Music City once again to record the *Nashville Skyline* album. Charlie McCoy and Kenny Buttrey were back to play bass and drums, respectively. Pete Drake played steel, while Norman Blake, Charlie Daniels, and Bob Wilson rounded out the lineup of Nashville studio musicians. In an attempt to pursue a more overtly country sound, Dylan smoothed the nasal edges from his distinctive singing voice and included a duet with Johnny Cash on the final LP. While Dylan's decision to record *Blonde on Blonde* and *John Wesley Harding* in Nashville upped the city's cool factor among musicians in the know, the title of *Nashville Skyline* shined a brighter spotlight on both the city and the genre of country music. As a significant pop-culture tastemaker, Bob Dylan caused the rock counterculture to reevaluate its perceptions of country music and the South.

"I think the albums Dylan did here did wonders for Nashville in terms of knocking down a bunch of barriers," Mac Gayden reflected. Session ringmaster and Escorts leader Charlie McCoy agreed. "His coming here was one of the biggest things that ever happened to Nashville," he explained. "It opened the door for all these other people to come down—the Byrds, Joan Baez, Buffy Sainte-Marie, and so forth. It was like, 'Hey, if it's OK for Dylan then it must be OK down there.'" ★

CHAPTER 20
Southern Delight:
Area Code 615 and Barefoot Jerry

★ ★

 NE OF THE MANY artists who flocked to Nashville in Bob Dylan's wake was the Monkees' Mike Nesmith. He traveled there in 1968 to record songs for a planned Monkees double album that would spotlight each of the four members' solo explorations. Escorts and Dylan veterans Charlie McCoy, Wayne Moss, and Kenny Buttrey were joined by pedal-steel guitarist Weldon Myrick and former Muscle Shoals sidemen David Briggs and Norbert Putnam for the Nesmith sessions. As had happened with Bob Dylan, the musicians found themselves with considerable free time as they waited in the studio for Nesmith to finish his songs. To pass the hours, they spent time jamming together and working up arrangements of rock songs.

The young Nashville studio musicians enjoyed the rare moments they had to jam together outside the confines of strictly

scheduled recording dates. "We were sittin' around waiting on Mike Nesmith to work on lyrics," Moss remembered. "David Briggs started playing 'Lady Madonna' and singin' X-rated lyrics to it. We had a lot of fun just goofin' around."

Before long, the cream of Nashville's instrumentalist crop was forming into a band that would allow the members to explore beyond the boundaries of the commercial sessions they played each day to make a living. "Area Code 615 evolved out of the Mike Nesmith sessions," Wayne Moss explained. Mac Gayden, who doesn't recall playing the Nesmith sessions himself, soon joined the lineup. "I was only brought into Area Code as kind of like a semi–Neil Young influence to give it some kind of street cred or something," Gayden laughed. "Elliot Mazer, who had done the producing on Linda Ronstadt's *Silk Purse* album [which was recorded at Wayne Moss' Cinderella Sound studio in Nashville], got this idea for a band, and approached Kenny with it. The two of them, actually, kind of produced Area Code 615."

Named in reference to the telephone area code for middle Tennessee, the group landed a recording contract with Polydor Records and released their self-titled debut album in 1969. In addition to Mac Gayden, Wayne Moss, Charlie McCoy, Kenny Buttrey, Bobby Thompson, Norbert Putnam, Weldon Myrick, Buddy Spicher, and David Briggs, the album credited producer Elliot Mazer—who did not play an instrument on the LP—as a member of the band. *Rolling Stone* called the finished product "one of the most enjoyable and stimulating instrumental albums to appear in quite a while."

Given the unique professional situation of the band's members, touring was not a viable option. "We were making a whole lot more money playing sessions than we would out promoting a record," Wayne Moss recalled. "They sent a guy down from the William Morris Agency in New York. He said, 'How many dates a year do you guys want to work?' We all said 'none' in unison. He said, 'Well, that's a wrap.' He told the label, 'You need to drop those guys. They're never going to amount to anything.' And that's when we cut a Grammy-nominated album."

Their follow-up album, the Grammy-nominated *Trip in the Country*, was released in 1971. "We knew the importance of what we were doing," Gayden said of their increased profile as musicians, "because it was scaring the crap out of the main people here in the music business. They did everything they could behind the scenes to undercut what we were doing. The labels didn't want us to have any power

AREA CODE 615

- ▸ CHARLIE MCCOY harmonica, vocals
- ▸ WAYNE MOSS guitar, bass
- ▸ MAC GAYDEN guitar, vocals
- ▸ KENNY BUTTREY drums
- ▸ BOBBY THOMPSON banjo, guitar
- ▸ NORBERT PUTNAM bass
- ▸ WELDON MYRICK pedal steel guitar
- ▸ BUDDY SPICHER violin
- ▸ DAVID BRIGGS piano

whatsoever. There's a lot of territorial stuff that happens in Nashville."

The only live concert that Area Code 615 ever played was an appearance at Bill Graham's Fillmore West in San Francisco. "Linda Ronstadt introduced us to the Bay Area crowd," Gayden explained. "She sang about three or four songs with us, and then we played with Country Joe & the Fish and Sons of Champlin. Area Code was off the charts. We didn't rehearse together. We didn't have time with everybody's schedule. There's nine people in the band! So we just said, 'Everybody rehearse the songs as they are on the album, and when we get to California we'll just go through them briefly in soundcheck.' And that's what we did. The music we played that night was unrehearsed, but it was almost to-the-letter perfect."

Despite making an appearance on *The Johnny Cash Show*, Area Code 615 simply weren't able to sustain a high profile that would result in significant album sales. "We weren't dedicated enough to devote our lives to playing live," Moss confessed. "I think we could have probably done a lot of things we didn't do, and made our way to the top real fast. It takes dedication on the part of everyone involved, and we didn't really have that. We had it from a musical standpoint, as far as making records were concerned, but not from the standpoint of devoting your life to something."

But there was more than scheduling and personal commitment behind the breakup of Area Code 615. In truth, the musical tastes—and personal tastes—of the band members were not always aligned. "We weren't a jam band," Gayden explained.

I tried to get 'em to jam more, but they wouldn't. Those guys were such sticklers for knowing every note that they're gonna play. There was also a cultural difference. Several of us had started using cannabis, and that drove a wedge between those of us who were doing that and those

that weren't. In those days, it was the alcohol people against the cannabis people, and there was no in between. I went places where, actually, the marijuana people would not allow anyone with a beer to even come in the room. It was that distinct of a line drawn. It wasn't that way down in Macon, Georgia. They didn't see the difference, but we did up here, for some reason. That's just the way it was. I was one of those to step over the line and they didn't like it. Charlie McCoy was put out by that a little bit. It kinda just took the legs out of one of the best bands that was ever assembled here in Nashville.

Following the breakup of Area Code 615, Wayne Moss, Mac Gayden, and Kenny Buttrey recruited keyboardist John Harris, a practicing medical doctor, and began jamming together. "John was always a huge fan of Charlie McCoy and the Escorts," Gayden explained. "We knew he played some piano, but we didn't know how good he was or anything. . . . We started hanging out and playing. He had a spontaneous, almost spiritual, abstract kind of playing that you can't teach."

Before long they'd put together an official group. "For three years I lived in a place called Townsend, Tennessee," Gayden continued, "which is in the Smoky Mountains. Right next door to my cabin was a little store called Barefoot Jerry's Grocery. You could go in there sometimes and he would skiffle dance for you and play his fiddle and sing.

One day I was back in Nashville, jamming around with the guys, and we did a forty-six-minute nonstop jam. I went back to the mountains, and I thought, 'I'm going to ask Barefoot Jerry if he'll let us use his name.'"

Gayden served as the main songwriter and vocalist, while Moss was the group's producer. They set up shop in Moss' Cinderella Sound studio to begin work on the debut release. "We went crazy cutting the greatest album the world had ever heard," Moss recalled, "giving very little thought to ever having to play it live with just four guys."

At first, Barefoot Jerry was going to be a five-man operation, including Charlie McCoy. But though he seemed like an obvious fit, McCoy quit after recording only one selection, "Hospitality Song," the lead track on the debut LP. According to band lore, the others slipped Charlie some marijuana-laced fudge, and he wasn't pleased. Charlie, who was still accustomed to working quickly, didn't care for the band's approach to the process, either. "We spent eleven studio hours doing the first cut of the first album and nearly drove McCoy crazy," Moss recalled. "He said, 'I love you guys, but I don't like to make records this way.'"

The group completed the remainder of the sessions as a four-piece, and the album, *Southern Delight*, was released in 1971 on Capitol Records. "Many groups play country music," Moss explained at the time, "but with us it is different. Country music we know, because we have all worked in Nashville for years, but we originally come from all over,

Barefoot Jerry, in the mid-1970s, before a show at Tennessee Tech University in Cookeville, Tennessee. *Left to right:* WSMT DJ John Powell, Russ Hicks, Si Edwards, Wayne Moss, and Terry Dearmore (front), Warren Hartman, and Jim Colvard. (Courtesy of John Powell)

A mid-1970s publicity photo of Barefoot Jerry, *left to right:* Si Edwards, Jim Colvard, Wayne Moss, Terry Dearmore, Russ Hicks, and Warren Hartman.

BAREFOOT JERRY

- WAYNE MOSS guitar, keyboards, bass, multi-instrumentalist, vocals
- MAC GAYDEN guitar, vocals
- KENNY BUTTREY drums
- JOHN HARRIS keyboards
- CHARLIE MCCOY keyboards, harmonica
- RUSS HICKS guitar, pedal steel guitar, horns, vocals
- KENNY MALONE drums
- BOBBY THOMPSON bass, guitar
- FRED NEWELL banjo, harmonica, vocals
- DAVE DORAN guitar, bass, vocals
- BUDDY SKIPPER keyboards
- SI EDWARDS percussion
- TERRY DEARMORE guitar, bass, vocals
- JIM COLVARD guitar, bass
- WARREN HARTMAN keyboards
- BUDDY SPICHER violin
- DALE SELLERS guitar
- BARRY CHANCE guitar
- STEVE DAVIS keyboards, guitar, vocals
- MIKE MCBRIDE guitar, percussion, mandolin
- BUDDY BLACKMON banjo

and we brought with us our rock and blues influences." Though the members of Barefoot Jerry continued to play studio dates as backing musicians, their embrace of musical exploration was accompanied by growing out their hair and adopting the hippie persona. While Area Code 615 had been a step beyond the old ways of doing things, Barefoot Jerry was a giant leap. Things were changing in Nashville, as Gayden recalled:

I was on a session one time, and I was stoned. I remember a couple of beer cans being thrown at me from across the studio. They were just trying to make a point, you know. It was weird. There wasn't any violence or anything going on between the two factions, but definitely a vibe going on.

We were looking to break some boundaries. In Nashville at that time, we were maybe five years behind California, in terms of cultural changes. Some of us in the band were kind of where California was, and that just didn't go down good with a lot of people, you know. It was like a tidal wave hit Nashville, and the residual effect of Dylan coming several years before just took time to hit. The main song on our first album was "The Minstrel Be Free at Last." That was about session players breaking out of the studio.

The *Southern Delight* album wasn't a big seller, as Barefoot Jerry were plagued by the same problem that had led to the collapse of Area Code 615. "The band just didn't want to tour," Moss explained. Not surprisingly, Cap-itol Records dropped the group. Kenny Buttrey departed to play drums with Neil Young's band, and Gayden departed soon after.

Wayne Moss and John Harris stuck with it, with Moss covering the lead-guitar slot vacated by Gayden while continuing to play bass on the recordings. They recruited Russ Hicks to play steel guitar and Kenny Malone to replace Kenny Buttrey on drums. From that point on, Barefoot Jerry would become a revolving door of Nashville's finest studio musicians, with Moss the only constant member. "Barefoot Jerry personnel is whoever I say it is at a given time," Moss laughed.

In May of 1972, Barefoot Jerry began work on their second album. Released on Warner Bros. Records, the self-titled LP was recorded at Moss' Cinderella Sound facility, with Moss and John Harris co-producing. Additional side musicians appeared on the album, including Bobby Thompson and Buddy Spicher, both of whom had been members of Area Code 615.

By the time Barefoot Jerry's 1974 album *Watchin' TV* was released, the band had moved on to yet another label, Monument Records, and experienced further lineup changes. Though they didn't tour extensively, they did play regional gigs, and it was becoming increasingly difficult to replicate their sound live. Without additional personnel, it wouldn't be feasible to perform their material in front of an audience. Bobby Thompson, who was a guest player on the previous album, joined as the newest member of Barefoot Jerry. Dave Doran—who'd been a member of the group Moby Grape—took over the lead-guitar spot, while Fred Newell became the new bassist. As with previous albums, however, most band members served as multi-instrumentalists for the recording process.

Before the album was complete, John Harris departed to concentrate on his medical practice, and was replaced by Buddy Skipper on keyboards. Drummer Kenny Malone left soon after, and was replaced by Si Edwards on drums and percussion. By the time the LP was released, Dave Doran had also departed, to be replaced by Jim Colvard, who'd been a member of the Nashville Guitar Group on the Monument label.

The following year, Monument released *You Can't Get off with Your Shoes On*, featuring the lineup of Moss, Hicks, Thompson, Newell, Skipper, Edwards, and Colvard, with the addition of new member Terry Dearmore. Dearmore became the official lead singer. "We decided that we needed a lead singer, even if he couldn't play," Moss explained. "We were known for our musical abilities but not our singing talents. I don't fantasize myself to be a singer at all—a songwriter, maybe—and we had a lot of insecurities about our live singing."

Charlie McCoy appeared as a guest musician on harmonica, flute, piano, and vocals. When Skipper departed during the sessions, he was replaced by Warren Hartman. And when Fred Newall departed the group, Dearmore took over the bass duties on the live shows.

Barefoot Jerry's music was topical and socially conscious. Several songs extolled the virtues of marijuana, which was controversial for a group of Nashville pickers. "We don't lay a lot of heavy messages on the people," Moss said of the band's style at the time. "Rather, we try and indicate what they might be missing.

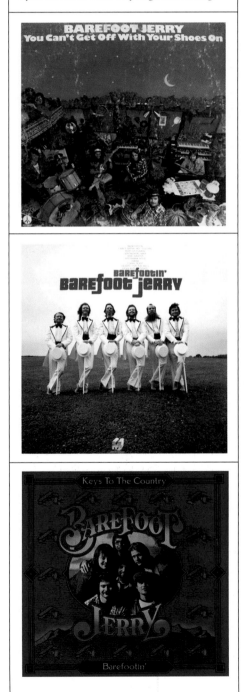

A lot of folks miss out on nature. The tremendous progressive strides we've made are killing the countryside. The mass transit of highways is eliminating the fields with folks taking the speed limits to the level where you couldn't enjoy the scenery if your life depended on it. 'Slowin' Down' is about that."

The following year, Monument released *Keys to the Country*, which featured a similar lineup to the previous album. Before the recording was completed, Colvard departed, and was replaced by Barry Chance, son of longtime *Grand Ole Opry* bassist Lightnin' Chance, who played bass and guitar. Around the same time, Hartman left, and was replaced by Steve Davis on keyboards. The formula was beginning to grow stale, and *Keys to the Country* was not one of the better Barefoot Jerry albums. Tragically, Colvard took his own life that same year. It was beginning to feel like Barefoot Jerry were stalling out.

"We don't get offered a lot of gigs outside the state," Wayne Moss explained at the time. "The companies bit their nails over our dope songs, and just want us to stick to ballads or the social comment.... The papers never give us coverage. *Rolling Stone* won't touch us, and we've done no TV in two years. There's too much business and not enough music in American rock companies. Unless you have an aggressive image or an aggressive label, you stay put."

Though various configurations of Barefoot Jerry released independent albums for decades, their final major-label release was 1977's *Barefootin'*. After the lackluster *Keys to the Country*, the album was a refreshing return to form. Dearmore left and was replaced by bassist Mike McBride. Steve Davis also left, with banjoist Buddy Blackmon taking his place. Charlie McCoy finally joined as an official member of Barefoot Jerry, bringing the band full circle.

"You would put us in the Southern rock genre," Wayne Moore affirmed years later, "but we went in a lot of different directions than the Allman Brothers or Marshall Tucker. You would know them on the radio if you heard them, but our music was so diverse. If you tried to compare a song like 'Two Mile Pike' with 'Only Time for Love,' it just didn't fit at all. We were going in so many different directions, but our income as session players gave us the money and the freedom to pursue what we wanted. It helped a lot that, when we went through the budget the label gave us, we'd just keep going until we were happy. I owned the studio, and as long as we were going to shoot for excellence, we figured, we'd go for it." ★

BLACK AND WHITE: TONY JOE WHITE
—

WHEN SOULFUL SOUTHERN troubadour Tony Joe White appeared in Nashville in late 1966, his signature blend of R&B, country, and rock—"swamp music," he called it—contributed to the winds of change that had begun stirring in the country-music capital with the arrival of Bob Dylan just a few months prior. Unlike Dylan, White was a product of the region, and served as a link between the bayou, Nashville, Muscle Shoals, Macon, Memphis, and the early stirrings of what would blossom into the Southern rock movement.

Tony Joe White was raised on a cotton farm in the swamps of northeast Louisiana. The youngest of seven siblings in a musical family heavily rooted in white gospel and country sounds, Tony Joe enjoyed a personal artistic awakening in his teen years. "When I was about fifteen, my brother brought home an album by Lightnin' Hopkins," he recalled. "That introduced me to the blues, and I started sneaking my dad's guitar into my bedroom at night, and started learning the blues licks."

White soon discovered that his peers were drawn to the same music. "Me and the rest of the river kids, as I called 'em, listened to the blues at house parties," he remembered. "Then came Elvis, and that changed it around again. Elvis was kind of bluesy, but he was white." Before long it was Tony Joe, accompanied by a drummer, who was providing the entertainment at house party gatherings.

After graduating high school, White began playing clubs, and eventually landed steady work in Corpus Christi, Texas. He played cover songs by Lightnin' Hopkins, Elvis, and others before penning his own tunes. "When I heard 'Ode to Billy Joe' by Bobbie Gentry on the radio," he recounted, "I said, 'Man, how *real* that is!' I thought to myself that if I ever write anything I'm gonna try to write about something I know. Well, I knew about rainy nights in Georgia and I knew about polk salad, so I started writing down the truth."

By 1966, Tony Joe had amassed a pile of original songs and saved up enough money to travel to Memphis to try to work his way into the music business. "When I got to Memphis," he explained, "I just kept on going toward Nashville. I don't know why. The car kind of veered right on 40 East, almost on its own. I said to myself, 'Man, why are you headed up there? The worst place you could go with your music is Nashville, Tennessee. That's a country and western place!'"

While in town, White managed to get a meeting with Bob Beckham, who ran Combine Music, the publishing arm of Monument Records. Beckham, who nurtured the careers of Kris Kristofferson, Dolly Parton, and others, had a reputation as an open-minded supporter of songwriters. "I had no idea where this guy was going to fit," Bob later recalled to Ben Edmonds about the black-sounding Tony Joe, "but I sure liked what he was doing." White signed with Monument and released a single, "Georgia Pines," in early 1967.

White returned to Corpus Christi, but he was back in Tennessee in 1968 to record his first album. The sessions were produced by fellow songwriter Billy Swan in Nashville with some of the early Muscle Shoals musicians—Norbert Putnam, David Briggs, and Jerry Carrigan—who'd relocated to the Music City by that time. "They were having to play a lot of country sessions just to make a living," White explained, "so I was almost like a relief sent in to 'em. All of a sudden they could get down, get funky, and let it go."

When Tony Joe White's debut album, *Black and White*, was released in 1969, the label issued two unsuccessful singles. The third, "Polk Salad Annie," then slowly began to gain traction throughout the Southeast. "'Polk' hadn't really clicked yet," he recalled, "but it was getting a lot of play, and Phil Walden had heard it down in Geor-

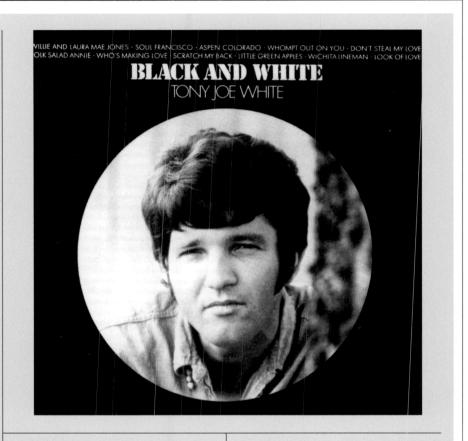

gia. Phil flew to Corpus Christi and he said, 'Man let's hook up and let me see if I can get this thing pushed.' That's when the tours began, the rock music began. He had me on tour with people like Sly & the Family Stone, or playing at the Isle of Wight. He got me in some really big spots."

Thanks in part to Walden's managerial assistance, "Polk Salad Annie" became a Top 10 single and established Tony Joe White as a master of blue-eyed soul. In turn, White turned Walden on to the band Eric Quincy Tate. "They played in some of the same clubs I played in at that time in Corpus Christi, and we all became good friends," Tony Joe recounted. "I was glad the world was gonna get to hear some of the stuff I'd been hearing them do down there since I'd been in Texas." Walden landed the band a deal with Atlantic's Cotillion label, and White co-produced the first album.

Tony Joe's second album, partially recorded in Memphis, included "Rainy Night in Georgia," which found its way to Brook Benton and became a major hit for the R&B singer in 1970. After White cut a third LP for Monument, Phil Walden orchestrated his move to Warner Bros.,

where he released a handful of critically acclaimed LPs in the 1970s.

Following his stint with Warner Bros., White continued to record for a variety of labels, including Arista, Casablanca, and Columbia. Though he never had another hit as big as "Polk Salad Annie," his songs were recorded by a long list of luminaries, including Ray Charles, Dusty Springfield, Elvis Presley, Waylon Jennings, Jerry Lee Lewis, Hank Williams, Jr., Tina Turner, and Etta James.

In launching White's professional career from Nashville, he and Bob Beckham did much to shake up the spirit of the city's music industry. "Beckham's studio and his office was filled with people like Kristofferson and Chris Gantry and long-haired boys," Tony Joe recalled. "You could see the people changing a good bit. Donnie Fritts, up from Muscle Shoals; Spooner Oldham. It was a hang-out for all the late-nighters, the little-bit-different types, and those of us that didn't so much fit into the Nashville system."

By operating outside that system, Tony Joe White played a crucial role in connecting the dots between the country music business, the Muscle Shoals sound, mainstream R&B, Phil Walden, and Nashville's emerging Southern rock sensibilities.

(GAB Archive/Redferns/ Getty Images)

CHAPTER 21
Uneasy Riders:
The Charlie Daniels Band

★ ★

 N ADDITION TO paving the way for Area Code 615 and Barefoot Jerry, Bob Dylan's arrival in Nashville helped bolster the career of Charlie Daniels. Daniels, who is today a member of the *Grand Ole Opry* and widely regarded as a country singer, was a leading Southern rock champion in the 1970s who transformed himself from a bar-band guitarist and studio musician to an elder statesman of the Southern rock movement.

Born in Wilmington, North Carolina, in 1936, Charles Edward Daniels was an only child whose father worked in the timber industry. "Work back then was hard to come by," he recalled, "so we moved around a bit when I was younger." Charlie and his family spent time in a handful of locations in Georgia and the Carolinas. He learned to make friends in the various working-class communities of the South, and developed a warm and friendly personality. "I come from a blue-collar background," he explained to *American Cowboy* magazine in 1994. "When I think about things, I think about them in the vernacular, in a way. All of my people were farmers, timber people, that sort of thing."

Like many budding musicians, Charlie grew up listening to the *Grand Ole Opry* on Saturday nights. "I can't begin to tell you what an impact the *Grand Ole Opry* had on the rural southeast," he wrote in his book *The Devil Went Down to Georgia: Stories*. "650 WSM came booming down our way all the way from Nashville, Tennessee, sounding for all the world like a local station." Charlie first picked up a guitar as a teenager while hanging out at his friend Rus-

CHARLIE DANIELS BAND

- CHARLIE DANIELS vocals, guitar, fiddle, mandolin, banjo, multi-instrumentalist
- "TAZ" DIGREGORIO keyboards, vocals
- JERRY CORBITT guitar
- BILLY COX bass
- JEFFREY MYER drums, percussion
- EARL GRIGSBY bass
- FRED EDWARDS drums
- BUDDY DAVIS drums
- MARK FITZGERALD bass
- BARRY BARNES guitar
- GARY ALLEN drums
- TOM CRAIN guitar
- DON MURRAY drums
- CHARLIE HAYWARD bass
- JAMES MARSHALL drums

sell Palmer's house. "He casually pulled out a Stella guitar," Charlie remembered, "and proceeded to play about two and a half chords. Well, I immediately went crazy. I had had a secret desire to play a guitar almost all my life." Charlie soon began learning to play mandolin, and he and Russell joined forces with a friend named Joe Phillips, who played the banjo. They dubbed themselves the Misty Mountain Boys and started playing local gigs.

Soon after graduating from high school, Charlie took a factory job, but he continued to

pursue his music. The Misty Mountain Boys landed a weekly half-hour radio show at 6:30 on Saturday mornings and picked up a handful of gigs playing at square dances. By this point, Daniels had taught himself to play the fiddle, in addition to the mandolin and guitar. When Charlie's parents moved yet again, however, he said goodbye to the Misty Mountain Boys and followed his family back to their hometown of Wilmington, North Carolina.

"I started playing with a lady named Little Jill," he recalled of his return to Wilmington. "She paid me $50 a week, which was good money back then. It was the first time I considered myself a real, professional musician." By the mid-1950s, rock and roll had captured Charlie's attention, so when Little Jill eventually left the band, Charlie developed the group into a guitar-driven outfit called the Rockets. "I basically started out playing beer joints," he confirmed. "There was hardly any place to play in Wilmington because they didn't have open bars. They had two or three beer bars, but there was just not that kind of nightlife going on, except for the one place up in Jacksonville, North Carolina. That was the home of the 2nd Marine Division. Those guys were out there partying until they ran out of money, so we started working there six nights a week."

After a couple of years, Charlie decided to dedicate himself exclusively to the music, as he revealed in an interview with Ron Johnson:

> I was working a day job with my father at the Taylor Colquitt Creosoting Company, and around 1958, I think it was, they had some layoffs. There was a fella there, Louis Frost, who had been there longer than me,

The Charlie Daniels Band in 1974, as shown inside the *Fire on the Mountain* LP. *Left to right*: Mark Fitzgerald, Taz DiGregorio, Charlie Daniels, Freddie Edwards, Gary Allen, and Barry Barnes. (Kama Sutra Records)

and because he was black, you see, he was chosen to be let go. Well, he had a family to feed and I had my music, so I went to the foreman and offered to go if he'd let Louis stay on. He was fine with that arrangement, so Louis stayed on until he retired. Anyway, that's when I made the jump to being a full time musician.

By the end of the 1950s, the Rockets were touring a circuit of US cities. A chance meeting in

Texas on one such trip opened the door for the group to make a record of their own.

When I played in Jacksonville, I met a guy by the name of Bill Belcher who was from Ft. Worth. We became good friends. When he got out of the marine corps he went back to Texas. Well, I was taking my first trip to play some dates out in California in 1959, and our route took us through Ft. Worth. We said, "We'll just stop and

see Bill." Well, Bill knew Bob Johnston, who was working at Bell Helicopter and trying to get something going, recordwise. Bob said, "You guys want to go in the studio and cut something?" I said, "We don't have anything to cut." He said, "Well, let's write something." So we did. We wrote an instrumental called "Jaguar" and went in and recorded it.

Epic Records released the "Jaguar" single

The classic lineup of the Charlie Daniels Band, as pictured on the back of the *Nightrider* LP. *Left to right*: Don Murray, Taz DiGregorio, Charlie Hayward, Freddie Edwards, Tommy Crain, and Charlie Daniels. (Epic Records)

but wanted to change the name of the band to match the song title. "The Rockets became the Jaguars," Charlie laughed. With one foot in the door of the music industry, Daniels continued on as a working musician while honing his songwriting skills. In 1964, Elvis Presley recorded "It Hurts Me," which was co-written by Charlie and Bob Johnston. "It was by far the biggest thing that had ever happened to me in my life," Daniels said.

After spending the better part of a decade slogging it out with the Rockets and the Jaguars—including an extended stay in Washington, D.C.—Daniels was ready for a change of pace. "I went to Nashville in 1967," he recalled. "I had been on the road for a long time, and was not really getting anywhere. Bob Johnston . . . had taken over Columbia [Records] in Nashville. He asked me if I wanted to come down."

Because of his relationship with Johnston, Daniels was invited to be a part of Bob Dylan's *Nashville Skyline* sessions. "I was lookin' for that withdrawn, surly sort of person you hear about," Charlie confessed, of his first experience recording with Bob Dylan, "but he was fun to work with." Like the future Area Code 615 and Barefoot Jerry personnel who played with Dylan, Charlie cited that period as a turning point in both his own—and Nashville's—creative development. "I didn't fit in so well until Bob Dylan came to town," he remarked.

In addition to his work on *Nashville Skyline*, Daniels would also go on to play on Dylan's controversial *Self Portrait* album, as well as the *New Morning* LP. "I felt I had a lot

in common with Charlie," Dylan noted, in his memoir. "The kind of phrases he'd use, his sense of humor, his relationship to work, his tolerance for certain things. . . . When Charlie was around, something good would usually come out of the sessions."

By the end of the 1960s, Daniels began working on the other side of the studio glass. "The Youngbloods were looking for a producer, and they had called Bob Johnston," Charlie recalled. "He had a full agenda, so he said, 'I don't have time to do it, but I've got a guy that works with me here that's got time if you'd like to talk to him.' I flew out to L.A. and went to RCA studios. We sat down and talked, and decided to give it a shot."

The Youngbloods' folk-rock-flavored *Elephant Mountain* LP, produced by "Charles E. Daniels," was released in 1969 to favorable reviews. As the 1970s dawned, Charlie contin-

ued to cement his reputation as a fine session musician for the left-of-center projects that were cropping up more frequently for Nashville's best players. He worked on Al Kooper's *Easy Does It* album in 1970, and appeared as a guitarist on Ringo Starr's *Beaucoup of Blues* LP the following year.

Charlie returned to work with the Youngbloods once again on their 1971 live album *Ride the Wind*. It was partially recorded at a music festival in Baton Rouge, Louisiana, where Charlie was inspired to write "Uneasy Rider," which would become his first Top 10 single. "All the San Francisco bands were there," Charlie recounted, "the Grateful Dead and the Jefferson Airplane and all these people. . . . A lot of 'em were really terrified about being in the South. I think they'd seen this movie [*Easy Rider*]. They were afraid if they stopped at a 7-Eleven store somebody's gonna run out with a pair of shears and cut their hair or something. . . . I thought it was a funny attitude to have, and I think that's where the song came from."

By the time "Uneasy Rider" became a hit in 1973, Charlie had already gone through several incarnations of his band and recorded three albums as a solo artist. Working with Jerry Corbitt—who had been a member of the Youngbloods, but left the group before Charlie began working with them—led to Daniels' own artist career. Corbitt, like his old bandmates, was looking for a producer, Charlie recalled:

He had talked to the guys in the Youngbloods, his friends. They said, "We've got this guy Charlie Daniels we're really enjoying working with." He said, "Let's talk," so we did, and I ended up doing a record on him. He was on Capitol, and we had gone down to Capitol in L.A. to play some of our songs for the powers that be there. Jerry's manager said, "Charlie, why don't you play them some of your songs?" I had a backlog of stuff I'd written, so I

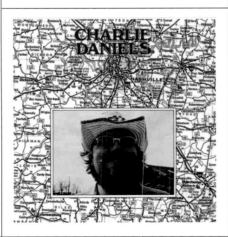

Charlie Daniels at an autograph signing session in New Haven, Connecticut. (Courtesy Carl Lender)

acclaim, however, the album failed to catch on. "It was a well-kept secret, actually," Daniels laughed, years later.

Moving to Kama Sutra Records, Charlie released *Te John, Grease, & Wolfman* in 1972, which featured a new lineup of the Charlie Daniels Band. Taz DiGregorio and Jeffrey Meyer played keyboards and drums respectively, while Earl Grigsby handled bass guitar duties. Though the album was again credited to Charlie solo, the title referred to the band members' nicknames. "Charlie loves to give people nicknames," DiGregorio explained to Michael Buffalo Smith. "That was one of those Southern rock cultural things." Bassist Earl Grigsby was "Te John," drummer Jeffrey Meyer was "Wolfman," and keyboardist Taz DiGregorio was dubbed "Grease" for his greasy hair.

The *Te John, Grease & Wolfman* album was originally intended to be a collaboration with Jerry Corbitt as Corbitt & Daniels, but while the band were on tour in 1970, opening for Delaney & Bonnie at Carnegie Hall, Jerry Corbitt abruptly departed. "I am not sure what happened, but something happened with Corbitt and he quit the band," DiGregorio recalled. "Charlie was really very upset.... The contracts had been signed, and the money had been put up, and Corbitt quit."

When *Te John, Grease & Wolfman* debuted, the label released "Great Big Bunches of Love" as a single. It failed to make a dent on the national charts. Drummer Jeffrey Meyer departed, and was replaced by Buddy Davis and Freddie Edwards, who provided the dual-drummer lineup that the Allman Brothers Band had popularized in Southern rock circles.

Charlie and his band soon returned to the studio to record the *Honey in the Rock* album, released in May of 1973. The group then spent nearly a year on the road promoting the LP. Their efforts paid off when "Uneasy Rider" climbed to #9 on the *Billboard* pop chart. While touring that year, the Charlie Daniels Band often shared the bill with other up-and-coming Southern rock performers with whom they formed lasting friendships. "We met the Marshall Tucker Band for the first time in Kansas," Freddie Edwards recalled. "We kicked ass. Then it was time for Tucker. Wow. After they played, it became a new era for us. They wanted to tour with us because they liked us so much. So we did thirty days with them, back-to-back... Tommy and Toy Caldwell were always hanging out with Charlie and David Corlew, our road manager, so we all partied every night."

Despite the success, bassist Earl Grigsby departed. He was replaced by Billy Cox, Jimi Hendrix's old bassist, who was in the origi-

picked up a guitar and played some songs. They signed me on the spot.

Though his self-titled debut was billed as a solo record, Charlie began putting together the original incarnation of the Charlie Daniels Band around the same time. The first recruit was Joel "Taz" DiGregorio, who had played with Charlie in the latter days of the Jaguars, following a stint with Paul Chaplain & His Emeralds (best known for the 1959 hit "Shortnin' Bread"). "I came to Nashville," DiGregorio told interviewer Bronson Herrmuth, "and he was in the studio with Leonard Cohen. I didn't even know who Leonard Cohen was. I had just got out of the army, and the whole

world had changed. I hadn't been in the United States in eighteen months and everything had changed. Everybody had long hair and they were acting strange."

"Basically," he continued, "the original band was Charlie, Jerry Corbitt from the Youngbloods, Billy Cox from Band of Gypsys, and Jeffrey Meyer and myself. That band did not stay together but about six months, then it just dissolved." By the time the album came out, the band had already splintered. *Rolling Stone*, in its glowing review, said Charlie's voice was "a synthesis of the lechery of Levon Helm and the sensuality of Van Morrison. Put 'em all together, they spell an excellent album of Southern badass rock and roll." Despite the

nal version of the Charlie Daniels Band. The group began work on the follow-up album, *Way Down Yonder*, but both Billy Cox and drummer Buddy Davis left the group before it was completed. The Charlie Daniels Band lineup was reconfigured yet again with Barry Barnes on guitar, Barry's friend Gary Allen joining Freddie Edwards to complete the dual-drummer configuration, bassist Mark Fitzgerald replacing Billy Cox, and the ever-faithful Taz DiGregorio on keyboards. "We rehearsed six hours a day until we were ready to go on the road," Edwards recalled.

Though *Way Down Yonder* was not a commercial success, the Charlie Daniels Band hit their stride in 1974 when they recorded the landmark *Fire on the Mountain* LP in Macon, Georgia. The album's producer, Paul Hornsby, had recently made an arrangement with the Capricorn label to produce outside acts that were not signed to Walden's label. "In August, I went in with the Marshall Tucker Band and cut *Where We All Belong*," Hornsby recalled, "one of the biggest albums of my career. And following on its heels was *Fire on the Mountain* with Charlie Daniels. Being that I was not exclusive, I could produce anybody I damn wanted to. Charlie Daniels was my first outside act."

Macon had exactly the vibe Charlie was looking for. "Capricorn is made to accommodate a band instead of a band accommodate it," Daniels remarked to the *Lyon County Reporter* in 1976. "You can walk in off the street and play there, and the damn engineer don't get mad at you, 'cause you got your amp over 2 ½. They don't pull their hair out 'cause we got two drummers. . . . It's just relaxed. When you walk out of the studio you're through with show business. You go drink some beer in a redneck bar or something. It's a trusting atmosphere, a good atmosphere to make a record."

When *Fire on the Mountain* was released, in November of 1974, it was credited to the

Charlie Daniels Band. "I am a band-type person," Daniels explained. "I always have been, and I just thought that's the way it should be." The album included the classics "The South's Gonna Do It Again" and "Long Haired Country Boy." The former entered the Top 30 on the pop chart, while the latter, which featured dobro work by Dickey Betts, became a rock-radio classic. "I just wanted to write a song in tribute to my friends," Charlie recalled. "They were all from the South, and they're all playing, and we were playin' together, and we were all cookin' and kickin'."

The final two tracks on the *Fire on the Mountain* LP were recorded live on October 4, 1974, and gave birth to an annual concert event known as the Volunteer Jam. Daniels explained:

> We wanted to do "Orange Blossom Special" and "No Place to Go" in front of a live audience. We did it in Nashville. It was supposed to be a one-time thing. I casually invited some of my friends to come up and play with us. Three members of the Marshall Tucker Band came that first year. Dickey Betts was in town, and he came. It just took on a life of its own. We moved from a 2,200-seat hall to a 13,000-seat hall the next year. It was a

unique show at that time because there were no other things like that.

Named in reference to Tennessee's designation as the "Volunteer State," the second Volunteer Jam was held in 1975 at Middle Tennessee State University in Murfreesboro, Tennessee. The Charlie Daniels Band were riding high on the success of the *Fire on the Mountain* LP, and Charlie accepted his first Gold record onstage that evening. The album would eventually be certified Platinum. Capricorn released a live LP from the show that included performances by the Charlie Daniels Band, Chuck Leavell, the Marshall Tucker Band, Wet Willie's Jimmy Hall, and Dickey Betts. The performance was also captured on film, and was released theatrically.

Starting in 1977, the Volunteer Jam took place every January, featuring an array of guest artists, including Wet Willie, Willie Nelson, the Marshall Tucker Band, Rufus Thomas, James Brown, and many others. "The jams were always a good time, as well as a time for seeing other musicians," Grinderswitch's Dru Lombar recalled, in an interview with the online magazine *Road to Jacksonville*. "When you're on the road, sometimes you don't see anyone but the guys you work with. The Southern music circle was a pretty tight-knit group. Everybody

Publicity photo from the Million Mile Reflections Tour, 1979. *Left to right*: Jim Marshall, Fred Edwards, Charlie Hayward, Charlie Daniels, Taz DiGregorio, and Tommy Crain. (Epic Records, courtesy of CDB, Inc.)

was friendly with each other. The Jam gave us a chance to visit and catch up on each other's lives. I miss that the most, the brotherhood."

Charlie Daniels emerged as a colorful spokesman, ringleader, and unifying force of the Southern rock community, thanks to the success of the Volunteer Jam concerts and the *Fire on the Mountain* LP. One of the more memorable tracks on the album was the ready-made Southern rock anthem "The South's Gonna Do It Again," which name-checked Grinderswitch, the Marshall Tucker Band, Lynyrd Skynyrd, Dickey Betts, Elvin Bishop, ZZ Top, Wet Willie, and Barefoot Jerry.

Because Charlie was slightly older than some of the others—and because he was eager to encourage the talents of others—his fellow musicians looked up to him as a friend and mentor. He appeared on countless albums by other artists and truly believed in the community aspect of the genre. "The whole Southern rock thing was a brotherhood," Taz DiGregorio explained, "a family."

In 1976, Charlie Daniels left the Kama Sutra label and signed a substantial $3 million contract with Epic Records. The future held promise, but Charlie found himself having to reorganize his band yet again. Guitarist Barry Barnes, drummer Gary Allen, and bassist Mark Fitzgerald departed, leaving only DiGregorio and Edwards.

Nashville native Tommy Crain, who was buddies with Barefoot Jerry founder Mac Gayden, played in a local group called Flat Creek with his brother Billy. Flat Creek's road manager, David Corlew, went on to work as the road manager for the Charlie Daniels Band when Flat Creek broke up. Following that group's demise, Tommy formed a band called Buckeye that, thanks to the connection with Corlew, functioned as the opening act at the inaugural Volunteer Jam. "I actually played the first musical note of any Volunteer Jam ever, because it started with a guitar riff," Tommy explained. "I had met Charlie that night, and he told me that he was losing both his guitar player and drummer, and asked me if I would be interested. . . . I told him that I was still playing with my brother Billy, and I didn't want to leave him. . . . One year later, we played at another Volunteer Jam, and at that time my band had broken up. He asked me again, and I gladly accepted." Tommy's brother Billy went on to play with Bobby Whitlock, of Derek & the Dominos fame, before joining the Henry Paul Band. He then went on to work with the Bellamy Brothers for the better part of a decade.

With guitarist Tommy Crain in place, the Charlie Daniels Band added Don Murray on

drums and Charlie Hayward on bass. Hayward had been a part of the Tuscaloosa group that formed Sundown in Macon before going on to tour with Alex Taylor and Dr. John. By the time Chuck Leavell joined the Allman Brothers Band, Hayward had returned to his hometown of Tuscaloosa, where he played in a local band for fraternity parties and club gigs. "I joined Charlie Daniels' band in March of 1975," Hayward recalled. "I came in the house and my mom said some guy named Charlie Daniels had called. I didn't have any idea who he was, but

Paul Hornsby had recommended me to him. Charlie told me about the *Fire on the Mountain* album. Here I am trying to learn this song 'Cabal Diablo.' Talk about a learnin' curve!" Hayward met up with Daniels at a local show and was immediately hired. "I went from this band in Tuscaloosa, playing clubs," he recalled, "to playing 10,000-seat halls. It was intimidating, but also kind of exciting."

With the classic lineup of Taz DiGregorio, Fred Edwards, Charlie Hayward, Tommy Crain, and Don Murray, the Charlie Dan-

iels Band released four albums in a two-year period between November of 1975 and October of 1977. *Nightrider*, *Saddle Tramp*, *High Lonesome*, and *Midnight Wind* were all produced by Paul Hornsby. Thanks to their chosen producer and recording venue, the Charlie Daniels Band became a central part of the scene in Macon, Georgia. All four albums sold well, with *Saddle Tramp* and *Midnight Wind* earning Gold Records. Epic also rereleased the 1974 *Way Down Yonder* album as *Whiskey* in 1977.

Hayward recalled:

> Charlie had a real work ethic. When we would work on albums, we would go in a rehearsal hall for six or seven hours a day and work on the same couple of songs over and over and over to get them really tight. The first four albums I did with him, we would do that, and then all load up and go down to Macon to record at Capricorn. We would have all the stuff down to a T. We'd be down there recording, and then when we'd get done with it, we'd go back to touring. And we were probably doing 250 dates a year.

By that period, the Charlie Daniels Band were part of the upper echelon of Southern rock royalty. "Charlie had that really strong camaraderie with Toy and Tommy Caldwell, and with Dickey Betts, and with Ronnie Van Zant," Charlie Hayward explained. "I think it was that we were all a bunch of guys that wasn't gonna get great success because of great looks or anything. But we had worked hard our whole lives and been in clubs and spent all that time grindin' it out doin' four sets a night. Once you've done that, and then gotten to the level of playin' these huge venues, there was just a shared experience."

Community was important to Daniels, and he made it a priority to be a positive presence in the Southern rock culture, while fostering a family atmosphere in his professional organization. "People don't take pride in their work," he observed in 1976. "You can't blame 'em, because they're considered like machines—they're numbers. Somebody comes in and punches the time card. The boss don't know what the fuck they look like and don't care. Don't know their wife's first name or anything. And that's just not the way it is with us. . . . It's more important to me to have a happy band, have a happy organization, people that are *really* into what they're doing and *know* they've got a future here."

Daniels' paternal impulses engendered loyalty from the band. "Charlie was kind of like a

Tommy Crain, Charlie Daniels, and Charlie Hayward onstage at Austin City Limits (PBS)

father figure to us," Hayward explained. "He started calmin' down in the late '70s. We were all under the influence of stuff, but he never fired us or gave up on us. He knew we were committed to him musically." The rest of the band members felt the same way. "As far as the writing goes," Tommy Crain told Michael Buffalo Smith, "we would go out to Charlie's and put all our ideas together and start rehearsing, and this would all gel and get put together. He would give us 50 percent, and he took the other 50 percent. And this was so nice of him, because he wrote most of the stuff, and we all just added to it. He was super cool to let everyone be a part of the music. That was really big of him, and there is no other man like him alive."

By the latter part of the 1970s, Charlie was increasingly identified as both a rock artist and a country artist. "I've been called a hillbilly in a derogatory manner," he complained to journalist Joe Nick Patoski in 1976, "and a dumb rebel and all that bullshit from people who think ladies from the South still wear hoop dresses." Despite the caricaturing of his persona, Charlie did not fit the prevailing country mold of the day. "There was very little country about us at that time," he recalled, of the band's early years. "We were doing stuff that probably could have been called country music *today*, but would certainly have not have fit in at that time."

Though *Honey in the Rock* and *Fire on the Mountain* had appeared on *Billboard*'s pop album chart, 1975's *Nightrider* was the first Charlie Daniels Band release to appear on the country rankings. The later *Nightrider*, *Saddle Tramp*, *High Lonesome*, and *Midnight Wind*

LPs all charted on both the country and mainstream *Billboard* rankings, but each charted higher in the country category, marking a shift in the band's identity, from Southern rock to country. It wasn't so much that the Charlie Daniels Band had changed. Instead, the Charlie Daniels Band were helping to change the definition of country music.

The Charlie Daniels Band reached their pinnacle in 1979 with the international pop and country smash hit "The Devil Went Down to Georgia," which appeared on the band's *Million Mile Reflections* LP. Tommy Crain recalled the album's recording sessions:

> We had cut our last track, and then Charlie's eyes got real wide and he said to Taz and I, "Boys, we don't have a fiddle song on this album. We have to have a fiddle song." Then he asked Taz and I to come out into the studio room, and he said that he had this idea about the Devil and this kid having a fiddling contest. I immediately came up with the beginning lick, and Taz and I and Charlie sat down, and we put the music together in about thirty minutes. We went home that night, and overnight Charlie had written the lyrics out, and he came in and we recorded it the next day. And then won a Grammy award for it.

Charlie and the band appeared in the film *Urban Cowboy*, and "The Devil Went Down to Georgia" was included on the hit soundtrack. "*Urban Cowboy* was probably the biggest and best thing that ever happened to the Char-

An early 1980s publicity photo. *Left to right*: Tommy Crain, Fred Edwards, Taz DiGregorio, Charlie Hayward, and Charlie Daniels. (Epic Records)

lie Daniels Band," Taz DiGregorio explained to Bronson Herrmuth. "I mean, 'Devil Went Down to Georgia' was doing OK, but when the movie came out—even though the movie wasn't a blockbuster—it took this song all over the world." In the US, "The Devil Went Down to Georgia" reached #1 on the country chart and #3 on the pop rankings. The *Million Mile Reflections* album went triple Platinum.

By the time *Million Mile Reflections* hit the stores, Freddie Edwards' friend Jim Marshall had replaced Don Murray as the second drummer. The slightly altered lineup continued to find success as the 1980s dawned. The 1980 *Full Moon* LP and 1982 *Windows* album were certified Platinum and Gold, respectively, and produced hit singles including "In America" and "Still in Saigon." The latter, an insightful exploration of post-traumatic stress faced by returning soldiers, failed to chart on the country rankings, but reached #22 on the mainstream *Billboard* chart. The second single from Windows, "Ragin' Cajun" stalled at #109 on the pop listings. It was the Charlie Daniels Band's last charting rock release. They would appear on the country singles rankings more than twenty times in the next twenty years, solidifying the group's transition—in perception, if not as dramatically in sound—into a country band. The quadruple Platinum *A Decade of Hits* compilation from 1983 marked the conclusion of the band's Southern rock era and the birth of their second phase as country hit-makers.

In February of 1980, Charlie was hospitalized after his sleeve was caught in a piece of equipment on his farm. He broke his right arm in five places, which required surgery and a hospital stay of a week. The accident caused

Charlie to renew his Christian faith. Taking stock of his life, he became serious about eternity, morality, and the preservation of conservative values. In some ways, this shift in worldview was more compatible with country audiences than with the spirit of rock and roll. "I am very opinionated and will make no bones about it, and have no qualms speaking about the way I feel about things," Charlie explained to *Gritz* magazine in 2003.

Starting in 2000, Charlie launched a "Soapbox" section on his website, as a forum to sound off on politics, culture, faith, and freedom. Often controversial, Daniels has become known for his outspoken musings as much as his music. In 2006, the First Amendment Center at Nashville's progressively oriented Vanderbilt University awarded Charlie their annual "Spirit of Americana" Free Speech Award.

Though Daniels is happy to share his blunt cultural assessments—his 2003 book *Ain't No Rag: Freedom, Family, and the Flag* was a popular collection of his philosophies—he has always prided himself, first and foremost, on being a solid performer with a strong band that doesn't care to draw boundaries around music. "Somebody once asked me if my music was country or bluegrass or rock," he recalled. "I said, 'Yeah.' It's all of those. I don't believe in strongly categorizing music. What difference does it make? Just let it breathe; let it be." Like his old friend Bob Dylan, Charlie Daniels ultimately became a spokesman, whether purposefully or not, for his musical genre. "I don't see myself as an influence or having a certain image to live up to," he insisted. "I am just an entertainer that goes and plays shows and makes records and tries to entertain people." ★

I CAN'T HELP IT: THE WINTERS BROTHERS BAND
—

BROTHERS DONNIE AND Dennis Winters moved to Tennessee as young children when their father, Don, relocated the family from Miami. "Dad came to Nashville to get into country music," Donnie recalled. Don eventually hit #10 on the *Billboard* country chart with his single "Too Many Times" in 1961. Soon after, Marty Robbins hired him as a singer. "Growing up backstage at the *Grand Ole Opry* in the late '50s and '60s influenced us a lot," Donnie explained. "Marty [Robbins] was like an uncle to my brother Dennis and me."

Despite their love for country music, the Winters brothers' ears were attuned to new sounds. "Barefoot Jerry started before Charlie Daniels," Donnie recalled, "so we started seeing more and more rock-type music coming out of Nashville. We started going out and seeing more shows, local acts. There was the Gentrys, who were real big, and Charlie McCoy was a family friend."

With Jack Pruett and Bruce Campbell joining Dennis and Donnie on bass and drums, respectively, the Winters Brothers Band booked club dates and started building up a reputation in the region. Around that time, Charlie Daniels was just beginning to break through to national prominence, following the release of *Fire on the Mountain*. "My dad told Charlie about us and actually set up an appointment for us to go visit with him and his wife," Donnie explained. "We had a meeting, and we asked Charlie if he'd produce an album or a demo on us or something to help us get where we were really wanting to go." Because he was already over-committed, Charlie connected the boys with his keyboard player, Taz DiGregorio.

"About the time that Taz started working with us," Donnie recounted, "Charlie Daniels' band was working on their *Nightrider* album. They were auditioning musicians, and Don Murray, who actually played on *Nightrider*, came down and brought his best friend, Gene Watson. Gene auditioned for the gig with Charlie, but he was a little too funk and jazz oriented for what Charlie was looking for. Taz turned us on to Gene Watson, and it was like he just blew us all away." Gene came aboard to replace Jack Pruett, while Otis Harris was recruited to replace Bruce Campbell on drums.

Thanks largely to Taz's influence, the Winters Brothers Band soon adopted a second drummer, Steve DellaVecchia, and added keyboardist Terry Huff. It was a short-lived lineup. "We had pictures taken with Steve and Terry Huff," Donnie recalled, "but then Terry and Steve wanted an equal cut of the money. My brother and myself had other ideas. We let them go." Still in need of a keyboard player, Spig Davis was hired to round out the five-man lineup.

In 1976, Capricorn executive Dick Wooley established Rabbit Records, the Macon-based label that signed the band Grinderswitch. Rabbit's second signing was the Winters Brothers Band. They recorded a self-titled album for the label that was released through Atlantic's Atco imprint. Co-produced by Taz DiGregorio and engineer Sam Whiteside at Capricorn Studios, the LP featured Charlie Daniels on fiddle. The first single, "Sang Her Love Songs," garnered regional attention, and afforded the band the opportunity to open shows for a who's who of Southern rock royalty, including Lynyrd Skynyrd, the Allman Brothers Band, the Marshall Tucker Band, Wet Willie, and many others.

The Winters Brothers Band signed a deal with Phil Walden's Paragon Agency at the

Publicity photo of the Winters Brothers Band. *Left to right:* Donnie Winters, Terry Huff, Dennis Winters, Steve Della Vecchia, Kent "Otis" Harris, and Gene Watson. (Rabbit Records)

start of 1977. The following year, Donnie recalled, they began work on another album:

Taz was going to produce, but we couldn't get back into Macon, because Marshall Tucker was in the studio doing an album. Our record label president, Dick Wooley, got a deal at Bayshore recording studio in Miami, which was right down the street from Criteria. Bayshore was the studio the Eagles did *Long Run* in. We went down there and spent ten days to two weeks, and things got crazy. Taz had just come in off the road and he still wasn't wound down or serious about wanting to do the album with us. He was old friends with the engineer, so they were sittin' back there, smokin' pot and tellin' jokes and shit, while we were trying to work.

We let Taz go, but the management made us fire Otis, too. Otis didn't have any reason to be fired. He didn't do nothing wrong. The worst thing about Otis was that he was overweight, and he wasn't "commercially appealing," but he was a great musician and a great guy. It still breaks my heart. But we had no choice.

Otis was replaced by drummer Bill Connell, who'd played with both the 5 Men-Its and the Allman Joys. After rehearsals, the band headed to Macon to work with Paul Hornsby on what was to be their second album, *Coast to Coast*. "It came off really great," Donnie recalled, "but the Atco/Atlantic Records guys came down and they had a listen to the final mixes, and they said that they didn't hear any hits. That kind of left us in limbo. Dick Wooley tried to shop it to

a couple of other places to no avail, and it never got released."

After that, the band began to unravel. "We tried, but we had gotten in on the tail end of the Southern rock movement anyway," Donnie lamented. "We had worked some clubs that had mechanical bulls, and when we got back, those clubs had either turned into punk clubs or disco clubs. We watched it all change right before our eyes."

Younger brother Dennis concurred. "When the Southern rock scene started to fade, work dropped off dramatically," he told Michael Buffalo Smith. "We had to pay the bills, so we went to work doing what we could in order to take care of our families. Donnie got into construction, and I started driving tractor trailers and buses for Waylon Jennings, the Oak Ridge Boys, and others."

A promotional poster for a Charlie Daniels Band concert featuring the Winters Brothers Band, 1977.

WINTERS BROTHERS

- ‣ DONNIE WINTERS guitar, vocals
- ‣ DENNIS WINTERS guitar, vocals
- ‣ JACK PRUETT bass
- ‣ BRUCE CAMPBELL drums
- ‣ GENE WATSON bass
- ‣ KENT "OTIS" HARRIS drums
- ‣ STEVE DELLAVECCHIA drums
- ‣ TERRY HUFF keyboards
- ‣ DAVID "SPIG" DAVIS keyboards
- ‣ BILL CONNELL drums
- ‣ BOB TUCCILLO drums
- ‣ BOBBY MILLER drums

CHAPTER 22
Family Tradition: The Southern Rock Rebirth of Hank Williams, Jr.

★ ★

 N DECEMBER 1975, MGM Records released *Hank Williams, Jr. and Friends*, an LP that *Rolling Stone* called "one of the very finest country-rock albums to emanate from either side of that hyphen." Though the label had issued at least twenty-five albums by Hank, Jr., since 1964, *Friends*, as Hank called the project, represented a significant turning point. Recorded in Muscle Shoals and Macon—with guest musicians including Toy Caldwell, Chuck Leavell, and Charlie Daniels—the album showcased Hank's growing Southern rock sensibilities, and helped set the stage—along with Charlie Daniels' records—for mainstream country music's wholehearted embrace of Southern rock.

When Hank Williams, Sr. died at the age of twenty-nine on New Year's Day 1953, he left behind a powerful country music legacy. Though the elder Hank's marriage to his first wife Audrey was a tumultuous relationship that ended in divorce, she became the driving force behind the preservation of his legacy, and she carefully groomed their young son, Randall Hank Williams, to continue the family tradition. By the time he was eight years old, Randall had been dubbed Hank, Jr., and was performing his father's songs in concert, wearing miniaturized replicas of his dad's stage suits. "I became a part of that legend," Hank explained, in his memoirs. "I grew up surrounded by the myth, and I accepted my place in it. . . . I knew that I would never grow up to be a cowboy or a fireman or the president of the United States. I knew I'd grow up to be a singer."

Though the stage may have been his destiny, Hank was indifferent. "I had *no* hunger for it,"

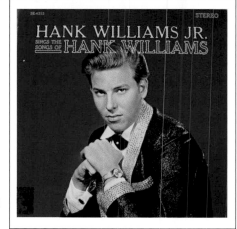

he confessed. "I mean, come on, I'm eight years old. I don't know what the hell I'm doing. I'm out there with my hands in my pockets with my little suit and my crew cut, with at least ten hillbillies on the show. Then, everybody's looking at me, and they're breaking into this hysterical cry. That will have a hell of an effect an eight-, nine-, or ten-year-old kid."

By the time Hank turned eleven, he was performing on the *Grand Ole Opry*. By sixteen, his highly driven mother had secured him a recording contract with MGM Records, the same label that helped make his father a star. "My mother was a complex, troubled woman," Hank reflected in his 1979 autobiography, "and more than anything else, she believed in the glamour of the country music business." Audrey pushed hard, and her efforts to mold Hank into what was predominantly a tribute act proved successful. Between the mid-1960s and mid-1970s, Hank, Jr., enjoyed seventeen Top 20 country singles.

Deep down, however, Hank Williams, Jr., felt an alternate musical identity that was scratching to get out. From his youngest years, he was more interested in listening to rock and roll than country music. "I was sleeping up in the back of these Oldsmobiles and Cadillacs, where the speakers used to be up in the back window," he recalled of his early days on the road. "They were playing the radio. I said, 'I don't want to hear the *Grand Ole Opry*. I wanna hear WLAC. I wanna hear John R. I wanna hear Bobby Blue Bland. I wanna hear John Lee Hooker.'"

Like his father, Williams was drawn to black music. It was an African American street musician named Rufus "Tee-Tot" Payne who taught the elder Hank to play guitar. "If it hadn't have been for Tee-Tot," Williams mused, "then maybe there's no Hank, Sr. He was the one giving my daddy the lessons." Hank, Jr., didn't see a need to draw racial distinctions any more than his father did. "Country music has always had a debt to the blues, to black music, that country has never wanted to acknowledge," he wrote. "The real guts of country, the real guts of Daddy's music, I think, came from that black tradition, both blues and gospel. But by the early 1970s, the country music establishment had succeeded in scouring country music of any black influence—can't take a chance on confusing country with rock and roll, they said."

Unbound by categories, Hank, Jr., worked at teaching himself to play several instruments. "I practiced those rock-and-roll licks," he recalled, "and I worked at singing those rock-and-roll songs—to myself, to my friends. If I'd gone onstage and sung 'Roll Over Beethoven,'

An early publicity photo of Hank Williams, Jr., and his band. (MGM Records)

I was convinced that my fans would have lynched me, right then and there."

Thanks to his family legacy, however, Williams had the opportunity to pick up pointers from many of the musicians he admired. "You had Elvis, Ray Charles, Fats Domino, Jerry Lee. They all had records of Daddy's songs," Hank pointed out. "So, guess what? They're gonna stop in at 4916 Franklin Road when they're in Nashville, and they're gonna see Audrey Williams, and they wanted to see Hank Williams' piano. And then, 'Oh, who's this little kid over here?' So there I am, and I've got Fats Domino at my house, for God's sake, when I was growing up. Jerry Lee Lewis. These people gave me pointers. They became my teachers." Inspired to make music for himself, Hank formed a teen combo called Rockin' Randall & the Rockets. "I'd go out on the road and be Hank Williams, Jr., and come back home and be Rockin' Randall," he recalled. "That's how I would do it—two worlds."

After years of playing the part his mother scripted for him, Hank began looking toward the future. "It sometimes bugs me that I'm so associated so strongly with my father," he confessed to a *Rolling Stone* reporter in late 1973. He wanted to make his own mark. Hank's ears were open, and he was drawn to the growing influence of Southern rock. "There was a new sound coming out of the South," he explained. "It came from people like Charlie Daniels and the Allman Brothers Band, and it owed a debt to

not only country but to blues as well.... Most people in Nashville went to great lengths to ignore this new voice from the South, but the first time I heard it, my ears perked up.... I could feel, even through the haze I was living in, that a fusion between rock and country music was not only possible, it was inevitable."

By the mid-1970s, Hank—like his father before him—was haunted by the demons of depression and substance abuse. Much of it was born from the feeling that his music was not his own artistic expression. Ultimately, Williams chose to step away from that pressure. "I looked up from my stupor long enough to get a reading on my music," he recalled, "and the bulk of it was shit, plain and simple. I'd been doing the same act for so long that I didn't really give a damn about it one way or the other, and the audience was catching on real fast."

Beset by personal troubles, and in desperate need of a change, Hank packed up his belongings and left Nashville for rural Alabama. Following a half-hearted attempt at suicide, he decided to put his career on the line and fully incorporate Southern rock sounds into his country material.

I wanted to do a special album of my own music, done my own way. It would be totally different from anything I'd ever done before.... Instead of the same old Nashville pickers who'd worked on every

one of my albums since Day One, I'd use Southern rock people.

I began talking to Phil Walden, the president of Capricorn Records, in Macon, Georgia ... and he arranged the introductions between me and the Brothers and the Tuckers. For whatever reason, the words "Hank Williams" will open the door to anyone. It could be the biggest English rock band in the world. I don't give a fuck who it is. The bottom line is, the door is open because of that name. Of course, if it's Dickey Betts or Toy Caldwell, it was, "Hell yeah, let's get in there." It didn't take them long to realize, "Hey, wait a minute! This kid can spank the plank. Him and Billy Gibbons were born under the same star."

Hank included two of Toy Caldwell's songs, "Can't You See" and "Losin' You," on his *Hank Williams, Jr. & Friends* LP. His vocals were recorded in Muscle Shoals, but the tracks were laid down both in Muscle Shoals and at the Capricorn studio in Macon. The album was completed in July of 1975. Hank attended the annual Capricorn Records picnic that summer, and was fully embraced by the Southern rock community. Williams and his new friends shared a common approach to music-making.

"The bottom line of the Southern rock thing is, we *play*," Hank explained. "We don't stand there and hold the mic like fucking Frank Sinatra. We write and play music from our soul.... The ones that inspired me were Dickey Betts and Toy Caldwell. I was listening to Goose Creek Symphony and Black Oak Arkansas, and of course Skynyrd. Those are the ones where I thought, 'I'm going to show them that I can do this.'"

Feeling like his life and his art were getting back on track, Hank—an avid outdoorsman—headed for Montana in August for some rest and relaxation, prior to introducing the world to the new and improved Hank Williams, Jr. While in Montana, he was hiking through a snow bank on Ajax Peak when he lost his footing and plummeted nearly 500 feet. By the time he landed, his skull was split open, and his face was virtually destroyed. Hank would spend months receiving multiple surgeries, healing through a slow and painful process of physical therapy, and relearning to speak and sing. In an effort to mask the scarring and disfiguration that resulted from the accident, he adopted a new look. For decades to come, Hank Williams, Jr., would be recognized by his trademark beard, sunglasses, and cowboy hat.

Given the dramatic circumstances of the experience, some observers attributed the brush with death to the change in Hank's style. "They say one guy went up the mountain, and another one went down," Hank explained. "That's a bunch of shit. What was so awful about it is that the musical change had already started. I was feeling good, and going down the home stretch. And then, I'm laying up there wondering how I can ever sing again with my face crushed, my jaw wired shut, and no teeth on the top or the bottom."

Hank Williams, Jr. & Friends was finally released in December of 1975. "FM progressive-rock stations picked up the album," Hank recalled, "and the cut they played the most often was 'Can't You See.' It was a first—a hard country artist like me making *any* inroads into that FM market." Despite prompting the rock audience's interest in a mainstream country artist, the album was not a major financial success. Hank urged MGM to release "Can't You See" as a single for the country market, but the label refused. With Hank's blessing, Waylon Jennings recorded his own version of the song for RCA, and it climbed to #4 on the country singles chart.

Displeased with his change of direction, MGM dropped Hank, Jr. from the roster. He soon landed at Elektra Records, and his debut for the label, *One Night Stands*, continued to marry the sounds of country and Southern rock. Hank did not consider it one of his better albums. The follow up, *The New South*, was co-produced by Waylon Jennings, and was a much more energetic effort. "I wanted to show my fans—what fans I still had left—that I was

An early-1980s Elektra/Asylum Records publicity photo.

getting ready to come out of the woods," Hank recalled, "and come out rocking."

The attempt to win traditional country fans to the Southern rock sound wasn't always easy. "I hit a few obstacles," Hank laughed. "They'd say, 'He's crazy!' 'He's nuts!' 'Why is he hanging out with those guys?' There I was, playing 'La Grange' standing on the piano at the Grand Ole Opry House. Roy Acuff was about to croak!"

Although Hank received personal fulfillment from doing *his* music *his* way, the new sound was not immediately embraced. Perhaps getting nervous, the label pushed him to try some music that fell outside the Southern rock sounds he'd grown to love. "They've got me in Wally Heider Studios in California," he recalled, "and they got me singing these disco-sounding songs like [Jackson Browne's] 'You Love the Thunder.' I said, 'Fuck this.' 'You Love the Thunder,' my fucking ass. I just couldn't stand it. I went to the airport and got the red eye and went back to Muscle Shoals."

Hank had no interest in recording music for which he had no passion. "*The New South* was a chance, and it was a good album," he wrote in his autobiography. "It didn't take off and make me a superstar overnight again. You can hash over the reasons for that until you're blue in the face, but what it comes down to is that there

really isn't a reason, except that change takes time. And it's scary. I've got to do what I've got to do. And I know that, in the end, I'll find that audience that appreciates just me. I'm prepared to wait."

He didn't have to wait long. Following the release of his book, Hank enjoyed two major country hits at the close of 1979 when "Family Tradition" and "Whiskey Bent and Hell Bound" made it to the Top 5. It was the start of a serious winning streak for Williams, who released eighteen studio albums from 1979 through 1992, all of which were certified Gold or Platinum. Starting in 1980, with the hit "Old Habits," every song Hank released as a single for the next six years became a Top 10 hit, with eight of them hitting the #1 position.

By the late 1980s, Hank was a country-music superstar. The country audience had embraced the Southern rock legacy that he incorporated into his music, and, thanks in large part to Williams' influence, most country fans were fans of Southern rock. "At first," Hank reflected, "it was, 'Oh, God. Why are you doing that? You're crazy.' Then we started to have some success, and those obstacles disappeared. Then, all of a sudden, the music industry people are saying, 'Oh, we're behind you 100 percent.' Believe me, I know how to recognize bullshit." ★

151

Part Six

HOLLER AND SHOUT: THE ODYSSEY OF PHIL WALDEN AND CAPRICORN RECORDS, PART TWO

THE ORIGIN OF the term "Southern rock" can be traced to Mo Slotin, who wrote for an underground newspaper in Atlanta called the *Great Speckled Bird*. Capricorn publicist Mike Hyland recalled:

> He coined the phrase "Southern rock" in the paper. Frank Hughes, who had a little management company and booking agency in Atlanta, had these little pins made up that said, "Support Southern Rock." He gave me one of 'em. I was wearing it at Capricorn, and they said, "What's that all about?" I told 'em about Moe and this whole bit. Before you know it, Capricorn had their own buttons that said, "Capricorn Records Supports Southern Rock." It became a movement, basically. It became, like, a marketing tool. We didn't even know what marketing was back then, we were just throwing shit out and hoping it worked. So, with that, we became a genre.

Spencer Kirkpatrick, who was a member of the Atlanta-based band Hydra, remembered the details differently. "We were sending out stuff on our postage from Frank Hughes' agency that booked us," he explained. "The slogan was 'Support Southern *Music*.' All of a sudden, the folks in Macon kind of pirated our little logo there. The way that our agency was using it, 'Support Southern Music' was referring to the geographic South, no matter what style you played. Capricorn kind of took it over and started using it to just mean bands like Marshall Tucker and the Allman Brothers."

Phil Walden, however, remembered the original intent of the Capricorn buttons being the same as what the Atlanta folks meant. "We had buttons made that said 'Support Southern Music,'" he recalled, "not Southern *Rock* Music. It has always been my thesis that all original American music originated in these sunny Southern states."

The fact that the details about the exact wording of the buttons has become obscured over the years is illustrative of the reality that most anything Capricorn released in the 1970s—and most any band that emerged from the region—was classified as "Southern rock."

Regardless of labels, by 1974 "Southern rock" was an established musical category, and Capricorn Records was its undisputed headquarters, and a force to be reckoned with in the US recording industry. In its first five years, the label released more than twenty LPs that appeared on the *Billboard* album charts. Following the Brothers' back-to-back successes with *At Fillmore East*, *Eat a Peach*, and *Brothers and Sisters*, both Gregg Allman and Dickey Betts hit the Top 20 with their respective solo debut albums. The Marshall Tucker Band's first three LPs were certified Gold, and the Capricorn studio had produced major Top 10 hit singles with the Allmans' "Ramblin' Man" and Wet Willie's "Keep On Smilin'." Charlie Daniels' "The South's Gonna Do It" solidified Southern rock's identity as a distinct genre, while name-checking a handful of groups who comprised the Southern rock roster. Most of them, of course, were signed to Capricorn Records.

By that point, Phil Walden drove a Rolls Royce and had a Picasso hanging on his wall. Suddenly, the Macon business community was embracing the longhaired musicians it had eyed with skeptical caution just a few short years prior.

"The old Capricorn office was right across from the police station," explained Mark Pucci, who went to work for Capricorn in July of 1974. "Phil became good friends with Mayor Ronnie Thompson, who was known as 'Machine Gun Ronnie.' He was a no-nonsense guy, but he loved the music business. He made things easier for Capricorn at the time. Because Phil was so entrenched in the city and got involved in philanthropic efforts, that kind of helped ease things. Once people there saw the attention that was getting focused on Macon, it was creating a nice little business and tourist industry."

PHIL WALDEN

Phil Walden. (Courtesy of Bill Stewart)

Despite the growth of its music industry, Macon was still a small town. Entertainment options were few. "I don't particularly care to be involved in the social aspects of the music business," Walden declared in a 1972 interview with *Creem* magazine, "and that's the only benefit I can see to living in New York or L.A. This way, it breaks down to you and your music; it just sort of cuts away all that superfluous crap."

Phil's attitude and the limitations that a small town imposed helped hold the tight-knit music community together even as the scale of the label's success grew exponentially. The various musicians still hung out at the Capricorn studio, or one of a handful of local businesses like the H&H Restaurant or Grant's Lounge.

After the clubs closed, the musicians would gather at a handful of late-night meeting spots. "Le Carousel had the famous hot chicken," Wet Willie's Jimmy Hall remembered. "It was open after the clubs were closed, so after we got through jammin' at Grant's Lounge, that's where we were hangin' out." The various houses and farms where specific groups maintained their multi-purpose rehearsal spaces, crash pads, and party-palace headquarters also remained frequent gathering places to get high and jam.

Nowhere was the sense of community on display more than at the Capricorn picnics. These annual invitation-only events were legendary celebrations that attracted music-industry luminaries and cultural movers and shakers to Georgia for waterskiing, volleyball competitions, pinball machines, live music by Capricorn acts, free-flowing booze, the famous red-hot chicken from Le Carousel, and a little recreational drug use.

"Phil's masterstroke," noted freelance journalist Tom Dupree, who wrote for *Rolling Stone* and other publications, "was that he was selling his home region, so he stayed there and made the L.A. execs come to *him*."

Launched in 1972, the event served to bolster the company's image. "It got to the point," explained Capricorn publicist Mike Hyland, "where everybody wanted to come. We had Jimmy Carter, Don King, Andy Warhol, Bette Midler, Cameron Crowe, Lester Bangs, and all these fuckin' people. It was great."

"It was one of the hottest tickets," Capricorn staffer Mark Pucci recalled. "There was such a great buzz about that thing. Everybody called it the Capricorn picnic, but the actual real name of it was the Capricorn Barbecue & Summer Games." With a bevy of activities to choose from, the festivities were always eventful. "It was," Johnny Sandlin noted, "a time when people who stayed inside all the time would go out and injure themselves; the day sometimes ended up with a short trip to the emergency room."

As Capricorn grew more successful, the picnics grew more elaborate. "The party would go on for two or three days," the Marshall Tucker Band's Doug Gray recounted, "and the headaches would go on for weeks. It was the party of a lifetime each year."

Even though Capricorn fueled the fire of the Southern rock craze by both building a community around it and carefully marketing it, Phil Walden and Frank Fenter never intended to exclusively peddle one genre. As it grew in the mid-1970s, the label released a diverse range of albums, including Queen of Country Music Kitty Wells' *Forever Young* LP. They expanded further into the country arena with the slogan "Kickin' Country," and set their sights on Nashville. Projects from the Tennessee capitol that found a home on Capricorn included LPs by Kenny O'Dell (who hit the country charts with Capricorn singles like "Soulful Woman" and "Come Out Lovin'"), Larry Henley (who would go on to write "Wind Beneath My Wings"), Johnny Darrell, songwriting troubadour Billy Joe Shaver, and a self-consciously rustic studio invention called the Blue Jug Band that sought to capture the rootsy aesthetic of the Band.

Aside from country releases, Capricorn put out albums such as Marcia Waldorf's folksy singer-songwriter LP *Memoranda*. A handful of albums emerged from Muscle Shoals, including titles by Percy Sledge, John Hammond, and Travis Wammack. Perhaps most surprising was Capricorn's decision to distribute the US releases of albums by harmonious British folksters Easy Street and South African rockers Rabbitt, a band that included Trevor Rabin, who would go on to join the band Yes in the early 1980s.

Despite all the activity, most everyone identified Capricorn almost exclusively with Southern rock. "Capricorn Records allowed us to have a lighthouse," explained the Marshall Tucker Band's Doug Gray, "because Southern bands didn't have a place to go to. Capricorn was always an open door, 'cause they'd listen to everybody."

A publicity image for Hydra's second album. *Left to right*: Orville Davis, Wayne Bruce, Spencer Kirkpatrick, and Steve Pace. (Capricorn Records)

CHAPTER 23
Rocking the World: Hydra

★ ★

N THE SUMMER of 1965, the Vox instrument and amplifier company staged a multi-week Battle of the Bands competition in Atlanta. The winning group, a teen ensemble called the Atlanta Vibrations, won an opening slot for the Beatles' August 18th performance at Atlanta's Fulton County Stadium. "Somebody had forgotten to tell the Beatles' manager, Brian Epstein, about the contest," laughed the Atlanta Vibrations' guitarist, Spencer Kirkpatrick. "He had a fit." Eventually, the group were allowed to perform instrumentally behind a planned "London Look" fashion show staged by Regenstein's, a local women's clothing store. "I was fifteen years old," Kirkpatrick added, "and, even with *that* arrangement, I felt like I was gonna pee my pants the whole time!"

When the Atlanta Vibrations broke up, Kirkpatrick played gigs with various groups in the Atlanta area. Ultimately, he wound up in a cover band called Strange Brew that made it all the way to Los Angeles in early 1968. They held down a steady gig for a month at a club called the Galaxy on the Sunset Strip. When Strange Brew splintered, Kirkpatrick and drummer Steve Pace returned home to Atlanta.

HYDRA

▸ **SPENCER KIRKPATRICK** guitar

▸ **STEVE PACE** drums

▸ **WAYNE BRUCE** vocals, guitar

▸ **TRIP BURGESS** bass

▸ **ORVILLE DAVIS** bass

Hydra, *left to right:* Wayne Bruce, Orville Davis, Steve Pace, and Spencer Kirkpatrick. (Capricorn Records)

"After coming back, Steve and I bummed around and ended up having a couple of other oddball bands that nobody's heard of," Spencer recalled. They soon recruited guitarist and lead vocalist Wayne Bruce and formed a new group called Noah Mayflower. The band's dynamic, which mixed a few original selections with cover versions of Jimi Hendrix, Eric Clapton, and Moody Blues songs, was shaped by both Southern and British sounds. "I came from a family that listened to Dixieland jazz, country, rhythm and blues, and early rock and roll," Wayne Bruce explained in an interview with Luc Brunot. "Then, of course, the British Invasion was a big influence."

Noah Mayflower became Osmosis in 1969 with the four-man lineup of Spencer Kirkpatrick, Steve Pace, Wayne Bruce, and bassist Jim Youmans, who later made his mark with

an Atlanta band called Kudzu. At the dawn of 1970, Osmosis moved Youmans to keyboards and brought in a new bass player named Trip Burgess. "Jim decided he couldn't do that because he couldn't dance behind the keyboard like he could with the bass," Kirkpatrick explained. "So he left, and we became Hydra."

"When we changed over from Osmosis to Hydra," Spencer recalled, "we were beginning to get a lot more regional recognition at that time, and started opening shows for people like Grand Funk." They also earned a reputation as one of the top bands at the Sunday jams in Piedmont Park that served as a rallying point for the emerging hippie scene in Atlanta. "It was like an all-day event," Kirkpatrick recalled of the weekly gatherings. "We had Bruce Hampton and that bunch that were the Hampton Grease Band. I'd met those guys because they

A ticket stub from the 1965 Beatles concert at which Spencer Kirkpatrick's band Atlanta Vibrations appeared.

had all been in the Vox Battle of the Bands back in 1965. Eric Quincy Tate was there. There was a group called Chakra that had Ron Norris and Deborah McColl in it. I think Deborah ended up doing backup with Jimmy Buffet for a number of years. It was just a local *scene*." It was there that Hydra first rubbed shoulders with their famous future labelmates. "The first time we saw the Allman Brothers was at Piedmont Park in Atlanta in 1969," Bruce remembered.

"Next thing we know, Spencer laughed, "Trip was married, and he wasn't gonna play anymore. That's when Orville came in." With Orville Davis holding down the bass guitar slot, Hydra created an even stronger buzz. "We had a reputation," Wayne Bruce recalled, "as one of the best unrecorded bands from the South. . . . We did many shows with big name acts at the time, and we were getting a lot of attention."

Throughout the 1970s, Hydra were picked to open performances for a wide array of bands. Kirkpatrick recalled:

We never had an actual tour, but rather played sporadic dates with a lot of people. We played several one-nighters with ZZ Top. . . . We played a lot with Lynyrd Skynyrd. . . . I should also mention Wet Willie, Marshall Tucker, Grinderswitch, and Charlie Daniels.

There was a club on Peachtree called Funnochios that was kind of a big deal. They would have a band in for, like, one week at a time. There was a little rotation. There were two bands from Florida, one called Boot who, I think, were from Miami, and Lynyrd Skynyrd. It was the first time we met the boys in Skynyrd. The band Mose Jones, which had originally come up to Atlanta as Stonehenge, was also in the rotation, and we were in the rotation. So there were these four bands. This is where Al Kooper discovered that all this stuff was going on in Atlanta.

Hydra's sound was lean, guitar-driven rock that was considerably heavier than many Southern groups of the era. "Wayne was sort of the Leslie West of Atlanta," Kooper mused, comparing Bruce with the hard-rock guitarist who founded Mountain. He offered Hydra a contract, which they were eager to sign. "We just wanted to get a record deal," Spencer remembered, "so we could start doing all of our own stuff." Their manager, however, had another plan. "Frank Hughes kind of pulled the high card," Kirkpatrick continued, "and said that since he had a relationship with Johnny Sandlin, who was the Allman Brothers' producer, that we would go ahead and go with Capricorn."

Hydra signed with Capricorn Records in 1973, but Sandlin was too busy to produce the album and recruited Dan Turbeville, a staff engineer at the Record Plant in New York, to go into the studio with them to begin work on their debut LP. "They started trying to get Steve and Orville to simplify the bass and drum parts to try to make it a little more cohesive," Spencer recalled, "but it kind of took a little of the spark out of some of the stuff. Plus, it made them real pissed off. We had been doing this stuff live for several years."

By August of 1974, Hydra's self-titled debut album appeared in stores. "It was a wide spectrum of stuff," Spencer recalled. "Stylistically, there were things that had a little bit to do with, like, real country stuff, but was presented in a rock vein. Some things had a little bit of a progressive edge to it. Some things had a blues edge to it." While the LP captured Hydra's diversity, it didn't necessarily capture the band's spirit. "Our live shows at that time were very high energy," Bruce explained, "so I think if the record had been more like our live sound, it would have been more raw, more of a hard rock sound. Some of our fans were actually disappointed in that first album. They were so used to hearing us live, and the record was more subdued—keeping in mind that we were all in our early twenties, and full of piss and vinegar."

While Hydra might not have set out to court the Southern rock audience, their debut release placed them firmly in that camp. In his review in *Phonograph Record* magazine, Alan Niester wrote, "They are obviously Southern, adhering perfectly to the characteristics of the latest worthwhile local scene, the South. . . . They are the equal of Marshall Tucker, Lynyrd Skynyrd, Wet Willie, Mose Jones, the Atlanta Rhythm Section, and all the rest, but they play strong, good music that sedates even the most crucial rock-and-roll need."

By the time Hydra started work on their second Capricorn album, *Land of Money*, the band began collaborating with producer Johnny Sandlin in the studio. "It was easier," Kirkpatrick explained, "because they'd already had the first thing with us, and knew we were sensitive about a whole lot of changes. It caused us to grow up a little bit and modify our approach to recording." The result was a more restrained collection of songs—in some ways, Capricorn's success as the home of Southern rock created a climate in which bands were pressured to fit into that particular culture. "They kept trying to make us sound more like everyone else," Wayne Bruce complained, in an interview with the French magazine *Bands of Dixie*.

Spencer Kirkpatrick onstage. (Courtesy of Spencer Kirkpatrick)

A Capricorn Records ad promoting new releases by Duane Allman, Dickey Betts, Kenny O'Dell, and Hydra. (Courtesy of Walter Vanderbeken)

Guitarist Spencer Kirkpatrick. (Courtesy of Spencer Kirpatrick)

Hydra onstage, *left to right*: Orville Davis, Wayne Bruce, Spencer Kirkpatrick, and Steve Davis.

With the passage of time, both *Hydra* and *Land of Money* would hold up as solid albums. When they were released, however, neither generated critical attention or significant sales. "I think we would have been better off with someone other than Capricorn," Bruce lamented. "We should have signed with Al Kooper in 1973. Al was a musician, and understood what we were doing. He came to see us several times in the early '70s—he even sat in with us on a couple of occasions. In other words, he had played music with us live, we had talked, had drinks, and we had a musician's relationship."

When it came time to record again, Hydra ended up parting ways with Capricorn. "We already had material to do a third album," Kirkpatrick recounted, "but Capricorn was hemming and hawing. We were [signed] with No Exit Publishing, which was their in-house publishing company. We ended up having to sign away our royalties just so we could get out of that contract so we could go ahead and get out of that deal."

In the end, they were victims of Capricorn's greater success. "We never got a tour with anybody," Kirkpatrick explained. "We never got to go out with the Brothers or Wet Willie or anybody. For a long time we went through a bitter spell where we felt like, 'Well, you know, there were people that could've helped and they didn't.' But, in retrospect, it's just the way it played out. Thank goodness we at least got to do two good records with them."

In 1976, Hydra hooked up with producer Michael Stewart, who had been the guitarist in the British glitter-rock band Sweet. He took the band to Atlanta's Sound Pit studio in November and recorded an album with them for Polydor Records. By that time, bassist Orville Davis had departed. "Wayne had been writing so much of Orville's parts on the second album that he just transitioned over from guitar to bass," Spencer explained. The resulting album, *Rock the World*, found the trio version of Hydra finally putting their live sound to tape. "After talking to Steve, Spencer, and speaking for myself," Bruce explained, "*Rock the World* is our favorite."

With the new album on Polydor came new opportunities to find a bigger audience outside the South. "We were gonna tour with Rush," Kirkpatrick recalled. "We went up in January of 1977 to Louisville to do a show with them. At the end of the show, Rush realized that we essentially had two three-piece bands with a fairly heavy format. They declined to let us do the tour with them, and from there it's kind of like every step up the ladder we took, we got to revisit that step on the way back down. Everybody got really upset. We were pissed with each other, and we were pissed with everybody else." The Polydor album didn't reverse Hydra's fortunes. "It turned out that we ended up being a tax write-off for Polydor," Spencer explained, "and that was kind of the end of it." In 1978, Hydra called it quits.

"Looking back on that Southern rock label being applied to Hydra," Kirkpatrick mused in 2013, "is like Woody Allen said in one of his movies, 'a travesty of a mockery of a sham.' I never thought that we were what they turned Southern rock into, but the people that loved us in town sure thought that it was Southern rock and that *we* were Southern rock. After this many years, the fans *still* think we're Southern rock. We're just glad that some people still remember us." ★

Grinderswitch publicity photo, *left to right*: Rick Burnett, Larry Howard, Steve Miller, Dru Lombar, and Joe Dan Petty. (Courtesy of Chuck Perkins)

CHAPTER 24
Pullin' Together: Grinderswitch

FTER PLAYING IN an Indiana band called the Jokers in the mid-1960s, Dickey Betts moved to Florida and formed a new group with the same name. Joe Dan Petty, a native of Bradenton, Florida, played drums in the band. "I could only play marginally when I started hanging out with Dickey," Joe Dan told *Vintage Guitar* magazine in 1996, "but he taught me a lot."

Thanks to his relationship with Betts, Joe Dan eventually took a job working for the Allman Brothers Band's crew in 1970. "We were down at Criteria Studios doing the second album," Brothers road crew member Kim Payne told author Scott Freeman, "and we were looking to hire another roadie. We'd tried out several people and they didn't last long. And then, here's Joe Dan, and he don't weigh ninety pounds. He was really skinny. I went to Dickey, and I said, 'This ain't gonna work.' . . . Dickey said that Joe Dan was tough, to give him a chance. And it worked out great."

Petty spent the early part of the 1970s as a faithful member of the Brothers' organization, appearing in the iconic photograph of the roadies that adorned the back of the *At Fillmore East* LP. But though he took pride in his work for the Allman Brothers Band, he was itching to get back to playing music of his own.

Guitarist Larry Howard was born in Winterhaven, Florida. His father was a bluegrass musician, but Larry was more interested in classical and jazz. As a teenager, he played trombone and spent two summers at a music program at the University of Miami, where he studied under Count Basie for six weeks. "After coming home from doing that," Larry recalled,

Grinderswitch at the Palace Theatre in Manchester, England, December, 1976. *Left to right*: Dru Lombar, Joe Dan Petty, and Larry Howard. (Courtesy of Peter Cross)

"some guy in town . . . came to me, and wanted me to play guitar in their band. I had never played a guitar but they convinced me to try it."

The group, United Sounds, included drummer Rick Burnett, with whom Larry had played in a Dixieland jazz band when they were both thirteen years old. They would later count guitarist Les Dudek as a member. "I played in the United Sounds, and then I played for a while in a band called Ron and the Starfires," Larry

GRINDERSWITCH

- ▸ **DRU LOMBAR** guitar, lead vocals
- ▸ **LARRY HOWARD** guitar, vocals
- ▸ **JOE DAN PETTY** bass, vocals
- ▸ **RICK BURNETT** drums
- ▸ **STEVE MILLER** keyboards
- ▸ **AUSTIN PETTIT** guitar

Larry Howard, Rick Burnett, Dru Lombar, and Joe Dan Petty. (Photo by Terry Milam, courtesy of Larry Howard)

Howard recalled. The group also included brothers Carl and Gerald Chambers, who went on to country music success, with Carl writing hits for the group Alabama and Gerald playing with the Bellamy Brothers and Ricky Skaggs.

Following his stint with the Starfires, Larry Howard formed Blue Truth with drummer Rick Burnett, guitarist Les Dudek, bassist Bob Hodge, and lead singer Ricky Erickson. "We started playing and touring then," Howard recalled. "We did all original music and toured with, and backed up, lots of bands coming through Florida." The members of Blue Truth even had the chance to make a record of their own. "We did some recording in Nashville with Dean Mathis," Larry recalled. "He was the lead singer in the band the Newbeats that had the song 'I Like Bread and Butter,' which was a big hit in the '60s. We got hooked up with him through a manager we had at the time, and he produced the first recording that me and Ricky Burnett and Les Dudek did. But we never got a deal out of it."

After Duane Allman's death, with the future of the Brothers still uncertain, Dickey Betts toyed with the idea of launching a side project, which he planned to call Solo. Naturally, he

turned to his familiar network of Florida musicians to find players who understood his influences. He recruited keyboardist Peter Schless, who had been in a band called Power with Les Dudek but had recently joined Blue Truth. Schless departed for Macon to play with Betts.

Once the Allman Brothers Band began working on the *Brothers and Sisters* album, however, the future of Solo was in question. "The record company and the people in the band did not want Dickey to do a solo project at the same time he was trying to keep the band going without Duane," Larry Howard recalled. Feeling bad about abandoning the players who had uprooted their lives to move to Macon, Dickey recruited Schless' Blue Truth bandmate Les Dudek to move to Macon and take his place as the guitarist for Solo. "The idea was that Dickey didn't want to dissolve the band until he saw what was gonna happen," Howard continued. "He was paying these guys as his band, and rather than break the band up, he hired Les to come up and practice and stuff while he was still doing the Allman Brothers Band." Meanwhile, back in Florida, the remaining members of Blue Truth—which included Larry Howard and Rick Burnett—broke up.

When he arrived in Macon, the nineteen-year-old Les Dudek moved in with Joe Dan Petty and immersed himself in the local scene, which he described to *Hittin' the Note*:

Back then, it was like, anything that would go on in that town, at the drop of a hat, let's back the truck up and jam, let's pull the gear out. It was a real big music scene for such a small town in the South. Man, we'd play all the time. We'd show up at Grant's Lounge, this little bar downtown. There'd be like ten people in the bar. By the time we finished the first tune, you couldn't move in there, it'd turn into one big jam session. I just wish they had camcorders back in those days. You could feel Duane's spirit everywhere

Impressed with his guitar prowess, Phil Walden signed Les to a management deal. He wound up playing memorable guitar parts on the songs "Ramblin'" Man" and "Jessica" when the Allmans were recording their *Brothers and Sisters* album. In the end, however, Dudek wasn't the right fit for the Brothers in the long term. Solo never got off the ground, and Les

Advertisement for the Straight Southern Rock tour of England, featuring Grinderswitch, Bonnie Bramlett, and the Marshall Tucker Band. (Courtesy of Peter Cross)

departed to play in former Macon resident Boz Skaggs' band. Before he left Macon, however, Dudek facilitated the introductions that led to his roommate, Joe Dan Petty, finally putting together a band of his own.

"I was hanging around Macon, and I thought I might like to get a band together," Petty explained. Dudek connected him with the old Blue Truth bandmates he'd left behind when he relocated to Georgia. Larry Howard recalled:

> Les called and said we should come up and meet with Joe Dan and jam and play with him and see what would happen. When Rick and I got there, we went out to the Allman Brothers' farm. We were out there riding horses, and we were gonna come back that evening and just jam together, the three of us. But Joe Dan fell off his horse and broke his collarbone. . . . So, we spent about three days together just *talking* about music concepts and what our philosophies were. After the conversation, we said, "Well, we don't need to play together, 'cause we all think alike." That was the beginning of Grinderswitch, just me and Ricky and Joe Dan.

After spending a few weeks in Macon, Larry and Rick decided to pull up stakes and relocate to Georgia to play with Joe Dan permanently. When the two returned to Florida to collect their belongings, tragedy struck the Allman Brothers Band once again. "We had been at the Big House hanging out for a month," Larry recalled, "and when we went home to Florida, Berry got killed. We left town to get our stuff, and when we got back Berry was gone."

Petty continued to work as a roadie with the Brothers while he, Larry Howard, and Rick Burnett were on the lookout for other musicians to finalize the lineup of their band. Howard recalled:

> We started working up some songs, and Joe Dan said, "I know this other guitar player from Florida named Dru Lombar," so he and Ricky took off to Florida to go find Dru to see if he might be interested in playing with us. He was playing in a band there. I didn't know Dru. He was from Jacksonville. They went to Jacksonville Beach looking for him, and while they were gone I was at Grant's Lounge, and there was this band called the King James Version playing there, with this guy playing guitar. I really liked his playing a lot and started talking to him afterward.

The guitarist turned out to be Dru Lombar. "I didn't know that it was who Joe Dan was looking for," Larry continued. "Dru said, 'This is the last night of the band. Our band is breaking up tonight.' I said, 'Well, why don't you come hang out with me for a few days?' Joe Dan and Ricky came back from Jacksonville, 'cause they couldn't find Dru. When they came back, he was asleep in the living room on the couch!" Knowing that it must be fate, the four joined forces. "We played together for about six days," Larry added, "and he went home and got his stuff and came to live at our house."

Dru Lombar grew up in Neptune Beach, Florida, where he cut his teeth on R&B. "Hossman Allen from WLAC," Lombar reflected, in an interview with Luc Bronot. "As a kid, I heard my first blues and soul music on his radio show based in Nashville." Inspired, Lombar learned to play guitar and formed his first band, the Soul Searchers, while still in high school. After a stint in a

group called Maji, he joined the King James Version and played clubs around Jacksonville, as well as the usual Southern circuit.

Dru Lombar officially moved to Macon in December of 1972. Early the following year, Dru, Joe Dan, Larry, and Rick relocated to a farm near Warner Robbins, Georgia. "We lived off of $25 a week Joe Dan would pay us," Lombar told Michael Buffalo Smith. "He was the only guy working, as a crewman for the Brothers, so he was keeping us in cigarette, beer, and food money." It was during this era that the band settled on a name. "Grinderswitch is a mythical town that Minnie Pearl is from," Howard explained. "She used it in her routine and stuff. I don't know how we decided on it. We just thought it was a neat name, plus we were into trains and stuff."

Joe Dan soon emerged as the group's spiritual leader, as Lombar explained to *Road to Jacksonville* in 2004:

> Joe Dan Petty exposed me to a lot of roots music—Lonnie Mack, Merle Haggard, Albert King, etc.—and it really helped shape my style. Being a teenager in the '60s, I was influenced by a lot of the English bands—Stones, Animals, Manfred Mann—as well as instrumental groups like the Ventures and Duane Eddy, and soul artists like Otis Redding, Wilson Pickett, and Ray Charles. By the time I did the first album I had these different kinds of music in my head. I still do today. Anyway, Joe Dan also taught me about commitment and keeping your values in order. He was kind of like a musical Vince Lombardi. He was a very honorable man!

The months spent squirreled away writing and rehearsing did much to solidify the bond upon which the members of Grinderswitch built their band dynamic. "We had our differences and each one of us was stubborn," Howard acknowledged, "but when we walked onstage it was like magic. At the risk of sounding weird, we had a sixth sense between us when it came to music."

Ultimately, the hard work paid off when producer Paul Hornsby started hanging out and jamming with the band at the farm. "I went down and we played all night," Hornsby recalled. "I did that several times. Then they'd come to the studio, and we turned the tape machines on a few times and cut a few things. I went up and played it for Phil and Frank, and they dug it. They said, 'Go on and cut some more stuff on 'em.'"

After a showcase at Grant's Lounge, Phil

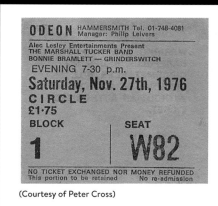

(Courtesy of Peter Cross)

Grinderswitch around the time of their *Redwing* album, 1977: Joe Dan Petty, Steve Miller, Rick Burnett, Dru Lombar, and Larry Howard. (Rabbit Records)

Walden and Frank Fenter signed the band on the spot. Grinderswitch released their debut LP, *Honest to Goodness*, in 1974. The songs had been carefully crafted during the months they spent woodshedding in preparation for their chance to enter the studio. The sound was organic and rootsy, with strains of R&B and laid-back country-rock laying a foundation for consistently crisp blues licks. "I think the title of their first album said it all," Paul Hornsby enthused. "It was just honest to goodness non-pretentious, just havin' a good time playin' down-home music."

The LP opened with "Kiss the Blues Goodbye," featuring some fine guitar work courtesy of Dickey Betts. It sounded like the Allman Brothers Band infused with a soulful shot of joy. Skilled musicians, the members of Grinderswitch glided effortlessly through the solid collection of songs. Producer Paul Hornsby operated as a de facto fifth member of the group. "Paul played keyboards on the first two Grinderswitch albums," Larry Howard confirmed, "and played many live dates with us, including the early Charlie Daniels Volunteer Jam recordings."

Though they were highly respected by their peers, Grinderswitch didn't sell a lot of albums. "Capricorn put it out, and that's about all that happened with it," Hornsby lamented. "I don't know if they put it out or if it *escaped*. It didn't cost 'em anything to make it. It probably cost 'em to press it up. I know it didn't cost 'em to promote it, 'cause they didn't promote it."

By the time Grinderswitch had completed recording *Honest to Goodness* at the Capricorn studio, Joe Dan Petty had left his job with the Allman Brothers Band to dedicate himself full-time to his own group. "The last show I did as an Allman Brothers roadie was on a New Year's Eve at the Cow Palace in San Francisco," he recalled. "When the Brothers went back out on the road the next March, Grinderswitch went out as their opening act."

Touring with the Allmans provided a nurturing environment for the new group. "On the road," Dru Lombar explained to Michael Buffalo Smith, "there are some bands that feel like, 'You can't use this monitor,' or, 'You can't use these lights, You can't do this, You can't do that.' But the Brothers said, 'Go out there and use whatever you want.' And if we got an encore, they'd say, 'Go out there and take your encore.' They were real supportive guys, man."

In addition to the Allmans, Grinderswitch toured extensively with Wet Willie, the Charlie Daniels Band, and Lynyrd Skynyrd. "It was a big family with all those bands," Lombar reflected. The support they received in the Southern rock community allowed them the freedom to enjoy long opening sets and stretch out with their musical exploration. "I had never played in a band as tight as we were musically," Larry Howard explained, "and I've never played in a band that tight since."

In 1975, just a year after releasing their debut album, Grinderswitch returned with their second effort, *Macon Tracks*. The opening song, "Mail Train Blues," featured Charlie Daniels on fiddle, adding some additional flavor to the Allman-like guitar licks. Whereas the first album sounded like a very accomplished blues-based bar band, *Macon Tracks* was a bit more nuanced. The arrangements were looser and felt more natural, with Larry Howard and Dru Lombar's guitar lines weaving in and out of one another.

Because the members of Grinderswitch drew from the same musical well as their peers, they often had to assert their validity as an original band. "There's only two things happening in Georgia," Atlanta Rhythm Section lead singer Ronnie Hammond declared from a Florida stage in 1975, in front of an audience of 5,000 concertgoers, "and that's Gregg Allman and the Atlanta Rhythm Section. Bands like Grinderswitch should go back to the car wash where they belong." The comment did not go unanswered. "I went onstage after him," Larry Howard laughed. "Me and him, and I think it was Robert Nix, got into it. We finally made it off to the side of the stage and continued on for a while back there. We made it back to the motel and started again in the parking lot. The road crew got us all in a room and barred the door and said, 'OK, finish it or put it to rest.' After that, Ronnie and I became real good friends. That was just a lot of liquor and cocaine talking is what that was."

After the release of the second album, Joe Dan Petty was at the Fillmore West in San Francisco when he met Stephen Miller, who was playing with Elvin Bishop's band at the time. "He asked Steve if he would like to join Grinderswitch," Dru Lombar told *Bands of Dixie*, "and Steve was ready for a change, so he moved to Macon, and we became a five-piece band."

The third album, 1976's *Pullin' Together*, was a positive reflection of the altered personnel. "My favorite Grinderswitch album was *Pullin' Together*," Lombar proclaimed. "It was the first album we did with Stephen Miller and it is so full of energy. The band really matured musically making this album." With Miller's organ and the increasingly complex dual guitar soloing between Lombar and Howard, the debt to the Allmans remained in evidence. But there was more to the band. "Grinderswitch . . . aren't just one more set of Allmans/Skynyrd imitators," critic Chas de Whalley noted. "[They] have a refreshingly different way of approaching the spaced out Southern boogie we have come to expect from Phil Walden's Capricorn label."

That same year, Grinderswitch accompanied the Marshall Tucker Band and Bonnie

Bramlett on a three-week tour of Europe that included appearances in the UK, Germany, Holland, France, and Belgium. They opened the shows and then functioned as Bonnie's backing band before the Tuckers took the stage and closed the evening. The European tour was the culmination of a hectic schedule. "That year we went out on the road with Skynyrd for a long tour from the East Coast to the West Coast," Larry Howard recalled. "Then we hooked up with Marshall Tucker and did the West Coast back to the South, and then went out with Charlie Daniels. We went home to rehearse with Bonnie for three or four days in Macon, and then went straight to Europe. . . . We were on the road for 120 days nonstop." The European exposure earned Grinderswitch some international fans if not international fortune. "We had a great time," Lombar explained to Brunot. "We came home broke, but what an experience."

By 1977, the Southern rock craze had begun to cool, and the members of Grinderswitch, like many of their peers, were expanding their musical boundaries. For the *Redwing* album, the band still had plenty of barn-burning blues-infused twin-guitar lines, but they also began stretching into other realms, with the country toe-tapper "Faster and Faster" and the mid-tempo rock of "You and Me." Despite the fact that it was another solid LP, however, Capricorn chose not to release it. Dick Wooley, the former Capricorn promotion man who'd left to launch his own Rabbit Records, picked up the album and released it via his distribution deal with Atco Records.

"The *Redwing* album was probably our most successful album," Larry remembered. "When we were out on the road after that album, *Saturday Night Fever* came out. That was the end of that for most everybody. I think *Redwing* had positioned us to move to the next level, but then the bottom fell out. Showcase clubs and stuff all turned into discos, so it was tough then."

By the time the decade came to a close, Grinderswitch had become a highly respected Southern rock band among fans in the know, but they had failed to break into the mainstream in a major way. With the genre's popularity waning, it seemed their moment had passed. Then, when it came time to record a follow-up to *Redwing*, the album met an unfortunate fate, as Larry Howard explained:

> We did another album for Rabbit called *Chasin' Wild Desires*, and I thought it was a great record. The guys from Atco/Atlantic, Ahmet Ertegun and Jerry Wexler, heard the album. One of the songs was a twelve-minute blues cover of Albert King's "You're Gonna Miss Me When I'm Gone." They said, "You can't put a twelve-minute blues song on a 'pop' album," as they called it. There was some discussion about that, and finally we said, "Well, we already did, and you paid for it!" At that point, they said, "You know, you're right. We *did* pay for it." So they took the album and put it in the vault in New York, and it's still there. That was the wrong thing to say to those two guys. We were making a power play, but we found out real soon that we had firecrackers and they had nukes.

The unreleased *Chasin' Wild Desires* would be the last album Larry Howard recorded with Grinderswitch. Though Joe Dan had gotten sober before Grinderswitch formed, drugs were a way of life for the other members, and they became a serious problem for Larry in particular. In December of 1979, Howard officially departed the group. "I left the band because I was a drug addict and was becoming a liability," he explained. "Also, I was tired of the whole lifestyle that went along with it. I took music seriously when I started, but all the politics and plain BS was stealing the very thing I loved."

With both the Capricorn and Rabbit/Atco deals behind them, Grinderswitch replaced Howard with Austin Pettit and signed with Auric Records to release the *Right on Time* LP in 1980. Album sales were minimal. The following year, they recorded *Have Band Will Travel* for Robox Records, but it, too, failed to make a splash.

By the end of 1981, Grinderswitch had broken up. "We did one final tour," Dru Lombar recalled, "and we went with Bonnie [Bramlett] and did a bunch of things in Canada and that was it. It was over. Boom! It was over." The members were never able to fully comprehend their inability to find sustained success. "Why it didn't happen for us in a financial way," Howard reflected, "in record sales and everything, nobody ever knows. I think everybody was as shocked as we were."

In 1980, Larry Howard finally got clean. "After a serious overdose in Florida, I just made a decision," he explained. "I said, 'That's it.' I became a Christian and stopped doing drugs. I've been straight since August of 1980." He later reemerged as a gospel blues artist, while Dru Lombar started a band called Dr. Hector & the Groove Injectors in 1986 that was regionally popular throughout the South. Joe Dan Petty ultimately returned to the Allman Brothers Band's road crew.

In the end, Grinderswitch left a legacy of excellent music, and a lifetime of memories. Dru Lombar recalled:

> Charlotte Speedway. The August Jam. We played with the Brothers and Emerson, Lake & Palmer, in front of 300,000 people. I've never seen so many people in one place at the same time. We flew in on a helicopter and said, "My God, look at this!" It looked like a sea of people. It was an incredible experience. And the Brothers' shows, especially Madison Square Garden and Long Island, they were just really great shows. And doing Central Park with the Tuckers—that was real cool, man. Right in the middle of New York City, all these guys in cowboy hats. I loved it. ★

Joe Dan Petty, Larry Howard, Dru Lombar, and Rick Burnett. (Photo by Terry Milam, courtesy of Larry Howard)

Elvin Bishop onstage at Richard's Club in Atlanta, 1974. (Photo by Tom Hill/WireImage)

CHAPTER 25
Juke Joint Jump: Elvin Bishop

★ ★

IN MAY OF 1976, Elvin Bishop's "Fooled Around and Fell in Love" hit #3 on the *Billboard* pop chart. With the exception of the All-mans' "Ramblin' Man," it was Capricorn's highest charting single. The song appeared on *Struttin' My Stuff*, the third LP Bishop made after inking a deal with the label in 1974. Though he'd been a celebrated blues guitarist since the mid-1960s, Bishop found his strongest audience after reinventing himself as a Southern rocker in Macon.

Elvin Bishop grew up in rural Iowa. "Until I was about ten or eleven, there was hardly any musical influence at all," Elvin recalled. "I lived out in the country, on a farm. There was no electricity, and we had this radio—this was primitive times—and the radio had a battery that weighed about ten pounds. It worked when the weather was right, and that was it." Just prior to his adolescent years, Bishop's family migrated south. "My dad went to Oklahoma," Elvin recounted, "because they had a big drought there, and they were payin' big prices for hay. He applied for a job in Tulsa, and we moved there. I lived in Tulsa until I graduated high school."

"When we moved to Tulsa," Bishop explained, "I got exposed to country music real heavy. This was the early '50s, when country was really strong and good, you know, like Hank Williams and Kitty Wells and Webb Pierce and Lefty Frizzell—people like that. Tulsa was a stronghold of Bob Wills and those kinds of guys. You got the country influence just by breathing the air."

In many ways, Elvin Bishop's teen years

The Paul Butterfield Blues Band, *left to right:* Billy Davenport, Mark Naftalin, Michael Bloomfield, Paul Butterfield, Elvin Bishop, and Jerome Arnold. (Elektra Records)

were similar to those of his musical peers in Georgia, Alabama, or Florida. "Oklahoma, in those days, was more like the South than you would think," he explained. "For one thing, there was really hardcore segregation. It was 'white' and 'colored' everything. There were no black people at my school. In Oklahoma, people are really conservative—too goddamn conservative for me. On the other hand—it's like a paradox, and I don't understand it—but they're the nicest people in the world."

Like so many American rock musicians of his generation, Bishop discovered the blues and R&B over the late night airwaves. "We'd get a lot of blues stations," he recalled, "because Tulsa's right in the middle of the plains. I loved WLAC out of Nashville—Herman Grizzard, Hoss Allen. I knew all the DJs, and I still remember most of the commercials. I used to

send off to Randy's Records in Gallatin, Tennessee, and get Howlin' Wolf, Jimmy Reed, and Muddy Waters records."

A bright student, Bishop earned a National Merit Scholarship in physics that gave him the freedom to choose what college to attend. Knowing that the blues music he loved was centered in the Windy City, Elvin packed his bags and headed to the University of Chicago in 1960. "Education was just my cover story," he confessed. The day he arrived in Chicago, Bishop met fellow student Paul Butterfield on campus. The two quickly discovered they shared a mutual love for the blues. "We gravitated right together," Elvin explained.

Playing with Paul Butterfield was enjoyable, but Bishop had gone to Chicago to encounter the blues masters he admired. "I'd made friends with the black dudes that worked in the cafeteria at the University," he told journalist Chip Eagle. "Within a couple of weeks, I was going down in the ghetto with them. The first blues band I ever saw was Muddy Waters, James Cotton, Otis Spann, Willie Smith, Pat Hair, and a bass player."

Before long, Elvin was getting a first-rate education, but it wasn't in a University of Chicago classroom. His scholastic studies fell down the priority list as he spent more and more time soaking up the local black music scene. Many of the musicians took the time to show Elvin their guitar techniques, and he honed his skills considerably. In 1963, he and Paul formed the Paul Butterfield Blues Band with drummer Sam Lay and bassist Jerome Arnold, who were veterans of Howlin' Wolf's group. The interracial band eventually signed with Elektra Records and

Capricorn promotional photo of Elvin Bishop. (Courtesy of Chuck Perkins)

added Mike Bloomfield to the lineup. After a few unsatisfactory attempts at recording, keyboardist Mark Naftalin joined the band, and they released their self-titled debut LP in mid-1965.

"The Paul Butterfield Blues Band really was modeled on our heroes," Elvin pointed out in an interview with Carl Wiser, "on Chicago blues guys, Muddy Waters and Howlin' Wolf, and people like that. Otis Rush, Little Walter. And we were doing mostly their tunes in the beginning.... It's sad but true, the white public will accept from young white faces what they will not accept from old black faces."

In 1966, the Paul Butterfield Blues Band released the groundbreaking *East-West* album. The instrumental title track was a thirteen-minute performance with overlapping and intertwining guitar parts by Elvin and Mike Bloomfield that captured the attention of future Southern rockers like the Allmans. "Duane was a big fan . . . and had the *East-West* album when we first got together as the Hour Glass," Johnny Sandlin noted. "He listened to it a lot and could play all the songs on the record."

Michael Bloomfield departed following the release of the *East-West* LP to form the Electric Flag. Elvin Bishop stuck around for the follow-up release, 1967's *The Resurrection of Pigboy Crabshaw*, an album whose title referred to Bishop's overall-wearing alter ego. The following year, however, he departed to form his own Elvin Bishop Group. Signing with Bill Graham's label, Fillmore Records, Bishop moved to San Francisco, where he jammed with a number of

eclectic musicians and appeared on *The Live Adventures of Mike Bloomfield and Al Kooper*.

Between 1969 and 1972, Elvin released a couple of LPs credited to either the Elvin Bishop Group or the Elvin Bishop Band that reflected an increasing exploration of genres beyond straight blues. "For a while, I thought that blues was the whole thing," he told *Rolling Stone* in 1970. "It was the first really intense music that I heard—but now I know it's just another kind of intense music. Gospel, country blues, Chicago blues, R&B, soul—they're all just different formats for the same feeling."

Elvin's group appeared with the Allman Brothers Band for the legendary run of shows at the Fillmore in March of 1971 that produced the Brothers' *At Fillmore East* double LP. Elvin joined them onstage to play a version of his song "Drunken Hearted Boy" that later appeared on the deluxe version of the album. "The Allman Brothers actually got me my contact with Capricorn," he remembered. "Our paths crossed a few times. Me and Duane really just fell right together, and I got along good with Dickey, too. They played a gig in San Francisco.... There was a party afterward, and Dickey grabbed Phil Walden and me, and we went in this room on the side, and Dickey said, 'Listen to this guy's songs.' I played three or four songs for him, and he signed me up. He offered me a deal on the spot."

Elvin was soon strongly associated with the Southern rock movement, and he grew close to many of the key players in that community. "I used to hang out a lot," he recalled. "Toy Caldwell and I were really good friends,

and I'd go fishing with him, or with Dickey. We'd all just hang together."

The Georgia community made a major impression on him, as he recounted to *Universal Music Tribe* in 2011:

> Macon was still like a part of the old South at the time. It hadn't been modernized the least damn bit.... You'd go to the barbeque stand and the guy in front of you would have a big ol' pistol strapped on. That cut out any urge you might have to say something smart. Once in a while they would take me out to one of these places way back out in the woods, and they would have picnic tables and sawdust on the floor and get some of that corn liquor. Capricorn Records was the only thing happening in town that was different from anything in a thousand other towns around the South at the time.

By the time he signed with Capricorn, Elvin had put together a consistent band that would remain with him for most of the 1970s. Jon Vernazza—known as Johnny V.—played guitar, while Michael "Fly" Brooks and Don Baldwin covered the bass and drums, respectively. Phil Aaberg was the keyboard player who replaced Stephen Miller when Miller departed Elvin's band to join Grinderswitch.

Bishop entered the Capricorn recording facility in 1974 to begin work on *Let It Flow*. With Johnny Sandlin in the producer's chair, a parade of Macon's musical elite headed to the studio to lend a hand to the newest member of the family. Charlie Daniels, Paul Hornsby, Toy Caldwell, Randall Bramblett, and a host of others participated in the sessions. "It wasn't a big plan or anything," Bishop said of the lineup of top-tier guest artists. "That was just a lot more of a jammin' time than it is now. Guys would just get together." One memorable moment occurred when Charlie Daniels got carried away during a recording session. "He wrecked a metal folding chair," Elvin laughed. "Charlie was a big boy, and he was rockin' away, sawin' on that fiddle, and the damn chair collapsed."

With key tracks like "Stealin' Watermelons" and "Travelin' Shoes," *Let It Flow* became Bishop's most successful album to date. "Travelin' Shoes," complete with its twin lead guitar parts, was his first charting single. "I love gospel music, and I love blues," Elvin declared, in a 2013 interview with Michalis Limnios, "and that is the recipe for Southern rock music—those little things right there. So, in that particular recording situation I got into, I was encouraged to do that." Having concentrated on the blues for so many years, Bishop was relieved to give vent to the other sides of his musical personality. "All the stuff from my country side was just kind of backed up," he explained, "and hadn't had an outlet until then."

Thanks to Bishop's association with Capricorn, he and his band were soon playing in front of Southern rock fans all over the country. "We didn't do any organized tours," Elvin explained, "but we ended up playing a lot of gigs with Skynyrd, and Marshall Tucker, the Allmans, Wet Willie." So completely was he embraced by the Southern rock community that within months of singing with Capricorn, Charlie Daniels mentioned Bishop in his signature tribute to the Southern rock genre, "The South's Gonna Do It." Singled out with the memorable line that "he ain't good lookin' but he sure can play," the song helped solidify Elvin's association with the Southern rock elite. "I guess it couldn't do any harm," Elvin laughed. "Of course, if a guy the size of Charlie tells you you ain't good lookin', you just kind of accept it. No sense trying to fight a guy that size. We never discussed it. I don't remember ever even mentioning it to Charlie."

In 1975, Elvin released the *Juke Joint Jump* album, featuring his second charting single, "Sure Feels Good." Though Johnny Sandlin produced the album, the sessions were conducted at the Record Plant in Sausalito, California, rather than at the Capricorn studio in Macon. The resulting LP lacked some of the more overt country overtones of Bishop's first Capricorn release, but it was generally well received. That same year, Elvin traveled to Criteria studio in Miami to record his third Capricorn album, *Struttin' My Stuff*, with producer Bill Szymczyk.

The *Struttin' My Stuff* sessions would produce Bishop's biggest hit, "Fooled Around and Fell in Love." Vocal duties on the song were handled by Mickey Thomas, who'd been singing with Elvin's band since before he signed with Capricorn. "We had ten or eleven songs," Elvin remembered, in an interview with William Westhoven. "[Szymczyk] said we need one more piece of material. 'What else you got laying around?' So I said, 'What about this?' . . . So we cut a track of 'Fooled Around and Fell in Love.'" The song wasn't the right fit for Bishop's vocal style. "I tried singing it," he remembered, "and I said, 'That's not buttering my biscuit, my vocal on this. Why don't we give Mickey a shot at this?'"

Once the label heard it, they knew "Fooled Around and Fell in Love" had the potential for a mainstream hit. "Frank [Fenter] must have played that song at least fifty times one day," Capricorn promotion man Dick Wooley recalled. By 1976, with "Fooled Around and Fell in Love" climbing the charts, Elvin and his band were touring aggressively. "We were on the road constantly," Mickey Thomas told Keith Gordon. "We got to do a lot of jamming and hanging out; we did a lot of shows with Lynyrd Skynyrd, the Marshall Tucker Band, ZZ Top, the Allman Brothers . . . I feel like I did my graduate work with the Elvin Bishop Band. It was an exciting time for music. We played everything from stadiums to bars."

It was a golden era for Capricorn, and Elvin was one of its biggest stars. "It was a great time," he recalled. "That's when they were having those big picnics, and there was a lot of drinkin' goin' on and gettin' high. It was just a big fun party." For his part, Bishop welcomed the boost,

Capricorn's Mike Hyland with Elvin Bishop. (Courtesy of Mike Hyland)

following a number of professional disappointments. "My heart's been broken so many times before," he told *Rolling Stone* magazine at the time, "I'm happier than a pig in shit."

The cover of the follow-up album, *Hometown Boy Makes Good*, depicted Bishop carrying sacks of money into a bank. Unfortunately, the LP failed to sustain the success of his previous release. The ballad "Spend Some Time," with Mickey Thomas again handling lead vocal duties, was an attempt to replicate the success of "Fooled Around and Fell in Love," while the reggae influenced cover version of "Twist and Shout" and the disco flavor of "Give It Up" carried Elvin farther from the rootsy influences of his earlier Capricorn efforts. But if the music was more reflective of the changing times, the musicianship was still top caliber. One critic called the album's closer, "D. C. Strut," "an irresistible slice of layered funk, a maze of solo patterns so goddamn intricate it pins me to the wall."

A live double LP, *Raisin' Hell*, was released in 1977 to mixed reviews. By the time Elvin issued his final Capricorn album, *Hog Heaven*, in 1979, bassist Fly Brooks, vocalist Mickey Thomas, and drummer Donny Baldwin had departed the band. Thomas and Baldwin resurfaced in the group Jefferson Starship, which morphed into Starship in the mid-1980s, and featured Thomas' voice on the #1 pop hits "We Built This City," "Sara," and "Nothing's Gonna Stop Us Now."

Though continued chart success would elude Bishop, his 1970s sojourn as a Southern rock all-star would define his career legacy. "Nobody knew how to describe me," Elvin said of his categorization as a Southern rock artist. "What it amounts to is that it was the one and only time in history that there was an official category that writers and media people and radio programmers could comfortably stuff my ass into. It was the only recognized category that ever seemed to fit at all. Otherwise, I'm just a different dude. ★

Dickey Betts and Elvin Bishop backstage in Atlanta, Georgia, in 1976. Capricorn publicists Mark Pucci (*far left*) and Mike Hyland (*far right*) present Bishop with a framed copy of his *Guitar Player* magazine cover photo. (Courtesy of Mike Hyland)

Grinderswitch backing
Bonnie Bramlett at
the Palace Theater in
Manchester, England,
1976. (Courtesy of
Peter Cross)

CHAPTER 26
Lady's Choice: Bonnie Bramlett

★ ★

EFORE THERE WAS a Southern rock community, there was the roots-oriented musical family that formed around Delaney and Bonnie Bramlett in Los Angeles during the late 1960s. Proudly flaunting their gospel, R&B, and country influences, the fluid lineup of Delaney & Bonnie & Friends included Leon Russell, Rita Coolidge, Eric Clapton, Duane Allman, King Curtis, Traffic's Dave Mason, and future Derek & the Dominos members Bobby Whitlock, Carl Radle, and Jim Gordon. By the early 1970s, Delaney and Bonnie's musical and marital partnership had crumbled. Moving to Macon for the better part of that decade, Bonnie reinvented herself as the maven momma of soul-drenched Southern rock.

She may not have been born a Southerner, but Bonnie Lynn O'Farrell converted as soon as she could:

> I grew up in *southern* Illinois. My people were Southerners. My dad was an Ozark Mountain man who came to Granite City to work in the steel mill, so I was raised with a country feel.
>
> I was mostly raised by my great-aunt and my great-grandmother. I was a very difficult child. I probably would have been diagnosed *at least* ADD, if not something a little more severe. It was the hardest thing in the world to have me sit still and be quiet. It's a good thing I had the expression of music in my life, because my feelings are way too big to fit "normal." If I were a kid today they would have medicated me and I would have never been a singer.

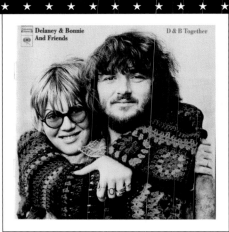

> We were from a very racist town, but because we were Christians we weren't allowed to behave ugly or say that nasty word that starts with an "n." I didn't *know* to hate anyone. Nobody taught me that. The first year of integration in Madison, Illinois, was major. I got to see black gospel singers for the first time, and it blew my mind. All of a sudden, I fit in. It was the *expression*.

For the first several years of her young life, church music was the only music Bonnie knew. "I didn't hear any secular music until I was six or seven years old," she recalled, "and I started going to the bars with my real father when he'd pick me up on the weekends. He was a drunk, and in those days you could take your kids to the bars. That's where I heard jukebox music." With the encouragement of the adult patrons, little Bonnie became the free entertainment at her dad's favorite watering holes. "They'd get drunk," she recalled,

"and they'd give me quarters and I'd play the jukebox and sing Kay Starr songs."

By the time she was a teenager, Bonnie was soaking up the music scene that centered on St. Louis' Gaslight Square. "When we went to dance," she explained to journalist Jill McLane Smith, "we got to dance to Little Milton, Ike & Tina, Albert King, Chuck Berry. Those were local groups for me." More than just entertainment, the performers became an inspiration. "I looked at some of these people . . . Tina Turner, when I was about fifteen, and she was all of about twenty, and I just knew that was what I wanted to do," Bonnie remembered. "I thought, 'What they're doing to me, I want to do to other people.' And I knew in my inner-most feelings that I could. . . . I found that freedom in the black churches, and in those black neighborhoods where I began performing onstage."

At fifteen, Bonnie was invited to become an Ikette for a few days when Ike Turner found himself in a bind after losing a female backup singer. Bonnie's mother consented to let her daughter go on the road, but it was a short-lived arrangement. "I was an underage white girl going across state lines in the South [with black musicians]," Bonnie explained to journalist Barry Gilbert, "and he had to send me back home." Bonnie still managed to pick up some important lessons from Tina. "She sang from every cell in her freaking body," Bramlett recalled. "I vomited trying to growl and sound like Tina." Offstage, the seasoned singer offered her teen protégé a few pointers. "Tina would tell me things like, 'Honey, you're not in a beauty contest. To sing right, you breathe from that belly and you got to get ugly to be soulful—go ahead and sweat.'"

Back in St. Louis, Jimmy O'Donnell, who operated a club called the Living Room in Gaslight Square, became Bonnie's legal guardian, so she could work in the club despite being underage. It was there that she first encountered the Allman brothers, back when they were still touring as the Allman Joys. "They played right across the street from where I was playing at the Living Room at a place called Pepe's a Go Go," Bonnie explained. "I used to work with Albert King, and Duane would come across and jam with us. Then we'd go out and sing blues with him on breaks." Johnny Sandlin, who was playing with the Allmans at the time, recalled that Bonnie had a strong reputation in St. Louis. "I remember hearing about this girl singer, Bonnie Lynn, that was just great," he recalled. "I went to the club where she was singing and saw her one night. I know Gregg and Duane hung out with her some, too."

One night in 1967, a band called the Enemies caught Bonnie's set at a club where she was working in Wisconsin. Their manager left her his contact details and encouraged her to move to Los Angeles. "Well, that was my ticket to ride," she chuckled. "As soon as I found someone that was dumb enough to go with me, my girlfriend and I went to California to make me a big star. Those guys in the Enemies turned out to be Three Dog Night. It was Danny Hutton, Corey Wells, and Chuck [Negron]. So, Three Dog Night brought me to California and made me a star. Well, they gave me my first step. All I had to do was sing. I took over that town!"

A few months after relocating to Los Angeles, Bonnie was booked on a three-week series of performances with the Shindogs, who had been the house band on the ABC television show *Shindig!* Leon Russell was the group's keyboardist, and the bassist was Mississippian Delaney Bramlett. "On the very last night I gave him my phone number," Bonnie recalled. "He came over and never left. Seven days later, we got married." Almost immediately, the two discovered a personal and musical chemistry. "It was very romantic," Bonnie explained to interviewer Randy Patterson. "Very cool. Very righteous. We had so much in common musically, but also spiritually— our religion and our upbringing. It was like we were perfect for each other. And when we sang, it was absolute magic from the first note we ever hit together until the last one."

"I was the Yoko Ono of the Shindogs," Bonnie laughed. "I broke that band slap up. I told him, 'You need to be the lead singer. You need to be the lead guitar player. You know what you're *doing*, Delaney.' When he got his wings, that sucker flew. He was meant to put

a band together, and he put a *monster* band together." The pair's Southern musical influences made for a powerful combo. "I was totally blues and gospel, and he was totally country," Bonnie explained. "That's the same with the Southern rock. It was that coming together of the black and white expression, and the spiritual and the secular." For Bonnie, it all tapped into a common root. "Country music and blues are the same thing," she elaborated in an interview with Mark T. Gould. "It's just a different expression of the same frustration, the same homegrown, uneducated way of expressing pain."

Stax Records' Donald "Duck" Dunn heard the Bramletts singing in Los Angeles and secured them a recording contract with the Memphis label in 1968. The resulting album left Delaney dissatisfied, and Stax shelved the project. Returning to California with Memphis Musician Bobby Whitlock in tow, Delany & Bonnie assembled a ten-piece band and began working the Los Angeles clubs. "They actually started out as Bonnie & Delaney," Whitlock recalled in his autobiography. "Everyone always called them that until Delaney raised so much hell that nobody could stand it."

It was in Los Angeles, at a small Laurel Canyon performance venue called Snoopy's, that Delaney & Bonnie got their next break. "We were discovered by Gram Parsons in a club," Bonnie explained to Jill McLane Smith. "He introduced us to our management and brought George Harrison to hear us." Harrison attempted to sign them to the Beatles' Apple label, but Delaney had recently contractually bound them to Elektra Records after the Stax deal crumbled. Elektra released *The Original Delaney & Bonnie & Friends (Accept No Substitute)* with a band that included Whitlock, Leon Russell, Carl Radle, Jim Keltner, Bobby Keys, and Rita Coolidge. Critic Nick Logan called it "the quintessen-

tial fusion of gospel, country, and soul influences that was easily the most exciting sound of its time." In response to the attention the LP attracted, Stax decided to release the previous year's *Home*, giving fans the impression that it was actually their second album.

At George Harrison's suggestion, Eric Clapton took Delaney & Bonnie & Friends on the road to open for Blind Faith in the summer of 1969. "For me," Clapton recounted in his memoirs, "going on after Delaney & Bonnie was really, really tough, because I thought they were miles better than us. Their band had all these great Southern musicians, who put out a really strong sound and performed with absolute confidence." Eric started sitting in during Delaney & Bonnie's opening sets and continued to play with them following the tour. After he helped them secure a new record deal with Atco, Delaney & Bonnie & Friends released *On Tour with Eric Clapton* in 1970. The album went Gold.

The *On the Road* album captured the trademark stew of Southern influences that Bobby Whitlock called "a melting pot, including rock, gospel, hillbilly, country, blues, and soul." The no-frills aesthetic and embrace of traditional American musical forms was a direct precursor to the Southern rock movement. "We kicked the dang door open," Bonnie proclaimed of the role she and Delaney played in that transition. "We crossed the line boldly."

Around the same time, Delaney produced Eric Clapton's debut solo album and used his "Friends" as the backing band. Many of the same players would leave Delaney & Bonnie to back Joe Cocker on his *Mad Dogs & Englishmen* tour, George Harrison on his *All Things Must Pass* album, and Eric Clapton in Derek & the Dominos.

Despite losing so many great players, Delaney & Bonnie continued to attract the upper echelon of rock royalty. Three more albums—

Signing with Capricorn Records. *Left to right:* Phil Walden, Bonnie Bramlett, Mike Hyland, and Dick Wooley. (Courtesy of Mike Hyland)

at the moment when Bonnie most needed rescuing. "Phil Walden came and got me," she remembered. "I loved Phil Walden. Phil was a good guy. He really was a *good* guy."

In Georgia, Bonnie found acceptance at her lowest point. "Bonnie Bramlett just showed up in Macon and immediately became one of us," explained Dru Lombar of Grinderswitch, in an interview with Michael Buffalo Smith. "Not only is she one of the best female singers of all time, she is also a real honest down to earth person."

The welcoming community was exactly what Bonnie needed:

> They loved me. I was *Southern*, man. I thrive here and everybody here, I'm telling you, from Charlie Daniels' family, the Allman Brothers, Ronnie Van Zant, all of 'em, saw me beat-up and wounded. I was a hurt little puppy, honey. They just embraced me and kept the rest of the world from kickin' the shit out of me. They protected me. It was way more than musical. I was dying and they helped me. They joined hands and made a circle around me, metaphorically speaking, and didn't let anybody hurt me until I could heal enough to defend myself. . . . I was born in Illinois and raised there, but I didn't grow up there. I grew up down here. Everybody was, like, holding the net under me, if you will. I've never felt more loved in my life.

When Dickey Betts moved to Florida, Bonnie took up residence on the Allman Brothers' farm, where she lived for about four years. "We had a freakin' ball," Bonnie laughed. "We had money, and no rules." Though she was in need of some light heartedness following her tumultuous relationship with

To Bonnie from Delaney, *Motel Shot*, and *D&B Together*—were issued, each of which featured a long list of "Friends" that always included Duane Allman. "When we could not find Duane," recalled Capricorn's Mike Hyland, "somebody would say, 'Well, find Delaney & Bonnie's itinerary. He's probably out with them.' And he would be!"

Behind the scenes, Bonnie and Delaney's marriage was crumbling due to drug abuse and an explosive clash of personalities. "I was drunk," Bonnie confessed, in Mitchell D. Lopate's *Rock 'n Blues Stew*, "coked out of my brain, hoarse, up for three days, hardly no chops—and everybody looks at that point in time and says, 'Listen to her voice crack—how soulful.' That wasn't soulful, it was just getting the note out, man!"

The end of Delaney and Bonnie's musical and marital relationship came in 1972. For Bonnie, it seemed to end as quickly as it had started. "We met, and we were married seven days later," she recounted. "We were in love, had children, put a band together, went right to the top, got introduced to cocaine, and fell right back to the bottom, in about three seconds."

Bonnie left behind a half-dozen solid albums with Delaney, as well as songwriting credits on classics like Eric Clapton's "Let It Rain," and "Groupie (Superstar)," which became a major hit by the Carpenters. With a strong track record behind her, she released one solo album for CBS and threw herself into background singing work with artists such as Carly Simon, Elvin Bishop, the Everly Brothers, and Little Feat. "I always say I'm like cow shit in Texas," Bonnie laughed. "You can dang near find me anywhere." Though her name was closely associated with rock royalty, offstage Bonnie struggled with the considerably less glamorous demons of substance abuse and a broken heart. It was time for a change.

Bonnie Bramlett soon found a caring community in Macon, Georgia. "Duane always said that if anything ever happened to Delaney, that I would be in the Allman Brothers Band with them," Bonnie recalled. Duane's old Hour Glass bandmate and fellow Maconite Johnny Sandlin shared his appreciation for Bonnie's voice. "I saw her in New York at A&M Recording Studio when Delaney & Bonnie did that thing with Duane," Sandlin remembered. "I loved her voice, and I asked Phil Walden, 'Please sign Bonnie.' And he did." It happened

Joe Cocker and Bonnie in the studio with producer Johnny Sandlin (*far left*) during the recording of the *Lady's Choice* LP. (Courtesy of Johnny Sandlin)

Bonnie in 1978. (Capricorn Records)

Delaney, Bonnie was also ready to get to work. She entered the studio to begin crafting her Capricorn debut, 1974's *It's Time*.

The album was a team effort. "All the Allman Brothers helped me, and everybody," Bonnie remembered. "Scott Boyer wrote the title song, which is just a monster, wonderful, beautiful song called 'It's Time.'" With producer Johnny Sandlin at the helm, the cream of Macon's musical crop formed the backing band. "I believe in him as a producer like I believe in God," Bramlett said of Sandlin, in an interview with Michael Buffalo Smith. "He can do anything." Though the album was a consistently strong effort, it was the Gregg Allman–penned closing track that most excited Bonnie. "I think my favorite performance . . . in the studio is 'Oncoming Traffic,'" she acknowledged. "With Gregg Allman performing on the piano, it is special."

In 1976, Capricorn released Bonnie's second album for the label, another Sandlin production called *Lady's Choice*. Ironically, the duet concept album wasn't exactly the lady's choice. "To be honest," Sandlin revealed, "neither Bonnie nor I particularly wanted to do a duets album. Phil and Frank were insistent, so we started putting together songs that would work for the concept."

The album was recorded at Muscle Shoals Sound but mixed and overdubbed at Capricorn. The final *Lady's Choice* LP was a combination of solo performances and duet efforts with Dobie Gray, Gregg Allman, Wet Willie's Jimmy Hall, Bobby Whitlock, and Mickey Thomas, who'd sung lead vocals

on Elvin Bishop's "Fooled Around and Fell in Love." Joe Cocker came to a session but passed out drunk on the studio floor and did not appear on the finished product. In the end, the album garnered positive reviews and brought Bonnie renewed attention.

That same year, Bonnie headed overseas with the Marshall Tucker Band and Grinderswitch. Despite rave concert and album reviews, and a dedicated core of ardent in-the-know fans, *Lady's Choice*—like *It's Time* before it—did not see impressive sales figures. In 1978, Bonnie released her third Capricorn collection, *Memories*, which was produced by Deke Richards, rather than Sandlin. "I think that was a favor that Phil Walden screwed up on," Bonnie mused, regarding the choice of producer. "He was shady at the time, I think. Richards wanted to produce me. That's all right. I'm not crazy about that album. He was trying to find a new me instead of embracing the one that he had." It would be Bonnie Bramlett's last Capricorn Records release.

In the spring of 1978, Bonnie completed an alcohol rehabilitation program and embraced sobriety. "Charlie Daniels calls me Sister Bonnie, and he prayed for me when I was getting sober and dying of alcohol abuse," she revealed. "He would say, 'Aren't you tired little Sister, aren't you ready to come home now?' He knew that I had been raised in the church and knew I had done too much to get back righteously. I feel like it was Charlie . . . that prayed me back home."

Physically and spiritually renewed, Bonnie appeared as an "Allman Sister," singing a duet of "Crazy Love," on the Allman Brothers Band's *Enlightened Rogues* LP. She took to the road as a member of the group for their tour the following year.

By the close of the decade, Bonnie had moved out of Macon, but she was still a quintessential part of the family. "Some people get Grammy awards . . . but to me, to get on the Allman Brothers stage, or the Charlie Daniels Band, or Toy and the Tucker boys, those are like real men. . . . You know there [is] certain acceptance by these men in the Southern rock business that I wear like a badge of merit. . . . They always treated me like a lady, whether I acted like one or not. They put me way up on a pedestal and make me feel more than an equal."

Though she spent time in Los Angeles and other locales following her era of rebirth in Macon, Bonnie eventually re-settled south of the Mason-Dixon Line for good. "I'm in the South," she reflected in 2012. "I feel like I belong here, and I mean something to Southern rock music." ★

ONE OF A KIND: BOBBY WHITLOCK
—

BY THE TIME Bobby Whitlock rolled into Macon, Georgia, in early 1975, he'd already lived the rock-and-roll dream, both as a solo artist and in collaboration with luminaries including Eric Clapton, George Harrison, Duane Allman, Dr. John, Stephen Stills, and others.

Whitlock spent his formative years in Tennessee, Arkansas, and Kansas City. His grandmother played the dobro, and Bobby showed an aptitude for music from an early age. "I always knew what I was going to do," he recalled. "It was in my spirit."

Immediately after high school graduation in 1965, the budding singer and multi-instrumentalist headed for Memphis, where he hung out at Stax Records. "The first performance of mine that was ever recorded," Bobby recalled, "was clapping hands with Isaac Hayes and David Porter on Sam & Dave's 'I Thank You.'" Before long, Stax bassist Donald "Duck" Dunn was producing sides by Whitlock for the label's pop-oriented Hip imprint.

Bobby was playing at Memphis' Cabaret nightclub in 1968 when Dunn showed up. "He brought Delaney & Bonnie to hear me one night," he recounted. "It was a Thursday, and they heard me and said, 'We're gonna put a band together. Would you like to come to California?' I said, 'Yeah!' and I was gone on Saturday. I just packed my doo-wah diddy bag, and I had my Nehru jacket on, and got off the plane in California."

When Eric Clapton started sitting in with Delaney & Bonnie during the 1969 tour with Blind Faith, the legendary guitarist was struck by Whitlock's skills. "[Bobby] was without a doubt the most energetic sideman I had ever seen," Eric Clapton recalled, in the introduction to Whitlock's biography. By the time of 1971's *Motel Shot*, Whitlock had tired of the drugs and the fighting. He departed the group as Delaney & Bonnie's relationship crumbled.

With no solid career prospects, Bobby contacted Eric Clapton in England. "I had $120 in my pocket," Whitlock remembered. "I called Eric and I said, 'Hey, man, do you mind if I come over and visit for a minute?'" Once he arrived in England, Bobby also reunited with former Delaney & Bonnie bandmates Carl Radle and Jim Gordon. The three moved into Clapton's house and began jamming and writing songs. Eventually, they'd be known to the world as Derek & the Dominos. "It was during this period [that] I learned what little I do know about writing songs," Clapton continued, "and most of that I learned from Bobby Whitlock."

In 1970, the Dominos entered Criteria Studios in Miami, where they collaborated with Duane Allman on *Layla and Other Assorted Love Songs*. Contributing guitar, piano, organ, and vocals—as well as receiving songwriting credits on nearly half the album's songs, including "I Looked Away," "Why Does Love Got to Be So Sad," and other standout tracks—Whitlock was an integral part of the band's success. Nevertheless, Derek & the Dominos eventually imploded, and Bobby found himself a musical wanderer once again.

At the invitation of former Delaney & Bonnie sideman Bobby Keys, Whitlock traveled to France to hang out with Keys and Gram Parsons while the legendary saxophonist worked with the Rolling Stones on the *Exile on Main Street* album. After returning to America, Whitlock hooked up with Stephen Stills, and appeared on the album *Down the Road* with Stills' band Manassas. He recorded a couple of strong albums for the ABC/Dunhill label, but they didn't garner the same attention as his work with the Dominos.

With no record deal and no manager, Whitlock eventually headed back to Memphis. "One day I picked up a *Rolling Stone*," he recalled, "and was sitting on the patio, smokin' a cigarette and drinkin' a cup of coffee, and there was a thing about the Allman Brothers in it. I looked and I said, 'Oh, Phil Walden.' I didn't even think about calling him before."

Whitlock contacted Phil in Macon:

The cover of Whitlock's *Rock Your Sox Off* album, 1976.

Promotional image of Bobby Whitlock in Macon, Georgia. (Courtesy of Light in the Attic Records/Bobby Whitlock personal collection)

I said, "You're the only music that's happening in the world that makes any sense to me, this Southern rock." He said, "Man, come on down, let's talk." I took that as a "Yes." I went and got a truck and loaded up my dog and my pregnant girlfriend and took off to Macon, Georgia.

I actually moved down there and just became a part of that scene, and it was really cool. They were a bunch of good people, and I made friends with all of 'em. The next thing you know, here I've moved into this giant family in Macon, Georgia.

As a true Southern musician, Bobby loved to jam. He spent hours at the Allman Brothers' farm, talking music and swapping licks. "I stayed at the cabin there many a night," he remembered, "drinking whiskey, and shooting guns, and playing guitar with Dickey Betts."

The backing musicians for Whitlock's Capricorn debut, *One of a Kind*, included Dickey Betts, Chuck Leavell, Johnny Sandlin, and Grinderswitch guitarist Dru Lombar. "Dru and I were real close," Bobby reflected. "He was a good friend. There was a lot of local players. The camaraderie of Capricorn, I believe, is really what held it together."

The day that *One of a Kind* hit the stores was a special day for Bobby. "My daughter was released the same day that my first record down there came out," he laughed. "They both came out the same day, August the 16th." While biding his time in the waiting room, Bobby was comforted by a Brother bearing a six-pack of Heineken. "Gregg was the only person who came to sit with me when my daughter was born," Whitlock

noted. As a result, Gregg Allman became baby Ashley's godfather.

Whitlock's second album, *Rock Your Sox Off*, was produced by Paul Hornsby. The backing musicians included guitarist Les Dudek, Grinderswitch's Larry Howard and Dru Lombar, Wet Willie's Jimmy Hall and Ricky Hirsch, and Chuck Leavell. One of the theories about the album's failure was the artwork. "*Rock Your Sox Off* was one of the best records out on Capricorn that year," Lombar declared in a 2001 interview, "but they put the ugliest cover on it, so that killed it." The artwork, a drawing by comedian and Capricorn artist Martin Mull, was mortifying to Bobby. "We usually had great covers," Johnny Sandlin recalled, "but that one? Oh, man."

Following the Capricorn period, Whitlock entered semi-retirement from the music business to concentrate on his family. Though he played on occasional recording sessions, he didn't resume his critically acclaimed solo career until 1999.

Capricorn didn't make Bobby Whitlock a superstar, but the label did give him a home in the Southern rock family at a time when he needed a musical community. "Phil Walden gave me an opportunity when nobody else would," he reflected. "Now, I may not have made a dime to this day, or never seen a royalty statement, but the point is Phil Walden gave me the opportunity to keep me in the mainstream of the music world, and to have my product out there, and gave me the absolute creative freedom to do so. When it was over, it was over. And I was a better man for it."

Part Seven

GREEN GRASS AND HIGH TIDES: RIDING THE SOUTHERN WAVE

The Outlaws in 1975. *Left to right:* Monte Yoho, Henry Paul, Hughie Thomasson, Frank O'Keefe, and Billy Jones. (Courtesy of John Gellman)

WHILE MACON, GEORGIA, became the logical focal point for the genre, significant bands emerged from across the South in the 1970s. Alongside Muscle Shoals, Nashville, and Jacksonville, places like rural Arkansas, Texas, Atlanta, and Tampa produced important players on the scene that had little or no connection to Southern rock's more prominent centers.

The members of Black Oak Arkansas, a band that was practically a genre unto itself, emerged from the Land of Opportunity and named themselves after their hometown. After starting their recording career in Memphis and Los Angeles, they eventually settled into a communal living arrangement in the Ozark Mountain region of their home state.

Similarly, the members of ZZ Top closely associated themselves with *their* home state, referring to themselves as "that little ol' band from Texas" and coming up with album names like *Rio Grande Mud* and *Tejas*. Their 1976 Worldwide Texas Tour was an over-the-top spectacle of state pride that was a major success with concert audiences. Point Blank, who shared a manager with ZZ Top, were another of the small group of Texas-based Southern rock bands to make a splash in the 1970s.

The city of Atlanta played a pivotal role in the history of Southern rock thanks, in part, to the Piedmont Park concerts that began in the late 1960s with the Allman Brothers Band, and continued with local groups like Hydra and Eric Quincy Tate. It was also in Atlanta where Al Kooper first met Lynyrd Skynyrd and launched his Sounds of the South label. But the Allmans were based in Macon, and Kooper's label was more of an imprint, with the business run primarily out of MCA's Los Angeles headquarters. The Atlanta Rhythm Section, however, were *based* in Atlanta, *recorded* in Atlanta, and *ran their business* from Atlanta.

Around the time the Atlanta Rhythm Section were enjoying a breakthrough in popularity, the Outlaws emerged from Tampa, Florida. While Jacksonville seemed to be a breeding ground for Southern rock bands, Tampa, 200 miles to the south, was not as well known for its music scene. It was from there that the Outlaws established a strong following before signing with a national label and finding themselves an integral part of the Southern rock community.

Likewise, the Amazing Rhythm Aces formed in Knoxville, Tennessee, located about 200 miles east of Nashville. After relocating to Memphis they began their recording career, and eventually found success with a wide audience.

"A lot of times they just fit people into that category 'cause of where they came from, or some other reasons besides the music that they played, for better or worse. It was more of an industry label than anything else, but I must say that Southern rock has held on for all these years."

—J. R. COBB, THE ATLANTA RHYTHM SECTION, 2013

Jim "Dandy" Mangrum and Rickie Lee Reynolds in 1975. (Courtesy of Frank White)

CHAPTER 27
Jim Dandy to the Rescue: Black Oak Arkansas

★ ★

IM MANGRUM IS unremittingly obnoxious onstage," John Mendelsohn wrote in a 1971 *Rolling Stone* review of Black Oak Arkansas' self-titled debut. "He introduces songs by reproducing the sounds of tumultuous orgasm, is fond of shaking his ass in little girls' faces, perpetually wears a demented wide-eyed smirk, and chews gum insolently. Cocky, randy, and gross beyond exaggeration, he gets away with it all because he's very beautiful, with luxurious chest-length golden hair and delicate features. . . . I think Black Oak Arkansas are one fantastic rock-and-roll band."

Black Oak Arkansas, best remembered for the 1973 hit "Jim Dandy," were the brainchild of lead singer and instigator Jim "Dandy" Mangrum. Dandy was an unselfconscious wild man. Raucous and raunchy,

BLACK OAK ARKANSAS

▸ JIM "DANDY" MANGRUM **lead vocals**

▸ RICKIE LEE REYNOLDS **guitar**

▸ HARVEY JETT **guitar, banjo, piano**

▸ PAT DAUGHERTY **bass**

▸ WAYNE EVANS **drums**

▸ STANLEY KNIGHT **lead guitar, organ**

▸ TOMMY ALDRIDGE **drums**

▸ RUBY STARR **vocals**

▸ JIMMY HENDERSON **guitar**

he strutted around the stage shirtless, wearing spandex pants and playing a washboard. Dandy's testosterone-fueled swagger gave the band a distinct visual identity, and his flamboyant antics captivated rock audiences.

"A lot of the Southern musicians think they're so good that they can just stand there like a cardboard cutout and not even move," Mangrum complained. "But we're here to entertain you. We give the people a *show*. Used to be that Elvis, James Brown, Jerry Lee Lewis, Tina Turner, these people would come out and move and sweat and bleed and entertain. We were trying to keep that alive a little bit." But the show didn't stop with the music. Between songs—or backstage, or giving interviews, or talking with fans, or wherever he happened to be—Jim Dandy was a verbal tornado of free association, words flowing out with a manic rhythm at least four times the speed of the average Southern drawl. Like a rock-and-roll preacher, Dandy held court on every topic from politics to religion to the nature of the universe—and all points in between. "I always said Jim would make a really good preacher or politician, 'cause he loves to talk," guitarist Rickie Lee Reynolds laughed. "He is a wordsmith!"

"I am the most profound radical nonconformist of our time," Mangrum declared to journalist Marty Jones, "and I've always upset people like that. They either love me like nothin', or I upset them greatly. And that doesn't bother me. I kind of like it. See, I was a leader and spokesman of a reactionary group, and that's far out when you consider I was from a place where people were afraid to speak their own mind, even inside their own living rooms."

Between 1971 and 1978, the highly prolific

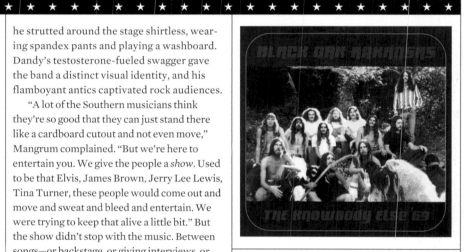

Black Oak Arkansas released eleven studio albums and two collections of live material. With three Gold albums and one hit single, they carved out a unique niche on the Southern rock scene of the 1970s.

Guitarist and songwriter Rickie Lee Reynolds was born in Arkansas but grew up in California. "I moved back to Arkansas at the first part of the tenth grade," Reynolds explained, "and that's where I met Jim Dandy. We were the only longhairs in Arkansas at that time, in a little town called Monette. Black Oak was so small it didn't have its own school, so the kids from Black Oak went to school in Monette. We were attracted to each other 'cause we were the ones that was always gettin' picked on by rednecks."

"I was the first longhair in Arkansas," Mangrum laughed. "Then these people I thought liked me last year started hating me for what I 'stood' for—whatever that was. It was the *way* they said it. My dad didn't know

Harvey Jett, Rickie Lee Reynolds, Tommy Aldridge, Jim "Dandy" Mangrum, Pat Daughtry, and Stanley Knight. (Courtesy of Mark Pucci)

he was raisin' a radical nonconformist. My mama didn't either. They thought they was raisin' a good American, which they *were*."

By refusing to conform to the haircut standards of the day, Jim was forced to learn to use his fists. "I was having five fights a week," he explained to writer Adam Sheets, "because I was a longhair, and people thought they could whoop me. But no one ever knocked me out." Though they were regularly hassled, Jim and Rickie didn't usually start the confrontations. "We were probably the most peace-loving boys in the South," Jim told *Rolling Stone* in 1971, "but we were always fighting—always just to protect ourselves. We had a reputation as hell-raisers, but it was always the rednecks who started the trouble."

Finally, Jim got an idea, which he related to interviewer Gary James: "I told Rick one day, 'Don't you know three chords?' He said, 'I know four.' I said, 'Well, let's just have a band. I can't fight these motherfuckers one at a time. We'll win them over.'" Though he'd played drums previously, Jim Dandy now switched to vocals. In a 2002 interview with *Carbon 14* magazine, Mangrum explained the moment he left the drums behind. "One of these fights I had," he recalled, "was over forty-five minutes

long and I couldn't hold my hands tight long enough anymore. I broke every finger on both hands except for one thumb. I couldn't hold the drumsticks, so I went out front. . . . I realized I had some kind of talent—not so much for singing—I learned how to sing and talk between songs just because I love to communicate with the audience. I love to agitate change. I love to say the things that they're afraid to say."

Recruiting a handful of musicians—including J. R. "Artis" Brewer, Sam Schattenberg, and Rickie's brother Danny on bass—Reynolds and Mangrum soon had a real band. "At that time," Rickie explained, "there was nobody else around Arkansas like us, so we named ourselves the Knowbody Else. . . . We'd play little fairs, little bitty clubs, American Legion huts, school proms, little things like this." Being longhairs was one thing, but long-haired *musicians* in rural Arkansas in the mid-1960s were regarded as troublemakers. Jim and his fellow musicians were constantly hassled by school authorities. The only place they could be themselves was in the grain elevator behind Jim's parents' place, where they spent hours practicing. All they lacked was decent equipment. In 1966 they hatched a plan to procure the necessary components of a proper rock-band arsenal.

"Me and Jim, my brother Danny, and a couple of J. R.'s friends were all drunk one night," Rickie explained, "and we had very little equipment. We were mad at principals and school superintendents and this, that, and the other thing for hassling us. It was in the dead of winter, and we went into the high-school PA system and took their little power amp and these two little speakers they had." Mangrum rationalized the theft in a 1973 *Rolling Stone* interview. "We hit the schools 'cause we figured they were stealin' from our parents, so we had the right." The band members may have had the heart for the job, but their burglary skills were a bit shaky. "We was wearin' all black, like the cat burglar," Jim laughed. "They had these old school windows on the school with six big panes. I hit it with a crowbar and that thing just rattled. I said, 'Back up, Rickey, I'm gonna break it this time.' He said, 'Wait, wait, wait.' He pushed on the window, and it wasn't even locked!"

"We used 'em for rehearsal a couple of times," Rickie remembered of the speakers, "and they went out and didn't work anymore, so we just kind of left them laying around. The school, being as small as it was, didn't even use these things until next spring, when basket-

ball season rolled around. They had all the kids in the auditorium. The principal said, 'Will you please stand now for the Pledge of Allegiance and the National Anthem?' We stood there and stood there and stood there. After five minutes, nothing happened. Finally, the principal comes out. 'We won't have the Pledge of Allegiance, as it looks like our PA system is missing.'"

It was Mangrum's father who would ultimately solve the case of the missing equipment. "What we actually got caught for," Reynolds explained, "is that Jim's daddy was the caretaker for the cotton gin over there at the grain elevator where we rehearsed. Jim got into the cotton gin one night and got a bunch of Cokes out of the machine there. His daddy found a case of those Cokes in his trunk and thought he would teach Jim a lesson. He turned him in for stealing a case of Cokes. Then the cops started looking into stuff and realized that we had that PA system, too."

"They got the meanest judge in Arkansas," Jim told writer Ray Shasho. The boys were found guilty of grand larceny. Later band publicity touted the twenty-six years to which they were sentenced at Tucker Prison Farm. In reality, it was a cumulative figure, and they didn't actually serve hard time. "I think I got an eight-year suspended sentence," Rickie recalled. "Jim got a twelve-year suspended sentence. My brother, myself, and Jim, we all added up to that big number. They had no ankle bracelets and stuff at that time. We could leave the state, but if we got arrested for anything during that time we'd be sent back to Arkansas to serve the rest of our remaining sentence. We had to wait until that was over with. We had to be good, and for us that's not an easy task!"

The band members' academic careers came to an end after their run-in with the law. "They finally kicked us out," Mangrum explained to Adam Sheets. "They said I was an agitator.... Fuck 'em if they can't take a joke." Rickie was a promising honor-roll student, but his intellectual abilities didn't seem to matter as much as his rebellious reputation. "I was the valedictorian of my class," Reynolds confirmed. "I got Rickie kicked out of every public school in the state of Arkansas," Mangrum added, "and I ruined his life." The band moved to the hills outside of town where they could rehearse their music in peace. Thanks to their status as convicted felons, they were ineligible for the draft and so avoided having to go to Vietnam.

It was during this era that the Knowbody Else honed their live show, which included a healthy dose of Jim Dandy philosophizing from the stage. "They can't keep me from being who I am," he declared. "They try to break

you in school. If they can't do it there, they try to break you in the military. If they can't do it there, they're gonna break you in prison. If they can't do it there, they're gonna put you in the ground, but that never bothered me. I wanted to talk to the people. I thought everybody was talking to the audience. We didn't see concerts until we started playing them."

According to Rickie Reynolds, Mangrum's charismatic rock-and-roll personality was fully formed from the band's earliest days. "What you saw onstage in the 1970s," he explained, "was the same as what we were doing in 1965. It was just who we were. There's no 'persona' put on. Jim Dandy is that character. Being from Arkansas, it was like a joke that we made it as far as we did. We thought it was funny as hell, so we just became funny as hell guys."

In the late 1960s, the Knowbody Else built up a regional reputation as an entertaining live act and moved to the nearest metropolis. "We were playing all over West Memphis," Reynolds recounted. "We became one of the top rock bands in Arkansas, playing clubs and stuff. Well, the only big town in Arkansas is Memphis, Tennessee. So we were living there." In 1968, Jim Stewart of Stax Records signed the band to his label's Hip subsidiary, which also signed fellow Memphis musician Bobby Whitlock.

Hip released the self-titled Knowbody Else album in 1969. The cover art featured a cosmic space scene glimpsed through a rustic cabin window. It was an apt visual representation of the blend of country-rock and psychedelic influences that defined the band's music in that era. When the LP failed to gain much attention, the Knowbody Else decided to relocate. "We were getting a lot of trouble from the heat in Memphis," Reynolds recalled. "We'd have helicopters circling overhead in the night with spotlights on us and stuff. Even if you weren't doing anything, that kind of gets to you. But we *were* doing something. Pot was like a killing

offense in Memphis, and we smoked pot. So we went down to Long Beach, Mississippi, which was only a half-hour or so from New Orleans." Mangrum laughed at the goal of their relocation. "We tried to stay out of trouble by going to New Orleans," he explained, "but that's right out of the pan and into the fire."

"We got a job on Bourbon Street," Rickie remembered. "We played every night at a club called the Gunga Den. We would play for a half-hour, and then another band would play for a half-hour. We'd go back and forth from seven o'clock at night until six o'clock the next morning. We did this for almost 500 days straight. During Mardi Gras, it was so crazy we had to sleep in the club. You couldn't get out to get back home again."

By 1970, Jim Dandy Mangrum decided to head to Los Angeles. Though they'd traveled there a couple of times before, they were determined to stick it out this time, until their band got the big break it needed to move to the next rung on the ladder of rock-and-roll dreams. Knowbody Else members Artis Brewer and Sam Schattenberg decided to step away, and were replaced by Wayne Evans on drums and Stanley Knight on lead guitar.

After arriving in California, Mangrum and Reynolds decided it was time for a name change. "Nobody else was like us back here," Jim told Gary James of the band's Arkansas beginnings. "When we got to California, everybody else was like us." The group began seeking out a new identity that would set them apart from the crowd. "A good friend of ours named Jerry Cohen was managing Jefferson Airplane and two or three other groups," Reynolds continued. "He said, 'Where are your roots at?' We told him that the first place we practiced was in a grain elevator in Black Oak Arkansas. He said, 'That's what you ought to call yourself.' We said, 'Grain elevator?' He went, 'No! Black Oak Arkansas!'"

By late 1970, Black Oak Arkansas had taken the Los Angeles club scene by storm. Audiences didn't know what to make of the kinetic Jim Dandy as he stomped around the stage like a wild-eyed sexually charged evangelist. One of the more unique aspects of the band was Jim Dandy's use of a washboard as a percussion instrument. "Back in the old days," Rickie recalled, "you'd be sitting there writing a song, and it helps to have somebody creating a beat while you're creating a song. So, there was a scrub board lying around, and Jim started playing that with his mom's thimbles. It sounded cool, so after we used it on a couple of songs he got known for being the only rock guy that was playing scrub board. It's like being type cast in a movie. You can't stop it once you've started it."

Following an encounter with Turkish-born Atlantic Records' chief Ahmet Ertegun, Black Oak Arkansas found the break they'd been working toward. "It took about a year for us to get Ahmet Ertegun to come out to see us," guitarist Harvey Jett recalled, "but when he finally came out to the Corral in Topanga, where we were playing, he was dancing and clapping his hands and generally raising hell all night long." Ertegun spoke with the band after the show. "At the start, we couldn't even understand each other," Rickie Reynolds confessed to *Rolling Stone* in 1971. "Ahmet's got his accent, you know, and it was like Turkey talking to Arkansas."

The band signed with Atlantic Records and recorded for the label's Atco subsidiary. At the time the group inked the deal, the lineup consisted of Jim Mangrum, Rickie Lee Reynolds, Harvey Jett, Pat Daugherty, Wayne Evans, and Stanley Knight. As with many Southern rock groups, Black Oak Arkansas included dual lead guitars. "The reason we had two lead players," Jim explained, "was because Harvey, when we went to California, he found this girl he thought he wanted to grow old with. He quit the band, so we got Stanley and brought him out there. Then Harvey came back and said, 'That bitch tried to stab me with a butcher knife. Can I come back to the band?'"

The self-titled debut album was released in 1971. The first track, "Uncle Lijah," started with a rustic, acoustic introduction before kicking in with Jim Dandy Mangrum's trademark gravel-voiced vocals. "Jim's voice is so strange," Reynolds later pointed out, "nobody ever thought he'd be a lead singer." Once listeners recovered from the shock of hearing Mangrum's raspy growl, they were likely singing along to the instantly catchy refrain. "I don't want to live forever, and I don't want to deny myself the adventure of life," Jim said of the song. "Uncle Elijah lived to be 105 and never left the state of Arkansas. I can't even fathom that. . . . I'm a lover of life. I love living life. If I could only have life if I had to be in hell, I'd say, 'Well, give me hell and I'll find a way to have fun there.'"

With standout songs like "Lord Have Mercy on My Soul" and "When Electricity Came to Arkansas," *Black Oak Arkansas* slowly caught on with rock fans. The album eventually achieved Gold status three years after its release. One of the most popular tracks was "Hot and Nasty," an anthem to Dandy's amorous impulses. Randy and raucous as he was, Jim Dandy was still a country boy at heart. The only cover song on the album was a version of Marty Robbins' "Sin-gin' the Blues," which was Jim's dad's favorite song. "At the very end," Rickie explained, "Jim says, 'This is for you, J. C.!' J. C. Mangrum is Jim's daddy. Everybody thought, 'Oh, he's dedicating it to Jesus Christ!'"

From the rock-and-roll swagger of "Hot and Nasty" to the gentle steel guitar of "Singin' the Blues," the LP covered a lot of musical ground. "It was a country sound with a little bit of a Southern rock to it, blues rock, or whatever," guitarist Harvey Jett reflected. "They called it confused," Mangrum reflected, "what we called versatile . . . We were just worried about covering all of the areas of our liking and from our heritage."

The band's second album, *Keep the Faith*, was released in early 1972, with legendary producer Tom Dowd at the helm. Mike Saunders, in his *Rolling Stone* review, was perplexed by Jim Dandy. "On first hearing," Saunders noted, "he is just absolutely, indescribably awful." He went on to call the lyrics "moronic" but conceded that he was won over by the "crass, brash, raunchy, energetic, and rocking" feel of the second side of the record. In the final analysis, Saunders couldn't resist the band's simplistic rock-and-roll sleaze.

Just four months after releasing *Keep the Faith*, Black Oak Arkansas put out their third album, *If an Angel Came to See You, Would You Make Her Feel at Home?* Like its predecessor, the LP was produced by Tom Dowd, but it featured a new drummer. "We ended up having to let Wayne go," Rickie recalled. "He had a birth defect that nobody knew about. His sternum was right up against his heart, so he couldn't stand a lot of stress. With us being on the road 300 days a year, the strain just got to be too much."

The replacement drummer was Tommy Aldridge, who would later go on to play with Pat Travers Band, Ozzy Osbourne, and Whitesnake. When Tommy joined, they were already in full-tilt party mode. "There was heavy pot smoking going on at the time," he told writer Mike Dolbear, "some serious chemical abuse, although not coke and heroin. . . . These guys just pummeled massive amounts of hash." After Aldridge came aboard, Black Oak Arkansas released an excellent live album in 1973 called *Raunch 'n' Roll Live*. Four of the seven tracks were previously unrecorded songs and, like the band's debut release, the album was eventually certified Gold.

That same year, Black Oak Arkansas relocated from a ranch in the Santa Monica Mountains to an eight-acre compound, surrounded by 1,300 additional acres, back in Arkansas. "We figured if we all went together and got

Stanley Knight, Tommy Aldridge, Harvey Jett, Pat Daughtry, Jim "Dandy" Mangrum, and Rickie Lee Reynolds. (Photo by Michael Ochs Archives/Getty Images)

Publicity photo of Black Oak Arkansas with Ruby Starr.

a place, like we were living anyway, it would be a communal thing," Rickie explained. "We found a place in the Ozarks that used to be a hunting and fishing lodge. People started bringing in girlfriends that turned into wives. People started having babies. It was more like a family than a band." Black Oak Arkansas even became a corporate entity, with the goal of sharing the spoils of their success among themselves and their manager. There was a pension plan, real estate investments, and significant philanthropic activity.

With their hectic touring and recording schedule, however, there wasn't much time for the band to spend at the lodge. "In 1972 and 1973, Black Oak Arkansas did 300 and 310 one-nighters," Rickie recalled. "And we did four albums in those two years." Before the end of 1973, they returned to the studio with Tom Dowd to begin work on *High on the Hog*. Thanks to a fateful phone call from Elvis Presley, the LP included the band's biggest hit, "Jim Dandy."

"We had a friend who grew up with Elvis," Rickie explained. "George Klein was a disc jockey on an AM station in Memphis called WHBQ, and he would play a lot of Black Oak stuff. He called us up one time and said, 'Man,

y'all are fixin' to get a phone call from Elvis.'" The idea made Jim immediately nervous. "I said, 'Well, have I done something wrong?' He said, 'No, it's something you *haven't* done.' I thought, 'God, what could *that* be?' George said, 'He'll call you in two hours.' And it was exactly two hours. He was punctual as hell. Of course, I was scared to death, you know."

Elvis called to suggest that, since Mangrum already used the name, Black Oak Arkansas should record the song "Jim Dandy," as popularized by LaVern Baker in 1956. "My daddy called me Jim Dandy since I was nine years old," Mangrum recalled, "but I never heard the song. You missed a lot in Arkansas and the South." Nevertheless, Jim quickly agreed with Elvis' idea. "I told him, 'You don't say no to the King of Rock and Roll,'" he elaborated to journalist Ray Shasho, "and then I thought, 'That was corny, what did I say that for?' Elvis said, 'Rock and roll was created by a disc jockey for his own pocketbook. I play rhythm and blues and gospel, and there ain't but one King, and I ain't him.' But the coolest thing he said at the end of the conversation was . . . 'Jim Dandy, it comes through us, not from us, we just got the best seat in the house.' I thought, 'How noble.'"

Black Oak Arkansas' version of "Jim Dandy"

peaked at #25 on the *Billboard* chart on February 16, 1974, and the *High on the Hog* LP became another Gold album for the band. "Jim Dandy" included a female vocalist named Ruby Starr, who was born with the considerably less rock-and-roll name Constance Henrietta Mierzwiak, in Toledo, Ohio. Once Black Oak Arkansas stumbled upon her vocal talents, she became an important part of the family.

"We was in Evansville, Indiana, playing at a baseball stadium at this festival thing, and we went downtown to eat," Jim recalled. "After we ate at this restaurant, we was walking back, instead of riding. We wanted to stretch our legs. We heard this girl with this local band called Ruby Jones practicin' in a downstairs basement kind of auditorium. They were gonna play that night, so they were doing a soundcheck, and she was wailin'. She was like a mix between Brenda Lee and Janis Joplin. She was a spitfire."

Rickie elaborated:

At that time, we had started to diversify. We decided to use some of our money to help other groups around this area do what we did—come out of the South and make a hit. We said, "If you'll come with us, we'll get you a record deal." While Ruby was

doing her record, we were looking for a girl to sing the "Go Jim Dandy" part, and she was perfect for it. She and Jim Dandy were actually dating at that time. She was like a sister to all of us. At the lodge we had in Arkansas, we ended up buying another hunting lodge across the street and moving Ruby and her whole band over there.

Thanks to the boost from Black Oak Arkansas, Ruby Starr signed with A&M Records, while remaining an important part of Black Oak at the same time. "She sang on several tunes in the studio with me and Rickie and Pat," Mangrum told Gary James. "We did two European tours with her and two or three US tours with her." It was a golden era for Black Oak Arkansas. They were finally achieving notoriety through televised appearances and ample coverage in the rock press.

Despite the band's growing success, Harvey Jett left the band at the beginning of June 1974, immediately following a thirty-day tour of Europe opening for Black Sabbath, after experiencing a religious conversion. The last album on which he appeared was 1974's *Street Party*, another Tom Dowd production that included highlights like "Everybody Wants to See Heaven, Nobody Wants to Die" and the band's version of "Dixie."

The decision to record "Dixie," and the confederate flag motif that adorned both the front of Stanley's custom-made Les Paul electric guitar and the front of the drum risers, put Black Oak Arkansas firmly in the Southern rock camp in the mid-1970s. "The song 'Dixie' was just part of the image that we were at the time," Mangrum explained, in an interview with Philippe Archambeau. "We felt it was a good traditional remake. Southern rock is a category of music they put us in, like Skynyrd, Allman Brothers, etc. We were a little of rock, blues, and country."

Jim Dandy wasn't always entirely comfortable with the label or the image. "I was born in Michigan," he explained, "and spent my first seven years there. I don't see any of these imaginary lines. . . . If that term means something to the fans, though, I'm not going to knock it."

"We're not big flag wavers," Rickie Lee confessed, "but there is a vibe among Southern people about the rebel flag. The confederacy, before the Civil War, was a whole different thing in the South. I'm not talking about slavery. I'm talking about manners, Southern belles, gentlemen. It was a thing that should be remembered. Of course, there was terrible things about it, but there was also good things about it. Stanley was one of those people where the Confederate flag meant something to him, so he had it put on one of his guitars."

It only solidified the band's reputation as rebellious working-class rockers. "Some people think we're not the elite listeners' choice," Jim admitted to journalist Chet Flippo. "We don't claim to be. But we do have a following of people that relate to us, common people, the silent majority's sons and daughters, and they ain't had a voice in a lotta things, and they ain't been able to get the chances to learn a lotta things about the elite side of life." Black Oak Arkansas weren't attempting to impress the critics as much as the fans. "The main thing is the people," Mangrum affirmed, "because if it wasn't for them, we wouldn't have this great job. The gathering is a sacred gathering. It's a ritual, and I'm the master of the ceremony of that sacred gathering."

In 1975, no fewer than four Black Oak Arkansas albums appeared on the market. *Ain't Life Grand* was their final album for Atco. Recorded in Los Angeles, it was the first LP with Jimmy Henderson playing guitar, following Harvey Jett's departure. Richard Podolor was at the helm. "Richard did Steppenwolf, Three Dog Night, and so much great stuff," Rickie said. "He did a lot of production for MCA, and he was a great idea man." The album wasn't as dynamic as some of their earlier efforts, however. An unnecessary cover of the Beatles' "Taxman" and some other missteps lead critic Martin Popoff to evaluate the album as "all vine and no taters, chest-thumping but powerless."

The band then signed with MCA Records and, with Podolor still at the helm, released *X Rated*. With songs like "Bump 'n' Grind," "Flesh Needs Flesh," and "Too Hot to Stop," the LP was the band's raunchiest effort yet. Jim chalked up the sexual preoccupation with his small-town upbringing. "There were 272 people there," he pointed out in an interview with

Denver Westword. "They were all farmers, and it was mostly boys around my age. There were no girls around, and that's why sex had so much to do with my music."

Before the year was out, Atco released another live album, called *Live! Mutha*, and the Stax label rereleased the old Knowbody Else material as *Early Times* under the name Black Oak Arkansas. "Our manager had us doing two albums a year," Jim pointed out. "That's like competing against yourself. I asked Billy Gibbons once, 'Hey, when do you put out an album, Billy?' He said, 'When the one I've got out there quits selling.' Duh."

Two more MCA albums followed. *Balls of Fire*, from 1976, was a mixed bag. Highlights like "Leather Angel" contrasted with a handful of disco-oriented numbers. The band's final MCA recording, *10yr Overnight Success*, emerged in 1977, but was a largely sanitized attempt to stay relevant in a marketplace that was moving further and further away from Southern rock. At that point, the band began to splinter.

"We were incorporated," Rickie explained, "and our manager had power of attorney and kept us on the road all the time. I left because I started looking at the books and figures, and it wasn't adding up. The *10yr Overnight Success* album I'm on, and I wrote a bunch of those songs, but I left before it came out. They took my picture off the cover and reshot it, and didn't put my name on any of the credits." It was a turning point for the band. "Rickie Lee Reynolds left the band on July 4th 1976," Mangrum recalled, in an interview with *Road to Jacksonville*. "It just wasn't the same without him and his songs."

Tommy Aldridge eventually wanted out, too, but it wasn't an easy proposition:

I was an equal owner of a very successful band. I really didn't want to be there, and I said, "Just keep all that. Let me have my contractual freedom and I'll go." But they wouldn't have it. The roadie had become the manager and an equal member, and he was very, very homespun and seat-of-the-pants. He had some issues, and liked to keep everyone under his thumb. . . . When I told him I was unhappy, and it would be best for everybody if I respectfully bow out, he said, "That's like you coming into my kid's bedroom in the middle of the night and putting a .357 Magnum into her mouth!" I said, "Excuse me?!" So that was his perspective.

Eventually, Aldridge had to sneak away from the compound under cover of night.

Jim Dandy with Black Oak and the staff of Capricorn Records, 1978. (Courtesy of Mike Hyland)

In 1977, Jim Dandy signed with Capricorn Records, changed the name to Black Oak, and recorded two albums, backed by studio musicians. Only Jimmy Henderson remained from the previous incarnation of the band. The first Capricorn release, *Race with the Devil*, was a moderately solid album. The follow-up, *I'd Rather Be Sailing*, was an abysmal collection of impotent soft rock. "Jim Dandy hates *I'd Rather Be Sailing*," Rickie explained. "He calls that album, *I'd Rather Be Doing Anything Else Than This Album*."

Though observers were wondering what had happened to Jim Dandy, the reality behind the scenes was that the band's toxic manager had made life so miserable that Mangrum, too, was looking for a way to extricate himself. "I was the biggest fool of all," Jim admitted, "but I was the last one to notice. I was having too much fun on the road.... When we signed the deal with Capricorn, I was already in a state of mind where I was just tryin' to pay all the bills and leave. He'd run off all my guys, like a lot of these trophy managers who just want the one star and hire the musicians."

With millions of dollars unaccounted for, Black Oak Arkansas devolved into a series of lawsuits and lost investments. The band members were devastated. "When we wanted to begin enjoying life," Rickie recounted, "we were left high and dry. We all lost our homes, cars, publishing, and almost lost our band name. It got blamed on bad investments. All I know is some of us had to pawn our Gold albums to feed our families." When the band compound burned down, Mangrum was investigated for arson and fraud. "I'm the one that burned the lodge," he said in 2013. "I don't care who knows it. They can only try you once.... The irony was that I had more fun, more friends, and more pussy than the guy that took my money."

While they might not get much credit for it today, Black Oak Arkansas helped set the pattern for the rock bands to follow. "David Lee Roth is a friend of ours," Rickie explained. "And David admits to studying Jim really closely before he ever got with Van Halen." There's no question that Jim Dandy had a hand in shaping the rock-and-roll archetype of the outrageously sensual lead singer with flowing feminine locks and raw sexual energy.

"I wasn't tryin' to show off my dick in them pants," Mangrum laughed. "I just had a lot of balls. It's like a woman that's got big tits but don't wear a bra. They kind of hang!" The unique image set them apart from their musical brethren. "Black Oak was never considered a Southern band by Southern bands," Rickie reflected. "We were weird. We were like a burr under the saddle or something."

"In the end," Mangrum added, "freedom of speech and individuality is what the Dandy is all about. I was proud of what we did and proud of where we was from. Things happened, but when you have personality ... even if they take all your money you can get more, as long as you keep your personality and your sense of humor. They can't get you down unless you let 'em."

In 2013, Atlantic Records re-signed Black Oak Arkansas and released *Back Thar N' Over Yonder*, a mix of unreleased masters from the 1970s, as well as new songs. The band hit the road once again, embarking on an unexpected new chapter with a renewed sense of purpose. The unlikely re-association of a classic-era Southern rock band with a major record label was no surprise to Mangrum. "My dad used to say, 'Son, *can't* never could do nothing and *can* always will,'" Jim related. "He'd say, 'What are you?' And I'd say, 'I'm a *can* man, dad!'" ★

Dusty Hill and Billy Gibbons onstage at the Macon Coliseum in Macon, Georgia, 1974. (Photo by Tom Hill/ WireImage)

CHAPTER 28
Hot, Blue, and Righteous: ZZ Top

★ ★

 N 1983, ZZ TOP released *Eliminator*. Accompanied by vivid videos packed with beautiful women and tailored to the MTV age, the singles "Gimme All Your Lovin'," "Sharp Dressed Man," and "Legs" propelled the album to sales of more than ten million copies, and made band members Billy Gibbons, Dusty Hill, and Frank Beard iconic superstars of the 1980s. But before taking over the world with their trademark beards, spinning guitars, and synthesizer-pulsing beats, the members of ZZ Top had already established themselves as one of the finest Southern blues and boogie bands of the 1970s.

"Texas being its own planet, it's certainly fair to say that it maintains its own degree of Southernness," guitarist and primary vocalist Billy Gibbons reflected in 2013, "as well as its own independent state of mind." In much the same way, ZZ Top is a band that formed with a strong regional identity before going on to represent what can only be described as a category unto itself. "Without question, we've embraced the term Southern rock," Gibbons continued. "I think the term was coined as a convenience

ZZ TOP

- ▸ BILLY GIBBONS guitar, vocals
- ▸ DAN MITCHELL drums
- ▸ LANIER GREIG keyboards
- ▸ BILLY ETHRIDGE bass
- ▸ FRANK BEARD drums
- ▸ DUSTY HILL bass, vocals

tool to point out the activities on the rock scene that had previously been either overlooked, or perhaps not taken as seriously."

Though Billy was born in Houston and raised in the nearby suburb of Tanglewood, his father, Fred, was a New Yorker who relocated to the Lone Star State in the 1930s. Establishing himself as an accomplished pianist and bandleader, the elder Gibbons eventually became the conductor of the Houston Philharmonic orchestra. While Fred encouraged his son's artistic impulses, he was not personally a fan of R&B or rock and roll. Those influences entered the Gibbons home through the family housekeeper, Stella Matthews.

Since they were involved in the local music community, Billy's parents were frequently away from home in the evenings. "Three nights a week, we got to stay overnight with Big Stella," he remembered. "She had four kids of her own. Little Stella, who was around eighteen, was the oldest. Big Stella would go to sleep early, and it was Little Stella that grabbed me by the hand and swooped up my sister and walked us down the street where there was a great club. I was gettin' to see Jimmy Reed, B. B. King, Little Richard.... It was exciting, and something kind of cool, but you look back now and go, 'Wow! We actually got to see that stuff!'"

Piecing together Gibbons' early musical development is a challenge, given his penchant for embellishment and intentional myth-making. "Spending a day with Gibbons is like diving into a novel co-written by Mark Twain, Hunter S. Thompson, and Phillip K. Dick to a psychedelicised Robert Johnson soundtrack," *Guitar Aficionado*'s Pete Makowski wrote in 2010, before going on

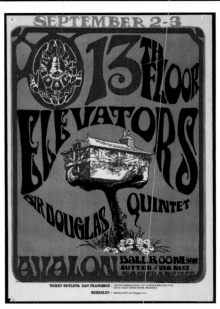

A concert poster for the 13th Floor Elevators, a key influence on Billy Gibbons and the Moving Sidewalks.

to describe the guitarist as "musically a shaman, visually a conceptual work of art in progress, verbally a snake-oil salesman mixed with beatnik philosopher and Indian mystic."

Billy Gibbons has always been a prankster. His propensity for self-amusement derived from spinning yarns and telling tall tales to journalists over the years has created an official narrative of the band's history that's part truth, part exaggeration, part imagination, and *all* entertainment. Like a rock-and-roll P. T. Barnum, Gibbons has presided over the ZZ Top fanfare and folklore for so many years that even he has likely lost sight of where reality ends and the show begins.

Moving Sidewalks publicity photo, *left to right*: Dan Mitchell, Tom Moore, Don Summers, and Billy Gibbons.

And that's the point. ZZ Top is about loud guitars, fast cars, greasy barbecue, beautiful women, and every larger-than-life testosterone-fueled fantasy that a working-class Texas boy could dream of. "Their music is rock and roll at its most powerful," Glenn O'Brien proclaimed in a 1985 *Spin* magazine article. "Heavy metal is a joke. ZZ Top is a joke, too—but they're in on it."

By the time Billy Gibbons was in his early teens, he began trying his hand at making music. "I got my first guitar on Christmas Day, right after I turned thirteen," he explained. "Six months later, I was cuttin' it up with my pals down the street. We had a little teen band, the Saints, that got hired to play the frat parties because we were cheap and we knew all the fast numbers. It was loud, man."

Over the years, Gibbons has told journalists about other bands he was in with names like the Mangy Mutts or Billy G. & His Ten Blue Flames, but his Houston peers didn't recall such outfits. What *is* certain is that the Saints morphed into an R&B group called the Coach-

men, and honed themselves into an excellent cover band. "Growing up in Texas," Billy reflected in a 1984 interview with Barney Hoskyns, "there just seemed to be so much time on your hands, and that was a factor, that plus the old tradition of the Texas gunslinger. In other words, if you didn't have a six-shooter, you used six strings."

When the psychedelic movement began to take hold, Gibbons took notice. "All of a sudden," he recalled, "out of nowhere, came this mind blowing band called the 13th Floor Elevators, with this manic singer named Roky Erickson. I said, 'Hold on! This is what's doing it for me.'" Billy and Coachmen drummer Dan Mitchell formed a group called the Moving Sidewalks, in tribute to their new heroes. "I said, 'Well, if they're going to be the Elevators,'" Gibbons recounted, "they go up, and the sidewalks go forward. That's good enough for me." It was a marked shift from the R&B classics they'd been recreating as the Coachmen. "We made the jump from soul band to psychedelic band early in the summer of 1967,"

Gibbons told *Rolling Stone*'s Kurt Loder. "That's when the line was drawn. All of a sudden, nobody could understand what we were doing." With the shift came an openness to both musical and chemical exploration. In his book *Rock + Roll Gearhead*, Gibbons described the Moving Sidewalks as "a more experimental sound, with new stuff—new gear, different effects, things to step on, things to plug into. And strange new visions . . . things altering one's mind, so to say . . . you know."

In 1968, the Moving Sidewalks released a single on the Texas-based Tantara label called "99th Floor." It became a sensation on Houston radio at a time when regional hits could produce local stars. The single was picked up by the Wand label in New York, and the Moving Sidewalks eventually began touring beyond Texas before releasing a full length LP called *Flash*.

"We started stretching out and playing in Louisiana and Mississippi, and somehow we got hired to join the Jimi Hendrix Experience tour," Gibbons recounted. Joining the lineup of the Hendrix tour for four shows in Texas earned the Moving Sidewalks new fans as they gained musical confidence. Hendrix himself singled out the Sidewalks as a solid band to watch when he was interviewed on a New York radio station soon after the short tour.

"We finally wound up on the West Coast," Billy continued, "and we took residency there in Los Angeles. The two famous joints in '68 and '69 were Gazzari's, and even more popular was a joint called the Galaxy, which was next door. We were kind of keeping one foot back in Texas. It was a thirty-six-hour nonstop drive to haul ass between L.A. and Houston, and we were making that trip constantly." Despite the Moving Sidewalks' forward momentum, Uncle Sam put an end to the band when two members received their draft notices in 1969. "That left me and the drummer, Dan Mitchell," Billy recalled.

Gibbons enrolled at the University of Texas and continued making music with Mitchell and a keyboard player named Lanier Greig, who played the bass parts with foot pedals on his organ. "The first incarnation of ZZ Top," Gibbons explained, "came out of the Moving Sidewalks. When we added this third guy, we changed the name." Various legends explain the origin of the band name, including the plausible theory that it was a combination of the names of two popular brands of rolling papers, Zig Zag and Top. Gibbons has generally maintained it was a nod to their blues roots. "I said, 'Well, we have Z. Z. Hill at this end of the alphabet,'" Billy recounted in 2013, "and we've got B. B. King.' We were first called ZZ King, and I said, 'No, it's too much like B. B. King, but king is, like, at the *top* of the heap, so let's call it ZZ Top.'"

Around the same time Lanier Greig came into the picture, Billy hooked up with Bill Ham, a local record distributor who was looking to make his mark as a music manager. While holding onto his steady job at Daily Record Distributors, Ham inked a deal with Billy to become ZZ Top's manager. From that point forward, the driving force behind the band was the duo of Gibbons and Ham. They got a boost when Ham's bosses, the Daily brothers, agreed to help finance them in their early stages.

With Bill Ham producing, ZZ Top recorded their first single, "Salt Lick," on Ham's own Scat label in 1969. Though the song was driven by the organ, Gibbons and Dan Mitchell soon decided they needed a proper bassist. Lanier Greig was excised, and bassist Billy Ethridge joined the fold. "Billy had been playing in a band with Jimmie Vaughan and the great, late drummer Doyle Bramhall, Sr.," Gibbons explained. "We knew Billy from his Dallas group. They were called the Chessmen. We got Billy to fill in on bass and he introduced me to Frank Beard, also from Dallas."

When Dan Mitchell gave up ZZ Top (or was pushed out of the band, depending on who's telling the story) at the end of 1969, Frank Beard took his place. Frank had been in a popular Dallas group called American Blues that he formed with brothers Rocky and Joe Michael "Dusty" Hill. As a gimmick, each member of the American Blues dyed his hair blue. "All it ever got us was into fights," Frank confessed to *Rolling Stone* in 1974. By the end of 1968, the American Blues had broken up. Frank auditioned for ZZ Top the following year and landed the gig.

"I picked up on the fact that Billy was a little strange from the beginning," Frank remarked in later years. But Beard had a Texas-sized personality all his own. He may have been a Southern boy, but Dallas was no rural outpost. "Frank liked everything that went with city life," former ZZ Top roadie David Blayney observed, "particularly fast cars, fast women, fast chemicals, and fast living." Though he'd dropped out of high school at age fifteen to marry his pregnant eighteen-year-old girlfriend, Frank's partying ways prevailed, and he ended up devoting himself to rock and roll rather than family life. "It was pretty much a shotgun wedding," he admitted, in Scott Nance's *Recycling the Blues*. "Her family hated me. I hated them. I hated her. She hated me. My parents hated her, and her parents hated my parents. Everybody hated everybody."

Not long after Frank came aboard, Billy Ethridge, who regularly clashed with manager Bill Ham, departed the group. In early 1970 they recruited Frank's old American Blues bandmate, Dusty Hill, and the permanent lineup of ZZ Top was finally set in stone. "We'd gone through four or five guys who wanted to throw their hat in the ring," Gibbons remembered. "When Dusty strapped up and took the stage we wound up playing a blues shuffle for three

Dusty Hill, Frank Beard, and Billy Gibbons at the Little Cypress–Mauriceville High School prom in Orange, Texas, 1971. (From the Little Cypress–Mauriceville yearbook)

hours, and I said, 'Well, I think this pretty much speaks for itself!'"

In contrast to Billy's family, Dusty's parents embraced rock and roll and R&B. "When I was a kid, eight years old," Hill recounted in a 1990 *Q* magazine profile, "my mother was playin' Lightnin' Hopkins around the house and stuff. And I thought everybody did! I'd go 'round other kids' houses and say, 'Where's your Lightnin' Hopkins? Where's your Muddy Waters?' And their parents were upset that their kids would come to my house and hear this!"

Billy Gibbons, Frank Beard, and Dusty Hill holed up in Billy's garage for a couple of weeks to get comfortable playing together. Gibbons recalled:

> I think it's fair to say that blues was the preferred style that we leaned to. However, you can't be in Texas without being impacted by what was going on in country music, hillbilly music, Western swing music. And it all draws from a fairly simplistic backbone. Rock and roll, country, so many of the types of music have a common thread with that great artistic American art form called the blues. It was no different for us. In fact, that's one of the threads that brought the three members of ZZ Top together. We discovered that we'd all been listening to the same records and the same radio station that was playing those records.

The new lineup of ZZ Top played its first gig on February 10, 1970, in Beaumont, Texas. They put the pedal down and didn't let up, gigging all over the state.

Bill Ham was eventually able to land

ZZ Top a recording contract with London Records. Early recordings were done at Brians Studios in Tyler, Texas, where owner and engineer Robin Hood Brians produced commercial jingles in his modest home-based facility. "Being a musician himself," Gibbons said of Brians, in an interview with *Music Radar*, "he had a lot of empathy for anybody who wandered into his place. He knew how to make everyone feel at home."

The band's debut LP, aptly titled *ZZ Top's First Album*, was recorded for $12,000 and released in January 1971. The liner notes read, "In this day of homogenized rock, synthesized music, retakes, overdubbing, multi multi-tracking, an honest recording by accomplished musicians is a rewarding pleasure." The few critics who bothered to take notice of the band's first album pointed out that it sounded muffled and unprofessional. Gibbons, however, insisted he was going for an authentically lo-fi bluesy vibe.

The album's lone single, "(Somebody Else Been) Shakin' Your Tree," failed to chart. But while ZZ Top may not have found fame with their first outing, they expanded their regional audience in the South with their crunchy guitar riffs, and humorously suggestive lyrics. "We called the record *ZZ Top's First Album* because we wanted everyone to know that there would be more," Billy explained to Joe Bosso in a 2013 interview. "We weren't certain if we'd get another chance in the studio, but we had high hopes."

While touring in support of their debut LP, ZZ Top encountered the Allman Brothers Band for the first time, and were impressed. "They broke the whole thing wide open," Gibbons remarked in 2013. The first time ZZ Top opened for the Allmans was at the Warehouse in New Orleans, and Billy was mesmerized by Duane's playing. "There was a closer kinship between us and the Allman Broth-

ers," Gibbons pointed out, "because we had those strong Texas roots, and they were from Florida, Georgia, and Mississippi." Some observers have noted that, after hearing Duane, Billy's own playing became more precise, nuanced, and disciplined.

By the early 1970s, Billy Gibbons got into transcendental meditation, which created something of a relational chasm with Dusty and Frank, who were quintessential Texas party boys at heart. Regardless of what was going on behind the scenes, however, Gibbons and Ham were masters at presenting an image of the band as misogynist hell-raisers who lived for every pleasure—carnal and otherwise—that life had to offer. In the spring of 1972, ZZ Top released *Rio Grande Mud* to mixed reviews. Driven by the single "Francine"—a wildly inappropriate declaration of love for a thirteen-year-old girl that sounded similar to the Rolling Stones' "Brown Sugar"—the LP sold better than their previous effort.

The picture on the back of *Rio Grande Mud* showed the band onstage at the Coliseum in Houston, at the first show after they met the Allman Brothers Band. By that point, the stage had become their natural habitat. ZZ Top toured relentlessly, spending up to 300 nights per year on the road. Manager Bill Ham—who had developed himself into a charismatic, forceful, and intimidating presence in the mold of Elvis Presley's hard-charging manager Colonel Tom Parker—kept them touring, but cheered them on with evangelical fervor. "At his best," roadie David Blayney recalled, "Bill Ham could make the Reverend Billy Graham look like he needed a refresher course in motivational oratory and faith."

In the early 1970s, Ham booked them into opening slots for bands like Uriah Heep, Alice Cooper, Mott the Hoople and Deep Purple. In many cases, these groups' more successful days were behind them, and their stage shows lacked the energy of younger, hungrier

bands. In contrast, ZZ Top's energetic, grab-'em-by-the-throat opening performances garnered them a hard-won new fan base. One of their more high-profile opportunities as an opening act came when they warmed up for the Rolling Stones in Hawaii in 1973. "It was a little terrifying," Dusty recalled, "because I remember reading on that tour that nobody wanted to see any of the opening bands." Their populist appeal as first-rate Southern blues rockers won the crowd over, however. "We are a people's band," Frank Beard told *Rolling Stone*'s Chet Flippo in 1976, "even when we opened for the Rolling Stones . . . the curtain came up and there we were in cowboy clothes, and a hush fell over the crowd—they thought we were a country band. So we jumped quick—1-2-3-4!—into 'Thunderbird' and that crowd was ours."

By 1973, ZZ Top's hard work was beginning to pay off as the album *Tres Hombres* began its slow climb up the charts. By the following year, it was in the Top 10, earning ZZ Top their first Gold record. Driven by the single "La Grange," the FM radio staple "Waitin' For the Bus" / "Jesus Just Left Chicago," and the crowd-pleasing "Beer Drinkers and Hell Raisers," *Tres Hombres* was a commercial breakthrough, and ZZ Top's first great album. Thanks largely to the participation of a new engineer, Terry Manning, the band sounded crisper and cleaner, without losing their gutsy, blues-rooted guitar riffs.

Half of *Tres Hombres* was recorded in Tyler, Texas, at Brians Studios. The other half was done at the famed Ardent Studios in Memphis, Tennessee, where the band would

London Records promotional poster. (Courtesy of Walter Vanderbeken)

An early ZZ Top publicity photo. *Left to right*: Frank Beard, Billy Gibbons, and Dusty Hill. (Courtesy of Mark Pucci)

As the stage show became more elaborate, the situation at the home office grew more complicated. By early 1975, Ham and the Daily brothers acrimoniously parted ways over what percentage of profits the brothers should receive from the increasing popularity of ZZ Top. Following a tangle of lawsuits, the Dailys took their settlement and launched Cactus Records, which became Houston's best-known music retail store.

In the spring of 1975, ZZ Top released *Fandango!* The first side of the LP consisted of live performances, while the second side was comprised of a half-dozen new studio recordings. Like its predecessor, *Fandango!* entered the Top 10 on the album charts and earned Gold status. "Tush" brought the group their first Top 20 hit. It was one of the handful of songs on which Dusty handled the lead vocals instead of Billy. "As for the lyrics," Billy quipped, "well, it's not exactly Bob Dylan." In fact, at the time it was released, this ode to the pursuit of the female backside raised the eyebrows of more than a few radio listeners. The single was banned in some markets. "In Dallas 'tush' meant plush," Dusty explained. "Something fine. . . . But it could mean what you think of back east— 'tushy.' It could have a double meaning, like that's a 'tush tush.'"

Two other songs from *Fandango!*, "I Heard It on the X" and "Mexican Blackbird," paid tribute to two of the band's musical influences. "The X is Mexican radio," Gibbons explained. "All Mexican stations' call letters begin with X. The X stations used to be heard everywhere, because of their enormous power. . . . It was just outrageous." Growing up, both Billy and Dusty were mesmerized by the wide variety of entertainment they heard on the X stations. The song featured Gibbons and Hill trading lead vocals, which they would do onstage more often than on the band's albums.

"Mexican Blackbird" was an intentionally sloppy country-and-western song about a prostitute. "It all comes back to paying homage to that simplistic thread," Billy explained of their country dabbling. "It doesn't have to be very complex, as long as it touches you in that Southern soulful spirit. If you can ignite that, you're on your way."

In 1975, ZZ Top embarked on the Thank You, Texas tour, hitting the major Texas markets with a stage set consisting of cacti, fake boulders, prairie fencing, a cow skull, and other Texas-themed décor. It gave birth to the over-the-top Worldwide Texas Tour of 1976, which included a veritable traveling zoo that consisted of a longhorn steer, a buffalo,

record most of their material going forward. Though it was not a major hit on the pop charts, "La Grange" stirred controversy. In 1985, Dusty asked a *Spin* magazine journalist:

> Did you ever see the movie, *The Best Little Whorehouse in Texas*? That's what it's about. I went there when I was thirteen. A lot of boys in Texas, when it's time to be a guy, went there and had it done. Fathers took their sons there. You couldn't cuss in there. You couldn't drink. It had an air of respectability. Miss Edna wouldn't stand for no bullshit. That's the woman that ran the place, and you know she didn't look like Dolly Parton, either. I'll tell you, she was a mean-looking woman. But oil-field workers and senators would both be there.

The B-side to "La Grange" was "Just Got Paid," which had originally appeared on the band's first album. Its appearance on the single made it a popular song in the band's live show, but they ultimately retired it from the set list after enthusiastic fans began pelting the band with change when they performed it live.

With the group's popularity on the rise, however, critics still regarded ZZ Top as primarily a Southern rock band. "They've given the kids of the South what they want to hear—a steady stream of high-power, no-nonsense blues-boogie—and the kids have rewarded them by making them Dixie's most popular band since the Allman Brothers," *Rolling Stone* declared in 1974.

On Labor Day 1974, the band hosted ZZ Top's First Annual Texas Size Rompin' Stompin' Barndance and Barbecue at the University of Texas' Memorial stadium in Austin. More than 80,000 fans showed up to witness them debut a new stage set that consisted of a wagon wheel, hay bales, and live chickens. Billy wore a rhinestone-encrusted Nudie suit—a look that was soon adopted by the whole band. Visually, they were evolving into larger-than-life Texas cartoon characters with down-home appeal.

Promotional photo of Frank, Billy, and Dusty, taken shortly after the band's late-1970s hiatus. (Warner Bros. Records)

live rattlesnakes, tarantulas, buzzards, and a trained wolf. The Texas-shaped stage set was 3,000 square feet and weighed 35 tons. It took five big rigs—painted with Texas scenery—to transport all the equipment and staging to the more than one hundred US dates on the grueling schedule. When the dust had settled, the unprecedented Worldwide Texas Tour had grossed over $11 million.

The nature of the tour's outlandish presentation ensured media attention at every stop along the route, a masterstroke of Bill Ham's marketing prowess that raised the band's profile even further. Critics were often surprised by the sophisticated marketing machine behind ZZ Top. "Onstage they look like nothing other than a bunch of dumb shits from Texas," journalist John Tiven wrote in a condescending 1976 piece that adhered to the all-too-familiar formula of assuming that Southerners were ignorant rubes. He was surprised to find Billy Gibbons reflective and articulate. "Now if you've been paying close attention," Tiven pointed out, "you'll notice that he said some words which exceed one syllable, and in fact many a word

which you wouldn't even find in the vocabulary of your average college grad-u-ate."

Following the triumph of the Worldwide Texas Tour, the next album, *Tejas*, which was released in December of 1976, was not as strong as the band's previous two efforts. Other than the singles "It's Only Love" and "Arrested for Driving While Blind," the songs were largely forgettable. Nevertheless, it made the Top 20, and was certified Gold. "It's fair to say that this is a transitional record," Billy Gibbons noted years later, "although I'm not really sure what we were transitioning from and what we were becoming. It may be representative of how rapidly things were changing in the studio."

After the completion of the Worldwide Texas Tour in 1976, the band members went on a nearly three-year hiatus until the release of their next album, *Deguello*, in 1979. As with much of the ZZ Top story, mystery surrounds the exact circumstances of the break. Band members told the press that they planned to take six months off to rest, but that they allowed more time to elapse than originally expected. It's unusual that the hard-charging Bill Ham wouldn't concentrate on pushing

them into new areas following the successful tour, and it's not entirely clear what, exactly, they were doing. The break only helped build the mystique and anticipation on which Billy Gibbons and Bill Ham thrived. "Billy was a chameleon," David Blayney noted in his 1994 memoir of working with the group. "He could sidestep probing questions by getting people to talk about things *they* were interested in. . . . Billy had a broad enough range of knowledge to be completely convincing while discussing any topic, even when he was out-and-out bullshitting. . . . One could never be sure when Billy was being truthful, borrowing from something he'd read, or recalling someone else's experiences as if they were his own."

What *is* certain is that when ZZ Top returned in 1979, there were several notable changes. Bill Ham had successfully extricated them from their London Records contract and brokered a lucrative deal with Warner Bros. All three band members grew long beards during the time off, though Frank shaved his soon after they reunited. Journalists were delighted by the fact that the one guy in the band whose name was Beard didn't have a beard, and it's virtually impossible to find an article about them from that era forward that doesn't make the observation.

"It just turned into this thing," Gibbons said of the beards, in an interview with Glenn O'Brien. "It was never questioned. We didn't question it until my friend Zack, who is a massage therapist, said, 'What's really the reason behind that beard?' I said, 'What do you mean?' He said, 'You know it's kind of like your breast plate. In the old days, guys would protect themselves by wearing this armor.' He said, 'It's your protection isn't it? You're really watching out for yourself by wearing it.' I said, 'Yeah, OK. Sure.' So I don't know that you could get to the bottom of it, but maybe."

Another change that marked ZZ Top's reemergence in 1979 was that Frank Beard had kicked the nasty substance abuse problem that had developed over the previous decade. He got clean and switched his addiction from drugs and alcohol to golf.

Warner Bros. released *Deguello* in August 1979. The album title referred to "El Deguello," a Mexican bugle call signaling "no quarter" that is most commonly associated with Santa Ana's attack at the Alamo. Like the epic Texas showdown, the album was an all-out attack. The band were ready to pick up where they left off and push themselves to the next level of success. The LP was recorded more deliberately and painstakingly than anything they'd done before. Gibbons spent countless hours overdubbing guitar parts and tinkering with the sound at Ardent. Anchored by the singles "Cheap Sunglasses" and a remake of the Isaac Hayes–penned Sam & Dave song "I Thank You," it was more layered than their previous records. *Deguello* became ZZ Top's first Platinum record.

In the fall of 1981, the band's seventh studio album, *El Loco*, was released. It included a pop-oriented mid-tempo ballad called "Leila" but was otherwise heavily weighted with the juvenile sexually charged innuendo of songs like "Tube Snake Boogie," "Ten Foot Pole," and "Pearl Necklace." Their live show remained a raucous affair. "We tried playing 'Leila' once," Dusty recalled, "and to hell with that. It feels better playing the harder stuff live." Critic Deborah Frost characterized ZZ Top's lyrics as reflecting an attitude of "boys getting together and being silly about girls." Of course, it was all part of the carefully crafted image. "See, for white boys playing the blues," Gibbons told *Rolling Stone* in 1980, "you can only get away with it if it's amusing." As an entertainer, Gibbons was a genius. "Billy's a pretty funny guy," Frank Beard pointed out to journalist Charles Shaar

A 1983 Warner Bros. advertisement for the "Sharp Dressed Man" single.

Murray. "I mean, when you look like a cartoon, you act like a cartoon."

The more notable aspect of the *El Loco* album, however, was the band's embrace of new technology. When Frank Beard decided to install a demo studio in his home in Houston, he hired a former DJ, musician, computer whiz, and audio engineer named Linden Hudson to build and maintain it. "He was a gifted songwriter and had production skills that were leading the pack at times," Gibbons said of Hudson thirty years later. "He brought some elements to the forefront that helped reshape what ZZ Top were doing, starting in the studio and eventually to the live stage.... Linden had no fear and was eager to experiment in ways that would frighten most bands. But we followed suit, and the synthesizers started to show up on record."

Though ZZ Top were just beginning to experiment with technology, some purists complained. "In a really, really simplistic way, it's like rockabilly in the early days," Dusty Hill observed, in *Guitar World* magazine, "when they wouldn't use a drummer on *Grand Ole Opry* for how long? It sounds silly now, but to those guys it wasn't. At that time, I'm sure there were people who thought that would change everything, and you won't be playing with the same feeling, but that's bullshit. The technology is a tool that we use, and whatever we play is going to sound like this band." By the time ZZ Top hit the road for the El Loco tour, their live sound was augmented by pre-recorded parts. "We're more than roots," Billy joked. "We've got leaves and bark."

By 1982, ZZ Top had fully embraced synthesizers and drum machines as an integral part of

their sound for a new generation. Through data analysis, Linden Hudson had discovered that most hit songs were within a beat or two of 124 beats per minute. He and Billy Gibbons set out to capitalize on the formula, resulting in songs like "Sharp Dressed Man" and "Legs," which are both 125 beats per minute. The resulting album, *Eliminator*, was released in 1983, and led ZZ Top to the pinnacle of their success.

The subsequent music videos and international tour were built around the theme of a customized 1934 Model T—appropriately named "Eliminator"—that Billy paid more than $50,000 for. Frank told *Kerrang!* magazine:

Billy saw the movie *The California Kid*, and it had a cool black hotrod in it, and he wanted to build himself a car. So he built the Eliminator. Then it was time to make the first video, and we said, "Man, we ought to use that car. That car's cool!" It was one of those right place at the right time, magic moment things, because I don't think we could have sat around with the video director and come up with all the success that has been attached to the car and the keychain and the ZZ girls and the whole image that came about from that.

The MTV audience agreed. The Tim Newman–directed videos for "Gimme All Your Lovin'," "Sharp Dressed Man," and "Legs"—with their spinning, fur-covered instruments, resplendent facial hair, and carefully crafted story lines of whimsical male fantasies—helped catapult ZZ Top to the highest echelon of rock superstardom. The *Eliminator* tour was a big production, with laser lights, an enormous replica of the car, and each show ending with the detonation of a smoke bomb, exploding scenery, and a dummy "light man" collapsing to the stage from the rigging above. *Eliminator* was

Billy Gibbons in 2008. (Courtesy of Alberto Cabello)

Dusty, Frank, and Billy during the band's most successful era. (Warner Bros.)

nominated for a Grammy, and became one of the best-selling albums in history.

Amazingly, ZZ Top had never even performed live on US television, but they suddenly found themselves as true American icons. Billy claimed that the Gillette razor company offered him and Dusty $1 million to shave their famous beards in 1984, but they refused. Though influential critic Barney Hoskyns referred to the group as "three cosmic-hill-billy stooges" in a 1983 profile on the band, that year was actually when they went from being a *Southern* band to an *American* band. "A lot of our earlier work was chronicles of Texana and events that were of substance for the guy living in Texas," Billy explained to journalist Steve Rosen in 1986. "Certain things you experienced when you're coming up there. But our appeal has broadened so much, because we've just gotten honest and started singing about things that were not so regional."

"In England," Frank Beard observed, following the massive success of *Eliminator*, "they used to lump us in with the Southern rock bands—Lynyrd Skynyrd, the Allmans. Now they say we're like John Fogerty. It's weird." Though the band transcended the "Southern rock" label in the 1980s, they always recognized its influence. "That solo was truly the successful marriage of a techno beat with bar-band blues-style overtones from the guitar department," Billy Gibbons revealed to Alan Paul of his "Sharp Dressed Man" guitar work, "and that certainly includes a wide range of Southern inspiration. We were becoming increasingly

attracted to the beats, you see, and yet the Allman Brothers remain some of our biggest heroes. On 'Sharp Dressed Man,' we brought those two worlds together."

Though ZZ Top were characterized by mainstream stardom and teenage devotees in the mid-1980s, they were still good ol' Texas boys at heart. They occasionally found themselves embroiled in the shenanigans of Southern rock lore. In December of 1984, for instance, Dusty Hill was shot in the abdomen. The official story was that the woman he was with was pulling off his boots when a .38 caliber derringer fell out and accidentally discharged. The rumor, however, was that she shot him in a fit of anger. Ultimately, he was fine, after undergoing two-and-a-half hours of surgery. Whatever really happened, it's a story that's tailor made for one of the band's tall tales.

In the final analysis, ZZ Top were one of the few Southern rock bands able to successfully adapt to the changing musical landscape of the 1980s. They continued to release Platinum-selling albums through the mid-1990s, and were inducted into the Rock and Roll Hall of Fame in 2004. As their record sales and radio airplay eventually began to decline, they remained a perennial favorite on the touring circuit, and Billy even reunited the Moving Sidewalks in 2012. Even though ZZ Top ultimately returned to their guitar-driven blues roots, they were rarely re-categorized as a Southern rock band. Nevertheless, with Gibbons regarded as a guitar hero in the league of Duane Allman, ZZ Top are a key component of Southern rock's foundation. ★

ROCK-AND-ROLL SOLDIERS: POINT BLANK

—

POINT BLANK CAME together in 1974 under the tutelage of music impresario and ZZ Top mastermind Bill Ham. Guitarist Rusty Burns was playing at a club called the Cellar in Houston when he first caught the enigmatic manager's attention. At the same time, singer John O'Daniel was working in Oklahoma. "I got a call from a buddy of mine in Houston," he recalled, "who said, 'There's a guitar player here who's left handed and plays upside down. This guy's incredible. He's got a deal with ZZ Top's manager, and they're looking to put a band together. . . . I went down to Houston to meet Rusty at the Cellar club. When I walked offstage, he said, 'I think we can do something!'"

The two began performing under the name Southpaw with bassist Phil Petty and drummer Buzzy Gruen. Kim Davis was soon added as a second guitarist. "Kim was more of a blues-oriented type player," O'Daniel explained, "and Rusty is a little more of the—I guess you'd call it from the Hendrix school, or the rock-and-roll school of music. It was the combination of the two that made us what we were."

When Burns wasn't playing gigs he worked as Billy Gibbons' guitar technician. "The plan was to put this education to work on the band I was beginning to form," he recalled. After spending 1973 playing under the name Odessa, Ham started actively booking Rusty's band beyond the Cellar. "Our very first show," O'Daniel remembered, "was at a 110-seat club on a Friday night in Dallas. Ham called Saturday morning, and we got in the truck and drove to New Orleans to open for Marshall Tucker at the Warehouse that night. We had no clothes to wear. We had to go shopping before we could play!"

"Bill had called us Blue Tail Fly," O'Daniel laughed. "That's how we were introduced in New Orleans. When we got back, we were all standing in Ham's office, and we had a Texas map out. Somebody noticed this town named Point Blank." Something clicked. "We began touring as Point Blank in September 1974," Rusty recounted.

"We were on the road two years before

we did an album," O'Daniel added. "We played a lot with ZZ, Marshall Tucker, Lynyrd Skynyrd, the Elvin Bishop Band, Charlie Daniels, the Allman Brothers." To win over audiences, Point Blank rocked harder than their peers. "We weren't very pretty," Rusty recalled, "so in order to compete with pretty bands, we had to try and blow them off of the stage."

The band's self-titled first album was released on Arista Records in 1976, showcasing them as a blues-drenched powerhouse in the ZZ Top tradition. With two guitarists, however, Point Blank were able to stretch out with some dazzling dual-lead solos that hit listeners in the chest with both barrels.

By 1977, they had released a follow-up album, *Second Season*, when the band suffered a major setback. "We had sixty-two dates booked with Skynyrd," O'Daniel explained. "About halfway back to Houston, we got the news that they had crashed. That put us out of work for about six months. That kind of screwed us up, and I think it screwed the whole Southern rock thing up."

By the time Point Blank started work on their third album, they had been dropped by Arista Records, and had replaced bassist Phil Petty with Bill Randolph. Steve Hardin was added on keyboards. The resulting LP, released on MCA, was titled *Airplay*. "The addition of the keyboard softened the music in many ways," Buzzy Gruen admitted, "and we were experimenting." For Burns' part, he was growing uncomfortable with Ham's vision. "I began feeling we were boxed in as a ZZ clone," he confessed, "though we were anything but. Don't get me wrong, I love ZZ, but I cannot be ZZ any more than I can be Bonnie Raitt, whom I love also.'"

By the time Point Blank released their fourth album, *The Hard Way*, in 1980, keyboardist Hardin had been replaced by Karl Berkebile. "Nobody could spell it," O'Daniel laughed, "so they just called him Berke." Featuring a handful of live tracks mixed with studio cuts, the album lacked a cohesive direction. "For *The Hard Way*, we were under pressure to produce," Rusty admitted, "but there was not enough material that passed the test."

"After the fourth album," O'Daniel recalled, "everybody kind of panicked. The rest of the guys kinda wanted to go for the smoother, Journey-sounding thing. My contention was that all these years we'd built up a fan base with the common guy, the average redneck. . . . I just said, 'I think you guys would be better off to get you a little sissy to sing that stuff, and I'm gonna go on and sing real music.' We split ways."

Berkebile departed, too, and the band recruited keyboardist Michael Hamilton and lead vocalist Bubba Keith. With Point Black now focusing on the burgeoning AOR radio format, their pursuit of FM success finally paid off when the 1981 MCA album *American Exce$$* spawned the Top 40 single "Nicole."

Point Blank failed to recapture that radio success with their sixth album, 1982's *On a Roll*, however. "I think the process was becoming stale," Gruen observed, in an interview with *Sweet Home Music*. MCA dropped the band. "We were what you'd call a rowdy Southern rock band," John O'Daniel confirmed. "We drank a lot of whiskey and snorted a lot of foreign countries and did a lot of crazy stuff back in the day. . . . When MCA dropped them, the bottom just dropped out of everything."

In the fall of 1982, Rusty was injured in a skydiving accident. The combination of his recuperation time, changing public tastes, and a falling out with Ham that resulted in a lawsuit led to the band's breakup in 1984. Though they never garnered the recognition or success of ZZ Top, Point Blank were a major force on the Texas-based Southern rock scene of the 1970s.

Point Blank's *Second Season* from 1977. *Left to right*: Rusty Burns, Kim Davis, Buzzy Gruen, Phillip Petty, and John O'Daniel. (Arista Records)

POINT BLANK

▸ JAMES "RUSTY" BURNS guitar

▸ JOHN O'DANIEL lead vocals

▸ PHILLIP PETTY bass

▸ PETER "BUZZY" GRUEN drums

▸ KIM DAVIS guitar

▸ STEVE HARDIN keyboards

▸ BILL RANDOLPH bass

▸ KARL BERKE keyboards

▸ BUBBA KEITH vocals

▸ MIKE HAMILTON keyboards

The Atlanta Rhythm Section's
Ronnie Hammond onstage for the
Champagne Jam at Georgia Tech's
Grant Field in Atlanta, 1978.
(Photo by Tom Hill/WireImage).

CHAPTER 29
The Boys from Doraville:
The Atlanta Rhythm Section

 N 1977, the Atlanta Rhythm Section scored a major pop hit with "So into You," a laid-back mid-tempo keyboard-driven jam that had more in common with Steely Dan's mainstream hits than the guitar pyrotechnics of the more hard-edged Southern rock bands. Successful singles in a similar vein followed, including "I'm Not Gonna Let It Bother Me Tonight" and "Imaginary Lover." Though the band came to represent the softer side of '70s Southern rock, the members' roots stretched back much further.

The history of the Atlanta Rhythm Section revolves around Buddy Buie, a songwriter, producer, and manager who hailed from Dothan, Alabama. "I started having dances at the recreation center and things like that when I was a senior in high school," Buie recalled. "I loved bands, and I loved music. If I was bookin' my own shows, I could be in charge of who I wanted to have play." Eventually, Buie began managing a group called the Webs that featured John Rainey Adkins and Bobby Goldsboro.

Though not a proficient musician himself, Buie began writing lyrics and coming up with melodic ideas. "My love was writing songs, but I was ashamed to show 'em to anybody," he confessed. "I had 'em in my head. The person that helped me most was John Rainey Adkins. He was the first guy . . . We'd sit out in front of his house in a '56 Chevrolet, and he would humor me, writin' songs. I'd hum the melodies I was thinkin' up, and he'd play them on the guitar."

Around the same time, Buie found his way into the studio where, through trial and error,

THE ATLANTA RHYTHM SECTION

▸ J. R. COBB guitar
▸ BARRY BAILEY guitar
▸ PAUL GODDARD bass
▸ RODNEY JUSTO vocals
▸ DEAN DAUGHTRY keyboards
▸ ROBERT NIX drums
▸ RONNIE HAMMOND vocals
▸ ROY YEAGER drums
▸ BUDDY BUIE producer, songwriter

he sharpened his skills as a producer. "Bobby Goldsboro and I started fooling around with recording," Buie recalled, "and I was in the studio a lot with Bobby. In fact, we cut our first record at a place over a blood bank called Heart Records in Birmingham."

Buie continued to work as a promoter, which led to him connecting with Roy Orbison in the early 1960s. "Buddy promoted a date in Dothan, Alabama," explained future Atlanta Rhythm Section lead singer Rodney Justo, "and agreed to supply the backup band. Roy said, 'Does your band read music?' He said, 'Oh, yeah, sure they read music.' This was not true, but he had everyone learn those songs *perfectly*. After the gig, Roy said, 'Man these guys are good. I wonder if they'd want to come on the road with me?' Buddy, as a young man, was very much an opportunist. He said, 'They'll agree, but I've got to come along, too, as the

road manager.'" It proved to be a successful partnership. "I was on the road with Roy Orbison for three years as his road manager," Buie explained in 2013.

By 1964, Bobby Goldsboro had left Orbison to pursue a successful solo career. Following his departure, Rodney Justo—a Tampa singer who fronted a group called Rodney & the Mystics—came into the band. Orbison had gotten to know Justo in the early 1960s, and had already produced a record for him. It was a natural fit. "When Bobby left," Justo explained, "the band said, 'We can't just rely on working when Roy works.' They said, 'We'd like to work, when he's not working, as a band, and we need a singer.'"

"Time evolves," Justo pointed out. "Pop music was all single artists, but then bands started having hits, and Roy wanted to seem more current. He decided to be part of a band, Roy Orbison & the Candymen. They put that on the record, and it became part of the lie that we played in the studio. But we didn't. We only played the live dates. We lied about that for so long, we almost remember the sessions!" Eventually, the Candymen began making records of their own for the ABC label. By that time drummer Robert Nix and keyboardist Dean Daughtry had joined the group.

In 1967, the Candymen released their self-titled debut album, which was recorded in Atlanta with Buddy Buie producing. More than half the songs on the LP were credited to Buie as a writer, including "Georgia Pines," which became a minor hit. Concentrating on their own career, the Candymen ultimately parted ways with Orbison. "There was not a better band in America than the Candymen," Rodney

Justo declared. "There might have been one as good, but there was no band any better. We were the darlings of the South and East Coast." Though not blatant, Southern influences were part of the Candymen sound. "The first time I ever know of the term 'country-rock' being used was about the Candymen," Justo explained. "There was an article about us in the *New York Times*, back when they did *not* write about rock and roll. We didn't know it was such a big deal. We're a bunch of hillbillies from the South. We thought it was like being written about in the *Dothan Herald* or something."

Along the way, the band picked up further inspiration from their Southern homeland. "When I was in the Candymen," drummer Nix told Alison Heafner, "we would tour all over the world and come back home and play clubs all over Dixie. One group that impressed me more than any was the Allman Joys. Duane and Gregg had something that you just knew would someday explode on the world."

When the second Candymen LP was released in 1968, nearly half the selections were credited to Buddy Buie and J. R. Cobb. Buddy and J. R. had forged a fruitful writing partnership that helped define the Classics IV, a band that Cobb was associated with from its earliest days. Cobb explained:

> I was born in Birmingham, Alabama, but I moved to Jacksonville, Florida, when I was about five years old. I had an uncle who played guitar, and he showed me a couple

of chords when I was seven, eight, or nine years old. But most of my musical influence at that time was the radio, which was playin' all the time in my house. I remember early Les Paul and Hank Williams and all kinds of stuff. I can remember that the radio was so varied in those days. They'd play a Ray Charles song one hour, and the next thing you'd hear would be Hank Williams, and the next thing you'd hear would be Hugo Winterhalter or something.

By the time Cobb was finishing high school in Jacksonville—where he and Candyman Robert Nix graduated together—he was playing guitar seriously.

> I knew the guys in the Classics. They worked in a place called the Golden Gate Lounge. Their guitar player got drafted, and one of the guys said, "Would you consider being our guitar player?" Well, where they were workin' it was six nights a week, and I think you made about $80. That was considerably more than I was makin' as an apprentice welder at a place called Florida Steel, so that became my first real music job. At the time, it was just called the Classics. We had some horns and an organ. We did a lot of rhythm-and-blues stuff, and we had a great band. But we couldn't make any money. We were tryin' to live off what we were makin', so we cut it down to four pieces.... That led us to a lot of work.

After a failed stint with Capitol Records, the Classics IV signed with the Imperial label. "We played a place in Daytona Beach at a hotel called Daytona Plaza," J. R. continued. "While we were workin' there one summer, somebody from Bill Lowery's office came in and heard us, and invited us to come up to Atlanta to make a demo or something. We did that and got associated with Bill Lowery. He had a recording studio, a booking agency, and a publishing company, all out of the same building."

It was in Atlanta, around 1966, where Buie and Cobb began working together regularly, though they had known one another previously. In 1967, the Classics IV released "Spooky," which became a major hit and climbed to #2 on the *Billboard* charts. Cobb, who wrote the song with Buie, stopped traveling with the Classics IV and stayed in Atlanta, where he wrote subsequent hits for the band, including "Stormy," "Traces," and "Everyday with You Girl."

"The main reason we ever had a band like the Classics IV was to have an outlet for songs,"

Cobb explained. "After we'd had some success, I wanted to concentrate on songwriting, so I left the group and they went on." Though lead singer Dennis Yost's voice was a consistent presence, the Classics IV increasingly morphed into a studio entity, with Buie at the helm. As was true of the Beach Boys during that period, the producer freely augmented the band's recordings with additional musicians, including drummer Robert Nix and keyboardist Dean Daughtry, both from the Candymen.

Buddy Buie's textured production technique proved to have wide commercial appeal. "I was cuttin' the Classics IV and B. J. Thomas and Billy Joe Royal at that time," Buie recalled. "I had this band that I used, which was Robert Nix and John Rainey from the Candymen. They became my studio musicians, along with Emory Gordy." In addition to the Classics IV hits, Buddy was scoring with successful singles such as "Cherry Hill Park" by Royal and "Most of All" by Thomas. "I was hotter than a two-peckered goat from 1966 until 1970," he laughed.

Initially, Buie was working out of Bill Lowery's Atlanta studio:

> Bill had a studio called Master Sound. The guy that was his partner, Bob Richardson, and I had a big argument about a bass guitar. There was a bass that Emory Gordy played on every session I had with the Classics IV. That bass was on every hit that I was ever associated with. One day, the studio was booked, cuttin' a commercial or something, and I needed to get in there. I said, "That's fine. I'll go over to LeFevre," which was another studio in Atlanta. I said, "I just need the bass." Bob said, "This bass don't go out of the building." I said, "Say *what*?" He said, "It don't go out of the building." I said, "Let me tell you something. I *need* it." He said no, so I said, "Well, I've cut my last fuck-

Dean Doughtry · Barry Bailey · Robert Nix

J. R. Cobb · Paul Goddard · Rodney Justo

Atlanta Rhythm Section

DECCA

The Lowery Group
P.O. Box 9687
Atlanta, Ga. 30319
(404) 233-0101

The Atlanta Rhythm Section in their original incarnation (Decca Records)

ing record here. No more!" So I went to Lowery, and I said, "Hey, I ain't cuttin' no more in there. I'm going to build a studio, and I need your help." So he and I and J. R. Cobb and Paul Cochran, the four of us, started Studio One. It was a studio to be used exclusively for *my* music.

By the time Studio One was underway, the Candymen had been disbanded for about a year. Singer Rodney Justo had returned to Tampa, to sing with a band called Noah's Ark, while Dean Daughtry and Robert Nix teamed with former Classics IV guitarist J. R. Cobb to form the core of the band that would become the Studio One stalwarts. Barry Bailey and Paul Goddard, who had played together in a Georgia group called Joint Effort, rounded out the Studio One team. "The story of how the Atlanta Rhythm Section really began is that I had these guys that played on all my sessions," Buie explained. "We worked together every day. But then I heard the Allman Brothers and I just went nuts. I said, 'Shit, that is what I should do with my studio musicians, is make them into a band!'"

"One day, I got a call from Buddy Buie," Rodney Justo recalled, "and he'd been listening to an album called *Super Session* with Al Kooper, Steve Stills, and Michael Bloomfield. He said, 'If there can be a *Super Session*, why can't there be a super group? He said, 'I want to get the best musicians in the South

and start a band. We're building a studio. We can make money in the studio playing other people's records until we get our own thing going.' So I headed up there."

Buie recruited engineer Rodney Mills from LeFevre Sound Studios to join him as the staff engineer in his new venture. Once they secured a location in the Oak Cliff Industrial Park, in the Atlanta suburb of Doraville, the two were free to design their dream facility. "Rodney and I just drew up what we wanted," Buddy recalled. "One unique feature was that the control room jutted out into the studio, like a 'V' shape. I had a piece built on the front of it where I could walk around, see the musicians, and communicate."

Buie secured a recording contract with Decca Records, and put the musicians on a salary as they began work on their first album. "We were recording for the stars, and we wanted to be recording for our own selves," Dean Daughtry explained to Gary James in 1979. "Besides, we figured we could make more money as well." But it would take a while before that money began rolling in. "We stayed alive doing outside projects for B. J. Thomas, Joe South, Billy Joe Royal, Tommy Roe, and a friend of ours named Richard Supa," Justo recalled. "Then we would kinda work on our own stuff on the side. It took two years for that first record to get made and come out."

Atlanta Rhythm Section was released in 1972 and featured the soft but funky feel that

Buie had perfected in his work with the Classics IV. Without attempting to imitate the Allman Brothers Band, Buddy successfully took inspiration from the group to cast his unique vision for Southern rock with a delicate touch. "Bill Lowery named us the Atlanta Rhythm Section," Robert Nix remembered.

While waiting for the Atlanta Rhythm Section to catch on, Buddy occasionally allowed the studio to be used for outside projects:

> I had a manager named Jeff Franklin in New York City. He represented me as a producer, and he also represented Al Kooper. He said, "Kooper really loves your studio." Well, I usually cut at night, so I said, "Al, I'll tell you what I'll do. I'll cut at night and you can have the daytime." We made the deal and he came down. That's where he cut Lynyrd Skynyrd.... We were all buddies. They'd come in in the morning and I'd play them what I cut the night before. When I'd come in, Al would play me what they'd cut during the day.

On at least one occasion, one of Buie's stable of musicians was recruited to assist Skynyrd. "I played the drums on 'Tuesday's Gone,'" Robert Nix explained. "Ronnie told that it was one of his favorite tracks. I was very honored that Ronnie Van Zant and Al Kooper asked me to play on the record."

Eventually, the goings-on in the studio caused some strain within the band, as Rodney Justo recounted:

> I didn't want to be a studio singer. I wanted to work on the road. We were working our first tour in California. Buddy was with us, and he came backstage and he said, "You're not going to believe the deal I signed today. I just came back from Hanna-Barbera." I knew that was a cartoon company, but I thought maybe they were startin' a label or something. He said, "I just signed a deal so we can cut all the tracks for a new cartoon show called *Butch Cassidy and the Sundance Kids*." The first thing I'm thinkin' is, "Where does little Rodney fit in on cuttin' the cartoon tracks?" I said, "Dude, I'm not down for that. I thought we were gonna take this band on the road." This is our first tour. We're gonna work the road and build a following and all that. The next thing I know, they're talking about cartoon shows. I said, "Buddy, if I'm gonna be singing background on records, if that's gonna be my station in life, I'm

197

goin' somewhere where I can make some money doin' it." So I wished 'em the best of luck, and I headed for New York.

With Rodney Justo gone, and a second album due to the label, the Atlanta Rhythm Section were in need of a new singer. "We got Ronnie Hammond, who was an engineer at LeFevre Studio," Paul Goddard explained, in a 1977 interview with Cliff White. "I'd heard him sing, and I told Buddy, 'You gotta get him, he's great.' I never will forget that night. He was living underneath me at the time—we were in real dumps. And one of our roadies went down and said, 'Hey Ronnie, guess what, you just became the new singer with the Rhythm Section.'"

In 1973, the Atlanta Rhythm Section released their second album, *Back up Against the Wall*, with Ronnie Hammond handling the lead vocals. Though it, too, featured, a smooth and sophisticated sound, the band members were still the object of suspicion in the Georgia suburb, thanks to their appearance. One of the tracks, Joe South's "Redneck," lambasted small-town bigots who dismiss "darkies, dagos, and Jews" and harass "the hippies and the weirdoes." Punctuated with a defiant "screw you," the song's lyrics illustrated the tension that still existed between "rednecks" and long-haired Southern rock musicians in the early 1970s.

The locals had plenty of time to look, since the Atlanta Rhythm Section stayed close to home rather than spending long stretches on the road playing live. They continued to balance their time between working on their own material and backing other groups in the studio. "We were also playing on a lot of jingle/commercials," Robert Nix told *Sweet Home Music*. "Coke, Dr. Pepper, Kentucky Fried Chicken, and sports teams like the Atlanta Braves baseball team." Without hav-

The Atlanta Rhythm Section, shown here at the time of their *Third Annual Pipe Dream* album. *Left to right*: Ronnie Hammond, Barry Bailey, J. R. Cobb, Paul Goddard, Dean Daughtry, and Robert Nix.

ing built a major live following or appearing on either the singles or album charts after two LPs, Decca dropped the band. "My manager, Jeff Franklin, said, 'You don't worry about this one bit,'" Buddy recalled. "He said, 'You just keep cuttin' your records.' Then he got us a new deal with Polydor."

After the Polydor deal was signed, the Atlanta Rhythm Section got serious about gearing up as a live band. "To promote the records and do what you need to do," J. R. Cobb explained, "we went on the road. We quit doing the other stuff because we were on the road all the time, tryin' to promote the Atlanta Rhythm Section and their records."

"I stayed on their ass about touring," Buddy laughed. "I said, 'Guys, you gotta go out and play dates.' None of them ever cared anything about that. They weren't like the boys in the Allman Brothers, where everybody was livin' together and all that. These guys had separate homes and families and stuff. At first, they weren't that excited about going out on the road, but then they got into it. They definitely weren't the world's great-

est concert act. They stood there and played their songs. You wasn't gonna get any dancin' around or wearin' special clothes or anything. But they were all *great* musicians."

"We had to hone the live part," Barry Bailey admitted to journalist Hunter Pope in 2000. "It was a conscious effort by all involved." They were helped along, however, by one of Southern rock's greatest motivators. "Ronnie Van Zant had a major impact on us really going on the road more," Robert Nix recalled. "He would hang out with us at Studio One.... He would listen to us and say, 'Shit man, y'all got to take it to the people.' A lot of our first gigs were on the road with Skynyrd." As a result, the Atlanta Rhythm Section were embraced by the Southern rock audience. "We played a *lot* with Skynyrd," Cobb observed. "Because we were from the South and played rock and roll, everybody thought we were a Southern rock band!" The associ-

ation was further reinforced when the group aligned themselves with the key movers and shakers in Southern rock's spiritual homeland of Macon. "We even called Phil Walden and Alex Hodges at Paragon late one night to see if they would book the band," Nix remembered. "They said yes, and the rest is history."

With the switch to Polydor Records in 1974, and a newfound commitment to touring, the Atlanta Rhythm Section began appearing on the lower rungs of the album charts. Critics appreciated the band's instrumental prowess and often commented on the great sound of the records. "Rodney Mills played a very important part in our whole story," Buddy explained. "He was a big part of Skynyrd. He was probably the most underrated engineer and producer around."

Mills had come to Atlanta in 1966 with his own band, the Bushmen, who were rivaled only by the Candymen in terms of regional popularity. "There were only four studios in Atlanta then," he recalled in the mid-1970s, "and the big local artists were Billy Joe Royal, Joe South, and Dennis Yost. There was no conception of a 'Southern sound' then. Record companies wouldn't pick up on Southern acts. No matter what acts are signed out of the South now, it's tied in with the Allman Brothers. Before them, nobody cared."

Thanks, in part, to Mills' sharp ears and Buddy Buie's singular vision, the group were building a formidable reputation. Their humorously titled *Third Annual Pipe Dream* was a well-polished collection of songs that sounded as much like a product of Southern California as central Georgia. The song "Doraville," written by Buddy Buie, Robert Nix, and Barry Bailey, was a celebration of their Dixie homeland, and became the band's first Top 40 single. In 1975, the Atlanta Rhythm Section released *Dog Days*, another mixed bag of pop polish and tasteful Southern guitar licks.

The following year, the band stretched out with *Red Tape*, a more adventurous effort that, though still anchored by pop elements, included some serious guitar theatrics. "Another Man's Woman" was a nine-minute jam that gave album buyers a window into the feel of the band's live spontaneity. They often explored extended jams in their live shows, despite the fact that their studio sound was highly controlled and honed to perfection. "I think you'll be surprised at the way we approach recording," Paul Goddard told journalist John Swenson, who sat in on a 1975 recording session. "We cut unlike any group you'll see. We play a song night after night until it comes out right."

The Atlanta Rhythm Section found their greatest success between 1976 and 1979 with a trio of albums that each went Gold or Platinum. *A Rock and Roll Alternative* brought the band their first big hit with "So in to You," a Top 10 mid-tempo ballad that was as reminiscent of the band Chicago as it was anything coming from south of the Mason-Dixon Line. "I noticed when I was playing the song in the studio," J. R. Cobb observed, "that the chord patterns are almost exactly the same as 'Stormy.' It wasn't a conscious thing, but it did come out that way." If anything, it illustrated the consistent approach to music-making that Cobb, Buie, and their band of top notch musicians had perfected.

As the most successful era for the band dawned, the distinctive strands of Southern rock influence increasingly faded into the background. As was common with many groups at the time, they incorporated light disco elements into their sound starting with *A Rock and Roll Alternative*. They also began to explore a sanitized version of progressive rock that drew their attention away from a regional focus. "I'd cut my dick and nuts off to play with Kansas, and their bass player knows it," Paul Goddard exclaimed to *NME* in 1977. "He's a good friend of mine. To me, they are the best band that has ever functioned in the world.... We worked two shows with 'em, and it impressed our band so much that I think it's the best thing that ever happened to us."

The Atlanta Rhythm Section's only million-selling album, *Champagne Jam*, hit the stores in 1978. Anchored by hit singles like "Imaginary Lover" and "I'm Not Gonna Let It Bother Me Tonight," the band found themselves enjoying the commercial success that had eluded them for so long. That same year, 50,000 fans filled Grant Field at Georgia Tech University to hear their hometown boys. By 1978, the Atlanta Rhythm Section achieved enough notoriety that they were invited to play for President Jimmy Carter at the White House. "There was a lot of people there," Daughtry told *Ink 19* magazine. "Relatives, daughters and sons of the Congress and the Senate and all that. It was his birthday, and it was really nice. I felt real safe there, you know, even though there was snipers.... One time we had to use the bathroom. Ronnie couldn't wait. The bus was locked. We couldn't get back to the bathroom in time, so guess what Ronnie did? The grass died!"

The Atlanta Rhythm Section were riding high, but success took a toll on the band. "We had started to be famous enough, if that's the right word, to play for larger audiences," Cobb recalled. "I guess '77, '78, '79, those three years were probably, as far as the career went, the highlight. It was also one of the most strenuous, 'cause we were on the road all the time. I had a family. They were OK with it, and they knew that's what I did, but I felt bad about not bein' there to see my son grow up."

As popular acceptance of the band increased, however, critics accused the music of turning bland. When they began

work, in 1978, on the album that would become *Underdog*, Robert Nix was frustrated with the increasingly fluffier direction. "Buddy comes from more of a softer side of rock than me," he admitted to Alison Heafner. "Every time I could influence things my way, I would. We actually got in a fight one time, because I called him Pat Boone and told him I was more like Elvis Presley.... I was in total disagreement with the direction we went in after *Champagne Jam*. A lot of things happened after that record that caused Buddy, the band, and me to disagree. I was pretty much over the edge with a lot of creative depression. Drinking and drugging really entered the picture."

Ultimately, Nix found himself outside the band. "*Underdog* seems to me to be where we lost our sight of where we should have been headed," he admitted. "I personally would have liked to have gone more rock, à la *Red Tape*. I truly believe that record was our downfall. That's just my opinion.... I was very hard to live with, and was given my 'marching orders.'" J. R. Cobb, however, recalls that Nix left voluntarily. "Robert wasn't particularly happy with the direction the band was going," he explained. "I think he wanted to be more kind of Southern rock, or more like Lynyrd Skynyrd, for better or worse. For whatever reason, he just wanted to leave."

After Nix departed at the end of 1978, Roy Yeager took over the drum spot. The *Underdog* album, which was released in 1979, featured Nix on some tracks and Yeager on others. While the album was certified Gold, it lacked much bite. The LP led critic Martin Popoff to observe that the band's sound had become "like Poco and Elton John doing 'Witchy Woman' with Steely Dan twiddling the knobs nearly half as conscientiously as they might for themselves." Nevertheless, the Atlanta Rhythm Section scored a couple of Top 20 hits from the

album, "Do It or Die" and a remake of the Classics IV hit "Spooky."

Around the time the Atlanta Rhythm Section hit their commercial stride, original lead singer Rodney Justo reemerged on RCA Records with an eclectic Southern rock band of his own called Beaverteeth. After a period working as a commercial jingle singer and backup vocalist, Justo had become B. J. Thomas' bandleader. Rodney ultimately recruited original Candyman John Rainey Adkins' band, which was already known as Beaverteeth, to work as Thomas' backing group. They eventually returned to working as a unit independent of Thomas, and Justo joined them for two years. "It was Southern rock meets Paul McCartney," Justo laughed. "My strength is my flaw. There's a lot of people that sing prettier than me, and a lot of people that rock harder than me, but I'm fortunate in that I do a lot of things *pretty* well. Those Beaverteeth albums are all over the place, but if you put both of them together you'd get one pretty good album, I think."

After a great burst of success, Justo's old Atlanta Rhythm Section bandmates weren't able to hold on to their audience. In 1980, they released an album called *The Boys from Doraville* that represented bland pop music at its worst. They moved to CBS for 1981's *Quinella*, an album that, though it started promisingly with some nice guitar driven selections, quickly descended back into the bland adult contemporary realm. The band didn't know what else to do to stay afloat in a changing marketplace.

"Different kinds of music were coming along," J. R. Cobb pointed out, "punk rock and disco. MTV came along and bands were expected to be a lot more visual than maybe we were. Compared to a lot of other bands we weren't all that flashy. We were more interested in making the music than we were

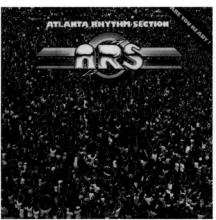

Atlanta Rhythm Section publicity photo. *Left to right*: Ronnie Hammond, Dean Daughtry, Barry Baily, Robert Nix, Paul Goddard, and J. R. Cobb. (Polydor Records)

in being a visual type entertainer." With sales declining and inter-band personalities clashing, Buddy Buie stepped aside. "Buddy had had enough," Justo confirmed. "I think he stopped managing them in '80 or '81. He just walked away."

Drummer Roy Yeager departed in 1982, and Ronnie Hammond soon followed. "It was kind of a relief that the band broke up for a little while," Bailey told *Smokey Mountain News*. "Egos by now were a little out of whack, and to pardon the standard band cliché, there were artistic differences. It was kind of scary for a while. Dean and I kept some form of the group together. There were different lineups, and a record deal fell apart. Like I said, it was scary, but it was a relief at the same time. We had new approaches to things. There was no real stress."

With that lack of stress came lower-paying gigs and a scramble to keep a full band together. Following Hammond's departure, Rodney Justo was called to participate once again. "I went back in 1983 when Ronnie left the band," he recounted. "I hadn't sung in five years, but I went back with the deal that I'd only work weekends. I had a regular job at an alcoholic beverages distribution company. The band was going to put together something with Chips Moman producing them. There was only one problem: I didn't like Chips Moman, and Chips didn't like me. I stepped aside again." The Moman album failed to materialize, and various members floated in and out of the band, as the Atlanta Rhythm Section slogged it out on the club circuit. By the mid-2000s, only Dean Daughtry remained from the original group.

Perhaps they'd had a better run than anyone ever expected from the beginning, however. "Playing music is not a purpose in life," Ronnie Hammond told journalist Cliff White in 1977. "The Rhythm Section won't last forever.

I'll enjoy it while it does, and possibly make enough money to open a business—my brother-in-law and I are thinking of buying a liquor store. I love music, but when it's over for me as a rock-and-roller, I'm gonna go back home."

In the final analysis, the surviving band members are proud of their achievements, even if they're dubious about their classification as a Southern rock band. "That was a label that disc jockeys and other people in the music business kind of put on us," Cobb reflected, "'cause we were from the South, and we did play rock and roll. The records we had success with were not particularly stereotypical Southern rock. We had two guitars but we didn't do the same things with two guitars that other people were doing. We figured that the Allman Brothers and Molly Hatchet and several other groups in the South had that base covered anyway, so we just kinda did what we did." ★

Hughie Thomasson and Billy
Jones backstage in Santa
Monica, California, 1975.
(Courtesy of John Gellman)

CHAPTER 30
Playin' to Win: The Outlaws

★ ★

 N 1975, Arista Records released the Outlaws' self-titled debut LP, featuring the Top 40 single "There Goes Another Love Song." Though they distinguished themselves from other Southern rock bands with their complex vocal harmonies, the Outlaws were particularly proficient at executing the three-guitar assault that came to be associated with Southern rock, and they worked closely with the top Southern rock bands of the era. "During the '70s, we toured with the Marshall Tucker Band, the Allman Brothers, the Charlie Daniels Band, and Lynyrd Skynyrd," singer and guitarist Henry Paul explained. "We were fiercely proud of our Southern heritage, and we banded together to form friendships, both musical and personal."

The Outlaws emerged from the Tampa music scene of the late 1960s. "The exact time lines are hard," acknowledged drummer Monte Yoho, who moved to Tampa in 1965 when his father became the principal of a local high school.

When we get into 1970 and '71, that's when the group known as the Outlaws with the five of us—myself, Henry Paul, Hughie Thomasson, Frank O'Keefe, and Billy Jones—was starting to come together. I'm not gonna say it's controversial, but that generic name, the Outlaws, was around all over the place at that time. We did have a little group prior to what you know as the Outlaws in the late '60s. I was a part of that. Hughie was certainly a part of it, Frank O'Keefe, Billy Jones. Then, me and Billy Jones had a group, and

THE OUTLAWS

- ▸ HUGHIE THOMASSON guitar, vocals
- ▸ FRANK O'KEEFE bass, vocals
- ▸ MONTE YOHO drums, percussion
- ▸ HENRY PAUL guitar, vocals
- ▸ BILLY JONES guitar, keyboards, vocals
- ▸ BUZZY MEEKINS bass
- ▸ HARVEY DALTON ARNOLD bass, vocals
- ▸ DAVID DIX drums, percussion
- ▸ FREDDIE SALEM guitar, vocals
- ▸ RICK CUA bass, vocals
- ▸ MIKE DUKE keyboard, vocals

it would all swap. You didn't know who was gonna play with who back then. It was all the teen centers and little frat parties up at the University of Florida.

"The Outlaws actually started in 1968," Thomasson remembered in an interview with Jeb Wright. Having played with a variety of local bands with names like the Rogues and the Four Letter Words, Thomasson joined forces with a guitarist named Frank Guidry in late 1967. Guidry had been in an earlier band that was also called the Outlaws. When he and Thomasson got together, they revived the name and recruited a revolving door of musicians that included, among many others, drummer David Dix, bassist Frank O'Keefe, and drummer Monte Yoho. Atlanta Rhythm Section vocal-

ist and Tampa native Rodney Justo quipped, "In Tampa, you can't walk out your front door without stepping on a former Outlaw!"

In the early days, the various lineups known as the Outlaws appeared regularly on the usual circuit for young cover bands. "We played teen gigs where you paid $1 on a Friday night and you could see five bands," Hughie explained. "We played Battle of the Bands contests, and we actually won one of them. It paid us $500, and we got to record our first record at Tower Records. . . . That was in '69." The two-sided single didn't sell. "One of them was called 'Goodbye,'" Thomasson recalled. "The flip side was 'At the Triple Feature in Cinema Scope and Color at the Drive in Movie Tonight.' I am proud to say that we didn't write those songs."

As with most Southern bands of the era, and particularly those in Florida, they took inspiration from Duane and Gregg Allman. "We played a show with them as the Outlaws at a place called The Electric Zoo in St. Petersburg, Florida," Thomasson recounted. "I stood there and literally did not move the whole time they were playing. I was blown away." It would prove a pivotal moment in Thomasson's musical development. "I wanted to be like them," he confessed. "I wanted to be that good and I wanted to have that kind of an impact on people."

The Outlaws eventually joined forces with a Tampa musician named Dave Graham, who was heavily influenced by the harmonious strains of Southern California country-rock groups like Poco. It was Graham who brought guitarist Billy Jones into the fold. "He had really just started playing guitar," Yoho recalled, "but he was one of those gifted people who could pick up anything and make it work."

Henry Paul backstage at Alex Cooley's Electric Ballroom in Atlanta in the mid-1970s. (Courtesy of John Gellman)

By 1971, with limited bookings, the group had fallen apart. Hughie Thomasson headed for New York, where he gigged around Greenwich Village, unaware that another Tampa musician, Henry Paul, was in the area pursuing a career as a folk singer. Paul recalled:

I was born in upstate New York in the foothills of the Catskill Mountains. We had a family farm there, so I grew up in a rural environment, so to speak, with a bunch of crusty German immigrants who had work ethic forever. My mom and dad ultimately split up, and she and my sisters and I relocated to Lakeland, Florida in 1957 when I was eight. Back then it was just a little town thirty-five miles east of Tampa. Growing up in Lakeland was really, really fun. There were a lot of lakes and phosphate pits and orange groves, and a whole different culture for me. I would

spend summers up there with my dad working on the farm, but lived with my sisters and my mom and went to elementary and junior high in Florida. Then we moved to Tampa, and I went to high school there. So, Florida was really home to me.

When Henry was still in his mid-teens, he found his excursions to his father's farm in Kingston, New York, becoming more frequent. "My stepbrother and I would take a bus from my house up in Kingston to midtown," he recalled, "and we'd walk down to Greenwich Village. This was around '65. I went to the folk music stores and bought records by Leadbelly, Woody Guthrie. I became a student of folk music, and I learned how to Travis pick. I started writing songs."

When he returned to Tampa, Henry began finding opportunities to perform. "There was a famous coffeehouse over in Pinellas County

called Beaux Arts," he explained. "I would hitchhike over there late Friday afternoon and hang out at the coffeehouse, and sit in the back row with the other performers and eventually work up the stones to get up onstage and sing songs into a microphone in front of a small audience." The venue, which had played host to Woody Guthrie, Ramblin' Jack Elliott, and Jim Morrison, was a key Florida stronghold of the folk movement. "It was a countercultural sort of outpost," Paul added.

"By 1969, I had graduated high school," Henry continued. "I had made the decision that I was going to gather up all my stuff and move to New York. I was going to go to Greenwich Village and make a career for myself in the music business. I started to audition at all of the folk music clubs like the Gaslight, Folk City, the Bitter End—I made the rounds at these places, and I got a job at the Strand Bookstore in the Village."

Within a short time, Henry captured the attention of some music-industry insiders.

> I ended up in the office of Don Ellis, the head of A&R at Epic Records. I auditioned for him, he dug it, and then he scheduled me into the midtown Columbia Studios to cut some demos. Word had gotten back to Tampa that I was startin' to get a little somewhere. . . . I put a little band together, and we came down and played a show at the Armory in Tampa in 1970 in front of a couple thousand people. That was an exciting moment, and it dawned on me that I could really do it.

After his triumph in Tampa, Henry returned to New York where he put together a four-piece band called Sienna, with the goal of returning to Florida for good. Upon arriving in Tampa, however, Sienna began to disintegrate. "That's when I met Monte," Henry recalled. "He became the drummer in our group. The bass player wound up getting homesick and went back to New York. Then Frank O'Keefe came into the band, because Monte knew Frank."

By the time Sienna's original guitarist departed, Hughie Thomasson was back in Tampa. "Hughie and I," Monte Yoho recounted, "had been playing with Bertie Higgins [who would have a Top 10 single with 'Key Largo' in the early 1980s] over on the beach somewhere, and we did a lot of session work at a studio in Tampa. But Hughie was in New York at the time the Tampa version of Sienna was coming together. He was playing with a folk artist named Milton Carroll. Hughie finally came back to Florida, and we eventually got him in the band."

Before joining Sienna, however, Thomasson took a brief musical detour. "Leon Wilkeson, Skynyrd's bass player, and I were in a band called the King James Version," he told Jeb Wright. "We were playing at the Jet Airport Lounge in Fort Lauderdale. We played literally at the end of the runway. Jets would fly over and drown out the music. Leon got a call one night and he told me that Skynyrd had called and that they were going to record their first album, and that he had to go. I told him to go, told him I loved him and that I wished him the best. I left the band at the same time."

At some point in the early 1970s, Sienna dusted off the Outlaws name once again. "Hughie said, 'You know, we were in a band called the Outlaws,'" Henry explained. "If we want to try to get more work, we could use that name to see if we could get more club owners to book us, and that sort of thing.'" The Outlaws soon booked an entire season's worth of steady work in 1972. "We had an opportunity to go over to the beach," Monte recalled, "and work for the whole summer at this club called the Pillow Talk Lounge at the Satellite Motel in Cocoa Beach, Florida. That's where we lived, and that really formed the band into who we were."

Before getting deep into the gig at Cocoa

Hughie Thomasson and Billy Jones onstage. (Courtesy of Carl Lender)

Hughie Thomasson, Harvey Dalton Arnold, Monty Yoho, Henry Paul, and Billy Jones. (Arista Records)

Beach, there was still one more piece of the puzzle that would complete the picture of the Outlaws. "We wanted to add a guitar player," Yoho continued. "Everybody, except probably Henry, knew Billy Jones, and had worked with Billy. He had moved out to Colorado at that time. We called Billy when we were first getting to Cocoa Beach around 1971. He'd just about had it out in Colorado, and said he'd love to come back. He hopped in his Datsun 260 convertible and drove back from Colorado. He pulled into Cocoa Beach and that's when the whole band was complete." When Billy Jones rolled into town with a $25 amplifier and no money in his pocket, the Outlaws kicked into high gear. "Before Billy joined, I thought we were gettin' pretty good," Henry explained to journalist Barbara Charone in 1976, "but Billy gave us that extra somethin'. Billy gave us that parsley on the side of the plate, the garnish. We were *hot*."

When the summer was over, the Outlaws returned to Tampa. "It was the southeastern version of the California scene," Henry Paul recalled. "There was a lot of pop culture activity, on a musical level. It was really fast, and by that I mean it was constantly changing. Bands went from being Beatle cover bands to Allman Brothers type bands in a moment. It was weird. It happened from 1970 to 1975."

"We spent a good year and a half with the five-piece group in Tampa, really growing an audience," Henry remembered. "We continued to write songs, and we did some really cool cover songs. It was kind of a country-rock band." The group's influences were artists that employed intricate vocal harmonies. "The Eagles are quite special in this field," he explained to *Bands of Dixie* magazine. "Crosby, Stills & Nash were enormously influential in this area and, before them, the Beatles, the Byrds, and the Buffalo Springfield were very important stylists." Combining vocal harmonies with an "outlaw" image made the band unique. "We adopted this sort of cowboy-rock image thing," he recalled. "We all wore hats and boots, and it was a significant departure from David Bowie and all the glam-rock thing that was going on."

By 1974, the Outlaws had built up considerable interest in music-business circles. Much of their early success was an outgrowth of their manager's tireless promotion efforts. "We had played at the University of South Florida," Monte recalled, "and Charlie Brusco was down there going to school, doing some grad work, I believe. He saw us and just flipped over us. He became our manager. Charlie knew what he was doing, and he knew how to build a little network of industry people."

Brusco, who started out promoting horse shows and karate exhibitions, was a tenacious advocate for the Outlaws. "He put us on the road for five months at a time once," Henry remembered. "We didn't get home in five months, almost six. Man, we were so burnt when we got back we couldn't see straight. I thought I was going in the front door and I'd be banging 'round the side of the house. Everybody was blitzed."

Everyone in the band knew it was hard work, but each man was committed, and the

hard work was paying off. "We got to do a show with Lynyrd Skynyrd in '74 in Nashville at a club called Mothers," Monte explained. Van Zant loved what he heard. "Ronnie's role in getting us noticed was paramount," Henry declared. "We had friends in very influential places, thanks to Ronnie's endorsement." Van Zant did not forget about the group. He sang their praises to people who had the power to help them. "It was Ronnie Van Zant who put the bug in the ear of a lot of record-industry people about us," Monte confirmed. Within months of meeting Ronnie, the Outlaws were working with Skynyrd's manager Alan Walden, and had signed a major recording contract. Ronnie Van Zant, in a 1976 interview with *Creem* magazine, proudly touted his discovery of the group: "Did you know I found the Outlaws? I got them signed with Walden, and then talked to Clive Davis at Arista about them."

When Alan Walden entered the picture, the Outlaws found a way to work with him while still remaining loyal to Brusco. "Charlie partnered up with Alan, who was managing Lynyrd Skynyrd at that point," Monte explained. "He managed to get us with Paragon Booking Agency in Macon, and we were the only unsigned band being booked by them. . . . With Alan and Charlie working together, that's when the doors really started opening. We were touring all over the South and getting real nice opening spots with Charlie Daniels, Marshall Tucker, and the Allman Brothers."

"We were kind of a buzz at that time," Henry Paul explained. "Clive [Davis] sent Bob Feiden to see us. We were doing a show with Lynyrd Skynyrd in the old Sportatorium in Orlando. It was an old metal building that you could probably put 3,000 people in." It was the big break the Outlaws had been working for. "Bob was impressed with the band's vitality and musicianship," Henry added. "He went back to Clive and told him he found us. This was in late 1974 or early '75.

I think Arista wanted a Southern rock band to go along with MCA's Lynyrd Skynyrd, and everything at Capricorn. It was in style."

Soon after, the legendary record executive headed south to hear the Outlaws for himself. "Clive flew out to Columbus, Georgia, to see us play a show with Skynyrd," Monte recalled. "He was blown away, and he signed us that night."

Touting the Outlaws as Arista's "first full-tilt rock-and-roll band," Clive Davis hired Paul Rothchild, best known for his work with the Doors and Janis Joplin, to produce their first album. Released in 1975, the LP was generally well received by critics and fans. "Clive was very smart in putting us with Paul Rothchild," Monte reflected. "He was a good teacher, and I don't know if the Outlaws would have existed the way we did without his teachings. Paul Rothchild just took us in and told us how it was done." "There Goes Another Love Song," with lead vocals by Hughie, was released as a single and climbed to #34 on the *Billboard* chart. "Arista really worked hard to break the band because they had a new label at stake," Henry explained. "They were very committed."

"Green Grass & High Tides," another Hughie song, became an FM-radio staple. Clocking in at nearly ten minutes, it was a well-constructed Southern rock anthem that ranks with "Freebird" as one of the enduring epic masterpieces of the genre. "I wrote that song in St. Augustine, Florida," Thomasson remembered, in an interview with William Turley. "We went to a cookout on the beach and everybody forgot to bring their guitars. I was standing by the ocean, and there was a breeze, and the words kept coming to me. It's about all the rock stars I liked that died had come back and were playing a show just for me—like Jimi Hendrix, Janis Joplin, and Jim Morrison." Rumors circulated among fans that the "green grass" of the title was a reference to marijuana, though Henry Paul denied it, telling Shawna Ortega:

There was an album out, the best of the Rolling Stones, called *High Tide and Green Grass*. That was the name of the Rolling Stones' greatest hits. This is like 1966. And I think it was a manifestation of that title turned in reverse, 'Green Grass & High Tides.' I know that much. And I know that it was a song written for rock-and-roll luminaries . . . A lot of it is just sort of a collage of words that really don't have all that much to do with anything. They just fit and sounded right. But I have to say it's one of my favorite lyrics.

In time, "Green Grass & High Tides" became the group's signature song. "It went from being three minutes long," Thomasson explained, "to what you hear on the first record, to the seventeen-minute version on the live record. The band helped it evolve—I didn't do that all myself. We kept expanding it, and it kept getting bigger and bigger."

In addition to "There Goes Another Love Song" and "Green Grass & High Tides," the best-known title on the album was "Song for You." These were the only three songs on which Hughie Thomasson sang lead vocals. Henry Paul and Billy Jones handled the remaining vocal duties, but most listeners regarded Hughie as the leader of the band, given the higher profile of his three songs on the album. Hughie was, of course, a force to be reckoned with. A *Rolling Stone* review of the group's appearance at the Bottom Line in New York City on August 2, 1975, singled him out as the "inventive lead guitarist . . . whose quiet

Billy Jones onstage. (Courtesy of Carl Lender)

Hughie Thomasson onstage. (Courtesy of Carl Lender)

power was the band's greatest strength." But a critic for *NME* identified Henry as the one who "stomps round the stage, driving home any nails that might be sticking up from the stage by pounding away with his Cuban heel till there's nothing there but splinters. He's the focal point of the group."

The truth was, the Outlaws included three fine lead vocalists in Hughie, Henry, and Billy—each of whom was also capable of wrapping the melodies of his bandmates with rich harmonies. While consciously drawing on inspiration from their Southern rock brethren, the band members were creating a unique sound of their own. "Lynyrd Skynyrd really were fighters," Henry mused. "The Allman Brothers were like a . . . trip. Somewhere in the middle were the Outlaws. We sang like the Eagles and played like the Allman Brothers." The album was certified Gold, and almost immediately, the band's audiences began to grow larger. "The first time we played in New York was in 1975 in Central Park with over 100,000 people there," Monte recalled. "It was Jefferson Airplane's twelfth anniversary show. I think that's when it all started to sink in for me."

In December of 1975, the Outlaws began work on their follow-up album. Paul Rothchild remained at the helm, but the group kept the recording sessions in their home state of Florida. "Once we got up and running" Henry explained, "we had a little more control, and we wound up recording down in Miami at Criteria Studios for the second record." Released in 1976, *Lady in Waiting* was another solid collection of harmony-laden folk-rock vocals, combined with the triple guitar attack of Paul, Thomasson, and Jones. "Our gimmick is no gimmick," Paul told *Sounds* that year. "These days, in the world of rock and roll, no gimmick is a gimmick."

The Outlaws continued to tour relentlessly, winning over most audiences for whom they had the opportunity to play. "We work hard for what we get," Henry declared in 1976. "Something inside us wants to relate to the audience in any way possible. Sometimes I just feel like taking my guitar off, my shirt, and everything else, and just jumpin' into the crowd." They were driven to rise to the upper echelon of Southern rock royalty. "The Outlaws," observed Lynyrd Skynyrd crew member Rock Eckerman, "saw themselves as the 'new' Skynyrd, so there was heated competition between the bands."

Soon after the release of *Lady in Waiting*, the Outlaws traveled overseas. "In about '76 we did a tour in Europe with the Who and Little Feat," Yoho explained. "We were playing some

of the big football stadiums, like Wembley, and it was just incredible." Nobody in the band had ever traveled outside the US or even had a passport prior to the European shows.

When they returned from Europe, the Outlaws played a homecoming gig in their native Tampa on July 4, 1976, at which they were awarded a key to the city. The band members would consider it the golden era of their career, a time when they were experiencing solid success and bonding together as a musical family. "The Allman Brothers had tattoos," Henry recalled, "and we were like, 'Wow, *that's* weird!' The only guys I knew that had tattoos were in the army. So we all went out and got tattoos. It was funny as shit. We just got our logo tattooed on our arm. Hughie and Monte and Frank got one, and then Billy's wife wouldn't let him get one. We used to give him a hard time about that. All the guys in the road crew got one, too."

The camaraderie extended beyond the band members themselves to the other Southern rock musicians with whom the Outlaws were often sharing the stage. "I would say Tommy Caldwell and Charlie Daniels were the two biggest influences on me as band leaders and as cultural icons," Henry told Michael Buffalo Smith. "They were two people who were worthy of imitation. We had this brotherhood. It was us against the world. It was, 'Fuck L.A. Fuck the Eagles.' I remember feeling it was us and Tucker and Charlie against L.A., the Eagles, and Linda Ronstadt, and Loggins and Messina. It was 'The South's Gonna Do It Again' and 'Dixie.'"

"It was sort of a very, very tight-knit social group of the lucky few that were able to rise up to that level of exposure," he later added. "There was competition between bands, but there was also a unique brotherhood and affectionate and respectful relationship amongst us toward the other people, especially the people

like Dickey Betts, who was higher up in terms of real significance. . . . It was uniquely consistent from one group to the next. There was a like-minded sense of friendship and support of one another, and it was pretty damn fun."

While the members of the Outlaws placed themselves firmly in the Southern rock camp, they were not interested in limiting their audience. "We're not strictly Southern," Billy Jones told *Melody Maker* in 1976, "it's just an all-American sound." As the band branched out beyond the Southern rock community, they found themselves opening dates for one of the biggest groups in the world. "We did one of the legs of the Rolling Stones' tour in the US," Monte recalled. "We did maybe a half-dozen string of dates. It's just unbelievable when you're out there sharing the stage with someone you've idolized your whole life. Mick walked into the dressing room, and I'm almost thinking, like, this really isn't happening. And he was so pleasant and down to earth, and so business-like, checking to make sure we were happy. They were so gracious."

By 1977, bassist Frank O'Keefe had departed the band and was replaced by a North Carolina bassist and vocalist named Harvey Dalton Arnold. Harvey's recording debut with the group came with the Outlaws' third release, *Hurry Sundown*, which hit stores that same year. Produced by Bill Szymczyk at Florida's Bayshore Studios, it was another collection of strong material. Though vocals were still shared by various bandmates, it was Thomasson's "Hurry Sundown" that became a minor radio hit.

The Outlaws had released three very strong albums within a two-year period, but the bonds within their brotherhood were beginning to fracture following the release of *Hurry Sundown*. "In some bands, everyone wants to be a star," Billy Jones had observed in a 1976 interview with Barbara Charone, "everyone wants to have the spotlight on them, and nobody's willing to settle back and make the rest of the guys sound good. *We* got over ego problems a long time ago with fist fights." Henry Paul agreed. "If we see somebody gettin' a little weird and they want to take over," he added, "we beat the shit out of them. If someone gets heavy, we harass them to the point where they feel like an outcast."

They weren't being completely honest, however—either with the journalist or with themselves. Or perhaps the situation shifted rapidly within a year. Whatever the case, co-leader Henry Paul abruptly departed the group. "Hughie wanted me out of the band in '77," Paul recounted, "because he wanted to go in more of a rock-and-roll direction, and I was sort of the country-rock guy in the band." Sadly, the Outlaws had fallen prey to the pitfalls that so many groups encounter once they achieve success. "It was the typical in-band, ego-driven control issues," Henry lamented. "One's view of one's self changes, and there were internal struggles for control. It's a pretty common story."

Freddie Salem was brought into the band to replace Henry Paul. While Henry had always played rhythm guitar behind Hughie and Billy's twin leads, Salem was another lead player. With three lead guitarists, the Southern California country-rock sound that had characterized the first trio of albums gave way to a more aggressive aesthetic. Additionally, drummer David Dix—who had played in one of the very early lineups of the Outlaws in the late 1960s—was brought in as a second drummer, alongside Monte Yoho. In 1978, they released a double live album called *Bring It Back Alive* that hit #29 on the *Billboard* album chart and was certified Gold.

In November 1978, the Outlaws issued their fourth studio album, *Playin' to Win*. Produced by Mutt Lange—who would go on to helm enormously successful records for Def Leppard and Shania Twain—the LP marked a shift in the band's sound. Gone was the ragged edge of their organic country-rock sound. Instead, the album was polished to a slick sheen that didn't suit the group's charm. Fans didn't embrace the LP as eagerly as they had the previous three efforts.

When they returned with *In the Eye of the Storm* in 1979, the Outlaws' sound had fully transitioned to hard rock. Produced by Capricorn stalwart Johnny Sandlin at Criteria Studios in Miami, it was a much better album than *Playin' to Win*. Like its predecessor, however, it fell far short of the Top 40.

That same year, Henry Paul reemerged on Atlantic Records with his own Henry Paul Band. The debut LP, *Grey Ghost*, was not a major success, but was highly regarded by Southern rock aficionados. The title track was a tribute to Ronnie Van Zant, who had done so much for the Outlaws. "Being forced out of the Outlaws in 1977 was painful," Henry acknowledged. "I was determined to be resilient in the face of my rejection, so to speak, that came from certain factions in the group. I was able to establish my own name and put a very competitive group on the road, and cut an artistically pertinent and relevant record. The *Grey Ghost* record was something I thought was pretty damn special. That was something I was really proud of." The Henry Paul Band would go on to

The early-1980s lineup of the Outlaws. *Left to right:* Freddie Salem, David Dix, Hughie Thomasson, Billy Jones, and Rick Cua. (Arista Records)

release three more albums, culminating with a 1982 LP credited to Henry Paul solo. The strongest of Paul's Atlantic output was 1979's *Feel the Heat*, which embraced the guitar-heavy feel of his best work with the Outlaws.

By 1980, Outlaws drummer Monte Yoho had departed the group to join the Henry Paul Band. With David Dix remaining, the Outlaws returned to a single-drummer configuration. Bassist Harvey Dalton Arnold left and was replaced by Rick Cua. "We tried out bass player after bass player after bass player," Hughie Thomasson told Gary James, "and he walked in and went 'Boom! Boom! Boom!' and I went, 'OK, that's it. You don't have to play any more songs—you're hired!'" Finally, former Wet Willie keyboardist Mike Duke came into the band to round out the lineup.

While the heavy-rock *Ghost Riders* album of 1980 sounded virtually nothing like the country-rock flavored Outlaws of the mid-1970s, it was a very strong release and reached #25 on the *Billboard* chart. It was the band's highest-charting LP, and it spawned the #31 single "(Ghost) Riders in the Sky." It was the only Outlaws title, other than the debut album

and the first live LP, to go Gold. A triumph for Thomasson, the successful LP made the Outlaws one of the rare Southern rock bands to experience greater commercial success in the 1980s than in the 1970s.

When the follow-up, 1982's *Los Hombres Malo*, was released, however, it became the band's lowest-charting album to date. With a title and cover reminiscent of ZZ Top, it continued the hard-rocking tradition into which the Outlaws had transitioned, following the departure of Henry Paul. Longtime guitarist Billy Jones was gone by this point, as was keyboardist Mike Duke. Bassist Rick Cua departed after the album was recorded to launch a career as a contemporary Christian music artist. *Los Hombres Malo* would be the Outlaws' final effort for Arista Records, as they were dropped from the label soon thereafter. For all intents and purposes, it was the end of the Outlaws' golden era.

"The writing was on the wall about that time for the Southern bands," Monte pointed out. "It was over, and everybody was struggling. Record companies were dropping everybody, and work was getting scarce, and the

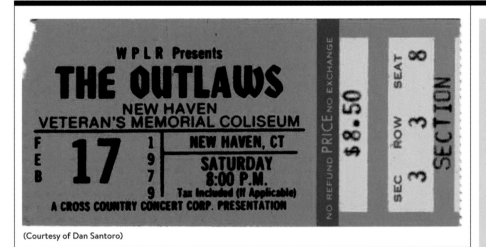

(Courtesy of Dan Santoro)

money wasn't the same. That was just about the end of it. Disco, Michael Jackson—a lot of that stuff just sent us spinning out of the landscape. We were just gone, and what a sad time."

"At one point," Henry recalled, "Alan Walden called me up and suggested that Hughie and I talk about getting back together, because he saw that when Hughie and I were together in the band that the band had more significant success. He thought perhaps the magic of the earlier days could be recreated." They released one album, *Soldiers of Fortune*, in 1986 on the independent Pasha label, but by then Hughie and Henry were the only original members left. Heavily produced and featuring synthesizers and drum machines, the album failed to deliver on the imagined possibilities of reuniting the group's primary leaders. "With the advent of MTV and new-wave rock," Henry observed, "the landscape was completely different. We were irrelevant. Lynyrd Skynyrd was gone. Marshall Tucker lost its creative and leadership center when Tommy Caldwell died. The Allmans were in and out of business, and it just fragmented."

"Hughie and I had a parting of the ways again right at the end of '88," Henry explained. "New Years Eve of '88 was my last show with the band." Paul eventually found his way to Nashville, where he experienced his greatest career success with the country group Blackhawk. The band's self-titled debut album from 1994 was a major success, and yielded four hit country singles. "I put out a multi-Platinum record," Henry recalled, "and it was like, 'Yee-fuckin'-ha.' It felt great."

Two years after Henry Paul found success with Blackhawk, Hughie Thomasson joined the reconstituted Lynyrd Skynyrd, where he stayed for nine years. "The Outlaws and Skynyrd toured together back in 1975, '76, and '77—right up until the time of the plane crash," Hughie recalled. "We played together, got to

know each other, and became friends. When I went to play with Skynyrd, it wasn't like I was going to play with strangers."

"The rock-and-roll band business, by nature, is a very tough game," Henry reflected in later years. "Some of the stories, whether it be John and Paul, or Don Henley and Bernie Leadon . . . it is a tough marriage. To make it really work, and work well, is difficult and very rare." Henry and Hughie were no different than so many other rockers who had to balance competing visions within the same band. "He and I struggled for control many times," Henry confessed. "It's the same old tale, and every time I discuss it—it never comes across as complex emotionally as it really was. There are some difficult parts to the story, and there are some really wonderful parts. I try to focus on the good stuff." Despite all the ups and downs, however, the Outlaws bond was never fully broken. "My affection for Hughie, Frank, Billy, and Monte is something that I know we all shared," Henry explained. "There was never animosity to one another to the point where it overrode our affection for one another."

The surviving band members are at peace with the Outlaws' place in Southern rock history. "I've read interviews where we denounced the term Southern rock," Henry laughed. "There must have been a reason, but I don't know why. It was really a cultural thing. . . . It was an eclectic cultural undercurrent and backdrop that transcended just the music."

"It was just something that we were termed with," Monte Yoho added. "I don't think it really mattered to us either way. As long as we were in the company of who they considered Southern rock—with the Allmans, Charlie Daniels, and Marshall Tucker—we figured we were in fine company. That term is probably overused, but it seemed to catch on. . . . For me, when I hear Southern rock, I just think of a real Southern brotherhood." ★

BURNING THE BALLROOM DOWN: THE AMAZING RHYTHM ACES
—

IN 1975, the Amazing Rhythm Aces fell just shy of the Top 10 on both the country and mainstream charts with "Third Rate Romance." The critically acclaimed *Stacked Deck* album on which it appeared captured a soulful Southern authenticity that crossed genres. "I would embrace the term Southern rock," lead singer and primary songwriter Russell Smith, conceded, "as long as I didn't have to stay in that corral the entire time. Part of our problem, as far as labeling us, was that we liked all the influences behind Southern rock almost equally."

Russell Smith played in various bands in Knoxville, Tennessee, in the late 1960s with bassist Jeff "Stick" Davis and drummer Butch McDade. Eventually, Davis and McDade departed for Canada to work with singer-songwriter Jesse Winchester as the Rhythm Aces. Around the same time, Smith took a trip to Muscle Shoals, where he hooked up with a keyboard player from Tennessee named Billy Earheart. "I was a young hippie in '67 or '69, when everybody got psychedelic," Earheart laughed. "I saw the Hour Glass with Gregg and Duane and Johnny Sandlin and Pete Carr, and that was a huge inspiration to me."

Smith and Earheart played well together, and Russell convinced Billy to move to Knoxville, where they put together a band. "We called ourselves Beaucoup Dap," Billy remembered. "That's Vietnamese for 'You're looking good, motherfucker!'" Butch McDade and Jeff Davis eventually returned from Canada, joining forces with Beaucoup Dap and reviving the Rhythm Aces name.

McDade contacted Barry "Byrd" Burton, a guitarist in Memphis who was working for Sam Phillips Recording. The band relocated there, and Burton and pianist James Hooker officially joined the group. "It was late '73—may have even been November or December—when we started recording a song or two here or there," Billy recalled. "We ended up doing about twenty tunes. That's when Sam Phillips helped us out. He knew everybody in the business from his Sun Records days, and he got his son, Knox Phillips, to talk to Don Gant at ABC Records in Nashville. They signed us in the spring of '75. We were an oddity right off the bat, plus we all had long hair down to our waist."

The Rhythm Aces' label discovered another band already had claim to the name, so a minor adjustment was made. "It was the time of the *Fabulous* Thunderbirds and the Ozark Mountain *Daredevils*, and all these dashing names," Russell explained, "so we just added the 'Amazing,' and it worked!" When *Stacked Deck* was released in 1975, the band members found their lives quickly transformed. "Not long ago," Smith told journalist Jeff Burger in 1976, "we all had day jobs. Jeff worked in a mortuary. I did construction, and so on. At night, we played in little clubs where the audiences got drunk and the managers told us to do Top 40. Now we're doing national tours and putting records on the charts."

After "Third Rate Romance" ran its course, the label released "Amazing Grace (Used to Be Her Favorite Song)." It was perceived by some to be a parody, but that was never Smith's intention. "If George Jones had sung that song," he speculated to *Rolling Stone* in 1976, "I don't think it would have come up as funny. Because we're not a straight country band, we've either got to have our tongue in our cheek or our finger up our ass to do a song like that."

The follow-up to the *Stacked Deck* LP, 1976's *Too Stuffed to Jump*, featured "The End Is Not in Sight (The Cowboy Tune)," which won a Grammy award for Country Vocal Performance by a Group. In 1977, they released *Toucan Do It Too*, followed by *Burning the Ballroom Down* the following year. Both albums were critically acclaimed, but sustained commercial success continued to elude the band.

By the close of 1978, Byrd Burton had departed the Amazing Rhythm Aces. He was replaced by Duncan Cameron. "Barry didn't want to be on the road no more," Smith explained. "He was six-foot-four. He hated traveling in buses and stuff. I didn't mind it so bad, cause I'm short. I could just duck up in a bunk and be comfortable. Plus, we were doing OK, but we weren't making a ton of

The Amazing Rhythm Aces, *left to right:* James Hooker, Butch McDade, Barry "Byrd" Burton, Russell Smith, Jeff "Stick" Davis, and Billy Earheart. (ABC Records)

money on the road. Also, Barry didn't drink and didn't party at all."

By the time the Amazing Rhythm Aces began work on their self-titled fifth LP, the group's sound was beginning to evolve away from country influences toward R&B. They traveled to Muscle Shoals, where Jimmy Johnson produced them. "Musically speaking, Muscle Shoals is in that no man's land between country and blues and soul and rock and all that other stuff," Russell enthused. Critics didn't always get it. *Rolling Stone*'s Daisann McLane profiled Russell Smith in an article about the band from that era. "He shrugs, struts, bugs his eyes out," McLane wrote, "in a way that leaves you wondering if he's evil or nuts. Or both."

The band's next album, 1980's cleverly titled *How the Hell Do You Spell Rythum?*, only went to #175 on the mainstream album charts. Russell Smith soon recorded a solo album for Capitol Records, and the Amazing Rhythm Aces began to splinter. "A lot of different things led to the breakup," Smith acknowledged. "It's the same story as everybody else's rock-and-roll band, and is just as boring." By the dawn of 1982, the band was finished. Smith reinvented himself as a hit

Nashville songwriter, while Earheart went on to join Hank Williams, Jr.'s band. Duncan Cameron reemerged as a member of the country group Sawyer Brown, before eventually leaving to pursue a career as a pilot for Southwest Airlines.

Though the Amazing Rhythm Aces defied easy categorization, their Southern rock roots always showed. "We were big on Southern music," Billy Earheart reflected in 2013. "We liked the Southern R&B a lot, the Muscle Shoals and Memphis hard soul kind of thing, the country side. We loved it all."

THE AMAZING RHYTHM ACES

- ‣ RUSSELL SMITH lead vocals, guitar
- ‣ JEFF "STICK" DAVIS bass
- ‣ BUTCH MCDADE drums
- ‣ BARRY "BYRD" BURTON guitar
- ‣ BILLY EARHEART keyboards
- ‣ JAMES HOOKER piano
- ‣ DUNCAN CAMERON guitar

Part Eight

TAKE NO PRISONERS: JACKSONVILLE'S SOUTHERN ROCK ASSAULT

"Jacksonville, Florida, was a navy town, and we all played sailor clubs, making a hundred bucks a week. You'd cut your teeth playing these songs and watchin' sailors get drunk and fight each other. Every single one of us, Duane Allman, Gregg, Ronnie Van Zant, everybody played those sailor clubs."

—DON BARNES, 38 SPECIAL, 2013

DESPITE THE CENTRAL role that Georgia played in the history of Southern rock, northern Florida was a hotbed for the biggest names in the genre. The Sunshine state was "a very creative place, musically," Henry Paul of the Outlaws explained to interviewer Jeb Wright. "There were a lot of places to play. It was a very hot, Sunbelt part of the world, and people were outside congregating. It wasn't like New Jersey, where you were in a little township and isolated. It was very open, and bands could gain a foothold on a regional level if they demonstrated exceptional qualities." Paul's bandmate Hughie Thomasson concurred. "I think it all started with Skynyrd," he told *Classic Rock Revisited*. "They started the ball rolling. Maybe there is something in the water. Molly Hatchet is from Florida. Tom Petty is from Gainesville. A lot of great bands came from Florida. Maybe it's the heat."

Don Barnes, Larry Junstrom, and Jeff Carlisi of 38 Special. (Photo by Charlyn Zlotnik/Redferns)

While several Florida cities produced noteworthy bands, it was Jacksonville, more than any other place, that gave the world a bumper crop of Southern rockers. The Classics IV, who later gave birth to the Atlanta Rhythm Section, originated in Jacksonville. The members of Lynyrd Skynyrd grew up there. The Allman Brothers first came together after a jam session there. Other important Capricorn acts like Cowboy and Grinderswitch came from Jacksonville, too.

Going back even further, Jacksonville boasted a rich musical heritage that stretched back decades prior to the birth of rock music. In the 1920s and '30s, the LaVilla neighborhood emerged as the cultural center for African American life in Jacksonville. It nurtured a thriving music scene that hosted the major black touring acts of the day in its Ritz Theater. Local clubs and venues showcased regional talent on and around Ashley Street, earning the area a reputation as the Harlem of the South.

Though the precise biographical details of his life are shrouded in mystery, blues guitarist Blind Blake, known as the King of the Ragtime Guitar, is believed to be one of the earliest professional musicians to have emerged from Jacksonville. His 1926 recording of "Ashley Street Blues" referred to the storied LaVilla area. In 1945, Ray Charles relocated to Jacksonville and spent a year there playing with tenor saxophonist and bandleader Tiny York, who was a major local attraction. Singer Billy Daniels, best remembered for his hit recording of "That Old Black Magic," emerged from LaVilla, as did trumpeter Teddy

Washington, who spent several years playing in James Brown's backing band. By the mid-1960s, however, the Harlem of the South had fallen quiet, as most of the promising musicians left for New York or other musical capitals.

By the 1950s, Jacksonville began to attract attention in the country field. Slim Whitman scored several Top 10 country hits in the 1950s with songs like "Indian Love Call," "Secret Love," and "Rose Marie." He moved to the Jacksonville area in 1957 and remained there for the rest of his career, racking up nearly thirty more charting singles. Former *Life* magazine writer Mae Boren Axton relocated to Jacksonville with her husband and children in 1949, where she worked as a publicist and part time country music DJ. She and steel guitarist Tommy Durden wrote "Heartbreak Hotel," which Axton played for Elvis Presley and convinced him to release as his first single on RCA Records. Her son Hoyt later made a splash as a songwriter, with credits including "Greenback Dollar" by the Kingston Trio and the Three Dog Night classics "Joy to the World" and "Never Been to Spain."

By the early 1970s, it seemed that virtually every Southern rock band had a Jacksonville connection. "There is no doubt about it," Grinderswitch guitarist Dru Lombar reflected, "90 percent of the Southern rock bands started in Jacksonville. . . . Jacksonville has always been a breeding ground for musicians." Following the first wave of Jacksonville bands, a crop of harder-edged rock groups emerged, the most prominent being Blackfoot, Molly Hatchet, and 38 Special.

Blackfoot onstage, *left to right*: Charlie Hargrett, Rickey Medlocke, Jakson Spires, Greg T. Walker. (Jeff Windwer Collection/Frank White Photo Agency)

CHAPTER 31
Born to Rock and Roll: Blackfoot

★ ★

 NE OF THE MORE influential local musicians in Jacksonville, Florida, was Shorty Medlock. Born in 1910, Shorty was a master of the Delta blues and an accomplished bluegrass picker who toured with Roy Acuff's band early in his career. The first generation of Jacksonville's Southern rockers got to know Shorty's legacy through his grandson, Rickey Medlocke, who added an *e* to the end of the family name and made a reputation for himself as a member of both Blackfoot and Lynyrd Skynyrd.

Medlocke was raised by his grandparents, and considered Shorty to be his dad. "He was on a TV show out of Jacksonville," Rickey explained to writer Ted Drozdowski. "*The Toby Dowdy Show*, a weekly country-music show. He had the idea to teach me banjo when I was three years old, and then we appeared on the show together." The elder Medlock was

an inspiration to his grandson. "Shorty taught me how to play and taught me the values of music," Rickey told Michael Buffalo Smith, "and that is why I really owe him everything. He really was the cat's ass to me when it came to being a real musician. He lived it, breathed it, and loved it." In fact, Medlock is rumored to be the inspiration for one of Skynyrd's best-known songs. "Ronnie and Gary and Alan and myself, when I was with the band in the early '70s, they'd go to my folks' place and hang out on the porch with my dad, because he played the blues," Medlocke explained. "And that's kind of where they got that song 'Curtis Lowe.' It's actually about my dad, Shorty."

"Jacksonville was a very transient town," explained Medlocke. "It was a stopover for vacationers going down to Miami and Ft. Lauderdale. There were three Naval bases. It was an industrial city with shipyards. So it was a big community with a small-town feel. And all of those people passing through or coming from other places to live there brought their interests and influences."

Rickey Medlocke, Greg T. Walker, Jakson Spires, and DeWitt Gibbs were long-time friends who'd known one another since kindergarten and grew up playing in various bands together. By 1969, Medlocke and Walker were in a group called Fresh Garbage with guitarist Charlie Hargrett. "When he came in to audition," Walker recalled in an interview with Fred Capitelli, "he played 'Badge' by Cream, and when he did that middle guitar section, we were like, 'Oh, you've got the job!'" Spires and Gibbs were playing in a competing band called Tangerine. When Fresh Garbage's keyboard player left around

Jakson Spires, Rickey Medlocke, Charlie Hargrett, and Greg T. Walker. (Atco Records)

BLACKFOOT

▸ **RICKEY MEDLOCKE** vocals, guitar, drums

▸ **GREG T. WALKER** bass

▸ **JAKSON SPIRES** drums, percussion

▸ **DEWITT GIBBS** keyboards

▸ **CHARLIE HARGRETT** guitar

▸ **LENNY SADLER BASS** guitar

▸ **DANNY JOHNSON** guitar

▸ **PATRICK JUDE** vocals

▸ **KEN HENSLEY** keyboards, guitar

▸ **BOBBY BARTH** vocals, guitar, keyboards

the same time Tangerine's lead guitarist departed in September, the two groups joined forces, forming a band called Hammer.

"We would have these be-ins in Jacksonville," Rickey Medlocke told *Goldmine* magazine, "and six or seven bands would get together and all set up their gear at the same time, and everyone would get up and jam. You would look up and see Duane, Gregg, Dickey, and Berry playing together. Then Skynyrd would play, and we would play. It was really the breeding ground for Southern rock." Unlike other Southern musical centers like Muscle Shoals, Macon, or Nashville, Jacksonville's bands tended to be harder and more aggressive. "It's a mean city," Medlocke

Blackfoot onstage in 1970. (Courtesy of Charlie Hargrett/siogo.com)

explained to the Jacksonville TV show *Back-street* in 1981. "It's the Transylvania of Florida. Anything that comes out of here is gonna be mean and right to the point."

Hammer relocated to Gainesville, an hour and a half south, where the boys landed a steady gig at a topless bar called Dub's in the fall of 1969. The nightly performances gave them ample opportunity to hone their sound. "That whole British Invasion was a huge influence on the band," Greg T. Walker recalled. "We would go buy import albums—you know, Deep Purple, Uriah Heep, before they ever broke in America, were unknown over here. And we would do a lot of their material back when we were doing five sets a night, you know, seven nights a week. You had to come up with a lot of songs."

Hammer's local popularity grew, and they scored a slot on the Miami International Rock Festival's lineup. Soon after, a Gainesville native named Nancy O'Connor, who was working for a music-publishing house in New York City, happened to catch the band's New Year's Eve set while she was in town for the holidays. She liked what she heard and convinced her boss, Ira Sokoloff, to give them a shot. After listening to their tape, he invited them to move to New York and agreed to

help manage their career. "There were not that many places for us to play in the South," Jakson Spires explained, "because we were too heavy for what was going on."

It was in New York that Hammer would be reborn as Blackfoot. After discovering that there was another band named Hammer on the West Coast, they changed their name to Free. Within weeks, "All Right Now" by Paul Rodgers' British rock quartet of the same name was released, leaving the hungry Florida rockers nameless once again. The search was on for a new moniker.

"Jakson Spires and I, you know, being of native descent, wanted something to do with our heritage," Greg T. Walker explained. "I'm Muscogee Creek. He was Cheyenne and Cherokee, so none of our tribal names sounded like a band name. And one night, watching Johnny Cash in New York City in 1970, on his variety show—he always had about a five- or ten-minute segment to honor native Americans—and we're sitting there and Jakson said, 'Blackfoot,' and we went, 'Yeah!'"

Blackfoot eventually landed at the Royal Hotel in Mt. Freedom, New Jersey. The once-grand resort had devolved into a rundown hippie haunt that had fallen into serious disrepair. Doing maintenance work and playing for free

in the hotel's "ballroom" to cover their rent, the band members were barely scraping by. For his part, though, Walker was committed to seeing their dream realized. "I said, 'Nobody can get married, nobody can buy a car, nobody can buy a house,'" he recalled to journalist Steve Wildsmith. "I told them we'd all live in one house and drive one van, and if anybody wasn't ready to do that until we made it, to speak up." DeWitt Gibbs wasn't ready. By the end of the summer of 1970, he departed.

By the fall, however, Blackfoot had begun to gain traction on the New Jersey college circuit, and were playing once or twice a week. They moved into a farmhouse outside Hackettstown and honed their sound as a four-piece band. Rickey Medlocke began playing rhythm guitar, filling in the space left by the departure of DeWitt's keyboard, and Blackfoot gained a solid following in the area. As the school year wound down in the late spring of 1971, the guys found themselves back in the same position they'd been in the previous year. With no money coming in, they moved from their farmhouse and tried to figure out how to survive. "I can remember eating Cheerios with water, because that was all we could afford," Walker recalled.

"For me," Medlocke explained to Michael Buffalo Smith, "I was just frustrated, not going anywhere or doing anything, and everything just going awry. I actually called Ronnie [Van Zant] up after I had gotten a hold of Allen Collins first and told him that I needed a gig. I told him that I would be able to drive a truck, load equipment, or whatever y'all need done. Then Ronnie asked me if I still played drums, and I told him, sure, I could do that, but in reality I had not sat on drums in a long time." Greg T. Walker soon followed Rickey, joining Skynyrd as their bassist. Jakson moved back to Florida, and Charlie stayed in New Jersey. It had been a fun ride, but Blackfoot simply hadn't gotten the break they

needed. They all figured it was the end.

In August of 1972, Charlie Hargrett was coaxed to North Carolina to join a band called Blackberry Hill that featured a bassist named Lenny Sadler. Unbeknownst to Sadler, however, Charlie had been talking with Rickey Medlocke and Jakson Spires, who were interested in getting Blackfoot back together. By that fall, Blackfoot had reformed in North Carolina with Saddler on bass. Wanting to concentrate on vocals alone, Medlocke set down his guitar and the band recruited Danny Johnson, from a Louisiana group called Axis, to join the lineup. It was a

short-lived arrangement, though, and Rickey soon returned to playing guitar.

Within a year, Blackfoot were playing regular dates in big clubs in Charlotte and Greensboro, and had landed gigs opening shows for more established bands like Poco and Black Oak Arkansas. In the summer of 1973, bassist Lenny Sadler experienced a spiritual conversion following a major health scare. He became a born-again Christian, left Blackfoot, and dedicated his life to the ministry. That fall, Greg T. Walker rejoined the band, and the core lineup of Rickey Medlocke, Greg T. Walker, Jakson Spires, and Charlie Hargrett was back together. They moved to New Jersey once again, and from then on, except for a brief period when Rickey was diagnosed with vocal nodules and sidelined from vocal duties, the lineup remained stable. Patrick Jude joined the band as lead singer during Medlocke's vocal problems, but the formally trained vocalist's style wasn't a good fit, and Rickey was soon able to return. Blackfoot spent the next year playing gigs, rehearsing, and writing songs.

Word began to spread that Blackfoot had become a really tight band with strong material, and Jimmy Johnson—the Muscle Shoals producer and musician who recorded Lynyrd Skynyrd's earliest material, back when Rickey and Greg were in the group— was interested in working with them again. "Ed King and I was workin' in the studio together," Johnson remembered. "I knew Ed was goin' back out to join Skynyrd, so I said, 'When y'all go through Jersey or New York, if you see Rickey Medlocke, tell him to call me.' Well, he called me, man, and I told him, 'I want to hear this new band you're in.'"

After so many years of slogging through gig after gig, trying to eke out a meager living, it looked like Blackfoot might finally get a shot. "We sent Jimmy and David a tape of our material," Charlie recalled, "and they made us an offer we couldn't refuse: if we could get from New Jersey to Alabama and back, they would house us and produce and record an album on speculation, at no cost to us, recouping their money only when they got a record deal for us."

Blackfoot temporarily made Alabama their home in early 1975 and started work on what would become their first album, *No Reservations*. Eight of the nine songs were written by Jakson Spires, with the final track, "Railroad Man," penned by Shorty Medlock. The album was released on Antilles Records, a subsidiary of Chris Blackwell's Island label, and "Railroad Man" was issued as the debut single. Though it was not a commercial success, the album's release gave the band an opportunity to expand

Greg T. Walker, Charlie Hargrett, Rickey Medlocke, and Jakson Spires.

their touring base. At the end of the year they moved to Gainesville and started working on songs for their follow-up album.

Returning to Muscle Shoals in 1976, Blackfoot recorded their second LP, *Flyin' High*. Island discontinued its relationship with the group, and the second album was released by Epic Records. Landing opening slots for acts like Ted Nugent, Kiss, and Peter Frampton, Blackfoot continued to win audiences over with their live shows. Their records, however, weren't selling. "They didn't do anything," Medlocke recalled. "They came out and fell short, you know." By the fall of 1977, Blackfoot found themselves without a record deal, and with fewer and fewer bookings. They went on the road backing former Black Oak Arkansas darling Ruby Starr under the billing Ruby Starr and Blackfoot. The shows ran through January 1978, before the relationship with Ruby soured and Blackfoot returned to Florida with few prospects for their next move.

In the early summer, they hooked up with Al Nalli, who managed Brownsville Station (of "Smokin' in the Boys' Room" fame) and owned a music store in Ann Arbor, Michigan. Nalli was impressed by the band's live show and took over their management. They returned to New Jersey once again and began working on songs for their third album. Nalli's sister Rene was a vice president at Atco Records and convinced the label's president, Doug Morris, to sign the band. In January of 1979, Blackfoot's third album, produced by Al Nalli, was completed. It was released in April as *Strikes*. The singles "Highway Song" and "Train Train" made it into the Top 40, and the album was eventually

certified Platinum. "Train Train" was nominated for a Grammy award.

Blackfoot hit the road opening for Ted Nugent. "Touring with Nugent, playing to 12,000 people a night, we quickly became a ten-year overnight success," Walker laughed. Blackfoot spent 1979 touring relentlessly and, in September, the band finally upgraded from a van to a tour bus.

In late 1979, Blackfoot returned to Ann Arbor to work on the next album, and opened for the Who at the Silverdome in Pontiac. The band subsequently went on the road with the Who in the spring of 1980, releasing their fourth album, *Tomcattin'*, in June. Though "Fox Chase" became a fan favorite, Blackfoot didn't appear on the charts with either of the singles from the album. Staying on the road, they supported AC/DC in the US before embarking on their first UK tour, where they opened for the Scorpions at twenty dates in October.

Late in 1980, Blackfoot returned to Ann Arbor to begin work on their fifth album, *Marauder*. The album was comprised of the straight-ahead rock sound that characterized the group's golden era, but it failed to catch on when it was released in July of 1981. They played the Monsters of Rock show in England with AC/DC and Whitesnake in August before setting out on a headlining tour—with Def Leppard serving as the opening band—in October and November. The two bands struck up a strong rapport and began pulling pranks on each other on the road, with each jokingly threatening to sabotage the other on the last night of the tour. "When Leppard hit

the stage in the San Antonio Convention Center at 7:45 p.m. on November 22, all hell broke loose," Charlie remembered fondly, in a posting on his official website. "A large 'DIK LIK-KER' backdrop unfurled behind the band. Riggers in the lighting trusses dropped ping pong balls to the stage, first two or three at a time, then handfuls, then bushel baskets full, followed by flaming streamers of flash paper. Fumes from stink bomb fluid on a towel thrown in front of drummer Rick Allen's electric fan filled the stage.... The audience had no idea what to make of all this mayhem."

In the winter of 1981–82, Blackfoot holed up in Florida to work on songs for their next album. Having recently toured with groups like AC/DC and Def Leppard, the band's members could see that Southern rock's popularity was waning, and that heavy-metal bands were gaining traction as the MTV era dawned. They attempted to write songs that would connect to a more metal-oriented audience, but it was a struggle, and they weren't satisfied with the material. In the spring of 1982, they traveled to Europe for a French tour with Iron Maiden, a headlining jaunt through the UK, and a German leg with the Scorpions. In the hope of updating their sound, Blackfoot recruited Ken Hensley, Uriah Heep's keyboard player, in 1982.

With Hensley on board, Blackfoot went to Ann Arbor to begin work on their sixth studio album. *Siogo* was released in May 1983. The band told the label the name was an Indian word that meant "closeness" or "togetherness," although that wasn't entirely true, as Charlie explained:

> Actually, our road crew had coined the
> word during previous tours, an acro-
> nym taken from a sign they had put in the
> front lounge of their tour bus. The sign
> said something like this: "If you are read-

Blackfoot onstage, *left to right*: Rickey Medlocke, Charlie Hargrett, and Greg T. Walker. (Courtesy of Charlie Hargrett/siogo.com)

ing this, you must be a slut, since, otherwise, this sign would have been taken down before you got here. Suck It Or Get Out!" . . . The folks at Atco Records discovered the true meaning of "siogo" soon after the album was released in early 1983, when their publicist was calling all the Atco field reps to tell them all about the new Blackfoot record. One of the reps who had been on the road with us for a while and knew the truth began laughing hysterically when she told him "Siogo" meant "closeness," and he told her the real story. Atco was not amused.

Siogo was the first album to picture the band on the LP cover. "As well as the new musical influences Ken added," Charlie Hargrett explained, "he also brought in new fashion ideas. Soon, for the most part, Rick stopped wearing his trademark hat, boots, and duster, and more often wore the same kind of tight, wide vertical striped yellow-and-black or pink-and-black pants and Capezio dance shoes that Ken wore. I have to admit that I also tried wearing weird shirts with all the zippers and buckles and crap, but I felt pretty stupid about it." Medlocke later conceded it was a mistake. "It was the beginning of the end when we started listening to the record label," he admitted to interviewer David Iozzia. "We should have told them to take Blackfoot as we were, or don't take us at all." At the time, however, they were eager to try to adapt to changing times, even making two music videos—for "Teenage Idol" and "Send Me an Angel"—in an attempt to appeal to the MTV generation.

In the fall of 1983, Blackfoot took time off the road to write songs and do preproduction work for their next release. Both Charlie and Greg were left out of some of the preparations and were told that their contributions lacked the modern edge that was necessary to move the band forward. In interviews, Rickey began talking about moving away from macho-oriented material and embracing more sensitive themes, as the Police had done with "Every Breath You Take." Onstage, his movements reminded audiences of David Lee Roth. As the band dynamic descended into a desperate scramble to connect with young audiences, finger-pointing and blame-shifting began to tear at the fabric of the group's unity.

Tensions were high by the time the band started work on their *Vertical Smiles* album in Atlanta in November 1983. The album was completed in early January and submitted to the label, which wanted the band to re-record the entire second side. "Record-

Blackfoot promotional photo from the early 1980s. *Left to right*: Charlie Hargrett, Jakson Spires, Rickey Medlocke, and Greg T. Walker.

industry people said Southern rock was dying," Charlie Hargrett mused, in his written account of the band's history. "Quiet Riot was coming up to be the next big thing. They were people who wanted the band to change to try to become new. We've been in the same band for fourteen years, thirteen years. I thought, 'Do what you do.' It comes, it goes, you know. But stay true to yourself. It was not what I thought we should be doing and, by *Vertical Smiles*, it was time for me to go."

The *Vertical Smiles* album was, indeed, re-recorded, with Rickey handling all guitar duties. The band hit the road in 1984 to support the release, but tensions continued to flair. By the end of the summer, keyboardist Ken Hensley had quit. Bobby Barth, the singer and guitarist for Axe—another band managed by Al Nalli—was recruited to join Blackfoot's changing lineup. By December, however, Greg T. Walker and Jakson Spires were out. "We were slipping by then, and one night Rickey decided to end the band," Walker recalled to writer Todd K. Smith. "I don't know why, but we all agreed. Next thing we know, Rickey's back out on the road with a whole new band and calling it Rick Medlocke & Blackfoot. That wrecked us."

Now the only member from the original lineup, Rickey Medlocke took full legal control of the group's name. "For whatever reason, it all unraveled," Medlocke told Michael Buffalo Smith in 2004. "I do know that there has been things in the press said about whose fault it was, but to be honest, it was all of our faults. I don't think that it was any one person. . . . The record business is the most ruthless busi-

ness that I can even think of. . . . It took people downhill. There were some hurtful things exchanged between some of us."

For diehard fans, Blackfoot died in 1984. For the next decade, Rick Medlocke & Blackfoot continued on with a revolving cast of more than a dozen different supporting musicians. Rickey released three more Blackfoot albums, with virtually no commercial or critical acceptance. One critic wrote a particularly unforgiving summary of the group's 1991 album *Medicine Man*: "After running out of steam on Atlantic with a string of increasingly overproduced albums, this bloated effort comes across as nothing more than very bad hair metal released approximately five years after the genre had peaked." The critic in question was Cub Koda, former front man for Brownsville Station who played harmonica on "Train Train" from Blackfoot's 1979 *Strikes* album.

By 1996, Medlocke returned as a guitarist to the revamped Lynyrd Skynyrd, where he became a fixture with the band. "I think the Southern rock movement was really kind of an innocent thing," he later mused, while reflecting on his years in Blackfoot. "It just happened, you know. It just all of a sudden was *there*. What was really kind of cool is that we happened to be there in it." While embracing their Southern rock heritage, the members of Blackfoot were always careful to distinguish themselves as a hard-rock band with wide appeal who always played fast and aggressive. When asked by interviewer Dave Iozzia to sum up the band, Medlocke described Blackfoot, as only he could: "We were bad-ass sons-of-bitches who loved taking it to the hilt." ★

Molly Hatchet onstage in 1979. *Left to right:* Steve Holland, Duane Roland, Banner Thomas, and Dave Hlubek. (Photo by Michael Putland/Getty Images)

CHAPTER 32
Flirtin' with Disaster: Molly Hatchet

★ ★

 NE OF THE HEAVIEST-rocking and hardest-living of the Southern rock groups was Jacksonville's Molly Hatchet. "I have to tell you," guitarist and band founder Dave Hlubek observed in an interview with Philip Anderson, "even though we were tagged 'Southern rock,' it was only because of the location, the geographics. Us and Blackfoot, we were actually metal from the South. We certainly weren't anything like an Allman Brothers."

Produced by Tom Werman, best known for his work with Ted Nugent, Cheap Trick, and the Blue Oyster Cult, Molly Hatchet's early albums retained some distinctively Southern influences that were matched with arena-rock bombast. Their 1979 album *Flirtin' with Disaster* was certified triple Platinum and catapulted the band to stardom. It was a slow

MOLLY HATCHET

▸ **DAVE HLUBEK** guitar, vocals

▸ **STEVE HOLLAND** guitar

▸ **BANNER THOMAS** bass

▸ **BRUCE CRUMP** drums

▸ **DANNY JOE BROWN** vocals

▸ **DUANE ROLAND** guitar

▸ **JIMMY FARRAR** vocals

▸ **RIFF WEST** bass

▸ **B.B. BORDEN** drums

▸ **JOHN GALVIN** keyboards

▸ **BOBBY INGRAM** guitar

build, however, that was rooted in a long history on the Jacksonville music scene.

"Dave Hlubek *is* Molly Hatchet," lead singer Danny Joe Brown told *Gritz* magazine in 1999. "I was born in Jacksonville at the Naval air station," Hlubek explained, "but then I lived in Hawaii for six years because my father got stationed at Hickam Field in Oahu. I was a navy brat." By the time Dave was in third grade, the elder Hlubek, a naval aviator, was transferred to Moffett Field in Sunnyvale, California. The family bounced around California for a few years, ultimately landing in San Jose.

"The first time I saw the Beatles," he recalled, "I said, 'Wow!' The British explosion—with all those bands like the Stones, Gerry & the Pacemakers, and everyone that came from Europe in that British Invasion—I was hooked. When the Beatles started doing the movies like *A Hard Day's Night*, I said, 'That is for me. I want that!'" He put together a three-piece group called Something Else with a pair or brothers named Jesse and Ed. "Jesse and Ed's dad was a custodian at an insane asylum," Dave explained. "I guess he was also our agent, because the first gig we ever played was playing there during their lunch hour. We split $50. That was pretty good money back then!"

Something Else turned out to be a short-lived group when Dave's mother decided to return to Florida from California.

My mom and dad's marriage had gone the way of the dodo. Mama wanted to come back home, which was Jacksonville. When I got to Jacksonville, there was a culture shock right away. I was very West Coast, with bell-bottom pants, long hair, and loud,

colored clothes and stuff. I moved to the South, to Jacksonville, where the back of your hair didn't touch your collar, and all this other stuff. I got sent home because my bell-bottoms were too loud—orange and green paisley. To this day I don't understand what my pants had to do with my brain matter.

Dave's mother was a newly single mom with five children to support, so the family moved into her mother's home when they first settled in Jacksonville. "We were staying at my grandmother's house," Dave recalled, "and across the street—literally right across the street—the future Lynyrd Skynyrd was rehearsing. They were the One Percent then. I used to hear them rehearsing over there, and that was my first exposure to a music scene in town. They were already good back then!"

Like the members of the One Percent, Hlubek was preoccupied with the popular

Publicity photo of the original lineup of Molly Hatchet. *Left to right*: Bruce Crump, Banner Thomas, Dave Hlubek, Steve Holland, Danny Joe Brown, and Duane Roland. (Courtesy of Herb Kossover)

hard rock groups of the time. "I loved Cream," he told Michael Buffalo Smith, "anything by Clapton, the Doors. Early Hendrix stuff blew me away. Pretty much anything *loud* would do." Listening to music was one thing, but Hlubek was itching to put together another band of his own. He eventually assembled the Mind Garden, a four-piece group that included bassist Tim Lindsey, who later went on to play in the Rossington Collins Band, and a latter day incarnation of Lynyrd Skynyrd. "The Allman Brothers were getting started in Jacksonville at that period of time," Hlubek continued. "There was a Battle of the Bands, and Mind Garden took on the Allman Brothers. We sucked something terrible. Let's just say 'massacre' isn't even a strong enough word!"

Dave graduated from high school in 1971, the same year he met the guitarist with whom he would start Molly Hatchet.

> I was downtown at a place called Paula's Music Company. It was a music store where the now-famous Dickey Betts had worked as a salesman. You haven't lived 'til you've seen Dickey Betts in a Gant shirt, H.I.S. slacks, and loafers. That's a vision, I'm telling you. Anyway, I was up there playing a guitar and I hear this voice behind me go, "Ooh, that sucks!" It was Steve Holland, who had just moved from Virginia Beach with his new wife, three cats, and everything he owned in a van. We got to talking, and he said, "I play guitar. You wanna form a band?"

Hlubek and Holland left the store and headed to Steve's house. "We started rehearsing that very afternoon," Dave recalled, "and that band is what went on to become Molly Hatchet." Several musicians came and went, but the next future Molly Hatchet member to join was bassist Banner Thomas. After that, Dave explained, they auditioned for a drummer:

> We put the word out, and there was probably about sixteen drummers, all with their own kits, who showed up to try out. We'd let two or three in at a time while the others were waiting out in this area. At one point, we told one of our guys to go out there and call in the next drummers to come in for the audition. He said, "Dave, there's nobody out there but this blond-haired kid. Everybody's gone. The parking lot's empty." I said, "How is that possible? There were fifteen, sixteen guys out there before!"
>
> What happened was—and this is a true story—Bruce Crump came in. His mother worked for civil defense as a nurse, so he brought this megaphone with him to the audition, and goes up to the top of the stairs. He said, "Attention! Attention! You can all go home. We thank you for coming by, but we have found our new drummer." He hadn't even been in the main building yet!

With that, Bruce Crump became the band's drummer. "He was sixteen," Dave explained. "That was the first band he was ever in. He wasn't ever even in a garage band. He was a surfer. . . . He couldn't play drums worth shit, but he had an arrogance I loved."

In the early days, Hlubek handled the lead

vocal duties himself. A chance encounter in a late night club, however, resulted in Danny Joe Brown becoming the band's front man. "We were playing at an after-hours place called Dino's Disco," Dave recounted, "and in walks this guy who looks like Elvis Presley." At the break, Danny approached Dave. "He said, 'Can I tell you something? You're the greatest guitarist I have ever heard, but you can't sing to save your ass.' I said, 'Well, thank you very much.' He said, 'You need me.' I said, 'Who are you?' He said, 'Nobody you've ever heard, but I'm a singer, and I'm going to be your singer.' I said, 'Is that right? Well listen there, hot dog. We're going to be playing Jacksonville Beach next week. Why don't you come on out there and get onstage? You can audition in front of the audience.'"

Brown showed up at La Vita's Lounge the following week to sit in with the future Molly Hatchet. It happened to be ladies' night at the club. "He walked in there," Dave laughed, "and he got up and did about five songs—'Gimme Three Steps' and a few Skynyrd songs. There was not a pair of dry panties in the house. We took a break, and he said, 'So, when do I start?' I said, 'You just did.'"

By 1975, Duane Roland had become the sixth and final member of the original Molly Hatchet lineup. "He looked like Duane Allman," Dave recalled. "He was a great, great guitarist. We started playing local clubs and rehearsing and forming a Molly Hatchet sound."

Molly Hatchet continued to hone their skills in bars around Jacksonville. "Back in those days," Dave told Philip Anderson, "you could make a comfortable living, playing in Jacksonville. There were twelve nightclubs to play. When we finished the twelfth one, we'd go back to the first one. It was a cycle." At first, however, the group suffered from an identity problem. "We were changing the name of the band every two weeks," Dave recalled. "Nobody knew who the fuck we were! They would just get used to the name of the group, and we would finish the twelfth club and start over as the fucking Imbeciles or something! People would not know who we were. This is the same band that packed the place a few weeks before. Finally, we said, 'This is bullshit. We need to come up with a name for the group!'"

It was Dave who suggested the name Molly Hatchet. "I got the name from a book," he explained. "I was going to work in the funeral business. I started out as an apprentice at Hardage & Sons funeral home as a teenager. I went to the University of Florida in Gainesville, and was going for my journeyman's license so I could get a pay increase. I saw the name Hatchet Molly in the library there, and I thought it would be a bizarre enough name to describe six bizarre guys." Though it was rumored the name referred to a murderous prostitute, Hatchet Molly doesn't appear to have been an actual historical figure. Nevertheless, the name stuck.

As their regional notoriety increased, the

Backstage with record label representatives at Madison Square Garden, 1979. (Courtesy of Bruce Crump)

boys in Molly Hatchet hooked up with an established manager. "Pat Armstrong was a Jacksonville native who moved to Macon, Georgia, where Capricorn Records was," Hlubek explained. "Phil and Alan Walden were set up there, and Pat moved there because it was the Southern rock capital of the world. . . . He was our manager, and he turned out to be the seventh member of the band."

Pat Armstrong had previously been involved with Lynyrd Skynyrd's management. Dave told *Goldmine* magazine:

In the summer of '77, our manager arranged for us to meet Ronnie Van Zant—most of us already knew Ronnie from the Jacksonville music scene—and Ronnie took an interest in us and offered to produce our first demo tapes, and let us go into Skynyrd's private recording studio that they had on Riverside Avenue, in Jacksonville. And he took us in there and made us be there at nine o'clock every morning, or some ridiculous hour like that, and rehearsed with us for about a week. . . . He and his sound engineer, Kevin Nelson, recorded us in Skynyrd's recording studio there. And those were our first demo tapes.

According to Hlubek, Van Zant helped make Molly Hatchet a tighter band. "Ronnie made the songs on our first album make sense. He helped us get down to the nitty-gritty. He made suggestions. . . . We were gonna be his first rock band other than Skynyrd that he was gonna take under his wing. He was going to produce us. He left for the *Street Survivors* tour, where the plane crashed, and of course, it never happened."

At the end of 1977, Molly Hatchet got a break when Epic Records producer Tom Werman spotted them at a live show in Atlanta. "They literally left an imprint of my body on the wall, they played so hard." Werman recalled. He signed them to Epic in December of that year. "Epic didn't know

Publicity photo of Hatchet backstage with Ted Nugent. *Left to right:* Steve Holland, Bruce Crump, Ted Nugent, Duane Roland, Danny Joe Brown, and Dave Hlubek. (Epic Records)

what they'd signed," Hlubek laughed. "They thought Molly Hatchet was a big-tittied bitch. They didn't know. They hadn't heard us. It was like, 'Where's the girl in the band?'"

The band's debut album, *Molly Hatchet*, was recorded at the Sound Pit Studios in Atlanta, and released in September 1978. One of highlights was "Gator Country," a song that namechecked Lynyrd Skynyrd, Charlie Daniels, Richard Betts, Elvin Bishop, the Marshall Tucker Band, and the Outlaws. Unlike Charlie Daniels' "The South's Gonna Do It"—which references many of the same performers in a unified celebration of Southern musicians—the lyrics to "Gator Country" dismissed the various locales where these performers were based in favor of declaring regional pride in Florida.

While Molly Hatchet's members considered themselves ruder, louder, and edgier than many of the other Southern rock groups, it's noteworthy that they chose to include a cover of Gregg Allman's "Dreams" on their debut album. Appearing under the title "Dreams I'll Never See," their recording is a solid up-tempo interpretation that gives a unique slant to the song. The Allmans aren't the only Southern rock presence that shines through. "It is not by chance," Dave Hlubek pointed out, "that Molly Hatchet's first album sounds a lot like Skynyrd, because we used their equipment in the studio."

Renowned science-fiction and fantasy artist Frank Frazetta provided the album cover with his iconic *Death Dealer* painting. "We'd just finished our first album, and we had to pick a cover real quick," Dave told *Kerrang!* magazine. "We were running out of time, and Banner had this set of paintings by this dude called Frazetta. Pat Armstrong came up with this real neat logo to go on top." It looked like the cover of a heavy-metal album, and broke with the typically rootsy images that adorned many Southern rock releases.

While Molly Hatchet were heavier than most other Southern rock bands, however, their recorded sound was more akin to arena rock. In their live shows, they played harder and rawer. "We were more aggressive," Dave confirmed. "We'd just as soon go ahead and take your fucking head off. We were street fighters and barroom brawlers, for sure. We had that reputation because we certainly earned it." The band capitalized on their bad-boy image to help create an identity, relying on any press they could get to promote their reputation. "I don't care if it's good or bad, just spell the fucking name right," Hlubek said. "Our manager, Pat Armstrong, was an opportunist. He knew marketing. He said if we wanted to get on the cover of the *National Enquirer* or

Steve Holland, Bruce Crump, Banner Thomas, Jimmy Farrar, Dave Hlubek, and Duane Roland. (Epic Records)

any national magazines, we'd go [out] there and pick a fight in a bar. Whatever it took to go ahead and keep our name in the press."

Despite the bad boy image, the band members insisted they were good ol' Southern boys underneath it all. "What we are onstage and what we are offstage are two different animals," Hlubek declared to *Rolling Stone* in 1980. "Would you believe that we really are a bunch of sweethearts? We're good, solid people that were raised right." Promoting a rowdier image paid off, however. *Molly Hatchet* sold more than one million copies and was certified Platinum. The band toured relentlessly, building up a sizable following across the US. It wasn't until the following year, however, that they reached the pinnacle of their success.

Just over a year after the release of their first LP, Molly Hatchet returned to the charts in the fall of 1979 with a new album called *Flirtin' with Disaster*. Recorded at Bee Jay Studios in Orlando, the second effort had more energy and variety than the previous album. Featuring another Frank Frazetta cover, titled *Dark Kingdom*, it reached the Top 20, and was eventually certified triple Platinum.

Sales of the LP were driven largely by the popularity of the title song on FM radio. "The song's about me almost being killed in a car wreck," Hlubek explained:

> The Outlaws and 38 Special and Molly Hatchet were all gonna play at the Omni in Atlanta. Hughie Thomasson and myself were going to do a midday TV talk show about the show coming up that evening. He was gonna go on from 12:00 to 12:30,

Jimmy Farrar.

Promotional ad for a Jimmy Farrar–era Molly Hatchet concert in Mobile, Alabama, 1981.

and then I'd be on from 12:30 to 1:00. They wanted me there at 11:45.

Well, I was seein' a lady in Atlanta. I was over at her house, and I was doing some of my best work. She was bouncin' all over that bed. I happened to look at the clock, and it's 11:45. I said, "Whoa! Get dressed. We gotta go!" We had taken a cab to her house the night before. I said, "You got a car?" She said, "Yeah, but I don't drive it much." We ran outside, and she had a lime green four-cylinder Chevy Vega. I said, "When was the last time you started this car?" She said, "About six weeks ago." I said, "Oh shit." That thing was firing on three cylinders. She said, "Get in! I know some shortcuts!"

We were moving along and were in the middle of an intersection in this neighborhood. I looked to my right, and this canary-yellow long-ass El Dorado is coming straight for yours truly's damn door. They say your life flashes before your eyes? Bullshit. I didn't have time to make amends with the big boss. I said, "Get us out of this!" She slammed her foot down hard on that accelerator, and it was the first time that thing fired on all four cylinders. It actually threw me back in the seat. I couldn't believe it. She did some fancy swerving, and we hit the front porch of a house on the corner. She was a little tiny thing. She wasn't big, except for her boobs. Let me tell you what, she was hauling ass, running down the road, yelling after that guy in the Cadillac, "You son of a bitch! Get your ass back here! You don't want to fuck with me! You're flirtin' with disaster!"

Dave went home and used the phrase as the title to some music he'd been toying with for months. "Flirtin' with Disaster" would go on to become Molly Hatchet's best-known song.

"I'm as surprised as anybody," he told *Rolling Stone* in 1980, when asked about his group's success. "The band didn't expect it, the record company didn't expect it." While they sometimes distanced themselves from the term Southern rock, Hlubek viewed his band as part of an evolution of Southern music. As he reflected to journalist Xavier Russell in 1985:

I think you have to go back to the early bluesers, you know. To me, the origin of it would be these people sitting on a back porch . . . the real Southern blues artists. Then the Allman Brothers came along and made the sound heavier and started churning out these fifteen-minute songs. Next, Lynyrd Skynyrd came along and

refined that sound: made it more powerful and crunchier. Then you had Marshall Tucker and Grinderswitch, and they added a country flavor to it, and then came Molly Hatchet, and we were the first to put an almost metal edge to it. That was the evolution of the things that were taking place then.

As is often the case in the familiar rise-and-fall rock-and-roll story, Molly Hatchet began to splinter at the very moment they achieved stardom. While still riding high on "Flirtin' with Disaster," Danny Joe Brown departed the band. The official story was that he'd been diagnosed with diabetes and needed to step away from his fast lifestyle to take care of his health. While Brown's diabetes did play a role, he and Hlubek had begun to clash.

Nearly thirty-five years after the fact, Hlubek remained vague about what really happened with Brown. "There were just differences between different members," he cautiously explained. "Differences of opinions, differences in lifestyle. It was a sad thing. We were on tour when it happened. We were in Detroit, and that's when it happened." For his part, Brown told *Rolling Stone* that one of the issues was his questioning the band's manager regarding song publishing royalties he believed he was due.

Molly Hatchet weren't ready to call it quits, but they needed to come up with a solution fast. Jimmy Farrar had recently signed a contract with Hatchet's manager, Pat Armstrong. "About a month later," Farrar recounted, in an interview with Clyde Bradley, "he called

me up at about two o'clock in the morning and asked how I would feel about auditioning for another band. I told him I had a bar band and I didn't need another one because I had a damn good one now. So I said, 'Who is it?' And he said, 'I can't tell you.' So I said, 'Well then, I'm as sorry as I can be, but I can't come to Macon then.' Then he said, 'Well, it's Molly Hatchet.' And I said, 'I'll be there.'"

"We hired him over the telephone," Hlubek recalled. "He said, 'There's got to be a mistake.' He said, 'I can sing, but I'm ugly.' He said, 'I can sing everything. I love your band, but I'm not gonna win any fashion contests.' When he came into rehearsal, he walked into the room, and Steve Holland, with live mics on the stage, looked over at me and said, 'Hlubek, you have got to be fucking kidding!'"

Rolling Stone magazine later declared Farrar to be possibly the "meanest-looking man in the business." But to many observers, he

Dave Hlubek, Banner Thomas, Steve Holland, Duane Roland, Danny Joe Brown, and Bruce Crump.
(David Gahr/Epic Records)

was the perfect fit. "Larry Stessel, our product manager at Epic Records, told me I'd fit right in," Farrar recalled. "He said, 'You're dirty, raw, raunchy and disgusting—just like the rest of 'em. You'll go far."

Almost right away, the band returned to Bee Jay Recording Studios in Orlando to start work on their third album, *Beatin' the Odds*. "I think it's going to be a new side to Molly Hatchet," Dave told *Rolling Stone*. "This year we're goin' for double Platinum, which will be no small feat, given the economy and the state of the record business. But we are going to go out there and work and work and, in fact, we are going to beat the odds. If I have to do 300 dates this year, I'll do it. I have a lot to prove with this record. Molly's a mean bitch, and we don't take no for an answer."

The fact that a new vocalist had entered the fold was not emphasized. "What we did was make no public announcement," Hlubek commented. "We cut the third album hot on the heels of *Flirtin' with Disaster*, which went multi-multi-Platinum. We released a third album, *Beatin' the Odds*, with a new voice on there. People went, 'What the fuck?'"

Released in September, 1980—and featuring another Frank Frazatta cover—the LP still managed to climb to #25 on the album charts and was eventually certified Platinum. The album opened with an exceptionally heavy guitar riff that suggested a harder-rocking Molly Hatchet for the new decade. A mid-tempo ballad, "The Rambler," appeared on the singles charts, but was not a major hit. Farrar's clear-voiced performance stood in contrast to Danny Joe Brown's menacing growl.

The following year, Molly Hatchet recorded another album, *Take No Prisoners*, at Compass Point Studios in the Bahamas. AC/DC had recorded *Back in Black* there and recommended the facility to Hatchet when the two bands were touring together. Having spent the previous year on the road, however, the band weren't really ready to record. "*Take No Prisoners* was my least favorite," Hlubek confessed. "I got real lazy in my songwriting—the band was lazy overall—and I think the album reflects that. We were not focused."

Released in November 1981, *Take No Prisoners* entered the Top 40 but failed to achieve Gold certification. The cover was an unintentionally humorous painting of muscle-bound versions of the band members wearing *Conan the Barbarian*–style garb while subduing a dragon. Although it was somewhat reminiscent of Frank Frazetta's style, it obviously was not his work. "It was good working with Frazetta on the first three albums," Hlubek explained

to *Kerrang!*, "but by the time we came to the *Beatin' the Odds* cover, the price had tripled. His business manager was also his wife. I asked her why so much for the third cover, and she said, 'My husband's paintings made your band!' Well, we've never had a hit album cover played across the radio waves, so we stopped doing business with her."

Take No Prisoners is perhaps most memorable for featuring backup vocals by singer and actress Katey Sagal, best known today for her roles on *Married with Children* and *Sons of Anarchy*. As far as the public's acceptance of Jimmy Farrar was concerned, though, record buyers seemed to be pining for the days of Danny Joe Brown, as Dave recalled:

> We managed to pull the wool over the public's eyes for one album, but, after that, they wouldn't buy it anymore. Hatchet were going downhill fast, and Jimmy couldn't handle the pressures. We started to lose millions of dollars, and I got into drugs real heavy—I really did—because I figured we were losing everything, you know, and I didn't give a shit anymore because we were going into 17–20,000-seat coliseums and filling about a quarter of them. That's when the world started telling us, "We ain't buying it no more. The fat man has gotta go, or you're gone!"

Bassist Banner Thomas departed halfway through the *Take No Prisoners* tour in 1982, as he explained to journalist Philippe Archambeau:

> We all started thinking we were stars, and that drove wedges into the cracks that started forming. I was as guilty as anybody else. I got into an argument with Dave, got mad, and quit. Do I regret it today? Yes and no. I'm sorry I quit the way I did, when I did, but it looks like I picked a good time to

get out. Not long after, under pressure from management and the record company to produce more hit singles, the band started to lose its identity, and started to look like Loverboy. I'm glad I wasn't there for that.

That same year, Danny Joe Brown released his debut album, *Danny Joe Brown & the Danny Joe Brown Band*. Like Hatchet, it was a three-guitar band, featuring Steve Wheeler, Kenny McVay, and Bobby Ingram. John Galvin played keyboards, while Jimmy Glenn and Buzzy Meekins covered the drum and bass positions, respectively. In an interview with *Gritz* magazine, Brown recalled:

> They came out with *Beatin' the Odds* and I came out with my solo thing, and their album sales fell off. I mean just dropped off. We were a Platinum act before that. But when my solo album came out, I didn't do but a couple of hundred thousand records. And they dropped off from Platinum back down to Gold. And it took them a long time to get back up to Platinum. And they realized we weren't going anywhere separated. The company didn't push my record, and they didn't back Hatchet. And I remember going to the bathroom with the president of the record label. He said, "Danny, you guys have to get back together."

In the spring of 1982, after the *Take No Prisoners* tour concluded, drummer Bruce Crump and vocalist Jimmy Farrar both departed. Danny Joe Brown soon returned. "Danny was the singer for Molly Hatchet and will always be the voice for Molly Hatchet," Hlubek declared.

Bruce Crump, Dave Hlubek, Duane Roland, Riff West, Danny Joe Brown, and John Galvin. (Courtesy of Bruce Crump)

By the time Molly Hatchet began work on their fifth album, a new rhythm section consisting of Riff West and B. B. Borden was in place.

Released in March 1983, *No Guts ... No Glory* was the first Molly Hatchet record to use an actual photo of the band on the cover. Instead of the fantasy themes of previous covers, they appeared in a scene designed to look like the Old West. The album wasn't quite as heavy as some of the band's other work, and featured a few standout tracks including "The Peacemakers" and the instrumental "Both Sides," which closed the record. Dru Lombar from Grinderswitch appeared as a guest guitarist. In the end, however, the album only reached #59 on the charts, and like its predecessor it failed to achieve Gold status.

The following year, Molly Hatchet issued *The Deed Is Done*. Bruce Crump returned to the drums, but Steve Holland departed the band before the album was completed, leaving Molly Hatchet without a third guitarist for the first time since their official formation. With the change in lineup came a change in producers. Terry Manning, who'd engineered ZZ Top's highly successful albums, took over production duties from Tom Werman. The resulting LP, released in late 1984, was a calculated and slickly overproduced grab for commercial success. It only reached #120 on the album chart.

With one less guitar in the group, John Galvin, who had played keyboards in the Danny Joe Brown Band, came aboard to add new color to the sound. "If it wasn't for Danny," Galvin told Michael Buffalo Smith in 2002, "I wouldn't have been in Molly Hatchet. He frequently read the Bible, and treated everyone that came his way with respect. He has a good-ol'-boy persona that's almost Elvis-like. He was a 'yes ma'am, yes sir' kind of guy that appealed to both young and old."

Though Danny might have been regarded as a Southern rock bad boy, he wasn't interested in the darker side of the heavy-metal audience that embraced Molly Hatchet. "I think Lucifer's a piece of shit, you know, and that's how I was brought up," Brown reflected, in an interview with *Kerrang!* "The Big Boss is up there, and I'm against it 100 percent. I don't care if these so-called satanic bands can play or not, 'cause kids take their albums home, run them back and forth, and analyze the lyrics. It's sick, man!"

With the band unwilling to embrace certain aspects of the metal crowd, and recognizing that Southern rock's popularity was on the wane, the original Molly Hatchet era came to an end in the mid-1980s. The lifestyles of a few band members contributed to the decline as much as changing musical tastes. "At times

Riff West, John Galvin, Duane Roland, Danny Joe Brown, Bobby Ingram, and Bruce Crump. (Courtesy of Bruce Crump)

we could be a hell-raising band," John Galvin admitted to Smith, "some members more than others. I think that would have to fall into Danny and Dave's lap. They were the hardcore party men, the ones that would take the most risks, and hang with the riskiest of people.... We have always had a strong biker following, so it was not unusual to see the Hells Angels, Outlaws, Banditos, or any other bike club at our shows, and occasionally onstage with us."

"I had a horrendous, horrendous cocaine problem," Hlubek confessed. "All I did in a twenty-four-hour day, there was only two hours that I was working, and that was in a coliseum. The rest of the time I was coked up.... I'd like to think that I'm a strong person, but even a tanker truck runs out of gas."

Looking back from the perspective of many years, Hlubek lamented the money wasted and the toll taken by addiction. "Drugs are never a positive, good thing with any organization," he reflected, "and it certainly was not for ours. In the '70s, drug use ran rampant." Molly Hatchet limped along for the rest of the 1980s, but Hlubek left in 1987 and was replaced by for-

mer Danny Joe Brown Band guitarist Bobby Ingram. The band officially broke up in 1990, though Danny Joe Brown and Bobby Ingram continued to use the name with various lineups.

As with many bands that were embraced by fans of Southern rock, members of Molly Hatchet were never completely comfortable with the label. "As to country-flavored rock-and-roll songs about trains and alligators," Banner Thomas pointed out, "I think we've pretty much said everything that needs to be said on those subjects a long time ago. We should leave it to the old masters like Charlie Daniels and the Allman Brothers to handle that. They still do that better than anyone else. They still make it sound real. The rest of us just sound like copycats in their shadow."

Hlubek ultimately made peace with the classification. "I don't think there's a definitive sound to Southern rock," he explained in 2013, "but I'm real proud of my heritage. All we ever wanted was to hear ourselves on the radio one time. I never could have imagined we'd achieve everything we did. If it's Southern rock, well ... OK." ★

Donnie Van Zant onstage in Philadelphia, 1981. (Courtesy of Frank White)

CHAPTER 33
Wild-Eyed Southern Boys: 38 Special

★ ★

N 1989, JACKSONVILLE'S 38 Special reached #1 on *Billboard*'s Adult Contemporary singles chart with the song "Second Chance," a carefully crafted slice of melodic pop-rock. With a sound akin to Mr. Mister, John Waite, or Richard Marx, there was virtually no trace of the 38 Special that emerged in the 1970s amid criticism that they sounded too much like Lynyrd Skynyrd.

It all began in North Florida, where Ronnie Van Zant's younger brother Donnie, his partner and co-leader Don Barnes, guitarist Jeff Carlisi, and a rhythm section that featured two drummers came together to develop a winning pop formula. "We all grew up within a few blocks of each other," lead guitarist Jeff Carlisi told writer Scott Greene of the childhood

38 SPECIAL

- ▸ DON BARNES vocals, guitar
- ▸ DONNIE VAN ZANT vocals, guitar
- ▸ JEFF CARLISI guitar
- ▸ JACK GRONDIN drums
- ▸ STEVE BROOKINS drums
- ▸ KEN LYONS bass
- ▸ LARRY JUNSTROM bass
- ▸ CAROL BRISTOW backing vocals
- ▸ DALE KRANTZ backing vocals
- ▸ NANCY HENDERSON backing vocals
- ▸ LU MOSS backing vocals

he shared with the future members of Lynyrd Skynyrd. "I was in Cub Scouts with Billy Powell, and Leon [Wilkeson] lived two streets over from me. And I can remember jumping on my bike and riding over to Allen Collins' house, so yeah, we all knew each other and played around in different bands together."

Singer and guitarist Don Barnes' experience was very similar. "Allen and Leon were in my English class," he laughed. "I'd go over to Allen Collins' house and we'd trade guitar licks back and forth. He'd teach me a couple of blues licks from all these records that he had." Little did any of the boys know what kind of success they would eventually find. "I still look back in amazement," Carlisi added, "at all the people who lived so close that made such a difference in the musical world."

"My dad was a music minister at a Baptist church," Barnes explained, "so I learned about the structure of music and a little bit of theory from that. What was moving to me later on was guitar stuff like Muddy Waters, and then Hendrix and Clapton. As kids, we all wanted to *be* Clapton. My bedroom wall was full of Eric Clapton posters."

Don's love for music resulted in his first encounter with Donnie Van Zant, though the circumstances of their meeting were less than ideal:

> Donnie was in a band called Standard Production. When I was about fourteen, I rode my bike over to where they had a trailer with their gear in it. I broke into the thing and I got caught with my hand in the trailer trying to get a guitar out of it. They came running out and called the

police. I was just standing there, knock-kneed, just as nervous as can be. It all stemmed from just absolute poverty. I wanted to play music so bad I was willing to steal for it! Donnie told me years later how he kind of felt sorry for me.

When the police arrived, Barnes wasn't arrested, but he wasn't off the hook, either. "The cop told me, 'When I get off my shift, I'm gonna be coming by and telling your dad what happened here,'" Barnes remembered. "My dad came home and I said, 'Dad, sit down. I have something to tell you . . .' I told him the whole story, and he was so embarrassed. He said, 'Son, what were you *thinking*? I go to church with these people.' Well, after all that, the cop never showed up. He didn't come by at all."

The botched theft may have been an embarrassing situation for the Barnes family, but it was also a turning point in Don's musical development. "That's when my dad realized how

A mid-1970s shot of 38 Special. *Left to right:* Jeff Carlisi, Steve Brookins, Don Barnes, Jack Grondin, Donnie Van Zant, and Ken Lyons. (Courtesy of John Gellman)

bad I was wanting to do it," Barnes remembered, "so he took me to Sears and co-signed for an amplifier and guitar. I had to mow lawns to pay for it, and I worked it off."

By the time they were in high school, the Van Zants and other boys in the neighborhood were beginning to put together serious bands and find gigs around town. "We all played in teen clubs and sailor clubs," Don explained, in an interview with Melissa Parker. "This was a navy town. There are four navy bases there, and that's what we all did at fifteen years old." Though Don Barnes and Donnie Van Zant were initially in rival bands, they eventually joined forces. "One thing would fold and people would filter away," Barnes explained, "but Donnie and I kept trying. We had day jobs. I was mar-

ried at nineteen, with a kid, living in poverty. We kept thinking if we could *just* find the right people that were dedicated enough to show up for rehearsal and have that commitment like we did, we could get something going. We kind of scoured around and picked players from some of those other competitive bands."

Jeff Carlisi, who played in various rock outfits around Jacksonville during his teen years, headed to Atlanta for college in the early 1970s. He played in various country bands while in Georgia before returning home after graduation. Don and Donnie recruited him for their group, which finally came together with a lineup that also included bassist Ken Lyons and drummers Jack Grondin and Steve Brookins. "They were neighborhood guys and good

friends," Barnes laughed, "so we didn't have the heart to tell either one of 'em that we didn't really need 'em. It actually made a pretty cool visual thing, and added a good bit of power."

Before they were 38 Special, the band experimented with several names, including Sweet Rooster and Alice Marr. "Billy Powell was actually on the keyboards in that band," Don explained to Michael Buffalo Smith. "We offered for him to join us, and we played a few gigs, and then it was not long before he started being a roadie for Skynyrd."

Because the members of Alice Marr liked to play loud, finding a suitable rehearsal space was a challenge. Eventually, they found a spot north of Jacksonville in Yulee, Florida, near the Georgia border, as Don recalled:

Larry Junstrom, Jeff Carlisi, Donnie Van Zant, Don Barnes, Jack Grondin, and Steve Brookins. (A&M Records)

It was an old auto-parts warehouse. It was condemned, basically. The roof would leak so bad that we would put grocery store pallets down on the ground and put the equipment up on the pallets to keep it dry. We knew that, being out in the middle of nowhere with equipment in there, we had to secure it. We boarded up the windows and fortified this door with rebar and two-by-fours. By the time we were done, it was about a foot thick, like a vault door. We drilled a hole through it, and drilled a hole through the cinder block, and put a big tractor chain through the cinder block and the door with a giant lock on it.

Being as irresponsible as we were, we lost the key to the lock. There was a window up by the roof that was on hinges, so we found an old ladder that we'd keep out in the high weeds where you could lay it down and no one would know it was there. We'd all pool our money for gas—twenty-five cents apiece—and drive this old Buick with bald tires on it out there to the rehearsal spot. We'd pick up the ladder to climb up to that window, and then we'd climb down and rehearse.

One evening, the band received some unexpected visitors at the building that resulted in the confrontation that would provide the group's permanent name. "We were out there rehearsing one night," Donnie Van Zant recalled in a radio interview with Rod Zimmerman, "and heard the sirens and just, you know, wheels squealing and all that. Before we could actually get to the front door, the cops out there said, 'Hey, y'all come out of there with your hands up.'"

Apparently, someone had heard the noise and reported it, as Barnes recalled:

I guess they figured there were wild parties going on. We ran to the door and told 'em we didn't have a key to the lock, and we would have to climb out from the window. One of the cops out there said something about shootin' the lock off. He said, "I've got a .38 Special that'll do the talking for me," or some kind of Wild West–sounding thing like that."

We were just a bunch of unruly guys back then, and thought that was a funny story. Eventually, we got a club gig down in Gainesville, Florida, and we didn't have a name for the band, so we said, "Why don't we just call it 38 Special for now, and we'll come up with something better later." But we just actually never got around to changing it.

The name seemed to fit the prevailing Southern rock aesthetic of the time. "We figured it was a slightly ominous name," Barnes added, "and had a little bit of danger to it."

By the mid-1970s, 38 Special were playing non-stop in north and central Florida, as Don explained:

They used to have these places called bottle clubs that would open at two o'clock in the morning, after all the alcohol clubs were closed. Sometimes we'd play a regular club, get through, and go to a bottle club and play all the way until seven in the morning, with the sun bright in the sky and burning your eyes. This was the impetus for these long jams, which Skynyrd did a lot of. It was pretty much just to kill time. It was like, "You take a solo, then this guy over here takes a solo, while this guy smokes a cigarette." Songs like "Freebird" were born from these jams, and then they got edited down. We did a lot of that, too.

During the long hours in the clubs, the members of 38 Special began defining their own sound. "Donnie and I observed ZZ Top," Barnes recalled, "and saw how they traded vocal lines back and forth. We thought, 'You know, we can both be up there as two lead singers.' We started taking these songs and saying, 'You take this line, and I'll take this line,' and we just made it work."

It was during this era that Donnie's older brother, who had already found success with Lynyrd Skynyrd, began taking 38 Special under his wing to offer advice, encouragement, and constructive criticism. "Ronnie used to say, 'It doesn't matter if ten people are in a club. You don't know who's sitting out there,'" Barnes recounted. "He had a lot of great advice. He'd say, 'Don't go out there onstage after you've had a big meal, 'cause you won't be hungry enough to dig in.' That was kind of an esoteric way to say it, but it was good advice."

Ronnie was eager to help his brother, but he had no intention of letting the band take the easy road, as Don recalled:

Ronnie referred us to an agent out of Paragon Agency in Macon, just because we needed to be able to work. But, of course, he tells the guy, "Make sure they go through all the crap we went through." He said, "Book 'em in the worst places." There were plenty of times we would say, "Why did Ronnie do that to us?" We'd wake up in

Jeff Carlisi. (Courtesy of Carl Lender)

the back of a sticky van on a mattress, going to Kansas to play some crap-hole club, and we're thinkin', "Why couldn't it have been better?" Years later, you look back and you realize he *wanted* us to suffer. He wanted us to struggle, because you have to pay your dues and it makes you a stronger band.

In April 1976, guitarist Jeff Carlisi collaborated with Ronnie Van Zant on "Four Walls of Raiford," a rarity that fans regard as one of Van Zant's best songs. He told *Gritz* magazine:

At that time, 38 owned a rehearsal hall in Jacksonville, and there was a sandwich shop right next door that went out of business. So Skynyrd bought that space and made it into a recording studio, which was great, 'cause we could all hang out, and if we needed to record something, we could just walk next door and lay it down. Ronnie always wanted to have a project outside of Skynyrd, because he loved country music so much. One night . . . he asked me to stay, because he had another song he wanted to work on. . . . I heard it in a traditional American folk blues, and [it] just so happened Gary had a dobro sitting in the corner, so I picked it up and started playing this arrangement. At this point, it was 1 or 2

a.m., and Ronnie sat at a microphone in the middle of the room and sat two chairs face-to-face. He had a bottle of Jack Daniels. He opened it up and we spent about an hour working the arrangement out and getting in the right frame of mind, and recorded it in about three takes. It was a special moment, and one I will never forget.

The songwriting effort with Carlisi was evidence that Ronnie recognized that 38 Special's hard work had paid off. They were no longer Southern rock students who needed his guidance and advice but fully formed musicians and worthy collaborators. They were *ready*.

Don Barnes recalled:

Skynyrd's manager, Peter Rudge, took us under his wing, and he was the one who secured a record deal for us. Ronnie opened that door. Somebody can open a door for you, but you've gotta have something to back it up when you walk in there. There was a bidding war back then with Southern groups because it was kind of the hot thing happening. We came along after it was waning a *bit*, but there was still competition with CBS and Arista and A&M. Everybody wanted their own Southern rock group. I remember having dinner

with Clive Davis, and different people were trying to pitch us to sign with them. We eventually got a better deal with A&M.

The band were paired with producer Dan Hartman, who had written and sung the 1972 hit "Free Ride" as a member of the Edgar Winter Group. In later years, he would go on to score hits as both a performer ("I Can Dream About You" in 1984) and a songwriter (James Brown's "Living in America" in 1985). In early 1977, however, Hartman was a budding producer when 38 Special traveled to his studio in Westport, Connecticut, to begin work on their debut LP.

Before the album was completed, bassist Ken Lyons departed and was replaced by Larry Junstrom. Larry was another Jacksonville musician who'd played in local bands, including an early incarnation of Lynyrd Skynyrd. He had shared the same experiences as the other guys on the Jacksonville rock scene. "We had long hair," Junstrom recalled of his teen years, in an interview with Scott Greene, "and Jacksonville had a lot of rednecks at the time. So we fought our way out of a lot of places just because we had hair longer than they did. I remember one night some guys chased me and pulled a gun on me just 'cause I had long hair."

When *38 Special* was released in the summer of 1977, the unavoidable association with Skynyrd began immediately. "People would talk," Barnes remembered, "saying, 'Oh, they're Lynyrd Skynyrd, Jr.' It was like they thought there was nepotism and this kind of thing going on." Critics couldn't resist the opportunity to compare and contrast. "*38 Special* is technically a better album than any of Skynyrd's studio recordings," John Swenson wrote in his *Rolling Stone* review. "But where Ronnie's dilemma seems to cause him the pain that makes him one of rock's great angry young men, Donnie's persona is more innocent and hedonistic. He'll have to get past that if he wants to be more than a wan reflection of his brother."

With their first album available in stores, 38 Special hit the road in 1977 to prove to the world that they had something to offer. "We were always more of a live band," Barnes pointed out. "We did that better than we did the studio, so we just kept getting on those stages and hammering away. We'd be the first act on a show with three bands. We'd go on at seven o'clock, and there would be 500 people in an arena that held 10,000. But we were trying to prove to those 500 people that we had value."

By that point, the members of 38 Special had worked toward their goals for so long that they'd become a close fraternity. "We had the same mindset," Don continued. "We came from the same town and we struggled together, which builds character. It became like a second family, or a gang mentality. If somebody's depressed, the other guys are a supportive group. You go through so much starvation and sacrifice and you become a tighter knit group."

Initially, they were paired with Johnny Winter, Foghat, and similar guitar-driven acts, but they occasionally had the opportunity to open for Lynyrd Skynyrd. "My first show with 38 was the Super Bowl of Rock," Larry Junstrom told *Gritz*, "and it is, to this day, one of the biggest shows we have ever done. It was at Soldier field in Chicago, and there were about 100,000 people there. I will never forget it. The acts on the bill were Journey, Skynyrd, Ted Nugent, and several other bands. I was so nervous before that show that I could not sleep for three nights before."

Seeing the band on the big stage was gratifying for Ronnie Van Zant. "We . . . arrived at the gig in time to see 38 Special perform," Skynyrd crewmember Ron Eckerman recalled. "Ronnie even sneaked onstage and watched for a while. You could tell he was so proud of his younger brother."

Eager to prove themselves to anyone who would listen, 38 Special would accept any high-profile opportunity in the late 1970s. "We were an unknown band that opened for Kiss at the height of their success," Don laughed. "And, of course, nobody cares about the opening act. They're waitin' for all the explosions. They used to have these radio contests everywhere Kiss went, where fans would put grease paint on their face to look like their favorite member of the group. We'd come out, this group of Jacksonville, Florida, Southern cowboy-looking guys, and the first eighty rows was nothing but Kiss faces looking at us. You talk about strangers in a strange land!"

October 20, 1977, was the day Lynyrd Skynyrd's jet crashed into a Mississippi swamp, killing six people. "Our crew guys busted in on us when we were rehearsing," Barnes remembered, "and they pulled Donnie out. One of the guys, Dennis, was standing there, and I said, 'What happened?' He said that Skynyrd had been in a plane crash. I said, 'Oh man, but everybody's all right, though?' He said, 'No, Don, it's a *plane crash*. Everybody's *not* all right.

Don Barnes and Larry Junstrom. (Courtesy of Carl Lender)

Donnie Van Zant and Jeff Carlisi onstage at WPLR in New Haven, Connecticut. (Courtesy of Carl Lender)

Don Barnes and Larry Junstrom. (Courtesy of Carl Lender)

boardroom somebody didn't have the heart to do it, and they gave us one more chance."

For their third album, the band decided to record in the South, rather than in Connecticut. They set up shop at Studio One in Doraville with engineer-turned producer Rodney Mills. As Don explained:

> We were fans of the sound of the Atlanta Rhythm Section, and Rodney had been the engineer on those records all those years, not to mention some of the Skynyrd stuff that was cut in Doraville. Our album was his first foray into producing, so we were all a little green.... We finally learned the lesson that less is more. It's broad brushstrokes, just the basic emotional part of it. Before, we were trying to load up these tracks with overdubs and cleverness, and the listener just got bombarded with too much information. We had to learn to strip it down. We were able to find that sound that we called "muscle and melody." It was muscular guitars with a good story and a good melody, and it was a good formula. We were just glad to find something that created a stylized signature sound that was different from Skynyrd and everybody else down there.

The resulting album, *Rockin' into the Night*, yielded a moderate hit with the title track. "We started writing with outside songwriters," Donnie Van Zant explained, "not just ourselves, you know, and started really paying attention to what was happening with radio, you know, and then we put 'Rockin' into the Night' out, and we had the Top 40 single . . . which opened the door up completely for 38 Special."

Though the single actually peaked at #43 on the *Billboard* chart, it was enough to start building solid momentum. The song had come to the group through their manager, Mark Spector, as Don explained:

> The band Survivor had just formed, and they left "Rockin' into the Night" off their record. Mark Spector sent us the tape, and it was so foreign to us. We were in that same Southern rock mode. It had this chant kind of feel to it, and it was so strange. But we were desperate, and desperation figures in a lot of groups. When it's not working, and you're about to lose the record deal, and the record company sends you a song, you figure, "Look, we'll try anything at this point."
>
> When it came time to do the next album, Mark Spector said, "Why don't you go write

There were fatalities.' When something like that happens, you just don't want to believe it." Donnie Van Zant stayed in Jacksonville to comfort his mother while Don Barnes got on a plane with Ronnie and Donnie's father, Lacy, to head to the crash site. "All the way there," Don remembered, "Lacy kept saying, 'No, they've made a mistake. My son is not dead.'"

But Ronnie was gone. Though the experience was particularly hard on Donnie, all the guys in 38 Special regarded Ronnie as a brother. "It made us all stronger to drive forward with that tragedy," Don explained.

Without their mentor to cheer them on, 38 Special returned to Westport, where Dan Hartman produced their second album, *Special Delivery*. Like the first LP, however, it was not a success. "Our first couple of albums failed miserably," Barnes admitted. "We were at a point where we already had two albums, and now we were in debt with the label. It didn't really work out for us. We had a two-album deal, and I figured they were probably gonna drop us. When everything happened with the plane crash and the tragedy and everything, I think somewhere in that A&M

with the guy who made 'Rockin' into the Night?' Maybe you can come up with something." So, we did. We went to Jim Peterik's house and sat down at his kitchen table.

Before forming Survivor, Peterik had been a member of the Ides of March. When he was still a teenager, he wrote and sang the song "Vehicle," which carried the band all the way to #2 on the *Billboard* singles chart. Barnes continued:

> We didn't know him. We just met him, and we brought these little germs of ideas—a piece of this, or a melody here or there, or a title. At the time I was having some real bad problems. My marriage had gone bad. We were talkin' about relationship-oriented things, and I said, "What is it about people that they can't celebrate their differences and give each other room to be themselves? They always try to change each other." I said, "What do you think about this title, 'Hold On Loosely,' for an idea?" And he said, "Oh yeah, and don't let go." That was the first thing out of his mouth, and it was the perfect complement for that line.

Credited to Don Barnes, Jeff Carlisi, and Jim Peterik, "Hold On Loosely" reached #27 on the *Billboard* singles chart, and helped propel 38 Special's fourth album, *Wild-Eyed Southern Boys*, to Platinum status. Peterik was credited as a songwriter on four of the album's songs, including the title track, which he wrote by himself.

> Jim was very integral to our success. He was the one who kind of showed us that we can take our ideas and run with them, and not try to be like somebody else. He had that pop sensibility. Ronnie had told us years ago, "Don't try to be a clone of somebody else." We were trying to be Skynyrd, the Charlie Daniels Band, Mar-

shall Tucker, but it had already been done by the best. He was trying to tell us to be honest about our own influences, and we realized we were more pop-oriented. That kind of came through with those songs.

With charting singles and strong record sales, the band stayed on the road, winning over even more fans with their "muscle and melody" approach. "One of the things that differentiated us from a lot of Southern rock bands was they were blues-oriented," Barnes reflected, "but we sort of had this happier, positive element that people related to. It was the kind of brighter sound that makes you want to put the top down on the car and sing along with it."

By the time they stopped to take a breath, it was already time to begin work on a new album. "We came back from the tour," Barnes recalled, "and we didn't have an idea of one single note. I was dating a girl at the time and I said, 'I can't ever get any work done, 'cause I'm so caught up in you all the time.' It just sort of rolled out, and I thought, 'You know, that's not a bad title for a song.'" Barnes partnered with Peterik and Carlisi once again, and the trio came up with "Caught up in You," which became 38 Special's first Top 10 single, and the highlight of their Platinum-selling *Special Forces* album. As Barnes explained:

> At that time, the term Southern rock was not something that you wanted to be labeled. That kind of regionalized you, and people thought, "Oh, *another* Southern rock band." We were trying to break out of that mold and just be an American rock band. We were trying to take it down different avenues. We changed our style to more of an arena-rock sound. We liked Bad Company and a bunch of groups that were not from the South. We were a little tired of the twang by that time. You had Molly Hatchet singing about whiskey and alligators, but we wanted to do something fresh.

The new formula worked perfectly, though almost too perfectly for many Southern rock fans. When their next album, *Tour de Force*, came out in 1983, it was regarded by some as too polished. Author Martin Popoff described the LP as 38 Special's "slide into pure pop whoredom." In his review of *Tour de Force* for *Rolling Stone* magazine, critic Steve Futterman called the group "a closet West Coast AOR band." He clearly did not care for the group's evolving direction. "The band may have avoided all the excesses of

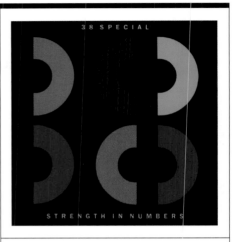

their Southern legacy," he wrote, " . . . but 38 Special have also left the guts behind."

The members of 38 Special refused to allow the criticism to hold them back. They had intentionally transformed themselves into a pop group, and they were skilled at constructing pop songs. "We still had the same underdog spirit as a lot of Southern rock bands," Barnes explained. "We had that desire to put those guitars in people's faces and really be aggressive about it, but at the same time we understood more of the melody." With that understanding came something that was slipping away from some of their Southern rock compatriots at the time—stardom.

"People always say . . . what kind of music, what category or niche do you put yourself in," Jeff Carlisi mused in an early 1980s interview.

> A great song is a great song no matter what the style is. It's the spirit. . . . Don and I have talked a lot of times before about how much of an influence, in a subtle way, the Cars were on us when they came out. Because it was all of a sudden this new sounding type of music that was a little bit foreign to your ear when you first head it, but that you could take a very simple and very elementary style of rock-and-roll music and put great melody to it, and make it something that's very successful and very unique. And you kind of learn that simplicity maybe is the best way sometimes.

In the end, 38 Special adapted in ways that allowed them to thrive during the 1980s when so many of their peers faded away. By the end of the decade they'd racked up a Gold album, three Platinum albums, and a dozen Top 10 singles on *Billboard*'s Mainstream Rock chart. Like ZZ Top, 38 Special were one of the few bands to emerge from the Southern rock scene of the 1970s to achieve greater stardom as a radio-friendly rock band with wide appeal. ★

Part Nine

HOLD ON LOOSELY: SOUTHERN ROCK IN CHANGING TIMES

Seal Level onstage, *left to right*: Chuck Leavell, Lamar Williams, Jimmy Nalls, Joe English, Davis Causey, and Randall Bramblett. (Sea Level Archives, courtesy of Chuck Leavell)

BY THE END of the 1970s, Southern was chic. The President was from Georgia, *Smokey and the Bandit* made Burt Reynolds the coolest guy in America, the outlaw antics of *The Dukes of Hazzard* made for popular television fare, and John Travolta was in Texas filming *Urban Cowboy*. Jeans and boots were adopted as high fashion, and the earthiness of Southern culture seemed to resonate with a significant portion of society.

At the same time, however, disco and new wave were on the rise. A shift in the musical landscape was underway, and loud electric guitars would seem passé in the face of sophisticated synthesizers and drum machines that dominated the pop music of the early 1980s. In 1981, MTV went on the air, fundamentally altering the importance of rock music's visual image. Almost overnight, the rural-themed fad seemed to collapse, and the commercial acceptance of Southern rock went with it.

By the beginning of the 1980s, Lynyrd Skynyrd were out of commission due to the plane crash, the Allman Brothers Band had broken up, Capricorn Records had declared bankruptcy, and Southern bands weren't getting radio airplay. It seemed as if everything had fallen apart as rapidly as it had come together. Within a five-year period, Southern rock went from the peak of popularity to an irrelevant joke. Many observers wondered if the genre would survive.

"I don't care if somebody wants to say I'm Southern rock. I'm proud of that. But to me there's only two kinds of music. And that's good and bad, honest and fabricated."

—DRU LOMBAR, GRINDERSWITCH

The Marshall Tucker Band's Toy Caldwell and George McCorkle, with presidential candidate Jimmy Carter (wearing a Marshall Tucker Band T-shirt) at a benefit concert in Atlanta, 1975. (Photo by Tom Hill/WireImage/Getty Images)

CHAPTER 34
The South's Gonna Do It: Jimmy Carter, Southern Rock President

'D LIKE TO SEE a liberal Democratic president," Duane Allman told a reporter from the New Orleans *Free Press* on New Years' Eve 1970, "and I think we will get it too, 'cause Nixon's fucked up so much, man." Within six years, a liberal Democrat *had* been elected president. On top of that, he was a *Southerner* that the Allman Brothers Band and their friends helped catapult to the White House by raising money and mobilizing young music fans.

Jimmy Carter was a naval veteran and peanut farmer from Plains, Georgia, who'd served two terms in the state senate before making an unsuccessful bid for governor in 1966. In the 1970 election, he finally seized the governorship, taking office in January of 1971. In stark contrast to his predecessor, Lester Maddox, Carter took a strong stand against racial inequality. "I've traveled the state more than any other person in history," Carter declared, "and I say to you, quite frankly, that the time for racial discrimination is over."

Carter openly expressed his enthusiasm for rock music and became a hero to the progressive-minded musicians in Macon. When he introduced anti-piracy legislation in Georgia that was designed to combat music bootlegging, Phil Walden enthusiastically lent his support to the effort. The two became fast friends. "I was really smitten with him," Walden was quoted as saying in *Music from Macon*. "I thought he represented our state and our region so well. He was part of that new South that I wanted the whole South to become part of. He was the kind of guy who had the respect for what

Jimmy Carter, Phil Walden, Johnny Sandlin, and Dickey Betts in the Capricorn Studios in Macon, Georgia. (Courtesy of Johnny Sandlin)

was good from our past, but a willingness to change what was bad for our region."

As his term as Georgia's governor progressed, Carter increasingly reached out to the music community. In early 1974, he hosted a reception for Bob Dylan to celebrate Dylan's Atlanta concert appearance. Gregg Allman was invited, but was delayed in the recording studio. By the time he arrived at the governor's mansion, the party had concluded. Gregg asked the guard at the gate to pass an apology note to Carter. "I turned around to go back to the limo," Gregg recalled in his autobiography, "and, just as I got my hand on the door, the guard said, 'Mr. Allman, please wait a min-

ute. The governor would like to see you up on the porch of the mansion right away.'" When Gregg approached the house he spotted someone out front. "I could see the silhouette of this guy standing on the porch," he recalled. "He didn't have on a shirt, he didn't have any shoes on, and he had on this old pair of Levi's.... I was thinking, 'I wonder who this damn hippie is, hanging out at the governor's mansion?' Well, it was him—Jimmy Carter himself."

Though the reception had ended, Governor Carter invited Gregg in for a visit. "He was a really nice guy and was really hip to music," Allman recounted. Carter told Gregg he was planning to run for president, but would have

Publicist Mike Hyland offers a plate to presidential candidate Jimmy Carter at the 1975 Capricorn Records Barbecue and Summer Games. Boxing promoter Don King is visible at the far left. (Photo by Tom Hill, courtesy of Mike Hyland)

to raise a lot of money. Though Allman had formed a favorable impression of Carter, he had doubts. "I certainly never believed he was going to make it to the White House," he later mused in a 2009 interview with Russell Hall. "A Southern president? You must be kidding."

By the end of January 1975, Carter had concluded his term as governor and began a grassroots effort to build national recognition. The fact that he was not well known ultimately proved advantageous. Following Richard Nixon's resignation in the wake of the Watergate scandal, the public was skeptical of Washington insiders. Charlie Daniels, who aligned himself with conservative politicians and causes in later years, explained Carter's appeal:

> Think back on the time. It was Watergate. We had been lied to. We had been deceived. We had been misled. We could no longer trust anybody inside the Beltway. This whole Nixon regime had people who went to jail for different reasons. I wanted

to see somebody get in office who would put some integrity and some honesty back into the office of president, and into politics. Here comes Jimmy Carter, who is an honorable person, and who I felt could be trusted. He's a guy from the South. He's one of us. He speaks with a Southern accent. He is an intellectual, but he does not come across as an intellectual-type person. He's not one of these people that's so far separated from the public that nobody gets it. He's just down home people.

Allman Brother Chuck Leavell agreed wholeheartedly. "Carter came on as a real individual that cared," he explained. "He was honest and true, a Christian man. We all just thought, 'This is the right guy for these times.'"

Phil Walden recalled Carter coming to him for help in the early days of the campaign. "He said, 'We're gonna be broke before our caucus, unless we can raise some money.' And he says, 'Can you do some con-

certs?'" Walden, who was a natural born promoter, kicked into high gear. "The Allman Brothers and the Marshall Tucker Band kept Carter's candidacy alive," journalist Michael Gross claimed in 1977, "and raised nearly half a million dollars, which was then matched by federal funds under the same election laws."

Carter gave the musicians credit for helping his campaign maintain its viability at an uncertain time. He was especially grateful for a crucial show the Allman Brothers Band staged in Rhode Island on November 25, 1975, during a challenging season for the campaign. The candidate himself took to the stage to introduce the band and mailed handwritten thank-you notes to the band members after the event. "There is no question," Carter remarked not long after, "that the Allmans' benefit concert for me in Providence kept us in that race."

Phil Walden staged four additional benefit concerts for Carter. "I just really believed that was part of our obligation," Walden mused, "to use the success of rock and roll." Carter

A presidential portrait of Jimmy Carter. (Courtesy of the National Archives)

do we rule the airwaves and the concert stage, but we get to have our own personal pal in the White House. The whole thing was crazy how much momentum there was."

Chuck Leavell agreed. "We were all enthralled with the guy," he enthused. "We really liked him. We thought, 'He probably doesn't have a chance in hell, but let's do this.' Much to our surprise, the rascal won the presidency!"

"It all started with a bunch of Southern rock-and-rollers helping a friend raise some money," Carter campaign staffer Tom Beard explained to documentarian Anne Fentress, "but giving him credibility at the same time." Carter agreed that associating himself with popular musicians was helpful. "I think that was one of the reasons I won," he reflected, "because I *did* align myself with characters like these, who were admired by millions of people around the world. It was a very popular thing to do."

The credibility ran both ways. "We raised a lot of money to help Jimmy Carter get elected," the Marshall Tucker Band's Doug Gray explained, "but, at the same time, it was helping twofold. It was helping Jimmy Carter to do it, [and] it was lettin' people know that the Southern bands really weren't a bunch of redneck 'cut ya and shoot ya' kind of guys."

Charlie Daniels, the Marshall Tucker Band, and members of the Allman Brothers Band appeared at the inauguration festivities. Gregg Allman was invited to join Carter for the new president's very first White House dinner.

While Carter's rise to the highest office was exciting, the campaign proved to be a distraction for Phil Walden that took his attention off Capricorn Records. "Phil more or less took a leave from the company to work on Carter's campaign," Johnny Sandlin recalled. "Phil was about the only one who could keep the various factions getting along and working together. . . . It was Phil's label, and he made it work because of his personality."

As Phil began to lose his grip on things at Capricorn, Carter's term was increasingly marred by serious challenges, including national economic woes, an energy crisis, and the Iran hostage situation. Though he'd taken office with a 66 percent approval rating, Carter's numbers fell by more than half of that within four years, and he lost the presidency to Ronald Reagan during his reelection bid. "It was heartbreaking for us to see him lose that election," Chuck Leavell recalled. "It was almost as heartbreaking as when we heard that Duane had died. It was a really big event, and not the way we thought it should have gone." ★

attended the annual Capricorn picnic in 1975 and was frequently spotted with Southern rock musicians. For his official campaign song, he adopted "The South's Gonna Do It" by the Charlie Daniels Band.

When Carter won his party's nomination in 1976, the Southern rock community was abuzz with excitement. "Jimmy Carter was a great governor," Chuck Leavell reflected. "All of us thought he was a very interesting and enigmatic figure. Before he ran for president, we were recording Dickey Betts' *Highway Call* record. The word came down

that the governor wanted to come to Capricorn and take a tour, and would like to stop in at a session." The visit formed the genesis of some strong personal relationships. "He was just going to drop by the studio and say hello," Dickey recalled, "and he stayed there about four hours. He was really intrigued by it. He really is into music."

The Capricorn crew's appreciation of Carter's friendship became a common sentiment among most Southern musicians. "That just underscored the geographical camaraderie," the Outlaws' Henry Paul reflected. "Not only

Gregg Allman onstage in the late 1970s. (Photo by Richard E. Aaron/Redferns)

CHAPTER 35
Win, Lose, or Draw: The Unmaking and Remaking of the Allman Brothers Band

★ ★

Y THE TIME Jimmy Carter was elected president, in November 1976, the Allman Brothers Band had broken up. Key members refused to speak to one another, while others made public pronouncements that they would never perform together again. It was the tragic result of a long, slow unraveling that had begun nearly two years prior.

In early 1975, Gregg Allman met Cher at the Troubadour nightclub in West Hollywood, California. Within days, they were dating, and Gregg was spending more time on the West Coast. His absence caused tension with his bandmates, particularly when it came time to start work on the follow-up album to the phenomenally successful *Brothers and Sisters*. "If somebody's in love, I can appreciate that," Chuck Leavell said of Gregg and Cher in a 1976 *Rolling Stone* story, "but I did not appreciate

Cher and Gregg onstage. (Courtesy of Peter Cross)

the lack of respect they showed for the band. You know, we'd record a day and he'd split for Los Angeles and never show up again."

The truth was, nobody felt particularly passionate about the material or the recording process. "It was just time to make a record," Chuck explained, "but a lot of it was like pulling teeth. I was as bad or worse than any of them. Dickey was having a little trouble. My old lady was pregnant. Gregg and Cher were going through their trip; he was off to L.A. every week. Jaimoe was having trouble with his back. It started dragging out and dragging out. It took six months to do the record. When you overdo something it shows—and it showed on the record *Win, Lose or Draw*."

Butch, too, noticed a shift during the making of the album. "Our music is spontaneous and the spontaneity was gone," he explained,

in *Midnight Riders*. "We sat down one day and had to start talking about our music and that was the beginning of the end."

"I was bouncing back and forth between Macon and L.A., which was not a good way to make a record," Gregg confessed, in *My Cross to Bear*. "Things started and stopped, in part because I wasn't always there. I overdubbed a lot of my vocals out in California at the Record Plant with Johnny Sandlin. He would bring out the tapes of the basic tracks, I would cut my vocal parts, and then he would take the tapes back to Macon."

For his part, Jaimoe—who had suffered from whiplash after a car accident—was dealing with severe pain during the recording sessions. "I look back now," he admitted, "and see how I was an asshole. . . . I was impatient and got irritated easily." At times, Sandlin had

THE ALLMAN BROTHERS BAND

▸ GREGG ALLMAN vocals, keyboards, guitar

▸ JAI JOHANNY "JAIMOE" JOHANSON drums and percussion

▸ BUTCH TRUCKS drums and percussion

▸ DICKEY BETTS guitar, vocals

▸ CHUCK LEAVELL keyboards

▸ LAMAR WILLIAMS bass

▸ DAN TOLER guitar

▸ DAVID "ROOK" GOLDFLIES bass

The Allman Brothers Band on tour. (Capricorn publicity photo, courtesy of Mike Hyland)

to recruit outside help just to keep the process moving forward. Capricorn musician Bill Stewart was brought in for two songs. "I played drums on 'Louisiana Lou and Three Card Monty John,' and I played timbales on 'High Falls,' which was an instrumental," he confirmed. "They were all pissed off at each other. It was really screwy around that time. They were legendary, but they were feuding."

The label was nervous that its biggest earner couldn't seem to get it together creatively. "After years of struggle, we've got one of the hottest bands," Capricorn's Frank Fenter remarked in 1975. "But now it's tough to get them into the studio. They've got homes, cars, and money coming, so it's hard to motivate them." Even Phil Walden, desperately hungry for new Allman Brothers material, was dismayed with the final album. "That son of a bitch was made with paste," he complained. "The drummer would go down and make a drum track, and then the other drummer would come in. They wouldn't want to be in there together. There's not a lot of feeling on that album. *Win, Lose or Draw* was definitely 'lose.' It was just an awful record."

Band members' shenanigans outside the studio didn't help matters, either. "I spent a lot of time cleaning up Butch's and Dickey's scrapes with the law," tour manager Willie Perkins remembered, "driving under the influence, drunk and disorderlies, and car wrecks. . . . Dickey attacking his wife Sandy Bluesky's unoccupied Mercedes with an axe after one of their numerous violent arguments."

Cher and Gregg were married in Las Vegas on June 30, 1975, just days after her divorce from Sonny Bono was finalized. Suddenly, the Brothers' lead singer was splashed all over the gossip magazines in every grocery store checkout line in the country. Gregg and Cher's relationship provided seemingly endless tabloid fodder as their unlikely relationship played out on a very public stage.

Nine days after exchanging vows, Cher filed for divorce after Gregg pulled a knife on her in a sloppy attempt to get alone so he could score heroin. He immediately entered rehab, and Cher soon returned. In his *Doonesbury* comic series, Gary Trudeau lampooned their relationship in a series of strips that lasted several days. Gregg's drug habit was raging out of control, but there was a genuine love between him and Cher. "I'd be dead now," he told an interviewer in 1997, "if it wasn't for Cher. That's almost definite." At the time, however, he was lost in a haze. One journalist who met with Gregg during his time in Hollywood called him "surly and arrogant." His bandmates, and probably his wife, would have fully agreed.

"When Gregg and Cher started happening," Capricorn publicist Mark Pucci recalled, "that brought it up to a whole different level. We started getting paparazzi coming down there to Macon, and everybody wanted to talk about Gregg and Cher. That was a tremendous pain in the ass, 'cause we wanted to talk about music." The more details of Gregg's heroin use and the couple's on-again-off-again relationship appeared in the press, the more out-of-control things became for Gregg, Cher, and the Allman Brothers Band.

Win, Lose or Draw hit the stores in late August. "No one," Gregg remembered, "was happy with that release—not the critics, not the fans, not the record company, not us. The six months of frustration in the studio ended with a frustrated album. And maybe the worst part was that the tour hadn't even begun." The band hit the road near the end of the summer, but nobody's heart was in the music. For his part, Gregg just wanted to be with Cher. "I won't let anything come between me and Cher," he told *Creem* magazine at the time. "I've never been this happy in my life."

That same year, Dickey started dating Cher's secretary and close friend Paulette Eghazarian, and she soon became pregnant.

Gregg couldn't shake the sense that Dickey was somehow messing with him by getting personally involved with someone in Cher's inner circle. Tensions escalated when Cher fired Paulette. Later that fall, Gregg filed for divorce, but when Cher discovered she was pregnant, the two reunited once again. The money, the drugs, the Hollywood marriage, the constant competition, and the trappings of stardom had erupted into a full-scale Southern rock soap opera.

The Allman Brothers Band played forty-one shows between August of 1975 and May of 1976, wallowing in every stereotypical rock-and-roll excess along the way. They leased their own Boeing 720 airliner, which had previously been used by the Rolling Stones, Led Zeppelin, Alice Cooper, and others. "When the Allman Brothers got that goddamn plane," Gregg noted, "it was the beginning of the end.... The first time we walked onto the plane, 'Welcome Allman Bros' was spelled out in cocaine on the bar."

The Allman Brothers Band played to a capacity crowd of around 80,000 at the newly opened Louisiana Superdome in New Orleans, headlined Madison Square Garden, and played some of the most high-profile performances of any American rock band of the era. "All hell broke loose," Butch Trucks reflected, in *Mojo* magazine. "All of a sudden we're flyin' around in these goddamn chartered planes, and everybody's got their own hotel suites ... and everybody's fucked up twenty-four hours a day. Women everywhere, cocaine everywhere. We absolutely lost sight of what we were all about."

Critics and fans soon began recognizing that the group's performances were suffering. "Allman's continually diminishing low profile in the band," one concert reviewer wrote of Gregg's performance in New Jersey on September 23, 1975, "deprives it of its most inspiring and charismatic member." The light had gone from Gregg's eyes, and though they were on top of the world, the Allman Brothers Band were careening downward at a rapid pace. "We had quit living together," Butch Trucks lamented to *Rolling Stone*, "which I think had a lot to do with our demise.... We were drifting further and further apart, until the last couple of years were pure bullshit. Actually, to me, they were just a blank. I was drunk twenty-four hours a day."

The Allman Brothers Band wrapped up the tour at the Roanoke Civic Center on May 4, 1976, and returned home to Georgia. "Technically, it took a couple of months to go through the formalities," Gregg explained, "but after we all saw the price tag for that tour, it basically was done."

Gregg Allman in an era of legal trouble and negative publicity. (Courtesy of Peter Cross)

But there was more to it than just the tour and the strained relationships. On May 28, 1976, Scooter Herring, who worked security for the band and was close with Gregg, was indicted on five counts of conspiracy to distribute narcotics. Scooter had been hired by Gregg in February of 1974 to work as his personal valet before moving on to become one of the band's assistant road managers. "I remember, quite distinctly, that the reason he was hired," recalled Capricorn engineer Jim Hawkins, "was 'cause he could get some good coke." Herring was associated with a local pharmacist named Joe Fuchs, who was supplying pharmaceutical cocaine and other pills. Once Gregg figured out where it was coming from, he often went directly to Fuchs.

Both Herring and Fuchs were swept up in a complex federal investigation into drug trafficking in Macon that was intertwined with the activities of a major organized crime ring known as the Dixie Mafia. Both Fuchs and Herring were arrested, but while Fuchs pleaded guilty, Scooter chose to fight the charges. Gregg's attorney contacted him to inform him that the federal prosecutor wanted Gregg to testify at Herring's grand jury hearing, which got underway in June of 1976. He could either cooperate or face prison himself. Gregg returned from California to Macon, where the trial attracted a tabloid frenzy.

"I went to the office one day," producer Johnny Sandlin remembered, "and people were talking about how the district attorney was investigating drug use as a way to bring down the record company. The DA was looking to make a big name for himself in Macon and wanted someone with star power. Of course, the biggest star would have been Gregg." Others in Macon theorized that more than an overzealous DA was behind the investigation. "I believe to this day," Willie Perkins confessed, "that part of this whole exercise had some connection with smearing Jimmy Carter's candidacy for president by indirectly linking him to a drug scandal."

Gregg, on the advice of his lawyer, told the truth about the nature of his relationship with Scooter, and on July 19, 1976, Herring was sentenced to seventy-five years in prison for selling cocaine to Gregg Allman. In the end, Herring only served eighteen months, but the tide

A Capricorn publicity image of Jaimoe, Dickey Betts, Gregg Allman, Butch Trucks, and Phil Walden, taken following the Great Southern concert in Central Park, New York City, August, 1978.

dramatically turned against Gregg for testifying. "He threw Scooter away just because he didn't need him anymore," Dickey Betts angrily told *Rolling Stone*.

Once the people of Macon turned on Gregg, the local scene began to collapse. In August, Jaimoe composed a letter that was published in a local paper, declaring that the Allman Brothers were finished. "I love Gregg Allman," Jaimoe wrote, "but for eight years I have seen him hurt the people who loved him. . . . I can no longer work with or for Gregg Allman." Butch, Chuck, and Dickey confirmed the announcement in subsequent interviews, with Dickey telling *Rolling Stone*, "There is no way we can work with Gregg again, ever." Gregg believed he was judged unfairly. "Not one of the Allman Brothers Band, not one of the men in that band, was at that trial," Gregg pointed out. "Therefore, I can only believe that they made up their minds on hearsay alone. I figured when the chips were down, if they were brothers, they wouldn't have turned me out like they did."

With time, the animosity toward Gregg softened. "Six months later," Dickey Betts confessed, "I read the court transcripts and said, 'Goddamn, this guy had his ass between a rock and a hard place.'" At the time, however, Gregg became the scapegoat for everything that was wrong with the band. "Truth is," he later wrote, "there ain't one thing or person alone that broke up the Allman Brothers. It was everything and everyone. Scooter, my recording *Laid Back*, my living in L.A., the drugs—they were all just easy excuses, ways of talking around the unavoidable truth: that none of us knew when or how to walk away."

Gregg released another solo album for Capricorn, *Playin' Up a Storm*, in May 1977. Later that year, Dickey released a self-titled album with his new band for the Arista label called *Dickey Betts & Great Southern*. One of the stronger tracks, "Bougainvillea," was written with Betts' pal and future *Miami Vice* actor Don Johnson. Fed up with the music business, Butch Trucks returned to Florida and enrolled at Florida State University to work on his degree.

In November of 1976, Capricorn had released an Allman Brothers Band double live album called *Wipe the Windows, Check the Oil, Dollar Gas*. Cobbling together a variety of performances spanning the years 1972 through 1975, it suffered from a poor mix and was unfairly compared to the impossibly high standard set by the classic Fillmore shows. It attracted little attention from fans at the time, and the critics generally ignored it. It was the first Allman Brothers Band album since

A reunited and revised Allman Brothers Band. *Left to right:* David "Rook" Goldflies, Dan Toler, Butch Trucks, Gregg Allman, Dickey Betts, and Jaimoe. (Capricorn Records)

Idlewild South that failed to register in the Top 40 on the *Billboard* album chart.

Around the same time Dickey debuted with Great Southern, Gregg and Cher put out a duet album called *Two the Hard Way*, billed as All-man and Woman and featuring a heavily air-brushed cover that looked like the front of a romance novel. One reviewer called the LP "the bottom of the barrel after a long fall for Gregg." Most everyone took for granted that Gregg and the Brothers would never rise up from the depths into which they'd fallen. As far as the critics and the fans were concerned, the Allman Brothers Band were never coming back.

By 1978, Cher had filed for divorce. Gregg was aimless, spending his evenings partying and sitting in with local bands. He wound up back in Daytona, where he tried to get work on a shrimp boat for $25 per day. When he refused to cut his hair and shave his beard, the cap-tain turned him away. He passed the time play-ing with a local group called the Nighthawks, and toyed with the idea of joining the surviv-ing members of Lynyrd Skynyrd as their lead vocalist in the wake of the plane crash.

In March of 1978, Dickey Betts and Great Southern released another album, *Atlan-ta's Burning Down.* It was not a major suc-cess. It had been nearly two years since the All-man Brothers Band broke up when Dickey and Gregg, with encouragement from Phil Walden, got together to talk about the possibility of re-forming. Everybody needed the money. Walden had borrowed millions of dollars from PolyGram Records, and he was hopeful he

could generate some serious revenue with a solid Allman Brothers reunion effort. Gregg was practically broke.

Around the same time, Scooter Her-ring's conviction was overturned by the Fifth Circuit US Court of Appeals. Herring got another trial, with a much less severe pun-ishment, and Gregg's reputation as a villain began to soften. "Gregg, he should have been hurt," Dickey said of the backlash following the Scooter Herring trial. "He deserved it. I think it's about time he was let off the fuck-ing hook. . . . Gregg's been paying for it and I think he's paid enough." Butch was soften-ing, too. "See, we didn't know the full story," he admitted to Scott Freeman. "We thought he'd just copped a plea. We just weren't talk-ing to each other, so we made our decision

Dickey Betts and Jaimoe onstage, 1979. (Courtesy of Dan Santoro)

Dan Toler onstage, 1979. (Courtesy of Dan Santoro)

based on newspaper headlines. Dickey and I, we felt like we'd given Gregg a raw deal."

In mid-August, Great Southern played a concert in Central Park in New York. At the end of the set, Dickey invited Butch, Jaimoe, and Gregg onstage to help close the show. The fans were ecstatic. A week later, they were all at the seventh annual Capricorn picnic, where they jammed together in a surprise appearance with the full lineup, including Chuck and Lamar. "I don't think any of us had realized how much we missed it all until right then," Gregg reflected. "Now we all knew for sure that we were getting back together for the music as much as for the money."

In the end, Chuck and Lamar chose not to participate, but Jaimoe returned to the Allman Brothers Band. Dan Toler came in on guitar, and David "Rook" Goldflies replaced Lamar on bass. Both had been members of Great Southern with Dickey, suggesting that Dickey would continue to be the driving force of the band's leadership in this renewed incarnation. "It took a lot of time for us to get some *fire* back into it, man," Gregg admitted at the

time. "Now we've got new blood in the band, which helps greatly. I mean Danny and David, they're real assets. I don't think we could have made a better choice." It was the first time since Duane's death that the Allman Brothers Band featured two full-time guitarists.

In December, the band traveled to Criteria Studios to work with Tom Dowd on the reunion album. They hadn't recorded with Dowd since the *Eat a Peach* sessions, and his presence was an asset. *Enlightened Rogues* was released in February of 1979 to favorable reviews. Gregg wrote only one song on the album, with Dickey contributing five of the LP's eight titles. One of Dickey's tunes, "Crazy Love," would become the band's second Top 40 single, which helped propel the album into the Top 10, earning them yet another Gold record. In addition, the song "Pegasus" was nominated for a Grammy for best instrumental performance.

The mid-1970s had been a time when Gregg "went from being an exceptional white blues singer and the leader of one of the best American rock bands, to being a laughingstock, a pathetic churl apparently unaware of the humiliation he suffered at the hands of Hollywood and the glitzy Cher," John Swenson wrote in his *Rolling Stone* review of the album. "The proposed Allman Brothers Band reunion," he continued, "promised to be a ghoulish joke." He went on, however, to say that *Enlightened Rogues* "ranks with the group's greatest albums." Nobody expected it, but after a decade of triumph and tragedy, the Allman Brothers Band were back on top. Unfortunately, before the end of the year, their record label would go bankrupt. ★

NOTHING MATTERS BUT THE FEVER: SEA LEVEL

—

"DICKEY, GREGG, AND BUTCH, I think, were exhausted," Chuck Leavell reflected, of the era when the Allman Brothers first broke up in 1976. But Jaimoe, Lamar, and Chuck weren't interested in hanging up their instruments. "We had a meeting one day to finalize some business with the Brothers," Leavell related to Michael Gross in 1977, "and the only cats who showed up was us three. We smiled and said, 'Let's go play.'"

Jimmy Nalls, who had played with Chuck in Alex Taylor's band, was quickly added to the group that became known as Sea Level. "There was other labels that wanted us," Chuck explained, "but Capricorn gave us the best offer."

The band released their self-titled debut album in 1977. "*Sea Level* was an experiment to try to put a little distance between the term Southern rock and the music that we were doing," Leavell explained. "Fusion was really big at the time. It was an attempt to go out of the box into that realm, and still maintain some Southern heritage. I'm not sure the experiment worked!"

Before the end of 1977, Sea Level had nearly doubled in personnel and released a second album, *Cats on the Coast*. Guitarist David Causey was added, and Randall Bramblett came in to lend his songwriting, vocal, keyboard, and saxophone talents.

Bramblett grew up in Jesup, Georgia, where he became obsessed with the black music he heard on the radio. "We didn't know about Howlin' Wolf and Muddy Waters and people like that, and I don't know how I would've heard 'em if not for WLAC," he explained. Bramblett headed to Athens, Georgia, for college before relocating to Macon. "I camped out with Tommy Talton and Scott Boyer out at Idlewild South," he recalled, "where the Allman Brothers used to live."

It was in Macon that Randall first got to know Chuck Leavell. "I was with Cowboy for one record, for maybe a year," Bramblett continued. "When Gregg Allman did his first couple of solo tours, they asked Chuck and Cowboy to be the backing band.

I was the leader of the horn section, so I got to be friends with Chuck."

Around the same time, Bramblett was working on a solo career, and he ultimately recorded two albums for Polydor Records. "After my solo stuff started comin' out, we must have been on the same bill with Sea Level," Bramblett recalled. "When Chuck heard our band, I think he was pretty impressed with me and Davis, the guitar player. We went down and stayed at Chuck's house and did a lot of rehearsing, and then we started recording *Cat's on the Coast*. It turned out to be a pretty good record."

Though Jaimoe appeared as a percussionist on the second album, he was already working himself out of the band. "After we'd made some personnel changes," Chuck recalled, "Jaimoe wasn't entirely happy with the musical direction in which the band was heading. At the end of the touring, Jaimoe announced that he wanted to resign. He had already thought of a replacement, a drummer he knew from his R&B days named George Weaver."

By the time Sea Level returned to the studio to begin work on a third LP, Weaver, too, had departed. Looking for a replacement, the members of Sea Level thought of Joe English. The skilled drummer had relocated to Macon from upstate New York in the 1970s with his band Jam Factory. They took up residency at Grant's Lounge, ultimately transforming into a group known as Tall Dogs. In 1975, English was tapped to join Paul McCartney's band Wings. "We thought, 'Oh man, he would be the perfect guy, but geez, he's with Paul McCartney,'" Leavell laughed. "We said, 'Well, what the heck, let's ask him, and maybe he can do a record with

Left to right: Davis Causey, Jimmy Nalls, Joe English, Chuck Leavell, Randall Bramblett, and Lamar Williams. (Capricorn publicity photo, courtesy of Chuck Perkins)

us or something.' So we asked him, and he quit McCartney to join us! We were like, 'Are you kidding?'"

The band released *On the Edge* in 1978, but the tone of the album was less experimental and lacked some of the freshness of their first two releases. "We just kind of ran out of material after a while," Randall Bramblett confessed, "because nobody was really bearing down. Everybody was partying pretty heavy, so we started recycling some of my solo songs."

By the time of 1979's *Long Walk on a Short Pier*, the band sounded a bit slicker and more sanitized. As the album neared completion, however, Capricorn Records was facing bankruptcy, and the LP wasn't released in the United States.

After switching to Arista for 1980's *Ball Room* album, Sea Level faced a lukewarm reception. "Clive [Davis] didn't like it," Chuck admitted, "and it failed to garner much attention." On top of that, personality clashes in the group were causing friction, and Randall and Davis wanted Lamar Williams out of the band. "He was late for rehearsals and just didn't seem to be into the band," Chuck recalled, "and when we played live, he certainly didn't contribute what he always had in the past. It caused a lot of heartbreak, but we did it."

With Lamar's exit, Sea Level recruited bassist Paul Broudour and began working on material for another Arista release. Just as they headed into the studio, however, Brou-

dour was diagnosed with cancer. "We shut down production with the hope that Paul might bounce back," Chuck recalled, "but he died within a matter of weeks." After one more attempt to record a single, with studio players backing Chuck and Davis Causey, Sea Level called it quits in 1980.

Despite going on to become a successful sideman with the Black Crowes, Eric Clapton, and the Rolling Stones—with whom he served as keyboardist and unofficial musical director from the early 1980s on—Leavell always regretted that Sea Level didn't break through to a wider audience. "We thought we had a serious chance," he admitted, "of breaking the mold of what people considered 'Southern' rock."

Chuck Leavell. (Sea Level Archives, courtesy of Chuck Leavell)

SEA LEVEL

- ▸ CHUCK LEAVELL keyboards, vocals
- ▸ JAIMOE drums, percussion
- ▸ LAMAR WILLIAMS bass, vocals
- ▸ JIMMY NALLS guitar, vocals
- ▸ RANDALL BRAMBLETT saxophone, keyboards, multi-instrumentalist, vocals
- ▸ DAVIS CAUSEY guitar
- ▸ GEORGE WEAVER drums
- ▸ JOE ENGLISH drums, vocals
- ▸ PAUL BROUDOUR bass

Phil Walden.
(Courtesy of
Mike Hyland)

CHAPTER 36
Long Walk on a Short Pier: The Sinking of Capricorn Records

HEN CAPRICORN Records released Sea Level's *Long Walk on a Short Pier* to the Canadian market in 1979, it marked the final LP to appear from the label before it collapsed in bankruptcy amidst a flurry of audits and lawsuits. Capricorn had begun unraveling three years earlier due to a confluence of factors, including the distraction of Jimmy Carter's Presidential campaign, the breakup of the Allman Brothers Band, increased drug use, and ill-advised business partnerships that eroded the foundation of the house that Phil Walden built.

"Phil's focus was not in the music by 1976," former Capricorn artist Bobby Whitlock reflected, years later. "His focus was in politics." Most of the artists and staffers recognized that, though they loved Carter, his campaign marked a shift in the culture at Capricorn. Producer Paul Hornsby put it matter-of-factly:

> I can tell you what led to the downfall of Capricorn Records: Jimmy Carter. Phil wanted to do greater things, and greater things, and greater things. Well, here was an American President that he helped get elected. In the meantime, his damn bands are broken down on the side of the Interstate in Arizona. Every time I'd call to talk with Phil, they'd say, "Oh, he's out. He's in Washington." Nobody else that he left behind seemed to be able to make a decision. This went on for over a year or two, but it doesn't take very long of neglecting something for the whole thing to fall apart.

Chuck Leavell. (Courtesy of Carl Lender)

Having a direct line to the president was a crowning achievement for a man who had already made the money—but still craved the respect—of the upper class. "Phil was incredibly charismatic," recalled Mike Hyland. "You couldn't help but like the guy. He had a great personality. He had a great sense of humor. He could be very funny. He could also tear your head off, just cussin' you out. But he was very charming, and he really wanted to get along with the snobs of Macon. Probably just to say he did it."

In 1975, Walden and the label were profiled in the September issue of the prestigious *Fortune* magazine. In the article, titled "How Phil Walden Turns Rock into Gold," journalist Luis Kraar called his subject a "hip southern impresario," detailing the scene in Macon where Phil, then a thirty-five-year-old art collector who was chauffeured in his own Mercedes limousine, maintained a freewheeling atmosphere where "business meetings frequently begin with a round of J&B scotch highballs."

Mike Hyland observed warily as the luxuries that began to surround Capricorn Records slowly moved toward bloated excess. "Phil

bought Debbie Reynolds' 1960 white Rolls Royce for his wife, Peggy," Hyland recalled. "Seeing that in Macon was very weird. Then there was the Capricorn jet. At first, they had a little prop plane. Then we got a jet and were using it to move Phil around and all this other stuff, and be cool boys." Having worked exceedingly hard to build his kingdom, Phil had every intention of enjoying the spoils. "I like to see 200,000 people on their feet cheering for a group I built up from nothing," he told *Fortune*. "If you can make money and have fun and power, that's what it's all about."

But the darker side of success began catching up with Capricorn Records in the late 1970s. "Greed and substance abuse and everything else just sort of led where it always does," observed Cowboy co-founder and Capricorn mainstay Tommy Talton. "Everybody partied too much. It was too easy. There was lots of money floating around. It's just what happens when people get too into drugs and greed and ego."

"There seems to have been an evolution of drugs in Macon that started innocently with marijuana," producer Johnny Sandlin noted. "Cocaine came later, and was expensive, and until everyone started making money, we couldn't afford to buy it. When the good money started coming in, it was easy to get, and we were all doing it. Cocaine helped us stay up a long time, and we thought it gave us an edge— although the project was usually compromised, because the work wasn't as good as it might have been if we'd not been doing drugs."

Those closest to Phil watched helplessly as drugs took a toll. "For many, many years, Phil was a great personal friend of mine," explained

Dick Wooley, who spearheaded the label's promotion department, "but Phil was a very troubled man. In addition to having his genius for music, he had a well-publicized drug and alcohol addiction that made him have a violent temper and, ultimately, that made him a target for a self-inflicted disaster. In the year I left Capricorn, it was sad for me to see him wreck himself and the company."

In many respects, changing public tastes were also a major factor in the deterioration of a label that's greatest financial success was built upon the Southern rock of the Allman Brothers Band and the Marshall Tucker Band. "Oddly enough," remarked Grinderswitch's Larry Howard, "I would say probably the drugs wasn't the reason for the decline as much as disco."

The shift away from Southern rock couldn't have come at a worse time for Capricorn. When Phil left Atlantic and signed a five-year distribution deal with Warner Bros. Records in 1972, Capricorn had entered a golden age of prosperity and success. The Allman Brothers Band rose to prominence as perhaps the biggest group in America, and the label was raking in approximately $16 million a year. When it came time to renew the deal in 1977, however, Phil shopped around for better terms, and wound up signing with PolyGram instead.

"What killed 'em was the PolyGram deal," Mike Hyland observed. "What killed 'em was not renewing with Warner Bros. for another five years. Phil tried to get a better deal. They got more money out of PolyGram, but then they had to hire their own promotion staff. PolyGram wasn't going to do the promotion or the sales, which Warners had handled previously. So, Capricorn had to hire all these new people."

With interest in Southern rock waning, the investment didn't pay off, as Mark Pucci recalled:

When I went to work for Capricorn in July of '74, the office was just the original location at 535 Cotton Avenue. Later on, we expanded. There was an alley between

Sound engineer Billy Wendt with Capricorn staffers Herb Kossover, Gail Giddens, Mike Hyland, and Mark Pucci. (Courtesy of Mike Hyland)

Capricorn staffers at the height of the label's success. *Left to right:* Mike Hyland, Dick Wooley, Gail Giddens, David Young, Frank Fenter, and Phil Walden. (Courtesy of Rose Lane White Leavell/Center for Public History, University of West Georgia)

the original building and what became the second Capricorn building, which Phil restored. It was a beautiful old brick building, and that became Phil's executive offices. Frank Fenter and all the accounting people were all there. Phil even had an exercise room and a sauna and stuff put in up in the top. The company was expanding, and you had the different people who were hired to do regional and local promotion in a lot of cities around the United States. Probably, at its height, there were fifty or more people. These were Capricorn employees, not freelancers. When I started, there were, maybe, twenty or twenty-five people, so it grew quickly.

"We were spreading ourselves too thin," Hyland admitted. "It was too crazy. If they were a little more focused . . . but none of us were focused. Frank was bringing stuff in from Europe and all over the place that he could get either for nothing or very little, and he just kept throwin' it out. We had a band called Fringe Benefit that was dreadful. We had a band from Canada—that I can't even remember the name of—that was dreadful. Just really, really bad records."

Though Phil and Frank had started branching out into the country-music market as early as 1974, they expanded the country activity following the PolyGram deal. Many of the country artists were recorded in Nashville, where studio time was a hefty expense.

In addition to the political distractions, the drugs, the haphazard expansion of the artist roster, and the bad deal with PolyGram, Capricorn was subjected to a barrage of audits and lawsuits, beginning in 1978. Several people associated with the label believed they weren't receiving the royalties they were due. Producer and vice president Johnny Sandlin was the first to initiate legal action. "The lawsuit I filed," he explained, "was my way of saying, 'Let's work on this; let's come to an understanding.'" Instead, Sandlin, who had been there since the beginning, was fired. Dickey Betts also filed suit to collect unpaid royalties that totaled $873,000, while Chuck Leavell was suing the Allman Brothers Band for unpaid royalties of his own. The entire empire was crumbling.

Capricorn owed more than $5.5 million to PolyGram. Word began to leak out that the label was in trouble, but the company attempted to dismiss the rumors while scrambling to find new financing. They told the press that over-shipping of their releases in late 1978 resulted in a high volume of unexpected returns, but that they were getting back on track. In reality, the situation had spun out of control.

By the summer of 1979, PolyGram sued Capricorn to recover "assets used as collateral for over five million in loans." What they were seeking was the recorded masters, the artists that were under contract, and any other valuable holdings that would cover the label's debt. The Allman Brothers Band, Sea Level, and the

Marshall Tucker Band had already each sued for breach of contract, and were in various stages of securing new record deals.

Phil still believed he could turn things around. Some of the label's recent signings showed strong promise, including a group from Oklahoma named Two Guns. Their *Balls Out* album was one of the final Capricorn releases, and it showcased some excellent hard-edged Southern rock in the Molly Hatchet/Blackfoot tradition. Paul Hornsby's excellent production, the layered guitars, and strong female backup singers made for an album that could have attracted serious attention. But it was too late. By the end of October, Phil Walden's lawyer filed a petition for bankruptcy in federal court in Macon.

At the time, Johnny Sandlin was on the road with Delbert McClinton, who had signed with the label in 1978 and recently released his second Capricorn effort *Keeper of the Flame*. "Delbert called Capricorn to see what they were doing to promote the album," Sandlin recalled, "but the phone had been disconnected."

"People knew that things were not in great shape," Mark Pucci explained, "but when it finally went down, I think it was a shock for a lot of people." Even as the phones were cut off, Walden insisted the office was open. "I had a lot of meetings after that happened," Pucci recalled. "I remember a lot of times we were meeting at Frank Fenter's house with Frank and Phil, discussing how we're going to address all of this. They were trying to get it together to continue to operate. There wasn't a whole lot

of positive spin you could put on that. When everything went down, and the bankruptcy was declared, that was it."

Capricorn's assets were listed at over $12 million, with debts of over $9 million. Poly-Gram, alone, was owed nearly $6.5 million. Dickey Betts won his arbitration agreement but was unable to collect during the bankruptcy. The documents also revealed that the label owed producer Tom Dowd over $100,000. By that point, Gregg Allman was completely disgusted with Phil. "Not even the strong performance of *Enlightened Rogues* or our tour that followed was enough to save that label," Gregg lamented, in his memoirs. "He only thought of himself, and, in doing so, he broke the damn company."

"They still had those buildings in Macon," Mark Pucci recalled, "and even though Phil had lost everything, he was trying to get something going. Right in there was when Frank Fenter died. After that, everything just pretty much dissolved." Frank had a fatal heart attack in his office on July 21, 1983. He had recently begun negotiations with Mo Ostin at Warner Bros. Records to try to re-launch Capricorn, but the deal died with Fenter.

Walden began representing several clients, including actors Jim Varney, who popularized the Ernest P. Worrell character, and Billy Bob Thornton. He finally relaunched Capricorn Records from Nashville in 1991, signing a new generation of performers including Widespread Panic, 311, Kenny Chesney, Cake, Screamin' Cheetah Wheelies, and Gov't Mule. Walden eventually sold off his assets after a nine-year run. He died in 2006.

Even after his passing, Phil Walden remains an enigmatic figure, and one who is the object of both admiration and scorn. According to Johnny Sandlin:

> Phil had a legendary temper, but he never directed it toward me.... Someone would make him mad and he'd go nuts. He'd get on the phone and start cussing someone, and it would just go on and on. I was in the office a couple of times when those calls came in; I'd sit there almost afraid to move. I'd be afraid he was going to kill himself because his face would turn red and I thought he was about to have a heart attack. He'd get up, pace, and pound on the desk.... Just when you thought he couldn't get any more intense, he'd hit another gear and it would be just unbelievable.

"Many years later," Mark Pucci explained, "Phil was diagnosed as being bipolar. I think

some of the drugs and things that were going on really affected him and exacerbated the problems that he was having. But if Phil was your friend, he would give you anything. He really was a very generous guy in a lot of ways. I do know that I saw the side of him where he was giving things to people. And he had a great sense of humor. He was a funny, funny guy."

"I have nothing but respect and love and wonderful memories of Phil Walden," Chuck Leavell explained. "He was a tough guy. He stood up for the artist. Of course, he was very clever and was interested in making money. There was a time he had his fingers in the management, the record company, and the booking agency. That's probably a little too much for one man to be involved in. You want checks and balances, but on a personal level, I thought Phil was talented. He knew no fear. He would fight for his artists."

As went the Allman Brothers Band, and as went Capricorn Records, so went Southern rock. "Looking back on it now," Gregg recalled, "there wasn't much that went right for us during these times. The hangover was long and it was bleak. These were some rough years, and the end of Capricorn was just the start." ★

Press coverage of the Capricorn barbecues in happier times.

The Rossington Collins Band onstage in 1980. *Left to right*: Billy Powell, Allen Collins, Dale Krantz, Gary Rossington, Leon Wilkeson, Derek Hess, and Barry Harwood. (Photo by Larry Hulst/Michael Ochs Archives/Getty Images)

CHAPTER 37
Free Fall:
The Sound of the End of an Era

I **N 1978,** nearly a year after Lynyrd Skynyrd's plane crashed in Gillsburg, Mississippi, MCA Records released *Skynyrd's First and . . . Last.* The LP collected nine of the songs the band recorded with Jimmy Johnson in Muscle Shoals in 1971 and 1972. The album quickly went Platinum. Without Ronnie, however, the surviving members didn't see any way they could carry on as Lynyrd Skynyrd. "We were very bitter about what happened," keyboardist Billy Powell admitted. "Personally, I dove into a bottle for a while. I didn't find any answers, but it numbed the pain of losing my career. It had a major psychological effect on all of us."

Guitarists Gary Rossington and Allen Collins spent most of their time hanging out at Ronnie's house with his widow, Judy, in a booze- and cocaine-fueled attempt to process their grief. As with Billy, the accident plunged them into a depth of physical and emotional pain that they could only medicate with alcohol, powder, and pills. "We got hooked after the plane crash," Gary explained to VH1, "'cause they gave us every kind of pain pill there was, and you could get 'em anywhere."

One night at the Van Zant house, Allen and Gary agreed they would never try to reassemble the band. They drew up an agreement with Judy, which they all signed. Eventually the other surviving members signed it, too. Rather than drawing the band members closer together, however, the agreement, and the aftermath of the tragedy, seemed to pull them further apart. "We were bitter over losing Skynyrd," Billy Powell observed, years later, in *Mojo* magazine. "That's when the drinking and

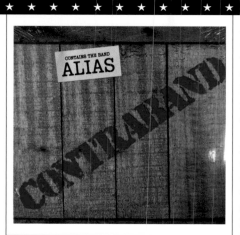

the fighting was the worst." To make matters worse, there was little support from the music industry that profited from the band's success. "Peter Rudge and our management company and all of our lawyers and everybody," Artimus Pyle recalled, "they just dropped us the next day after the crash, like we were dead."

With both Lynyrd Skynyrd and the Allman Brothers Band broken up at the start of 1978, and with Capricorn on the brink of serious financial trouble, it appeared that the Southern rock era was finished. Before it disappeared into the mist of 1980s new-wave pop, however, a final flowering of bands emerged to try to carry on the magic of Southern rocks' quickly fading golden era, while searching for an angle to stay relevant in the face of a changing musical landscape. Though personally damaged, the former members of Lynyrd Skynyrd rallied, in various configurations, to lead the charge of keeping the genre alive.

A brief article appeared in the February 23, 1978, issue of *Rolling Stone*, announcing that

Gary Rossington and Allen Collins were hoping to gather the Skynyrd survivors for a new band with a different name. "I've been getting together and messing around with Allen," Rossington revealed. "We're doing a little playing and a little thinking, but we're not worried about making any big rock-and-roll moves."

In 1979, several of the old Skynyrd bandmates gathered onstage at Charlie Daniels' Volunteer Jam, but they had yet to emerge with a tangible group. "Gregg [Allman], Allen, and I were going to form a band with Robert Nix of the Atlanta Rhythm Section on drums," Gary Rossington revealed, "but that fell through." In the meantime, Billy Powell, Artimus Pyle, and Leon Wilkeson put together a band called Alias, releasing one album, *Contraband,* for the Mercury label. With vocals handled by both Jimmy Dougherty and former Skynyrd backup singer JoJo Billingsley, the album maintained the classic Southern rock aesthetic that Skynyrd had helped pioneer. It was a solid effort, but the band was a short-lived enterprise.

Finally, a blurb in the November 29, 1979, issue of *Rolling Stone* confirmed that all the Skynyrd survivors were reuniting under the banner of the Rossington Collins band. It was reported that they were rehearsing and working on songs with Billy Powell, Leon Wilkeson, Artimus Pyle, and newcomer Barry Harwood, but had not yet found a vocalist.

In truth, they were already courting Dale Krantz, a former backup singer for Leon Russell, who was performing with 38 Special at the time. Choosing a female vocalist would help avoid comparisons with Ronnie, but Artimus didn't agree with the vision. He was already feuding with Rossington and Col-

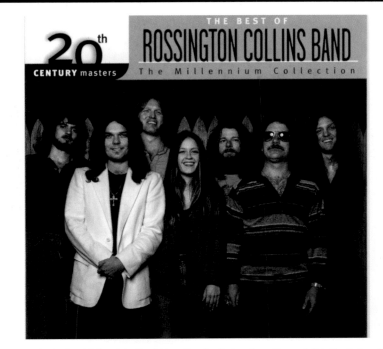

The Rossington Collins Band, *left to right*: Derek Hess, Gary Rossington, Barry Harwood, Dale Krantz, Leon Wilkeson, Billy Powell, and Allen Collins. (MCA Records)

lins over the decision before he crashed his Harley-Davidson motorcycle while swerving to avoid a drunk driver, breaking his leg in a dozen places. There was little hope that he would be able to play drums in the near future. Barry Harwood suggested drummer Derek Hess, who had played with Harwood in a locally popular Jacksonville band called Runnin' Easy, and the Rossington Collins Band lineup was completed without Artimus.

"38 Special had the same management as Lynyrd Skynyrd," Dale Krantz explained to *Musician* magazine, "so when the plane went down, it stopped everything. While the management stuff was being worked out, I spent a year in Jax, not doing much music. Gary and Allen took a big chance with me. They'd seen me around clubs in Jacksonville and I'd sung one lead duet with Donnie on the third 38 Special album, but that was it." When the Rossington Collins Band made their live debut in Orlando in February of 1980, the group ended the evening with an instrumental encore of "Freebird." It was the only Lynyrd Skynyrd song they played that night.

When the band released their first MCA album, *Anytime Anyplace Anywhere*, in July, record buyers got a chance to hear new material from Allen and Gary for the first time in almost three years. Rooted in the Skynyrd tradition, but softened for changing radio tastes, the music sounded like the next logical step in the band members' evolution. The album was a success, climbing just shy of *Billboard*'s Top 10 and earning the group a Gold record.

The Rossington Collins Band followed it with a second album, *This Is the Way*, in October of 1981. Within weeks of its release, however, tragedy struck the Skynyrd family once again, when Allen Collin's pregnant wife died of a hemorrhage while at the movies with her two young children. Allen was heartbroken. "After his wife died," Rossington recalled to

Jaan Uhelszki, "he became real bitter, even with me." The tour was eventually put on hold. Allen descended deeper into his grief, while Gary and Dale, who had fallen in love and gotten married in May of 1982, decided to take time off to start a family.

In 1982, Artimus Pyle reemerged with an album for MCA called *A.P.B.*, which stood for Artimus Pyle Band. Produced by a trio of Marshall Tucker Band refugees—Doug Gray, George McCorkle, and Jerry Eubanks—the album adhered to the Skynyrd formula of muscular rock but incorporated a touch of 38 Special's radio-friendly shine. By the time the A.P.B. released a follow up, 1983's *Nightcaller*, they were obviously reaching for mainstream pop success. The addition of female vocalist Karen Blackmon added new texture, but the sound, in general, was representative of the careful smoothing of the edges that had taken place in Southern rock by the early 1980s.

The remaining members of the Rossington Collins Band regrouped as the Allen Collins Band in 1983 and recorded a one-off album for MCA called *Here, There & Back*. The group consisted of everyone from the Rossington Collins Band minus Gary and Dale. Jimmy Dougherty, who had sung lead in the band Alias, was recruited to handle the vocal duties, while Randall Hall came in on guitar. Unfortunately, tragedy continued to plague Collins. He was involved in a traffic accident while driving drunk in 1986 that left him paralyzed and killed his girlfriend. He pleaded no contest to DUI

manslaughter, but avoided prison due to his physical condition.

While none of the Skynyrd offshoot projects of the late 1970s and early 1980s became classics, they were generally quality releases that represented the struggle to remain faithful to a Southern rock heritage, while moving the music toward mainstream public tastes that were rapidly shifting from a hard-edged guitar assault to a more sophisticated pop sound. These were difficult waters to navigate, but the guys were trying to hold on, as the final wave of the original Southern rock era crashed around them.

While the members of Lynyrd Skynyrd had a solid track record to fall back on, new Southern rock bands were emerging at the same time and attempting to establish themselves in a genre with fading popularity. "I think, if anything, a number of the key Southern groups of the '70s got trapped into the very thing that they tried to avoid when they started making records," Phil Walden later reflected, in an interview with Robert Gordon. "They started making records in the Southern rock formula, and it lost a lot of its fire and its spirit." If the new groups were to survive, they would have to find ways to tweak the formula to stay fresh.

New Southern rock bands of the late 1970s not only faced scrutiny from fans but also from the very pioneers who defined the genre. "We are tired of all this 'Southern scene' crap that follows us in newspapers," Ronnie Van Zant complained to one journalist as early as 1974.

The Artimus Pyle Band in 1982. *Left to right*: Artimus Pyle, John Boerstler, Steve Lockhart, Steve Brewington, and Darryll Otis Smith. (MCA Records)

"It's gotten so that a great band from New York has less of a chance now than an average band from the South. People have come in and started to make money, and there are folks now that'll snap you up just because you're from Dixie. That ain't good and it ain't fair."

By the latter part of the decade, a few quality bands—the Dixie Dregs, Stillwater, Cooder Browne, and Doc Holliday among them—would briefly appear on the scene to make closing arguments for the decade-long

Southern rock revolution before it retreated into hibernation.

The Dixie Dregs released their first major album in 1977, but the members traced their roots back to a five-piece band called Dixie Grit that was formed in 1970 in Augusta, Georgia. When founding guitarist Steve Morse departed for the University of Miami in 1971, Dixie Grit split up. He would occasionally team with Dixie Grit bassist Andy West for duo performances under the name Dixie Dregs. Assembling a new lineup of musicians, the Dixie Dregs recorded their first album, *The Great Spectacular*, on the University of Miami campus in 1975, and self-released it the following year. The band became a regional favorite among local musicians who admired their skills, but they did not attract a wide audience.

Unlike most Southern rock bands, the Dixie Dregs were an instrumental group that incorporated sophisticated jazz-fusion influences and virtuosic musical chops into a Southern-fried version of Rush or Steely Dan. "We began blitzing the record companies with demos," Morse revealed in a 1978 interview with Jas Obrecht. "People said, 'Wow, that's a weird band,' but nobody was

willing to do anything with it because it was instrumental music."

The Dixie Dregs finally began to gain traction at the end of 1976. "We got on a gig with Sea Level in Nashville," Morse recalled, "and freaked out Chuck Leavell and Twiggs Lyndon. So when we finished playing, I talked to Twiggs about working for us. I was feeling sort of depressed, because I knew we couldn't afford him, but he said, in short, that he'd work for nothing, or whatever we could give him."

Lyndon, who had been a key member of the Allman Brothers Band organization, came aboard as both the Dixie Dregs' road manager and unofficial mentor. He was pictured on the back of their first album, 1977's *Free Fall*, which appeared on the Capricorn label. The cover depicted the band members superimposed on an aerial scene designed to look like they'd just stepped out of a flying plane. The album art took on an eerie tone when Twiggs died in a skydiving accident two years later, while on tour with the Dixie Dregs.

The music on *Free Fall*, all credited to Morse, was intricate and exciting. While the sound was adventurous, the Dixie Dregs maintained a light-hearted spirit that was missing from many fusion-oriented bands. Critics loved it, but the public didn't know what to make of an instrumental group that relied on dazzling skill rather than pop-leaning radio hits.

The follow-up, 1978's *What If*, was received even more enthusiastically by critics. Incorporating a wide range of eclectic influences, from classical to country to funk, the second LP was more fully realized than its predecessor, with the standout tracks including the awe-inspiring "Odyssey." The Dixie Dregs earned a loyal following among appreciative musicians, if not widespread commercial success.

In 1979, the band released *Night of the Living Dregs*, which was made up primarily of studio recordings but also included live tracks that showcased the addition of keyboard-

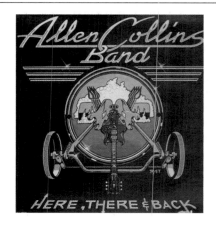

The Dixie Dregs in 1978. *Left to right*: Andy West, Mark Parrish, Rod Morgenstein, Allen Sloan, and Steve Morse. (Capricorn Records)

ist T. Lavitz. As the band moved toward a new decade, they would incorporate the synthesizer into their sound, while never dumbing down their instrumental prowess. The album was nominated for a Grammy for Best Rock Instrumental Performance.

When Capricorn filed for bankruptcy in 1979, the Dixie Dregs signed with Arista Records. In 1980, they released another Grammy-nominated LP, *Dregs of the Earth*. They followed it with 1981's *Unsung Heroes*, a well-executed album that lacked the energy and excitement of the band's previous efforts. By that point, Steve Morse and his bandmates were simply calling themselves the Dregs, in hopes of downplaying their regional affiliation and broadening their appeal.

Switching gears for 1982's *Industry Standard*, the group incorporated vocals into their sound for the first time. Former Santana singer Alex Ligertwood and Doobie Brother Patrick Simmons were recruited to lend their singing talents. Virtuoso violinist and future Nashville studio musician Mark O'Connor joined the band for *Industry Standard*, but despite another Grammy nomination and

tweaks to the lineup, sales were minimal. Arista dropped them from its roster, and the members went their separate ways into various prestigious projects. Though they would reunite in the 1990s to great critical acclaim, the Dixie Dregs discovered in the early 1980s that instrumental pyrotechnics would not be the salvation of Southern rock.

Another act that first emerged from the troubled Capricorn Records roster in 1977 was Stillwater. The members of the band grew up playing in various local outfits around War-

ner Robbins, Georgia, in the early 1970s, before signing a management deal with Phil Walden and ultimately working their way onto his label. Their debut album, *Stillwater*, was produced by Atlanta Rhythm Section mastermind Buddy Buie at Studio One in Doraville, Georgia.

Drummer Sebie Lacey was the band's lead vocalist, though he shared the duties with Jimmy Hall, a percussionist who happened to have the same name as Wet Willie's front man. Featuring the nuanced touch of Buie's production, the band's first LP was generous with the folky, Southern California influence that had been popularized by the Eagles. A single, "Mind Bender," fell just shy of the Top 40, but the album remains well regarded by Southern rock treasure hunters. While Buie's production work was tasteful, the LP ended with the predictable Southern rock convention of an epic twin-guitar overdose.

Stillwater released their second LP, *I Reserve the Right*, in 1978. The album showed considerable promise, and featured a guest appearance by Bonnie Bramlett on the final track. Within months, however, the label was out of business. "Capricorn records went bankrupt after our second album," guitarist Bobby Golden recounted to Luc Brunot. "We turned down a record offer, hoping to get signed with a new label on the West Coast, which fell through. We played and continued recording until the end of 1983. I left the group to go back to college. The band quit playing shortly after."

Yet another lesser-known Southern rock group to emerge in the waning years of the late 1970s was a Texas quartet known variously as the Cooder Browne Band and Cooder Browne. Drummer Dale Bolin, bassist Skip Tumbleson, keyboardist David Haworth, and multi-instrumentalist Larry Franklin—who played fiddle, guitar, and mandolin—got together in 1976. The vocal duties were shared by Tumbleson, Haworth, and Franklin, who drew from the same well as the Marshall Tucker Band and the Charlie Daniels Band, with a heaping dose of Western swing–style Texas fiddling.

The group's sole self-titled album was released in 1978 on Lone Star Records, an imprint of the Mercury Label that was spearheaded by Willie Nelson. "We formed in north Texas and moved to Austin when the whole Willie Nelson/Austin music scene started taking off," Larry Franklin told *Fiddler* magazine. "Willie kind of took us under his wing and signed us to his Lone Star Records, and we did one album, put it out, and toured with Willie."

Produced by Paul Hornsby at the Capricorn studio in Macon, the album featured electric guitar work by Jimmy Nalls. The Marshall Tucker Band's Toy Caldwell played pedal steel. Though they were particularly impressive instrumentalists, the members of Cooder Browne came along at the wrong time, and couldn't come to a unified decision on the band's focus following the first album. "We later disagreed on some directions that we wanted to go," Franklin explained. "I also play guitar, and the group was asking me to get away from the fiddle. I was wanting to play the fiddle, and I was trying to find guitar players to fill that spot. They never accepted anybody I brought in. That was the whole reason that fell apart." The group disbanded without ever connecting in any significant way with a national audience.

"We turned that record out pretty quick," producer Paul Hornsby recalled, "and the life of the label was nearly as quick. I don't know all of the business behind the label folding, but anyhow, there went the career of the band." Larry Franklin went on to join the legendary Texas swing revivalists Asleep at the Wheel before moving to Nashville, where he became an in-demand session musician.

A Stillwater publicity photo. Back row, *left to right*: Bobby Golden, Jimmy Hall, and Michael Causey. Middle row, *left to right*: Bob Spearman, Rob Walker, and Al Scarborough, with Sebie Lacy (front). (Courtesy of Chuck Perkins)

Perhaps the last legitimate band to emerge out of the original Southern rock era was Macon, Georgia's Doc Holliday. Originally formed in 1971 by brothers Bob and Bruce Brookshire as a blues band called Roundhouse, the group earned a reputation as a popular regional club band before landing a deal with A&M Records in 1980. By that time, Bob had departed to work as a backing musician for soul legends like Solomon Burke, Clarence Carter, and Johnny Taylor, leaving Bruce to front the band as lead vocalist and guitarist. At the time they were signed, Roundhouse also included bassist John Samuelson, keyboardist Eddie Stone, guitarist Ric Skelton, and drummer Herman Nixon.

When A&M Records discovered another group were using the name Roundhouse, Bob and his bandmates had to come up with an alternative. The name Doc Holliday was selected from a short list of options suggested by listeners who called in to vote as part of a Georgia radio station contest. It referred to legendary Wild West gunfighter and Wyatt Earp associate John Henry "Doc" Holliday, who originally hailed from Georgia. With a nod to both their outlaw attitude and Georgia roots, it proved a fitting name for the band.

The debut album, *Doc Holliday*, was recorded at Bee Jay Studios in Orlando in 1980. Producer Tom Allom, best known for his work with Judas Priest, was hired to oversee the sessions. Featuring loud guitars, rough-hewn vocals, and a raw rock sound, Doc Holliday doubled down on an edgy brand of Southern rock with ample twin-lead guitars in an era when 38 Special and similar bands were turning to softer sounds. The LP reached the Top

Cooder Browne, *left to right*: Larry Franklin, Dale Bolin, Jimmy (Skip) Tumbleson, and David Haworth. (Courtesy of Larry Franklin)

40 on the *Billboard* charts and is regarded as a classic of the later Southern rock era.

Doc Holliday toured aggressively, opening shows for everyone from the Charlie Daniels Band to Black Sabbath. By the time their second album, *Doc Holliday Rides Again*, was released, near the end of 1981, they had smoothed their sound somewhat. The changes were appealing, and they created a Southern rock classic with "Lonesome Guitar," a fairly pedestrian mid-tempo ballad that suddenly erupts into an explosive Southern rock dual-guitar showdown at the three-and-a-half-minute mark. It was Doc Holliday's "Freebird," and it helped cement the second album as a fan favorite.

By the time the group released their third effort, *Modern Medicine*, in 1983, they'd wandered far from the Southern rock reservation. "It got to the point in America where getting airplay on radio was crucial," Bruce Brookshire explained to journalist Xavier Russell, "and we couldn't get arrested with our music. And the charts back then were full of claptrap like Culture Club and Cyndi Lauper." Recording at Musicland Studios in Germany, the band embraced an entirely new sonic palette. "We used techniques on that record we never had tried before," Brookshire recalled, in an interview with Michael Buffalo Smith. "Click tracks and loops, replacing recorded drum tracks with

new tracks, things that are very common now [but] were new to us then." The producer, Mack, was best known for his work with Queen, ELO, and Billy Squier. "Mack scared us and intimidated us a little," Bruce confessed, "but we were pretty strung out on drugs, so he did what he could. We intentionally tried to combine techno music with Southern rock, and we failed miserably. That album went cardboard—not Gold or Platinum. We lost our record deal, our house and tour bus, our equipment, everything. Techno was raging in 1983, and a drugged-out Southern band was not big business."

Though they came together again in 1986 and continued to perform in a Southern rock

vein for years to come, Doc Holliday found that their legacy was better preserved in Europe than in the United States. Perhaps arriving a bit too late to the game, their high-quality first two albums remain frequently overlooked contributions to the Southern rock canon.

Despite the appearance of quality bands like Doc Holliday, Cooder Browne, Stillwater and the Dixie Dregs in the late 1970s and early 1980s, the tide of public taste had already turned, and Southern rock was against the ropes. Even the godfathers of the genre found it impossible to survive.

Once Capricorn collapsed, the Allman Brothers Band signed a new contract with Arista Records, with which Dickey Betts had had a relationship from his work with Great Southern. They recorded two albums, *Reach for the Sky* and *Brothers of the Road*. Taken together, the two projects are regarded by even the most diehard of fans as the lowest creative point in the group's history. "The musical trend turned away from blues-oriented rock towards more simple synthesizer-based, dance music arrangements," Dickey Betts explained to Alan Paul. "That forced the record company to dictate what type of record we could make, and we got caught up in that whole thing."

The label retained the right to choose the producer, and would not allow the Brothers to work with Tom Dowd. The results showcased a misguided attempt to update the band's sound with the slick studio technology that would mark some of the worst pop music of the 1980s. "It was like a whole different band made those records," Gregg confessed in his autobiography. "We had background singers, songwriters, synthesizers—fuck me, man. In truth, though, I was just too drunk most of the time to care one way or the other." Duane Allman's biographer, Randy Poe, aptly called the Arista albums

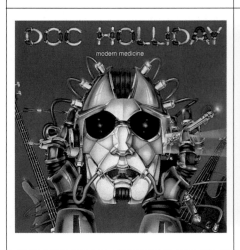

The Allman Brothers Band in 1980. *Left to right:* Butch Trucks, David "Rook" Goldflies, Dickey Betts, Frankie Toler, Gregg Allman, Jaimoe, and Mike Lawler. (Arista Records)

an example of a band "compromising rather than evolving."

Prior to recording *Brothers of the Road*, Jaimoe and Dickey got into a disagreement about band finances, and Betts fired him from the group. Jaimoe was replaced by Dan Toler's brother Frankie, also a veteran of Great Southern, effectively turning the Allman Brothers into Great Southern, with Butch Trucks and Gregg seemingly tagged on as an afterthought.

On January 23, 1982, the Allman Brothers Band played *Saturday Night Live*. After that, the members went their separate ways. Gregg's drinking was out of control, Gregg and Dickey were once again locked in a power struggle, and the record company was fundamentally trying to change the group's identity. "I think you remember that fiasco with Arista Records in 1980," Butch mused in later years, "when disco was king and Southern rock was anathema, and we decided to try something different .... Now we *did* have a small group of fans that really loved what we played and were sticking with us. And rather than just sticking with them and pulling back—you know, we were used to playing Madison Square Garden—we kept trying to change ourselves and write hits and do this, that, and the other, and it was a mistake."

"All of a sudden," Betts remembered, in an interview with *Hittin' the Note*, "managers and record company people were telling us that we should no longer use terms like 'Southern rock,' or that we couldn't wear hats or boots onstage, that it was embarrassing to a modern audience. We finally decided we couldn't meet the current trends—that if we tried we were going to make fools out of ourselves and ruin

any integrity we had left. Looking back, splitting up was the best thing we could have done."

The second breakup of the band did nothing to help Gregg clear his head, as he descended again into crippling alcoholism and drug abuse. He went on the road with the Gregg Allman Band, but he didn't record again for several years. Dickey recorded a straight country album in 1982 that wasn't released. "It was during the '80s, when we were trying to survive the disco thing by playing in beer joints," Dickey said of a new group he formed called BHLT that stood for (Dickey) Betts, (Jimmy) Hall, (Chuck) Leavell, and (Butch) Trucks. Rounded out by Danny Parks and David "Rook" Goldflies, BHLT were primarily relegated to club bookings. "It sounded like a deli sandwich, but

it was a pretty good band," Dickey quipped, in *One Way Out*. "But it died. I mean, nobody would even let us record an album."

Things remained bleak for the Brotherhood for most of the decade. On January 21, 1983, former bassist Lamar Williams died of lung cancer at the age of thirty-four. Doctors believed he most likely became sick as the result of exposure to Agent Orange when he was in the army in Vietnam. "I remember his beautiful smile," Chuck Leavell said of Lamar. "He had really kind eyes, and when he would smile, his eyes would smile along with him. He was an engaging guy. He had a nice laugh, and you just couldn't help but like him."

In the mid-1980s, when he was forty years old, Gregg started dating a sixteen-year-old girl named Shannon Wilsey, who became an adult film star, performing under the name Savannah, before eventually taking her own life. Her death, along with that of Lamar and the loss of Twiggs Lyndon in his skydiving accident a couple of years prior, seemed to demonstrate that the air of tragedy that frequently surrounded the Allman Brothers Band showed no sign of letting up. Though they'd survived the deaths of Duane Allman and Berry Oakley to become one of the biggest American bands of all time, there seemed to be no bouncing back from the confluence of factors that faced them at the dawn of a new decade. Changing musical tastes, poor creative choices, substance abuse, and personal tragedy all took a toll. By 1982, the Allman Brothers Band was gone, Capricorn Records was a memory, and Southern rock was dead. ★

BHLT publicity photo, *left to right:* Rick Hall, Dickey Betts, David Goldflies, Butch Trucks, Chuck Leavell, and Dan Parks.

Part Ten

NEVER GONNA CHANGE: AN ENDURING LEGACY

Derek Trucks and Warren Haynes of the Allman Brothers Band. (Courtesy of Carl Lender)

"THE FIRST BIG slam to Southern rock was the death of Skynyrd," Point Blank's Buzzy Gruen told Rick Flynn in 2012. "That was a shock. That was a culture shock. And then, after that, rock and roll, in general, and the music we enjoyed listening to on the radio, changed. . . . The Bee Gees had a big part in changing that. When we came back home, after ten years on the road, the clubs weren't even hiring live bands anymore. I'd go into a club, and they'd be playing disco and they'd have a drummer on a set with a pair of headphones playing along with the damn record!"

By the mid-1980s, popular music was dominated by acts like Culture Club, Lionel Richie, Madonna, Wham, Whitney Houston, and Mr. Mister. The radio airwaves were a barren wasteland for anything that could be remotely identified as Southern rock. Even the popularity of ZZ Top's pulsing video-driven pop hits and 38 Special's melodic mainstream ear candy was on the decline. Virtually every other band that had ever been associated with the Southern rock genre had either broken up or was now slogging it out in low paying beer joints.

"The general consensus, it would appear," Molly Hatchet's Dave Hlubek told *Kerrang!* magazine at the end of 1984, "is that Southern rock is over with. It's a dead issue as far as being a saleable commodity in big numbers is concerned. But everything goes in a circle. It will come around again someday, I believe, just like fashions do. I mean, my sister's now wearing clothes my mother used to wear. So I guess I gotta wait all those years 'til it comes back."

"There is no denying the Allman Brothers' influence is primary over all these folks. Their influence is pretty awesome. But I don't think any of these contemporary bands attempt to copy anything from the Allman Brothers. It's that wonderful influence of guys playing very well, and of talented people getting together and expressing themselves through their music."

—PHIL WALDEN, 1998

CHAPTER 38
Edge of Forever: How Southern Rock Rose Again

 AVE HLUBEK DIDN'T have to wait quite as long as he might have imagined for Southern rock to return. Suddenly, in 1987, the gods of rock and roll flipped a switch, and the floodgates opened for a Southern revival. It all began with a lone electric guitar playing a gritty guitar riff that announced the opening bars of the Georgia Satellites' "Keep Your Hands to Yourself." Singer Dan Baird's voice chimed in with an unmistakable twang before the whole band confidently crashed in, ripping through three and a half minutes of pure, boozy Southern swagger.

The Atlanta-based Georgia Satellites had signed with Elektra Records in 1986, releasing a self-titled debut album full of blazing guitars and top-notch barroom boogie. By the summer of 1987, "Keep Your Hands to Yourself" had climbed to #2 on the *Billboard* singles chart, and the album was certified Platinum. "I'm proud to be associated with people like Little Richard, Carl Perkins, the Allman Brothers, Lynyrd Skynyrd, Otis Redding," Baird told *Creem* magazine that same year. "We were afraid of being lumped in with other Southern bands because we have the word Georgia right in our name.... Now I like having that regional association in our name."

The Georgia Satellites' late-'80s success heralded a new era when the South would rise again to reclaim its place at the rock-and-roll table. The first major tour the band undertook was an opening slot with Nashville's Jason & the Scorchers, a group experimenting with the collision of sincere country reverence and pure punk power. While they never scored a major

Lynyrd Skynyrd in 1987. *Left to right:* Gary Rossington, Ed King, Johnny Van Zant, Artimus Pyle, Randall Hall, Billy Powell, and Leon Wilkeson. (Fox Theater)

hit, the Scorchers were representative of a new generation of Southerners who were drawing from the roots of country and blues but reinterpreting those sounds for a new era.

As younger Southern performers started incorporating the sounds of their region's history into their music in the mid-to-late 1980s, Lynyrd Skynyrd suddenly came roaring back to life. Following the demise of the Rossington Collins Band and the Allen Collins Band, the former members of Lynyrd Skynyrd spent the mid-1980s pursuing various solo projects. Gary Rossington and Dale Krantz-Rossington eventually reemerged as Rossington, an overproduced attempt to embrace the synthesizer-driven sounds of the era, while Billy Powell and Leon Wilkeson joined a Christian rock band called Vision. In 1987, Vision toured with former Grand Funk front man Mark Farner.

"Every night, in between songs," Powell told author Marley Brant, "people would start yelling, 'Skynyrd!' [That's] when a lightbulb finally went off in my head." Recognizing the audience demand, Powell reached out to the other surviving members.

The original plan was to reunite for a one-time appearance at Charlie Daniels' Volunteer Jam on September 6, 1987. By the 24th, they were embarking on a five-week tour. Gary Rossington, Leon Wilkeson, Billy Powell, and Artimus Pyle signed on. Allen Collins had been paralyzed following his 1986 car crash, but he went on the road as musical director and selected Randall Hall from the Allen Collins Band to take his place onstage. Guitarist Ed King, who had left the group prior to the plane crash, returned to the fold to reconstitute the three-guitar army. Dale Krantz-Rossington and Carol Bristow became the new Honkettes.

Re-forming Lynyrd Skynyrd without Ronnie Van Zant had seemed like an impossibility until Ronnie's youngest brother, Johnny Van Zant, was recruited to give voice to his brother's lyrics once again. Johnny had debuted as a recording artist in 1980 with his own Johnny Van Zant Band. The group's first album, *No More Dirty Deals*, was released on Polydor Records, with production by Al Kooper. While it was fairly well received, the band's two subsequent Polydor releases were generally watered-down efforts that went largely ignored. They were still far better than a 1985 outing on the Geffen label that was released under the band name Van-Zant. The half-hearted attempt to reinvent the group as a keyboard-drenched glam-rock entity ended as poorly as one would expect, and Johnny Van Zant left the music business to take a job driving a truck.

When Johnny signed on to front the reconstituted Lynyrd Skynyrd, fans showed up in droves for what was regarded as a tribute to the original Lynyrd Skynyrd band. A subsequent live album, *Southern by the Grace of God*, featured guest appearances by Donnie Van Zant and Jeff Carlisi from 38 Special, Toy Caldwell from the Marshall Tucker Band, The Dixie Dregs' Steve Morse, and Charlie Daniels. It was produced by Muscle Shoals' Jimmy Johnson.

Thanks to the success of the tribute tour, the band decided to carry on as Lynyrd Skynyrd. The reunion, however, was not without controversy. Judy Van Zant Jenness and Teresa Gaines Rapp, the widows of Ronnie and Steve, sued the group for using the name Lynyrd Skynyrd, and won the rights to what would have been the two musicians' shares of all merchandise income and music royalties. A new legal agreement was hammered out, and after being given the green light to soldier on, Lynyrd Skynyrd were reborn as a perennially popular touring behemoth on the classic-rock circuit. They returned to recording, beginning with the Tom Dowd–produced *1991*, which was released on the Atlantic label.

While Lynyrd Skynyrd achieved significant financial success in their second incarnation, they continued to experience their share of tragedy and instability. Allen Collins died in 1990 due to complications from pneumonia. Artimus left the band in 1991, and Leon Wilkeson was thrown in jail for beating up his girlfriend in 1993. In 1996, Billy Powell was also charged with domestic violence, though he was later cleared. That same year, Ed King took a break from the band following a heart attack, but was not allowed to return after his recovery. The snub resulted in a lawsuit. King was

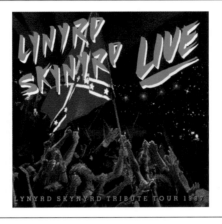

replaced by former Outlaws guitarist Hughie Thomasson. That same year, Blackfoot's Rickey Medlocke, who had briefly been a member of Lynyrd Skynyrd in the early 1970s as a drummer, rejoined the fold on guitar.

As Lynyrd Skynyrd moved into their fourth decade, the band's critical reception steadily declined. *Rolling Stone* offered a one-star review of 2003's *Vicious Cycle*, ripping it up as calculated pandering. "An echo of the Skynyrd sound is present," the reviewer noted, "but the soul is sure gone on these smug songs offering endless praise to Mama, flag-waving, and drinking." While the band's new albums earned little critical praise, the group's legacy was undiminished. On March 13, 2006, Lynyrd Skynyrd were inducted into the Rock and Roll Hall of Fame.

Hughie Thomasson left Skynyrd in 2005 to re-form the Outlaws, but he died of a heart attack two years later at the age of fifty-five. Billy Powell also died of a heart attack, on January 28, 2009. With Powell's death, Gary Rossington was left to preside over the Lynyrd Skynyrd name as the only original member from the classic era. Bob Burns, Ed King, and Artimus Pyle were effectively barred from participation after the mid-1990s, and the handful of surviving original band members continued to trade barbs in the press. "After 1987," Artimus Pyle complained, "Lynyrd Skynyrd became a crass commercial enterprise. Now it's Gary Rossington and ten people they hired yesterday. They call that Lynyrd Skynyrd and charge you $100,000? It's bullshit. If Ronnie Van Zant is not your lead singer, you're not in Lynyrd Skynyrd. Period." Nevertheless, fans continued to flock to the shows.

With the revived lineup of Lynyrd Skynyrd stoking interest in the band in 1987, Southern rock fans wondered if the Allman Brothers Band would do the same. In March of 1986, Gregg Allman and Dickey Betts had begun touring together. Dickey and his band would play, followed by Gregg. Both groups would then close the show with a selection of Allman Brothers Band songs. In July of that year, the Brothers came together at Charlie Daniels' Volunteer Jam with Jaimoe and Chuck Leavell. When the tour hit Macon, Chuck, Butch, and Jaimoe took the stage for a lengthy Allman Brothers Band set, but a full-fledged reunion would have to wait. Gregg signed with Epic Records, releasing two solo albums in the late 1980s. The first, *I'm No Angel*, reached #30 on the *Billboard* album chart, while the single of the same name became a hit. The second, *Just Before the Bullets Fly*, featured a title track written by guitarist Warren Haynes, who was playing in Dickey's band.

Left to right: Leon Wilkeson, Billy Powell, Gary Rossington, Johnny Van Zant, Owen Hale, Hughie Thomasson, and Rickey Medlocke. (Alliance Artists)

In 1989, Mercury Records released a four-disc Allman Brothers Band boxed set called *Dreams* that collected some of the group's most important recordings alongside a selection of early material and solo efforts from band members. It generated renewed interest in the band after almost a decade apart and created an opportunity to tour again. "Disco went out and the good old blues came back around," Gregg explained to Alan Paul, "so we got back together." Initially, the idea was to do a one-off tour to commemorate the twentieth anniversary of the band. Gregg and Dickey reunited with Butch and Jaimoe and picked new players to complete the lineup.

Dickey selected Warren Haynes as the second guitarist. "I liked him right away," Gregg

said. "I liked what he brought to the table, because he could play, write, and sing, so he helped make it desirable to put the band back together." Allen Woody, who had played in Artimus Pyle's band, came aboard as the bassist, and Johnny Neel, who'd played with both Dickey Betts and Gregg Allman's solo bands, joined them on keyboards. "By the time we finished that reunion tour in '89," Gregg explained, "there was no doubt that having Allen and Warren in the band put a good, fresh wind in our sails. Those two together made the band really click." Butch Trucks agreed. "Warren and Woody really reenergized us, and helped us get back to being the Allman Brothers Band," he remarked. For Warren Haynes it was a natural fit. "The fact that Dickey and I had played together for almost three years played a huge role in the band sounding so good from the start," he reflected, in an interview with Alan Paul, "because that relationship is central to the Allman Brothers."

Deciding to extend the band beyond a one-off reunion tour, the reconstituted Allman Brothers Band recorded a string of albums in the 1990s, including *Seven Turns*, *Shades of Two Worlds*, and *Where It All Begins*. They were all produced by Tom Dowd, and they were generally strong efforts. After Johnny Neel departed and former Spyro Gyra percussionist Marc Quiñones came aboard in 1991, the band's lineup remained fairly consistent for several years.

In 1995, the Allman Brothers Band were inducted into the Rock and Roll Hall of Fame. When he saw footage of himself drunkenly delivering his brief acceptance speech at the ceremony, however, Gregg was disgusted. It was the shocking wakeup call he needed. He

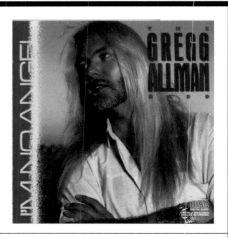

The 1989–90 lineup of the Allman Brothers Band. *Left to right*: Dickey Betts, Warren Haynes, Gregg Allman, Butch Trucks, Allen Woody, Jaimoe, and Johnny Neel. (Photo by Kirk West/Epic Records, courtesy of the Big House Museum, Macon, Georgia)

The 1991–97 lineup of the Allman Brothers Band. *Left to right*: Allen Woody, Gregg Allman, Jaimoe, Dickey Betts, Butch Trucks, Warren Haynes, and Marc Quinones. (Photo by Kirk West/Epic Records, courtesy of the Big House Museum, Macon, Georgia)

The 1997 lineup of the Allman Brother Band. *Left to right*: Gregg Allman, Butch Trucks, Jaimoe, Jack Pearson, Dickey Betts, Oteil Burbridge, and Mark Quinones. (Photo by Kirk West/Epic Records, courtesy of the Big House Museum, Macon, Georgia)

hired two nurses to live in his home around the clock and help him get sober for good. After nearly a dozen stints in rehab over the years, he was finally ready to hit the reset button. "And then it was all over," Gregg wrote of his getting clean in 1996. "I mean, it was over, man. It was flat over. I quit drinking, I quit smoking, I quit snorting anything—I quit all that. I had prayed to God, 'Man, get me off of this shit,' and he did. I thought, 'I have been released.'"

Unfortunately, Dickey continued to struggle with substance abuse, and after the *Where It All Begins* album in 1994, his problems grew worse. He was drinking heavily, and tensions were developing between him and other band members. Fed up, Warren Haynes and Allen Woody departed in 1997 to focus on their side project, Gov't Mule, which they'd originally successfully launched in 1994. Nashville musi-cian Jack Pearson and Oteil Burbridge, a for-mer member of Col. Bruce Hampton's Aquar-ium Rescue Unit, replaced Warren and Allen on guitar and bass, respectively.

After a couple of years, Jack departed, and the Allman Brothers Band once again found themselves in need of a guitarist. Back in 1990, while they were recording the *Seven Turns* album in Miami, Butch had taken Gregg, Allen, and Warren to a South Beach club called Tropics International to see his guitar-play-ing nephew Derek perform. The guys were blown away by Derek Trucks, who was eleven years old at the time. By 1999, he was nineteen, and playing with Butch Trucks and Oteil Bur-bridge in a side group called Frogwings. He sat in with the Brothers as a featured musi-cian on a number of shows, and was officially brought on for the entire summer tour. Trucks was the perfect fit for the band. "Where does Derek come from," Gregg wrote in his autobi-ography. "I don't know, man, but if you believe in reincarnation.... I mean, sometimes I look over and see my brother."

Though the addition of Derek Trucks was a breath of fresh air, things didn't get better with Dickey Betts. "Getting clean was like having my windshield washed," Gregg explained in his autobiography, "and it felt like me, Jaimoe, and Butchie were all too caught up with Dick-ey's bullshit. In the spring of 2000, we did an eight-show run that ended in Atlanta on May 7th; during this stretch, Dickey was drinking a ton of beer, and God only knows what else he was doing. He was in rare form, blowing song after song, and the worse he got, the louder he played. It was a total train wreck, and just embarrassing to the rest of us."

Jaimoe, Butch, and Gregg agreed that Dickey needed to go to rehab. It was a tough line to draw, especially considering the band had put up with Gregg's self-destructive behav-ior for much of the group's history. "Yes, Gregg struggled with alcohol for years," Butch Trucks told Alan Paul, "but when he had problems, he tended to get real quiet and almost shrink away. When Dickey drank, he got louder and more difficult to deal with ... just very mean." The dual personality had been an issue for years. "When he is an Indian, he is so spiritual," Bonnie Bramlett said of her experience touring with Dickey Betts in the early 1980s. "A great leader, he does not force opinions but he shares information. When he is a cowboy, he's not. Let's just say that he is not anything like the Indian when he is a cowboy. I love him either way. I always have and I always will."

Butch, Gregg, and Jaimoe signed a letter that was faxed to Dickey, informing him that they would do the 2000 summer tour without him. "It basically said," Dickey explained to the press at the time, "'We feel that your perfor-mances have been repeatedly disappointing for the fans and the band. So we have decided you will not tour with us this summer.'" Although the message left open the possibility of com-ing back once he got himself straightened out, Dickey would later tell the press that he'd been "fired by fax." He sued the band, resulting in a drawn-out arbitration process.

Derek Trucks' friend Jimmy Herring, who'd also played with Oteil in the Aquarium Res-cue Unit, joined the band as Dickey's replace-ment on the 2000 summer tour. After the tour concluded, he moved on to play with the Grate-ful Dead's Phil Lesh, and eventually joined Widespread Panic. Warren Haynes ultimately returned to the Allman Brothers Band to replace the departing Jimmy Herring.

By 2001, the band had settled into the lon-gest consistently running lineup in the group's history, with original members Gregg, Jaimoe, and Butch, along with Warren Haynes, Derek Trucks, Marc Quiñones, and Oteil Burbridge. Though Gregg battled Hepatitis C in 2007, which led to him undergoing a liver transplant in the summer of 2010, the band persevered. In 2009, they played fifteen shows at New York's Beacon Theater to celebrate their fortieth anni-versary. It was also the twentieth anniversary of the group taking up an annual residency at the Beacon for a run of shows at the venue that has come to be regarded as hallowed ground by fans. Special guests joined them onstage, including Billy Gibbons, Buddy Guy, Eric Clapton, Johnny Winter, Sheryl Crow, and members of the Grateful Dead. In early 2014, Warren Haynes and Derek Trucks announced that they would step away from the Allman Brothers Band at the end of the year. Gregg Allman confirmed in a subsequent interview with *Relix* magazine that the group would stop touring, though he left open the possibility of limited future perfor-mances. "Who's to say? We all may get together every five years and just do one play at a time."

With Skynyrd and the Allmans back in business, Southern rock influences returned to the mainstream in the 1990s. Chuck Leavell had been unable to rejoin the Allman Broth-ers Band due to his commitment to the Rolling Stones, but in 1989 he was tapped to play key-boards on a session by a young Atlanta band called Mr. Crowe's Garden that would intro-duce a new generation to the spirit of South-ern rock. Shortly after signing to Def Ameri-can Recordings, Mr. Crowe's Garden changed their name at the suggestion of the label. By the time their first album, *Shake Your Money*

Derek Trucks. (Courtesy of Carl Lender)

The Allman Brothers Band on their summer tour of 2000. *Left to right*: Jimmy Herring, Oteil Burbridge, Butch Trucks, Derek Trucks, Marc Quinones, Jaimoe, and Gregg Allman. (Photo by Kirk West/Epic Records, courtesy of the Big House Museum, Macon, Georgia)

Maker, was released in February of 1990, they were known as the Black Crowes.

Heavily influenced by British groups such as the Faces and the Rolling Stones, the Black Crowes, like Lynyrd Skynyrd before them, infused their fascination with British rockers with authentic Southern grit. With the success of the singles "Jealous Again," "She Talks to Angels," and a cover of Otis Redding's "Hard to Handle," the group's album rose to #4 on the *Billboard* chart and was eventually certified Platinum five times over. Conscious of negative assumptions about the South, the band members initially distanced themselves from that image. "We've tried so hard to stay away from Southern connotations," lead singer Chris Robinson declared in 1991. "It's bullshit—I've never had a Confederate flag."

By the time the Black Crowes released their second effort in 1992, however, they had come to embrace at least some Southern connotations. The album, which debuted at #1 on the *Billboard* chart, was titled *Southern Harmony and Musical Companion*. Embracing the Southern hippie aesthetic pioneered by the Allman Brothers Band, the group members sought to clarify that there was much more to their home region than one-dimensional caricatures would suggest.

In a 1995 interview with *Mojo*, guitarist Rich Robinson reflected on stereotypes he encountered while recording in Los Angeles:

> People would say, "Hey, do you have an airport down there? Do you live on a cotton field?" Weird shit like that. They don't realize Atlanta's a huge city of about four million people. Many Americans still har-

A publicity photo of what was revealed in 2014 would be the final touring lineup of the Allman Brothers Band. *Left to right*: Derek Trucks, Warren Haynes, Butch Trucks, Gregg Allman, Jaimoe, Marc Quinones, and Oteil Burbridge. (MSO)

bor a lot of preconceived notions, and some don't even know we're in the same country. It's just people's ignorance and stupidity. But the funny thing is, that's what the South is known for—"they're all ignorant stupid down there"—but who's really ignorant and stupid? The people who don't know what's going on but point fingers and judge before actually knowing, or people just trying to be who they really are?

By the late 1990s, the Black Crowes had evolved into a roots-oriented Southern jam band, with a revolving door of top-notch musicians joining brothers Chris and Rich Robinson in various on-again/off-again configurations. Nashville native Jeff Cease, who was in the original lineup of the group before being replaced by highly regarded guitarist Marc Ford, went on to perform with country star Eric Church. Ford was replaced by North Carolinian Audley Freed in 1998. Freed had emerged from the band Cry of Love, who recorded two Southern rock-influenced albums for Columbia in the early 1990s. Marc Ford later returned to the band,

A publicity photo of brothers Chris and Rich Robinson of the Black Crowes. (Paradigm Talent Agency)

while Freed went on to back up the Dixie Chicks, Jacob Dylan, Sheryl Crow, and others. From 2007–11, Luther Dickinson of the North Mississippi Allstars was dividing his time between the Black Crowes and his own band, while original Black Crowes bassist Johnny Colt joined Lynyrd Skynyrd in 2012.

Another Atlanta group with Southern rock influences, Drivin' n Cryin', was formed in 1985. After finding regional success with their debut independent release, the band landed a deal with Island Records in 1987 and brought guitarist Jeff Sullivan into the lineup. Sullivan had played guitar for Mr. Crowes' Garden before they became the Black Crowes. Drivin' n Cryin' found their greatest success with 1991's *Fly Me Courageous*, a guitar-heavy alternative-rock effort with a Southern accent that gained traction with college radio and was certified Gold.

That same year, Capricorn Records rose from the ashes when Phil Walden secured a new distribution deal with Warner Bros. Records and set up shop in Nashville. The revived label's first signing was Widespread Panic from Athens, Georgia. Though the group had formed in 1986 and released an independent album in 1988, their 1991 self-titled Capricorn debut was their first major effort. It was helmed by longtime Capricorn producer Johnny Sandlin, and helped carve out a niche for the skilled Southern musicians in the blossoming jam-band scene of the early 1990s.

The second album on the new Capricorn imprint was Col. Bruce Hampton & the Aquarium Rescue Unit's self-titled effort. Hampton's avant-garde Hampton Grease Band had formed in the late 1960s and been part of the scene around Piedmont Park in Atlanta, which also played host to groups like the Allman Brothers Band, Hydra, and Eric Quincy Tate. Hampton's original group signed with Columbia Records and released a double album, *Music to Eat*, in 1971. It has frequently been described as one of the worst-selling albums in the label's history, second only to an instructional yoga LP by the Maharishi Mahesh Yogi.

During Walden's second Capricorn run, he re-signed the Dixie Dregs and released one album by Lynyrd Skynyrd, 1994's *Endangered Species*. As with the original Capricorn label, however, the second incarnation was focused on more than just Southern rock. Walden and company released the first album by future country superstar Kenny Chesney, as well as launching the careers of the successful rock bands Cake and 311.

Two key bands that signed with Walden's revived label enthusiastically incorporated influences from the Southern rock era. The Screamin' Cheetah Wheelies, led by vocalist Mike Farris, formed in Nashville in 1990 and signed with Atlantic Records in 1993. The group's blend of classic rock riffs, Southern-fried boogie, and jam-band explorations earned a respectable following, thanks largely to an early single, "Shakin' the Blues." After their Atlantic debut, they moved over to Capricorn for a couple of albums in the late 1990s. But while the Capricorn single "Boogie King" gained some attention, and the group built a respectable following through nonstop touring, they never broke through to achieve consistent mainstream success.

Allman Brothers Band members Warren Haynes and Allen Woody formed Gov't Mule as a side project in the mid-1990s, teaming up with drummer Matt Abts, with whom both Haynes and Woody had played in the pre-

Allmans-reunion version of the Dickey Betts Band. Releasing their debut album in 1995, Gov't Mule carved out a respectable space on the live circuit as a Southern rock outfit with jam-band credibility. Though they only released a couple of albums for the Capricorn label in the late 1990s, their complete discography includes releases for a variety of independent record companies, as well as innumerable live performances that have been made available via the group's website. Both Haynes and Woody left the Allman Brothers Band in 1997 to concentrate full-time on Gov't Mule, but when bassist Allen Woody died unexpectedly in 2000, Haynes returned to the Brothers and continued to divide his time between the two groups. The band's 2003 release *The Deepest End: Live in Concert* was the only one of their albums to be certified Gold.

After the Black Crowes, Drivin' n Cryin', Widespread Panic, the Aquarium Rescue Unit, the Screamin' Cheetah Wheelies, and Gov't Mule injected Southern rock influences into their music in the 1990s, the trend continued into the next decade, as new bands emerged from the South that either intentionally incorporated those elements or unconsciously reflected the influence by virtue of having grown up in an environment where

A publicity photo for the Dixie Dregs' 1994 album *Full Circle*. (Courtesy of Lesley Bohm)

classic-rock radio leaned heavily on the Allman Brothers Band, Lynyrd Skynyrd, the Marshall Tucker Band, and others.

The North Mississippi Allstars formed in the mid-1990s and became fixtures on the north Mississippi blues scene, where legends like R. L. Burnside presided over a new generation of musical purists. Founding members and brothers Cody and Luther Dickinson were the sons of Memphis music legend Jim Dickinson, and were strongly rooted in traditional Southern sounds. The band's first album came out in 2000, with Luther Dickinson's blistering slide-guitar work capturing critics' attention. Three of the group's albums were nominated for Grammys in the Best Contemporary Blues Album category. Their dirty lo-fi blues-drenched brand of Southern rock paved the way for similarly configured but more commercially successful groups like the Black Keys. In addition to playing in his own band, Luther spent several years in the late 2000s as a member of the Black Crowes.

Another genre-stretching artist to emerge from the same community as the Dickinson brothers was Jimbo Mathus. Mathis was raised in Oxford, Mississippi, and his childhood nanny was Delta bluesman Charley Patton's daughter. After moving to North Carolina in the early 1990s, he formed Squirrel Nut Zippers, an ensemble that explored blues, swing, and gypsy jazz. He began collaborating with Jim and Luther Dickinson in the mid-1990s. After the disintegration of his band and his marriage, Mathus returned to Mississippi in the early 2000s, reclaiming his Southern blues roots for a critically lauded career as a genre-bending musician embracing the various strands that shaped the original Southern rock era.

The Drive-By Truckers, one of the most highly regarded bands of the 21st century's Southern rock revival, formed in Athens, Georgia, in the mid-1990s. Straddling the line between alternative country and Southern rock, the Truckers were built around Mike Cooley and Patterson Hood. Patterson's father, David Hood, was the bassist in Muscle Shoals' legendary Swampers studio band.

The Drive-By Truckers' breakout release was the 2001 double CD *Southern Rock Opera*. The sprawling and ambitious song cycle told the story of Lynyrd Skynyrd through the lens of a fictitious band. The superb song structures, three-guitar lineup, and insightful lyrical explorations about the complexities of life in the South garnered rave critical reviews and earned Drive-By Truckers the distinction of "Band of the Year" from *No Depression* magazine in 2002.

Songwriter and guitarist Jason Isbell joined the band in 2001, just before the *South-*

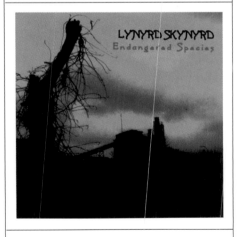

ern Rock Opera* tour, and began lending his songwriting talents to the group. Subsequent concept albums like *Decoration Day* and *The Dirty South* were highly regarded, demonstrating that the group could draw from Southern rock while forging a unique identity that transcended the genre. Emerging as

271

The Screamin' Cheetah Wheelies. *Left to right:* Terry Thomas, Mike Farris, Steve Burgess, Bob Watkins, and Rick White. (Courtesy of Danny Clinch)

KINGS OF LEON

YOUTH & YOUNG MANHOOD

Gov't Mule in 2010. *Left to right:* Danny Louis, Matt Abts, Jorgen Carlsson, and Warren Haynes. (Shore Fire Media)

up on the road, where they immersed themselves in the South's gospel strains before gravitating to rock music. Signed to RCA Records, Kings of Leon began gaining traction in the UK in the early 2000s before they broke through in the US. Their early work was the sound of a scrappy garage band, à la the Strokes, but with a Southern flair. By the time their fourth album, *Only by the Night*, went to #4 and was certified double Platinum in the US, they were already successful overseas. The popular single "Use Somebody" betrayed no distinctively Southern influences, and the band's regional association faded as their popularity increased.

Another group that has distanced itself from the Southern rock label is My Morning Jacket, led by Jim James and hailing from Louisville, Kentucky. The group's debut album, *Tennessee Fire*, was released in 1999. Though the band made a cameo, covering the song "Freebird," in Cameron Crowe's 2005 film *Elizabethtown*, James and the other band members have been resistant to the Southern rock label. While their music has extended far beyond the boundaries of Southern rock, they occasionally return to those influences in nontraditional ways.

With the rise of Americana in the 2000s, it's often difficult to determine where alternative country ends and Southern rock begins. A number of bands have emerged from the South in recent years that straddle the lines between alt-country, soul, blues, and Southern rock. The Memphis-based Lucero began building a steady following in the late 1990s with their Southern spin on Replacements-influenced garage rock. Similarly, the Old 97's emerged from Texas in the mid-1990s and represented a collision of carefully crafted guitar pop and Texas twang in the alt-country vein, while the Alabama Shakes emerged in 2012 with their brand of Southern

a refreshingly articulate Southern voice for a new era, the Drive-By Truckers are widely regarded as the next step in the evolutionary chain of Southern rock's development.

Green Hill, Alabama, native Jason Isbell departed the Drive-By Truckers in 2007 and released his solo debut record that same year. He then formed a band, the 400 Unit, with former members of Son Volt and Drivin' n Cryin'.

As a songwriter and performer, he earned a reputation, alongside former bandmate Patterson Hood, as a literate Southern voice for a new age.

Highly touted as a Southern rock band for a new generation, Nashville's Kings of Leon were formed in 1991 by brothers Anthony, Ivan, and Michael Followill, as well as cousin Cameron Followill. The Followill brothers' father was a traveling evangelist, and the boys grew

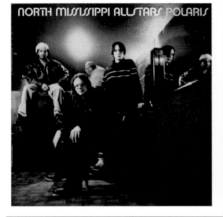

Alabama Shakes. (The Fun Star publicity photo by Joshua Black Wilkins)

soul-drenched blues rock. With heavy echoes of Memphis and Muscle Shoals, the group, from Athens, Alabama, were nominated for three Grammy awards in 2013. Thanks, in large part, to the raw appeal of singer Brittany Howard's lead vocals, the Alabama Shakes' debut album was certified Gold.

While some alternative rock- and alt-country-oriented bands have kept Southern rock influences alive in a new century, the genre has also cropped up in the music of some decidedly mainstream artists. Southern rock vocalist Bo Bice gained national attention as the runner up to winner Carrie Underwood on the fourth season of the televised singing competition *American Idol* in 2005. The Alabama-born Bice had been pursuing a music career in bands with names like Purge and SugarMoney when he auditioned for the show by singing "Whipping Post" by the Allman Brothers Band.

Following his run on *Idol*, Bice released his solo debut, *The Real Thing*, on RCA Records in December of 2005. A bland and generic update of the appealing '70s Southern rocker persona that made him popular with TV audiences, the album nonetheless went Gold. Plagued by medical concerns and longing to take control of his music, however, Bice enjoyed only a brief tenure with RCA. His subsequent independent releases were not as commercially successful as his debut, but they found him returning to his Southern rock roots and performing concerts with Lynyrd Skynyrd.

With Southern rock influences cropping up everywhere from classic-rock radio stalwarts, to exploratory jam bands, to edgy contemporary rock outfits, to scraggly Americana, and to middle-of-the-road televised singing competitions, Southern rock is no longer a distinct genre, but an attitude and set of influences that has found a home in a variety of musical settings. ★

Blackberry Smoke, *left to right*: Richard Turner, Brit Turner, Charlie Starr, Brandon Still, and Paul Jackson. (Big Hassle publicity photo by David McClister)

CHAPTER 39
Uncaged: Southern Rock Finds a Home in the Country

★ ★

"IF YOU LISTEN to today's country music," former Capricorn promotion man Dick Wooley remarked in a 2012 interview with Michalis Limnios, "it's not really authentic country music . . . it's '70s Southern rock!" In fact, though strains of Southern rock can be heard in many genres, the sound and aesthetic of the Southern rock era of the 1970s lives on most vigorously in the country market—despite the fact that the Nashville industry largely ignored Southern rock during its original heyday.

The roots of country music's embrace of Southern rock can be traced to Austin, Texas, in the early 1970s, where venues like the Armadillo World Headquarters played host to a mix of fans of traditional country and countercultural hippies. Open-minded country-rock troubadours like Jerry Jeff Walker, Doug Sahm, Michael Murphy, Kinky Friedman, and Ray Wylie Hubbard formed the core of a local scene of long-haired musicians who eschewed the strict musical boundaries of the Nashville establishment and formed an alternative country music community. "People down here move more slowly," singer-songwriter Steve Fromholz reflected in the early 1970s, "and drink lots of Lone Star beer and smoke a whole bunch of dope, and they play good music."

Starting in 1972, Austin radio station KOKE pioneered a "progressive country" format that catered to listeners with diverse tastes for both rock and country. "They were one of the first outfits that started blending George Jones, backed up with the Rolling Stones doing 'Wild Horses,' then back to a Merle Haggard track, then over to Van Morrison and Them," explained ZZ Top's Billy Gibbons, "just really an eclectic thing. They were really stirring the pot up. If it took the English guys to make it OK to play the blues, the KOKE FM guys made it OK to be playing country music." As the format gained traction, it began to spread to other US radio markets.

The undisputed spiritual leader and musical godfather of the bourgeoning Austin scene was Willie Nelson. Nelson had moved to Nashville in 1960, and made his mark as the songwriter of classics like Faron Young's "Hello Walls" and Patsy Cline's "Crazy." He recorded more than a dozen albums for the Liberty and RCA labels and charted a handful of moderately successful but unmemorable singles as a squeaky clean-shaven country crooner. Disillusioned by the Nashville music industry, Nelson moved to Austin in 1972 and reinvented himself as a scruffy countercultural singer-songwriter with traditional country roots.

Willie attracted a community of like-

Doug Sahm and his son Shawn. (Courtesy of Vanguard Records)

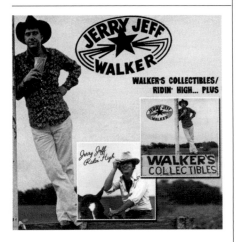

minded friends, including Waylon Jennings, another RCA recording artist who established a career as a clean-cut country-pop performer before growing a beard and embracing more artistically adventurous fare. With artists like Nelson, Jennings, and Kris Kristofferson pushing the boundaries of country music, the genre's fans slowly began to accept a new breed of long-haired, free-thinking, fast-living characters into the community. In January 1976, RCA Records released a compilation album called *Wanted! The Outlaws* that featured Nelson, Jennings, Tompall Glaser, and Jessi Colter. Celebrating what had come to be known as the outlaw country movement, the LP became country music's first Platinum-selling album.

Willie Nelson publicity photo. (Photo by Art Maillet, courtesy of Sony Music Entertainment)

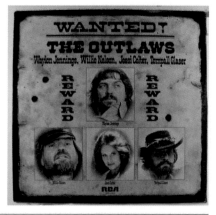

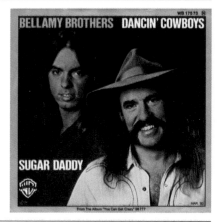

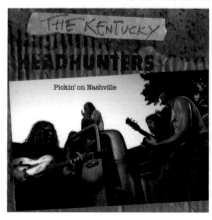

Charlie Daniels publicity photo, 1981. (Sound Seventy Management)

Hank Williams, Jr.—more so than any other mainstream country artist—actively incorporated the sound of Southern rock into his changing brand of rowdy outlaw country in the late 1970s. His initial efforts were not commercially successful, but with the *Family Tradition* album in 1979, Williams began a streak of seventeen albums that entered the Top 10 and went either Gold or Platinum. Williams became a country superstar and almost single-handedly redefined mainstream country music to include the sound of Southern rock.

While Willie, Waylon, and Hank emerged from within the country music mainstream and introduced their evolving tastes to listeners who were already familiar with them as artists, a handful of performers who initially established themselves in the rock field began to cross over to the country market, further confusing the barriers between what would be considered "country" and what would be categorized as "Southern rock."

Between 1975 and 1982, Charlie Daniels placed songs on both the country and mainstream charts, and was generally regarded as a rock performer with little regard for what country's conservative core audience might think of him. "I ain't got no image to protect or none of that bullshit," he told author Frye Gaillard in the late 1970s. "We don't wear no rhinestone Nudie suits; we don't have to worry about nobody knowing that we drink or smoke dope. I don't give a fuck, you know? The kind of people we appeal to don't give a damn. I ain't worried about the Baptists banning us, because they don't come to see us anyway. We're kind of a hard-livin' bunch of people. I think that reflects in our music. We just are what we are." By 1983, Daniels' chart activity had moved exclusively to the country category, even as his sound was unchanged. Despite Daniels' later born-again spiritual experience bringing his theological worldview in line with the Baptists he once shrugged off, his acceptance as a country artist can be attributed primarily to the fans' evolving notions of what constituted country music.

Similarly, David and Howard Bellamy, from Darby, Florida, crossed over from mainstream success to the country market in the same era. The Bellamy Brothers moved to Los Angeles in the 1970s and found pop success with the 1976 #1 hit "Let Your Love Flow." The song also reached #21 on the country chart, foreshadowing the duo's future country success with songs like 1979's #1 country single "If I Said You Had a Beautiful Body Would You Hold It Against Me." The song also charted in the Top 40 on the pop charts, but the Brothers, despite their long locks and ample facial hair, would soon be exclusively identified as a country act. Bringing an earthy visual image to their California-influenced country-rock sound, the Bellamy Brothers racked up twenty-six Top 10 country singles between 1979 and 1990.

Since the birth of commercial country music in the 1930s, most successful acts had either been solo performers or part of a duo or family act. While a few artists—like Ernest Tubb, Hank Thompson, Buck Owens, and Waylon Jennings—emphasized the importance of their bands, those musicians were still members of *backing* groups, whose primary role was to support the star whose name appeared on the marquee. In contrast, solo performers were a rare exception in the Southern rock genre, where the emphasis—as with most rock performers who came after the Beatles—was largely focused on groups. Country music's de-emphasis on bands began to change in 1980 with the emergence of Alabama, a wildly successful group that heralded Southern rock's full integration into mainstream country.

The group had originally formed under the name Wildcountry in Fort Payne, Alabama, in 1969. They became a popular club act in Myrtle Beach, South Carolina, in the mid-1970s, before singing with GRT Records in 1977. It was then that they changed their name to the Alabama Band, before eventually shortening it to Alabama. After making various independent recordings in the 1970s, Alabama signed to RCA Records in 1980. Their debut album spawned the hits "My Home's in Alabama" and "Tennessee River," and was certified double Platinum. The band members had long hair and beards, and incorporated light shows and other features more commonly associated with rock performers into their stage act. Alabama released eight more albums during the 1980s, with each rising to the #1 position and achieving at least Platinum status. Between 1980 and 1993, Alabama scored thirty-two #1 singles on the *Billboard* country chart.

"If you listen to Alabama," the Marshall Tucker Band's Doug Gray mused, "what they had to have was good songs that represented good Southern values and good relationships with people, and the ability to communicate with the people they were playing for. That's the same thing Marshall Tucker did. It's easy for me to sit here and bullshit and evaluate, but a lot of the later country artists were influenced by all of us—the Allman Brothers, Charlie Daniels, and other people like that."

By the mid-1980s, with the phenomenal success of artists like Hank Williams, Jr., and Alabama, country audiences simply took for granted that Southern rock was a crucial part of "their" working-class roots-music tradition. As the 1980s came to a close and the 1990s dawned, country music experienced an explosion in mainstream popularity. One of the elements that contributed to country's increased profile in the post–Garth Brooks era was the broadening definition of what was considered a legitimate part of the genre. Southern rock influences continued to play a crucial role in defining "country music" for a new generation of fans.

Raised in Texas, Steve Earle launched his recording career from Nashville in the mid-1980s. His 1986 debut album, *Guitar Town*, was certified Gold and went to #1 on the country album chart. In the fall of 1988, Earle released *Copperhead Road*, featuring a title track built around screaming electric guitars. By the time the album was released, Earle appeared as a menacing, long-haired tattooed rebel who looked like a member of a biker gang. Country music had come a long way from rhinestones and pompadours. The album climbed to the Top 10 and was awarded triple-Platinum status.

Another influential performer who brought Southern rock elements to country music was Lee Roy Parnell from Abilene, Texas. The highly respected slide guitarist cut his teeth on the Austin music scene of the mid-1970s before moving to Nashville in the late 1980s and signing with Arista Records. His distinctively blues-oriented, soulful take on country music earned him a string of Top 10 hits in the early and mid-1990s.

Following in the footsteps of Alabama—but cultivating a more rough-around-the-edges "redneck" persona—were the Kentucky Headhunters. Brothers Richard and Fred Young formed a group called Itchy Brother in 1968 that also included lead guitarist Greg Martin. After a hiatus in the early 1980s, they began performing as the Kentucky Headhunters with another pair of brothers, Doug and Ricky Lee Phelps. Signing with Mercury Records in 1989, the Headhunters released *Pickin' on Nashville*, which went double Platinum and spawned four Top 40 singles. As a result, the Kentucky Headhunters won Top New Vocal Duo or Group at the Academy of Country Music Awards, Vocal Group of the Year and Album of the Year at the CMA Awards, and Best Country Performance by a Duo or Group with Vocal at the Grammy Awards. More than any other country performers before them, the Kentucky Headhunters *looked* the part of a 1970s Southern rock band. Their influence continued as guitarist Greg Martin substituted for Ed King on Lynyrd Skynyrd's 1992 tour, while Richard Young's son, John Fred Young, co-founded Black Stone Cherry, a group that refined the classic metal side of Southern rock's contemporary legacy.

Southern rock–influenced country performers continued to dominate the charts as the 1990s progressed. "I used to have a lot of friends in Nashville that were studio musi-

Alabama, *left to right*: Mark Herndon, Jeff Cook, Randy Owen, and Teddy Gentry. (RCA Records)

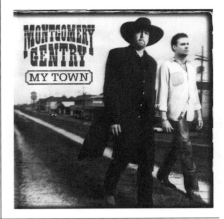

cians," the Atlanta Rhythm Section's J. R. Cobb explained. "Most of 'em came from pop and Top 40. They weren't country. The so-called country music of today is closer to pop and Southern rock than it is country." Hiram, Georgia, native Travis Tritt, for example, was one of the country stars of the 1990s to eschew a cowboy hat in favor of long hair and a leather jacket. He incorporated bluesy Southern rock into his music, and a gravelly soulful vibe into his vocal performances. Tritt released five consecutive Top 10 albums between 1990 and 1996, with each one certified at least Platinum, and enjoyed fifteen Top 10 singles during the same period.

Similarly, Brooks & Dunn incorporated loud electric guitars and rock-star showmanship into their performances, making them one of the most successful country acts of all time. Each of their releases—from their six-times-Platinum debut, 1991's *Brand New Man*, through 2007's *Cowboy Town*—went to #6 or higher on the country chart. After a remarkable run of singles that included twenty #1s, the duo's final charter, 2009's "Honky Tonk Stomp," was a collaboration with ZZ Top's Billy Gibbons.

Some of the other groups to emerge during the same period embraced the Southern rock sound and visual image to such an extent that traditional country elements were largely absent from some of country music's biggest hit-makers. The rock-edged Confederate Railroad from Marietta, Georgia, signed with Atlantic Records in 1992 and released four albums for the label. The first two went double Platinum and Platinum, respectively, and all four reached the Top 10 on the country album rankings. Similarly, the duo Montgomery Gentry, comprised of Kentuckians Eddie Montgomery and Troy Gentry, debuted on Columbia Records in 1999 with what critic Steve Huey described as "the sound and spirit of Southern rockers like Lynyrd Skynyrd, the Marshall Tucker Band, and Charlie Daniels, painting themselves as rowdy redneck rebels who still hold small-town values." In 2000, they won Favorite New Artist in the country category at the American Music Awards, Top New Vocal Duo or Group at the Academy of Country Music Awards, and Vocal Duo of the Year at the Country Music Association Awards. They recorded six albums for Columbia, with four of them going Gold or Platinum, and produced fifteen singles that reached the Top 10.

"Country music is now all about what we were doing in 1975 in some aspects," Outlaws guitarist Hughie Thomasson pointed out in a 2007 interview with Jeb Wright. "They have discovered the snare drum, the lead electric Fender guitar and three part harmonies. We did all of that stuff back then. We are called Southern rock and they are called Country." One of the trends that blurred those lines even further, however, was the conscious pursuit of the mainstream country market by performers who had already achieved success as Southern rockers. Thomasson's former Outlaws partner Henry Paul relocated to Nashville and won over the country market with his band Blackhawk, who found major success with a double-Platinum debut album in 1994. The group earned seven Top 10 singles in the 1990s, though country music's embrace of Southern rock was so complete by that point that Paul's music was not dissimilar to what he was producing in the 1970s. "If you take my first band, Sienna, and trace it to the Outlaws, to the Henry Paul Band, back to the Outlaws, and on to Blackhawk, that is a very straight line," he explained. "It's an unwavering musical personality, and it's musically consistent. It's vocally

Kix Brooks and Ronnie Dunn. (Courtesy of William Morris Endeavor)

Zac Brown Band publicity photo. *Left to right:* John Driskell Hopkins, Daniel de los Reyes, Coy Bowles, Zac Brown, Chris Fryar, Clay Cook, and Jimmy De Martini. (Courtesy of ROAR Management)

harmonious but aggressively guitar-driven, and it plays into my vision [of] trying to integrate country music into popular music."

Brothers Johnny and Donnie Van Zant, of Lynyrd Skynyrd and 38 Special respectively, teamed up in the late 1990s, releasing a rock album called *Brother to Brother* that failed to chart. It was followed in 2001 by *Van Zant II*, which also generated a lukewarm response. In 2005, however, they signed to Columbia Records and turned their focus to the country audience. The resulting *Get Right with the Man* went Gold on the country album chart and spawned a Top 10 country single with "Help Somebody." By comparison, the same single only hit #66 on the mainstream chart. A second Columbia album, 2007's *My Kind of Country*, also reached the Top 10. While contemporary rock audiences seemed to have little interest in Southern rock's past, country audiences enthusiastically adopted the Van Zant brothers into the family.

After more than three decades of absorption into the country genre, Southern rock influences show no sign of slowing. Country stars like Gretchen Wilson, Big & Rich, Jamey Johnson, and Waylon's son Shooter Jennings, have fully adopted the Southern rock visual image and many of its musical influences. Long-haired bearded country rock bands like the Shooter Jennings–produced Fifth on the Floor, or Texas' Whiskey Myers, are marketed as country groups now that their brand of Southern rock is hard pressed to find a large audience outside the country community. In 2013, Nashville's Big Machine Records—home to Taylor Swift, Rascal Flatts, and Tim McGraw—signed the Cadillac Three, a tattooed Southern rock band that—had they appeared thirty years earlier—would almost certainly have signed to Capricorn Records and been ignored by the country market as far too edgy.

The best of the latest crop of Southern rockers to find a home in country circles is Blackberry Smoke, a group that emerged from Atlanta with independent albums in 2004 and 2009 before breaking through with the Top 10 country album *The Whippoorwill* in 2012. Like the Cadillac Three, Blackberry Smoke look and sound more like they should be onstage in a biker bar than playing the *Grand Ole Opry*. As was the case when Dylan first traveled to Nashville in the '60s, the city's strict musical categories are being broken down and expanded.

Blackberry Smoke's breakthrough album was released by Southern Ground Records, a label that was launched by Georgia native Zac Brown. The Zac Brown Band formed in 2002 and toured relentlessly before releasing their first independent album in 2004. In 2008, Zac's label partnered with Atlantic Records, and the group saw their single "Chicken Fried" rise to the #1 position on the country singles chart. The album from which it emerged, *The Foundation*, went triple Platinum. Clay Cook, who had been a member of the latter-day Marshall Tucker Band, joined the Zac Brown Band in 2009. That same year, the group released "Toes," launching a string of seven consecutive #1 country singles. They won a Best New Artist Grammy in 2010.

The Zac Brown Band have been joined onstage by Gregg Allman and other Southern rock luminaries, the members recognizing that their influences stem directly from the Southern rock era. "It's not that we didn't want to be considered country," bassist John Driskell Hopkins explained to interviewer Nancy Dunham in 2012. "We've been embraced by the country community and we're very pleased. It's just that we are a little too schizophrenic to be under one name, in our minds.... We are all a product of all our influences, mostly Southern rock. We are all country boys from the South, in one way or another." ★

Epilogue
REBEL SOUL: THE ROAD GOES ON FOREVER

★ ★

Kid Rock. (Atlantic Records publicity photo by Jeremy Deputat)

WHEN THE POPULARITY of Southern rock dipped in the 1980s, public perceptions of the region had already improved dramatically. Thanks in part to ambassadors like the Allman Brothers Band and President Jimmy Carter—who heralded a New South of progressive idealism—popular notions of Southern life were being reexamined. Media stereotypes of Southerners that helped contribute to the impulse to categorize Southern rock as a distinct genre didn't quite disappear but softened considerably.

In the 1990s, the region maintained an alluring mystique. The values and characters that populated the South of popular imagination were informed by the novels—and subsequently by films inspired by the novels—of Southerner John Grisham. Cineplex versions of Southerners were often eccentric, but they generally lacked the condescending simplicity or the frightening menace of the media portrayals of earlier eras. Films like *Fried Green Tomatoes*, *Sling Blade*, *The Apostle*, *O Brother, Where Art Thou*, *Crazy Heart*, and *Beasts of the Southern Wild* presented Southerners who were idiosyncratic but not inauthentic.

Similarly, television portrayals brought Southerners further into the mainstream with the success of shows like *Designing Women*, *Evening Shade*, *Friday Night Lights*, *Justified*, *The Walking Dead*, and *Hart of Dixie*.

What is significant is that, while the South is still regarded as a unique region, Southern-oriented entertainment draws much more than a regional audience. On the political front, three of the five presidents to have held office since Jimmy Carter emerged from the South. Today, the South is mainstream America, and Southern rock is mainstream music. The lines are no longer as distinct as they once were.

In fact, the man most responsible for raising the profile of Southern rock in the 2000s and beyond isn't really a Southerner. Initially, he wasn't even a rocker. Bob Ritchie first emerged from the Detroit area in the late 1980s as a break-dancer, rapper, and DJ known as Kid Rock. After releasing a rap album on Jive Records in the early 1990s, followed by several subsequent independent releases, Ritchie finally broke through to the mainstream as a rap-rocker with his phenomenally successful *Devil Without a Cause* in 1998. The album made Kid Rock a superstar in the rap-metal mold, and eventually achieved Platinum status eleven times over.

The follow-up, 2001's *Cocky*, continued the same musical direction, but included a few surprising deviations. "You Never Met a Motherfucker Quite Like Me" sampled Lynyrd Skynyrd's "Freebird" and featured Hank Williams, Jr., in the official video, while "Picture" was a straight country duet with Sheryl Crow. The latter became Kid Rock's highest charting single to date, and his first song to appear on the country chart.

With the release of 2003's *Kid Rock*, the former rapper fully remade himself in the Southern rock mold as a working-class hero who drew liberally from country, classic rock, hip-hop, and Southern sounds. Rock appealed to a new generation of blue-collar hell-raisers who grew up on a musically diverse diet. His transformation was perhaps best illustrated by his selection as the artist to induct Lynyrd Skynyrd into the Rock and Roll Hall of Fame in 2006. Two years later, Rock's "All Summer Long" incorporated the intro from "Sweet Home Alabama" and became another major cross-genre hit.

While Kid Rock did much to revive a South-

Zac Brown and Kid Rock perform on a USO tour at Ramstein Air Base in Germany. (Photo by Chad J. McNeeley/ Department of Defense)

ern attitude in rock music, what was perhaps most surprising was his whole-hearted embrace by mainstream country fans. "All Summer Long" climbed to #4 on the country singles chart in 2008, and Rock went on to host the CMT (Country Music Television) awards in 2010 and 2011. While he certainly would never be mistaken for Johnny Cash or George Jones, it was precisely his celebration of Southern rock that endeared Kid Rock to contemporary country audiences. His adoption into the country music mainstream is illustrative of the fact that the roots of modern country are much more likely to be found in the music of Lynyrd Skynyrd than Hank Williams.

As he began to find success in the country market, Kid Rock bought a house in Nashville, and he has continued to associate himself with both country and rock artists. By the end of 2013, he had scored nineteen Top 40 hits on *Billboard*'s Mainstream Rock charts, as well as seven charting country singles. In other words, he'd earned credibility as a rapper, a rock star, a country singer, a tough Detroit homeboy, and an adopted Southerner. His 2011 song "Care" featured guest vocals by both rapper T.I. and mainstream country songstress Martina McBride. It was his embrace of Southern rock sounds and attitudes that allowed Kid Rock to bridge the gaps of musi-

cal genre and celebrity personas that were previously regarded as completely incompatible. Southern rock was the glue that made Kid Rock's cross-genre appeal possible.

In late 2012, Kid Rock released *Rebel Soul*, his sixth straight Top 10 album. More than that of any other artist, Kid Rock's commercial success illustrates the full absorption of Southern rock into the American musical mainstream. While critics and music-industry observers felt the need to designate Southern rock as a distinct subgenre in the 1970s, today it lives on in various permutations. Southern rock is alive and well—it's just no longer set apart as a distinct category.

For those who might be waiting for Southern rock to rise again, it has already risen. Its influence is all around us, but it no longer needs its own box. You hear it on classic-rock radio, see it on *American Idol*, sense its spirit in contemporary country, recognize its scrappy sincerity in alternative roots music, and enjoy its influence in virtually every realm of popular music. From the visceral sustained notes of Duane Allman's Les Paul, all the way through to the latest hit by the Zac Brown Band, what started of necessity as an organic musical movement has finally found its sweet home as an integral part of the rich and diverse patchwork that is the best of American music. ★

Acknowledgments

HE PROCESS OF putting this book together was a remarkable learning experience, and I'm truly grateful to each person who took the time to share stories, give insights, provide source material, and offer encouragement along the way. Thanks to those who paused from their busy schedules to answer my questions, including: Gregg Allman, Don Barnes, Elvin Bishop, Randall Bramblett, Bonnie Bramlett, Buddy Buie, David Cantonwine, J. R. Cobb, Bruce Crump, Charlie Daniels, Billy Earheart, Mac Gayden, Billy Gibbons, Doug Gray, Jack Hall, Jimmy Hall, Jim Hawkins, Charlie Hayward, Dave Hlubek, Paul Hornsby, Larry Howard, Mike Hyland, Jimmy Johnson, Rodney Justo, Ed King, Spencer Kirkpatrick, Al Kooper, Chuck Leavell, Jim "Dandy" Mangrum, Wayne Moss, John O'Daniel, Henry Paul, Mark Pucci, Artimus Pyle, Rickie Lee Reynolds, Johnny Sandlin, Russell Smith, Bill Stewart, Tommy Talton, Tony Joe White, Bobby Whitlock, Donnie Winters, Hank Williams, Jr., and Monte Yoho. Distilling a subject as big as Southern rock into a single book was a challenge. There are countless quotes, tidbits, and tales that I had to leave behind in the interest of space, but that I hope will have the opportunity to resurface for a future project. Whether I quoted a single line from our conversation, or multiple lengthy passages, each of these people was invaluable in helping me understand how I wanted to present the story.

Thanks are also due to the publicists, managers, lawyers, and various music industry folks who provided information, coordinated interviews, and helped me pull everything together, especially Woody Bomar of Green Hills Music Group, Jerry Butler, Craig Campbell of the Campbell Entertainment Group, Mark Case at the Gibson Custom Shop, Blain Clausen of Sanctuary Artist Management, Steve Dixon of Delta Groove Productions, Sean Gilday at Blue Raven Artists, Norman Gillis, Tammy Helm of Universal Music Publishing, Tammy Hensley, Michael Lehman, Don Murry Grubbs at Absolute Publicity, Paul Marshall, Bob Merlis, Chank Middleton, Connie Moss, Terry Reeves at Music Matters Entertainment, Toby Silver and Tom Tierney at Sony Music, Kendall Small, Tom Soares at SC Publicity, Paula Szeigis with Charlie Daniels' office, Tammy Taylor of Artists International Management, Kirt Webster of Webster & Associates Public Relations, Leann White, Trey Wilson at Vector Management, and CoCo Carmel Whitlock.

The process of tracking down and assembling photos for this book would not have been possible without the help of the photographers, fans, collectors, institutions, and musicians who held on to some great images over the years. Thanks to Joe Bender, Dave Brichler at Lone Wolf Productions, Lesley Bohm, Alberto Cabello, David Cantonwine, Peter Cross, Bruce Crump, Tim Davis and Michael Gray at the Country Music Hall of Fame and Museum, Mark Estabrook, Robin Fenter, Larry Franklin, John Gellman, Getty Images, Rodney Hall at Fame Studios, Charlie Hargrett, Jim Hawkins, Paul Hornsby, Larry Howard, Mike Hyland, Bob Johnson, Spencer Kirkpatrick, Herb Kossover, Carl Lender, Chuck Leavell, Rose Lane White Leavell, Clay Patrick McBride, David McClister, the Middle Georgia Archives at the Washington Memorial Library in Macon, Georgia, Terry Milam, Kenny Nemes of Jampol Artist Management, Helge Øverås, Chuck Perkins, Randy Poe, John Powell, Mark Pucci, the estate of Otis Redding at *OtisRedding.com*, Johnny and Anathalee Sandlin, Dan Santoro, Bill Stewart, Paula Szeigis, Tommy Talton, Carter Tomassi at messyoptics.com, the University of West Georgia's Center for Public History, Walter Vanderbeken, Kirk West, the Frank White Photo Agency, Bobby Whitlock, and Ron Wray. Pete Howard has an amazing collection of rare and original concert posters and memorabilia at PosterCentral.com. If you're a fellow collector, or have something to sell, take a moment to connect with him via his website. Extra special thanks to Jared Wright at the Big House Museum in Macon, Georgia, who went well above and beyond the call of duty, and was an absolute pleasure to work with. If your travels take you to Macon, be sure to visit the Allman Brothers Band Museum at the Big House (*thebighousemuseum.org*), and check out their fantastic collection.

I am especially appreciative of Gregg Barron and Clemens Morgenroth, of BMG Rights Management, for their flexibility and support. Thanks to Patrick Cleary, who's always good for a music talk, and extra special thanks to Chris Miles, who deserves special recognition for his patience and insight as an unwitting sounding board. Thanks, also, to Joe Bell, Michael Gray, Frank Friedman, Jennifer Wiley, Scott Moore, and Patrick Hamilton. He knows why.

There has been much written about Southern rock over the years, and this project would not have been possible without the men and women who came before me who helped preserve the history, especially Lee Ballinger, Marley Brant, Chris Charlesworth, Cameron Crowe, Tom Dupree, Candice Dyer, Ron Eckerman, Jim Esposito, Chet Flippo, Scott Freeman, Robert Gordon, Scott Greene, Barney Hoskyns, Martha Hume, Gary James, Mark Kemp, Kurt Loder, Pete Makowski, Daisann McLane, John Mendelsohn, Jas Obrecht, Alan Paul, Martin Popoff, Anathalee Sandlin, John Swenson, Jann Uhelszki, Kirk West, Kirsten West, and Jeb Wright of Classic RockRevisited.com. Luc Brunot of the French *Bands of Dixie* magazine, and Philippe Archambeau, Ron Johnson, John Molet, and Yves Phillippot, of the French *Road to Jacksonville* webzine, have all conducted important interviews with key Southern rockers. John Lynskey and the staff and writers at *Hittin' the Note* magazine have done so much to preserve the story of the Allman Brothers Band and related artists, and their back issues proved to be invaluable resources in my own education.

When it comes to celebrating, chronicling, and promoting the history of Southern rock, nobody is more passionate than Michael Buffalo Smith. Whether in his original *Gritz* magazine, on the *Swampland* website, in his *Kudzoo* digital magazine, on the Kudzoo Radio show, or through his countless freelance articles, liner notes, and blog posts, Smith is a one-man Southern rock history preservation machine. I would not have been able to even think of putting this book together without his truly invaluable pioneering efforts.

Several people read various passages in early stages and were notably generous with their time in responding with suggestions. My good friends Tim Bernsau, Mike Bunn, Paul Cope, Randy Fox, Andrew Lyons, Heather Thomson-Bunn, and John Warren helped me clarify my thoughts. And I couldn't possibly say "thank you" enough times to express my deep appreciation for Carol Cherman, who read most every word of the very long original draft. She has an otherworldly ability to spot mistakes, and her eye for excellence was critical to helping me whip the original manuscript into a something approaching coherence.

Peter Guralnick was a great help and encouragement to me as I navigated the very first steps of the process, and I am so appreciative of his guidance. My editor, Mike Edison, probably got more than he bargained for, but his patience, collaborative spirit, and cool demeanor kept us (mostly) on track. Thanks, also, to Carol Bomar for cheering me on, and Patrick Crowley for making me look good. Much appreciation to Jessica Burr, John Cerullo, Bernadette Malavarca, Tom Seabrook, and Wes Seeley at Backbeat.

My deepest appreciation goes to Randy Poe, Duane Allman's biographer, who recommended me for this project. He has been a consistent sounding board, encourager, cheerleader, and supporter, both personally and professionally. I could never find the right words to express my gratitude to this wonderful man who has done so much for me.

Finally, I wish to thank my wife, Melanie. My life filled up with unexpected commitments soon after I signed on to write this book, and our time together grew increasingly rare as the deadline approached. I will always treasure her unselfish support and encouragement, even when she had to compete with the computer screen for my affections. I'm so grateful to have such an amazing partner with whom to share life.

Sources

AUTHOR INTERVIEWS

Barnes, Don. 38 Special, October 16, 2013.

Bishop, Elvin. Capricorn recording artist, August 1, 2013.

Bramblett, Randall. Singer/songwriter/musician, August 20, 2013.

Bramlett, Bonnie. Capricorn recording artist, August 9, 2013

Buie, Buddy. Atlanta Rhythm Section, September 9, 2013.

Cantonwine, David. Eric Quincy Tate, August 28, 2013.

Cobb, J. R. Atlanta Rhythm Section, September 12, 2013.

Crump, Bruce. Molly Hatchet, November 1, 2013.

Daniels, Charlie. The Charlie Daniels Band, December 7, 2012.

Earheart, Billy. The Amazing Rhythm Aces, September 9, 2013.

Gayden, Mac. Area Code 615 and Barefoot Jerry, July 5, 2013.

Gibbons, Billy. ZZ Top, August 23, 2013.

Gray, Doug. The Marshall Tucker Band, August 27, 2013.

Hall, Jack. Wet Willie, May 16, 2013.

Hall, Jimmy. Wet Willie, September 26, 2013.

Hawkins, Jim. Capricorn Studios engineer, August 19, 2013.

Hayward, Charlie. The Charlie Daniels Band, August 20, 2013.

Hlubek, Dave. Molly Hatchet, September 5, 2013.

Hornsby, Paul. Hour Glass and Capricorn producer, August 10, 2013.

Howard, Larry. Grinderswitch, August 14, 2013.

Hyland, Mike. Capricorn staff, September 19, 2013.

Johnson, Jimmy. Muscle Shoals musician and producer, October 10, 2012.

Justo, Rodney. Atlanta Rhythm Section, September 16, 2013.

King, Ed. Lynyrd Skynyrd, December 12, 2012.

Kirkpatrick, Spencer. Hydra, July 29, 2013.

Kooper, Al. Musician and producer of Lynyrd Skynyrd, September 23, 2013.

Leavell, Chuck. The Allman Brothers Band and Sea Level, September 25, 2013, September 30, 2013.

Mangrum, Jim "Dandy." Black Oak Arkansas, September 9, 2013.

Moss, Wayne. Area Code 615 and Barefoot Jerry, July 5, 2013.

O'Daniel, John. Point Blank, September 30, 2013.

Paul, Henry. The Outlaws and Blackhawk, September 12, 2013.

Pucci, Mark. Capricorn staff, September 16, 2013.

Pyle, Artimus. Lynyrd Skynyrd, August 19, 2013.

Rickie Lee Reynolds. Black Oak Arkansas, August 22, 2013.

Sandlin, Johnny. Hour Glass and Capricorn Records producer, August 30, 2013.

Smith, Russell. Amazing Rhythm Aces, October 1, 2013.

Stewart, Bill. Capricorn Studios drummer, August 9, 2013.

Talton, Tommy. Cowboy and Capricorn musician, August 5, 2013.

Whitlock, Bobby. Derek & The Dominos and Capricorn recording artist, July 29, 2013.

White, Tony Joe. Recording artist, January 3, 2014.

Winters, Donnie. The Winters Brothers Band, August 5, 2013.

Williams, Hank Jr. Recording artist, September 30, 2013.

Yoho, Monte, The Outlaws. September 10, 2013.

OTHER INTERVIEWS

Allman, Duane. Interview by Dave Herman, WABC-FM. New York, New York. December 9, 1970.

Bramlett, Bonnie, and Charlie Daniels, Mike Hyland, Ed King. "Brothers and Sisters: The Rise of Southern Rock." Country Music Hall of Fame and Museum Panel Discussion. Nashville, Tennessee. Moderated by Michael McCall. October 29, 2011.

Fogerty, John. Interview by Bob Santelli. The Grammy Museum. Los Angeles, California. September 26, 2013.

Medlocke, Rick and Shorty Medlock. Interview by Rich Langlois. *Backstreet* TV show. Jacksonville, Florida. 1981.

Medlocke, Rickey. Interview by Elliot Levin. *New York Hard Rock Examiner*. November 18, 2009.

Walker, Greg T. Interview by Fred Capitelli. *The Music and Entertainment Buzz*. Web series. Undated.

BOOKS

Allman, Gregg, and Alan Light. *My Cross to Bear*. New York: Morrow, 2012.

Altschuler, Glenn C. *All Shook Up: How Rock 'n' Roll Changed America*. Oxford: Oxford University Press, 2003.

Bane, Michael. *White Boy Singin' the Blues: The Black Roots of White Rock*. London: Da Capo, 1992.

Berry, Chuck. *Chuck Berry: The Autobiography*. New York: Harmony Books, 1987.

Bordowitz, Hank. *Bad Moon Rising: The Unauthorized History of Creedence Clearwater Revival*. New York: Schirmer Books, 1998.

Ballinger, Lee. *Lynyrd Skynyrd: An Oral History*. New York: Spike, 1999.

Blayney, David. *Sharp Dressed Men: ZZ Top Behind the Scenes from Blues to Boogie to Beards*. New York: Hyperion, 1994.

Brant, Marley. *Freebirds: The Lynyrd Skynyrd Story*. New York: Billboard Books, 2002.

Brant, Marley. *Southern Rockers: The Roots and Legacy of Southern Rock*. New York: Billboard Books, 1999.

Cash, W. J. *The Mind of the South*. New York: A.A. Knopf, 1941.

Clapton, Eric. *Clapton: The Autobiography*. New York: Broadway Books, 2007.

Cobb, James C. *Away Down South: A History of Southern Identity*. Oxford: Oxford University Press, 2005.

Daniels, Charlie. *The Devil Went Down to Georgia: Stories*. Atlanta: Peachtree Publishers, 1985.

Du Noyer, Paul. *The Illustrated Encyclopedia of Music*. London: Flame Tree Publishing, 2003.

Dyer, Candice. *Street Singers, Soul Shakers, Rebels with a Cause: Music from Macon*. Macon, Georgia: Indigo Custom Publishing, 2008.

Dylan, Bob. *Chronicles: Volume One*. New York: Simon & Schuster, 2004.

Eckerman, Ron. *Turn It Up!* Marina Del Rey, CA: Restless Artists, 2011.

Escott, Colin and Martin Hawkins. *Good Rockin' Tonight: Sun Records and the Birth of Rock 'n' Roll*. New York: St. Martin's Press, 1991.

Freeman, Scott. *Midnight Riders: The Story of the Allman Brothers Band*. Boston: Little, Brown, 1995.

Frost, Deborah. *ZZ Top: Bad and Worldwide*. New York: Collier Books, 1985.

Gaillard, Frye. *Watermelon Wine: Remembering the Golden Years of Country Music*. Montgomery: New South Books, 2004.

Gibbons, Billy F, Tom Vickers, and David Perry. *Billy F. Gibbons: Rock + Roll Gearhead*. St. Paul, MN: MBI Pub, 2005.

Goad, Jim. *The Redneck Manifesto: How Hillbillies, Hicks, and White Trash Became America's Scapegoats*. New York: Simon Schuster, 1998.

Guralnick, Peter. *Last Train to Memphis: The Rise of Elvis Presley*. Boston: Little, Brown, and Co., 1994.

Guralnick, Peter. *Sweet Soul Music: Rhythm and Blues and the Southern Dream of Freedom*. New York: Harper & Row, 1986.

Hedge, John T. "The Allman Brothers: The Only Place They Really Felt at Home was Mama Louise Hudson's Soul-Food Restaurant." *The Oxford American Book of Great Music Writing*, Marc Smirnoff, ed. Fayetteville: University of Arkansas Press, 2008.

John, Dr. (Mac Rebennack) with Jack Rummel. *Under a Hoodoo Moon: The Life of the Night Tripper*. New York: St. Martin's Press, 1994.

Jones, Roben. *Memphis Boys: The Story of American Studios*. Jackson: University Press of Mississippi, 2010.

Kemp, Mark. *Dixie Lullaby: A Story of Music, Race, and New Beginnings in a New South*. New York: Free Press, 2004.

Kooper, Al. *Backstage Passes & Backstabbing Bastards: Memoirs of a Rock 'n' Roll Survivor*. New York: Backbeat Books, 2008.

Leavell, Chuck and J. M. Craig. *Between Rock and a Home Place*. Macon: Mercer University Press, 2004.

Logan, Nick and Bob Woffinden. *The Illustrated Encyclopedia of Rock*. New York: Harmony Books, 1978.

Lopate, Mitchell D. *Rock 'n Blues Stew*. Bloomington, IN: AuthorHouse, 2005.

Malone, Bill and David Stricklin. *Southern Music / American Music*. Lexington: University of Kentucky, 2003.

Marsh, Dave, and John Swenson. *The Rolling Stone Record Guide: Reviews and Ratings of Almost 10,000 Currently Available Rock, Pop, Soul, Country, Blues, Jazz, and Gospel Albums*. New York: Random House, 1979.

Nance, Scott. *Recycling the Blues: ZZ Top*. Las Vegas: Pioneer Books, 1991.

Norman, Philip. *Rave on: The Biography of Buddy Holly*. New York: Simon & Schuster, 1996.

Ownby, Ted. "Freedom, Manhood, and White Male Tradition in 1970s Southern Rock Music." *Haunted Bodies: Gender and Southern Texts*. Anne Goodwyn Jones and Susan V. Donaldson, eds. Charlottesville: University Press of Virginia, 1997.

Paul, Alan. *One Way Out: The Inside History of the Allman Brothers Band*. New York: St Martin's Press, 2014.

Perkins, Willie. *No Saints, No Saviors: My Years with the Allman Brothers Band*. Macon: Mercer University Press, 2005.

Poe, Randy. *Skydog: The Duane Allman Story*. San Francisco: Backbeat Books, 2006.

Reid, Jan W. *The Improbable Rise of Redneck Rock*. Austin: Heidelberg Publishers, 1974.

Roberts, Diane. "Lynyrd Skynyrd: Song of the South." *The Oxford American Book of Great Music Writing*, Marc Smirnoff, ed. Fayetteville: University of Arkansas Press, 2008.

Popoff, Martin. *Southern Rock Review*. Burlington, Ont: Collector's Guide Pub, 2001.

Richards, Keith and James Fox. *Life*. New York: Little, Brown and Co., 2010.

Sandlin, Anathalee. *A Never-Ending Groove: Johnny Sandlin's Musical Odyssey*. Macon: Mercer University Press, 2012.

Smith, Michael B. *Carolina Dreams: The Musical Legacy of Upstate South Carolina*. Beverly Hills: Marshall Tucker Entertainment, 1997.

Streissguth, Michael. *Outlaw: Waylon, Willie, Kris, and the Renegades of Nashville*. New York: It Books, 2013.

Till, Brian M. *Conversations with Power: What Great Presidents and Prime Ministers Can Teach Us About Leadership*. New York: Palgrave Macmillan, 2011.

Varesi, Anthony. *The Bob Dylan Albums: A Critical Study*. Toronto: Guernica, 2002.

Ward, Brian. *Just My Soul Responding: Rhythm and Blues, Black Consciousness, and Race Relations*. Berkeley: University of California Press, 1998.

Wells, Paul. "The Last Rebel: Southern Rock and Nostalgic Continuities." *Dixie Debates: Perspectives on Southern Cultures*. Richard H. King and Helen Taylor, eds. New York: New York University Press, 1996.

Whitlock, Bobby and Marc Roberty. *Bobby Whitlock: A Rock 'n' Roll Autobiography*. Jefferson, N.C.: McFarland, 2011.

Williams, Hank Jr. and Michael Bane. *Living Proof: An Autobiography*. New York: Putnam, 1979.

Willman, Chris. *Rednecks & Bluenecks: The Politics of Country Music*. New York: New Press, 2005.

Woodward, C. Vann. *The Burden of Southern History*. Baton Rouge: Louisiana State University Press, 1960.

Young, Neil. *Waging Heavy Peace: A Hippie Dream*. New York: Blue Rider Press, 2012.

ARTICLES

Abbott, Lee. "Oh Say Can't You See: Marshall Tucker Marches On." *Crawdaddy*. September 1978.

Abowitz, Richard. "Lynyrd Skynyrd: Vicious Cycle." *Rolling Stone* no. 924. June 12, 2003.

Aledort, Andy. "Big Brother." *Guitar World*. April 2007.

Anderson, Philip. "Dave Hlubek—Guitarist / Founder, Molly Hatchet." Kaos2000. 1999. Web. August 25, 2013.

Archambeau, Philippe. "Banner Thomas' Interview." Road to Jacksonville. November 2002. Web. August 25, 2013.

Archambeau, Philippe. "Jim Dandy." Road to Jacksonville. May 2008. Web. August 21, 2013.

Archambeau, Philippe, Jeff Lescene, and Ybes Philippot. "Charlie Hargrett Interview: Blackfoot." Road to Jacksonville. November 2009. Web. September 10, 2013.

Ayers, Tom. "Marshall Tucker's Favorite Toy." *Country Rambler*. March 10, 1977.

Bangs, Lester. "Heavy Metal Brontosaurus M.O.R." *Creem*, May 1976.

Bangs, Lester. "The Allman Brothers Band." *Rolling Stone* no. 52. February 21, 1970.

Bangs, Lester. "The Marshall Tucker Band." *Rolling Stone* no. 137. June 21, 1973.

Barnes, Ken. "Lynyrd Skynyrd: Gimme Back My Bullets." *Phonograph Record*. March, 1976.

Barnes, Ken. "The Outlaws: Outlaws." *Phonograph Record*. July, 1974.

Bashe, Philip. "Marshall Tucker at Home: Fast Food, Fast Cars, and Easy Living." *Circus*. 1980.

Bell, Max. "Elvin Bishop: Hometown Boy Makes Good." *NME*. January 15, 1977.

Bell, Max. "Little Feat/The Outlaws: Hammersmith Odeon, London." *NME*. June 26, 1976.

Bell, Max. "The Outlaws." *NME*. November 1, 1975.

Binelli, Mark. "The Lost Brother." *Rolling Stone* no. 1082/1083. July 9–23, 2009.

Boucher, Caroline. "Who the Hell Are Lynyrd Skynyrd?" *Disc and Music Echo*. February 16, 1974.

Bosso, Joe. "Billy Gibbons Talks ZZ Top: The Complete Studio Albums (1970–1990). *Music Radar*. June 3, 2013. Web. September 2, 2013.

Branin, Jeb. "Interview: NDN." *In Music We Trust* no. 13. October 1998. Web. September 9, 2013.

Bradley, Clyde. "An Interview with Jimmy Farrar." *Classic Rock Revisited*. 2004. Web. August 25, 2013.

Brant, Marley. "George McCorkle." *Original Marshall Tucker*. Web. June 4, 2013.

Breznikar, Klemen. "Point Blank Interview with John O'Daniel & Rusty Burns." *It's Psychedelic Baby*. June 21, 2011. Web. October 20, 2013.

Browne, David. "Where Are They Now: Alex, Kate, and Livingston Taylor." *Rolling Stone* no. 508. September 10, 1987.

Brunot, Luc. "Bobby Golden: Stillwater." *Bands of Dixie* no. 31. March–April 2003.

Brunot, Luc. "Doc Holliday: The Last Ride." *Bands of Dixie* no. 82. September–October 2011.

Brunot, Luc. "Dru Lombar: Grinderswitch." *Bands of Dixie* no. 36. January–February 2004.

Brunot, Luc. "Jimmy Hall." *Bands of Dixie* no. 58. September–October 2007.

Brunot, Luc. "Larry Howard: Grinderswitch." *Bands of Dixie* no. 38. May–June 2004.

Brunot, Luc. "Paul Hornsby: Capricorn Records, Hourglass." *Bands of Dixie* no. 37. March–April 2004.

Brunot, Luc. "Wayne Bruce: Hydra." *Bands of Dixie* no. 48. March–April, 2006.

Burger, Jeff. "Amazing Rhythm Aces: Third-Rate Romance, First-Rate Rock." *Jeff Burger Blog*. December 1, 1976. Web. August 29, 2013.

Cahill, Tim. "Nothing Matters but the Fever." *Rolling Stone* no. 178. January 16, 1975.

Calverley, Bob. "They Banded Together for Pediatric's Center." *Sun-Sentinel*. February 14, 1975.

Cecolini, Vinny. "Henry Paul: Rock's Outlaw Rebels Still Rolling. *JAM Magazine Online*. Web. August 26, 2013.

Charlesworth, Chris. "Allman Brothers Band: Leavell Headed Allman." *Melody Maker*. February 16, 1974.

Charlesworth, Chris. "Elected! Rock and US Politics." *Melody Maker*. November 13, 1976.

Charlesworth, Chris. "Gregg Allman." *Melody Maker*. January 26, 1974.

Charlesworth, Chris. "Lynyrd Skynyrd: Rainbow Theatre, London." *Melody Maker*. December 14, 1974.

Charlesworth, Chris. "Memories of Lynyrd Skynyrd and Peter Rudge." Rock's Back Pages. Web. May 6, 2013.

Charlesworth, Chris. "Southern Rock: Under the Sign of Capricorn. *Melody Maker*. February 2, 1974.

Charone, Barbara. "The Outlaws: Dixie Chickens." *Sounds*. June 19, 1976.

Charone, Barbara. "Lynyrd Skynyrd. *Zoo World*. April 25, 1974.

Chebatoris, Jack. "Band of Brothers." *Town* vol. 1 no. 5. July 31, 2011.

Crowe, Cameron. "Lynyrd Skynyrd: Hell on Wheels Puts on the Breaks." *Los Angeles Times*. October 24, 1976.

Crowe, Cameron. "Marshall Tucker: The South Also Rises." *Rolling Stone* no. 156. March 14, 1974.

Crowe, Cameron. "The Allman Brothers Story." *Rolling Stone* no. 149. December 6, 1973.

De Whalley, Chas. "Grinderswitch: Pullin' Together." *Sounds*. December 18, 1976.

Demeslay, Didier and Luc Brunot. "Henry Paul: Outlaws—Henry Paul Band—Blackhawk— Brothers of the Southland." *Bands of Dixie* no. 88. September–October 2012.

DeMeyer, Trace A. "An Interview with Blackfoot Bass Player Greg T. Walker, Back on the Scene: Blackfoot Strikes Again!" *Yahoo! Contributor Network*. April 13, 2010. Web. September 10, 2013.

Devokaitis, E. J. "Bobby Whitlock: A Rock 'n' Roll Autobiography." *Hittin' the Note* no. 68. 2011.

Doell, Paul. "In a Family Way: The Long, Joyous Ride of Wet Willie." *Hittin' the Note* no. 72. 2012.

Doherty, Harry. "Lynyrd Skynyrd: Gimme Back My Bullets." *Melody Maker*. January 31, 1976.

Doherty, Harry. "Lynyrd Skynyrd: Skyn Flick." *Melody Maker*. September 4, 1976.

Dolbear, Mike. "One from the Archives: Interview with Tommy Aldridge." MikeDolbear.com. 2008. Web. August 21, 2013.

Drozdowski, Ted. "Rickey Medlocke's Gibson-Powered Trip from Lynyrd Skynyrd to Blackfoot and Back Again." Gibson Guitars official site. June 18, 2008. Web. September 9, 2013.

Dubro, Alex. "Them Vino-Lovin' Allman Brothers." *Rolling Stone* no. 77. March 4, 1971.

Dunham, Nancy. "Exclusive Q&A: Zac Brown Band's John Driskell Hopkins Talks Music, Eats, and Garth Brooks." *Our Stage*. January 31, 2012. Web. October 26, 2013.

Dupree, Tom. "Macon Breakin'." *You and Me, Dupree* Blog. September 7, 2009. Web. July 27, 2013.

Dupree, Tom. "Wet Willie: No More Jr. Allmans." *Rolling Stone* no. 180. February 13, 1975.

East, Jon. "Toy Caldwell." Unknown newspaper clipping. Sunday, April 8, 1979. Posted to originalmarshalltucker.com. Web. May 14, 2013.

Edmonds, Ben. "Snapshots of the South: The Allman Brothers and Capricorn Records." *Creem*. 1972.

Edwards, Gavin. "Nothing Weighs as Much as a Heartache: Thirty Years of Ups and Downs with the Allman Brothers Band." *Rolling Stone* no. 826. November 25, 1999.

Ellis, Blake. "Mobile Natives Wet Willie Set to Celebrate Mardi Gras at Workplay." *AL.com*. February 6, 2013. Web. April 18, 2013.

Esposito, Jim. "Elvin Bishop: The Bourbon Street Irregulars." *Rock's Back Pages*. 1975. Web. September 18, 2012.

Esposito, Jim. "Lynyrd Skynyrd: The 100 Proof Blues." *Creem*. October 1975.

Evans, Michael. "Online Mercury's Conversation with Elvin Bishop." *Online Mercury*. August 5, 2000. Web. July 29, 2013.

Fletcher, Gordon. "ZZ Top: Hombres Riding North." *Rolling Stone* no. 162. June 6, 1974.

Flippo, Chet. "Black Oak: Rauch & Roll at the 8-Acre Spread." *Rolling Stone* no. 141. August 16, 1973.

Flippo, Chet. "ZZ Top: Power to the People." *Rolling Stone* no. 220. August 26, 1976.

Flynn, Rick. "Point Blank: The Bio." *Rick Flynn Productions*. February 6, 2012. Web. October 2, 2013.

Forte, Dan. "Elvin Bishop: Cultivating the Blues." *Vintage Guitar*. Web. August 6, 2013.

Forte, Dan. "Tommy Caldwell: Innovative Bassist for the Marshall Tucker Band." *Guitar Player* vol. 13. February 1979.

Francis, Miller Jr. "Nothing but the Blues: An Interview with Johnny Jenkins." *Great Speckled Bird* vol. 3 no. 38. September 28, 1970.

Friskics-Warren, Bill. "Family Tradition: The Legacy of Ol' Hank." *New York Times*. October 30, 2008.

Futterman, Steve. "Tour de Force." *Rolling Stone* no. 415. February 16, 1984.

Garner, Rick. "Alabama Soul Man: Interview with Jimmy Hall." *Hittin' the Note* no. 16. Spring 1997.

Gibbons, Billy. "The Allman Brothers Band." *Rolling Stone* no. 972. April 21, 2005.

Gilbert, Barry. "Bonnie's Back." *St. Louis Today*. April 24, 2004.

Gill, Andy. "The Black Crowes." *Mojo*. January, 1995.

Goodman, Mark. "Sittin' in with Jimmy Hall, Part Two." *Blues Wax*. May 15, 2012. Web. April 18, 2013.

Gordon, Robert. "The South Rises Again: The Improbable Return of Redneck Rock." *Creem*, 1995.

Gould, Mark T. "Bonnie Bramlett: She's 'Still the Same,' And Better!!" *Sound Waves*. August 2004. Web. August 9, 2013.

Greenblatt, Michael. "Set for the Big Sendup: That's Southern Rock's New Powerhouse, the Marshall Tucker Band." *Photoplay*. November 1977.

Greene, Scott. "Charlie Hargrett, From Blackfoot to Black Molly Charlie Hargrett Is Still Rocking Hard." *Swampland: Cultures of the South*. January 2001. Web. September 10, 2013.

Greene, Scott. "Jeff Carlisi (38 Special): The Guitarist Talks About 38 Special, Lynyrd Skynyrd, and Big People." *Swampland: Cultures of the South*. October, 2001. Web. October 16, 2013.

Greene, Scott. "Larry Junstrom Recalls His Days with Lynyrd Skynyrd and Talks About His Band, 38 Special." *Swampland: Cultures of the South*. July 2003. Web. November 19, 2013.

Grissim, John. "Area Code 615." *Rolling Stone* no. 48. December 13, 1969.

Gordon, Keith A. "Mickey Thomas Interview." *About.com Guide*. 2010. Web. July 29, 2013.

Gross, Michael. "The Death of the Allman Brothers Band." *Swank*. 1977.

Guy, Paul. "Lynyrd Skynyrd: Rickey Medlocke & Johnny Van Zant." *Fuzz*. 2007. Web. September 10, 2013.

Hall, Russell. "Gregg Allman Talks About Duane, Southern Rock and Role as Elder Statesman." Gibson.com. March 11, 2009. Web. January 9, 2013.

Hare, Sam. "Slowhand Remembers Skydog—Eric Clapton Comments on Duane Allman." *Hittin' the Note* no. 26. 2000.

Harrell, Scott. "A Treasured Find: Singer Bonnie Bramlett on Hangin' with Clapton, Harrison, the Allmans . . . and Roseanne." *Creative Loafing Tampa Bay*. January 12, 2005. Web. August 9, 2013.

Harris, Art. "Allmans Still Brothers—Win, Lose or Draw." *Rolling Stone* no. 195. September 11, 1975.

Henke, James. "Molly Hatchet's 'Beatin' the Odds' Due This Month. *Rolling Stone* no. 324. August 21, 1980.

Henke, James. "Molly Hatchet's Mistaken Identity." *Rolling Stone* no. 327. October 2, 1980. Hermmuth, Bronson. "My Interviews: William Joel "Taz" DiGregorio." Bronsonmusic.com. 2007. Web. July 20, 2013.

Herron, Amanda. "An Exclusive Interview with Charlie Daniels, Country Music Legend." *Yahoo! Contributor Network*. April 6, 2007. Web. July 20, 2013.

Hiatt, Brian. "Q&A, Eric Clapton." *Rolling Stone* no. 1178. March 14, 2013.

Himes, Geoffrey. "The Rossington Collins Band: Southern Rock Survival Among the Alligators." *Musician*. February 1982.

Hinkle, Sally. "10,000 Applaud Gala Daniels Homecoming." *Billboard*. January 27, 1979.

Hirsiger, Madeleine. "New Carolina Group Believes Macon is South's Music City." *Macon News*. 1972.

Hoskyns, Barney. "Alabama Shakes: The Saga of Southern Rock." *The Guardian*. April 6, 2012.

Hoskyns, Barney. "Southern Men: The Long Tall Saga of the Allman Brothers Band." *Mojo*. December 2002.

Hoskyns, Barney. "The Cats' Whiskers: Down Home with ZZ Top." *NME*. November 17, 1984.

Hoskyns, Barney. "The Strange Story of Eddie Hinton." *Soul Survivor*. 1987.

Hoskyns, Barney. "ZZ Top: The Marquee, London." *NME*. 1983.

Huey, Steve. "Montgomery Gentry: Artist Biography." *All Music*. Web. November 24, 2013.

Hughes, Rob. "Lynyrd Skynyrd: Sultans of Swamp." *Uncut*. May 2006.

Hume, Martha. "Bonnie Bramlett's Gospel." *Rolling Stone* no. 226. November 18, 1976.

Hume, Martha. "Marshall Tucker at Home." *Rolling Stone* no. 244. July 28, 1977.

Hurt, Edd. "Bob Johnston: The Cream Interview." *Nashville Scene*. September 18, 2012.

Ingham, John. "Lynyrd Skynyrd." *Sounds*. February 28, 1976.

Iozzia, David. "An Interview with Rickey Medlocke." *Rock Is Life*. 2006. Web. September 11, 2013.

James, Gary. "Gary James' Interview with Dean Daughtry of the Atlanta Rhythm Section." *Classic Bands*. 1979. Web. August 29, 2013.

James, Gary. "Gary James' Interview with Dru Lombar of Grinderswitch." *Classic Bands*. 1978. Web. July 31, 2013.

James, Gary. "Gary James' Interview with Hughie Thomasson of the Outlaws." *Classic Bands*. Undated. Web. August 26, 2013.

James, Gary. "Gary James' Interview with Jim 'Dandy' Mangrum of Black Oak Arkansas." *Classic Bands*. Undated. Web. August 21, 2013.

James, Gary. "Gary James' Interview with John O'Daniel of Point Blank." *Classic Bands*. Undated. Web. September 20, 2013.

James, Gary. "Gary James' Interview with Russell Smith of the Amazing Rhythm Aces." *Classic Bands*. Undated. Web. August 29, 2013.

Jeness, Judy Van Zant. "Name Changes and Ten Dollar Gigs." *Lynyrd Skynyrd History*. Web. June 9, 2013.

Johnson, Ron. "Charlie Daniels Interview." *Road to Jacksonville*. Web. July 21, 2013.

Johnson, Ron. "Interview with Elvin Bishop." *Road to Jacksonville*. April 14, 2004. Web. July 29, 2013.

Johnston, Donna. "Jonathan Edwards Full Biography." Jonathanedwards.net. July 2009. Web. May 13, 2013.

Jones, Marty. "Jim Dandy to the Rescue: The Southern-Rock Wildman on Sex, Politics, and Firing One up with the President." *Denver Westword*. May 21, 1998.

Kimball, George. "The Allman Brothers Band at Fillmore East." *Rolling Stone* no. 89. August 19, 1971.

King, Alan. "You Can't Stand Tall if You're Afraid to Fall: A Conversation with Black Oak Arkansas' Jim Dandy Mangrum." *Carbon 14* no. 23. 2002.

King, Bill. "Inside Wings: An Interview with Joe English." *Beatlefan*. December 19, 1978.

Klinger, Judson. "Rhythm Aces: Don't Call Them Country." *Rolling Stone* no. 220. August 26, 1976.

Kraar, Louis. "How Phil Walden Turns Rock into Gold." *Fortune* volume XCII, no. 3. September, 1975.

Krause, Tim. "Livingston Taylor Is 20." *Rolling Stone* no. 73. December 24, 1970.

LaRose, Michelle. "Stillwater: Michelle LaRose Talks with Bobby Golden." *Road to Jacksonville*. Web. October 24, 2013.

LaRose-Hasselbach, Michelle. "Atlanta Rhythm Section." *Ink 19*. July 2005. Web. August 29, 2013.

Landau, Jon. "Bandleader Duane Allman Dies in Bike Crash." *Rolling Stone* no. 96. November 25, 1971.

Lewis, Grover. "Hitting the Note with the Allman Brothers Band." *Rolling Stone* no. 96. November 25, 1971.

Limnios, Michalis. "An Interview with Legendary Elvin Bishop, an Artist Who Has Been Travelling the Blues Road Longer Than Most." *Blues at Greece*. April 6, 2013. Web. July 28, 2013.

Limnios, Michalis. "Legendary Dick Wooley Talks About Allmans, Capricorn, Clapton, King Mojo, Southern Rock, & Jimmy Carter." *Blues at Greece*. March 12, 2012. Web. October 14, 2013.

Loder, Kurt. "Marshall Tucker's Solid Future." *Circus*. July 6, 1978.

Loder, Kurt. "ZZ Top: The Boys Just Wanna Have Fun." *Rolling Stone* no. 419. April 12, 1984.

Lopate, Mitch "Layla, and Many Other Songs of Love: Bobby Whitlock Talks About Derek & The Dominos, Duane Allman, Gram Parsons, Eric Clapton and More." *Swampland: Cultures of the South*. Winter, 2000. Web. July 29, 2013.

Lynskey, John. "Gregg Allman, Low Country Blues." *Hittin' the Note* no. 68. 2011.

Lynskey, John. "Reflections—The World According to Jaimoe." *Hittin' the Note* no. 21. 1998.

Lynskey, John. "Reflections 2—The World According to Jaimoe." *Hittin' the Note* no. 22. 1999.

Makowski, Pete. "Billy Gibbons: An Interview." *Guitar Aficionado*. Fall, 2010.

Makowski, Pete. "Lynyrd Skynyrd: If I Leave Here Tomorrow." *Sounds*. March 15, 1980.

Makowski, Pete. "Lynyrd Skynyrd: Saturday Night Special." *Sounds*. October 30, 1976.

Makowski, Pete. "Lynyrd Skynyrd: The Wild Bunch." *Sounds*. February 12, 1977.

Marx, Jonathan. "Rock in a Hard Place." *Nashville Scene*. November 30, 1995.

McGee, David. "Amazing Rhythm Aces: The Other End, New York, June 2nd, 1976." *Rolling Stone* no. 218. July 19, 1976.

McGee, David. "Jaded and Joyless in Jersey: The Allman Bros. Draw a Blank." *Rolling Stone* no. 198. October 23, 1975.

McGee, David. "The Bottom Line, New York City, August 22nd, 1975." *Rolling Stone* no. 197. October 9, 1975.

McLane, Daisann. "Amazing Rhythm Aces: Playing with a Full Deck." *Rolling Stone* no. 294. June 28, 1979.

McLane, Daisann. "ZZ Top is Nationwide Again." *Rolling Stone* no. 316. May 1, 1980.

Mendelsohn, John. "Black Oak Arkansas." *Rolling Stone no.* 83. May 27, 1971.

Mendelsohn, John. "Turkey Talking to Arkansas." *Rolling Stone* no. 96. November 25, 1971.

Miles. The Outlaws: Southernly Last Summer. *NME*. July 3, 1976.

Molet, John. "Dave Hlubek's Interview." *Road to Jacksonville*. Web. August 25, 2013.

Molet, John. "Hydra Interview (Spencer Kirkpatrick)." *Road to Jacksonville*, 2004. Web. July 27, 2013.

Moseley, Willie G. "Joe Dan Petty: 'Techin' It Twice.'" *Vintage Guitar*. November 1996.

Moseley, Willie G. "Toy Caldwell Goes Back to Thumbin'." *Vintage Guitar*. Posted to originalmarshalltucker.com. Web. May 14, 2013.

Mulhern, Tom. "Dusty Hill: Low Down Bottom for ZZ Top." *Guitar Player Magazine*. February, 1981.

Mullins, Jesse. "Sentiments of a Simple Man." *American Cowboy*. September/October, 1994.

Murray, Charles Shaar. "ZZ Top: Welcome to Weirdsville." *Q*. November 1990.

Niester, Alan. "Hydra." *Phonograph Record*. September 1974.

Nobles, Barr. "More Talk of Allman Brothers Band Breakup." *Rolling Stone* no. 221. November 9, 1976.

O'Brien, Glenn. "ZZ Top: Life at the Top." *Spin*, 1985.

Obrecht, Jas. "Duane Allman Remembered." *Guitar Player*. October 1981.

Obrecht, Jas. "Twiggs Lyndon Talks Gear: An Unpublished 1978 Interview." *Jas Obrecht Music Archive*. 2010. Web. January 16, 2013.

Obrecht, Jas. "Young Duane Allman: The Bob Greenlee Interview." *Jas Obrecht Music Archive*. 2010. Web. 16 Jan. 2013.

Obrecht, Jas. "Young Duane Allman: The Jim Shepley Interview." *Jas Obrecht Music Archive*. 2010. Web. January 16, 2013.

Ogden, John. "The Hoochie Coochie Man, Berry Oakley." *Hittin' the Note* no. 22. 1999.

Ortega, Shawna. "Charlie Daniels Interview." *Songfacts*. Web. August 7, 2013.

Ortega, Shawna. "Henry Paul of the Outlaws, Blackhawk." *Songfacts*. 2006. Web. August 26, 2013.

Patterson, Randy. "The Bonnie Bramlett Interview." *Boomer City*. July 2011. Web. August 9, 2013.

Parker, Melissa. "Don Barnes Interview: Legendary Rockers 38 Special Release 'Live from Texas.'" *Smashing Interviews*. October 19, 2011. Web. November 19, 2013.

Paul, Alan. "Looking Back with Billy Gibbons." *Guitar School*. March, 1995.

Paul, Alan. "Low Down and Dirty, Gregg Allman: Looking Back . . . Looking Forward." *Hittin' the Note* no. 26. 2000.

Paul, Alan. "Low Down and Dirty: Shades of Dickey Betts." *Hittin' the Note* no. 22. 1999.

Palmer, Robert. "The Allman Brothers: A Great Southern Revival." *Rolling Stone* no. 290. May 3, 1979.

Phillippot, Yves, and John Molet. "Rusty Burns Original Interview." *Road to Jacksonville*. November, 2009. Web. October 3, 2013.

Pope, Hunter. "Into the Rhythm." *Smokey Mountain News*. April, 2000.

Rademacher, Brian. "Interview with Don Barnes." *Rock Eyez*. April, 2008. Web. November 19, 2013.

Rollins, Kenneth. "Legend of the Lounge." *The Eleventh Hour*. Web. April 26, 2013.

Rosen, Steven. "Billy Gibbons: Sittin' On Top of the World." *Guitar World*. November 1986.

Russell, Xavier. "Doc Holliday." *Cult Heroes* no. 39. November 25, 2010. Web. October 25, 2013.

Russell, Xavier. "Rebel Yell! No Drop in Standard from Molly Hatchet." *Kerrang!* Issue 86. January 24–February 6, 1985.

Saunders, Mike. "Keep the Faith, Black Oak Arkansas." *Rolling Stone* no. 109. May 25, 1972.

Schilling, Mary Kaye. "The Marshall Tucker Band Begins Again." *US*. June 10, 1980.

Scoppa, Bud. "Lynyrd Skynyrd: Nuthin' Fancy." *Rolling Stone* no. 189. June 19, 1975.

Scoppa, Bud. "Lynyrd Skynyrd: Second Helping (MCA)." *Crawdaddy*. September, 1974.

Scoppa, Bud. "The Amazing Rhythm Aces: Stacked Deck." *Rolling Stone* no. 200. November 20, 1975.

Scoppa, Bud. "Wet Willie." *Rolling Stone* no. 93. October 14, 1971.

Shasho, Ray. "Interview: Jim 'Dandy' Mangrum: Southern Rock Pioneer with Black Oak Arkansas." *Examiner*. December 4, 2012. Web. August 21, 2013.

Shaw, Russell. "Once Again, the South Rises." *Circus*. 1976.

Sheets, Adam. "Jim Dandy to the Rescue: An Interview with a Southern Rock Icon." *No Depression*. March 14, 2011. Web. August 19, 2013.

Shelasky, Paul. "Larry Franklin: Nashville Session Man, Texas Hall-of-Famer." *Fiddler*. Fall 2002.

Shipp, Michael R. "Rusty Burns: Point Blank's Lead Guitarist Talks About Texas, Touring with ZZ Top, and His Faith in God." *Kudzoo* online magazine vol. 1 no. 3. November–December 2012.

Shuster, Fred. "Bluesman Ends 25-Year Drought: Georgia's Jenkins Still Harbors Bad Feelings, but the Man Whose Style Influenced Hendrix Is Ready to Give the Music Biz Another Shot." *Daily News* (Los Angeles). August 28, 1996.

Simmons, Sylvie. "All the Things You Ever Wanted to Know About ZZ Top." *Creem*. March 1986.

Simmons, Sylvie. "ZZ Top." *Kerrang!*, 1995.

Smith, Jill McLane. "Bonnie Bramlett. Don't You Remember You Told Me You Loved Me Baby? A Conversation with Bonnie Bramlett." *Swampland: Cultures of the South*. Summer 2000. Web. August 8, 2013.

Smith, Michael Buffalo. "Alan Walden: Skynyrd, The Allmans and Otis, Alan Walden's Career in Rock and Soul." *Swampland: Cultures of the South*. January 2002. Web. April 24, 2013.

Smith, Michael Buffalo. "Blackfoot Reunited: An Exclusive Interview with Jakson Spires, Charlie Hargrett, Greg T. Walker, and Bobby Barth." *Gritz* no. 10. March 2005.

Smith, Michael Buffalo. "Charlie Hayward: Playing in the Charlie Daniels Band. *Swampland: Cultures of the South*. June, 2002. Web. July 20, 2013.

Smith, Michael Buffalo. "Checking in with Dennis Winters of the Winters Brothers Band." March, 2000. *Swampland: Cultures of the South*. Web. 24 Jul 2013.

Smith, Michael Buffalo. "Danny Joe Brown: Still Beatin' the Odds." *Swampland: Cultures of the South*. November 1999. Web. August 25, 2013.

Smith, Michael Buffalo. "Don Barnes—There's Still Something Special About 38." *Swampland: Cultures of the South*. February 2000. Web. November 19, 2013.

Smith, Michael Buffalo. "Dru Lombar Recalls Grinderswitch, Joe Dan and Southern Rock of the Seventies." *Swampland: Cultures of the South*. June 2001. Web. July 31, 2013.

Smith, Michael Buffalo. "Elvin Bishop: The GRITZ Interview." *Swampland: Cultures of the South*. Web. July 28, 2013.

Smith, Michael Buffalo. "Eric Quincy Tate's Dave Cantonwine: The GRITZ Interview." *Swampland: Cultures of the South*. Web. April 24, 2013.

Smith, Michael Buffalo. "Freddie Edwards: The Charlie Daniels Band." *Swampland: Cultures of the South*. August 2003. Web. July 20, 2013.

Smith, Michael Buffalo. "Galvinized Metal: An Exclusive Interview with Molly Hatchet's Keyboard Wizard John Galvin." *Swampland: Cultures of the South*. May 2002. Web. August 26, 2013.

Smith, Michael Buffalo. "Jakson Spires: On Blackfoot and the Southern Rock Allstars." *Swampland: Cultures of the South*. June 2001. Web. September 10, 2013.

Smith, Michael Buffalo. "Just as Wet as Ever: Wet Willie Front Man Jimmy Hall." *Swampland: Cultures of the South*. Summer 1998. Web April 18, 2013.

Smith, Michael Buffalo. "Larry Howard. The Southern Rock of Ages." *Swampland: Cultures of the South*. April 2001. Web. August 1, 2013.

Smith, Michael Buffalo. "Love the Spider: Taz DiGregorio on Thirty-Plus and Counting Years in the Charlie Daniels Band and His New Solo Album." *Swampland: Cultures of the South*. December 2001. Web. July 20, 2013.

Smith, Michael Buffalo. "Once an Outlaw: An

Interview with Henry Paul." *Universal Music Tribe*. May 2011. Web. August 26, 2013.

Smith, Michael Buffalo. "Paul Hornsby: An Ear for Southern Rock." *Swampland: Cultures of the South*. January 2001. Web. October 21, 2013.

Smith, Michael Buffalo. "Playin' in the Allstar Band: Dave Hlubek Talks About Molly Hatchet, The Southern Rock Allstars and TV." *Swampland: Cultures of the South*. May 2001. Web. August 26, 2013.

Smith, Michael Buffalo. "Rickey Medlocke." *Swampland: Cultures of the South*. June 2004. Web. September 10, 2013.

Smith, Michael Buffalo. "Scott Boyer on Cowboy, the Decoys, and a Lifetime of Southern Music." *Swampland: Cultures of the South*. Web. April 22, 2013.

Smith, Michael Buffalo. "Still Jammin' for Danny Joe: Riff West's Life in Molly Hatchet, Foghat, White Witch, and Service to All Creatures Great and Small." *Swampland: Cultures of the South*. October 2000. Web. August 25, 2013.

Smith, Michael Buffalo. "The Bonnie Bramlett Interview." *Swampland: Cultures of the South*. 2008. Web. August 8, 2013.

Smith, Michael Buffalo. "The Heart & Soul of Charlie Daniels." *Gritz Magazine*. December 2003.

Smith, Michael Buffalo. "The Church of What's Happening Now: A Conversation with Elvin Bishop." *Universal Music Tribe*. March 2011. Web. July 28, 2013.

Smith, Michael Buffalo. "Tom Wynn of Cowboy: The GRITZ Interview." *Swampland: Cultures of the South*. Web. April 22, 2013.

Smith, Michael Buffalo. "Tommy Crain." *Swampland: Cultures of the South*. December 2002. Web. July 20, 2013.

Smith, Michael Buffalo. "Tommy Talton and the Cowboy Reunion." *Swampland: Cultures of the South*. Web. April 22, 2013.

Smith, Michael Buffalo. "What's Up, Doc? Doc Holliday and Bruce Brookshire's Southern Spirit." *Swampland: Cultures of the South*. October 2001. Web. October 25, 2013.

Smith, Michael Buffalo, with Roxanne Crutcher. "The Most Important Things in Life Are Rock and Roll, and a Hot Carr . . . An Interview with Muscle Shoals Guitar Legend, Pete Carr." *Swampland: Cultures of the South*. May, 2000. Web. April 24, 2013.

Smith, Todd K. "The Outlaws 2009: Rising from the Ashes, the Flame Still Burns—Our Exclusive Interview with Henry Paul." *The Cutting Edge*. 2009. Web. August 26, 2013.

Smith, Todd K. "The Spirit of Southern Rock Takes Flight Once Again: Our Exclusive Interview with Bassist Greg T. Walker." *The Cutting Edge*. 2009. Web. September 10, 2013.

Snow, Mat. "The Black Crowes: Guilty!" *Q*. August 1991.

Snyder, Patrick. "The Sorrowful Confessions of Gregg Allman." *Rolling Stone* no. 225. November 4, 1976.

Specker, Lawrence. "Wet Willie to Celebrate 40 Years of Dixie Rock on Saturday." AL.com. May 27, 2012. Web. June 3, 2013.

St. Pierre, Roger. "The Allman Brothers: A Rock Tragedy." *NME*, December 9, 1972.

Stewart, Tony. "Lynyrd Skynyrd: I See the Bloodbath that Was Hamburg." *NME*. October 25, 1975.

Spangler, Kevin and Ron Currens. "Butch Trucks, the Different Drummer." *Hittin' the Note* no. 15. Fall 1996.

Spangler, Kevin and Ron Currens. "Jaimoe on Butch . . . and a Whole Lot More!" *Hittin' the Note* no. 15. Fall 1996.

Strange, Jay. "Barefoot Jerry: A History and Critical Review." *Art into Dust* Blog. June 15, 2010. Web. July 16, 2013.

Swenson, John. "38 Special." *Rolling Stone* no. 245. August 11, 1977.

Swenson, John. "Atlanta Rhythm Section: Back to the Classics." *Rolling Stone* no. 240. June 2, 1977.

Swenson, John. "Backtalk: Venerated Bluesman Elvin Bishop Stays Sharp." *Offbeat: Louisiana Music and Culture*. October 1, 2012.

Swenson, John. "Southern Rock: Gone with the Trend." *Crawdaddy*. July 1975.

Tamaerkin, Jeff. "Georgia Satellites: Fire the Retro Rockets." *Creem*. April 1987.

Tannenbaum, Ron. "Tom Petty on Retiring the Hits, Teasing the Heartbreakers, and Smoking Medical Weed." *Rolling Stone* no. 1184. June 6, 2013.

Thames, Bill. "Tommy Talton: Back to a Time." *Hittin' the Note*. Web. July 14, 2013.

Thomas, Alun. "In the Spotlight, Point Blank: Interview with Guitarist and Founder Rusty Burns." Rusty Burns official website. June 2, 2002. Web. October 2, 2013.

Thomas, Jimmy. "MTB: We're in This Together." *Gwinnett Life*. September 24, 1978.

Tiven, Jon. "The Allman Brothers Band: Rapping with Duane Allman and Berry Oakley." *New Haven Rock Press*. December 10, 1970.

Tiven, Jon. "ZZ Top A Go Go." *Blast*. August 1976.

Tobler, John. "Al Kooper: Sweetheart of the South." *Melody Maker*. March 2, 1974.

Trucks, Butch. "A Strange Tale of Tragedy." *The World According to Butch Trucks* Blog. August 5, 2011. Web. December 14, 2012.

Trucks, Butch. "Duane Allman." *The World According to Butch Trucks* Blog. July 17, 2011. Web. December 14, 2012.

Turley, William. "Hughie Thomasson Reforms the Outlaws." *Swampland: Cultures of the South*. Spring, 2005. Web. August 26, 2013.

Uhelszki, Jann. "Beat the Devil: The Allman Brothers." *Creem*. December 1975.

Uhelszki, Jann. "Lynyrd Skynyrd: Fifths and Fists for the Common Man." *Creem*. March 1976.

Uhelszki, Jann. "How the South Rose Again: The Soaring Flight and Tragic Fall of Lynyrd Skynyrd." *Mojo*, November 1997.

Uncredited. "A Moment Captured in Time: The *Crawdaddy* Interview with Duane." *Hittin' the Note* no. 26. 2000.

Uncredited. "An Interview with Duane Allman of the Allman Brothers Band." *Free Press* (New Orleans) no. 1. February 1, 1971.

Uncredited. "Backstage Pass: Molly Hatchet Flirtin' with Greatness. *Goldmine*. June 10, 2008. Web. August 25, 2013.

Uncredited. "Billboard Album Reviews: Eric Quincy Tate, Drinking Man's Friend." *Billboard*. June 24, 1972.

Uncredited. "Black Oak Arkansas Sign with Atlantic/Atco Records After 40 Years. New Album, "Back Thar N' Over Yonder" Set for October 15th Release." Press Release, Atlantic Records. July 29, 2013.

Uncredited. "Blackfoot, Skynyrd Vet Rickey Medlocke Celebrates Southern Rock Roots." *Goldmine*. June 20, 2008. Web. September 10, 2013.

Uncredited. "Buzzy Gruen: Point Blank." *Sweet Home Music*. Web. September 20, 2013.

Uncredited. "Capricorn Records Declares Bankruptcy. *Rolling Stone* no. 311. February 21, 1980.

Uncredited. "Capricorn Struggles to Survive; A&M to Discontinue Horizon Label." *Rolling Stone* no. 301. October 4, 1979.

Uncredited. "Charlie Daniels." *Digital Interviews*. August, 2000. Web. July 20, 2013.

Uncredited. "Charlie Daniels: Three Million Dollars' Worth of Fiddlin'." *Lyon County Reporter*. August 20, 1976.

Uncredited. "Dru Lombar." *Road to Jacksonville*. November 20, 2004. Web. July 31, 2013.

Uncredited. "Hughie Thomasson (The Outlaws, Lynyrd Skynyrd): Interview from the Archives." *The Backstage Pass*. July 2, 2010. Web. August 26, 2013.

Uncredited. "Interview: Bonnie Bramlett." *Music-Illuminati*. September 21, 2012. Web. August 9, 2013.

Uncredited. "PolyGram Sues Capricorn." *Rolling Stone* no. 302. October 18, 1979.

Uncredited. "Robert Nix: Candymen, Atlanta Rhythm Section, Alison Heafner." *Sweet Home Music*. Web. August 29, 2013.

Uncredited. "Veteran Guitarist Johnny Jenkins Dies." *Billboard.com*. Web. May 8, 2013.

Unknown. "Reflections on the Macon Scene & More: An Interview with Les Dudek." *Hittin' the Note*. June 19, 2004. Web. July 31, 2013.

Van Matre, Lynn. "Marshall Tucker Band: Hometown Boys Mine Gold." *Chicago Tribune*. March 27, 1977.

Washburn, Dennis. "'Real Serious About Playing' Is Marshall Tucker Success." *Los Angeles Daily News*. 1977.

Welch, Chris. "Marshall Tucker Band, Grinderswitch, Bonnie Bramlett: Hammersmith Odeon, London." *Melody Maker*. December 4, 1976.

Welch, Chris. "The Outlaws: Outlaw Country." *Melody Maker*. June 12, 1976.

West, Kirk. "Dickey Betts: The Early Years." *Hittin' the Note* no. 67. 2010.

West, Kirk. "Dickey Betts: The Early Years 2." *Hittin' the Note* no. 69. 2011.

West, Kirk. "Dickey Betts: The Early Years, Part 3." *Hittin' the Note* no. 70. 2011.

West, Kirsten. "Inside the Elusive Mr. Betts." *Hittin' the Note* no. 10. Fall 1994.

Westhoven, William. "Elvin Bishop and His 'Red Dog' Gibson ES-345—Together Almost 50 Years." *Guitar World*. October 7, 2011. Web. August 3, 2013.

White, Cliff. "Baby You Can't Drive My Car." *NME*. April 30, 1977.

Wilcock, Don. "BluesWax Sittin' in with Elvin Bishop, Part One: The Day the Blues Was Reborn." *Blues Review*. December 10, 2010. Web. July 29, 2013.

Wildsmith, Steve. "A Lifetime of Memories and a Love for the Music Keeps Blackfoot Founder Going." *The Daily Times*. August 31, 2011. Web. September 11, 2013.

Wiser, Carl. "Songfacts Songwriter Interview with Elvin Bishop." *Songfacts*. Web. July 28, 2013.

Wirtz, Ella. "Interview with Dru Lombar: The Conductor of the Ghost Train." *Rocktimes: The Online Rock Music Magazine*. December 19, 2004. Web. July 31, 2013.

Wosahla, Steve. "Redneck Rock and Tough as Hell!!!" Posted to originalmarshalltucker.com. Web. June 4, 2013.

Wright, Jeb. "Silver Stages & Golden Curtains: An Interview with the Late Hughie Thomasson." *Classic Rock Revisited*. 2007. Web. August 26, 2013.

Wright, Jeb. "Southern Pride: An Interview with Outlaw Henry Paul." *Classic Rock Revisited*. 2012. Web. August 26, 2013.

Yamada, Paul. "Wet Willie: Kiel Center, St Louis." *Concert News*. July 1974.

LINER NOTES

DeYoung, Bill. *Eric Quincy Tate*. Cotillion Records / Rhino Handmade, 2006.

Edmonds, Ben. *Swamp Music: Tony Joe White, the Complete Monument Recordings*. Rhino Handmade, 2006.

Hoskyns, Barney. "Sumpn' Funky Goin' On: True Tales of Blue-Eyed Backwoods Soul." *Country Got Soul*. Casual Records, July 2003.

O'Brien, Ron, with Andy McKaie. "American by Birth . . . (Southern by the Grace of God)." *Lynyrd Skynyrd*. MCA Records, 1991.

Swenson, John. *The Allman Brothers Band: Dreams*. Polygram Records, 1989.

Wynn, Ron. "Tuning In: The Promised Land." *Night Train to Nashville: Music City Rhythm & Blues: 1945–1970*. Country Music Foundation / Lost Highway Records, 2004.

FILM / VIDEO

American Revolutions: Southern Rock. Dir/Prod. Anne Fentress. CMT, 2005.

Behind the Music: Lynyrd Skynyrd. Prod. Daniel Bowen. VH1 Television, 2007.

Freebird: The Movie. Dir. Jeff G. Waxman. Cabin Fever Entertainment, 1996.

Interview with Livingston Taylor. Living Legends Music, January 12, 2008. Web. June 7, 2013.

Lynyrd Skynyrd's Uncivil War. Dir. Cali Alpert. VH1 Productions, October 15, 2002.

Respect Yourself: The Stax Records Story. Dirs. Robert Gordon, Morgan Neville. 2007.

Sweet Home Alabama: The Southern Rock Saga. Dir. James Maycock. BBC, 2012.

What Happened to Joe English? Word of Faith Video Testimony. Word of Faith Fellowship.

WEB

Charlie Hargrett official site. siogo.com.

Donnie Winters official site. donniewintersmusic.com.

Hittin' the Note. hittinthenote.com

Lynyrd Skynyrd History. lynyrdskynyrdhistory.com.

Paul Hornsby official site. paulhornsby.com.

Pure Southern Rock. puresouthernrock.com.

Rick Hirsch official site. ktb.net/~insync/wet_willie.

Rusty Burns official site. rustyburns.com.

The Ed King Forum. edking.proboards.com.